Race, Ethnicity, and Gender

To Kaya O'Brien-James, Benjamin Healey, and Caroline Healey,
in the hope that the issues of our world will be resolved in theirs.

Race, Ethnicity, and Gender

Selected Readings

Edited by

Joseph F. Healey

Christopher Newport University

Eileen O'Brien

College of William and Mary

PINE FORGE PRESS
An Imprint of Sage Publications, Inc.
Thousand Oaks • London • New Delhi

For information:

 Pine Forge Press
A Sage Publications Company
2455 Teller Road
Thousand Oaks, California 91320
E-mail: order@sagepub.com

Sage Publications Ltd.
6 Bonhill Street
London EC2A 4PU
United Kingdom

Sage Publications India Pvt. Ltd.
B-42, Panchsheel Enclave
Post Box 4109
New Delhi 110 017 India

Printed in the United States of America

Library of Congress Cataloging-in-Publication Data

Race, ethnicity, and gender: Selected readings / [edited by] Joseph F. Healey, Eileen O'Brien.
    p. cm.
Includes bibliographical references and index.
ISBN 0-7619-8820-3 (pbk.: alk. paper)
    1. Minorities—United States. 2. United States—Race relations.
3. United States—Ethnic relations. 4. Racism—United States.
5. Ethnicity—United States. 6. Minority women—United States.
7. Sex role—United States. I. Healey, Joseph F., 1945– II. O'Brien,
Eileen, 1972–
E184.A1 R277 2004
305.8′00973—dc22

                                    2003016742

This book is printed on acid-free paper.

03   04   05   06   10   9   8   7   6   5   4   3   2   1

Acquisitions Editor:	Jerry Westby
Editorial Assistant:	Vonessa Vondera
Production Editor:	Denise Santoyo
Developmental Editor:	Denise Simon
Copy Editor:	Pam Suwinsky
Typesetter:	C&M Digitals (P) Ltd.
Indexer:	Teri Greenberg
Cover Designer:	Janet Foulger

CONTENTS

PREFACE

Relations between ethnic and racial groups in U.S. society today are fairer and more open than they have ever been before. This may not be saying much, however, given a national history that features slavery, segregation, attempted genocide, racist immigration restrictions, and unrelenting political, economic, legal, and sexual assaults on minority group members. The improvements in group relations during the past several decades are real and should be celebrated: they have opened up opportunities for millions of people and have moved us closer to the ideal of a truly color-blind society. However, we cannot mistake these improvements for final resolutions. As real as the progress has been, many long-standing minority group problems and grievances remain, and they are joined by new issues with great regularity.

Even as we acknowledge the improvements, it is clear that the dominant-minority group issues that remain are complex and difficult to resolve. They range from affirmative action to immigration policy, from discrimination in the criminal justice system to urban poverty and welfare reform, and from racism in the classroom to residential segregation. Furthermore, they affect virtually every aspect of the social system, from the halls of the Supreme Court to the meanest back alleys of our cities and towns. Solutions are not obvious and, indeed, there are no guarantees that the society will be able to address the issues honestly, let alone resolve them successfully. It is certain, however, that we will never succeed in building a truly open multigroup society unless we confront the problems openly and examine them critically.

This book is intended to help students understand and analyze the dominant-minority group issues that permeate our society. It emerges from decades of teaching and interacting with students and a continual monitoring of their responses to information, perspectives, and arguments. While the book presents no final answers or easy solutions, it will help students develop their understanding by presenting crucial background information and a variety of perspectives on the issues.

The book is divided into four parts. Part I introduces basic concepts and perspectives, and Part II presents an overview of the development of dominant-minority relations in the United States. Part III, the bulk of the text, is organized by racial-ethnic group and examines a variety of issues for each group. Part IV presents some of the best contemporary thinking on antiracist strategies for the present and for the future.

The chapters include three sections. The "Narrative Portraits" present the insights and experiences of the victims of racism and racial oppression and are intended to personalize the concepts used in the text and to give them a human face. The "Readings" present the views of a variety of leading scholars and analysts and represent some of the most important thinking and research currently being conducted. The readings were selected not only for their importance but also for their accessibility to students and for their diversity of approach and perspective. Finally, the "Current Debates" section presents opposing views on current issues, including affirmative action, reparations, and immigration policy. These selections are intended to help students develop their own thinking and come to a fuller understanding on these issues.

This reader has a companion textbook, *Diversity and Society* by Joseph F. Healey, also available from Pine Forge Press. The chapters in this reader have been designed to parallel the chapters in the text and to extend its analysis and broaden its perspective. Both books emphasize the diversity of each racial-ethnic group's experience and, especially, the ways in which that experience has been mediated and shaped by gender. In combination or singly, these texts present an analysis that is comprehensive, diverse, cogent, contemporary, and highly accessible to students.

ACKNOWLEDGMENTS

First and most important, we would like to thank our students who, over the years, have helped us identify the approaches, ideas, and readings that would be most helpful for teaching a subject matter that is often complex, misunderstood, and emotionally charged. We thank our colleagues for their support and guidance. We also owe a great debt of gratitude to Lynn Maycroft and Stacy Stratton of Christopher Newport University and Gloria Condoluci, Danielle Lessard, Lindsay Bork, Brittany Buck, and Andrea Born of SUNY-Brockport for their invaluable support.

For permission to reprint from the following, grateful acknowledgment is made to the publishers and copyright holders.

Narrative Portraits

Chapter 1: "Rooster," from *Life on the Color Line,* Gregory Williams. Copyright © 1995 by Gregory Williams. Used by permission of Dutton, a division of Penguin Group (USA) Inc.

From *Kaffir Boy,* Mark Mathabane. Copyright © 1986 by Mark Mathabane. Used with the permission of Scribner, an imprint of Simon & Schuster Adult Publishing Group.

Chapter 2: *Choosing a Dream: Italians in Hell's Kitchen,* Mario Puzo. Reprinted by permission of Donaldio & Olson, Inc. Copyright ©1993 by Mario Puzo.

From *Always Running: La Vida Loca, Gang Days in L.A.* by Luis Rodriguez. (Curbstone Press, 1993). Reprinted with permission of Curbstone Press. Distributed by Consortium.

Chapter 3: *Life as a Slave Girl,* Harriet Jacobs. Reprinted by permission of the publisher from *Incidents in the Life of a Slave Girl Written by Herself* by Harriet A. Jacobs and with an introduction by Jean Fagen Yellin, pp. 27–30, Cambridge, Mass.: Harvard University Press, Copyright © 1987, 2000 by the President and Fellow of Harvard College.

Narrative of the Life and Adventures of Henry Bibb, Henry Bibb. Edited by Osofsky, Gilbert. (1969). *Puttin' on Ole Massa.* New York: Harper and Row, pp. 64–65, 80–81. Reprinted with permission of Marcia Osofsky, Ph.D.

Chapter 4: *Death on the City Pavement,* Richard Wright. From Wright, R. (1988). *12 Million Black Voices* (pp. 105–111). New York: Thunder's Mouth Press.

Readings

"Southern Women, Southern Households," Elizabeth Fox-Genovese. From *Within the Plantation Household: Black and White Women of the Old South* by Elizabeth Fox-Genovese. Copyright © 1988 by the University of North Carolina Press. Used by permission of the publisher.

Chapter 4: *The Meaning of Emancipation According to Black Women,* Angela Davis. From *Women, Race, and Class* by Angela Davis. Copyright © 1981 Angela Davis. Used by permission of Random House, Inc.

Distinguishing Five Models of Affirmative Action, David B. Oppenheimer. Copyright © 1988–1989 by the Regents of the University of California. *Berkeley Women's Law Journal, 4,* 42–61. Reprinted by permission of the University of California, Berkeley.

Chapter 5: *'I Am Not a Racist But…': Mapping White College Students' Racial Ideology in the USA,* Eduardo Bonilla-Silva and Tyrone A. Forman. In *Discourse and Society, 11,* 50–85. Copyright © Sage Publications Ltd., 2000. Reprinted by permission of Sage Publications Ltd.

Race and Criminalization: Black Americans and the Punishment Industry, Angela Y. Davis. Copyright © 1997 by Angela Y. Davis, from *The House That Race Built* by Wahneema Lubiano. Copyright © 1997 by Wahneema Lubiano. Used by permission of Pantheon Books, a division of Random House, Inc.

The Elephant in the Living Room: The Issue of Race in Close Black/White Friendships, Kathleen Odell Korgen. In *From Black to Biracial: Transforming Racial Identity Among Americans* by Kathleen Odell Korgen. Reproduced with permission of Greenwood Publishing Group, Inc., Westport, CT.

Chapter 6: *Trends Among American Indians in the United States,* Russell Thornton. Reprinted with permission from N. Smelser, W. Wilson, and F. Mitchell (Eds.). (2001). *America Becoming: Racial Trends and Their Consequences.* (Vol. 1, pp. 135–169). Washington, DC: National Academies Press. Copyright © 2001 by the National Academy of Sciences, courtesy of the National Academies Press, Washington, DC.

Growing Up Indian, Leonard Peltier. Copyright © 1999 by Leonard Peltier. From *Prison Writings* by Leonard Peltier. Reprinted by permission of St. Martin's Press, LLC.

Angry Women are Building: Issues and Struggles Facing American Women Today, Paula Gunn Allen. From *The Sacred Hoop: Recovering the Feminism in American Indian Tradition.* Copyright © 1986–1992 by Paula Gunn Allen. Reprinted by permission of Beacon Press, Boston, MA.

Chapter 7: *Mock Spanish: A Site for the Indexical Reproduction of Racism in American English,* Jane H. Hill. Reprinted by permission of Jane Hill.

Seeing More Black Than White: Latinos, Racism, and the Cultural Divides, Elizabeth Martinez. Reprinted by permission of Elizabeth Martinez.

Chapter 8: Hurh, Won Moo and Kim, Kwang Chung. (1989). The "Success" Image of Asian Americans: Its Validity, and Its Practical and Theoretical Implications, *Ethnic and Racial Studies, 12*(4), 512–538. Reprinted by permission of Taylor & Francis Ltd. www.tandf.co.uk/journals/routledge/01419870.html

The Interrelationship Between Anti-Asian Violence and Asian America, Victor Hwang. Originally published 21 *Chicano Latino Law Review* 12 (2000).

Chapter 9: *How Jews Became White,* Karen Brodkin. From *How Jews Became White Folks and What That Says About Race in America* (pp. 25–52) by Karen Brodkin.

Current Debates

African American Culture Was Created by an Interplay of Elements From Africa and America, John Blassingame. From Blassingame, John W. (1972, 1979). *The Slave Community: Plantation Life in the Antebellum South.* New York: Oxford University Press, pp. 20, 21, 47, 48.

The Experiences of Female Slaves Has Been Under-Researched and Under-Reported, Deborah Gray White. From White, Deborah Gray. (1985). *Aren't I a Woman? Female Slaves in the Plantation South.* New York: Norton, pp. 17–18, 21–25. Copyright © 1985 by Deborah Gray White.

Chapter 4: *Affirmative Action Casts Suspicions on Legitimate Black Achievement and Depicts African Americans as Incapable,* Thomas Sowell. Reprinted by permission of Forbes Magazine. Copyright © 2003 Forbes Inc.

Why We Still Need Affirmative Action, Orlando Patterson. From *Ordeal of Integration* by Patterson, Orlando. Copyright © 1997 by Perseus Books Group. Reproduced with permission of Perseus Books Group in the format Textbook via Copyright Clearance Center.

Kahlenberg, Richard. (1996). Affirmative Action Should Be Based on Class Rather Than Race. In *The Remedy: Class, Race, and Affirmative Action* (pp. 83–86). New York: Basic Books. Copyright © 1996 by Richard Kahlenberg. Reprinted by permission of Basic Books, a division of HarperCollins Publishers, Inc.

Chapter 5: *Reparations for African Americans in Historical Context,* Joe R. Feagin and Eileen O'Brien. From *When Sorry Isn't Enough: The Controversy Over Apologies and Reparations for Human Injustice* by Roy L. Brooks. Reproduced by permission of New York University Press.

Reparations Are an Idea Whose Time Has Come, Manning Marable. From *Newsweek,* August 27 2001. Copyright © 2001 *Newsweek,* Inc. All rights reserved. Reprinted by permission.

Why I Don't Want Reparations for Slavery. From McWhorter, John. (2001). "Blood Money: An Analysis of Slavery Reparations," *The American Enterprise,* 12:5, p. 18. Reprinted with permission.

Chapter 6: *Columbus Day Should Be Celebrated,* Christopher Hitchens. Reprinted with permission from the October 19, 1992 issue of *The Nation.* For subscription information, call 1-800-333-8536. Portions of each week's *Nation* magazine can be accessed at www.thenation.com

Why Columbus Day Celebrations and Parades Should Be Opposed, Glenn Morris and Russell Means. www.dickshovel.com/colum.html Russell Means and Glenn Morris wrote this position statement in 1991 on behalf of the American Indian Movement of Colorado, 1574 South Pennsylvania St., Denver, CO. Reprinted with permission.

Momaday, N. Scott. (1999). The Value of Native American Culture and Indian Identity. In P. Nabakov (Ed.)., *Native American Testimony* (Rev. Ed., pp. 437–440).

Chapter 7: *Immigration Is Harmful,* Peter Brimelow. From *Alien Nation* by Peter Brimelow, Copyright © 1995 by Peter Brimelow, Maps and Illustrations Copyright © 1995 by John Grimwade. Used by permission of Random House, Inc.

Immigration Is Not Harmful, Reynolds Farley. From Reynolds, F. (1996). *The New American Reality* (pp. 199–207). New York: Russell Sage. Copyright © 1997 Russell Sage Foundation, New York, New York.

We Need to Reframe the Immigration Debate, George Borjas. From Borjas, G. (1999). *Heaven's Door: Immigration Policy and the American Policy* (pp. 4, 15–16).

Part I

An Introduction to the Study of Minority Groups in the United States

1

Diversity in the United States

Questions and Concepts

This chapter introduces several concepts crucial to the study of dominant-minority relations in the United States. The selections emphasize prejudice and racism but also call attention to the widely misunderstood concept of race.

The topic of race is addressed in two places. First, the Narrative Portrait by Gregory Williams recounts a young boy's reaction to a startling revelation: At the age of ten, he learns that he is black, not white, and this new identity changes his social world completely and forever. His story illustrates the point that race is fundamentally a *social construct:* a way of thinking about ourselves and others that is socially determined and a reflection of our experiences in a highly race-conscious society. Race is important because we are trained to think it's important, not because of some essential quality inherent in the concept.

The biological and social realities of race are further explored in the Current Debate. Why do African American (and African) athletes dominate in so many sports? Jon Entine's answer to this question assumes that race is a meaningful biological reality and that the dominance of African American athletes is, in some sense, "natural." Jonathan Marks, on the other hand, questions not only Entine's logic and assumptions but the reality of the concept of race itself.

The concepts of prejudice and racism are addressed from a number of perspectives. The Narrative Portrait by Mark Mathabane recounts an incident from his childhood in South Africa during the days of Apartheid. In this memoir, we see how prejudice and racism (and the "knowledge" that race is a biological reality) are carefully taught in highly race-conscious societies and how prejudicial thinking can be reinforced even by people who believe they are trying to combat it. The reading by Yetman distinguishes among prejudice, discrimination, and racism—concepts that are at the core of the sociological analysis of dominant-minority relations. Researchers Van Ausdale and Feagin explore how these concepts are used by young children in their interactions with each other. Again, we see the realities and results of race-conscious thinking and careful training in prejudice.

In the final reading, Rosenblum and Travis shift our attention to the dynamics of privilege and stigma. People who view the world from a more privileged status (for example, males versus females, whites versus blacks) tend to see their own views and experiences as "normal," the standard against which the experiences and views of others can be measured. Thus, the perceptions implicit in prejudice and racism (and sexism) interlock with the power relationships that separate the privileged from the stigmatized.

NARRATIVE PORTRAITS

THE SOCIAL CONSTRUCTION OF RACIAL IDENTITY

Race is both a biological and a social concept. Biologically, race is linked to a set of physical and anatomical traits (skin color, hair shape, and so forth), but socially it is a matter of perception and convention.

Today, extensive and long-term scientific investigation has resulted in the nearly unanimous conclusion that, biologically, race is a triviality. Racial typologies (black, white, yellow, and so on) are hopelessly arbitrary, and even the most ambitious attempts have failed to find unambiguous dividing lines between the so-called races. The biological concept of race has been largely abandoned as a serious concern.

On the other hand, race continues to be a matter of great importance in everyday social life. Its significance, however, derives from perception and social convention, not from biology or anatomy. Race is a social construction: a matter of importance only because of our perceptions of it, not because of its independent reality. The way in which we identify ourselves and others racially is subjective and negotiable, not fixed and permanent. Racial identity is a part of the self-image that is constructed during socialization, not a simple or direct function of one's genetic heritage.

The social nature of race is illustrated in the following excerpt from *Life on the Color Line* (1995). The author of this memoir, Gregory Williams (known then as Billy), grew up in the white community of Virginia in the 1940s and 1950s, a time when the South was highly race conscious and almost completely segregated. The separate, unequal position of African Americans was mandated by law. At the age of ten, in the midst of a bitter divorce between his parents, Billy learns that his father is "half-colored." In accordance with common American perceptions of race, this makes Billy "colored." The dichotomous perception of race in the United States has been described as the "one-drop rule": Any nonwhite ancestry disqualifies a person from the Caucasian race.

In the following passage, Billy, his brother Mike, and his father are traveling by bus to Muncie, Indiana, when his father breaks the news about the divorce and his race. The boys resist their new racial identity, but Billy gradually begins to sort out the implications of his transformed status in society. Note that what changes are Billy's perceptions of himself and his father, not his biology or his genes.

LIFE ON THE COLOR LINE

Gregory Williams

He leaned closer and spoke very softly. "There's something else I want to tell you."

"What?" I groaned.

"Remember Miss Sallie who used to work for us in the tavern?"

Dad's lower lip quivered. He looked ill. Had he always looked this unhealthy, I wondered, or was it something that happened on the trip? I felt my face, skin like putty, lips chapped and cracked. Had I changed, too?

"It's hard to tell you boys this." He paused and then slowly added, "But she's really my momma. That means she's your grandmother."

"But that can't be, Dad! She's colored!" I whispered, lest I be overheard by the other white passengers on the bus.

"That's right, Billy," he continued. "She's colored. That makes you part colored, too, and in Muncie you're going to live with my Aunt Bess."

I didn't understand Dad. I knew I wasn't colored, and neither was he. All of us are white, I said to myself. But for the first time, I had to admit that Dad didn't exactly look white. His deeply tanned skin puzzled me as I sat there trying to classify my own father. Goose bumps covered my arms as I realized that whatever he was, I was. I took a deep breath. I couldn't make any mistakes. I looked closer. His heavy lips and dark brown eyes didn't make him colored, I concluded. His black, wavy hair was different from Negroes' hair, but it was different from most white folks' hair, too. He was darker than most whites, but Mom said he was Italian. That was why my baby brother has such dark skin and curly hair. Mom told us to be proud of our Italian heritage! That's it, I decided. He was Italian. I leaned back against the seat, satisfied. Yet the unsettling image of Miss Sallie flashed before me like a neon sign.

Colored! Colored! Colored!

He continued, "Life is going to be different from now on. In Virginia you were white boys. In Indiana you're going to be colored boys. I want you to remember that you're the same today as you were yesterday. But people in Indiana will treat you differently."

I refused to believe Dad. I looked at Mike. His skin, like mine was light, almost pallid, white. He had Dad's deep brown eyes, too, but our hair was straight. Leaning towards Dad, I examined his hands for a sign, a black mark. There was nothing. I knew I was right, but I sensed something was wrong. Fear overcame me as I faced the Ohio countryside and pondered the discovery of my life.

"I don't wanta be colored," Mike whined, "I don't wanta be colored. We can't go swimmin' or skatin'," he said louder. Nearby passengers turned towards us.

"Shut up, Mike." I punched him in the chest. He hit me in the nose. I lunged for him. We tumbled in the aisle. My knee banged against a sharp aluminum edge. The fatigues ripped. I squeezed his neck. His eyes bulged. I squeezed harder. *Whap!* Pain surged from the back of my head. Dad grabbed my shirt collar and shoved me roughly into my seat. Mike clambered in beside me, still sniffling.

"Daddy, we ain't really colored, are we?" Mike asked quietly.

No! I answered, still refusing to believe. I'm not colored, I'm white! I look white! I've always been white! I go to the "whites only" schools, "whites only" movie theaters, and "whites only" swimming pools. I had never heard anything crazier in my life! How could Dad tell such a mean lie? I glanced across the aisle to where he sat grim-faced and erect, staring straight ahead. I saw my father as I never had seen him before. The veil dropped from his face and features. Before my eyes he was transformed from a swarthy Italian to his true self—a high-yellow mulatto. My father was a Negro! We were colored! After ten years in Virginia on the white side of the color line, I knew what that meant.

SOURCE: Williams, Gregory. (1995). *Life on the Color Line* (pp. 32–34). New York: Dutton.

The Cultural Sources of Prejudice

Kaffir Boy*, Mark Mathabane's best-selling memoir of growing up in racist South Africa, provides abundant illustrations of the importance of culture and conformity in developing individual prejudice. Prior to recent social and political reforms, South Africa was the most rigidly race conscious and segregated society on Earth. Black South Africans were kept economically and politically powerless and were used as a source of cheap labor for the benefit of white South Africans. White South Africans of even modest economic means were able to afford domestic help (cooks, gardeners, maids, and such) or other amenities because of this system of exploitation and discrimination.

This elaborate system of racial privilege was stabilized in part by a strong, government-sanctioned ideology of antiblack prejudice and racism. Black and white South Africans had little contact with each other except in situations in which the black person was clearly subordinate. What "knowledge" the white community had of blacks came from constrained,

---

* In South Africa, *Kaffir* is a derogatory term for blacks, roughly equivalent to *nigger*.

lopsided interactions or from the racist content of their culture. For example, the idea that blacks are inferior was taught in school as part of the official curriculum.

In the following passage, Mathabane recalls a day when he went to work with his grand-mother, a gardener for an affluent white family named Smith. Clyde Smith was roughly the same age as Mark and clearly demonstrates the results of being socialized in a culture in which racism is both "normal" and government supported. Note that Mrs. Smith challenges her son's attitudes with antiracist values and beliefs—even blatantly racist cultures are not monolithic in their commitment to bias. How does she also reinforce racial inequality in her actions and words?

KAFFIR BOY

Mark Mathabane

"This is Mrs. Smith's house," Granny remarked as she led me up a long driveway of a beautiful villa-type house. . . . We went to a steel gate at the back of the yard, where Granny rang a bell.

"I'm here, madam," she shouted through the gate. . . . A door creaked open, and a high-pitched woman's voice called out, "I'm coming, Ellen." . . . Presently the gate clicked open, and there appeared a short, slender white woman. . . . "I'm just getting ready to leave for tennis," she said to Granny.

"Madam, guess who I have with me today," Granny said with the widest smile. . . .

"My, what a big lad he is! . . . Is he really your grandson, Ellen?" The warmth in her voice somehow reduced my fears of her; her eyes shone with the same gentleness of the Catholic Sisters at the clinic.

"Yes, madam," Granny said proudly; "this is the one I've been telling you about. This is the one who'll some day go to university." . . .

"I believe you, Ellen," said Mrs. Smith. "He looks like a very smart pickaninny." . . .

Toward early afternoon Mrs. Smith returned. She called me to the car to remove several shopping bags from the backseat. . . . As we were talking, a busload of white schoolchildren stopped in front of the house and a young boy [Mrs. Smith's son, Clyde] alighted and ran up the driveway. . . . "Who is he, Mother?"

"That's Ellen's grandson. . . . Now run along inside and change and . . . then maybe you can play with pickaninny."

"I don't play with Kaffirs," the white boy declared. "At school they say we shouldn't."

"Watch your filthy mouth, Clyde," Mrs. Smith said, flushing crimson. "I thought I told you a million times to leave all that rubbish about Kaffirs in the classroom." . . .

Turning to Granny, . . . Mrs. Smith said, in a voice of someone fighting a losing battle, "You know, Ellen, I simply don't understand why those damn uncivilized Boers from Pretoria teach children such things."

"I agree, madam," Granny said, "All children, black and white, are God's children." . . .

"I'm afraid you're right, Ellen," Mrs. Smith said, somewhat touched. . . .

Shortly, Clyde emerged. . . . He called to me. "Come here, pickaninny. My mother says I should show you around."

I went.

I followed him around as he showed me the things his parents regularly bought him. . . . I couldn't understand why his people had to have all the luxuries money could buy, while my people lived in abject poverty. . . . We finally came to Clyde's playroom. The room was roughly the size of our house, and was elaborately decorated. . . . What arrested my attention were the stacks of comic books on the floor and the shelves and shelves of books. Never had I seen so many books. . . .

Sensing that I was in awe of his magnificent library, Clyde said, "Do you have this many books in your playroom?"

"I don't have a playroom."

"You don't have a playroom," he said bug-eyed. "Can you read? . . . My teachers tell us that Kaffirs can't read, speak or write English like white people because they have smaller brains, which are already full of tribal things. My teachers say you're not people like us, because you belong to a jungle civilization. That's why you can't live or go to school with us, but can only be our servants."

"Stop saying that rubbish," Mrs. Smith said angrily as she entered the room. . . . "How many times have I told you that what your teachers say about black people is not true?"

"What do you know, Mama?" Clyde retorted impudently, "you're not a teacher. Besides, there are textbooks where it's so written."

SOURCE: Mathabane, Mark. (1986). *Kaffir Boy* (pp. 187–192). New York: New American Library.

READINGS

In this section, we examine the development and application of many key concepts related to the understanding of diversity in the United States. The first reading, "Prejudice, Discrimination, and Racism," examines in depth three concepts that are often confused and used interchangeably in everyday language, yet have very distinct and specific meanings in the sociological study of majority–minority group relations. The author, Norman Yetman, begins by introducing sociologist Robert K. Merton's typology of *prejudice* and *discrimination*, which illustrates how prejudice and discrimination are not the same thing. Although discrimination is often motivated by prejudice, it does not have to be, as it can sometimes be a result of social pressure and conformity. Likewise, prejudice does not always have to result in discrimination, for similar social reasons. This discussion reminds us that prejudice and discrimination are not simply psychological in nature. Thus, simply "educating" folks to be "more open-minded" as a strategy of prejudice reduction is hardly enough to eliminate inequality, although many well-meaning Americans seem to think so. Driving home this point further, the author then develops a definition of *racism* that has both ideological and behavioral components, stressing the necessity of holding societal power in order for racism, by definition, to occur. Yetman's essay concludes by exploring the differences between *attitudinal discrimination* and *institutional discrimination*, providing many examples of each. Incidents with high media exposure, such as the beating of Rodney King and the refusal to serve black customers at places like Denny's and Shoney's, serve as examples of attitudinal discrimination. However, institutional discrimination refers to policies and practices that are not nearly as obvious in their intent. Examples such as jury selection from only registered voters, referral of employees by word of mouth, and different penalties for crack and powder cocaine users alert us to how covert and far-reaching the dynamics of prejudice, discrimination, and racism are in the United States.

The second selection, "Using Racial and Ethnic Concepts: The Critical Case of Very Young Children," takes us into a research setting where the concepts of prejudice, discrimination, and racism are put into practice by some of the most seemingly innocent citizens of the United States—preschool-aged children. Using the method of participant observation, authors Debra Van Ausdale and Joe R. Feagin investigate how young children negotiate racial and ethnic boundaries on their own terms with each other, rather than in response to any preformulated questions by adults. This essay presents numerous firsthand examples of how children use racial and ethnic concepts to include each other as well as to control each other, and also to demarcate their own and others' identities. Far from innocently parroting words they might have overheard from adults, these children are quite savvy at putting racial and ethnic dividing lines into practice. Also interesting are the adult reactions to children's racial transgressions, since the adults are quick to deny that the children learned it from them. Thus, society at large has already given them clear messages about who the in-groups and out-groups are in their communities, and they have learned these lessons well enough to begin putting them into practice, even at such young ages.

After focusing mainly on the dynamics of exclusion of racial and ethnic minorities, the third reading turns our attention not only to those who are excluded, but also to those who are included and thus advantaged by that inclusion—those who have majority group *privilege*. In their essay, "Experiencing Difference," authors Karen Rosenblum and Toni-Michelle Travis explore racial identity as well as gender, social class, and sexual orientation as both privileged and stigmatized statuses, thus broadening our understanding of how these concepts can be applied to other minority and majority groups in the United States. Using sociologist Erving Goffman's concept of *stigma*, the authors point out how we are usually more aware of the stigmatized statuses we hold than we are of being privileged. We tend not to notice privileged experiences by seeing them as the norm or the standard, as in the example of "doctor" versus "woman doctor" given in the reading. This means privileged individuals often engage in *rereading* or *looping*—that is, they tend to dismiss accounts given by stigmatized persons about the discrimination they face, seeing them as hypersensitive or overreacting. We can find this occurring often in today's society when whites describe African Americans as "complaining too much" about racism, or when men patronizingly tell women to just "calm down" if women point out the mistreatment and inequality that they face. Seeing their own experiences as the norm leads the privileged to discount the reality of discrimination. This discussion points us to the "we-ness" of minority groups, since they share an awareness of the stigma that they face as a collective. Another dimension of minority group status is typically visibility, yet the authors problematize this as a uniform criterion, because although stigma can be visible (*discredited/flaming*), it can alternatively be invisible (*discreditable*) as the stigmatized can be *passing* as a member of the majority group in order to attain some of the privileges associated with that status. After exploring these multiple dimensions of majority–minority group dynamics in the United States, the authors conclude by returning to a "point of contention" also made in the first reading—that the relative *power* of these different groups in society is a crucial distinguishing factor in analyzing the impact of prejudice and discrimination.

PREJUDICE, DISCRIMINATION, AND RACISM

Norman Yetman

Prejudice and discrimination are important elements in all majority-minority relations. The term *prejudice* derives from two Latin words, *prae* "before" and *judicum* "a judgment." It denotes a judgment before all the facts are known. According to Gordon Allport, *prejudice* is "an avertive or hostile attitude toward a person who belongs to a group, simply because he [or she] belongs to that group, and is therefore presumed to have the objectionable qualities ascribed to the group" (Allport 1958:8). Prejudice thus refers to a set of rigidly held negative attitudes, beliefs, and feelings toward members of another group.

Prejudice often involves an intense emotional component. Thus, many white Americans consciously and rationally reject the myths of African American inferiority but react emotionally with fear, hostility, or condescension in the presence of African Americans. The forms of prejudice range from unconscious aversion to members of the out-group to a comprehensive, well-articulated, and coherent ideology, such as the ideology of racism.

Discrimination, on the other hand, involves unfavorable treatment of individuals because of their group membership. Prejudice and discrimination should not be equated. Prejudice involves attitudes and internal states, whereas discrimination involves overt action or behavior. Discrimination may be manifested in a multitude of ways: mild slights (such as Polish jokes); verbal threats, abuse, and epithets; intimidation and harassment (such as threatening phone calls); defacing property with ethnic slurs, graffiti, or symbols; unequal treatment (such as refusing to hire or promote qualified applicants); systematic oppression (such as slavery); or outright violence (vandalism, arson, terrorism, lynching, pogroms, massacres).

. . . Attitude surveys conducted in the United States since the 1940s have shown a significant decline in antiblack prejudice; increasingly, white Americans have come to support broad principles of racial integration and equal treatment in public accommodations, employment, public transportation, schools, housing, and marriage. For example, in 1942, 32 percent of whites agreed that whites and blacks should attend the same schools; by 1982, this figure was 90 percent. When asked in 1958 whether they would object to sending their children to schools in which half the children were black, nearly half (47 percent) responded affirmatively; by 1997, this figure had declined to 12 percent. In 1944, 45 percent thought that blacks should have as good a chance as whites to get any kind of job; and by 1972, 97 percent agreed. The percentage approving integration in public transportation rose from 46 percent in 1942 to 88 percent in 1970. Moreover, whites have indicated increasing willingness to participate personally in desegregated settings. In 1958, four-fifths of whites said they would move if blacks moved into their neighborhood "in great numbers"; in 1997, those indicating they would move declined to 12 percent. Finally, whereas only 4 percent of whites said they approved of interracial marriages in 1958, more than three-fifths (61 percent) expressed their approval in 1997 (Schuman, Steeh, and Bobo 1985; Hochschild 1995; Gallup Poll Social Audit 1997). These changes are a result of two factors. First, they reflect attitude changes among individuals over their lifetimes. Second, younger people generally exhibit less racial prejudice than their elders, and as younger, more tolerant cohorts have replaced older, more prejudiced ones, overall racial prejudice has declined (Firebaugh and Davis 1988).

However, among white Americans, the same striking agreement on how to combat discrimination or segregation does not appear. Although today white Americans endorse broad principles of nondiscrimination and desegregation in important areas of American life, they are much less likely to support policies for translating these principles into practice. For example, despite the strong support among white Americans for the principle of integrated education, the percentage of whites who felt that the federal government should ensure that black and white children attend the same schools declined between the 1960s and 1980s. Moreover, widespread white opposition was raised to busing as a means of desegregating schools (Schuman, Steeh, and Bobo 1985).

The substantial gap between white people's support for broad principles of equality and their support for specific programs to implement these principles indicates the complexity of racial attitudes. The relationship between prejudicial attitudes and discriminatory behavior is equally complex. Prejudice does not always produce discrimination, although it has frequently been treated as the cause of discrimination. An individual, however, may be prejudiced without *acting* in a discriminatory manner. In recent years it has become less fashionable to express racial prejudice publicly. Overt forms of discrimination, such as exclusion from public accommodations, jobs, and colleges and universities—behaviors that in the past were tolerated by most whites—are now often prohibited by law and condemned by public opinion.

The distinction between prejudice and discrimination and the interrelationship between these two phenomena were first systematically developed by Robert Merton (1949) in his classic article, "Discrimination and the American Creed." "Prejudicial attitudes," Merton argued, "need not coincide with discriminatory behavior." Merton demonstrated the range of possible ways in which prejudice and discrimination interact by distinguishing among four types of individuals:

1. The unprejudiced nondiscriminator—the all-weather liberal

2. The unprejudiced discriminator—the fair-weather liberal

3. The prejudiced nondiscriminator—the fair-weather bigot

4. The prejudiced discriminator—the all-weather bigot

The unprejudiced nondiscriminator consistently adheres to the American creed of equality for all in both belief and practice. The unprejudiced discriminator, on the other hand, internalizes and may even articulate the ideals of the American creed but may acquiesce to group pressures to discriminate. Similarly, the prejudiced nondiscriminator conforms to social pressures not to discriminate despite harboring prejudices toward ethnic minorities. Finally, the prejudiced discriminator is, like the unprejudiced nondiscriminator, consistent in belief and practice, rejecting the American creed and engaging in personal discrimination.

Merton's discussion was critical to the recognition that whether prejudice becomes translated into discriminatory behavior depends on the social context. From this perspective it becomes impossible to understand the dynamics of majority-minority relations by examining prejudice alone; prejudice is most appropriately considered not as a causal factor but as a dependent variable. As Richard Schermerhorn has cogently suggested, prejudice "is a product of situations, historical situations, economic situations, political situations; it is not a little demon that emerges in people because they are depraved" (Schermerhorn 1970:6).

Thus, discrimination is much more likely to occur in a social setting in which acts of ethnic and racial bias are accepted or are not strongly condemned. This principle was underscored in a study undertaken at Smith College, where in 1989 racial tensions erupted after four black students received anonymous hate messages. Researchers asked students how they felt about these incidents. Before a student could answer, a confederate, arriving at the same time, would respond by strongly condemning or strongly justifying the incidents. The researchers found that the students' opinions were strongly influenced by the opinions they heard expressed by the confederates. Hearing others express strongly antiracist opinions produced similar sentiments, whereas students who first heard

expressions more accepting of racism offered "significantly less strongly antiracist opinions" (Blanchard, Lilly, and Vaughn 1991:105). Clearly, the social climate affects whether personal prejudices are translated into discriminatory acts; to explain the dynamics of ethnic and racial relations fully, it is necessary to analyze the historical, cultural, and institutional conditions that have preceded and generated them.

During the past quarter century, the conceptualization of American race relations has undergone several significant changes. These changes have been profoundly influenced by the changing nature of race relations in the United States. Before the advent of the Black Protest Movement during the 1950s, social scientists focused their attention primarily on racial attitudes, because prejudice was thought to be the key to understanding racial and ethnic conflict. This perception of the essential dynamics of race relations is perhaps best illustrated in Myrdal's classic *An American Dilemma,* in which he defined race prejudice as "the whole complex of valuations and beliefs which are behind discriminatory behavior on the part of the majority group . . . and which are contrary to the egalitarian ideals in the American Creed" (Myrdal 1944:52). This model of race relations was predicated on the assumption that racial conflict in the United States was a problem of ignorance and morality that could best be solved by changing—through education and moral suasion—the majority's prejudicial attitudes toward racial minorities. "A great majority of white people in America," Myrdal wrote, "would be better prepared to give the Negro a substantially better deal if they knew the facts" (Myrdal 1944:48).

The black protest era of the 1950s and 1960s challenged the assumption that change in the patterns of racial inequality in American society could be brought about through a reduction in prejudicial attitudes alone. Sociologists and social activists focused increasingly on the dynamics of discrimination and sought means of eliminating discriminatory behavior. The numerous forms of direct protest, such as nonviolent sit-ins, boycotts, and voter registration drives, were tactics designed to alter patterns of discrimination. In keeping with this emphasis on discrimination were the legislative efforts undertaken to secure enactment of the Civil Rights Act of 1964, which outlawed discrimination in public accommodations and employment, and the 1965 Voting Rights Act, which provided federal support to ensure that African Americans had the right to vote throughout the South.

However, the greatest racial unrest of the black protest era occurred after these legislative victories had been achieved. Whereas the earlier civil rights phase of the Black Protest Movement had been directed primarily against public discrimination and especially its manifestations in the South, the outbreak of urban riots in northern cities focused attention on the nature of racial inequalities affecting African Americans throughout the entire nation. For several summers during the late 1960s, the nation was torn with racial strife. Parts of cities were burned, property damage ran into the millions of dollars, and the toll of dead—primarily, although not exclusively, blacks—numbered almost a hundred (National Advisory Commission on Civil Disorders 1968:116). In July 1967 President Lyndon Johnson appointed a national commission (the Kerner Commission) to investigate the causes of these urban riots. In 1968 the commission issued its report, which concluded the following:

> What white Americans have never fully understood—but what the Negro can never forget—is that white society is deeply implicated in the ghetto. White society condones it. . . . Race prejudice has shaped our history decisively in the past; it now threatens to do so again. White racism is essentially responsible for the explosive mixture which has been accumulating in our cities since the end of World War II. (National Advisory Commission on Civil Disorders 1968:203)

Racism

Especially because the Kerner Commission concluded that the ultimate responsibility for the racial disorders of the 1960s should be attributed to "white racism," the term has been widely invoked to explain racial inequalities and conflict in American society. However, the term is extremely imprecise and ambiguous.

This imprecision enabled President Johnson, who had created the Kerner Commission, to ignore its findings, and his successor, Richard Nixon, to condemn and deny them. Consequently, the term *racism* is in urgent need of clarification.

First, *racism* is a general term, subsuming several analytically distinct phenomena— prejudice and several forms of discrimination. Stokely Carmichael and Charles Hamilton distinguished between individual racism and institutional racism:

> Racism is both overt and covert. It takes two closely related forms: individual whites acting against individual blacks and acts by the total white community against the black community. . . . The second type is less overt, far more subtle, less identifiable in terms of specific individuals committing the acts. But it is no less destructive of human life. . . . When white terrorists bomb a black church and kill five black children, that is an act of individual racism, widely deplored by most segments of the society. But when in that same city, Birmingham, Alabama—five hundred black babies die each year because of the lack of proper food, shelter, and medical facilities, and thousands more are destroyed and maimed physically, emotionally, and intellectually because of the conditions of poverty and discrimination in the black community, that is a function of institutional racism. (Carmichael and Hamilton 1967:41)

However, as I will note more fully later, prejudicial attitudes are causal factors in Carmichael and Hamilton's conceptualization of institutional racism. Moreover, they do not distinguish between psychological and sociological factors in its operation.

Another problem in the use of the word *racism* is that although it lumps together all forms of racial oppression, it is not sufficiently inclusive. It does not encompass majority-minority situations based on criteria other than race—criteria such as religion, tribal identity, ethnicity, or gender. Therefore, in the following discussion, I have analytically distinguished the terms *racism, prejudice,* and *discrimination.*

The term *racism* has traditionally referred to an *ideology*—a set of ideas and beliefs—used to explain, rationalize, or justify a racially organized social order. There are two essential parts of racism: its content and its function. Racism is distinguished from ethnocentrism by insistence that differences among groups are biologically based. The in-group is believed to be innately superior to the out-group, and members of the out-group are defined as being "biogenetically incapable of ever achieving intellectual and moral equality with members of the ingroup" (Noel 1972:157). Howard Schuman has offered a commonly accepted definition of racism:

> The term racism is generally taken to refer to the belief that there are clearly distinguishable human races, that these races differ not only in superficial physical characteristics, but also innately in important psychological traits, and finally that the differences are such that one race (almost always one's own, naturally) can be said to be superior to another. (Schuman 1969:44)

Racism's primary function has been to provide a rationale and ideological support—a moral justification—for maintaining a racially based social order. In other words, the assertion of the innate "natural" superiority or inferiority of different racial groups serves to justify domination and exploitation of one group by another. As Manning Nash has written, "no group of [people] is able systematically to subordinate or deprive another group of [people] without appeal to a body of values which makes the exploitation, the disprivilege, the expropriation, and the denigration of human beings a 'moral' act" (Nash 1962:288). In addition, not only does an ideology of racism provide a moral justification for the dominant group of their positions of privilege and power, but it also discourages minority groups from questioning their subordinate status and advancing claims for equal treatment.

. . . As noted before, there has been a substantial decline in professions of racist attitudes among white Americans in the past half century; especially since 1970, white Americans have increased their approval of racial integration (Schuman, Steeh, and Bobo 1985; Gallup Poll Social Audit 1997). In 1942 only 42 percent of a national sample of whites reported that they believed blacks to be equal to whites in innate intelligence; since the late 1950s, however, around 80 percent of white Americans have rejected the idea of inherent black inferiority. The Kerner Commission was therefore misleading in lumping all white antipathy toward blacks into the category of racism.

Rather than believing that African Americans are genetically inferior, whites often employ a *meritocratic ideology* to explain the substantial gap that continues to separate black and white income, wealth, and educational attainment. The basic element in a meritocratic ideology is the assumption of equality of opportunity—that all people in the United States have equal chances to achieve success, and that inequalities in the distribution of income, wealth, power, and prestige reflect the qualifications or merit of individuals in each rank in society. In other words, in a meritocratic society, all people are perceived to have an equal opportunity to succeed or fail—to go as far as their talents will take them—and the system of social ranking that develops is simply a "natural" reflection of each person's abilities or merit. Affluence is perceived as the result of the personal qualities of intelligence, industriousness, motivation, and ambition, while the primary responsibility for poverty rests with the poor themselves. Therefore, in this aristocracy of talent, those in the upper strata deserve the power, prestige, and privileges that they enjoy, while those lower in the social ranking system are placed according to their ability. Such a belief system is not inherently racist, but rather is a general judgment about human nature that can be applied to all sorts of human conditions or groups. However, it can have racist effects when it is used to explain racial inequalities in the United States without recognizing or acknowledging the external disabilities (such as prejudice and discrimination) that racial minorities experience. Thus, by this definition, African Americans are still considered inferior people; otherwise, they would be as well-off as whites. (See Hochschild 1995 for an excellent discussion of the conflicting perceptions of whites and blacks regarding opportunity in American society.)

If the term *racism* referred merely to the realm of beliefs and ideology and not to behavior or action, its relevance for the study of race relations would be limited. To restrict the meaning of racism to ideology would be to ignore the external constraints and societally imposed disabilities—rooted in the power of the majority group—confronting a racial minority. If one group does not possess the power to impose its belief system on another, ethnic stratification cannot occur (Noel 1968). During the late 1960s and 1970s, when critics charged that the ideology of Black Power was "racism in reverse," African American spokespersons responded that their critics failed to consider the components of differential power that enabled the ideology of white supremacy to result in white domination:

> There is no analogy—by any stretch of definition or imagination—between the advocates of Black Power and white racists. Racism is not merely exclusion on the basis of race but exclusion for the purpose of subjugating or maintaining subjugation. The goal of the racists is to keep black people on the bottom, arbitrarily and dictatorially, as they have done in this country for over three hundred years. (Carmichael and Hamilton 1967:47)

Recently Feagin and Vera (1995) have taken a similar stance against the contention that "black racism" is equally as critical an issue as white racism. They contend that "black racism does not exist" because

> Racism is more than a matter of individual prejudice and scattered episodes of discrimination. There is no black racism because there is no centuries-old system of racialized subordination and discrimination designed by African Americans to exclude white Americans from full participation in the rights, privileges and benefits of this society. Black (or other minority) racism would require not only a widely accepted racist ideology directed at whites but also the power to systematically exclude whites from opportunities and rewards in major economic, cultural, and political institutions. (Feagin and Vera 1995:ix-x)

Therefore, the crucial component of a definition of racism is behavioral. Racism in its most inclusive sense refers to actions on the part of a racial majority that have discriminatory effects, preventing members of a minority group from securing access to prestige, power, and privilege. These actions may be intentional or unintentional. This broader conception of racism therefore entails discrimination as well as an ideology that proclaims the superiority of one racial grouping over another.

As noted earlier, *discrimination* refers to the differential treatment of members of a minority group. Discrimination in its several forms comprises the means by which the unequal status of the minority group and the power of the majority group are preserved. In the ensuing discussion, I distinguish between *attitudinal* discrimination, which refers to discriminatory practices attributable to or influenced by prejudice, and *institutional* discrimination, which cannot be attributed to prejudice, but instead is a consequence of society's normal functioning. Both of these types can be further elaborated according to the sources of the discriminatory behavior. In reality, these types are at times interrelated and reinforce each other. Seldom is discrimination against a minority group member derived from one source alone.

ATTITUDINAL DISCRIMINATION

Attitudinal discrimination refers to discriminatory practices that stem from prejudicial attitudes. The discriminator either is prejudiced or acts in response to the prejudices of others. Attitudinal discrimination is usually direct, overt, visible, and dramatic. Despite increasing white acceptance of principles of nondiscrimination and racial segregation, ethnic minorities, especially African Americans, continue to be confronted with incidents of attitudinal discrimination. . . . [Joe] Feagin distinguished five categories of . . . discrimination: avoidance, rejection, verbal attacks, physical threats and harassment, and physical attacks. Despite increasing verbal acceptance by whites of the principles of nondiscrimination and racial integration, African Americans have been confronted with attitudinal discrimination in almost every public aspect of their lives. Many of these discriminatory acts appear trivial, insignificant, and unimportant to white observers: a white couple's crossing the street to avoid walking past a black male, a "hate stare," receiving poor service at restaurants, stores, and hotels. Many whites also trivialize discrimination that takes the form of racial and ethnic slurs and epithets. Incidents of this kind are seldom reported in the press, yet they are demeaning realities to which minorities of all social classes are consistently exposed.

Much more dramatic incidents of discrimination are reported almost daily in the news media. For example, the brutal beating of Rodney King, a black motorist, by members of the Los Angeles Police Department in 1991 was captured on videotape, was widely publicized, and drew widespread attention to the vulnerability of blacks to police harassment. The subsequent acquittal of four police officers who had been videotaped beating him unleashed the most destructive American urban disorders of the twentieth century. Yet the King incident was only one of 15,000 complaints of police brutality filed with the federal government between 1985 and 1991 (Lewis 1991). Moreover, during the 1980s and 1990s hundreds of incidents of discrimination, intimidation, harassment, and vandalism as well as physical attacks against racial and religious minorities were reported. These included the burning of over 65 black churches in 1995 and 1996 alone; although investigators concluded that there was no evidence of an organized national racist conspiracy, they did find that racial hatred was a motive in most cases (Sack 1996; Butterfield 1996).

Similarly, cases of racial discrimination in education, in housing, in public accommodations, and in the workplace continue to be widely reported. Some of the most widely publicized cases of discrimination in the workplace and in public accommodations involved nationally prominent corporations—Denney's, Shoney's, Avis, Circuit City, and Texaco (*Time* 1987; Ehrlich 1990; U.S. Commission on Civil Rights 1990; Jaffe 1994; Feagin and Vera 1995; Eichenwald 1996; Myerson 1997). Yet these cases were among only the most widely publicized; between 1990 and 1993 the Equal Employment Opportunity Commission (EEOC), the federal agency responsible for enforcing civil rights laws in the workplace, resolved an average of 4,636 cases in favor of individuals charging racial discrimination. In most instances, however, discrimination is

extremely difficult to prove, and the burden of filing charges and the recourse to legal remedies are so cumbersome and time-consuming that many people are discouraged from pursuing them. Nevertheless, by 1995 the EEOC had a back log of about 100,000 cases charging racial discrimination in employment alone (Kilborn 1995; Myerson 1997).

Thus, despite the enactment of antidiscrimination legislation and contrary to white perceptions that discrimination has been eradicated and that, as a consequence of affirmative action programs, minorities receive preferential treatment in hiring, recent "bias studies" have demonstrated that African Americans and Hispanics continue to experience discrimination. In a study of employment discrimination, for example, pairs of white and black men with identical qualifications applied for 476 jobs advertised in Washington and Chicago newspapers. Whereas 15 percent of the white applicants received job offers, only 5 percent of the black applicants did. Moreover, white applicants advanced further in the hiring process and in the Washington area were much less likely to receive rude, unfavorable, or discouraging treatment than were their black counterparts. These findings were similar to an earlier study of the hiring experiences of Hispanics and Anglos in Chicago and San Diego in which whites were three times as likely both to advance further in the hiring process and to receive job offers as were Hispanic applicants (Turner, Fix, and Struyk 1991).

What are the consequences of these continuing encounters with attitudinal discrimination? In his study involving interviews with African Americans throughout the United States, . . . Feagin found that despite antidiscrimination legislation and changing white attitudes, even middle-class blacks remain vulnerable to discrimination and that incidents of discrimination against them are far from isolated. Instead, they are *cumulative;* that is, a black person's encounters with discrimination are best described as a "lifelong series of such incidents."

The cumulative impact of constant experiences of discrimination—what writer Ellis Cose (1993) has characterized as "soul-destroying slights"—and the energy expended in dealing with them was clearly articulated by one of the respondents in Feagin's study:

... if you can think of the mind as having one hundred ergs of energy, and the average man uses fifty percent of his energy dealing with the everyday problems of the world—just the general kinds of things—then he has fifty percent more to do creative kinds of things that he wants to do. Now that's a white person. Now a black person also has one hundred ergs: he uses fifty percent the same way a white man does, dealing with what the white man has [to deal with], so he has fifty percent left. But he uses twenty-five percent fighting being black, [with] all the problems of being black and what it means. Which means he really only has twenty-five percent to do what the white man has fifty percent to do, and he's expected to do just as much as the white man with that twenty-five percent. . . . So, that's kind of what happens. You just don't have as much energy left to do as much as you know you really could if you were free, [if] your mind were free.

Anthony Walton, an African American who grew up in a comfortable middle-class home in the Chicago suburbs, has referred to these "petty, daily indignities that take such a toll on the psyches of American blacks" as a "black tax," "the tribute to white society that must be paid in self-effacement and swallowed pride" (Walton 1996:7).

Attitudinal discrimination does not always occur in so virulent or so direct a manner. It may be manifested less dramatically merely by the acceptance by members of the dominant group of social definitions of traditional subordinate group roles. Malcolm X, the charismatic black protest leader who was assassinated in 1965, recalled how his well-intentioned white high school English teacher, Mr. Ostrowski, was bound by cultural norms concerning the "proper" caste roles for blacks:

I know that he probably meant well in what he happened to advise me that day. I doubt that he meant any harm. . . . I was one of his top students, one of the school's top students—but all he could see for me was the kind of future "in your place" that almost all white people see for black people. . . . He told me, "Malcolm, you ought to be thinking about a career. Have you been giving it any thought?". . . The truth is, I hadn't. I have never figured out why I told him, "Well, yes, sir, I've been thinking I'd like to be a lawyer." Lansing certainly had no lawyers—or doctors either—in those days, to hold up an image I might have aspired to. All I really knew for certain was that a lawyer didn't wash dishes, as I was doing.

Mr. Ostrowski looked surprised, I remember, and leaned back in his chair and clasped his hands behind his head. He kind of half-smiled and said, "Malcolm, one of life's first needs is for us to be realistic. Don't misunderstand me, now. We all here like you, you know that. But you've got to be realistic about being a nigger. A lawyer—that's no realistic goal for a nigger. You need to think about something you can be. You're good with your hands—making things. Everybody admires your carpentry shop work. Why don't you plan on carpentry? People like you as a person—you'd get all kinds of work." (Malcolm X 1966:36)

Here we should recall Merton's distinction between the prejudiced discriminator and the unprejudiced discriminator. According to the definition advanced earlier, discrimination involves differential treatment of individuals because of their membership in a minority group. The term has traditionally referred to actions of people who arbitrarily deny equal treatment (for example, equal opportunity to obtain a job or to purchase a home) to minority group members because of their own personal prejudices. Such is the behavior of the prejudiced discriminator or all-weather bigot.

But discrimination can occur without the discriminator's necessarily harboring prejudices. As Merton points out, an unprejudiced discriminator—the fair-weather liberal—can discriminate simply by conforming to existing cultural patterns or by acquiescing to the dictates of others who are prejudiced. Such discrimination can be attributed to the actor's conscious or unconscious perception of the negative effects that nondiscriminatory behavior will have. An employer or a realtor may genuinely disclaim any personal prejudice for having refused a minority group member a job or home. Perhaps the person felt constrained by the negative sanctions of peers, or by the fear of alienating customers. In this case, the discriminatory actor's judgment would be based on the prejudicial attitudes of a powerful reference group.

Although the heart and mind of the actors in our hypothetical situations may be devoid of any personal prejudice, nevertheless, the consequences—no job, no home—for the minority-group applicant are no different than if they were old-fashioned, dyed-in-the-wool bigots. . . .

INSTITUTIONAL DISCRIMINATION

Both forms of attitudinal discrimination just defined are ultimately reducible to psychological variables: the actor is prejudiced, defers to, or is influenced by the sanctions of a prejudiced reference group or the norms of a racially biased culture. Institutional discrimination, on the other hand, refers to organizational practices and societal trends that exclude minorities from equal opportunities for positions of power and prestige. This discrimination has been labeled "structural" by some scholars *(Research News* 1987:9). Institutional or structural discrimination involves "policies or practices which appear to be neutral in their effect on minority individuals or groups, but which have the effect of disproportionately impacting on them in harmful or negative ways" (Task Force on the Administration of Military Justice in the Armed Forces 1972:19). The effects or consequences of institutional discrimination have little relation to racial or ethnic attitudes or to the majority group's racial or ethnic prejudices.

The existence of institutional inequalities that effectively exclude substantial portions of minority groups from participation in the dominant society has seldom been considered under the category of discrimination. According to J. Milton Yinger, discrimination is "the persistent application of criteria that are arbitrary, irrelevant, or unfair by *dominant standards,* with the result that some persons receive an undue advantage and others, *although equally qualified,* suffer an unjustified penalty" (Yinger 1968:449, italics added). The underlying assumption of this definition is that if all majority-group members would eliminate "arbitrary, irrelevant, and unfair criteria," discrimination would, by definition, cease to exist. However, if all prejudice—and the attitudinal discrimination that emanates from it—were somehow

miraculously eliminated overnight, the inequalities rooted in the normal and impersonal operation of existing institutional structures would remain. Therefore, the crucial issue is not the equal treatment of those with equal qualifications but rather is the access of minority-group members to the qualifications themselves.

Consider the following additional examples of institutional discrimination:

• An employer may be genuinely willing to hire individuals of all races but may rely solely on word-of-mouth recommendations to fill job vacancies. If Hispanics had previously been excluded from such employment, they would be unlikely to be members of a communications network that would allow them to learn about such vacancies.

• Jury selection is supposedly color-blind in most states, with jurors randomly selected from lists of registered voters. However, because they are more likely to be poor and geographically mobile (and thus ineligible to vote), blacks are less frequently selected as jurors. Similarly, a recent study found that, because a disproportionate number of black males are in prison or have been convicted of a felony, 14 percent of black men—nearly 1.5 million of a total voting age population of 10.4 million—are ineligible to vote, thus substantially diluting African American political power (Butterfield 1997).

• City commissions are often selected on either an at-large or a district basis. In at-large elections, all voters select from the same slate of candidates. By contrast, when elections are conducted on a district basis, the city is divided into geographically defined districts, and a resident votes only for candidates within his or her district. When an ethnic or a racial group constitutes a numerical minority of a city's population, its voting power is likely to be diluted and its representation in city government is likely to be lower than its proportion of the population under an at-large system of voting. Thus, under an at-large system, a city with a population that is 40 percent black could have no black representation on the city commission if voting followed racial lines. Because of patterns of residential segregation, this situation would be much less likely in a system organized on a district basis.

• In Minnesota a judge ruled unconstitutional a law that punished possession of crack more severely than possession of comparable amounts of powdered cocaine. Testimony indicated that crack is used mainly by blacks, whereas whites are much more likely to use cocaine. Although there was general agreement that the Minnesota legislature had enacted the penalties for the two crimes without any intent of targeting a specific minority group, the judge contended that the absence of racial prejudice or negative intent in the law's enactment was less relevant in considering the constitutionality of the crack law than whether enactment affected blacks disproportionately and thus had the practical effect of discriminating against them. "There had better be a good reason for any law that has the practical effect of disproportionately punishing members of one racial group. If crack was significantly more deadly or harmful than cocaine that might be a good enough reason. But there just isn't enough evidence that they're different enough to justify the radical differences in penalties" (London 1991).

The issue of racial disparities in sentencing for crack and powdered cocaine has become a hotly contested part of the national debate over mandatory federal sentences for drug offenses, where blacks were 90 percent of those convicted in Federal court crack offenses but only 30 percent of those convicted for cocaine. Studies show that the physiological and psychoactive effects of crack and powered cocaine are similar, and the independent U.S. Sentencing Commission recommended that Congress scrap laws that establish dramatically harsher sentences (by a ratio of 100 to 1) for possession of crack than for possession of cocaine. Nevertheless, in 1995 both the Clinton Administration and Congress refused to modify the disparate sentences given for possession of the two drugs, and in 1996 the Supreme Court rejected the argument that the dramatic racial differences in prosecution and penalties for crack possession reflected racial discrimination. However, the consequence of these decisions was to reinforce and maintain the dramatically disproportionate number of African Americans under the control of the criminal justice system

(Morley 1995; Jones 1995; Greenhouse 1996; Wren 1996).

Institutional discrimination is central to two important recent interpretations of inequalities in American life that focus on opportunities in two institutions in American life—the economy and education. In a series of books—*The Declining Significance of Race* (1978), *The Truly Disadvantaged* (1987), and *When Work Disappears* (1996), William Julius Wilson has identified several broad social structural factors that have dramatically transformed the economic opportunity structure for African Americans. He contends that the overall economic and social position of the inner-city poor has deteriorated in the past quarter century not only because of attitudinal discrimination but also because of impersonal structural economic changes—the shift from goods-producing to service-producing industries, increasing labor market segmentation, increased industrial technology, and the flight of industries from central cities—that have little to do with race. Earlier in the twentieth century, relatively uneducated and unskilled native and immigrant workers were able to find stable employment and income in manufacturing. Today, however, deindustrialization has created an economic "mismatch" between the available jobs and the qualifications of inner-city residents. On the one hand, manufacturing jobs, which in the past did not require highly technical skills, have either been mechanized or have moved from the inner cities to the suburbs, the sun belt, or overseas. Unskilled blacks in central cities are especially vulnerable to the relocation of high-paying manufacturing jobs. On the other hand, the jobs now being created in the cities demand highly technical credentials that most inner-city residents do not have. The economic opportunities of the African American urban poor, who lack the educational and occupational skills necessary for today's highly technological jobs, are therefore rapidly diminishing. The result is extremely high levels of unemployment.

These broad structural changes have triggered a process of "hyperghettoization" in which the urban poor are disproportionately concentrated and socially and economically isolated. As many stable working-class and middle-class residents with job qualifications have moved from inner-city neighborhoods, the stability of inner-city social institutions (churches, schools, newspapers, and recreational facilities) has been undermined, and the social fabric of neighborhoods and the community has deteriorated. As Wilson argues . . . , "A neighborhood in which people are poor but employed is different from a neighborhood in which people are poor and jobless."

Although the lack of educational and occupational skills among the African American urban poor reflects a historical legacy of attitudinal discrimination, institutional factors—the broad structural changes in the economy that were just mentioned—play a crucial role in sustaining black economic inequality. Even if all racial prejudice were eliminated, inner-city African Americans would still lack access to high-paying jobs that provide security and stability for both families and the black community (Wilson 1987; 1996).

Similar impersonal factors play a critical role in creating and sustaining dramatic racial disparities in educational opportunities. In his powerful book, *Savage Inequalities,* Jonathan Kozol (1991) has focused on the dramatic differences in the quality of public education in poor and in wealthy school districts in the United States and on the way in which these differences— these "savage inequalities"—affect educational opportunity. Focusing on the vast disparities in the quality of facilities, programs, and curricula that typically distinguish inner-city and suburban schools, Kozol contends that what is most glaringly apparent are the dramatic financial inequities among schools serving poor and affluent students, often in neighboring school districts; schools attended by poor students are invariably the most poorly funded, while those attended by students from affluent backgrounds have the highest per-pupil expenditures. Kozol reports that a study

of 20 of the wealthiest and poorest districts of Long Island [New York], for example, matched by location and size of enrollment, found that the differences in per-pupil spending were not only large but had approximately doubled in a five-year period. Schools in Great Neck, in 1987, spent $11,265 for each pupil. In affluent Jericho and Manhasset the figures were, respectively, $11,325 and $11,370. In Oyster Bay the figure was $9,980.

Compare this to Levittown, also on Long Island but a town of mostly working-class white families, where per-pupil spending dropped to $6,900. Then compare these numbers to the spending level in the town of Roosevelt, the poorest district in the county, where the schools are 99 percent non-white and where the figure dropped to $6,340. Finally, consider New York City, where in the same year, $5,590 was invested in each pupil—less than half of what was spent in Great Neck. The pattern is almost identical to that [in the Chicago and many other metropolitan areas] (Kozol 1991:120).

The principal source of these glaring financial inequities is the mechanism—local property taxes—that traditionally has been used to fund public schools. Reliance upon local property taxes to fund public schools, although perhaps initiated as public policy with no racial considerations in mind, has, given the history of racial residential segregation in American society, created dramatically different educational opportunities for white and for minority children. Recently these disparities have increased at precisely the same time that cities have undertaken extensive urban redevelopment programs; by offering tax abatements to businesses and corporations that locate in central city locations, the tax bases from which inner-city schools are funded lose an estimated $5 to $8 billion annually (Lewin 1997). Kozol contends that, because states require school attendance but allocate their resources inequitably, they "effectively require inequality. Compulsory inequity, perpetuated by state law, too frequently condemns our children to unequal lives" (Kozol 1991:56).

Similarly, in an analysis of school desegregation within and between American cities and their suburbs, David James (1989) has shown that the state, by creating political boundaries that separate school districts and by refusing to accept interdistrict desegregation, has been instrumental in creating school segregation, thereby reinforcing patterns of social inequality. Suburban rings surrounding major American cities tend to have multiple school districts, and black suburbanites tend to be concentrated in areas close to the central cities. Therefore, because the Supreme Court has ruled that racial segregation *within* school districts is unconstitutional but that segregation *between* districts is not, whites can avoid living in school districts with large proportions of black students. They are able to implement a form of attitudinal discrimination precisely because the structure of school districts (in many instances created without racial intent) provides such opportunities.

Institutional discrimination, although not intended to victimize racial groups directly, is thus more subtle, covert, complex, and less visible and blatant than attitudinal discrimination. Because it does not result from the motivations or intentions of specific individuals, but rather from

policies that appear race-neutral, institutional discrimination is more impersonal than attitudinal discrimination, and its effects are more easily denied, ignored, overlooked, or dismissed as "natural," inevitable, or impossible to change. Nevertheless, institutional discrimination has the same discriminatory consequences for minority group members. In examining institutional discrimination, therefore, it is more important to consider the *effect* of a particular policy or practice on a minority group than it is to consider the *motivations* of the majority group.

REFERENCES

Allport, Gordon W. 1958. *The Nature of Prejudice.* Garden City, NY: Doubleday.

Blanchard, Fletcher A., Teri Lilly, and Leigh Ann Vaughn. 1991. "Reducing the Expression of Racial Prejudice." *Psychological Science.* 2.

Butterfield, Fox. 1996. "Old Fears and New Hope: Tale of Burned Black Church Goes Far Beyond Arson." *New York Times.* July 21.

——. 1997. "Many Black Men Barred From Voting, Study Shows." *New York Times.* January 30.

Carmichael, Stokely and Charles Hamilton. 1967. *Black Power: The Politics of Liberation in America.* New York: Vintage.

Cose, Ellis. 1993. *The Rage of a Privileged Class.* New York: HarperCollins.

Ehrlich, Howard J. 1990. *Campus Ethnoviolence and Policy Options.* Baltimore: National Institute against Prejudice and Violence.

Eichenwald, Kurt. 1996. "Texaco Executives, on Tape, Discussed Impeding a Bias Suit." *New York Times.* November 4.

Feagin, Joe R. and Hernan Vera. 1995. *White Racism: The Basics.* New York: Routledge.

Firebaugh, Glenn and Kenneth E. Davis. 1988. "Trends in Antiblack Prejudice 1972–1984: Region and Cohort Effects." *American Journal of Sociology.* 94.

Gallup Poll Social Audit. 1997. *Black/White Relations in the United States.* Princeton, NJ: The Gallup Organization. June.

Greenhouse, Linda. 1996. "Race Statistics Alone Do Not Support a Claim of Selective-Prosecution, Justices Rule." *New York Times.* May 14.

Hochschild, Jennifer L. 1995. *Facing Up to the American Dream: Race, Class and the Soul of the Nation.* Princeton: Princeton University Press.

Jaffe, Amy Myers. 1994. "At Texaco, The Diversity Skeleton Still Stalks the Halls." *New York Times.* December 11.

James, David R. 1989. "City Limits on Racial Equality: The Effects of City-Suburban Boundaries on Public-School Desegregation, 1968–1976." *American Sociological Review.* 54.

Jones, Charisse. 1995. "Crack and Punishment: Is Race the Issue?" *New York Times.* October 25.

Kilborn, Peter T. 1995. "A Family Spirals Downward in Waiting for Agency to Act." *New York Times.* February 11.

Kozol, Jonathan. 1991. *Savage Inequalities: Children in America's Schools.* New York: HarperCollins.

Lewin, Tamar. 1997. "Seeking to Shield Schools from Tax Breaks." *New York Times.* May 21.

Lewis, Neil A. 1991. "Police Brutality Under Wide Review by Justice Department." *New York Times.* March 15.

London, Robb. 1991. Judge's Overruling of Crack Law Brings Turmoil." *New York Times.* January 11.

Malcolm X. 1966. *The Autobiography of Malcolm X.* New York: Grove Press.

Merton, Robert K. 1949. "Discrimination and the American Creed." In Robert MacIver, ed., *Discrimination and the National Welfare.* New York: Institute for Religious and Social Studies and Harper and Row.

Morley, Jefferson. 1995. "Crack in Black and White." *Washington Post.* November 19.

Myerson, Allen R. 1997. "As U.S. Bias Cases Drop, Employees Take Up Fight." *New York Times.* January 12.

——. 1997. "At Rental Counters, Are All Drivers Created Equal?" *New York Times.* March 18.

Myrdal, Gunnar. 1944/1962. *An American Dilemma: The Negro Problem and Modern Democracy.* New York: Harper and Row.

Nash, Manning. 1962. "Race and the Ideology of Race." *Current Anthropology.* 3:3.

National Advisory Commission on Civil Disorders. 1968. *Report.* Washington, DC: Government Printing Office.

Noel, Donald L. 1968. "A Theory of the Origin of Ethnic Stratification." *Social Problems.* 16.

Noel, Donald L. 1972. *The Origins of American Slavery and Racism.* Columbus, OH: Charles E. Merrill.

Research News. 1987. "The Costs of Being Black." 38.

Sack, Kevin. 1996. "Burnings of Dozens of Black Churches Across the South Are Investigated." *New York Times.* May 21.

Schermerhorn, Richard A. 1970. *Comparative Ethnic Relations: A Framework for Theory and Research.* New York: Random House.

Schuman, Howard. 1969. "Sociological Racism." *Transaction.* 7.

Schuman, Howard, Charlotte Steeh, and Lawrence Bobo. 1985. *Racial Attitudes in America: Trends and Interpretations.* Cambridge, MA: Harvard University Press.

Task Force on the Administration of Military Justice in the Armed Forces. 1972. *Report.* Washington, DC: U.S. Government Printing Office.

Time. 1987. "Racism on the Rise." February 2.

Turner, Margery Austin, Michael Fix, and Raymond J Struyk. 1991. *Opportunities Denied,* *Opportunities Diminished: Discrimination in Hiring,* Washington, DC: The Urban Institute.

U.S. Commission on Civil Rights. 1990. *Intimidation and Violence: Racial and Religious Bigotry in America.* Washington, DC: U.S. Government Printing Office.

Walton, Anthony. 1996. Mississippi: *An American Journey.* New York: Knopf.

Wilson, William Julius. 1978. *The Declining Significance of Race: Blacks and Changing American Institutions.* Chicago: University of Chicago Press.

——. 1987. *The Truly Disadvantaged: The Inner City, the Underclass, and Public Policy.* Chicago: University of Chicago Press.

——. 1996. "Work." *The New York Times Magazine.* August 18.

——. 1996. *When Work Disappears: The World of the New Urban Poor.* New York: Knopf.

Wren, Christopher S. 1996. "Study Poses a Medical Challenge to Disparity in Cocaine Sentences." *New York Times.* November 20.

Yinger, J. Milton, 1968. "Prejudice: Social Discrimination." In D. L. Sills, ed., *International Encyclopedia of the Social Sciences.* New York: Macmillan.

Discussion Questions

1. What is the difference between prejudice and discrimination? Why have declining degrees of prejudice in American society not resulted in the elimination of discrimination? Given these realities, what kinds of efforts might be more effective in reducing the discrimination described in this reading than are the current civil rights measures?

2. What are some of the key components of a definition of racism, and why has there been so much confusion around developing a definition of what racism is? Given this definition, blacks can be prejudiced or discriminate, but there cannot be "black racism." Why?

3. Examples of institutional discrimination given in the reading are difficult to identify and change. How would you restructure employment practices, jury selection, and educational funding procedures so that they are no longer discriminatory in the ways described?

Using Racial and Ethnic Concepts:
The Critical Case of Very Young Children

*Debra Van Ausdale
and Joe R. Feagin*

Since the 1930s social science has examined children's attitudes toward race. . . . The literature clearly demonstrates that racial identification and group orientation are salient issues for children (Ramsey 1987).

. . . Most research focuses on children over five years of age; very young children are rarely studied. . . .

Researchers have rarely sought children's views directly, beyond recording brief responses to tests. Few have interviewed children or made in-depth, long-term observations to assess social attitudes, limiting the ability to investigate more fully the nature of children's lives. . . . An emphasis on psychological testing is often coupled with the notion that children have limited understandings of race and ethnicity (Goodman 1964; Katz 1976; Porter 1971). Children are typically assumed to have temporary or naive views about social concepts until at least age seven. Prior to that age, children's use of concepts differs from that of adults in form and content.

Little attention has been devoted to how children create and assign meaning for racial and ethnic concepts. . . .

We provide data indicating that racial concepts are employed with ease by children as young as age three. Research based on the conception of children as incapable of understanding race (Menter 1989) presents an incorrect image of children's use of abstractions. Drawing on Willis (1990) and Thorne (1993), we suggest that notions of race and ethnicity are employed by young children as integrative and symbolically creative tools in the daily construction of social life.

The Research Approach

. . . Our data come from extensive observations of 58 three-, four-, and five-year-old children in a large preschool in a southern city. The school employed a popular antibias curriculum (Derman-Sparks 1989). Over an 11-month period in 1993, we systematically observed everyday interactions in one large classroom containing a very diverse group of children. The center's official data on the racial and ethnic backgrounds of children in the classroom are: White = 24, Asian = 19, Black = 4, biracial = 3, Middle Eastern = 3, Latino = 2, and other = 3.

Children's racial and ethnic designations, which were given by parents, were supplemented with information that we gained through classroom observation of a few children with mixed ethnic identities. We use a shorthand code to describe the racial and ethnic backgrounds of the children. For example, Rita is described as (3.5: White/Latina), indicating that she is three and one-half years old, was initially registered as White, but was later discovered to

have a Latino heritage. Michael is listed as (4: Black), indicating that he is four years old, was registered as Black, and that no additional racial or ethnic information was revealed through further observation. This code attempts to illustrate the complex identities of many of the children. In a few cases we have used a broad designation (e.g., Asian) to protect a child's identity. . . .

Like the children and teachers, the senior author (hereafter Debi), a White woman, was usually in the classroom all day for five days a week. As observer and playmate, Debi watched the children and listened to them in their free play and teacher-directed activities. Over 11 months Debi observed 370 significant episodes involving a racial or ethnic dimension, about 1 to 3 episodes per day. When children mentioned racial or ethnic matters, Debi noted what they said, to whom they spoke, and the context of the incident. Extensive field notes were entered immediately on a computer in another room when the children were otherwise occupied. This was done to preserve the details of any conversations and the accuracy of the data.

Using an approach resembling that of the "least-adult role" (Corsaro 1981; Mandell 1988), Debi conducted extensive participant observation. When children or adults asked, Debi identified herself as a researcher, and she consistently assumed the role of a nonauthoritarian observer and playmate. She was soon accepted as such by children and teachers, and the children spoke freely, rarely ceasing their activities when she was present. Children's interactions with her differed from their interactions with teachers and parents. Our accounts make clear Debi's natural, nonsanctioning role in discussing racial and ethnic matters initially raised by the children. In no case did Debi ask predetermined questions. Racial and ethnic issues arose naturally. Although Debi sometimes asked questions that might have been asked by other adults, she never threatened the children with a sanction for their words or actions. Thus, our interpretations of children's attitudes and behavior evolved gradually as Debi observed the children in natural settings.

We began with the assumption that very young children would display no knowledge of racial or ethnic concepts and that any use of these concepts would be superficial or naive. Our data contradicted these expectations.

USING RACIAL AND ETHNIC
CONCEPTS TO EXCLUDE

Using the playhouse to bake pretend muffins, Rita (3.5: White/Latina) and Sarah (4: White) have all the muffin tins. Elizabeth (3.5: Asian/Chinese), attempting to join them, stands at the playhouse door and asks if she can play. Rita shakes her head vigorously, saying, "No, only people who can speak Spanish can come in." Elizabeth frowns and says, "I can come in." Rita counters, "Can you speak Spanish?" Elizabeth shakes her head no, and Rita repeats, "Well, then you aren't allowed in."

Elizabeth frowns deeply and asks Debi to intercede by telling her: "Rita is being mean to me." Acting within the child-initiated framework, Debi asks Rita, "If only people who speak Spanish are allowed, then how come Sarah can play? Can you speak Spanish, Sarah?" Sarah shakes her head no. "Sarah can't speak Spanish and she is playing," Debi says to Rita, without suggesting she allow Elizabeth in. Rita frowns, amending her statement: "OK, only people who speak either Spanish or English." "That's great!" Debi responds, "because Elizabeth speaks English and she wants to play with you guys." Rita's frown deepens. "No," she says. Debi queries, "But you just said people who speak English can play. Can't you decide?" Rita gazes at Debi, thinking hard. "Well," Rita says triumphantly, "only people who speak two languages."

Elizabeth is waiting patiently for Debi to make Rita let her play, which Debi has no intention of doing. Debi then asks Rita: "Well, Elizabeth speaks two languages, don't you Elizabeth?" Debi looks at Elizabeth, who now is smiling for the first time. Rita is stumped for a moment, then retorts, "She does not. She speaks only English." Debi smiles at Rita: "She does speak two languages—English and Chinese. Don't you?" Debi invites Elizabeth into the conversation. Elizabeth nods vigorously. However, Rita turns away and says to Sarah, "Let's go to the store and get more stuff."

Language was the ethnic marker here. Rita defined rules for entering play on the basis of language—she was aware that each child not only did not look like the others but also spoke

a different language. . . . Here we see the crucial importance of the social-cultural context, in particular the development of racial and ethnic concepts in a collaborative and interpersonal context. Defending her rules, Rita realized her attempts to exclude Elizabeth by requiring two languages had failed. This three-year-old child had created a social rule based on a significant understanding of ethnic markers. The final "two languages" rule did not acknowledge the fact that Sarah only spoke English. Rita's choice of language as an exclusionary device was directed at preventing Elizabeth from entering, not at maintaining a bilingual play space.

Exclusion of others can involve preventing associations with unwanted others, as in Rita's case, or removing oneself from the presence of unwanted others, as in this next instance. Carla (3: White) is preparing herself for the resting time. She picks up her cot and starts to move it. The head teacher, a White woman, asks what she is doing. "I need to move this," explains Carla. "Why?" asks the teacher. "Because I can't sleep next to a nigger," Carla says, pointing to Nicole (4.5: African/biracial) on a cot nearby. "Niggers are stinky. I can't sleep next to one." Stunned, the teacher's eyes widen, then narrow as she frowns. She tells Carla to move her cot back and not to use "hurting words." Carla looks amused and puzzled but complies. Nothing more is said to the children, but the teacher glances at Debi and shakes her head.

Three-year-old Carla's evaluation of the racial status of another young child was sophisticated and showed awareness not only of how to use racial epithets but also of the negative stigma attached to black skin. Like most children we observed, Carla was not the unsophisticated, naive child depicted in the mainstream literature. She used material (e.g., the epithet) that she undoubtedly had learned from other sources, probably in interaction with other children or adults, and she applied this material to a particular interactive circumstance.

Later, after the children have been wakened and have gone to the playground, the center's White director approaches Debi and says, "I have called Carla's parents and asked them to come to a meeting with me and Karen [the teacher] about what happened." Neither Debi nor the director feel a need to clarify what he is referring to, as he adds: "If you want to attend I would really like to have you there. Karen will be there too." Debi tells him she will attend. "I suppose this is what you're looking for," he continues with a smile. "Well, no, not exactly," Debi replies, "but of course it is worth nothing, and I am interested in anything that the kids do with race." "Well," he shot back, "I want you to know that Carla did not learn that here!"

Although the observed children rarely used explicit racial slurs, the director's remark about the origin of Carla's epithet is typical of the responses adults gave when children at the center used negative terms. The center's staff was extremely interested in limiting children's exposure to prejudice or discrimination and used a multicultural curriculum to teach children to value diversity. The center's adults often seemed more concerned with the origins of child-initiated race-relevant behaviors than with the nuanced content or development of those behaviors.

The meeting with Carla's parents was informative. Carla's mother is biracial (Asian and White), and her father is White. Both parents are baffled when told of the incident. The father remarks, "Well, she certainly did not learn that sort of crap from us!" The teacher immediately insists that Carla did not learn such words at the center. Carla's father offers this explanation: "I'll bet she got that ["nigger" comment] from Teresa. Her dad is really red," When Debi asks what he means, the father responds, "You know, he's a real redneck." Then the director steps in: "It's amazing what kids will pick up in the neighborhood. It doesn't really matter where she learned it from. What we need to accomplish is unlearning it." He suggests methods for teaching Carla about differences and offers her parents some multicultural toys.

The reactions of the key adults illustrate the strength of adult beliefs about children's conceptual abilities. Their focus was on the child as imitator. The principal concern of teacher, parents, and administrator was to assure one another that the child did not learn such behavior from them. Thus adults reshape their conceptions as children do, collaboratively. Acting defensively, they exculpated themselves by suggesting someone else must be responsible. The director ended the blaming by attributing the source of the child's behavior to neighborhood—a diffuse, acceptable enemy—and initiated the task of unlearning.

USING RACIAL AND ETHNIC CONCEPTS TO INCLUDE

The children also used racial and ethnic understandings and concepts to include others—to engage them in play or teach them about racial and ethnic identities.

. . .

Jewel (4: Asian/Middle Eastern) uses her knowledge of different languages to draw an adult into a child-initiated game. Jewel, Cathie (4: White), and Renee (4.5: White) are trying to swing on a tire swing. Rob, a White college work-study student, has been pushing them but leaves to perform another task. Jewel starts to chant loudly, "Unche I, Unche I!" (an approximation of what she sounded like to Debi). The other girls join in, attracting Rob's attention. He begins to push the girls again. With a smile, he asks, "What are you saying?" Jewel replies, "It means 'pants on fire'!" All three girls roar with laughter. Rob smiles and urges Jewel, "Say it again." She begins to chant it again, now drawing Rob into the play. Rob asks, "Tell me some more." Jewel shakes her head, continuing to chant "Unche I!" and to laugh. Rob persists, asking Jewel to teach him how to "talk." Jewel obliges, making up new chants and repeating them until the others get them, then changing the words and repeating the behavior again. Cathie and Renee are delighted. The playing continues for a while, with the girls chanting and Rob pushing them on the swing.

Later, Debi learned that Jewel had developed sophisticated ethnic play around her understanding of language. When Jewel translated "Unche I" as "pants on fire," Rob accepted this and the game continued. Several weeks later, however, Debi heard Jewel's mother greet her daughter at the door by saying "Unche I!" It seemed strange that a mother would say "pants on fire" to greet her child, and Debi noted the incident in her field notes. Some time later, when Debi presented this scene to graduate students in a seminar, one student laughed, informing her that as far as he could tell Jewel was saying her own name. The phrase meant "Jewel."

Jewel's use of her native name illustrates Willis's (1990) notion of symbolic creativity among children. Jewel was able to facilitate and increase interaction with an adult of another cultural background by choosing word symbols that intrigued the adult. As the interaction continued, she elaborated on that symbol, creating a new world of ethnic meanings that accomplished her goal. She successfully shaped an adult's actions for some time by catching his attention with language she realized he did not understand. This required that she understand his perspective and evaluate his knowledge of language, activities requiring considerable interpretive capability.

USING RACIAL AND ETHNIC CONCEPTS TO DEFINE ONESELF

The use of racial and ethnic concepts to include or exclude others is often coupled with the use of these concepts to describe and define oneself. For most children, racial and/or ethnic identity is an important aspect of themselves, and they demonstrate this in insightful ways in important social contexts.

Renee (4.5: White), a very pale little girl, has been to the beach over the weekend and comes to school noticeably tanned. Linda (4: White) and Erinne (5: biracial) engage her in an intense conversation. They discuss whether her skin would stay that color or get darker until she became, as Linda says, "an African American, like Charles" (another child). Renee denies she could become Black, but this new idea, planted in her head by interaction with the other children, distresses her. On her own initiative, she discusses the possibility with Debi and her mother, both of whom tell her the darker color is temporary.

Renee was unconvinced and commented on her racial identity for weeks. She brought up the issue with other children in many contexts. This linking of skin color with racial identity is found in much traditional literature on children's racial understandings (Clark and Clark 1940). But this racial marking was more than a fleeting interest, unlike the interest mainstream

cognitive theorists might predict for such a young child. Renee reframed the meaning of skin color by questioning others on their thoughts and comparing her skin to others'.

Corinne (4: African/White) displays an ability to create meaning by drawing from her personal world. Corinne's mother is Black and is from an African country; her father is a White American. Corinne speaks French and English and is curious about everything at the center. She is a leader and often initiates activities with other children. Most children defer to her. One day Corinne is examining a rabbit cage on the playground. A teacher is cleaning out the cage and six baby bunnies are temporarily housed in an aluminum bucket that Corinne is holding. Three bunnies are white, two are black, and one is spotted black and white.

As Corinne is sitting at a table, Sarah (4: White) stuck her head into the bucket. "Stop that!" Corinne orders. Sarah complies and asks, "Why do you have the babies?" "I'm helping Marie [teacher]," says Corinne. "How many babies are there?" Sarah asks Corinne. "Six!" Corinne announces, "Three boys and three girls." "How can you tell if they're boys or girls?" Sarah questions. "Well," Corinne begins, "my daddy is White, so the white ones are boys. My mommy is Black, so the black ones are girls." Sarah counts: "That's only five." The remaining bunny is black and white. "Well, that one is like me, so it's a girl," Corinne explains gently. She picks up the bunny and says, "See, this one is both, like me!" Sarah then loses interest, and Corinne returns to cooing over the bunnies.

This four-year-old's explanation incorporates an interesting combination of color, race, and gender. While her causal reasoning was faulty, she constructed what for her was a sophisticated and reasonable view of the bunnies' sexes. She displayed an understanding of the idea that an offspring's color reflects the colors of its parents, a knowledge grounded in her experience as a biracial child. Strayer (1986) underscores how children develop appropriate attributions regarding situational determinants. Corinne's use of parental gender to explain the unknown gender of the bunnies was an appropriate explanation of how bunnies got certain colors. Skin color was a salient part of her identity, and it was reasonable in her social world to assume that it would be salient for the identity of others, even animals.

. . .

Racial and ethnic understandings involve many aspects of one's culture. Jie (4.5: Asian/ Chinese) brought her lunch of homemade Chinese dishes to school. When David, a White student employee, asks her what she has, she replies, "I brought food for Chinese people." Pointing to containers of Chinese food, she explains, "Chinese people prefer Chinese food." When David asks for a taste, she hesitates. "Well," she offers, "you probably won't like it. You're not Chinese." Here are the beginnings of explanations for differences between racial and ethnic groups.

Jie demonstrated not only that she recognized the differences between racial and ethnic groups, but also that she understood the socially transmitted view that physical differences are accompanied by differences in cultural tastes and behavior. Her interaction with the adult revealed a strong understanding of her culture by referring to her food as "for Chinese people" and wondering if non-Chinese people would enjoy it. Her explanation indicated that she was aware of what is *not* a part of her culture as much as what *is* a part of it, and that it is possible that outsiders would not enjoy Chinese food. . . .

USING RACIAL AND ETHNIC CONCEPTS TO DEFINE OTHERS

We observed many examples of children exploring the complex notions of skin color, hair differences, and facial characteristics. They often explore what these things mean and make racial and/or ethnic interpretations of these perceived differences. Mindy (4: White) insists that Debi is Indian. When queried, Mindy replies that it is because Debi is wearing her long dark hair in a braid. When Debi explains that she is not Indian, the child remarks that maybe Debi's mother is Indian.

These statements show not only awareness of the visible characteristics of race and ethnicity but also insight into how visible markers are passed from generation to generation. They demonstrate a child's ability to grasp salient characteristics of a racial and/ or ethnic category not her own and apply them to others in a collaborative and evolving way.

In another episode, Taleshia (3: Black) approaches the handpainting table. Asked if she wants to make a handprint, she nods shyly. A child with dark brown skin, Taleshia scans the paint bottles and points to pale pink. Curious about her preference, Debi asks, "Taleshia, is this the color that looks like you?" Taleshia nods and holds out her hand. Behind her, Cathie (3.5: White) objects to Taleshia's decision. "No, no," Cathie interjects, "She's not that color. She's brown." Cathie moves to the table. "You're this color," Cathie says and picks out the bottle of dark brown paint. Cathie is interested in helping Taleshia correct her apparent mistake about skin color. "Do you want this color?" Debi asks Taleshia. "No," she replies, "I want this one," touching the pink bottle. Regarding Taleshia with amazement, Cathie exclaims, "For goodness sake, can't you see that you aren't pink?" "Debi," Cathie continues to insist, "you have to make her see that she's brown." Cathie is exasperated and takes Taleshia by the arm. "Look," she instructs, "you are brown! See?" Cathie holds Taleshia's arm next to her own. "I am pink, right?" Cathie looks to Debi for confirmation. "Sure enough," Debi answers, "you are pink." "Now," Cathie continues, looking relieved, "Taleshia needs to be brown." Debi looks at Taleshia, who is now frowning, and asks her, "Do you want to be brown?" She shakes her head vigorously and points to pale pink, "I want that color."

Cathie is frustrated, and trying to be supportive, Debi explains that "Taleshia can choose any color she thinks is right." Cathie again objects, but Taleshia smiles, and Debi paints her palm pink. Then Taleshia makes her handprint. Cathie stares, apparently convinced that Taleshia and Debi have lost touch with reality. As Taleshia leaves, Cathie takes her place, remarking to Debi, "I just don't know what's the matter with you. Couldn't you see that *she is brown!*" Cathie gives up and chooses pale pink for herself, a close match. Cathie makes her handprint and says to Debi, "See, I am *not* brown."

Taleshia stuck to her choice despite Cathie's insistence. Both three-year-olds demonstrate a strong awareness of the importance of skin color, and their views are strongly held. This example underscores the importance of child-centered research. A traditional conceptualization of this Black child's choice of skin color paint might suggest that the child is confused about racial identity. If she chose pink in the usual experimental setting (Clark and Clark 1940; Porter 1971), she would probably be evaluated as rejecting herself for a preferred whiteness. Debi had several other interactions with Taleshia. The three-year-old had, on other occasions, pointed out how pale Debi was and how dark her own skin was. She had explained to Debi that she was Black, that she thought she was pretty, and that pink was her favorite color. One possible explanation for her choice of pink for her skin color in the handpainting activity relies on Debi's knowledge of Taleshia's personality, family background, and previous interactions with others. Taleshia may have chosen pink because it is her favorite color, but this does not mean that she is unaware that most of her skin is dark. Another explanation for Taleshia's choice of skin color representation is that, like other African Americans, Taleshia's palms are *pink* while most of her skin is very dark. Perhaps she was choosing a color to match the color of her palms, a reasonable choice because the task was to paint the palms for handprints. The validity of this interpretation is reinforced by another episode at the center. One day Taleshia sat down and held Debi's hands in hers, turning them from top to bottom. Without uttering a word, she repeated this activity with her own hands, drawing Debi's attention to this act. The three-year-old was contrasting the pink-brown variations in her skin color with Debi's pinkish hand color. This explanation for the child's paint choice might not occur to a researcher who did not pay careful attention to the context and the child's personal perspective. Taleshia's ideas, centered in observations of herself and others, were more important to her than another child's notions of appropriate color. Far from being confused about skin color, she was creating meaning for color based on her own evaluations.

USING RACIAL CONCEPTS TO CONTROL

The complex nature of children's group interactions and their solo behaviors demonstrates that race and ethnicity are salient, substantial aspects of their lives. They understand racial nuances that seem surprisingly sophisticated, including the power of race. How children use this power in their relationships is demonstrated in two further episodes.

Brittany (4: White) and Michael (4: Black) come to Debi demanding that she resolve a conflict. Mike tearfully demands that Debi tell Brittany that he "does too have a white one." As he makes this demand, Brittany solemnly shakes her head no. "A white what?" Debi asks. "Rabbit!" he exclaims. "At home, in a cage." Brittany continues shaking her head no, infuriating Mike. He begins to shout at the top of his lungs, "I do too have a white one!" Debi asks Brittany, "Why don't you think he has a white rabbit at home?" "He can't," she replies, staring at Mike, who renews his cries. Debi tries to solve the mystery, asking Mike to describe his bunny. "She white," he scowls at Brittany. "You do not," she replies. Mike screams at her "I DO TOOO!" Debi hugs Mike to calm him and takes Brittany's hand. Brittany says, "He can't have a white rabbit." Debi asks why, and the child replies, "Because he's Black." Debi tells Brittany, "He can have any color bunny he wants." Mike nods vigorously and sticks his tongue out at Brittany, who returns the favor. "See," he says, "you just shut up. You don't know." Brittany, who is intensely involved in baiting Mike, shakes her head, and says "Can't." She sneers, leaning toward him and speaking slowly, "You're Black." Mike is angry, and Debi comforts him.

Then Debi asks Brittany, "Have you been to Mike's house to see his bunny?" "No," she says. Debi asks, "Then how do you know that his bunny isn't white?" Debi is curious to find out why Brittany is intent on pestering Mike, who is usually her buddy. "Can't *you* see that he's Black?" she gazes at Debi in amazement. Debi replies, "Yes, of course I can see that Mike is Black, but aren't we talking about Mike's rabbit?" Debi is momentarily thrown by the child's calm demeanor. Brittany again shakes her head slowly, watching Debi for a reaction all the while. "Mike is Black." she says, deliberately forming the words. She repeats, "He is Black." Debi tries again, "Yes, Mike is Black and his bunny is white," now waiting for her response. Brittany shakes her head. "Why not?" Debi tries. "Because he is *Black*," Brittany replies with a tone suggesting that Debi is the stupidest person she has ever met. "Have you been to his house?" Debi asks her again. She shakes her head no. "Then," Debi continues, "how do you know that his bunny isn't white?" "I know," Brittany replies confidently. "How?" Debi tries one last time. "He can't have just any old color rabbit?" Debi asks. "Nope." Brittany retorts firmly, "Blacks can't have whites."

Brittany insisted that Mike could not own a white rabbit because he is Black. She "knew" it and belabored this point until he was driven to seek adult intervention. His plea for intercession was unusual because he is a large boy who was normally in charge of interactions with peers. In this instance, however, he was driven to tears by Brittany's remarks. "Blacks can't have whites" was her social rule. The power of skin color had become a tool in Brittany's hands that she used to dominate interaction with another child.

Brittany's ideas are strong—she creates a similar confrontation with a different child a week later. In this later case, Brittany and Martha (3.5: Black/White) are discussing who will get to take which rabbit home. Martha states that she will take the white one. Brittany again starts the "Blacks can't have whites" routine that she so successfully used with Michael. Martha becomes upset, telling Brittany she is stupid. This scene lasts about 10 minutes until it escalates into shouting, and Joanne, a teacher, breaks up the fight. Neither girl will explain to Joanne what the trouble is. They both just look at her and say "I don't know" when Joanne asks what is going on. Joanne tells them that friends don't yell each other. When the teacher leaves, Martha takes a swing at Brittany, who runs away laughing and sticking out her tongue.

Thus Brittany engaged two Black children in heated interactions based on skin color. In the classical Piagetian interpretation, she would be seen as egocentric and resistant to other interpretations. Contesting her social rule on skin color creates a disequilibrium for her that would

somehow be worked out as she seeks a rational, adult perspective on skin color. However, an interpretive analysis underscores the crucial collaborative context. Brittany's use of racial concepts involves her in intimate interaction with two other children. When a teacher got involved, Brittany stopped, and she and her victim refused to offer an explanation. In the first episode Brittany was willing to engage Debi, who was not a sanctioning adult, in a detailed discussion, taking valuable playtime to explain her reasoning. When confronted by a teacher, Brittany withdrew, refusing to disclose what was going on between her and the Black girl. Brittany had created a tool to dominate others, a tool based on a racial concept coupled with a social rule. In addition, all three children were highly selective about the adults with whom they shared their racially oriented views and behavior.

In another encounter, this time among three children, a White child demonstrates her knowledge of broader race relations, demonstrating her grasp of race-based power inequalities. During playtime Debi watches Renee (4: White) pull Ling-mai (3: Asian) and Jocelyn (4.5: White) across the playground in a wagon. Renee tugs away enthusiastically. Suddenly, Renee drops the handle, which falls to the ground, and she stands still, breathing heavily. Ling-mai, eager to continue this game, jumps from the wagon and picks up the handle. As Ling-mai begins to pull, Renee admonishers her, "No, no. You can't pull this wagon. Only *White Americans* can pull this wagon." Renee has her hands on her hips and frowns at Ling-mai. Ling-mai tries again, and Renee again insists that only "White Americans" are permitted to do this task.

Ling-mai sobs loudly and runs to a teacher complaining that "Renee hurt my feelings." "Did you hurt Ling-mai's feelings?" the teacher asks Renee, who nods, not saying a word. "I think you should apologize," the teacher continues, "because we are all friends here and friends don't hurt each others feelings." "Sorry," mutters Renee, not looking at Ling-mai, "I didn't do it on purpose." "OK," the teacher finishes, "can you guys be good friends now?" Both girls nod without looking at each other and quickly move away.

This interaction reveals several layers of meaning. Both children recognized the implications of

Renee's harsh words and demands. Renee accurately underscored the point that Ling-mai, the child of Asian international students, was neither White nor American. Her failure to be included in these two groups, according to Renee's pronouncement, precluded her from being in charge of the wagon. Ling-mai responded, not by openly denying Renee's statements, but by complaining to the teacher that Renee had hurt her feelings. Both children seem knowledgeable about the structure of the U.S. and global racial hierarchy and accept the superior position accorded to Whites. The four-year-old child exercised authority as a White American and controlled the play with comments and with her stance and facial expressions. Our findings extended previous research on young children's knowledge of status and power (Corsaro 1979; Damon 1977) by showing that children are aware of the power and authority granted to Whites. The children were not confused about the meanings of these harsh racial words and actions.

ADULT MISPERCEPTIONS

. . . Adults tend to control children's use of racial and ethnic concepts and interpret children's use of these concepts along prejudice-defined lines. Clearly, the social context of children's learning, emphasized in the interpretive approach, includes other children and adults, but our accounts also demonstrate the way in which children's sophisticated understandings are developed without adult collaboration and supervision.

Jason (3: White) and Dao (4: Chinese) have developed a friendship over a period of several weeks, despite the fact that Dao speaks almost no English and Jason speaks no Chinese. The two are inseparable. The adults at the center comment on the boys' relationship, wondering aloud about their communication. Yet the boys experience little trouble in getting along and spend hours engaged in play and conversation.

As this friendship develops, Jason's mother, several months pregnant at the time, comes to the head teacher with a problem. "Jason has begun to talk baby talk," she informs the teacher. "Oh, I wouldn't worry about it," the teacher

reassures her. "Kids often do that when their mom is expecting an other baby. It's a way to get attention." Jason's mother seems unconvinced and asks the teachers to watch for Jason's talking "gibberish" and to let her know about it.

Jason and Dao continue their friendship. Teachers remark on their closeness despite Dao's extremely limited command of English. One afternoon, Dao and Jason are playing with blocks near Debi. Deeply involved, they chatter with each other. Debi does not understand a single word either of them are saying, but they have no difficulty cooperating in constructing block towers and laugh together each time a tower collapses. Jason's mother arrives to take him home. He ignores her and continues to play. The head teacher joins the scene and begins a conversation with Jason's mother. When Jason finally acknowledges his mother's presence, he does so by addressing her with a stream of words that make no sense to the nearby adults.

"See, see? That's what I mean," Jason's mother says excitedly. "He talks baby talk. It's really getting bad." The teacher remarks that perhaps after the baby's arrival this will disappear. Debi, after a moment's thought, says to Jason, "Honey, would you say that again in English?" Jason nods and responds, "I want to check out a book from the library before we go home." The teacher and Jason's mother look at him and then at Debi. "Oh, my goodness!" the teacher exclaims, "How did you know to ask him that?" Debi gestures toward the boys and says, "It seemed reasonable. They talk all the time." "That's amazing," Jason's mother shakes her head. "What language do you think they are speaking?" she asks Debi. "I don't know," Debi responds. "I don't understand a word of it. Maybe it's invented."

With the cooperation of Dao's father, who listened in on the boys, Debi finally determined that Jason had learned enough Chinese from Dao and Dao had learned enough English from Jason to form a blended language sufficient for communication. What adults thought was "baby talk"—and what was thought by the teacher to be jealousy toward an unborn sibling—was an innovative synthesis of two languages formed by young children maintaining a cross-ethnic friendship. This is a normal human phenomenon and, if the boys were adults, would likely have been interpreted as a pidgin language—the simplified language that develops between peoples with different languages living in a common territory.

One of the powerful ethnocultural definers of Dao's social life was his inability to speak English, which caused him grief because it kept him from following his teachers' directions promptly. He experienced difficulty in creating friendships, for most other children were not patient enough to accommodate him. Dao was a quiet and cautious child, particularly when teachers were nearby. Jason's ability to develop a language in interaction with Dao was empowering for Dao: the language was the cement that bonded the boys together. The boys' collaborative actions were not only creative, but also reveal one of the idealized (at least for adults) ways that human beings bridge ethnic and cultural differences. The boys were natural multiculturalists.

CONCLUSION

Through extensive observation, this study has captured the richness of children's racial and ethnic experiences. The racial nature of children's interactions becomes fully apparent only when their interactions are viewed over time and in context. Close scrutiny of children's lives reveals that they are as intricate and convoluted as those of adults.

Blumer (1969:138) suggests that any sociological variable is, on examination, "an intricate and inner-moving complex." Dunn (1993) notes that children's relationships are complex and multidimensional, even within their own families. In the case of Jason and Dao, for example, the interactions were not only complex and incomprehensible to adults, but also evolved over time. By exploring the use of racial concepts in the child's natural world, instead of trying to remove the child or the concepts from that world, we glean a more complete picture of how children view and manipulate racial and ethnic concepts and understandings.

For most children, racial and ethnic issues arise forcefully within the context of their interaction with others. Most of the children that we observed had little or no experience with people from other racial or ethnic groups outside of the center. For these very young children, who are having their first extensive social experiences outside the family, racial and ethnic differences became powerful identifiers of self and other. . . .

To fully understand the importance of children's racial and/or ethnic understandings, the nuanced complexity and interconnected nature of their thinking and behavior must be accepted and recognized. Measures of racial and ethnic awareness should consider not only children's cognitive abilities but also the relationships that children develop in social situations.

. . .

Regarding the racial and ethnic hierarchy, young children understand that in U.S. society higher status is awarded to White people. Many understand that simply by virtue of their skin color, Whites are accorded more power, control, and prestige. Very young children carry out interactions in which race is salient. Racial knowledge is situational, and children can interact in a race-based or race-neutral manner, according to their evaluations of appropriateness. In children's worlds race emerges early as a tool for social interaction and quickly becomes a complex and fluid component of everyday interaction.

The behaviors of the children in this preschool setting are likely to be repeated in other diverse settings. The traditional literature accepts that children display prejudice by the time they arrive at school, but offers no explanation about the acquisition of this prejudice beyond it being an imitation of parental behavior. We expect continuity of children's racial and ethnic categories across settings, for children reveal a readiness to use their knowledge of race and ethnicity.

The observed episodes underscore problems in traditional theories of child development. When children fail cognitive tasks framed in terms of principles such as conservation and reciprocity, researchers often conclude that children lack the cognitive capability to understand race. However, surveys and observations of children in natural settings demonstrate that three-year-old children have constant, well-defined, and negative biases toward racial and ethnic others (Ramsey 1987). Rather than insisting that young children do not understand racial or ethnic ideas because they do not reproduce these concepts on adult-centered cognitive tests, researchers should determine the extent to which racial and ethnic concepts—as used in daily interaction—are salient definers of children's social reality. Research on young children's use of racial and gender concepts demonstrates that the more carefully a research design explores the real life of children, the more likely that research can answer questions about the nature of race and ethnicity in children's everyday lives.

REFERENCES

Blumer, Herbert. 1969. *Symbolic Interactionism: Perspective and Method*. Englewood Cliffs, NJ: Prentice-Hall.

Clark, Kenneth B. and Mamie P. Clark. 1940. "Skin Color as a Factor in Racial Identification and Preference in Negro Children." *Journal of Negro Education* 19:341–58.

Corsaro, William A. 1979. "We're Friends, Right?" *Language in Society*. 8:315–36.

——. 1981. "Entering the Child's World: Research Strategies for Field Entry and Data Collection in a Preschool Setting." Pp. 117–46 in *Ethnography and Language in Educational Settings*, edited by J. Green and C. Wallat. Norwood, NJ: Ablex.

Damon, William. 1977. *The Social World of the Child*. San Francisco, CA: Jossey-Bass.

Derman-Sparks, Louise. 1989. *Anti-Bias Curriculum: Tools for Empowering Young Children*. Washington, DC: National Association for the Education of Young Children.

Dunn, Judy. 1993. "Young Children's Understanding of Other People: Evidence From Observations Within the Family." Pp. 97–114 in *Young Children's Close Relationships: Beyond Attachment*, edited by J. Dunn Newbury Park, CA: Sage.

Goodman, Mary E. 1964. *Race Awareness in Young Children*. New York: Crowell-Collier.

Holmes, Robyn M. 1995. *How Young Children Perceive Race*. Thousand Oaks, CA: Sage.

Katz, Phyllis A. 1976. "The Acquisition of Racial Attitudes in Children." Pp. 125–54 in *Towards the Elimination of Racism*, edited by P. A. Katz. New York: Pergamon.

Mandell, Nancy. 1988. "The Least-Adult Role in Studying Children." *Journal of Contemporary Ethnography* 16:433–67.

Menter, Ian. 1989. "'They're Too Young to Notice': Young Children and Racism." Pp. 91–104 in *Disaffection from School? The Early Years*, edited by G. Barrett. London, England: Falmer.

Porter, Judith D. R. 1971. *Black Child, White Child: The Development of Racial Attitudes*. Cambridge, MA: Harvard University.

Ramsey, Patricia A. 1987. "Young Children's Thinking about Ethnic Differences." Pp. 56–72 in *Children's Ethnic Socialization: Pluralism and Development*, edited by J. S. Phinney and M. J. Rotheram. Newbury Park, CA: Sage.

Strayer, Janet. 1986. "Children's Attributions Regarding the Situational Determinants of Emotion in Self and Others." *Developmental Psychological* 22:649–54.

Thorne, Barrie. 1993. *Gender Play: Girls and Boys in School*. New Brunswick, NJ: Rutgers University Press.

Willis, Paul. 1990. Common Culture: Symbolic Work at Play in the Everyday Cultures of the Young. Buckingham, England: Open University Press.

DISCUSSION QUESTIONS

1. There is a T-shirt that reads, "No Child Is Born a Racist." Based on the preceding analysis, do you think this statement is true? Is prejudice an inborn personality trait, a case of children simply mimicking adults, or is it the result of a complex combination of social factors? If the latter is true, what are those social causal factors (for children)?

2. On the one hand, we see these children enacting boundaries that seem cruel, yet on the other hand, we see them breaking barriers that most adults never get past. How can both be happening simultaneously? What does this tell us about prejudice and discrimination?

3. Why do you think adults seek to attribute blame to someone outside of themselves when their child has made a racial slur? Would the adults engage in this type of behavior if the child had been reprimanded for any other sort of misbehavior? What kind of "unlearning" approach do you think would be most effective for such children? Is "We don't say that word" enough? What do you think needs to occur to enable children to unlearn negative stereotypes at this early age?

Experiencing Difference

*Karen E. Rosenblum
and Toni-Michelle C. Travis*

. . . What one notices in the world depends in large part on the statuses one occupies. . . .

[An] example of experiencing one's status is offered by Lorene Cary in her autobiography, *Black Ice* (1991). Describing her life as one of the first black students in an exclusive and previously all-white prep school, Cary recalls what it was like to hear "one [white] girl after another say, 'It doesn't matter to me if somebody's white or black or green or purple. I mean people are just people'."

> Having castigated whites' widespread inability to see individuals [apart from] the skin in which they were wrapped, I could hardly argue with "its the person that counts." I didn't know why they always chose green and purple to dramatize their indifference, but my ethnicity seemed diminished when the talk turned to Muppets (1991:83–84).

While Cary notices that they are trying to express a commitment to fair treatment irrespective of race, she also hears her own *real* experiences being trivialized in a comparison to fictional green and purple creatures: Cary's status helps explain what she notices.

Because status affects how one is treated, status shapes one's perspective. In all, you experience your social statuses, you live through them, they are the filters through which you see and make sense of the world, in large measure they account for how you are treated and what you notice. In the sections that follow, we will focus on the experiences of privilege and stigma associated with master statuses.

The Experience of Privilege

Just as Lorene Cary's status helps explain what she notices, status also explains what we *don't* notice. The following is an account of a classroom discussion between a black and a white woman. The white woman has argued that because she and the black woman share the status of being female, they should be allied. The black woman responds,

> "When you wake up in the morning and look in the mirror what do you see?"

> "I see a woman," replied the white woman.

> "That's precisely the issue," replied the black woman. "I see a black woman. For me, race is visible every day, because it is how I am *not* privileged in this culture. Race is invisible to you [because it is how you are privileged]" (Kimmel and Messner, 1989:3; emphasis added).

Thus, we are likely to be fairly unaware of the statuses we occupy that privilege us, i.e., provide us advantage, and acutely aware of those that are the source of trouble, i.e., that yield negative judgments and unfair treatment. The mirror metaphor used by the black woman in this conversation emerges frequently among those who are stigmatized: "I looked in the mirror and saw a gay man." These moments of suddenly realizing one's social position with all of its life-shaping ramifications are usually about recognizing how one is stigmatized and underprivileged—rarely about how one is privileged or advantaged by the statuses one occupies. But it is privilege that we will focus on in this section.

Examples of Privilege

This use of the term privilege was first developed by Peggy McIntosh (1988) from her experience teaching Women's Studies courses. In those courses she had noticed that while many men were willing to grant that women were disadvantaged (or "underprivileged") because of sexism, it was more difficult for them to acknowledge that they were themselves advantaged (or "overprivileged") because of it. Extending the analysis to race, McIntosh generated a list of the ways in which she, as a white woman, was overprivileged by virtue of racism. Her list of over forty white privileges included:

I can turn on the television or open to the front page of the paper and see people of my race widely represented.

When I am told about our national heritage or about "civilization," I am shown that people of my color made it what it is.

I do not have to educate my children to be aware of systemic racism for their own daily protection.

I can worry about racism without being seen as self-interested or self-seeking.

I can think over many options, social, political, imaginative, or professional, without asking whether a person of my race would be accepted or allowed to do what I want to do (McIntosh, 1988:5–8).

When McIntosh later presented her analysis to public audiences, she learned about other white privileges: "A black woman said she was glad to hear me 'working on my own people,' because if she said these things about white privilege, she would be seen as a militant." Someone else noted that one of the privileges of being white was being able to be oblivious to those privileges. "Those in privileged groups are educated [to be oblivious] about what it is like for others, especially for others who have to be in their presence" (McIntosh, 1988).

One feature of privilege is that it makes life easier—it is easier to get around, to get what one wants, and to be treated in a way that is acceptable. Columnist Tony Kornheiser (1990) provides an example of this in his description of traveling with an African American colleague when both were using complimentary airline tickets. After Kornheiser, who is white, turned in his ticket and was assigned a seat, he watched the white ticket agent ask his black colleague for some identification:

The black man handed over his ticket. The female agent glanced at it and asked, "Do you have some identification?" [Kornheiser had not been asked for any identification.]

"Yes, I do," the black man said, and he reached for his wallet. "But just out of curiosity, do you mind telling me why you want to see it?"

The agent grinned in embarrassment.

She said nothing in response.

"How about a credit card?" the black man said, and he pulled one out of his wallet.

"Do you have a work ID?" she asked, apparently hoping to see something with the black man's photo on it.

"No," he said, and whipped out another credit card.

"A driver's license would be fine," she said, sounding trapped.

"I don't have my driver's license with me," he said. "I'm taking the plane, not the car. . . ."

"That's fine sir, thank you," the agent finally said, shrinking a bit with each successive credit card. "Enjoy the flight."

The men rode the escalator up to the gate area in silence.

The white man shook his head. "I've probably watched that a hundred times in my life," he said. "But that's the first time I've ever *seen* it."

The black man nodded. He'd seen it more times than he cared to count. "You don't ever need to remind yourself that you're black," he said, "because every day there's somebody out there who'll remind you."

They walked on for a while, and the black man started to laugh to himself. Pirouetting, he modeled his outfit, an Italian-cut, double-breasted suit with a red rose in his lapel for Mother's Day. "I really can't look any better than this," he said sardonically. Then, he looked into his friend's eyes and said, "I had my driver's license. But if I show it, we may as well be in Soweto." (Kornheiser, 1990)

(In reading about Kornheiser's behavior during this exchange—he stands by and watches—one black student was particularly angered: "Whites will stand by and watch this happen, and either be oblivious to the slight or sympathize with you afterward, but they won't go to the mat and fight for you.")

Thus, Kornheiser noted for the first time a privilege that he has as a middle-class white: he is not assumed to be a thief. By contrast, his black colleague is presumed to have stolen the ticket no matter how upper-class or professional he may look. Similarly, many black and Latino students describe being closely monitored for shoplifting when they are in department stores—just as the students who work in security confirm that they are given explicit instructions to watch black and Latino customers for shoplifting. On hearing this, one black student realized why she had the habit of walking through stores with her hands out, palm open, in front of her: it was a way to prove she was not stealing.

Thus, one of the privileges of being white is that shoplifting is easier, since the security people in stores are busy watching the black and Latino customers. As Jeffrey Reiman discusses . . . one explanation for the higher crime rates among blacks and the poor is that those who are white and middle- to upper-class are less likely to be arrested, charged, or convicted for their crimes.

Just as whites are not assumed to be thieves, they are not presumed to be violent (at least by other whites). By contrast, many whites presume blacks are violent. Even recent survey data show that 50 percent of whites believe this to be the case (National Opinion Research Center; 1990). Whites' fear of blacks—especially males—is fairly widespread. But . . . it is *blacks* whose lives are in danger as a consequence. When people are assumed to be criminal or potentially violent their life is at risk from preemptive violence directed against them; indeed, the violence directed at them is considered justified. One of the privileges experienced by those who are white and apparently middle-class is that they are not presumed to be potentially criminal or violent. Thus, they need not closely monitor their behavior in public for fear that others will perceive them as threatening. . . .

. . . David Mura describes a privilege likely to be invisible to those in single-race families, namely, the privilege of being recognized as a family. In the following account, the failure to perceive a family is linked to the expectation of black criminality.

> When my son was home visiting from college, we met in town one day for lunch. . . . On the way to the car, one of us thought of a game we'd often played when he was younger.
>
> "Race you to the car!"
>
> I passed my large handbag to him, thinking to more equalize the race since he was a twenty-year-old athlete. We raced the few blocks,

> my heart singing with delight to be talking and playing with my beloved son. As we neared the car, two young white men yelled something at us. I couldn't make it out and paid it no mind. When we arrived at the car, both of us laughing, they walked by and mumbled "Sorry" as they quickly passed, heads down.
>
> I suddenly understood. They hadn't seen a family. They had seen a young Black man with a pocketbook, fleeing a pursuing middle-aged white woman. My heart trembled as I thought of what could have happened if we'd been running by someone with a gun.
>
> Later I mentioned the incident in a three-day diversity seminar I was conducting at a Boston corporation. A participant related it that evening to his son, a police officer, and asked the son what he would have done if he'd observed the scene.
>
> The answer: "Shot out his kneecaps." (Lester, 1994:56–7)

Despite whites' fear of violence at the hands of African Americans, crime is predominately *intraracial.* In 1992, 66 percent of the perpetrators of violent crime against whites were white and 21 percent were black; in the same year, 86 percent of the perpetrators of violent crime against blacks were black and 7 percent were white. The remainder in each category include cases in which the race of the assailant was unknown, or there were multiple assailants of different races (Updegrave, 1994).

. . .

Two privileges in particular appear common among non-stigmatized statuses: the sense of entitlement and the privilege of being "unmarked." The sense of entitlement—that one has the right to be respected, acknowledged, protected, and rewarded—is so much taken for granted by those in non-stigmatized statuses, that they are often shocked and angered when it is denied them.

> After a 1982 lecture by Barbara Smith at Yale's Afro-American Cultural Center, [whites in the audience] shot their hands up to express how excluded they felt because Smith's lecture, while broad in scope, clearly was addressed first and foremost to the women of color in the room. . . .

What a remarkable sense of entitlement must drive their willingness to assert their experience of exclusion! If I wanted to raise my hand every time I felt excluded, I would have to glue my wrist to the top of my head (Ettinger, 1994:51).

Like entitlement, the privilege of occupying an "unmarked" status is shared by most of those in non-stigmatized categories. "Doctor" is an unmarked status; *woman* doctor is its marked variant. As Deborah Tannen writes . . . , an unmarked status is "what you think of when you are not thinking of anything special." Unmarked categories convey the usual and expected distribution of individuals; the distribution that does not require any special comment. Thus, the unmarked category tells us what a society takes for granted.

Theoretically the unmarked category "doctor" might include anyone, but in truth it refers to white males. How do we know that? Because other occupants of that status are usually marked: woman doctor, black doctor, etc. While the marking of a status signals infrequency, e.g., female astronaut or male nurse, it may also imply inferiority. A "woman doctor" may indicate that one is not considered a full-fledged member of the profession; a "black politician" is often presumed to represent only his black constituents.

Thus, a privilege of those who are not stigmatized is that their master statuses are not often used to discount their accomplishments or imply that they serve "special interests." Someone described as "a politician" is presumed to operate from a universality that someone described as "a white male politician" is not. Because white male politicians are rarely marked as that, their anchoring in the reality of their own master statuses is hidden. In this way, those in marked statuses appear always to be operating from an "agenda," or "special interest," while those in unmarked statuses can appear to be agenda-free: "women/black/gay/Hispanic politicians" are presumed to have special interests that "politicians" do not. Being white and male thus becomes invisible, since it is not regularly being identified as important. For this reason, some recommend marking *everyone's* race and sex as a way to recognize that we are all grounded in our master statuses.

This use of marked statuses also applies to classroom interactions. At white dominated universities, white students are unlikely to be asked to speak on behalf of all white people or to explain the "white experience." In this way, those who are white, male, heterosexual, and middle class look as if they have no race, sex, sexual orientation, or social class, and thus have the privilege of not having to often suffer through classroom discussions about the problems of "their people."

The Stigmatized and the Experience of Privilege; the Privileged and the Experience of Stigma

We have described some of the privileges enjoyed by those in non-stigmatized statuses, but those with stigma also have some experience of privilege—it is just less frequent. For example, in 1991 the Urban Institute investigated racial discrimination in employment by sending pairs of black and white male college students (who had been coached to present virtually identical personal style, appearance, dialect, education, and job history) to apply for jobs in Washington D.C. and Chicago.

In 20 percent [of the 576 job applications], the white applicant advanced farther in the hiring process [from obtaining a job application, to interview, to hiring] than his black counterpart, and in 15 percent the white applicant was offered a job while his equally qualified black partner was not. Blacks were favored over comparable white applicants in a much smaller share of cases; in 7 percent of the audits the black advanced farther in the hiring process, and in 5 percent only the black received the job offer (Turner, Fix, and Struyk, 1991:18).

Thus, black and white applicants both had some experience of preferential hiring, but the white applicant had about three times more of it. A similar study of job discrimination against Latino males conducted in Chicago and San Diego indicated an even larger gap between the amount of privilege experienced by Anglos and Latinos (Cross, Kenney, Mell, and Zimmermann, 1990).

Thus, concerns about "reverse discrimination" often miss the mark. While blacks, Latinos, Asian Americans, or white women are sometimes favored in hiring, they are not favored nearly as frequently as white males. Discrimination continues in its historic direction as evidenced as well in the constancy of race and sex differences in income. In 1975, black per-capita median annual income was 58.5 percent that of whites, by 1990 that figure had risen to only 59.0. In 1975, the same measure for Latinos was 56.1 percent of whites; by 1990 it had dropped to 55.1 percent (U.S. Department of Commerce, 1993:454).[1]

In 1975, the median earnings of women working full-time year-round were 58.8 percent of men's; in 1992, they were 70.6 percent (U.S. Department of Labor, 1993). In no occupational category do women earn as much as men (Bergmann, 1986; U.S. Department of Labor, 1991). For example, "on the average, men earned almost 30 percent more than women in information-systems management, almost 7 percent more in marketing, and almost 4 percent more in finance" (Benokraitis and Feagin, 1995:4). About half of the male/female wage gap can be attributed to discrimination (Treiman and Hartman, 1981).

Because the focus is so frequently on how stigma affects those who bear it, it is easy to assume that only the targets of racism, sexism, homophobia, or classism are affected by it. But that is not the case. For example,

> Think of white slaveowners and their wives: the meaning of the sexual difference between them was constructed in part by the alleged contrast between them as whites and other men and women who were Black; what was supposed to characterize their relationship was not supposed to characterize the relationship between white men and Black women, or white women and Black men.... So even though the white men and women were of the same race, and even though they were not the victims of racism, this does not mean that we can understand the relationship between them without reference to their race and to the racism that their lives enacted (Spelman, 1988:104–5).

Similarly, the interaction between men is affected by sexism, even though they are not themselves subject to it.

For example, we can't understand the racism that fueled white men's lynching of Black men without understanding its connection to the sexism that shaped their protective and possessive attitudes toward white women. The ideology according to which whites are superior and ought to dominate Blacks is nested with the ideology according to which white men must protect their wives from attack by Black men.... That men aren't subject to sexism doesn't mean sexism has no effect on their relationships to each other, especially when the men are from different races in a racist society (Spelman, 1988:106).

. . .

Those in privileged statuses may be unaware of the impact of stigma on their lives, as they may be unaware of the impact of privilege. Being unaware of one's own privilege, however, also bears on one's reaction to other's complaints of discrimination. Because privilege is usually invisible to those who possess it, those in privileged statuses may conclude that everyone is treated as they are. They are sometimes shocked to learn how others without the privilege are treated and may try to dismiss the experience by arguing that the event was exceptional rather than routine, that the victim was overreacting or misinterpreting, or that perhaps the victim even provoked the encounter. Such responses do not necessarily deny that the event took place as it was described; rather, they deny the meaning attributed to the event.

Hearing dismissals like these is usually frustrating because they reduce the teller to a child inadequate to judge the world. Often, such dismissals are framed in terms of the very stigma about which people are complaining, e.g. in the conviction that people complain too much about racism, sexism, or homophobia. In this way, what a stigmatized person says about their status is discounted precisely because they are stigmatized. The implication is that those who occupy a stigmatized status are the ones least able to assess its consequence. While such dismissals assume that those least involved have the most potential to be objective, their effect is to dismiss precisely those who have had the most experience with the topic.

This process, called "looping" or "re-reading," is described by many who have studied the lives of patients in psychiatric hospitals (Rosenhan, 1973; Schur, 1984; Goffman, 1961, 1963). If a patient says, "The staff here are being unfair to me," and they respond, "Of course he would think that—he's crazy" they have re-read, or looped, his words through his status. His words have been heard through his stigma and dismissed for exactly that reason.

Through such dismissals, those operating from positions of privilege can deny the experience of those without privilege. For example, college students who are in their late teens and early twenties often describe university staff as unresponsive to requests for tuition billing correction, residence change, or financial aid until they have had their parents call and complain. If the parents later said "I don't know why you had such a problem with those people. They were very nice to me. Did you do something to antagonize them?" that would indicate they were oblivious to their own privileged place in these university procedures as well as unaware of their child's underprivileged status in them.

There is a function served by these dismissals. Dismissing another's experience of status-based mistreatment masks the possibility that one has escaped such treatment precisely because of one's privilege. If we do not acknowledge that their status affects their treatment, we need not acknowledge that our status affects our treatment. Dismissing others' claims of status-based mistreatment allows us to believe that our treatment in the world is responsive to our individual merit but indifferent to our status. It allows us to avoid the larger truth that those who are treated well, those who are treated ill, and all the rest in between, are always evaluated both as individuals and as occupants of particular esteemed and disesteemed categories. Still, privilege does not inevitably yield this effect, and most are able to recognize their privilege when it is brought to their attention. . . .

THE EXPERIENCE OF STIGMA

The previous section considered the privileges conferred by some master statuses; now we turn to the consequences of occupying stigmatized master statuses.

In his classic analysis of stigma, sociologist Erving Goffman (1963) distinguished between the *discredited,* whose stigma is immediately apparent to an observer (e.g., race, sex, some physical disabilities), and the *discreditable,* whose stigma can be hidden (e.g., sexual orientation, social class). Since stigma plays out differently in the lives of the discredited and the discreditable, each will be examined separately.

The Discreditable: "Passing"

The discreditable are those who are "passing," i.e., not publicly acknowledging the stigmatized statuses they occupy. (Were they to acknowledge that status, they would become discredited.) The term "passing" comes from "passing as white," which emerged as a phenomenon after 1875 when Southern states re-established racial segregation through hundreds of "Jim Crow"[2] laws. At that point, some African Americans passed as a way to get better jobs.

> [S]ome who passed as white on the job lived as black at home. Some lived in the North as white part of the year and as black in the South the rest of the time. More men passed than women . . . the vast majority who could have passed permanently did not do so, owing to the pain of family separation, condemnation by most blacks, their fear of whites, and the loss of the security of the black community. . . . Passing as white probably reached an all-time peak between 1880 and 1925 (Davis, 1991:56–57).

"Passing as white" is now quite rare and strongly condemned by African Americans, a reaction that "indicate[s] the resolute insistence that anyone with even the slightest trace of black ancestry is black, and a traitor to act like a white" (Davis, 1991:138). We will use the term "passing" here to refer to those who have not made their stigmatized status evident; it is similar to the phrase "being in the closet" which is usually applied to gays. Because it is among gays that passing is now most frequent—as well as most vehemently debated—many of our examples will focus on that stigmatized status.

One may come to be passing by happenstance as well as by choice. For example, the presumption that everyone is heterosexual can have the effect of putting gay people in the closet even when they had not intended to be. In the midst of a series of lectures on marriage and the family, one of our colleagues realized that he had been making assignments, lecturing, and encouraging discussion with the presumption that all of the students in the class had, or wanted to have, heterosexual relationships. Unless his gay and lesbian students wished to do something specific to counter his assumption, they were effectively passing. His actions forced them to choose between announcing or remaining silent about their status. Had he assumed that students in the class would only be involved with others of the same race, he would have created a similar situation for those in interracial relationships. Thus, assumptions about another's private life may have the effect of making them choose between silence or an announcement of something they may consider private.

Those who are gay especially face the problem of passing because others have mistaken their identity. Since most heterosexuals assume that everyone else is heterosexual, many social encounters either put a gay person in the closet or require they announce their status.

> Every encounter with a new classful of students, to say nothing of a new boss, social worker, loan officer, landlord, doctor, erects new closets [that] . . . exact from at least gay people new surveys, new calculations, new draughts and requisitions of secrecy or disclosure. Even an *out* gay person deals daily with interlocutors about whom she doesn't know whether they know or not [or whether they would care]. . . . The gay closet is not a feature only of the lives of gay people. But for many gay people it is still the fundamental feature of social life; there can be few gay people . . . in whose lives the closet is not a shaping presence (Sedgwick, 1990:68).

Inadvertent passing is also experienced by those whose racial status is not immediately apparent. An African American acquaintance who looks white is often in settings in which others do not know that she is African American—or in which she does not know if they know—and must regularly decide how and when to convey that information. This is important to her as a way to discourage racist remarks, since whites often assume it is acceptable to make racist remarks to one another (as men often assume it is acceptable to make sexist remarks to other men, or as straights presume it acceptable to make homophobic remarks to those they think are also straight). It is also important to her that others know she is black so that they understand the meaning of her words—so that they will hear her words through her status as an African American woman. In all, those whose stigma is not apparent must go to some lengths to avoid being in the closet by virtue of others' assumptions.

But passing may also be an intentional choice. For example, one of our students, who was in the process of deciding that he was gay, had worked for many years at a local library and became friends with several of his coworkers. Much of the banter at work, however, involved disparaging gay, or presumably gay, library patrons. As he grappled with a decision about his own sexual identity, his social environment reminded him that being gay is a stigmatized status in American society. The student did not so much face prejudice against himself (since he was not "out" to his work friends), but rather he faced an "unwilling acceptance of himself by individuals who are prejudiced against persons of the kind he can be revealed to be" (Goffman, 1963:42). Thus, he was not the person his friends took him to be. While survey research indicates that those who personally know a gay man hold consistently more positive feelings toward male homosexuals as a group (Herek and Glunt, 1993), the decision to reveal oneself as possessing a stigma that others have gone on record as opposed to is not lightly made.

The revelation of stigma changes one's interactions with "normals"—even those who are not particularly prejudiced against the group of which one is a member. The stigma itself, for a time, is there as something to be dealt with; the relationship is for a time changed. Revealing stigma risks permanently altering important relationships. Parents disown children who come out as gay, just as they do children involved in interracial relationships. Thus, the decision to pass or be "out" is not taken lightly. For the discreditable, what Goffman euphemistically described as "information management" is at the core of one's life. "To tell or not to tell; to let on or not to let on; to lie or not to lie; and in each case, to whom, how, when, and where" (Goffman, 1963:42). Such choices are faced daily by those who are discreditable, not just those who are gay and lesbian, but also those who are poor, have been imprisoned, attempted suicide, terminated a pregnancy through abortion, are HIV-positive, are drug or alcohol dependent, or have been the victims of incest or rape. Thinking back to the discussion of privilege, one item we might now add is that those who do not occupy stigmatized statuses needn't invest emotional energy in monitoring information about themselves; when they choose, they can talk openly about their personal history.

Still, there are both positive and negative aspects to passing. On the positive, passing lets the person with the stigma exert some power over the situation; they control the information, the flow of events, and their privacy. By withholding their identity until they choose to reveal it, they may create a situation in which others' prejudices are challenged. In some ways, passing is an effort to get one's "due"—to be judged as an individual rather than be discounted by virtue of one's stigma. Passing also limits one's exposure to verbal and physical abuse, allows for the development of relationships outside the constraints of stigma, and improves job and income security by reducing one's exposure to discrimination.

On the negative side, passing consumes a good deal of time, energy, and emotion in the management of personal information. It introduces a significant level of deception and secrecy into even close relationships. Passing also denies others the opportunity to prove themselves unprejudiced, and it makes one vulnerable to depredation from those who do know about one's stigma.

While the closet is a significant feature in the lives of all the discreditable, they do not all suffer similarly upon coming out. Literature professor Eve Kosofsky Sedgwick (1990) makes this clear in a comparison between coming out as a Jew and coming out as gay. Jews are unlikely to be told that it's a phase, that they are just angry at gentiles, that counseling might help them get over it, or that they aren't "really" Jewish—but responses such as these are the frequent reaction to those who come out as gay. In many ways, such reactions assume that those outside the stigmatized status are best able to judge the situation or that those who do not fit the stereotypes about the stigmatized group could not really be "full-fledged" members of it.

Continuing with Sedgwick's analogy, a person coming out as a Jew is unlikely to be told that they could control it if they wanted to, or that the hearer always knew that the person was Jewish and was just waiting for them to recognize it themselves (another claim that those without the stigma are best able to judge how it operates). Coming out as a Jew does not suggest that the one to whom this is revealed might also be Jewish or that it is their fault that you are Jewish, it is not likely to be construed as an invitation to an intimate relationship, nor is it likely to plunge the hearer into the closet as someone with a Jewish friend or relative. And at this point in history, one is unlikely to be beaten up or killed for revealing that one is Jewish.

The Discredited: Flaming

While the stigma experienced by the discreditable is complicated by invisibility, the experience of the discredited is complicated by visibility. As we shall see, those who are discredited suffer from being the subjects of a disproportionate share of attention and of being seen in terms of stereotypes. In the face of these difficulties it is not surprising that the discredited sometimes "flame."

Being discredited means that one's stigma is immediately apparent to others. As essayist bell hooks describes below, those who are discredited often have little patience for those who at least have the option of passing.

Many of us have been in discussions where a nonwhite person—a black person—struggles to explain to white folks that while we can acknowledge that gay people of all colors are harassed and suffer exploitation and domination, we also recognize that there is a significant difference that arises because of the visibility of dark skin. . . . While it in no way lessens the severity of such suffering for gay people, or the fear that it causes, it does mean that in a given situation the apparatus of protection and survival may be simply not identifying as gay. In contrast, most people of color have no choice. No one can hide, change, or mask dark skin color. White people, gay and straight, could show greater understanding of the impact of racial oppression on people of color by not attempting to make these oppressions synonymous, but rather by showing the ways they are linked and yet differ (hooks, 1989:125).

For the discredited, stigma is likely to be always shaping interaction with those who are not stigmatized, but its effect does not necessarily play out in ways one can easily determine. Those whose stigma is visible must daily decide whether the world is responding to them or their stigma. Florynce Kennedy, a black activist in the civil rights and women's movements once commented that the problem with being black in America was that you never knew whether what happened to you, good or bad, was because of your talents or because you were black (Kennedy, 1976). This was described in 1903 by sociologist W.E.B. Du Bois as the "double consciousness" of being black in America. The concept was key to Du Bois's classic, *The Souls of Black Folk,* for which he was rightfully judged "the father of serious black thought as we know it today" (Hare, 1982:xiii). Du Bois described double consciousness this way:

> the Negro . . . [is] gifted with a second-sight in this American world—a world which yields him no true self-consciousness, but only lets him see himself through the revelation of the other world. It is a peculiar sensation, this double consciousness, this sense of always looking at one's self through the eyes of others, of measuring one's soul by the tape of a world that looks on in amused contempt and pity. One ever feels his twoness . . . (1982:45).

. . . When those who are stigmatized view themselves from the perspective of the nonstigmatized, they have reduced themselves to objects. This theme of double or "fractured" consciousness can also be found in contemporary analyses of women's experience.

The greatest effect of being visibly stigmatized is on one's life chances—literally, one's chances for living. Thus, the readings in this text detail differences in income, employment, health, life span, education, targeting for violence, and the likelihood of arrest and imprisonment. In this essay, however, we will consider the more mundane difficulties created by stigmatization, particularly the sense of being "on stage."

The discredited often have the feeling of being watched or on display when they are in settings dominated by non-stigmatized people. For example, when women walk through male-dominated settings, they often feel on display in terms of their physical appearance. Asian, black, and Latino students in white/Anglo dominated settings often describe a feeling of being on display in campus dining facilities. In such cases, the discredited are likely to feel that others are evaluating them in terms of their stigmatized status.

As sociologist Rosabeth Moss Kanter (1980; 1993) has shown, these feelings are likely to be accurate. When Kanter studied corporate settings in which there was one person visibly different from the others, she found that person likely to get a disproportionate share of attention. In fact, people in the setting were likely to closely monitor what the minority person did, which meant that their mistakes were more likely to be noticed—and that the mistakes of those in the rest of the group were more likely to be overlooked, since everyone was watching the minority person. Kanter focused on work settings, but found that this excessive attention to those who were visibly different persisted in after-work socializing as well. Thus, even at the time designated for relaxation among colleagues, the visibly different found themselves still on stage.

In addition to receiving a disproportionate share of attention, Kanter also found that the minority person's behavior was likely to be interpreted in terms of the prevailing stereotypes about the members of that category. For example, when there were only a few men in a setting in which women predominated, the men were likely to be subject to intense observation and their behavior was likely to be filtered through the stereotypes about men irrespective of their actual behavior. That is, perceptions were distorted to fit the pre-existing beliefs.

Prior to the entrance of a visibly different person, members of a setting are likely to see themselves as different from one another in various ways, as not necessarily constituting a coherent "us" in any special sense. Through contrast with the visibly different person, however, they notice their similarities. In this way, majority group members may construct dichotomies out of settings in which there are a few who are different. It is not surprising that those who are visibly different may sometimes isolate themselves in response.

Still, none of this is inevitable. Kanter argues strongly that as there is more diversity in a setting these processes abate but that the proportion of those who are visibly different must rise to about 15 percent before that change takes place. Until that point, however, those who are in the minority (or visibly stigmatized) are the subject of a good deal of attention. As a consequence they are often accused of "flaming." "Flaming" popularly refers to acting in an effeminate manner, with the intention of letting observers know that one is gay. Most likely, the term originated as a criticism of gay men but has since been appropriated more positively by that community. We use the term here to describe an unabashed display of one's stigmatized status.

Flaming is a charge those who are not stigmatized often level at those who are stigmatized. Although there are certainly occasions in which the discredited may deliberately make a show of their status, Kanter's work makes clear that when their representation is low, the discredited are likely to be charged with flaming no matter what they do. Subjected to a disproportionate amount of attention and viewed through the lens of stereotypes, almost anything the discredited do is likely to be noticed and attributed to the category of which they are a member. Thus, one of the frequent charges leveled at those in discredited groups is that they are "so" black, Latino, gay, etc., i.e., that they make too much of a show of their status.

There are various ways that this charge might affect those in discredited statuses. Many are careful to behave in ways deliberately contrary to expectations. At other times, however, flaming may be a deliberate goal. In the first session of one class, a student opened his remarks by saying "Well, you all know I am a gay man, and as a gay man I think . . .". The informal buzz of conversation stopped, other students stared at him, and one asked "How would we know you were gay?" The student pointed to a button showing a pink triangle he had pinned to his book bag and explained that he thought they knew that someone wearing it would be gay. (Pink triangles were assigned to gay men during the Nazi era, black triangles to lesbians and other "unwanted" women. Both have been adopted as badges of pride among gay activists. Still, his logic was weak: Anyone supportive of gay rights might wear the button.)

This announcement—which moved the student from a discreditable to a discredited status—may have been intended to keep his classmates from making overtly anti-gay comments in his presence. If they should make such comments, at least then all would know they were intended for his ears and his response. In a way, his was a strategy designed to counter the problem of passing described earlier: To avoid being mistakenly identified as straight and put into a position of inadvertent passing, he was in effect required to flame. In order to avoid misidentification, he had to find an opportunity to announce his status.

Similarly, light-skinned African Americans are encouraged to "flame" as black, lest they be accused of trying to pass. In adolescence, light-skinned black men are often derided by their black and white peers as not "really" black and so go to great lengths to counter that. As an instance of this, writer Itaberi Njeri offered a moving description of her cousin Jeffrey, who looked like singer Ricky Nelson, spent his brief life trying to demonstrate that he was black and tough, and died violently as a result (Njeri, 1991). While many light-skinned black men indicate that, when they are older, their skin color puts them at an advantage in both the black and white communities, in adolescence that is certainly not the case and thus they must "flame" their identity (Russell, Wilson, and Hall, 1992). However, light skin appears to be an advantage for black women throughout their lives.

But flaming does not only have this tragic side. For example, many bilingual Latino students talk about how much they enjoy a loud display of Spanish among Anglos; some Asian American students have described their pleasure in pursuing extended no-English-used card games in public spaces on campus. Black students and gay students sometimes entertain themselves by loudly affecting stereotypical behavior and then watching the disapproving looks that follow. Those who do not occupy stigmatized statuses may better appreciate these displays by remembering their experience of deliberating flaming as "obnoxious teenagers" in public settings—an experience many remember fondly. Thus, flaming may also be fun.

In all, those who are visibly stigmatized—who cannot or will not hide their identity—generate a variety of mechanisms to try to neutralize that stigma. Flaming is one of those mechanisms: It both announces one's stigmatized status and one's disregard for those who judge it negatively. Flaming neutralizes stigma by denying there is anything to be ashamed of. Thus, it functions as a statement of group pride. . . .

POINTS OF CONTENTION, STAGES OF CONTENTIOUSNESS

This essay has focused on privilege and stigma and how they yield different treatment and different world views. In this final section we will focus on differing conceptions of exclusion and racism. Then we will consider the stages of identity development within which privilege and stigma are experienced.

As we said earlier, flaming sometimes leaves those who are not members of the stigmatized category feeling excluded. For example, when Latino students talked about their enjoyment of using Spanish, an Anglo friend immediately responded with a description of how excluded she felt on those occasions. While aware of this, the Latino students nonetheless made clear that they were not willing to forgo these opportunities. Non-Spanish-speaking friends would just have to understand that it wasn't anything personal against them. This may well mark the bottom line: Those not part of stigmatized categorizations will sometimes feel and be excluded by their friends.

But there is another question implied here: If the Hispanics exclude the Anglos, can the Anglos similarly exclude the Hispanics? As a way to approach this, consider the following two statements about gays and straights. In what ways are they similar, and in what ways different?

A heterosexual says, "I can't stand gays. I don't want to be anywhere around them."

A gay says, "I can't stand straights. I don't want to be anywhere around them."

While the statements are almost identical, they speak from very different positions of power. The heterosexual could likely structure his or her life so as to rarely interact with anyone gay, or at least anyone self-identified as gay. Most important, however, the heterosexual's attitude is consistent with major social, political, legal, and religious practices. Thus, the heterosexual in this example speaks from a position of some power, if only that derived from alignment with dominant cultural practices.

This is not the case for the gay person in this example, who is unlikely to be able to avoid contact with straights—and who would probably pay a considerable economic cost for self-segregation if that were attempted. There are no powerful institutional supports for hatred of straights. Analogously, the pleasure of exclusiveness enjoyed by bilingual Latino students exists against a backdrop of relative powerlessness, discrimination, stigmatization, and the general necessity of speaking English. The same might be said of men's disparagement of women compared to women's disparagement of men. As one student wrote, "As a male I have at times been on the receiving end of comments like, 'Oh, you're just like all men,' or 'Why can't men show more emotion?', but these comments or the sentiments behind them do not carry any power to affect my status. Even in the instance of a black who sees me as a representative of all whites, his vision of me does not change my privileged status."

Thus, the exclusiveness of those in non-stigmatized statuses has as its backdrop relative powerfulness, a sense of entitlement, infrequent discrimination based on master status, and a general ability to avoid those who might be prejudiced against people like oneself. The forms of exclusion available to minority group members are unlikely to tangibly affect the lives of those in privileged statuses. Being able to exclude someone from a dance or a club is not as significant as being able to exclude them from employment, residence, education, professional organizations, or financing.

This is what is meant when it is said that members of stigmatized categories may be prejudiced but cannot be racist or sexist, etc.; they do not have access to the institutional power by which to significantly affect the lives of those in non-stigmatized groups.

Apart even from this, however, the term *racist* carries different connotations for blacks and whites. . . . Among whites being a racist usually means being color conscious; those who are not color conscious are not racists. This understanding of what it means to be a racist has partly followed from the civil rights movement. If, as the civil rights movement taught, color should not make a difference in the way people

are treated, whites who make a point of not noticing race argue that they are being polite and not racist (Frankenberg, 1993).

But given America's historical focus on race, it seems unrealistic for any of us to claim that we are oblivious to it. While many consider it impolite to mention race, differential treatment does not disappear as a consequence. Further, a refusal to notice race conveys that being black, Asian, or Latino is a "defect" it is indelicate (for whites) to mention. Thus, it can be argued that color-blindness is not really a strategy of politeness, it is a strategy of power-evasion. Since race clearly makes a difference in people's lives, pretending not to see it is a way to avoid noticing its effect, which has the consequence of maintaining racism. The alternative would be a strategy of race cognizance, i.e., of systematic attention to the impact of race on oneself and others (Frankenberg, 1993). . . .

REFERENCES

Benokraitis, Nijole, and Joe R. Feagin. 1995. *Modern Sexism: Blatant, Subtle, and Covert Discrimination.* 2d ed. Englewood Cliffs, New Jersey: Prentice Hall.

Bergmann, Barbara. 1986. *The Economic Emergence of Women.* New York: Basic Books.

Cary, Lorene. 1991. *Black Ice.* New York: Knopf.

Cross, H., G. Kenney, J. Mell, and W. Zimmerman. 1990. *Employer Practices: Differential Treatment of Hispanic and Anglo Job Seekers.* Washington, D.C.: The Urban Institute.

Davis, F. James. 1991. *Who is Black? One Nation's Definition.* University Park, Pennsylvania: Pennsylvania University Press.

Du Bois, W.E.B. 1982. *The Souls of Black Folk.* New York: Penguin. (Originally published in 1903.)

Ettinger, Maia. 1994. The Pocahontas Paradigm, or Will the Subaltern Please Shut Up? *Tilting the Tower,* edited by Linda Garber, 51–55. New York: Routledge.

Frankenber, Ruth. 1993. *White Women, Race Matters: The Social Construction of Whiteness.* Minneapolis, Minnesota: University of Minnesota Press.

Goffman, Erving. 1961. *Asylums.* New York: Doubleday Anchor.

———. 1963. *Stigma: Notes on the Management of Spoiled Identity.* Englewood Cliffs, New Jersey: Prentice-Hall.

Hare, Nathan. 1982. W. E. Burghart Du Bois: An Appreciation, pp. xiii-xxvii in *The Souls of Black Folk.* New York: Penguin (Originally published in 1969.)

Herek, Gregory M., and Eric K. Glunt. 1993. Heterosexuals Who Know Gays Personally Have More Favorable Attitudes. *The Journal of Sex Research, 30:239–244.*

hooks, bell. 1989. *Talking Back: Thinking Feminist, Thinking Black.* Boston: South End Press.

Kanter, Rosabeth Moss. 1993. *Men and Women of the Corporation.* New York: Basic Books. (Originally published in 1976.)

Kanter, Rosabeth Moss with Barry A. Stein. 1980. *A Tale of 'O': On Being Different in an Organization.* New York: Harper and Row.

Kennedy, Florynce. 1976. *Color Me Flo: My Hard Life and Good Times.* Englewood Cliffs, New Jersey: Prentice Hall.

Kimmel, Michael S. and Michael A. Messner, eds. 1989. *Men's Lives.* New York: Macmillan.

Kornheiser, Tony. 1990. The Ordinary Face of Racism. *Washington Post.* May 16, pp. Fl, F9.

Lester, Joan. 1994. *The Future of White Men and Other Diversity Dilemmas.* Berkeley: Conari Press.

McIntosh, Peggy. 1988. *White Privilege and Male Privilege: A Personal Account of Coming to See Correspondences Through Work in Women's Studies.* Working Paper Number 189, Wellesley College, Center for Research on Women, Wellesley, Massachusetts.

National Opinion Research Center. 1990. *An American Profile: Opinions and Behavior 1972–1989.* Detroit: Gale Research.

Njeri, Itaberi. 1991. Who is Black? *Essence,* September, pp. 64–66, 114–16.

Rosenhan, D.L. 1973. On Being Sane in Insane Places. *Science* 179:250–258.

Russell, Kathy, Midge Wilson, and Ronald Hall. 1992. *The Color Complex: The Politics of Skin Color Among African Americans.* New York: Harcourt Brace Jovanovich.

Schur, Edwin. 1984. *Labeling Women Deviant: Gender, Stigma, and Social Control.* New York: Random House.

Sedgwick, Eve Kosofsky. 1990. *The Epistemology of the Closet.* Berkeley: University of California Press.

Spelman, Elizabeth. 1988. *Inessential Woman.* Boston: Beacon Press.

Treiman, Donald J. and Heidi I. Hartmann. 1981. *Women, Work, and Wages: Equal Pay for Jobs of Equal Value.* Washington, D.C.: National Academy Press.

Turner, Margery Austin, Michael Fix, and Raymond J. Struyk. 1991. *Opportunities Denied, Opportunities Diminished: Discrimination in Hiring.* Washington, D.C.: The Urban Institute.

Updegrave. Walter. 1994. You're Safer Than You Think. *Money*, June, pp. 114–124.

U.S. Department of Commerce. 1993. *Statistical Abstract of the United States. 1992.* Washington D.c.: U.S. Government Printing Office.

U.S. Department of Labor. Bureau of Labor Statistics. 1991. February 80. *Usual Weeklu Earnings of Wage and Salary Workers: Fourth quarter,* 1990.

U.S. Department of Labor. Bureau of Labor Statistics. 1993. *Employment and Earnings* Washington. D.C.: U.S. Government Printing Office.

Notes

1. Income figures exclude "money income received before payments for personal income, taxes, Social Security, union dues, Medicare deductions, food stamps, health benefits, subsidized housing, or rent-free housing and goods produced and consumed on the farm" (U.S. Department of Commerce, 1993:425).

2. "Jim Crow" was "a blackface, singing-dancing-comedy characterization portraying black males as childlike, irresponsible, inefficient, lazy, ridiculous in speech, pleasure-seeking, and happy, [and was] a widespread stereotype of blacks during the last decades before emancipation . . ." (Davis, 1991:51). "Jim Crow" laws were laws by which whites imposed segregation following the Civil War.

Discussion Questions

1. Why is privilege so difficult for members of the dominant group to notice? Consider your own race and gender statuses, and determine whether they carry a privilege or a stigma in American society. If both are privileged, have you considered this prior to this reading? If both are stigmatized, are both equally noticeable to you, or is one more prominent than the other in terms of your day-to-day life experiences? If you have one stigmatized and one privileged status, is your stigma more noticeable to you than your privilege, as the reading suggests?

2. Most of the examples given of "re-reading" or looping in the reading do not address race or gender directly. Can you think of some examples of how dominant group members "re-read" accounts of discrimination reported by women and people of color? What do you think the effects of this are on members of minority groups?

3. Why do the authors claim that the statement "I can't stand straights" spoken by a gay person does not have the same impact or meaning as "I can't stand gays" uttered by a straight person? How does this apply to race? Gender? What does this tell us about the sociological nature of prejudice and discrimination?

Current Debates

Race and Sport

How real is race? Is it a matter of biology and genes and evolution or a mere social fiction arising from specific historical circumstances, such as American slavery? Does knowing a person's race tell us anything important about them? Does it help us understand anything about their character, their medical profile, their trustworthiness, their willingness to work hard, or their intelligence? Does race play a role in shaping a person's character or their potential for success in school or on the job?

The debate about the significance of race and the broader question of "nature versus nurture" has been going on in one form or another for a very long time. One version of the debate has centered on the relationship between intelligence and race. Some have argued that biological or genetic differences make some races more capable than other races. Today, most scientists reject this argument and maintain that there is no meaningful connection between race and mental aptitude (for the latest round of arguments in this debate, see Herrnstein & Murray, 1994; Jacoby & Glauberman, 1995).

Another manifestation of this debate centers on the relationship between race and sport. The fact is that—contrary to their general status as a minority group—African Americans dominate several different sports in the United States today and are more prominent among professional athletes—and especially among the very elite—than in virtually any other sphere of American life. For example, African Americans are heavily over-represented at the highest levels of achievement in basketball, football, track and field, and to a lesser extent, baseball and soccer. In the late 1990s, blacks made up only 13 percent of the population but more than 75 percent of professional basketball players, two-thirds of professional football players, and at least 15 percent of professional baseball and soccer players (Population Reference Bureau, 2000). With Tiger Woods dominating professional golf, only the National Hockey League remains "white" among professional sports. The dominance of athletes of African descent in certain sports is repeated at the level of international sports, where athletes of African descent dominate both sprinting and long-distance running events.

Why is this so? What role has race played in establishing this pattern? Are people of African descent "naturally" better athletes? Or are there social, cultural, and environmental forces at work here that produce this extraordinary dominance? One thing we do know, after so many decades of debate on this topic, is that there is no simple choice between nature and nurture; virtually every scholar agrees that both genetic heritage and experience play a role in shaping a person's potential and their adult personality. The continuing debate is more about the *relative* significance of these two forces, which is more important and powerful.

In the selections that follow, journalist Jon Entine argues that the dominance of black athletes is due to biological and genetic factors. While he acknowledges that environment and experience play a role, he concludes that the genetic superiority of black athletes is the key characteristic that explains their dominance in sports.

Professor Jonathan Marks presents the opposing viewpoint. He argues that Entine's use of the concept of race is uncritical and careless. He attacks Entine's argument on scientific and logical grounds and concludes that Entine confuses the social and biological meanings of race. If the category "African American" is a social construction and not a scientific reality, can an argument that assumes a biological difference between the races be sustained?

REFERENCES

Herrnstein, Richard, & Murray, Charles. 1994. *The Bell Curve*. New York: Free Press.

Jacoby, Russell, & Glauberman, Naomi. 1995. *The Bell Curve Debate*. New York: Random House.

Population Reference Bureau. 2000. *Occupational Segregation*. Retrieved from the World Wide Web on June 18, 2002, at: http://www.prb.org/Content/NavigationMenu/Ameristat/Topics1/RaceandEthnicity/U_S_Occupational_Segregatio.htm.

The Dominance of Black Athletes Is Genetic

Jon Entine

[T]he evidence of black superiority in athletics is persuasive and decisively confirmed on the playing field. Elite athletes who trace most or all of their ancestry to Africa are by and large better than the competition. The performance gap is widest when little expensive equipment or facilities are required, such as running, the only true international sport, and in widely played team sports such as basketball and football. Blacks not only outnumber their nonwhite competitors but, by and large, are the superstars.

This disparity, which we can expect to increase as socio-economic barriers continue to erode, results from a unique confluence of cultural and genetic forces. The favored and socially acceptable explanation for this phenomenon—a dearth of opportunities elsewhere, does not suffice to explain the dimensions of this monopoly. The decisive variable is in our genes—the inherent differences between populations shaped over many thousands of years of evolution. Physical and physiological differences, infinitesimal as they may appear to some, are crucial in competitions in which a fraction of a second separates the gold medalist from the also-ran. . . .

Whether or not genes confer a competitive advantage on blacks when it comes to stealing bases, running with the football, shooting hoops, or jumping hurdles remains the $64,000 question. Since the first known study of differences between blacks and white athletes in 1928, the data have been remarkably consistent: in most sports, African-descended athletes have the capacity to do better with their raw skills than whites. Let's summarize the physical and physiological differences known to date. Blacks with a West African ancestry generally have:

- relatively less subcutaneous fat on arms and legs and proportionately more lean body and muscle mass, broader shoulders, larger quadriceps, and bigger, more developed musculature in general;
- smaller chest cavities;
- a higher center of gravity, generally shorter sitting height, narrower hips, and lighter calves;
- a longer arm span and "distal elongation of segments"—the hand is relatively longer than the forearm, which in turn is relatively longer than the upper arm; the foot is relatively longer than the tibia (leg), which is relatively longer than the thigh;
- faster patellar tendon reflex;
- greater body density, which is likely due to higher bone mineral density and heavier bone mass at all stages in life, including infancy (despite evidence of lower calcium intake and a higher prevalence of lactose intolerance, which prevents consumption of dairy products);
- modest, but significantly higher, levels of plasma testosterone (3 to 19 percent), which is anabolic, theoretically contributing to greater muscle mass, lower fat, and the ability to perform at a higher level of intensity with quicker recovery;
- a higher percentage of fast-twitch muscles and more anaerobic enzymes, which can translate into more explosive energy.

Relative advantages in these physiological and biomechanical characteristics are a gold mine for athletes who compete in such anaerobic activities as football, basketball, and sprinting, sports in which West African blacks clearly excel. However, they also pose problems for athletes who might want to compete as swimmers (heavier skeletons and smaller chest cavities could be drags on performance) or in cold-weather and endurance sports. Central West African athletes are more susceptible to fatigue than whites and East Africans, in effect making them relatively poor candidates for aerobic sports.

East Africa produces the world's best aerobic athletes because of a variety of bio-physiological attributes. Blacks from this region in Africa have more energy-producing enzymes in the muscles and an apparent ability to process oxygen more efficiently, resulting in less susceptibility to fatigue; they have a slighter body profile and a larger lung capacity than whites or West Africans, which translates into great endurance.

White athletes appear to have a physique between central West Africans and East Africans. They have more endurance but less explosive running and jumping ability than West Africans; they tend to be quicker than East Africans but have less endurance.

SOURCE: Entine, Jon. (2003). *Taboo: Why Black Athletes Dominate Sports and Why We're Afraid to Talk About It*. New York: Copyright Clearance Center.

THE ARGUMENT FOR GENETIC DIFFERENCES IS DEEPLY FLAWED

Jonathan Marks

Why does one kid become a boxer and another a doctor? That's a question for astrologers, not for scientists. Expectations, early tracking, ethnic or familial tradition, self-image, and of course opportunity, are all forces that work with the genetic endowment. Unless those variables are controlled, one simply cannot make a reasonable scientific case for the latter being the determining variable.

If anthropology has shown anything in this century, it's that a consistent observed group difference (from professional overrepresentation to skull shape) is not valid evidence of an innate [or genetic] basis for the difference. And the achievements of the few most extreme individuals are simply not a valid description of the population from which they are drawn.

The closest thing to scientific argument in [Entine's] book is that in a black athlete and a white athlete, uncontrolled for any other life-history variables except maybe age, one had more "fast-twitch" fibers than the other. But that's hardly credible support for a genetic argument about racial endowments.

Especially notable is what the book omits to make its case. Dominant non-black athletes, like boxer Rocky Marciano or marathoner Grete Waitz, don't get a mention, and thus can't possibly be represented as racial paragons. The discussion of women in basketball doesn't include either Nancy Lieberman or Rebecca Lobo. . . . The glorification of Michael Jordan as a black athlete is never matched by that of Mark Spitz or Sandy Koufax as Jewish athletes. . . . [Entine's book] thus exists in a universe of racialized lives and accomplishments, in which an athletic achievement is not the product of individual greatness, but merely a tally on a group scorecard.

Ultimately [Entine's] arguments . . . are so muddled that it is unclear just what the book is trying to say about race and athletics. Does the author think the very best blacks have a genetic advantage over the very best whites, that the average black has a genetic advantage over the average white, or that all blacks have the genetic potential to be better than all whites? All three propositions, of course, are unknowable and thereby metaphysical, but the first is trivial (for it says nothing about races or populations), the second is statistically intractable (for how do you find the average?), and the third ridiculous (for its racial essentialism).

Entine writes very casually about the body build of the black athlete, but empirical data are the nemeses of essentialism: William (Refrigerator) Perry, Reggie White, Barry Sanders, Sammy Sosa, Ben Johnson, and Kobe Bryant all have very different body builds. Whatever common genetic-athletic thread they share is pretty obscure.

That elite athletes—or elite anybodys—are in some sense constitutionally endowed with the ability to perform at a high level, can hardly be challenged. The interesting question, which [Entine] never actually articulates, is the manner in which such genetic variation may be patterned.

The classical answer was that patterns of genetic variation respect social, political, and economic boundaries, such that different groups of people have detectably different genetic constellations. To the extent that such a hypothesis can be tested, it has failed miserably. . . . It seems as though the vast bulk of detectable genetic variation in the human species is within-group, not between-group, variation. . . . If genes for sports ability exist, then presumably they ought to follow the same pattern [of greater variation within than between groups]. . . .

What would it take to establish that black athletes are really better endowed than white athletes from the zygote? . . . Well-controlled experiments and data that begin by acknowledging the complexities of life histories, the poverty of rigorous data on the subject, the ease with which cultural stereotypes can be made to look like natural differences, and the difficulty in generalizing about the properties of populations from a comparison of the performances of their most outstanding members. Otherwise, you present a lot of interesting fluffy mush which doesn't make the point you advance—which is ultimately the problem [with Entine's book].

SOURCE: Marks, Jonathan. (2000). Review of "Taboo: Why Black Athletes Dominate Sports and Why We're Afraid to Talk About It." *Human Biology* 72, p. 1074.

QUESTIONS TO CONSIDER

1. Is Entine using the social or biological definition of race? What does he mean by "athletes of African descent"? Is this the same thing as "African American"? Is it racist to see black athletic superiority as a "natural" gift?

2. What does Marks mean when he accuses Entine of living in a "universe of racialized lives and accomplishments"? What, according to Marks, would we need to do to settle the "nature versus nurture" debate once and for all?

3. If Entine is wrong, what social or environmental arguments might explain the dominance of African Americans in some sports?

2

ASSIMILATION AND PLURALISM

The United States is growing increasingly diverse in terms of ethnicity, race, language, and culture. How should we respond to the challenges of this diversity? Should we celebrate our pluralism and preserve our differences? Should we stress the traits we have in common and encourage everyone to "Americanize" or assimilate? How much diversity can we tolerate before societal unity is threatened? These are some of the questions raised in this chapter and debated, in one form or another, in U.S. society every day.

One approach to these issues is provided by what we can call "traditional" assimilation theory. This approach is based on decades of sociological research on the experiences of the great wave of European immigrants—and their descendents—who came from Europe between the 1820s and 1920s. It stresses the slow process of adjustment made by immigrants and their children and grandchildren, as they moved through a series of stages from disparaged outsiders to middle-class respectability. Many versions of this approach assume that assimilation is desirable, a necessity for national unity and stability, and that all groups and all people who put forth the effort will eventually find themselves accepted into the "in-group."

This "traditional" approach to assimilation has produced a body of knowledge that is complex, sophisticated, and valuable. However, it has some significant limitations. Most important, perhaps, is the fact that it was developed from the experiences of specific groups during a specific era in history. Do these insights apply to the immigrants who are entering the United States today? Contemporary immigrants come not from just Europe but from every corner of the globe, and they are much more diverse than previous waves of immigrants. Some are highly educated and skilled professionals; others bring nothing more than the clothes on their backs and a willingness to take any job, no matter how poorly paid or menial. Will all of these groups assimilate? Will they (or, more likely, their descendents) find a place in middle-class, suburban America?

This chapter presents a variety of perspectives on American assimilation and pluralism. Some are supportive of the traditional perspective and others are highly critical of that approach. The two Narrative Portraits illustrate the dichotomy. Mario Puzo, the son of Italian immigrants, writes about his faith that he will find a way to succeed in America and realize his dreams. Luis Rodriguez, also the son of immigrants, writes about a very different American reality, in which his chances for success are severely limited.

The Readings continue to explore diversity and unity in the United States. M. Patricia Fernández-Kelly and Richard Schauffler are critical of assimilation theory and argue that it is inadequate for explaining the realities faced by the contemporary immigrants they study. Ronald Takaki criticizes the traditional assimilationist view because it is exclusionary and disparages or ignores nonwhite groups. He argues for a pluralism that is inclusive and respectful of all traditions and histories, not just those that grant a privileged status to whites, males, and the middle class.

The Current Debate presents two views on a continuing controversy related to assimilation: Should the United States have an "English Only" policy? The position stated by Richard Lamm is consistent with the traditional view of assimilation and stresses the need for societal unity and the advantages of language conformity. Robert King, on the other hand, argues that language diversity is irrelevant in a society that is held together by a robust value system and a sense of "unique otherness."

NARRATIVE PORTRAITS

ASSIMILATION THEN AND NOW

Mario Puzo and Luis Rodriguez are both sons of immigrants, but they grew up in two very different Americas. Puzo, best known as the author of *The Godfather,* grew up in the Italian American community, and his memoir of life in New York City in the 1930s illustrates some of the patterns that are at the root of many theories of assimilation. Writing in the 1970s, Puzo remembers the days of his boyhood and his certainty that he would escape the poverty that surrounded him. Note also his view of (and gratitude for) an America that gave people (or at least white people) the opportunity to rise above the circumstances of their birth.

Rodriguez paints a rather different picture of U.S. society. He grew up in the Los Angeles area in the 1950s and 1960s and was a veteran of gang warfare by the time he reached high school. His memoir, *Always Running: La Vida Loca* (1993), illustrates the realities of assimilation for many contemporary immigrants. In this extract, he describes how his high school prepared Mexican American students for a life of limited opportunity and a marginal existence. Contrast his despair with Puzo's gratitude. Which sector of American society is Rodriguez being prepared to enter?

CHOOSING A DREAM: ITALIANS IN HELL'S KITCHEN

Mario Puzo

In the summertime, I was one of the great Tenth Avenue athletes, but in the wintertime I became a sissy. I read books. At a very early age I discovered libraries. . . . My mother always looked at all this reading with a fishy Latin eye. She saw no profit in it, but since all her children were great readers, she was a good enough general to know she could not fight so pervasive an insubordination.

And there may have been some envy. If she had been able to, she would have been the greatest reader of all.

My direct ancestors for a thousand years have most probably been illiterate. Italy, the golden land, . . . so majestic in its language and cultural treasures . . . has never cared for its poor people. My father and mother were both illiterates. Both grew up on rocky, hilly farms in the countryside adjoining Naples. . . . My mother was told that the family could not afford the traditional family gift of linens when she married, and it was this that decided her to emigrate to America. . . . My mother never heard of Michelangelo; the great deeds of the Caesars had not reached her ears. She never heard the great music of her native land. She could not sign her name.

And so it was hard for my mother to believe that her son could become an artist. After all, her one dream in coming to America had been to earn her daily bread, a wild dream in itself. And looking back, she was dead right. Her son an artist? To this day she shakes her head. I shake mine with her.

America may be a Fascistic, warmongering, racially prejudiced country today. It may deserve the hatred of its revolutionary young. But what a miracle it once was! What has happened here has never happened in any other country in any other time. The poor, who have been poor for centuries . . . whose children had inherited their poverty, their illiteracy, their hopelessness, achieved some economic dignity and freedom. You didn't get it for nothing, you had to pay a price in tears, in suffering, but why not? And some even became artists.

SOURCE: Puzo, Mario. (1993). Choosing a Dream: Italians in Hell's Kitchen. In W. Brown and A. Ling (Eds.), *Visions of America* (pp. 56–57). New York: Persea Books.

ALWAYS RUNNING: LA VIDA LOCA

Luis Rodriguez

Mark Keppel High School was a Depression-era structure with a brick and art deco facade and small, army-type bungalows in the back. Friction filled its hallways. The Anglo and Asian upper-class students from Monterey Park and Alhambra attended the school. They were tracked into the "A" classes; they were in the school clubs; they were the varsity team members, and lettermen. They were the pep squad and cheerleaders.

But the school also took in the people from the Hills and surrounding community who somehow made it past junior high. They were mostly Mexican, in the "C" track (what were called the "stupid" classes). Only a few of these students participated in school government, in sports, or in the various clubs.

The school had two principal languages. Two skin tones and two cultures. It revolved around class differences. The white and Asian kids . . . were from professional, two-car households with watered lawns and trimmed trees. The laboring class, the sons and daughters of service workers, janitors and factory hands, lived in and around the Hills (or a section of Monterey Park called "Poor Side").

The school separated these two groups by levels of education: The professional-class kids were provided with college-preparatory classes; the blue-collar students were pushed into "industrial arts." . . .

If you came from the Hills, you were labeled from the start. I'd walk into the counselor's office and looks of disdain greeted me—one meant for a criminal, alien, to be feared. Already a thug. It was harder to defy this expectation than just accept it and fall into the trappings. It was a jacket I could try to take off, but they kept putting it back on. The first hint of trouble and the preconceptions proved true. So why not be an outlaw? Why not make it our own?

SOURCE: Rodriguez, Luis. (1993). *Always Running: La Vida Loca* (pp. 83–84). New York: Curbstone.

READINGS

In both sociology and U.S. mainstream culture, there are different approaches to thinking about how diverse racial and ethnic groups can live together in one society. We can group these approaches broadly into two major categories: *assimilation* and *pluralism*. Assimilation refers to the traditional "melting pot" idea, whereby ethnic differences eventually disappear as groups conform to the dominant culture over succeeding generations. In contrast, pluralism is similar to the concept of "multiculturalism," which refers to different racial and ethnic groups coexisting in one society while still maintaining some degree of ethnic autonomy, ideally in a situation where no one culture is dominant and differences are equally valued. Although the assimilation approach most closely fits the experience of older white immigrants to the United States, neither approach as an ideal type describes the United States fully. However, the nation clearly draws upon both of these polar ideals as it struggles to make sense of its increasing diversity.

Because of its limited explanatory potential, traditional assimilation theory is considered outdated to many sociologists, including the authors of our first reading, Fernández-Kelly and Schauffler, who begin "Divided Fates" with a critique of traditional assimilation theory. Assuming that all immigrant groups will go through a similar stage-like assimilation process neglects the social class backgrounds they have when they arrive, the degree of their concentration in certain locations, and their mode of incorporation into the labor market, among other things. Comparing the situations of five different immigrant groups—Vietnamese and Mexicans in Southern California and Haitians, Cubans, and Nicaraguans in South Florida— the authors argue for the importance of social capital and networks in the assimilation process. Using both survey data and in-depth interviews with immigrant children and their families, the authors demonstrate that for these families, succeeding in American society does not depend on blending in with the dominant culture, but rather on being able to count on the social capital and networks developed in a certain geographic area within one's own ethnic group. We also can observe the striking distinction between *ethnicity* and *race*, since members of each group interviewed prefer to identify with their respective ethnicity (for example, Cuban, Haitian) in order to distinguish themselves from the race (Hispanic, black) into which society places them, especially when that race is associated with negative stereotypes in their minds.

It is the physical features of Ronald Takaki, Asian American author of the second reading, that a cab driver reacts to when he questions where Takaki is from, even though he was born and raised in the United States. This skewed conception of who is an American is what Takaki seeks to challenge in "A Different Mirror." Taking the position of a pluralist, he points out that many ethnic groups have been a part of the United States from its earliest beginnings, making contributions that are still with us today. Takaki also notes that there is a debate within educational institutions about whether to include multicultural curricula, with scholars like Bloom and Hirsch advocating for an assimilationist type curriculum and viewing the addition of ethnic diversity as somehow tarnishing the integrity of academics. Yet Takaki takes issue with such a position, since he does not view ethnic history as a special, separate topic, but instead as a fundamental part of American history. The key to resolving the United States' "racial crisis," Takaki argues, is for us to develop better understandings of each other, and to realize that, although we have crucial differences in our histories and how we were treated, we can usually find that we have more in common with each other than we expected. The similarities between the songs of Irish laborers and African slave spirituals serve as a powerful example of this point.

Although Takaki's pluralist vision is a noble one, it remains to be seen whether those in power would capitulate to such a remodeling of American history in which all groups are studied through their own lenses rather than those of the dominant group. But if accomplished, it would be a different mirror indeed.

Divided Fates: Immigrant Children in a Restructured U.S. Economy

M. Patricia Fernández-Kelly and Richard Schauffler

. . .

Assimilation, perhaps the most enduring theme in the immigration literature, unfolds into descriptive and normative facets. From an empirical standpoint, the concept designates a range of adjustments to receiving environments and points to the manner in which immigrants blend into larger societies. In a normative sense, assimilation is linked to an expectation that foreigners will shed, or at least contain, their native cultures while embracing the mores and language of the host country. Put succinctly, assimilation has always been more than a convenient word to enumerate the ways in which immigrants survive; it has also been a term disclosing hopes about how immigrants "should" behave.

In this article we revisit the descriptive and normative aspects of assimilation from the perspective of political economy and informed by insights from the field of economic sociology. The first section includes a review of approaches and a discussion of segmented assimilation, a term coined by Portes and Zhou (1993) to denote varying modalities of immigrant incorporation into distinct sectors of American society. The notion is serviceable in that it refines generalizations of the past by pointing to factors that can turn assimilation into an uplifting or a leveling force. At the heart of the discussion is the realization that becoming American encompasses various and sometimes conflicting meanings.

Optimistic accounts of assimilation—captured in the image of the melting pot—coexisted with the early stages of American capitalism when immigrants were the purveyors of labor for an expanding economy. Tales of weary but resolute arrivals at the shores of opportunity became part of collective self-definitions. Assimilation, conceived as the ideal path towards success, also emerged as the wellspring of national identity. Over the last two decades, economic internationalization has transformed the context in which assimilation takes place. In the Fordist era, workers could envision entry-level jobs as the first step in a journey towards prosperity. At present, when firms often subcontract services and even product assembly, many of the paths toward socioeconomic improvement have been blocked. Will the new immigrants—mostly from Asia and Latin America—replicate earlier patterns of success or face conditions of arrested progress?

Sketched in the second section is a theoretical framework that assigns priority to interpersonal networks and social capital, a process by virtue of which individuals use their membership in a particular group to gain access to valuable resources, including information and jobs. We maintain that, all the more so in a restructured economy, the outcomes of assimilation depend on a series of toponomical—that is, socially and physically situated—factors. Immigrants able to draw upon the knowledge of preexisting groups that control desirable economic assets will share an experience much different from those lacking a social nexus to opportunity and resources of high quality.

Collective identity is itself a significant resource in the process of assimilation. Although the fate of immigrants depends upon macrostructural changes like industrial restructuring, it also varies in congruence with the recasting of collective self-definitions. The immigrant condition forces individuals to observe themselves even as they are being observed by others. As a consequence, immigrants repeatedly engage in purposeful acts to signify their intended character and the way that character differs from, or converges with, that of other groups. A stigmatized identity can turn assimilation into an injurious transition unless immigrants resort to shared repertories based on national origin, immigrant status or religious conviction. Some identities protect immigrants; others weaken them by transforming them into disadvantaged ethnic minorities.

There is an ongoing relationship between migration and ethnicity: today's ethnics are the immigrants of the past and vice versa; present immigrants are already forging tomorrow's ethnic identities. New arrivals interact empirically and symbolically with their predecessors. At that juncture the African-American experience has strategic importance for the study of downward assimilation, a process defined by the incorporation of immigrants into impoverished, generally nonwhite, urban groups whose members display adversarial stances toward mainstream behaviors, including the devaluation of education and diminished expectations.

In defining themselves, immigrants of all nationalities hold the image of the urban underclass as a pivotal referent to delineate their own place in the larger society. Most African Americans were never international migrants in the conventional sense of the word. However, as migrants from the rural South during the first half of the twentieth century, they shared commonalities in profile and expectations with migrants from lands afar. In points of destination, blacks faced barriers that resulted in their arrested socioeconomic advancement. Ironically, current analyses focus not primarily on the migrant past of African Americans, but on the distressing behavioral complex surrounding concentrated poverty in the urban ghetto. Yet one way to reframe that phenomenon is as a product of migration under conditions of extreme hostility over extended periods of time.

In the third section, we pursue the argument through a comparison of five immigrant groups, Mexicans and Vietnamese in southern California and Nicaraguans, Cubans and Haitians in southern Florida. The data to sustain the comparison is drawn from two complementary sources: a national survey of children of immigrants between the ages of twelve and seventeen conducted in 1992 and a series of ethnographic case studies carried out in the latter part of 1993 and early 1994 with a small subset formed by 120 families of immigrant children in the original sample. By combining the strengths of quantitative and qualitative analyses, we draw a profile of diverging adaptations, emerging identities and segmented assimilation.

The concluding section summarizes findings and reconsiders the central questions in the light of those findings.

ASSIMILATION: OLD AND NEW

By the time the sociologists of the Chicago School turned their attention to immigration in the 1920s, observers of the American experience had been debating its two presumed outcomes—assimilation and pluralism—for almost 150 years.... Throughout that period, the chronicle of immigration excluded any mention of blacks and indigenous people, focusing primarily on Europeans.

The beginning of the twentieth century witnessed a new phenomenon. For the first time Americans of British origin represented less than half of the country's total population....

Early theories of assimilation were forged against a distinct socioeconomic background. In the early decades of the twentieth century, the Fordist economy generated millions of jobs, almost a third of which were in manufacturing and most of which required little or no previous skill. The economic expansion which promoted rising wages and mass consumption invested with plausibility the story of the widening mainstream. The expectation was that those still struggling on the river banks would soon be engulfed by the broadening waters of economic progress.

There was a major deviation from that optimistic forecast. As foreigners continued to arrive in the United States, the industrial growth of the North fueled a demand for labor which, at the time of World War I, began to be filled by black migrants from the rural South where cotton agriculture was declining. African Americans appeared in cities like Chicago, New York, Boston and Philadelphia under conditions which Robert Park (1950) regarded as optimum for assimilation. Yet the process did not bring about the anticipated effects. The experience of black Americans presented a compelling argument against the certain identification of assimilation with economic success. Although Park himself grew increasingly skeptical about assimilation as a beneficial prospect for all racial and ethnic groups, the concept became paradigmatic in the understanding of immigrant adaptation.

Despite efforts by Frazier (1957) and Gordon (1964), the notion of assimilation remained problematic in subsequent years for several reasons. First, it implied that immigrant and American cultures were mutually exclusive and bounded categories. Retaining one's native culture and becoming American were conceived as a zero-sum game; only by giving up ethnic identity could immigrants fully participate in American life.

Second, the question of agency in the process of assimilation remained ambiguous. Was it American society or the immigrant that was doing the absorbing, appropriating and amalgamating? For the most part, Park and his associates had suggested that the immigrant was the passive object of the host environment. In so doing, society appeared as an unchanging force and the immigrant as the pliant clay of a teleological—and quasi-evolutionary—process that transcended human agency.

Third, what was American took the form of an assumption not a subject for investigation. Since, for the most part, assimilation was not viewed as a reciprocal process, the American condition remained unchanged, stultified. Contestations of the dominant ideology were excluded from discussions about American identity, as were other aspects of the social structure—social class and labor markets in particular.

Finally, the relationship between individual and collective processes was often confused.

Park's general description of assimilation and his concept of the marginal man spoke to the plight of the individual. Yet a role was also reserved for communities as mechanisms necessary for individual transitions. This implied relatively autonomous group processes. The paradox entailed in that formulation—how would the last immigrant in a particular group assimilate when the community necessary to facilitate that transition had already disappeared—was not addressed.

In the 1960s and 1970s, the Civil Rights Movement focused attention on the persistent exclusion of African Americans, and new waves of immigrants from Asia, Latin America and the Caribbean provoked a renewed public debate. Pluralism and assimilation were now challenged by a variety of structural approaches of a neo-Marxist inspiration. Research on immigrant enclaves and middleman minorities turned the original conception of assimilation on its head by describing alternative, and often more effective, modes of incorporation. Self-employment, business formation, and the maintenance of shared cultural understanding outside the American mainstream were shown to enhance and accelerate economic mobility. Those views portrayed assimilation as a deflating pressure threatening immigrants' chances for success in counterposition to earlier, more optimistic, interpretations.

Structural perspectives, as well, acknowledged the importance of personal endowments and shared cultural assets, but they assigned equal priority to patterned arrangements that facilitate or impede economic advancement. Works by Blauner (1972) on internal colonialism, Portes and Bach (1986) on ethnic enclaves, and Bonacich (1980) on middleman minorities, privileged labor market inclusion and exclusion patterns, as well as their effect on social mobility. Persistent inequalities were viewed in close relationship to the location of immigrant groups and racial and ethnic minorities within the larger society.

In that context, consensus emerged that the outcome of migration depends on the interaction of three factors: 1) the internal composition of the groups to which immigrants belong, particularly in terms of social class; 2) their degree of concentration in specific locations;

and 3) their mode of reception and incorporation into specific labor market strata. The distinction between labor migration, as represented by Mexicans and African Americans, and the immigrant enclave, as illustrated by Cubans, proved to be especially instructive. Cuban success in business formation was partly due to favorable government policies aiding settlement, the presence of a critical mass of entrepreneurs among Cuban exiles, and high levels of concentration in southern Florida. By contrast, the Mexican and African-American migrations were characterized by low levels of internal differentiation, weak or nonexistent resources in the process of adjustment, and high levels of concentration in impoverished neighborhoods. Those differences led, in turn, to varying social profiles and a dissimilar capacity for socioeconomic attainment.

Immigrants have always faced a modicum of discrimination, but their potential for collective progress has depended on a minimal threshold of gradual acceptance. The movement away from the immigrant slum entailed becoming American; almost always, that also meant becoming white. For African Americans the portal leading to economic improvement was exceedingly narrow. Yet increasing opportunities, especially in manufacturing, enabled even those vulnerable groups to make strides during the first half of the twentieth century. Recent changes operating at the global level raise new questions about the nature of immigrant absorption.

As the economic base shifted from manufacturing to services and information processing, cities suffered a process of deterioration but, paradoxically, they also attracted professionals linked to lucrative sectors of the new economy—international banking and finance, communications, and software design, for example. The presence of a new technocratic class in urban centers invigorated the demand for labor-intensive products and services—ranging from domestic help to restaurants and customized furniture and apparel—creating interstices for the employment of new waves of immigrants, now from Asia, Latin America and the Caribbean, many of whom were undocumented. As a result, the global city emerged upon the ruins of the old industrial metropolis as a strategic location for the centralization of coordinating functions vis-à-vis the international economy (Sassen, 1992).

Largely on account of major changes operating at the international level and partly because of regional variations, the options of new immigrants will divide depending on their spatial location, their contact with specific social networks, and their differentiated access to economic and political resources. Those subdivisions are what the notion of segmented assimilation seeks to make comprehensible. The concept builds on structural approaches and applies their insights beyond what has been essentially a discussion of labor market incorporation. The assumption is that amalgamation does take place, but the question is restated to make problematic both the host society and the immigrant population: Assimilation to what? Assimilation by whom? The modifier segmented further underscores that it is not a single mainstream group which serves as the unique reference point for all immigrants. Before exploring these issues in further detail, we sketch a theoretical framework that assigns priority to social networks.

Social Capital and Immigrant Networks

Network analysis became popular in the 1960s and 1970s partly in reaction to the determinism of structural functionalism and the methodological individualism fostered by multivariate statistical inquiries. . . .

Here, we take a different approach by grounding our analysis of social networks in the new economic sociology. A central objective of that field is to elucidate the social underpinnings of economic action. The point bears significantly upon immigration research because, as indicated in the previous section, the character of immigrant assimilation depends largely upon social forces leading to differentiated economic outcomes. Indeed, one way to conceptualize immigration is as a phenomenon of labor mobility sustained by interpersonal networks bridging points of origin and points of destination. . . .

The importance of social networks is exemplified by the functioning of the immigrant enclave. In assembling a remarkable business conglomerate in Miami, Cubans relied on social contacts within and outside their own group. They avoided discrimination from mainstream financial institutions by obtaining loans to capitalize their firms from banks whose owners and personnel were Latin American and, therefore, Spanish speaking. Beyond their strong feeling of membership in the same community, Cubans benefited from their inclusion in a network characterized by high levels of class heterogeneity; that, in turn, enabled its members to establish multiple connections. The opposite is true about Mexicans and African Americans whose social networks are characterized by low degrees of internal differentiation in terms of class.

Those cases, as well, underscore the importance of social capital and its relationship to quality of resources. Several major writings lead to an understanding of social capital as an incorporeal but vital good accruing to individuals by virtue of their membership in particular communities (Coleman, 1988). Social capital is distinct from human capital in that it does not presuppose formal education or skills acquired through organized instruction. Instead, it originates from shared feelings of social belonging, trust and reciprocity. The concentration of immigrants of various nationalities in particular niches of the labor market occurs as a result of word-of-mouth recommendations. Those, in turn, are made possible by immigrants' membership in social networks whose members vouch for one another.

A dramatic illustration of the workings of social capital is Kasinitz and Rosenberg's (1994) study of business activity in an empowerment zone located in the notoriously destitute ghetto of Red Hook, Brooklyn. Although many businesses in the zone employ multiethnic workforces, including crews of West Indian security guards, they refuse to hire local blacks. Prejudice plays a role in this curious subdivision, but the causes of exclusion and inclusion are more complex. West Indians are joined to the employment structure through personal contacts and endorsements. Native blacks share the same physical spaces with the businesses in

question, but they are socially disconnected and, therefore, bereft of the necessary links to obtain jobs. In that case, the primary reason for ghetto unemployment is not the lack of nearby opportunities but the absence of social networks that provide entry into the labor market.

As important as social capital is the quality of the resources that can be tapped through its deployment. Interpersonal networks are distinguished as much by their ability to generate a sense of cohesion as by the extent to which they can parlay group membership and mutual assistance into worthwhile jobs and knowledge. What distinguishes impoverished from wealthy groups is not their different capacity to deploy social capital—survival of the poor also depends on cooperation—but their varying access to resources of high quality. Those resources are often embedded in physical locations not available to the impoverished. . . .

To summarize, social networks are complex formations that channel and filter information, confer a sense of identity, allocate resources, and shape behavior. Individual choices depend not only on the availability of material and intangible assets in the society at large, but also on the way in which the members of interpersonal networks interpret information and relate to structures of opportunity. . . .

The Various Meanings of Becoming American

The data for this analysis are drawn from a 1992 survey of 5,263 children of immigrants and from in-depth interviews conducted with a subsample formed by 120 of those children and their parents. For the original survey, eighth and ninth grade students in Dade County (Miami), Broward County (Fort Lauderdale), and San Diego schools were randomly selected who met the following definition of second generation: those born in the United States with at least one foreign-born parent or born abroad but having resided in this country for at least five years. Questionnaires were administered to these students in schools selected to include both inner-city and suburban settings and student populations with varying proportions of whites, minorities and immigrants. In the Miami sample, two predominantly Cuban private schools were also included. The sample is evenly divided between boys and girls; the average age of the youngsters was about fourteen.

The follow-up interviews were conducted with a subset of those originally surveyed. The national-origin groups were stratified on the basis of sex, nativity (U.S. born or foreign born), socioeconomic status based on father's occupation, and family structure (two-parent families consisting of the biological parents of the child or other equivalent care-providers). In Miami, the Cuban group was also divided between public and private school students. Names, within the cells thus created, were picked randomly by country of origin for the largest groups in the original sample—Cubans, Nicaraguans, Haitians and West Indians (mostly Jamaicans and Trinidadians) in Dade and Broward Counties; and Vietnamese, Mexicans, Filipinos, Cambodians and Laotians in San Diego. Our analysis begins with cursory descriptions of five illustrative cases.

An Ethnographic Sampler

Haitian Strivers

Being admitted into the home of Aristide Maillol in Sweetwater, Miami, transports the visitor into a transfixed space. The location is American but the essence is that of rural Haiti. Aristide's mother does not speak English. Her eyes drift to the floor when explaining in Creole that her husband is hospitalized and she had to leave her job as a janitor in a local motel to attend to his needs. There is consternation and reserve in her demeanor. (The names in these narratives are pseudonyms.)

In the tiny sitting area adjoining the front door, a large bookcase displays the symbols of family identity in an arrangement suitable for a shrine. Framed by paper flowers at the top is the painted portrait of Mrs. Maillol and her husband. Crude forms and radiant colors capture the couple's dignity. Below, in three separate shelves, several photographs show Aristide's brother and three sisters. The boy smiles

confidently in the cap and gown of a high school graduate. The girls are displayed individually and in clusters, their eyes beaming, their hair pulled back, their attires fitting for a celebration. Interspersed with the photographs are the familiar trinkets that adorn most Haitian homes. Striking, however, is the inclusion of several trophies earned by the Maillol children in academic competitions. At seventeen, Aristide's brother has already been recruited by Yale University. Young Aristide, who is fifteen and wants to be a lawyer, speaks eloquently about the future:

> We are immigrants and immigrants must work hard to overcome hardship. You can't let anything stop you. I know there is discrimination, racism . . . but you can't let that bother you. Everyone has problems, things that hold them back, but if you study . . . [and] do what your mother, what your father, tell you, things will get better. . . . God has brought us here and God will lead us farther.

In silence, Mrs. Maillol nods in agreement.

Nicaraguan Sliders

That evening, in little Havana, the Angulo family prepares for dinner in their shabby apartment. Originally from Managua, Nicaragua, Mr. Angulo holds a degree in chemistry and for a time was the manager of a sizable firm in his home country. His wife belongs to a family with connections to the military. They arrived in Miami in 1985 when their son, Ariel, was eight and their daughter, Cristina, was only two years old. Both think of themselves as exiles but are not recognized as such by the authorities. In earnest, Mr. Angulo explains:

> We came with high hopes, escaping the Sandinistas, thinking this was the land of opportunity . . . ready to work and make progress, but we were stopped in our tracks. We haven't been able to legalize our situation. Every so often, we get these notices saying we'll be thrown out of the country; it is nerve-wracking. As a result, we haven't been able to move ahead. Look around; this is the only place we've been able to rent since

we came [to Miami]. . . . I work for an hourly wage without benefits, although I perform the duties of a professional for a pharmaceutical company. They know they can abuse my condition because I can't go anywhere; no one will hire me!

Mrs. Angulo, who works as a clerk for a Cuban-owned clinic, worries that Ariel, who is approaching college age, will not be eligible for financial assistance. She does not expect him to go beyond high school, although she and her husband place a premium on education and have typical middle class aspirations. As it is, Ariel cannot even apply for a legal summer job given his undocumented status. He attends a troubled school, where he mingles primarily with other Central Americans and African Americans. Conflict is rampant and academic standards are low. He complains that other students ridicule Nicaraguans. Ariel feels that his parents are too demanding; they do not understand the pressures at school or give him credit for his effort. Even more distressing is the fact that he cannot speak either English or Spanish fluently. Almost seventeen, he shares with his mother a dim view of the future.

Cuban Gainers

Ariel's experience is in stark contrast with that of fifteen-year-old Fernando Gómez, whose family migrated to Miami in 1980 as part of the Mariel boatlift. Originally from Oriente (Manzanillo), Cuba, Mr. Gómez was employed as a heavy equipment operator and then as a clerk for the same metallurgical firm prior to his migration to the United States. Since his arrival, he has worked as a mechanic for Dade County. His wife, who used to be a teacher in Cuba, now works providing care for the elderly. Although they hold working-class jobs, the couple's tastes evince an upwardly bound thrust. Their home is part of a Cuban-owned residential development that combines pathways bordered by russet tile and luscious vegetation with pale exteriors, wrought-iron gates, and roofs of an Iberian derivation. The family's living room is embellished with new furnishings.

Proudly, Mr. Gómez states that he has never experienced discrimination; he is not the kind of man who would ever feel inferior to anyone. He expects Fernando, an even better student than his older brother, to go far. There is no doubt that he will finish college, perhaps work toward an advanced degree. Although Fernando wants to become a policeman like his brother, Mr. Gómez dismisses that intent as a passing whim; he would like his son to work with computers because "that is where the future of the world is."

Mexican Toilers

More than 3,000 miles away, in south central San Diego, Carlos Mendoza's home stands next to a boarded-up crack house. Prior to the police raid that shut it down, the Mendoza family had covered their own windows with planks to avoid witnessing what went on across the alley. The neighborhood is an assortment of vacant lots, abandoned buildings and small homes protected by fences and dogs. Fourteen years ago, the family entered the United States illegally in the trunk of a car. Their goal was to earn enough money to buy a house in their hometown in Michoacan, and although they succeeded—and purchased the house in San Diego as well—they laughingly note that somehow they never made it back to Mexico. The family has now achieved legal status under the amnesty program promoted by the 1986 Immigration Reform and Control Act.

For the past ten years, Mr. Mendoza has worked as a busboy in a fancy restaurant that caters to tourists, a position he secured through a Mexican friend. He is a hard-working and modest man who wants his son, Carlos, to study so that he can get a good job: "[I want him] to be better than me, not for my sake but for his sake and that of his own family." Mrs. Mendoza irons clothes at a Chinese-owned laundry, and complains bitterly that her employers are prejudiced toward her and other Mexicans.

Carlos is doing well in school; he was the only boy at Cabrillo Junior High to be elected to the honor society last year. He wants to become an engineer and go back to Mexico. Life in San Diego has been hard on him; the gold chain his parents gave him as a gift was ripped from around his neck by neighborhood toughs; his bicycle remains locked up inside the house, for to ride it would be to lose it to the same local bullies. His younger sister, Amelia, is not doing as well in school and dresses like a *chola* (female gang member), although she insists it is only for the style. Her parents worry but they feel helpless.

Vietnamese Bystanders

Forty blocks to the east, in another working-class neighborhood populated by Mexicans, Vietnamese and blacks, Mrs. Ly and her daughter Hoa sit in their tiny apartment surrounded by several calendars and clocks, a small South Vietnamese flag, two Buddhist shrines, and four academic achievement plaques. Two of Mrs. Ly's daughters have maintained perfect grades for two years in a row. Hoa, her mother explains, is behind; her grade point average is 3.8 rather than 4.0.

Since their arrival in the United States in 1991, neither Mrs. Ly nor her husband have held jobs; they depend on welfare, although Mrs. Ly is unclear about where exactly the money they receive comes from. Back in Vietnam, she and her husband sold American goods on the black market and supplemented their income by sewing clothes. Leaving their country was filled with trauma; they are still a bit in a daze. In San Diego, the family is isolated; people in the area resent the new arrivals. More than anything else, what keeps the Lys and other Vietnamese families apart is the language barrier: "We can't speak English," says Mrs. Ly, "so the girls don't go out much, they stay home. I raise my children here the same as I raised them in Vietnam: to school and back home."

Hoa's only friend is Vietnamese. Her mother would like her to have more American contacts so that she could learn the language and the culture of their new country. Eventually, she would like her daughter to get an office job or a job in retail sales. Hoa disagrees; she would like to be a doctor.

The cases sketched above provide a glimpse into dissimilar experiences and the variations are not arbitrary; they are representative of the groups to which the families belong. Nicaraguans expected the treatment afforded to Cubans under what they regarded as similar circumstances. For many, those expectations were

dashed as a result of the political complexities surrounding the relationship between the United States and Nicaragua. Bereft of supports in the receiving environment, many of these new immigrants are experiencing a rapid process of downward mobility although many have middle-class backgrounds. Those of humbler provenance are unable to advance. Especially disturbing is the predicament of children who, confined to immigrant neighborhoods but having spent most of their lives in the United States, cannot speak English or Spanish easily. Unable to regularize their immigrant status and facing acute economic need, many of those youngsters are choosing low-paying jobs over education. With an increasing number of high school dropouts and out-of-wedlock pregnancies, many Nicaraguan youth appear to be recapitulating aspects of the African-American trajectory (Fernández-Kelly, 1994).

Cubans, by contrast, represent an unusual case of immigrant success partly owed to conditions antithetical to those characterizing Nicaraguan migration. The first large cohorts arrived in Miami during the 1960s, prompting the customary response of more established populations: departure to the suburbs. In the beginning, Cubans, too, were perceived as an undesirable minority. Nevertheless, by contrast to other arrivals, they were a highly stratified mass that included professionals as well as an entrepreneurial elite. As a result, many were able to escape the pressures of the labor market through self-employment and business formation (Portes and Rumbaut, 1990). That, a shared and vehement opposition to the Castro regime, and assistance from the U.S. government allowed Cubans to form a cohesive community. They proceeded to reconstitute the social foundations to which they had been accustomed, including the establishment of a private school system for those who could afford it.

In 1980, the Mariel boatlift jolted Miami with new waves of mostly working-class immigrants, many of whom were of Afro-Caribbean descent. They, too, were received with a modicum of hostility that included the ambivalent feelings of older Cubans. Nevertheless, continued support on the part of the U.S. government and the preexisting ethnic enclave allowed the newcomers to adjust rapidly. To this day, the tribulations of every *balsero* (rafter) arriving in Miami, in flight from Communism, elicit admiration and reignite feelings about a shared historical experience.

Haitians represent a strategic case that contains, alternatively, elements akin to those found in the Cuban experience and others closer to the experience of Nicaraguans. Despite the ordeal of illegal migration and prejudice in the receiving environment, a substantial number of Haitians, like Aristide Maillol and his brother, are doing surprisingly well in the United States. There is evidence that their fledgling success is rooted in deliberate attempts to disassociate themselves from the stigma imposed upon black populations in the United States through an affirmation of their national identity and their religious fervor.

Other Haitians, however, appear to be blending into impoverished black groups living in ghettos such as Miami's Liberty City. A growing number of Haitian youngsters are showing up in alternative schools, detention centers and penal institutions (Stepick and Dutton-Stepick, 1994). Given their poverty-stricken status and recent arrival, Haitian immigrants were pushed into areas where rental properties were abundant and real estate prices were low. As a result, Little Haiti, a teetering concentration of Haitian homes and businesses, emerged in close proximity to inner-city neighborhoods, and it is from its dwellers that many Haitians are learning their place in American society.

As in the cases of Vietnamese and Mexicans, when Haitian children speak of discrimination, they are often thinking of the verbal and physical abuses they experience at the hands of native black Americans in their neighborhoods and schools. But by contrast to the first two groups, who attend schools characterized by higher levels of ethnic diversity, Haitians do not have alternative referents in their familiar environments. In those circumstances, the choices are clearly bifurcated: either conscious attempts at self-distinction or yielding to the norm through conformity. Insular and destitute environments can rapidly translate conformity into socioeconomic stagnation or decline.

Mexicans represent the longest unbroken migration of major proportions to the United States. Partly as a result of their widespread undocumented status and partly because of geographical proximity, many Mexicans do not see moving to the United States as a long-term decision; instead, they see themselves as sojourners, guided by an economic motive, whose real homes are south of the border. Expectations about the duration of their stay in areas of destination diminish Mexicans' involvement in entrepreneurship and business formation (Roberts, 1995). That attitude, as well, has an impact upon children's prospects because, as Portes (1993:27) puts it: "It is difficult to reach for the future when you are constantly confronting your past." With little differentiation in terms of social class, Mexicans do not hold enough power to resist the embattled conditions in the neighborhoods where they live.

The Vietnamese experience is marked by paradox. An early wave of exiles in the 1970s—many of whose members started small businesses in the United States—was followed by larger groups of peasants and unskilled workers who confronted harsher than usual journeys. In areas of destination they faced hostility, but their rapid legalization entitled them to public assistance and other benefits—up to 50 percent of Vietnamese in California are on welfare (Kitano and Daniels, 1988). Lack of English fluency and the absence of a larger and cohesive community to depend on have translated into acute degrees of isolation. However, in this case, isolation added to a widespread faith in education, discipline and family unity is producing children who are high achievers. The Vietnamese continue to be in, but not of, the United States.

Figure 2.1 summarizes the nonrandom character of the conditions experienced by the immigrant groups studied. Each group has been assigned a label that captures a distinctive experience (Cubans as Gainers; Vietnamese as Bystanders; Haitians as Strivers; Mexicans as Toilers; and Nicaraguans as Sliders). To complete the comparison, we have added a sixth group (native blacks as Survivors). The purpose of the classification is not to create yet another typology of migration, but to decouple the characteristics of segmented assimilation from national and ethnic referents, thus exposing the outcomes of migration as a function of the

	Gainers	Bystanders	Strivers	Toilers	Sliders	Survivors
Internal Differentiation by Class	+ + +	+ −	+ −	−	+ −	−
Type of Reception	+ + +	+ +	−	−	−	− − −
Quality of Resources	+ + +	+ −	−	−	−	− −
Degree of Spacial Concentration	+ +	+ −	+ +	+ +	+ −	+ + +
Length of Time in Area of Destination	+	− −	− −	+ +	− −	+ + +
	1960>	1975>	1980>	1930>	1980>	1630>

Figure 2.1

factors listed in the column on the left: Internal Differentiation by Class; Type of Reception; Quality of Resources; Degree of Spatial Concentration; and Length of Time in Area of Destination. The first four dimensions designate decisive toponomical factors underpinning the aftermath of various kinds of migration.

Although Figure 2.1 condenses the generalized experiences of the various groups, it does not capture their internal diversity, especially in terms of social class. Its sole purpose is to serve as a heuristic device for understanding the patterns of adaptation under discussion. The positions occupied by the types in the figure should be understood as approximate points along a continuum. Thus, Type of Reception ranges from highly positive—as indicated by three plus signs—to extremely hostile—as indicated by three minus signs.

Gainers, characterized by high levels of class differentiation, experienced a relatively hospitable reception, including prompt legalization, government support, and low levels of discrimination. For those reasons, they were able to tap resources of high quality, such as effective schools and adequate, affordable housing. Their spatial concentration worked advantageously, facilitating the use of social capital to gain access to information and other desirable assets. Their experience of socioeconomic mobility markedly diverges from that of Survivors, for whom spatial concentration in antagonistic environments translated into diminished connections to the larger society, resources of low quality, and diminished ability to parlay social capital into economic advantage. While Gainers thrive, Survivors endure. The other groups occupy intermediary positions within those two extremes.

The length of time in areas of destination bears a direct relationship to the consolidation of positive or negative behavioral outcomes. Over extended periods of time, low levels of class heterogeneity added to hostile modes of reception, resources of low quality, and high degrees of spatial concentration inevitably lead to a hardening of negative traits among the children and the grandchildren of internal and international migrants. In the case of African Americans, the time line extends beyond the period covered by The Great Black Migration from the rural South (1910–1970) to include a longer stretch which is part of that group's historical memory.

SURVEY FINDINGS

Survey materials contribute additional insights to the picture made vividly real by the testimonies of immigrant children and their families. Table 2.1 condenses information about school performance, parental human capital, and children's aspirations. Some differences and similarities are worth noting. Not surprisingly, Cuban children in private schools display high grade point averages and the highest standardized test scores, followed by the Vietnamese whose grades are better but whose scores lag due to lower English proficiency. Cuban students in private schools dramatically exceed the performance of those in public institutions, illustrating the critical effect of social class even within that highly integrated community. Although they are experiencing downward mobility, the scores of Nicaraguan children, many of whom have middle-class backgrounds, are relatively high. Haitians and Mexicans display comparatively low scores, as generally found in predominantly working-class populations.

Even with that in mind, the contrast between Haitians and Mexicans is noteworthy. On the aggregate, the Haitian indicators are consistent with the divided experience sketched earlier, and those of Mexicans confirm their characterization as a highly homogeneous and vulnerable group. Figures on parents' educational achievement, socioeconomic status and occupational aspirations are compatible with those profiles. And yet, regardless of national origin and social class, most immigrant children voice high educational aspirations, with Haitians second only to Cubans in private schools in their ambition to go beyond college. Again, it comes as no surprise that Mexicans constitute the only group a large proportion of whose members expect never to achieve a college education.

Table 2.2 provides information about the friendship networks of the various populations. Regardless of national origin, most children associate with members of their own group and a large number of their friends are foreign born. Within that context, nevertheless, Cubans have the highest degree of contact with members of their own group and the lowest proportion of friendships with outsiders. Oddly, Nicaraguans report a higher degree of relations with Cubans than Cubans voice with respect to Nicaraguans. Similar albeit smaller disparities are found in the contrasting testimonies of Haitians with respect to Cubans and of Mexicans with respect to the Vietnamese. Those discrepancies are explained by two tendencies: that of Cubans and Vietnamese to see themselves as enclosed communities and that of Haitians, Mexicans and Nicaraguans to be more permeable to other groups in their environments. In addition, the relationship between Nicaraguans, Haitians and Cubans is marked by status differences; often, the latter are reluctant to admit they know Nicaraguans and Haitians. That tendency is mirrored by Nicaraguans' generalized feelings that Cubans discriminate against them. In other words, Cubans and Vietnamese display the least degree of porousness of the groups studied.

Most revealing is the information contained in Table 2.3 on perceptions of discrimination and self-identification. Cuban youth report the least discrimination, a fact that is understandable; it is hard for anyone to feel rebuffed when, as Table 2.2 indicates, the overwhelming majority of his contacts are with members of his own group. Nevertheless, Cuban children in public schools experience higher levels of discrimination from both blacks and whites than those in private schools. In contrast to private institutions, public schools expose children to a plurality of ethnic and national groups and are, therefore, less able to shield them from friction. With the exception of the Vietnamese, all other groups report higher levels of discrimination from whites than from blacks.

Only Nicaraguans see Cubans as a significant source of discrimination. That may be related to a panethnic effect in Miami where the Hispanic community is internally diversified in terms of national origin, with the Cubans occupying a preeminent position and, therefore, becoming easily identifiable as a source of discrimination, particularly toward other Hispanics. On the other hand, the case of Mexicans in San Diego invites reflection because, despite the existence of a large coethnic community, membership in it does not shield Mexicans from discrimination. That, too, may be an effect of localized factors—a continued climate of hostility against Mexican immigration in California has been recently exacerbated by a severe economic downturn following a fiscal crisis of the State government and deep cuts in military spending. Mexicans have become convenient scapegoats for heightened rates of joblessness. Finally, the recently arrived Vietnamese report the most discrimination, a reflection of the negative public reception that greeted their arrival. In addition, they tend to live in working-class neighborhoods

Table 2.1 School Performance, Parental Human Capital, and Children's Aspirations[a]

	School Performance				Parental Human Capital				Child's Aspirations			
	GPA[b]	Std Math Test[c]	Std Reading Test[c]	English Index Score[d]	Percent Father College Grad	Percent Mother College Grad	Father Occup SEI[e]	Mother Occup SEI[e]	Occupational Aspirations[f]	Less Than College (%)	College (%)	Graduate School (%)
Cuban—private School (N = 183)	2.6	80	69	15.3	55	42	50.4	47.3	65.4	3	32	67
Cuban—public school (N = 1044)	2.2	56	45	15.4	24	18	37.5	36.9	62.9	18	37	46
Nicaraguan (N = 344)	2.3	55	38	14.8	45	31	39.2	30.5	62.7	21	34	45
Haitian (N = 178)	2.3	45	30	15.2	16	15	29.1	29.4	65.6	16	34	50
Mexican (N = 757)	2.2	32	27	13.9	9	5	26.3	24.9	58.3	39	32	29
Vietnamese (N = 371)	3.0	60	38	13.4	24	14	34.2	32.4	61.8	23	40	37

[a] All column differences between national origin groups significant at the .001 level.
[b] Grade Point Average as reported by school district.
[c] Stanford Achievement Test, 8th edition, percentile score.
[d] Self-rated proficiency in reading, writing, speaking, and understanding English.
[e] Duncan socioeconomic index score, based respectively on father's/mother's current occupation.
[f] Treiman occupational prestige index score for child's desired occupation.

Table 2.2   Friendship Networks[a]

| | Number of Close Friends From Abroad | | | Percentage With Friends Who Are[b] | | | | |
	None (%)	Some (%)	Many or Most (%)	Cuban (%)	Nicaraguan (%)	Haitian (%)	Mexican (%)	Vietnamese (%)
Cuban—private school (N = 183)	1.1	5.5	93.4	**98.9**	7.3	0	na	na
Cuban—public school (N = 1044)	2.5	23.2	74.2	**93.8**	*29.0*	*3.3*	na	na
Nicaraguan (N = 344)	5.1	18.8	76.2	*78.1*	**79.4**	*3.9*	na	na
Haitian (N = 178)	9.8	43.9	46.2	*26.1*	*4.2*	**87.3**	na	na
Mexican (N = 757)	6.6	44.6	48.8	na	na	na	**82.9**	*4.5*
Vietnamese (N = 371)	6.5	38.6	54.9	na	na	na	*17.2*	**83.1**

[a] All column differences between national-origin groups are significant at the .001 level.
[b] Percentage of those who report having close friends from abroad (i.e., excludes those with none). Numbers in **bold** represent the right-to-left axis of conationals. Numbers in *italics* represent the asymmetrical pairs of nationalities on left-to-right axes.

Table 2.3   Perceptions of Discrimination[a]

| | Percent Who Experience Discrimination | Percent of Those Discriminated Against Who Attribute It to: | | | Percent Residing in U.S. 5–9 Years | Percent Born in U.S. |
		Whites	Blacks	Cubans		
Cuban—private school (N = 183)	31.7	46.4	28.6	1.8	3.3	91.3
Cuban—public school (N = 1044)	39.1	31.6	28.9	3.7	10.1	67.6
Nicaraguan (N = 344)	50.6	27.8	22.2	25.0	57.8	7.6
Haitian (N = 178)	62.4	35.8	29.4	9.2	28.7	43.3
Mexican (N = 757)	64.3	42.2	34.4	na	28.4	60.2
Vietnamese (N = 371)	66.3	37.9	40.2	na	42.3	15.6

[a] All column differences between national-origin groups are significant at the .001 level.

populated by black Americans but without the benefit of a "Little Saigon" that might insulate them from conflict.

The data in Table 2.4 summarize selected characteristics of the schools attended by immigrant children in our sample. The patterns revealed are consistent with the descriptions offered earlier. Taken as a whole, Cuban families show a higher degree of class heterogeneity—as reflected in the proportions of children receiving free or subsidized lunch, a proxy measure for poverty. Mexican children are located in schools that mirror their position at the lower end of the class hierarchy. Most Haitian children are to be found in predominantly black, inner-city schools given the proximity of

Haitian residential settlement in contiguity to ghettos. Table 2.4 underscores the extent to which schools function as segregative forces sorting out children in terms of social class and location.

Ethnic Identities

Ethnographic chronicles underscore the vital role of collective identities in the process of assimilation. Even under auspicious conditions, migration is a jarring experience that pushes individuals and groups to acquire new knowledge as they negotiate survival and adjustment. Immigrants learn how they fit in the larger society through the contacts they establish in familiar environments. Whether youngsters sink or soar frequently depends on how they see themselves, their families and their communities. For that reason, the immigrant life is preeminently an examined life. Iterative processes of symbolic and factual association and detachment shape immigrants' self-definitions. Schools play a major role in that respect (Matute-Bianchi, 1986).

At school, children mingle with groups differentiated by their own self-perceptions and the perceptions of external observers. Especially when they equate success with localized power attained through conflict and physical force—as in the case of youth gangs—those groups can exert a strong downward pull upon immigrant children. The paths that lead youngsters toward specific clusters is complex. However, one of the most effective antidotes against downward mobility is a sense of membership in a group with an undamaged collective identity. The Méndez children illustrate that proposition.

But for the fact that they are illegal aliens from Nicaragua, sixteen-year-old Omar Méndez and his younger sister Fátima could not be closer to the American Dream. They have grown up in Miami since they were five and three years old, respectively. They are superb students full of spirit and ambition. They attend a school where discipline is strict and where teachers are able to communicate with parents in Spanish. Most decisively, they see themselves as immigrants and that identity protects them from negative stereotypes and incorporation

into more popular but less motivated groups in school. In Fátima's words: "We're immigrants! We can't afford to just sit around and blow it like others who've been in this country longer and take everything for granted." To maintain her independence, she withdraws from her peers and endures being called a "nerd." She does not mind because her center of gravitation lies within her family.

Mariá Ceballos, a Cuban mother, agrees with Fátima. She despairs about her daughter's interest in material trinkets and her low levels of academic motivation. "At Melanie's age," she states, "I was very determined; maybe because I was born in a different country, I wanted to prove that I was as good as real Americans. My daughter was born here and [therefore] she doesn't have the same push."

Among vulnerable groups, the ability to shift ethnic identity often provides a defense from stigma and an incentive to defy leveling pressures. How they define themselves depends on the context. Miguel Hernández, an illegal Mexican alien in San Diego since 1980, explains that he and his wife define themselves "[depending on] who we are talking to. If we are talking to American people and they don't know the difference, we say 'Latinos;' that's easier for them and we avoid hassles." Miguel consciously avoids being labeled a Chicano because "It's a slang word for lower class types who don't know who they are. They don't want to be Mexicans, but they don't want to just be Americans; they don't even speak English but they don't know Spanish either [and they] fight for and about everything."

In answering questions about who they are, immigrants resort to antinomies, defining other groups in terms opposed to the ones they use to define themselves. Others are generally symbolized by the casualties of earlier migrations, especially inner-city blacks. Typically, immigrants see blacks as the victims of their own individual and collective liabilities. Martin López, a Mexican father, explains:

> Blacks in this country . . . don't want to work; [they] feel very American. They know government has to support every child they breed. [As immigrants] we can't afford to slacken the pace; we have to work hard.

Table 2.4   Socioeconomic Status of National Origin Groups[a]

	Low SEI[b] (%)	Middle SEI(%)	High SEI (%)	% Attend Majority Black School[c]	% Attend Majority Latin School	% Attend Majority White School	% Attend Central City School[d]	%Attend >2/3 Poor School[e]	% Attend 1/3–2/3 Poor School	% Attend <1/3 Poor School
Cuban—private school (N =183)	7.7	49.2	43.1	0	100	0	0	0	0	100
Cuban—public school (N = 1044)	25.8	60.1	14.1	2.1	84.2	3.9	26.1	31.1	28.8	40.0
Nicaraguan (N = 344)	23.8	65.8	10.4	7.3	79.4	1.5	27.6	39.4	16.3	44.3
Haitian (N = 178)	31.0	61.9	7.1	66.9	3.4	2.8	83.7	66.9	12.9	20.2
Mexican (N = 757)	66.9	30.4	2.7	.4	17.7	.4	57.7	51.3	38.0	10.7
Vietnamese (N = 371)	45.3	46.9	7.7	.3	.8	0	50.3	39.2	18.8	41.9

[a] All column differences between national origin groups significant at the .001 level.

[b] Based on score on composite index using father's and mother's occupations, education, and home ownership. Corresponds to working class (*e.g.*, busboys, janitors, laborers), middle class (small business owners, teachers), and upper middle class (lawyers, architects, executives).

[c] Majority in these three columns means greater than 60% of students who attend the school. Note that we cannot distinguish within the Latin group between immigrants and U.S.-born students.

[d] Geographically located within the central city area of Miami and San Diego.

[e] "Poor" here is measured by the proxy variable of the percentage of the student body eligible for federally funded free or subsidized lunch.

Given phenotypical commonalities with black Americans and disadvantages derived from the locations where they live, the issue of identity is paramount among Haitians. Madeleine Serphy, an ambitious girl at fifteen, has strong feelings about African Americans:

It may be true that whites discriminate, but I have no complaints [about them] because I don't know many [whites] . . . but blacks, they're trouble; they make fun of the way we [Haitians] speak. . . . They call us stupid and backwards and try to beat us up. I was always scared, so I [tried] to do well in school and that's how I ended [in a magnet school]. There, I don't stand out as much and I can feel good about being Haitian. . . . Haitian is what I am; I don't think about color.

For working-class Cubans, the problem of identity is equally complex, but for different reasons. As members of a successful group, many resent being melded into the broader classification of Hispanic. Such is the case with Doris Delsol, an assertive divorcee who lives on welfare because of a disabling affliction. Although her daughter, Elizabeth, experienced some early setbacks in grade school, Mrs. Delsol doggedly sought paths to uplift her. "We Cubans are not used to failure," she explained. She does not like being called Hispanic because:

We all speak [Spanish] but there are differences. [Cubans] always had self-respect, a sense of cleanliness and duty towards children, a work ethic. Miami used to be a clean city until the Nicaraguans came and covered everything with graffiti.

About American blacks, Mrs. Delsol thinks they are adversarial to all kinds of people, disruptive, prone to ruin their homes, and lazy. In her view, both Nicaraguans and blacks evince attitudes opposite to those of Cubans.

Ironically, many Nicaraguans think of themselves as Hispanics precisely because they hold perceptions similar to those voiced by Mrs. Delsol. They experience a strong dissociational push away from their own national group. Sixteen-year-old Elsie Rivas avoids discrimination by shifting between a Hispanic and a Nicaraguan self-definition at school and at the

supermarket where she works. She doesn't like the way Nicaraguans speak:

They are vulgar, ignorant. . . . When I am with my Cuban friends I can speak to them normally, but some Nicaraguans make me feel ashamed and I am tempted to deny my nationality; they make all of us look bad because of the way they express themselves, with all the bad words and the cussing.

As the majority of immigrant children, Elsie's younger sister, Alicia, does not care for those distinctions. She feels "Nicaraguan-American because my parents came from Nicaragua and I like the food, but I am really American, more American than those born in this country; here is where I grew up and here is where I am going to stay."

The perceptions of immigrants and their children about themselves and other groups are not always accurate. However, what matters is that, as social constructions, those perceptions are an integral part of a process of segmented assimilation that will eventually yield what Bellah (1985) calls "communities of memory." In their journey, the immigrant children of today are already forging tomorrow's ethnic identities. Contact, friction, negotiation and their eventual incorporation into distinct sectors of the larger society will depend, in the final analysis, upon the insertion of immigrant children into various niches of the restructured economy. Collective self-definitions will improve or worsen depending upon the structure of opportunity.

CONCLUSIONS

Our purpose in this study has been to unfold the various meanings of assimilation for immigrants arriving into locations distinguished by an assortment of physical, social and economic characteristics. We have argued that a limited number of toponomical—that is, socially and physically situated—features determines the outcomes of migration. Our analysis was based on survey and ethnographic data about a small number of groups. However, we have noted that each group represents an experience associated not so much with cultural or national features, but with the attributes of its reception in areas of destination, the character of resources available to it, its degree of internal differentiation in terms of class, its degree of spatial concentration, and the length of time the group's coethnics have resided in the United States.

There is no mystery to tales of immigrant success or failure. The fates of immigrant children divide in consonance with the kind and quantity of economic opportunity. Economic globalization has fostered major transformations, including increasing demand for immigrant labor and the formation of transnational markets unlikely to disappear through purely legislative initiatives. The alternative for policy cannot be solely the regulation of immigrant streams to the exclusion of a more important aspect: the implementation of measures that facilitate the adjustment of new arrivals and increases their connection to the institutions of the larger society. The experience of Gainers shows that a welcoming reception in areas of destination—including government initiatives to facilitate immigrant adaptation—can have long-term benefits. The opposite is also true. Over extended periods of time, hostile receptions have had predictable results: isolation, social dismemberment and the concentration of behavioral pathologies. For policymakers the lesson is clear—the nightmare of an urban underclass need not be repeated among the protagonists of the new migration if we give attention to the lessons of the past.

Once established, immigrant networks acquire a degree of relative autonomy from market forces reducing the costs and risks of migration and promoting the flow of information. When they are internally stratified in terms of class, the spatial concentration of immigrants can yield advantages for the group to which they belong and for the larger society. This, too, has importance for immigration policy. In the 1960s, when the Cuban exile first began, millions of dollars were spent needlessly to scatter the banished around the United States in the belief that this best contributed to their social incorporation. Instead, Cubans gravitated back to Miami where the strength of numbers, connections and entrepreneurial know-how quickly translated into economic prosperity. Atomization and geographical dispersion could have had very different results.

Finally, we have begun a discussion of the ways in which immigrants shape identities through repeated interaction in empirical and symbolic fields with other ethnic groups. Our point has been to underscore the salience of collective self-definitions in the process of segmented assimilation. There is an interactive relationship between the opportunity structure and the way individuals and groups perceive themselves and others. The self-image of the immigrant is, ironically, a hopeful image often bolstered by negative definitions of other groups that have experienced arrested mobility. Whether those hopeful images survive will depend on whether immigrant children succeed or fail in the new economy.

REFERENCES

Baker, R. and W. Dodd, eds. 1926. *Public Papers of Woodrow Wilson.* New York: Harper.

Bellah, R. N. *et al.* 1985. *Habits of the Heart: Individualism and Commitment in American Life.* Berkeley: University of California Press.

Blauner, R. 1972. *Racial Oppression in America.* New York: Harper & Row.

Bonacich, E. 1980. "Class Approaches to Ethnicity and Race," *Insurgent Sociologist,* 10.

Bourne, R. 1916. *The Radical Will: Selected Writings.* New York: Urizen Books.

Coleman, J. 1988. "Social Capital in the Creation of Human Capital," *American Journal of Sociology (Supplement),* S95–121.

Fernández-Kelly, M. P. 1994. "Towanda's Triumph: Social and Cultural Capital in the Transition to Adulthood in the Urban Ghetto," *International Journal of Urban and Regional Research,* 18(1):89–111.

Frazier, E. F. 1957. *Race and Culture Contacts in the Modern World.* New York: Knopf.

Gordon, M. 1964. *Assimilation in American Life: The Role of Race, Religion, and National Origins.* New York: Oxford University Press.

Kasinitz, P. and J. Rosenberg. 1994. "Missing the Connection: Social Isolation and Employment on the Brooklyn Waterfront." Working Paper, Michael Harrington Center for Democratic Values and Social Change. Queens College of the City University of New York.

Kitano, H. and R. Daniels. 1988. *Asian Americans: Emerging Minorities*. Englewood Cliffs, NJ: Prentice Hall.

Matute-Bianchi, M. G. 1986. "Ethnic Identities and Patterns of School Success and Failure among Mexican-Descent and Japanese-American Students in a California High School," *American Journal of Education*, 95:233–255.

Park, R. 1950. *Race and Culture*. Glencoe, IL: The Free Press.

Portes, A. 1993. "The Longest Migration," *The New Republic*, 26:38–42. April.

Portes, A. and R. Bach. 1986. *Latin Journey: Cuban and Mexican Immigrants in the United States*. Berkeley: University of California Press.

Portes, A. and Rubén Rumbaut. 1990. *Immigrant America: A Portrait*. Berkeley: University of California Press.

Portes, A. and M. Zhou. 1993. "The New Second Generation: Segmented Assimilation and Its Variants," *Annals of the American Academy of Political and Social Science*, 530:74–96.

Roberts, B. 1995. "The Effect of Socially Expected Durations on Mexican Migration." In *The Economic Sociology of Immigration: Essays on Networks, Ethnicity, and Entrepreneurship*. New York: Russell Sage Foundation.

Sassen, S. 1992. *The Global City: New York, London, Tokyo*. Princeton, NJ: Princeton University Press.

Stepick, A. and C. Dutton-Stepick. 1994. "Preliminary Haitian Needs Assessment." Report to the City of Miami. June.

DISCUSSION QUESTIONS

1. Why do different ethnic groups, according to the authors, have such varied experiences in terms of how well they do economically upon arrival into the United States? Does a traditional assimilation model, which criticizes some groups for not doing well and praises others for being "model minorities," take these differences into account? Why or why not?

2. If varying social networks result in unequal opportunities for different ethnic groups, should the government intervene to level the playing field? Why or why not?

3. Why do members of some Hispanic groups prefer the label "Latino" while others identify more with their particular ethnicity (for example, Cuban, Nicaraguan)? How do negative racial stereotypes affect these identifications?

A DIFFERENT MIRROR

Ronald Takaki

I had flown from San Francisco to Norfolk and was riding in a taxi to my hotel to attend a conference on multiculturalism. Hundreds of educators from across the country were meeting to discuss the need for greater cultural diversity in the curriculum. My driver and I chatted about the weather and the tourists. The sky was cloudy, and Virginia Beach was twenty minutes away. The rearview mirror reflected a white man in his forties. "How long have you been in this country?" he asked. "All my life," I replied, wincing. "I was born in the United States." With a strong southern drawl, he remarked: "I was wondering because your English is excellent!" Then, as I had many times before, I explained: "My grandfather came here from Japan in the 1880s. My family has been here, in America, for over a hundred years." He glanced at me in the mirror. Somehow I did not look "American" to him; my eyes and complexion looked foreign.

Suddenly, we both became uncomfortably conscious of a racial divide separating us. An awkward silence turned my gaze from the mirror to the passing landscape, the shore where the English and the Powhatan Indians first encountered each other. Our highway was on land that

Sir Walter Raleigh had renamed "Virginia" in honor of Elizabeth I, the Virgin Queen. In the English cultural appropriation of America, the indigenous peoples themselves would become outsiders in their native land. Here, at the eastern edge of the continent, I mused, was the site of the beginning of multicultural America. Jamestown, the English settlement founded in 1607, was nearby: the first twenty Africans were brought here a year before the Pilgrims arrived at Plymouth Rock. Several hundred miles offshore was Bermuda, the "Bermoothes" where William Shakespeare's Prospero had landed and met the native Caliban in *The Tempest.* Earlier, another voyager had made an Atlantic crossing and unexpectedly bumped into some islands to the south. Thinking he had reached Asia, Christopher Columbus mistakenly identified one of the islands as "Cipango" (Japan). In the wake of the admiral, many peoples would come to America from different shores, not only from Europe but also Africa and Asia. One of them would be my grandfather. My mental wandering across terrain and time ended abruptly as we arrive at my destination. I said good-bye to my driver and went into the hotel, carrying a vivid reminder of why I was attending this conference.

Questions like the one my taxi driver asked me are always jarring, but I can understand why he could not see me as American. He had a narrow but widely shared sense of the past—a history that has viewed America as European in ancestry. "Race," Toni Morrison explained, has functioned as a "metaphor" necessary to the "construction of American-ness": in the creation of our national identity, "American" has been defined as "white."[1]

But America has been racially diverse since our very beginning on the Virginia shore, and this reality is increasingly becoming visible and ubiquitous. Currently, one-third of the American people do not trace their origins to Europe; in California, minorities are fast becoming a majority. They already predominate in major cities across the country—New York, Chicago, Atlanta, Detroit, Philadelphia, San Francisco, and Los Angeles.

This emerging demographic diversity has raised fundamental questions about America's identity and culture. In 1990, *Time* published a cover story on "America's Changing Colors." "Someday soon," the magazine announced, "white Americans will become a minority group." How soon? By 2056, most Americans will trace their descent to "Africa, Asia, the Hispanic world, the Pacific Islands, Arabia—almost anywhere but white Europe." This dramatic change in our nation's ethnic composition is altering the way we think about ourselves. "The deeper significance of America's becoming a majority nonwhite society is what it means to the national psyche, to individuals' sense of themselves and their nation—their idea of what it is to be American."[2]

Indeed, more than ever before, as we approach the time when whites become a minority, many of us are perplexed about our national identity and our future as one people. This uncertainty has provoked Allan Bloom to reaffirm the preeminence of Western civilization. Author of *The Closing of the American Mind,* he has emerged as a leader of an intellectual backlash against cultural diversity. In his view, students entering the university are "uncivilized," and the university has the responsibility to "civilize" them. Bloom claims he knows what their "hungers" are and "what they can digest." Eating is one of his favorite metaphors. Noting the "large black presence" in major universities, he laments the "one failure" in race relations—black students have proven to be "indigestible." They do not "melt as have *all* other groups." The problem, he contends, is that "blacks have become blacks": they have become "ethnic." This separatism has been reinforced by an academic permissiveness that has befouled the curriculum with "Black Studies" along with "Learn Another Culture." The only solution, Bloom insists, is "the good old Great Books approach."[3]

Similarly, E. D. Hirsch worries that America is becoming "a tower of Babel," and that this multiplicity of cultures is threatening to end our social fabric. He, too, longs for a more cohesive culture and a more homogeneous America: "If we *had* to make a choice between the *one* and the many, most Americans would choose the principle of unity, since we cannot function as a nation without it." The way to correct this fragmentation, Hirsch argues, is to acculturate "disadvantaged children." What do they need to know? "Only by accumulating shared symbols, and the shared information that symbols represent," Hirsch answers, "can we learn to communicate effectively with one another in our national community." Though he concedes the value of multicultural education, he quickly dismisses it by insisting that it "should not be allowed to supplant or interfere with our schools' responsibility to ensure our children's mastery of American literate culture." In *Cultural Literacy: What Every American Needs to Know,* Hirsch offers a long list of terms that excludes much of the history of minority groups.[4]

While Bloom and Hirsch are reacting defensively to what they regard as a vexatious balkanization of America, many other educators are responding to our diversity as an opportunity to open American minds. In 1990, the Task Force on Minorities for New York emphasized the importance of a culturally diverse education. "Essentially," the *New York Times* commented, "the issue is how to deal with both dimensions of the nation's motto: 'E pluribus unum'—'Out of many, one.'" Universities from New Hampshire to Berkeley have established American cultural diversity graduation requirements. "Every student needs to know," explained University of Wisconsin's chancellor Donna Shalala, "much more about the origins and history of the particular culture which, as Americans, we will encounter during our lives." Even the University of Minnesota, located in a state that is 98 percent white, requires its students to take ethnic studies courses. Asked why multiculturalism is so important, Dean Fred Lukermann answered: As a national university, Minnesota has to offer a national curriculum—one that includes all of the peoples of America. He added that after graduation many students move to cities like Chicago and Los Angeles and thus need to know about racial diversity. Moreover, many educators stress, multiculturalism has an intellectual purpose. By allowing us to see events from the viewpoints of different groups, a multicultural curriculum enables us to reach toward a more comprehensive understanding of American history.[5]

What is fueling this debate over our national identity and the content of our curriculum is America's intensifying racial crisis. The alarming signs and symptoms seem to be everywhere—the killing of Vincent Chin in Detroit, the black boycott of a Korean grocery store in Flatbush, the hysteria in Boston over the Carol Stuart murder, the battle between white sportsmen and Indians over tribal fishing rights in Wisconsin, the Jewish-black clashes in Brooklyn's Crown Heights, the black-Hispanic competition for jobs and educational resources in Dallas, which *Newsweek* described as "a conflict of the have-nots," and the Willie Horton campaign commercials, which widened the divide between the suburbs and the inner cities.[6]

This reality of racial tension rudely woke America like a fire bell in the night on April 29, 1992. Immediately after four Los Angeles police officers were found not guilty of brutality against Rodney King, rage exploded in Los Angeles. Race relations reached a new nadir. During the nightmarish rampage, scores of people were killed, over two thousand injured, twelve thousand arrested, and almost a billion dollars' worth of property destroyed. The live televised images mesmerized America. The rioting and the murderous melee on the streets resembled the fighting in Beirut and the West Bank. The thousands of fires burning out of control and the dark smoke filling the skies brought back images of the burning oil fields of Kuwait during Desert Storm. Entire sections of Los Angeles looked like a bombed city. "Is this America?" many shocked viewers asked. "Please, can we get along here," pleaded Rodney King, calling for calm. "We all can get along. I mean, we're all stuck here for a while. Let's try to work it out."[7]

But how should "we" be defined? Who are the people "stuck here" in America? One of the lessons of the Los Angeles explosion is the recognition of the fact that we are a multiracial society and that race can no longer be defined in the binary terms of white and black. "We" will have to include Hispanics and Asians. While blacks currently constitute 13 percent of the Los Angeles population, Hispanics represent 40 percent. The 1990 census revealed that South Central Los Angeles, which was predominantly black in 1965 when the Watts rebellion occurred, is now 45 percent Hispanic. A majority of the first 5,438 people arrested were Hispanic, while 37 percent were black. Of the fifty-eight people who died in the riot, more than a third were Hispanic, and about 40 percent of the businesses destroyed were Hispanic-owned. Most of the other shops and stores were Korean-owned. The dreams of many Korean immigrants went up in smoke during the riot: two-thousand Korean-owned businesses were damaged or demolished, totaling about $400 million in losses. There is evidence indicating they were targeted. "After all," explained a black gang member, "we didn't burn our community, just *their* stores."[8]

"I don't feel like I'm in America anymore," said Denisse Bustamente as she watched the police protecting the firefighters. "I feel like I am far away." Indeed, Americans have been witnessing ethnic strife erupting around the world—the rise of neo-Nazism and the murder of Turks in Germany, the ugly "ethnic cleansing" in Bosnia, the terrible and bloody clashes between Muslims and Hindus in India. Is the situation here different, we have been nervously wondering, or do ethnic conflicts elsewhere represent a prologue for America? What is the nature of malevolence? Is there a deep, perhaps primordial, need for group identity rooted in hatred for the other? Is ethnic pluralism possible for America? But answers have been limited. Television reports have been little more than thirty-second sound bites. Newspaper articles have been mostly superficial descriptions of racial antagonisms and the current urban malaise. What is lacking is historical context; consequently, we are left feeling bewildered.[9]

How did we get to this point, Americans everywhere are anxiously asking. What does our diversity mean, and where is it leading us? *How* do we work it out in the post–Rodney King era?

Certainly one crucial way is for our society's various ethnic groups to develop a greater understanding of each other. For example, how can African Americans and Korean Americans work it out unless they learn about each other's cultures, histories, and also economic situations? This need to share knowledge about our ethnic diversity has acquired new importance and has given new urgency to the pursuit for a more accurate history.

More than ever before, there is a growing realization that the established scholarship has tended to define America too narrowly. For example, in his prize-winning study *The Uprooted,* Harvard historian Oscar Handlin presented—to use the book's subtitle—"the Epic Story of the Great Migrations That Made the American People." But Handlin's "epic story" excluded the "uprooted" from Africa, Asia, and Latin America—the other "Great Migrations" that also helped to make "the American People." Similarly, in *The Age of Jackson,* Arthur M. Schlesinger, Jr., left out blacks and Indians. There is not even a mention of two marker events—the Nat Turner insurrection and Indian removal, which Andrew Jackson himself would have been surprised to find omitted from a history of his era.[10]

Still, Schlesinger and Handlin offered us a refreshing revisionism, paving the way for the study of common people rather than princes and presidents. They inspired the next generation of historians to examine groups such as the artisan laborers of Philadelphia and the Irish immigrants of Boston. "Once I thought to write a history of the immigrants in America," Handlin confided in his introduction to *The Uprooted.* "I discovered that the immigrants *were* American history." This door, once opened, led to the flowering of a more inclusive scholarship as we began to recognize that ethnic history was American history. Suddenly, there was a proliferation of seminal works such as Irving Howe's *World of Our Fathers: The Journey of the East European Jews to America,* Dee Brown's *Bury My Heart at Wounded Knee: An Indian History of the American West,* Albert Camarillo's *Chicanos in a Changing Society,* Lawrence Levine's *Black Culture and Black Consciousness,* Yuji Ichioka's *The Issei: The World of the First Generation Japanese Immigrants,* and Kerby Miller's *Emigrants and Exiles: Ireland and the Irish Exodus to North America.*[11]

But even this new scholarship, while it has given us a more expanded understanding of the mosaic called America, does not address our needs in the post–Rodney King era. These books and others like them fragment American society, studying each group separately, in isolation from the other groups and the whole. While scrutinizing our specific pieces, we have to step back in order to see the rich and complex portrait they compose. What is needed is a fresh angle, a study of the American past from a comparative perspective.

While all of America's many groups cannot be covered in one book, the English immigrants and their descendants require attention, for they possessed inordinate power to define American culture and make public policy. What men like John Winthrop, Thomas Jefferson, and Andrew Jackson thought as well as did mattered greatly to all of us and was consequential for everyone. A broad range of groups has been selected: African Americans, Asian Americans, Chicanos, Irish, Jews, and Indians. While together they help to explain general patterns in our society, each has contributed to the making of the United States.

African Americans have been the central minority throughout our country's history. They were initially brought here on a slave ship in 1619. Actually, these first twenty Africans might not have been slaves; rather, like most of the white laborers, they were probably indentured servants. The transformation of Africans into slaves is the story of the "hidden" origins of slavery. How and when was it decided to institute a system of bonded black labor? What happened, while freighted with racial significance, was actually conditioned by class conflicts within white society. Once established, the "peculiar institution" would have consequences for centuries to come. During the nineteenth century, the political storm over slavery almost destroyed the nation. Since the Civil War and emancipation, race has continued to be largely defined in relation to African Americans— segregation, civil rights, the underclass, and affirmative action. Constituting the largest minority group in our society, they have been at the cutting edge of the Civil Rights Movement. Indeed, their struggle has been a constant reminder of America's moral vision as a country committed to the principle of liberty. Martin Luther King clearly understood this truth when he wrote from a jail cell: "We will reach the goal of freedom in Birmingham and all over the nation, because the goal of America is freedom. Abused and scorned though we may be, our destiny is tied up with America's destiny."[12]

Asian Americans have been here for over one hundred and fifty years, before many European immigrant groups. But as "strangers" coming from a "different shore," they have been stereotyped as "heathen," exotic, and unassimilable. Seeking "Gold Mountain," the Chinese arrived first, and what happened to them influenced the reception of the Japanese, Koreans, Filipinos, and Asian Indians as well as the Southeast Asian refugees like the Vietnamese and the Hmong. The 1882 Chinese Exclusion Act was the first law that prohibited the entry of immigrants on the basis of nationality. The Chinese condemned this restriction as racist and tyrannical. "They call us 'Chink,'" complained a Chinese immigrant, cursing the "white demons." "They think we no good! America cuts us off. No more come now, too bad!" This precedent later provided a basis for the restriction of European immigrant groups such as Italians, Russians, Poles, and Greeks. The Japanese painfully discovered that their accomplishments in America did not lead to acceptance, for during World War II, unlike Italian Americans and German Americans, they were placed in internment camps. Two-thirds of them were citizens by birth. "How could I as a 6-month-old child born in this country," asked Congressman Robert Matsui years later, "be declared by my own Government to be an enemy alien?" Today, Asian Americans represent the fastest-growing ethnic group. They have also become the focus of much mass media attention as "the Model Minority" not only for blacks and Chicanos, but also for whites on welfare and even middle-class whites experiencing economic difficulties.[13]

Chicanos represent the largest group among the Hispanic population, which is projected to outnumber African Americans. They have been in the United States for a long time, initially incorporated by the war against Mexico. The treaty had moved the border between the two countries, and the people of "occupied" Mexico suddenly found themselves "foreigners" in their "native land." As historian Albert Camarillo pointed out, the Chicano past is an integral part of America's westward expansion, also known as "manifest destiny." But while the early Chicanos were a colonized people, most of them today have immigrant roots. Many began the trek to El Norte in the early twentieth century. "As I had heard a lot about the United States," Jesus Garza recalled, "it was my dream to come here." "We came to know families from

Chihuahua, Sonora, Jalisco, and Durango," stated Ernesto Galarza. "Like ourselves, our Mexican neighbors had come this far moving step by step, and waiting, as if they were feeling their way up a ladder." Nevertheless, the Chicano experience has been unique, for most of them have lived close to their homeland—a proximity that has helped reinforce their language, identity, and culture. This migration to El Norte has continued to the present. Los Angeles has more people of Mexican origin than any other city in the world, except Mexico City. A mostly mestizo people of Indian as well as African and Spanish ancestries, Chicanos currently represent the largest minority group in the Southwest, where they have been visibly transforming culture and society.[14]

The Irish came here in greater numbers than most immigrant groups. Their history has been tied to America's past from the very beginning. Ireland represented the earliest English frontier: the conquest of Ireland occurred before the colonization of America, and the Irish were the first group that the English called "savages." In this context, the Irish past foreshadowed the Indian future. During the nineteenth century, the Irish, like the Chinese, were victims of British colonialism. While the Chinese fled from the ravages of the Opium Wars, the Irish were pushed from their homeland by "English tyranny." Here they became construction workers and factory operatives as well as the "maids" of America. Representing a Catholic group seeking to settle in a fiercely Protestant society, the Irish immigrants were targets of American nativist hostility. They were also what historian Lawrence McCaffrey called "the pioneers of the American urban ghetto," "previewing" experiences that would later be shared by the Italians, Poles, and other groups from southern and eastern Europe. Furthermore, they offer contrast to the immigrants from Asia. The Irish came about the same time as the Chinese, but they had a distinct advantage: the Naturalization Law of 1790 had reserved citizenship for "whites" only. Their compatible complexion allowed them to assimilate by blending into American society. In making their journey successfully into the mainstream, however, these immigrants from Erin pursued an Irish "ethnic" strategy: they promoted "Irish" solidarity in order to gain political power and also to dominate the skilled blue-collar occupations, often at the expense of the Chinese and blacks.[15]

Fleeing pogroms and religious persecution in Russia, the Jews were driven from what John Cuddihy described as the "Middle Ages into the Anglo-American world of the *goyim* 'beyond the pale.'" To them, America represented the Promised Land. This vision led Jews to struggle not only for themselves but also for other oppressed groups, especially blacks. After the 1917 East St. Louis race riot, the Yiddish *Forward* of New York compared this anti-black violence to a 1903 pogrom in Russia: "Kishinev and St. Louis—the same soil, the same people." Jews cheered when Jackie Robinson broke into the Brooklyn Dodgers in 1947. "He was adopted as the surrogate hero by many of us growing up at the time," recalled Jack Greenberg of the NAACP Legal Defense Fund. "He was the way we saw ourselves triumphing against the forces of bigotry and ignorance." Jews stood shoulder to shoulder with blacks in the Civil Rights Movement: two-thirds of the white volunteers who went south during the 1964 Freedom Summer were Jewish. Today Jews are considered a highly successful "ethnic" group. How did they make such great socioeconomic strides? This question is often reframed by neoconservative intellectuals like Irving Kristol and Nathan Glazer to read: if Jewish immigrants were able to lift themselves from poverty into mainstream through self-help and education without welfare and affirmative action, why can't blacks? But what this thinking overlooks is the unique history of Jewish immigrants, especially the initial advantage of many of them as literate and skilled. Moreover, it minimizes the virulence of racial prejudice rooted in American slavery.[16]

Indians represent a critical contrast, for theirs was not an immigrant experience. The Wampanoags were on the shore as the first English strangers arrived in what would be called "New England." The encounters between Indians and whites not only shaped the course of race relations, but also influenced the very culture and identity of the general society. The architect of Indian removal, President Andrew Jackson told Congress: "Our conduct toward these people is deeply interesting to the national character." Frederick Jackson Turner understood the meaning of this observation when he identified the frontier as our transforming crucible. At first, the European newcomers had to wear Indian moccasins and shout the war cry. "Little by little," as they subdued the wilderness, the pioneers became "a new product" that was "American." But Indians have had a different view of this entire process. "The white man," Luther Standing Bear of the Sioux explained, "does not understand the Indian for the reason that he does not understand America." Continuing to be "troubled with primitive fears," he has "in his consciousness the perils of this frontier continent. . . . The man from Europe is still a foreigner and an alien. And he still hates the man who questioned his path across the continent." Indians questioned what Jackson and Turner trumpeted as "progress." For them, the frontier had a different "significance": their history was how the West was lost. But their story has also been one of resistance. As Vine Deloria declared, "Custer died for your sins."[17]

By looking at these groups from a multicultural perspective, we can comparatively analyze their experiences in order to develop an understanding of their differences and similarities. Race, we will see, has been a social construction that has historically set apart racial minorities from European immigrant groups. Contrary to the notions of scholars like Nathan Glazer and Thomas Sowell, race in America has not been the same as ethnicity. A broad comparative focus also allows us to see how the varied experiences of different racial and ethnic groups occurred within shared contexts.

During the nineteenth century, for example, the Market Revolution employed Irish immigrant laborers in New England factories as it expanded cotton fields worked by enslaved blacks across Indian lands toward Mexico. Like blacks, the Irish newcomers were stereotyped as "savages," ruled by passions rather than "civilized" virtues such as self-control and hard work. The Irish saw themselves as the "slaves" of British oppressors, and during a visit to Ireland in the 1840s, Frederick Douglass found that the "wailing notes" of the Irish ballads reminded him of the "wild notes" of slave songs. The United States annexation of

California, while incorporating Mexicans, led to trade with Asia and the migration of "strangers" from Pacific shores. In 1870, Chinese immigrant laborers were transported to Massachusetts as scabs to break an Irish immigrant strike; in response, the Irish recognized the need for interethnic working-class solidarity and tried to organize a Chinese lodge of the Knights of St. Crispin. After the Civil War, Mississippi planters recruited Chinese immigrants to discipline the newly freed blacks. During the debate over an immigration exclusion bill in 1882, a senator asked: If Indians could be located on reservations, why not the Chinese?[18]

Other instances of our connectedness abound. In 1903, Mexican and Japanese farm laborers went on strike together in California: their union officers had names like Yamaguchi and Lizarras, and strike meetings were conducted in Japanese and Spanish. The Mexican strikers declared that they were standing in solidarity with their "Japanese brothers" because the two groups had toiled together in the fields and were now fighting together for a fair wage. Speaking in impassioned Yiddish during the 1909 "uprising of twenty thousand" strikers in New York, the charismatic Clara Lemlich compared the abuse of Jewish female garment workers to the experience of blacks: "[The bosses] yell at the girls and 'call them down' even worse than I imagine the Negro slaves were in the South." During the 1920s, elite universities like Harvard worried about the increasing numbers of Jewish students, and new admissions criteria were instituted to curb their enrollment. Jewish students were scorned for their studiousness and criticized for their "clannishness." Recently, Asian-American students have been the targets of similar complaints: they have been called "nerds" and told there are "too many" of them on campus.[19]

Indians were already here, while blacks were forcibly transported to America, and Mexicans were initially enclosed by America's expanding border. The other groups came here as immigrants: for them, America represented liminality—a new world where they could pursue extravagant urges and do things they had thought beyond their capabilities. Like the land itself, they found themselves "betwixt and between all fixed points of classification." No longer fastened as fiercely to their old countries, they felt a stirring to become new people in a society still being defined and formed.[20]

These immigrants made bold and dangerous crossings, pushed by political events and economic hardships in their homelands and pulled by America's demand for labor as well as by their own dreams for a better life. "By all means let me go to America," a young man in Japan begged his parents. He had calculated that in one year as a laborer he could save almost a thousand yen—an amount equal to the income of a governor in Japan. "My dear Father," wrote an immigrant Irish girl living in New York, "Any man or woman without a family are fools that would not venture and come to this plentyful Country where no man or woman ever hungered." In the shtetls of Russia, the cry "To America!" roared like "wild-fire." "America was in everybody's mouth," a Jewish immigrant recalled. "Businessmen talked [about] it over their accounts; the market women made up their quarrels that they might discuss it from stall to stall; people who had relatives in the famous land went around reading their letters." Similarly, for Mexican immigrants crossing the border in the early twentieth century, El Norte became the stuff of overblown hopes. "If only you could see how nice the United States is," they said, "that is why the Mexicans are crazy about it."[21]

The signs of America's ethnic diversity can be discerned across the continent—Ellis Island, Angel Island, Chinatown, Harlem, South Boston, the Lower East Side, places with Spanish names like Los Angeles and San Antonio or Indian names like Massachusetts and Iowa. Much of what is familiar in America's cultural landscape actually has ethnic origins. The Bing cherry was developed by an early Chinese immigrant named Ah Bing. American Indians were cultivating corn, tomatoes, and tobacco long before the arrival of Columbus. The term *okay* was derived from the Choctaw word *oke,* meaning "it is so." There is evidence indicating that the name *Yankee* came from Indian terms for the English—from *eankke* in Cherokee and *Yankwis* in Delaware. Jazz and blues as well as rock and roll have African-American origins. The "Forty-Niners" of the Gold Rush learned mining techniques from the Mexicans; American cowboys acquired herding skills from Mexican *vaqueros* and adopted their range

terms—such as *lariat* from *la reata, lasso* from *lazo,* and *stampede* from *estampida.* Songs like "God Bless America," "Easter Parade," and "White Christmas" were written by a Russian Jewish immigrant named Israel Baline, more popularly known as Irving Berlin.[22]

Furthermore, many diverse ethnic groups have contributed to the building of the American economy, forming what Walt Whitman saluted as "a vast, surging, hopeful army of workers." They worked in the South's cotton fields, New England's textile mills, Hawaii's canefields, New York's garment factories, California's orchards, Washington's salmon canneries, and Arizona's copper mines. They built the railroad, the great symbol of America's industrial triumph. Laying railroad ties, black laborers sang:

> Down the railroad, um-huh
> Well, raise the iron, um-huh
> Raise the iron, um-huh.

Irish railroad workers shouted as they stretched an iron ribbon across the continent:

> Then drill, my Paddies, drill—
> Drill, my heroes, drill,
> Drill all day, no sugar in your tay
> Workin' on the U.P. railway.

Japanese laborers in the Northwest chorused as their bodies fought the fickle weather:

> A railroad worker—
> That's me!
> I am great.
> Yes, I am a railroad worker.
> Complaining:
> "It is too hot!"
> "It is too cold!"
> "It rains too often!"
> "It snows too much!"
> They all ran off.
> I alone remained.
> I am a railroad worker!

Chicano workers in the Southwest joined in as they swore at the punishing work:

> Some unloaded rails
> Others unloaded ties,
> And others of my companions
> Threw out thousands of curses.[23]

Moreover, our diversity was tied to America's most serious crisis: the Civil War was fought over a racial issue—slavery. In his "First Inaugural Address," presented on March 4, 1861, President Abraham Lincoln declared: "One section of our country believes slavery is *right* and ought to be extended, while the other believes it is *wrong* and ought not to be extended." Southern secession, he argued, would be anarchy. Lincoln sternly warned the South that he had a solemn oath to defend and preserve the Union. Americans were one people, he explained, bound together by "the mystic chords of memory, stretching from every battlefield and patriot grave to every living heart and hearthstone all over this broad land." The struggle and sacrifices of the War for Independence had enabled Americans to create a new nation out of thirteen separate colonies. But Lincoln's appeal for unity fell on deaf ears in the South. And the war came. Two and a half years later, at Gettysburg, President Lincoln declared that "brave men" had fought and "consecrated" ground of this battlefield in order to preserve the Union. Among the brave were black men. Shortly after this bloody battle, Lincoln acknowledged the military contributions of blacks. "There will be some black men," he wrote in a letter to an old friend, James C. Conkling, "who can remember that with silent tongue, and clenched teeth, and steady eye, and well-poised bayonet, they have helped mankind on to this consummation. . . ." Indeed 186,000 blacks served in the Union Army, and one-third of them were listed as missing or dead. Black men in blue, Frederick Douglass pointed out, were "on the battlefield mingling their blood with that of white men in one common effort to save the country." Now the mystic chords of memory stretched across the new battlefields of the Civil War, and black soldiers were buried in "patriot graves." They, too, had given their lives to ensure that the "government of the people, by the people, for the people shall not perish from the earth."[24]

Like these black soldiers, the people in our study have been actors in history, not merely victims of discrimination and exploitation. They are entitled to be viewed as subjects—as men and women with minds, wills, and voices.

> In the telling and retelling
> of their stories,
> They create communities
> of memory.

They also re-vision history. "It is very natural that the history written by the victim," said a Mexican in 1874, "does not altogether chime with the story of the victor." Sometimes they are hesitant to speak, thinking they are only "little people." "I don't know why anybody wants to hear my history," an Irish maid said apologetically in 1900. "Nothing ever happened to me worth the tellin'." [25]

But their stories are worthy. Through their stories, the people who have lived America's history can help all of us, including my taxi driver, understand that Americans originated from many shores, and that all of us are entitled to dignity. "I hope this survey do a lot of good for Chinese people," an immigrant told an interviewer from Stanford University in the 1920s. "Make American people realize that Chinese people are humans. I think very few American people really know anything about Chinese." But the remembering is also for the sake of the children. "This story is dedicated to the descendants of Lazar and Goldie Glauberman," Jewish immigrant Minnie Miller wrote in her autobiography. "My history is bound up in their history and the generations that follow should know where they came from to know better who they are." Similarly, Tomo Shoji, an elderly Nisei woman, urged Asian Americans to learn more about their roots: "We got such good fantastic stories to tell. All our stories are different." Seeking to know how they fit into America, many young people have become listeners; they are eager to learn about the hardships and humiliations experienced by their parents and grandparents. They want to hear their stories, unwilling to remain ignorant or ashamed of their identity and past.[26]

The telling of stories liberates. By writing about the people on Mango Street, Sandra Cisneros explained, "the ghost does not ache so much." The place no longer holds her with "both arms. She sets me free." Indeed, stories may not be as innocent or simple as they seem to be. Native-American novelist Leslie Marmon Silko cautioned:

> I will tell you something about stories . . .
> They aren't just entertainment.
> Don't be fooled.

Indeed, the accounts given by the people in this study vibrantly re-create moments, capturing the complexities of human emotions and thoughts. They also provide the authenticity of experience. After she escaped from slavery, Harriet Jacobs wrote in her autobiography: "[My purpose] is not to tell you what I have heard but what I have seen—and what I have suffered." In their sharing of memory, the people in this study offer us an opportunity to see ourselves reflected in a mirror called history.[27]

In his recent study of Spain and the New World, *The Buried Mirror,* Carlos Fuentes points out that mirrors have been found in the tombs of ancient Mexico, placed there to guide the dead through the underworld. He also tells us about the legend of Quetzalcoatl, the Plumed Serpent: when this god was given a mirror by the Toltec deity Tezcatlipoca, he saw a man's face in the mirror and realized his own humanity. For us, the "mirror" of history can guide the living and also help us recognize who we have been and hence are. In *A Distant Mirror,* Barbara W. Tuchman finds "phenomenal parallels" between the "calamitous 14th century" of European society and our own era. We can, she observes, have "greater fellow-feeling for a distraught age" as we painfully recognize the "similar disarray," "collapsing assumptions," and "unusual discomfort."[28]

But what is needed in our own perplexing times is not so much a "distant" mirror, as one that is "different." While the study of the past can provide collective self-knowledge, it often reflects the scholar's particular perspective or view of the world. What happens when historians leave out many of America's peoples? What happens, to borrow the words of Adrienne Rich, "when someone with the authority of a teacher" describes our society, and "you are not in it"? Such an experience can be disorienting—"a moment of psychic disequilibrium, as if you looked into a mirror and saw nothing."[29]

Through their narratives about their lives and circumstances, the people of America's diverse groups are able to see themselves and each other in our common past. They celebrate what Ishmael Reed has described as a society "unique" in the world because "the world is here"—a place "where the cultures of the world crisscross." Much of America's past, they point out, has been riddled with racism. At the same time, these people offer hope, affirming the struggle for equality as a central theme in our country's history. At its conception, our nation was dedicated to the proposition of equality. What has given concreteness to this powerful national principle has been our coming together in the creation of a new society. "Stuck here" together, workers of different backgrounds have attempted to get along with each other.

> People harvesting
> Work together unaware
> Of racial problems,

wrote a Japanese immigrant describing a lesson learned by Mexican and Asian farm laborers in California.[30]

Finally, how do we see our prospects for "working out" America's racial crisis? Do we see it as through a glass darkly? Do the televised images of racial hatred and violence that riveted us in 1992 during the days of rage in Los Angeles frame a future of divisive race relations—what Arthur Schlesinger, Jr., has fearfully denounced as the "disuniting of America"? Or will Americans of diverse races and ethnicities be able to connect themselves to a larger narrative? Whatever happens, we can be certain that much of our society's future will be influenced by which "mirror" we choose to see ourselves. America does not belong to one race or one group, the people in this study remind us, and Americans have been constantly redefining their national identity from the moment of first contact on the Virginia shore. By sharing their stories, they invite us to see ourselves in a different mirror.[31]

NOTES

1. Toni Morrison, *Playing in the Dark: Whiteness in the Literary Imagination* (Cambridge, Mass., 1992), p. 47.

2. William A. Henry III, "Beyond the Melting Pot," in "America's Changing Colors," *Time*, vol. 135, no. 15 (April 9, 1990), pp. 28–31.

3. Allan Bloom, *The Closing of the American Mind: How Higher Education Has Failed Democracy and Impoverished the Souls of Today's Students* (New York, 1987), pp. 19, 91–93, 340–341, 344.

4. E. D. Hirsch, Jr., *Cultural Literacy: What Every American Needs to Know* (Boston, 1987), pp. xiii, xvii, 2, 18, 96. See also "The List," pp. 152–215.

5. Edward Fiske, "Lessons," *New York Times*, February 7, 1990; "University of Wisconsin-Madison: The Madison Plan," February 9, 1988; interview with Dean Fred Lukermann, University of Minnesota, 1987.

6. "A Conflict of the Have-Nots," *Newsweek*, December 12, 1988, pp. 28–29.

7. Rodney King's statement to the press, *New York Times*, May 2, 1992, p. 6.

8. Tim Rutten, "A New Kind of Riot," *New York Review of Books*, June 11, 1992, pp. 52–53; Maria Newman, "Riots Bring Attention to Growing Hispanic Presence in South-Central Area," *New York Times*, May 11, 1992, p. A10; Mike Davis, "In L.A. Burning All Illusions," *The Nation*, June 1, 1992, pp. 744–745; Jack Viets and Peter Fimrite, "S.F. Mayor Visits Riot-Torn Area to Buoy Businesses," *San Francisco Chronicle*, May 6, 1992, p. A6.

9. Rick DelVecchio, Suzanne Espinosa, and Carl Nolte, "Bradley Ready to Lift Curfew," *San Francisco Chronicle*, May 4, 1992, p. A1.

10. Oscar Handlin, *The Uprooted: The Epic Story of the Great Migrations That Made the American People* (New York, 1951); Arthur M. Schlesinger, Jr., *The Age of Jackson* (Boston, 1945).

11. Handlin, *The Uprooted*, p. 3; Irving Howe, *World of Our Fathers: The Journey of the East European Jews to America and the Life They Found and Made* (New York, 1983); Dee Brown, *Bury My Heart at Wounded Knee: An Indian History of the American West* (New York, 1970); Albert Camarillo, *Chicanos in a Changing Society: From Mexican Pueblos to American Barrios in Santa Barbara and Southern California, 1848–1930* (Cambridge, Mass.,

1979); Lawrence W. Levine, *Black Culture and Black Consciousness: Afro-American Folk Thought from Slavery to Freedom* (New York, 1977); Yuji Ichioka, *The Issei: The World of the First Generation Japanese Immigrants* (New York, 1988); Kerby A. Miller, *Emigrants and Exiles: Ireland and the Irish Exodus to North America* (New York, 1985).

12. Abraham Lincoln, "The Gettysburg Address," in *The Annals of America*, vol. 9, *1863–1865: The Crisis of the Union* (Chicago, 1968), pp. 462–463; Martin Luther King, *Why We Can't Wait* (New York, 1964), pp. 92–93.

13. Interview with old laundryman, in "Interviews with Two Chinese," circa 1924, Box 326, folder 325, Survey of Race Relations, Stanford University, Hoover Institution Archives; Congressman Robert Matsui, speech in the House of Representatives on the 442 bill for redress and reparations, September 17, 1987, *Congressional Record* (Washington, D.C., 1987), p. 7584.

14. Camarillo, *Chicanos in a Changing Society*, p. 2; Juan Nepomuceno Seguín, in David J. Weber (ed.), *Foreigners in Their Native Land: Historical Roots of the Mexican Americans* (Albuquerque, N. Mex., 1973), p. vi; Jesus Garza, in Manuel Gamio, *The Mexican Immigrant: His Life Story* (Chicago, 1931), p. 15; Ernesto Galarza, *Barrio Boy: The Story of a Boy's Acculturation* (Notre Dame, Ind., 1986), p. 200.

15. Lawrence J. McCaffrey, *The Irish Diaspora in America* (Washington, D.C., 1984), pp. 6, 62.

16. John Murray Cuddihy, *The Ordeal of Civility: Freud, Marx, Levi Strauss, and the Jewish Struggle with Modernity* (Boston, 1987), p. 165; Jonathan Kaufman, *Broken Alliance: The Turbulent Times between Blacks and Jews in America* (New York, 1989), pp. 28, 82, 83–84, 91, 93, 106.

17. Andrew Jackson, First Annual Message to Congress, December 8, 1829, in James D. Richardson (ed.), *A Compilation of the Messages and Papers of the Presidents, 1789–1897* (Washington, D.C., 1897), vol. 2, p. 457; Frederick Jackson Turner, "The Significance of the Frontier in American History," in *The Early Writings of Frederick Jackson Turner* (Madison, Wis., 1938), pp. 185ff.; Luther Standing Bear, "What the Indian Means to America," in Wayne Moquin (ed.), *Great Documents in American Indian History* (New York, 1973), p. 307; Vine Deloria, Jr., *Custer Died for Your Sins: An Indian Manifesto* (New York, 1969).

18. Nathan Glazer, *Affirmative Discrimination: Ethnic Inequality and Public Policy* (New York, 1978); Thomas Sowell, *Ethnic America: A History* (New York, 1981); David R. Roediger, *The Wages of Whiteness: Race and the Making of the American Working Class* (London, 1991), pp. 134–136; Dan Caldwell, "The Negroization of the Chinese Stereotype in California," *Southern California Quarterly*, vol. 33 (June 1971), pp. 123–131.

19. Tomas Almaguer, "Racial Domination and Class Conflict in Capitalist Agriculture: The Oxnard Sugar Beet Workers' Strike of 1903," *Labor History*, vol. 25, no. 3 (summer 1984), p. 347; Howard M. Sachar, *A History of the Jews in America* (New York, 1992), p. 183.

20. For the concept of liminality, see Victor Turner, *Dramas, Fields, and Metaphors: Symbolic Action in Human Society* (Ithaca, N.Y., 1974), pp. 232, 237; and Arnold Van Gennep, *The Rites of Passage* (Chicago, 1960). What I try to do is to apply liminality to the land called America.

21. Kazuo Ito, *Issei: A History of Japanese Immigrants in North America* (Seattle, 1973), p. 33; Arnold Schrier, *Ireland and the American Emigration, 1850–1900* (New York, 1970), p. 24; Abraham Cahan, *The Rise of David Levinsky* (New York, 1960; originally published in 1917), pp. 59–61; Mary Antin, quoted in Howe, *World of Our Fathers*, p. 27; Lawrence A. Cardoso, *Mexican Emigration to the United States, 1897–1931* (Tucson, Ariz., 1981), p. 80.

22. Ronald Takaki, *Strangers from a Different Shore: A History of Asian Americans* (Boston, 1989), pp. 88–89; Jack Weatherford, *Native Roots: How the Indians Enriched America* (New York, 1991), pp. 210, 212; Carey McWilliams, *North from Mexico: The Spanish-Speaking People of the United States* (New York, 1968), p. 154; Stephan Thernstrom (ed.), *Harvard Encyclopedia of American Ethnic Groups* (Cambridge, Mass., 1980), p. 22; Sachar, *A History of the Jews in America*, p. 367.

23. Walt Whitman, *Leaves of Grass* (New York, 1958), p. 284; Mathilde Bunton, "Negro Work Songs" (1940), I typescript in Box 91 ("Music"), Illinois Writers Project, U.S.W.P.A., in James R. Grossman, *Land of Hope: Chicago, Black Southerners, and the Great Migration* (Chicago,

1989), p. 192; Carl Wittke, *The Irish in America* (Baton Rouge, La., 1956), p. 39; Ito, *Issei*, p. 343; Manuel Gamio, *Mexican Immigration to the United States* (Chicago, 1930), pp. 84–85.

24. Abraham Lincoln, "First Inaugural Address," in *The Annals of America*, vol. 9, *1863–1865: The Crisis of the Union* (Chicago, 1968), p. 255; Lincoln, "The Gettysburg Address," pp. 462–463; Abraham Lincoln, letter to James C. Conkling, August 26, 1863, in *Annals of America*, p. 439; Frederick Douglass, in Herbert Aptheker (ed.), *A Documentary History of the Negro People in the United States* (New York, 1951), vol. 1, p. 496.

25. Weber (ed.), *Foreigners in Their Native Land*, p. vi; Hamilton Holt (ed.), *The Life Stories of Undistinguished Americans as Told by Themselves* (New York, 1906), p. 143.

26. "Social Document of Pany Lowe, interviewed by C. H. Burnett, Seattle, July 5, 1924," p. 6, Survey of Race Relations, Stanford University, Hoover Institution Archives; Minnie Miller, "Autobiography," private manuscript, copy from Richard Balkin; Tomo Shoji, presentation, Ohana Cultural Center, Oakland, California, March 4, 1988.

27. Sandra Cisneros, *The House on Mango Street* (New York, 1991), pp. 109–110; Leslie Marmon Silko, *Ceremony* (New York, 1978), p. 2; Harriet A. Jacobs, *Incidents in the Life of a Slave Girl, written by herself* (Cambridge, Mass., 1987; originally published in 1857), p. xiii.

28. Carlos Fuentes, *The Buried Mirror: Reflections on Spain and the New World* (Boston, 1992), pp. 10, 11, 109; Barbara W. Tuchman, *A Distant Mirror: The Calamitous 14th Century* (New York, 1978), pp. xiii, xiv.

29. Adrienne Rich, *Blood, Bread, and Poetry: Selected Prose, 1979–1985* (New York, 1986), pp. 199.

30. Ishmael Reed, "America: The Multinational Society," in Rick Simonson and Scott Walker (eds.), *Multi-cultural Literacy* (St. Paul, 1988), p. 160; Ito, *Issei*, p. 497.

31. Arthur M. Schlesinger, Jr., *The Disuniting of America: Reflections on a Multicultural Society* (Knoxville, Tenn., 1991); Carlos Bulosan, *America Is in the Heart: A Personal History* (Seattle, 1981), pp. 188–189.

DISCUSSION QUESTIONS

1. Takaki feels that the many ethnic conflicts discussed in his essay could be reduced or eliminated if the groups involved had a better understanding of their shared histories. Choose a racial or ethnic conflict in the news today or going on at your campus and consider whether this kind of historical education could help the situation.

2. Why does Takaki argue that works such as Brown's book on Indian history, Howe's book on Jewish Americans, and Camillo's book on Chicanos do not go far enough in creating a multicultural history? What kind of approach does he advocate instead? Thinking back to your own educational experience, what kind of multicultural education, if any, did you receive?

3. What new information did you learn about the ethnic groups Takaki covers in this essay? Does it change your understanding of them? Are there more similarities than you thought among the groups?

CURRENT DEBATES

DOES LANGUAGE DIVERSITY THREATEN NATIONAL UNITY?

The United States is currently experiencing high levels of immigration, diversity, and pluralism. The current wave of immigrants comes from every corner of the globe, a kaleidoscope of different customs, lifestyles, races, and languages. Many believe that this diversity is a threat to societal unity and a challenge to traditional American values.

Among the many questions and issues spurred by immigration and diversity is the role of the English language. What role should learning English take in the process of adjusting to the United States? Should English-language proficiency be a prerequisite for full inclusion in the society? Should English be made the official language of the nation? To what extent is the present multiplicity of languages a danger for social cohesion and unity?

Following are two attempts to deal with some of these issues. Richard Lamm, a former governor of Colorado, believes that English is essential for maintaining societal unity and peaceful group relations in America. Robert King, a journalist, argues that America's strong sense of national unity—its "unique otherness"—is not threatened by language diversity.

EVERYONE SHOULD LEARN ENGLISH

Richard Lamm (with Gary Imhoff)

Official federal government policies that encourage bilingual and bicultural education delay the assimilation of new immigrants. . . . I believe that it makes no sense for the government to discourage foreign-language speakers from speaking English. I am concerned about the dangers of countries in which two language groups clash. I think about the problems caused by Quebec's separatist movement, founded upon the French language. I think about the tensions even within peaceful multilingual countries: the cantonization of Switzerland and the division of Belgium. Language is clearly the cause of some of the world's most severe tensions and disputes. And I know that the United States makes few demands upon its new citizens, has few common elements shared by all Americans—and the English language is the greatest of these common elements.

Our language embodies everything we believe, every aspect of our concepts and our culture. English is the glue. It holds our people together; it is our shared bond. We cannot communicate with those who do not share our language; we are reduced to signs and charades. Likewise, migrants to the United States who do not speak English also have an attachment to their languages that goes beyond mere sentiment. Giving up a language . . . is not like changing hairstyles or clothes styles in order to fit in with a new society. Giving up a language—even learning a new language just to use in the public sphere, among strangers—is giving up part of oneself. The problem of splintered Miami is that Cuban and other Latin immigrants insist on the right to live their lives in Spanish words and Spanish concepts, and English-speaking Americans react to the rejection of America and its language by the immigrants who are welcomed here and live here (and who call English-speaking Americans "Anglos" in our own country). In this era of massive immigration, it is everybody's problem.

Consider some actual problems faced in many classrooms throughout this country today: Imagine that you are a migrant child in a classroom. You know little or no English. Your parents know none. Your teacher and most of your classmates, on the other hand, know little or none of your language. It does not matter whether that language is Vietnamese, Portuguese, Tagalog, or Spanish. You will feel isolated, and you are likely to retreat to the safety, the warmth, the acceptance of your fellow immigrants. Only the understanding encouragement of your teachers and parents can make the transition to English easier, less painful. Assimilation, after all, is a bittersweet experience, and something of your parents' past must be given up if your American future is to be won.

Imagine that you are a school administrator who must deal with migrant children. You must provide for the children's learning English, making the linguistic transition, and also cope with the ethnic demands . . . that the children's home language and cultures be respected and—possibly—preserved. You may be in Brownsville, Texas, where 95 percent of the children come from Spanish-speaking homes and where nearly 18 percent of them are immigrants to the United States, many of them illegal immigrants. Or you may be in Alexandria, Virginia, where children from over sixty countries, speaking forty languages, constitute 14 percent of the students in elementary schools. Their assimilation will be a bittersweet process for you, too, and a difficult one.

SOURCE: Lamm, Richard D., and Imhoff, Gary. (1985). "Language: The Tie That Binds." In *The Immigration Time Bomb: The Fragmenting of America* (pp. 99–101). New York: E. P. Dutton.

LANGUAGE DIVERSITY IS NOT A THREAT

Robert D. King

Many issues intersect in the controversy over [making English the official language]: immigration (above all), the rights of minorities (Spanish-speaking minorities in particular), . . . tolerance, how best to educate the children of immigrants, and the place of cultural diversity in school curricula and in American society in general. The question that lies at the root of most of the uneasiness is this: Is America threatened by the preservation of languages other than English? Will America, if it continues on its traditional path of benign linguistic neglect, go the way of Belgium, Canada, and Sri Lanka—three countries among many whose unity is gravely imperiled by language and ethnic conflicts? . . .

In much of the world, ethnic unity and cultural identification are routinely defined by language. . . . The twentieth century is ending as it began—with trouble in the Balkans and with nationalist tensions flaring up in other parts of the globe. . . . Language isn't always part of the problem. But it usually is. . . .

Is there no hope for language tolerance? Some countries manage to maintain their unity in the face of multilingualism, [including two nations that] could not be more unlike as countries go: Switzerland and India. German, French, Italian, and Romansh are the languages of Switzerland. The first three can be and are used for official purposes; all four are designated "national" languages. Switzerland is politically almost hyper-stable. It has language problems (Romansh is losing ground), but they are not major, and they are never allowed to threaten national unity.

Contrary to public perception, India gets along pretty well with a host of different languages. The Indian constitution officially recognizes nineteen languages, English among them. . . . Why is it that India preserves its unity with not just two languages to contend with, as Belgium, Canada, and Sri Lanka have, but nineteen? The answer is that India, like Switzerland, has a strong national identity. The two countries share something big and almost mystical that holds each together in a union transcending language. That something I call "unique otherness." . . .

Belgium and Canada have never managed to forge a stable national identity; Czechoslovakia and Yugoslavia never did either. Unique otherness immunizes countries against linguistic destabilization.

America may be threatened by immigration; I don't know. But America is not threatened by language. The usual arguments made by academics against Official English are commonsensical. Who needs a law when, according to the 1990 census, 94% of American residents speak English anyway? Not many of today's immigrants will see their first language survive into the second generation. This is in fact the common lament of first-generation immigrants: Their children are not learning their language and are losing the culture of their parents. . . .

But empirical, calm arguments don't engage the real issue: Language is a symbol, an icon.

Nobody who favors a constitutional ban against flag burning will ever be persuaded by the argument that the flag is, after all, just a "piece of cloth." A draft card in the 1960s was never merely a piece of paper. . . . Language, as one linguist has said, is "not primarily a means of communication but a means of communion." . . .

America has that unique otherness of which I spoke. In spite of all our racial divisions and economic unfairness, we have the frontier tradition, respect for the individual, and opportunity; we have our love affair with the automobile; we have in our history a civil war that freed the slaves and was fought with valor; and we have sports, hot dogs, hamburgers, and milk shakes—things big and small, noble and petty, important and trifling. "We are Americans; we are different."

If I'm wrong, then the great American experiment will fail—not because of language but because it no longer means anything to be an American. . . . We are not even close to the danger point. I suggest that we relax and luxuriate in our linguistic richness and our traditional tolerance of language differences. Language does not threaten American unity. Benign neglect is a good policy for any country when it comes to language, and it's a good policy for America.

SOURCE: Robert D. King. (1997). Should English be the Law? *Atlantic Monthly* 279, pp. 55–62.

QUESTIONS TO CONSIDER

1. What assumptions are these authors making about the role of language in the process of assimilation? Can a group adjust successfully to U.S. society without learning English? Who are the authors referring to when they use words like *us*, *we*, and *our*? What does this reveal about their points of view?

2. How do you suppose other groups (recent immigrants, African Americans, Native Americans, white ethnics) would respond to this debate? What stake would they have in this policy issue? Visit the library and research reactions to "English Only" from representatives of different minority groups.

3. As you think about the issue of bilingualism and multilingualism, see if you can identify some social class aspects. Which economic classes benefit from the English-only position? Which economic classes are hurt? How? Why?

4. Is English the glue that holds us together, as argued by Lamm? Can we tolerate language diversity? How much? Is Lamm advocating discrimination? Is "English Only" just a subtle way of expressing prejudice and contempt for immigrants?

5. Should Spanish be made an official second language? Would this threaten societal unity or would it empower currently excluded Spanish speakers? How strong is our "unique otherness"? Can it overcome diversity and difference?

Part II

UNDERSTANDING THE EVOLUTION OF
DOMINANT-MINORITY RELATIONS IN
THE UNITED STATES

3

THE DEVELOPMENT OF DOMINANT-MINORITY RELATIONS IN PRE-INDUSTRIAL AMERICA

The Origins of Slavery

What was it like to be a slave? Why did colonial Americans create the institution of slavery? What impact did slavery have on the development of African American culture?

What role did gender play in southern society? What did black and white females have in common? How did they differ? How did slavery shape American social institutions? What echoes of slavery can be heard in present-day race relations?

These are some of the issues raised in this chapter. We begin with the memoirs of two of the victims of slavery: a male and a female slave. Both managed to escape to the North, where they devoted their lives to the abolition of the system that had imprisoned them and their families. The memoirs give us insight not only into the everyday lives of slaves but also into the gender issues that differentiated the experience of slaves.

The two Readings discuss the origins of slavery and its implications for the South and for society as a whole. Joe R. Feagin argues that slavery, racial inequality, and racism lie at the very heart of the American experience, along with our ideas about democracy, freedom, and equality. He explores the rationales for this system of bondage and compares it to other slave systems and argues that the American version was uniquely cruel. Elizabeth Fox-Genovese examines race and gender in the old South and argues that slavery separated not only blacks and whites but males and females as well. Furthermore, the dynamics of slavery separated black and white females, allowing little opportunity for the growth of a sense of sisterhood across racial lines.

The selections in the Current Debates section explore the effects of slavery on the growth of African American culture. Stanley Elkins argues that slavery severed all ties with African cultures and that African American culture was formed in reaction to the oppressive system of slavery. John Blassingame takes the opposite position and argues that connections to the motherland were never completely severed, while Deborah Gray White introduces the gender dimension into the debate.

NARRATIVE PORTRAITS

THE LIVES OF SLAVES

This section presents a vivid portrait of American slavery as experienced by two of its victims. Harriet Jacobs grew up as a slave in Edenton, North Carolina, and, in this excerpt, she recounts some of her experiences—especially, the sexual harassment she suffered at the hands of her master. Her narrative illustrates the dynamics of power and sex in the "peculiar institution" and the very limited options she had for defending herself against the advances of her master. She eventually escaped from slavery by hiding in her grandmother's house for nearly seven years and then making her way to the North.

The second memoir was written by Henry Bibb, who also was able to flee from the South. Bibb was married and had a child when he escaped to the North, where he spent the rest of his life working for the abolition of slavery. The following passage gives an overview of his early life and expresses his commitment to freedom and his family. He also describes some of the abuses he and his family suffered under the reign of a particularly cruel master. Bibb was unable to rescue his daughter from slavery and agonizes over leaving her in bondage.

LIFE AS A SLAVE GIRL

Harriet Jacobs (edited by Jean F. Yellin)

During the first years of my service in Dr. Flint's family, I was accustomed to share some indulgences with the children of my mistress. Though this seemed to me no more than right, I was grateful for it, and tried to merit the kindness by the faithful discharge of my duties. But I now entered on my fifteenth year–a sad epoch in the life of a slave girl. My master began to whisper foul words in my ear. Young as I was, I could not remain ignorant of their import. I tried to treat them with indifference or contempt. The master's age, my extreme youth, and the fear that misconduct would be reported to my grandmother made him bear this treatment for many months. He was a crafty man, and resorted to many means to accomplish his purposes. Sometimes he had stormy, terrific ways, that made his victims tremble; sometimes he assumed a gentleness that he thought must surely subdue. Of the two, I preferred his stormy moods, although they left me trembling. He tried his utmost to corrupt the pure principles my grandmother had instilled. He peopled my young mind with unclean images, such as only a vile monster could think of. I turned from him

with disgust and hatred. But he was my master. I was compelled to live under the same roof with him, where I saw a man forty years my senior daily violating the most sacred commandments of nature. He told me I was his property; that I must be subject to his will in all things. My soul revolted against the mean tyranny. But where could I turn for protection? No matter whether the slave girl be as black as ebony or as fair as her mistress. In either case, there is no shadow of law to protect her from insult, from violence, or even from death; all these are inflicted by fiends who bear the shape of men. The mistress, who ought to protect the helpless victim, has no other feelings towards her but those of jealousy and rage. The degradation, the wrongs, the vices that grow out of slavery, are more than I can describe. They are greater than you would willingly believe. Surely, if you credited on half the truths that are told you concerning the helpless millions suffering in this cruel bondage, you at the north would not help tighten the yoke. You surely would refuse to do for the master, on your own soil, the mean and cruel work which trained bloodhounds and the lowest class of whites do for him at the south.

Every where the years bring to all enough of sin and sorrow; but in slavery the very dawn of life is darkened by these shadows. Even the little child, who is accustomed to wait on her mistress and the children will learn, before she is twelve years old, why it is that mistress hates such and such a one among the slaves. Perhaps the child's own mother is among those hated ones. She listens to violent outbreaks of jealous passion, and cannot help understanding what is the cause. She will become prematurely knowing in evil things. Soon she will learn to tremble when she hears her master's footfall. She will be compelled to realize that she is no longer a child. If God has bestowed beauty upon her, it will prove her greatest curse. That which commands admiration in the white woman only hastens degradation of the female slave. I know that some are too much brutalized by slavery to feel the humiliation of their position; but many slaves feel it most acutely, and shrink from the memory of it. I cannot tell how much I suffered in the presence of these wrongs, and how I am still pained by the retrospect. My master met me at every turn, reminding me that I belonged to him, and swearing by heaven and earth that he would compel me to submit to him. If I went out for a breath of fresh air, after a day of unwearied toil, his footsteps dogged me. If I knelt by my mother's grave, his dark shadow fell on me even there. The light heart which nature had given me became heavy with sad forebodings. The other slaves my master's house noticed the change. Many of them pitied me; but none dared to ask the cause. They had no need to inquire. They knew too well the guilty practice under that roof; and they were aware that to speak them was an offense that never went unpunished.

I longed for someone to confide in. I would have given the world to have laid my head on my grandmother's faithful bosom, and tell her all my troubles. But Dr. Flint swore he would kill me, if I was not as silent as the grave. Then, although my grandmother was all to me, I feared her as well as loved her. I had been accustomed to look up to her with a respect bordering upon awe. I was very young, and felt shamefaced about telling her such impure

things, especially as I knew her to be very strict on such subjects. Moreover, she was a woman of a high spirit. She was usually very quiet in her demeanor; but if her indignation was once roused, it was not very easily quelled. I had been told that she once chased a white gentleman with a loaded pistol, because he insulted one of her daughters. I dreaded the consequences of a violent outbreak; and both pride and fear kept me silent. But though I did not confide in my grandmother, and even evaded her vigilant watchfulness and inquiry, her presence in the neighborhood was some protection to me. Though she had been a slave, Dr. Flint was afraid of her. He dreaded her scorching rebukes. Moreover, she was known and patronized by many people; and he did not wish to have his villainy made public. It was lucky for me that I did not live on a distant plantation, but in a town not so large that the inhabitants were ignorant of each other's affairs. Bad as are the laws and customs in a slaveholding community, the doctor, as a professional man, deemed it prudent to keep up some outward show of decency.

O, what days and nights of fear and sorrow that man caused me! Reader, it is not to awaken sympathy for myself that I am telling you truthfully what I suffered in slavery. I do it to kindle a flame of compassion in your hearts for my sisters who are still in bondage, suffering as I once suffered.

I once saw two beautiful children playing together. One was a fair white child; the other was her slave, and also her sister. When I saw them embracing each other, and heard their joyous laughter, I turned sadly away from the lovely sight. I foresaw the inevitable blight that would fall on the little slave's heart. I knew how soon her laughter would be changed to sighs. The fair child grew up to be a still fairer woman. From childhood to womanhood her pathway was blooming with flowers, and overarched by a sunny sky. Scarcely one day of her life had been clouded when the sun rose on her happy bridal morning.

How had those years dealt with her slave sister, the little playmate of her childhood? She, also, was very beautiful; but the flowers and sunshine of love were not for her. She drank the cup of sin, and shame, and misery, whereof her persecuted race are compelled to drink.

In view of these things, why are ye silent, ye free men and women of the north? Why do your tongues falter in maintenance of the right? Would that I had more ability! But my heart is so full, and my pen is so weak! There are noble men and women who plead for us, striving to help those who cannot help themselves. God bless them! God give them strength and courage to go on! God bless those, everywhere, who are laboring to advance the cause of humanity!

SOURCE: Jacobs, Harriet A. (1987). *Incidents in the Life of a Slave Girl, Written by Herself.* Jean F. Yellin, ed. (pp. 27–30). Cambridge, MA: Harvard University Press.

NARRATIVE OF THE LIFE AND ADVENTURES OF HENRY BIBB

Henry Bibb (Edited by Gilbert Osofsky)

I was born May 1815, of a slave mother, in Shelby County, Kentucky, and was claimed as the property of David White. I was brought up . . . or, more correctly speaking, I was *flogged up;* for where I should have received moral, mental, and religious instruction, I received stripes without number, the object of which was to degrade and keep me in subordination. . . . The first time I was separated from my mother, I was young and small. . . . I was . . . hired out to labor for various persons and all my wages were expended for the education of [my master's daughter]. It was then I first commenced seeing and feeling that I was a wretched slave, compelled to work under the lash without wages, and often without clothes to hide my nakedness. . . .

All that I heard about liberty and freedom . . . I never forgot. Among other good trades I learned the art of running away to perfection. I made a regular business of it, and never gave it up, until I had broken the bands of slavery, and landed myself safely in Canada, where I was regarded as a man, and not a thing.

[Bibb describes his childhood and adolescence, his early attempts to escape to the North, and his marriage to Malinda.] Not many months [later] Malinda made me a father. The dear little daughter was called Mary Frances. She was nurtured and caressed by her mother and father. . . . Malinda's business was to labor out in the field the greater part of her time, and there was no one to take care of poor little Frances. . . . She was left at the house to creep under the feet of an unmerciful old mistress, Mrs. Gatewood (the owner's wife). I recollect that [we] came in from the field one day and poor little Frances came creeping to her mother smiling, but with large tear drops standing in her dear little eyes. . . . Her little face was bruised black with the whole print of Mrs. Gatewood's hand. . . . Who can imagine the feelings of a mother and father, when looking upon their infant child whipped and tortured with impunity, and they placed in a situation where they could afford it no protection? But we were all claimed and held as property; the father and mother were slaves!

On this same plantation, I was compelled to stand and see my wife shamefully scourged and abused by her master; and the manner in which this was done was so violent and inhuman that I despair in finding decent language to describe the bloody act of cruelty. My happiness or pleasure was all blasted; for it was sometimes a pleasure to be with my little family even in slavery. I loved them as my wife and child. Little Frances was a pretty child; she was quiet, playful, bright, and interesting. . . . But I could never look upon the dear child without being filled with sorrow and fearful apprehensions, of being separated by slaveholders, because she was a slave, regarded as property. . . . But Oh! when I remember that my daughter, my only child, is still there, . . . it is too much to bear. If ever there was any one act of my life as a slave, that I have to lament over, it is that of being a father and a husband to slaves. I have the satisfaction of knowing that I am the father of only one slave. She is bone of my bone, and flesh of my flesh; poor unfortunate child. She was the first and shall be the last slave that ever I will father, for chains and slavery on this earth.

SOURCE: Osofsky, Gilbert. (1969). *Puttin' on Ole Massa* (pp. 54–65, 80–81). New York: Harper & Row.

READINGS

Although the chattel slavery that held African Americans in bondage officially ended in 1865, social scientists still produce new studies that explore many aspects of this "peculiar institution" in more depth than was previously understood. It is perhaps the brutality and inhumanity of slavery that makes it possible only now for such information to be heard and accepted. The two readings that follow explore gender and race relations during the time of slavery and challenge many myths surrounding the subject matter. The first reading, by Joe Feagin, examines slavery not as a slight temporary deviation from democratic ideals, but as the "bloody foundation" of the United States, forming the very basis for the new nation. Many signers of the Declaration of Independence, presidents, speakers of the house, and senators were slaveholders themselves and saw to it that the legal structure preserved slavery. But even those who were not of the wealthy slaveholding class received "ill-gotten gains" from the system of slavery, since all those who bought and sold plantation-made products benefited from their labor. Feagin also points out that the form of chattel slavery that existed in the United States was particularly brutal and dehumanizing, more so than any other slave or servant system existing elsewhere. It existed for the entire duration of a person's life, and she or he was denied most all of the basic human rights such as voting, reading, writing, and getting an education. Although African nations may have willingly given over some of their citizens to the United States, they had no idea that this was the type of fate that would befall them. Feagin touches upon only some of the many cruelties that slavemasters perpetrated against their slaves, including the forcible rapes that were regularly committed against black women.

The second reading, by Elizabeth Fox-Genovese, continues this focus on women by exploring the situation of Southern women, both black and white, during slavery. As both readings make clear, neither black nor white women were in control of their own fates during this time period, since white men dominated this patriarchal society. However, the situation of white and black women was hardly one of sisterhood. Fox-Genovese challenges the notion that white women likened their situation of inferiority to men to the situation of black slaves, thus seeing themselves as kindred spirits with the slaves. Instead, most southern white women celebrated the paternalistic culture that placed them on a pedestal as chaste guardian of the domestic realm, a position that race and class barriers prevented black women (and lower class white women) from reaching. Further, while northern white women may have seen their "separate sphere" as separate but equal to that of white men, southern white women indeed saw nothing wrong with certain forms of inequality. Paternalism in which white men "protected" those who were seen as incapable of doing so for themselves was indeed the very foundation of southern culture. Fox-Genovese also critiques any assertion that black women experienced some sort of strength or equality through slavery. Just because black men could not access the full force of patriarchy does not mean by default that black women were somehow "liberated." Fox-Genovese asserts that all people in the South—male or female, black or white—had lives shaped by the institution of slavery, the economic and social foundation of the plantation economy. She advocates for women's history that gives voice to this southern experience, rather than privileging the "New England model," and takes into account the interactions of race, class, and gender as central dictators of the southerner's experiences.

SLAVERY UNWILLING TO DIE: THE HISTORICAL DEVELOPMENT OF SYSTEMIC RACISM

Joe R. Feagin

A BLOODY FOUNDATION: GENOCIDE AND SLAVERY

This nation was born in blood and violence against the racialized "others." This grim historical reality must be understood well if we are to comprehend contemporary racism and inter-racial relations. As the European colonists established permanent settlements in North America, they intentionally drove off or killed the indigenous inhabitants and took their land. These colonists enriched themselves in a process of genocide against the indigenous peoples.

Attacking Native Americans

Article 11 of the United Nations Convention on the Prevention and Punishment of Genocide defines genocide as "acts committed with intent to destroy, in whole or in part, a national, ethnical, racial, or religious group." These acts specifically include "causing serious bodily or mental harm" and "deliberately inflicting on the group conditions of life calculated to bring about its physical destruction in whole or in part."[1] From the late 1400s to the first decades of the 1900s, the European colonizers and their descendants periodically and deliberately inflicted conditions of life that brought about the physical devastation, in whole or in part, of numerous indigenous societies across the Caribbean islands and North and South America. Indeed, the intentional attacks on indigenous peoples—and the effects of European diseases—are estimated to have cost as many as ninety to one hundred million casualties—the largest example of human destruction in recorded history.[2] The brutal and exploitative practices of whites were not aberrations; they were common practice in European colonialism.

The English colonists on the Atlantic coast relied on indigenous peoples to survive the first difficult years. Soon, however, these Europeans turned on the indigenous inhabitants. As early as 1637, a war with the Pequots in New England ended when whites massacred several hundred inhabitants of a village and sent the rest into slavery. The 1675–1676 King Philip's War with the Wampanoag society and its allies, precipitated by the actions of the colonists, resulted in substantial losses on both sides. The Native American leader, Metacom (known by the English as King Philip), was "captured, drawn, and quartered: his skull remained on view on a pole in Plymouth as late as 1700."[3] Again, the survivors were sold as slaves by European colonists who, ironically, saw themselves as a "civilized" people dealing with "savage" peoples. It is not well known that European colonists enslaved some Native Americans as part of their initial attempts to find exploitable labor. In the mid-eighteenth century about 5 percent of those enslaved in several of the North American colonies were Native American.

Recall James Madison's comment that the stereotyped "red race" was second only to the "black race" in the openly racist concerns of whites.[4] What should be done with these people who stood in the way of European lust for the land and riches of the Americas? Few European colonizers made an effort to understand the attempts of indigenous peoples to protect themselves from European invaders. While some leaders like Benjamin Franklin and Thomas Jefferson expressed admiration for Indian societies (even viewing them as "the white men of America"), most whites more than balanced their admiration with hostility and negative imagery.[5]

Until the middle decades of the nineteenth century the majority of Native American societies maintained a substantial degree of political and cultural autonomy. Europeans were frequently forced by the strength of Native American societies to negotiate with them for land and other resources. A process of gradual encroachment became the rule. Europeans would move into Native American lands (often violating treaties), Native Americans would respond with defensive violence, U.S. troops would put the rebellion down, and a new treaty securing much or all of the stolen land for whites would be made. There was at least a pretense of negotiation and legal treatymaking. However, by the 1830s—with President Andrew Jackson's decision to expel Cherokees and other Native American groups from the eastern states by force (the infamous "trail of tears" that cost at least 4,000 lives)—Native American societies increasingly faced a policy of overt displacement from white areas to western reservations or renewed attacks designed to eliminate whole societies. Even the pretense of legality was gradually disappearing.

Indeed, by 1831 the Supreme Court was moving to redefine indigenous societies as "domestic dependent nations."[6]

The Losing Struggle
for Social Independence

In the 1857 Dred Scott decision the U.S. Supreme Court showed that leading whites viewed the situations of Native Americans and African Americans as quite different. Indians, Chief Justice Roger B. Taney asserted, had "formed no part of the colonial communities, and never amalgamated with them in social connections or in government. But although they were uncivilized, they were yet a free and independent people, associated together in nations or tribes, and governed by their own laws. . . . But they may, without doubt, like the subjects of any other foreign Government, be naturalized by the authority of Congress, and become citizens of a State, and of the United States; and if an individual should leave his nation or tribe, and take up his abode among the white population, he would be entitled to all the rights and privileges which would belong to an emigrant from any other foreign people."[7] Whites, the judge asserted, had long viewed Native American groups as autonomous nations, though less civilized than whites. In contrast, in this decision about the status of an enslaved black American, the white judges viewed black Americans not as a nation to be negotiated with,

but rather as "beings of an inferior order, and altogether unfit to associate with the white race, either in social or political relations; and so far inferior, that they had no rights which the white man was bound to respect."[8] Whites' racist views of indigenous societies often allowed for more independence, albeit as groups only beyond white borders and as individuals only if assimilated. Moreover, over the centuries each Native American society has confronted whites on its own turf, with much strength arising from the indigenous cultural and geographical resources. In contrast, those peoples taken from the diverse societies of Africa had to face their white oppressors on white turf, completely severed from their families and home societies.

Native Americans lost their ability to make treaties in 1871. Over the next several decades, federal government policies forced many of the remaining Native Americans onto federally supervised and segregated reservations. With some oscillation, federal policies allowed whites to take more Native American land and pressured Native Americans to assimilate to white ways. By 1890, with most forced onto reservations, the number of Native Americans in North America had decreased to only about 250,000, sharply down from an estimated fifteen million people when the Europeans arrived in the late 1400s. The brutal and bloody consequences of the European conquests do indeed fit the United Nations definition of genocide.

SLAVERY AND MODERN CAPITALISM

In the Spanish colonies in Mexico and South America, Native Americans were the major source of labor, and thus they were central to the internal development of these colonial societies. This was not true for the English colonies. . . .

". . . The Indian played virtually no significant role in the internal functioning of the colonial society, but [did play] a crucial role in defining its frontier."[9] It was Africans who would play a central role in the functioning of colonial society. By the early 1700s people of African descent had become a major source of labor for the colonies, and the economic foundation for several centuries of undeserved enrichment for whites was firmly set in place.

The North American colonies developed two major modes of economic production. One type of production was the subsistence economy of small-scale farmers, who were either European immigrants or their descendants. Early on, the North American colonies became places to dump surplus peasants and workers displaced by the reorganization of agricultural economies in European societies. Alongside this subsistence farming economy was a profit-making commercial economy, much of which was rooted in the slave trade, slave plantations, and the commercial businesses essential to the burgeoning slavery economy. Slavery in the Americas was generally a commercial and market-centered operation, which distinguished it from slavery in the ancient world.[10]

With much farm land available for the new European immigrants coming into the colonies, it was frequently difficult for colonial entrepreneurs and development companies to secure enough white laborers, particularly for large-scale agriculture. At first, the larger landowners made use of white indentured servants, but it became clear that these laborers could be difficult to control. By the late seventeenth century the white elites were worried about periodic revolts from white laborers and small farmers. White indentured servants also worked off their terms of servitude and went into farming for themselves. The enslavement of African women, men, and children not only stemmed from a desire for profit but also from a concern with developing a scheme of social control that maintained bond-labor against the resistance of those enslaved. The color and cultural differences of Africans made them easier for whites to identity for purposes of enslavement and control.

The Legal Establishment of Slavery

The first Africans brought into the English colonies were bought by the Jamestown colonists from a Dutch ship in 1619. Laws firmly institutionalizing slavery were not put in place in the English colonies until the mid-seventeenth century. In the decades prior to that time some imported Africans were treated more like indentured servants than slaves. Some were able to work out from under their servitude. However, even in this early period those of African descent were by no means the social or legal equals of the Europeans. During the earliest decade, the 1620s, the Africans for whom we have records were often treated differently from the English colonists. For one thing, all African laborers and servants were brought in involuntarily, even if they were in some cases allowed to work out their servitude. Moreover, getting out of servitude usually meant converting to Christianity. As early as 1624, one court case made it clear that a "negro"—note the early naming of Africans and the lowercase spelling—could testify in court only because he was a convert to Christianity. A "negro" status was already socially and legally inferior to a European colonist's status.[11] Forrest Wood has argued that Christianity in this colonial period, as later in U.S. history, was highly dogmatic, Eurocentric, and antiblack "in its ideology, organization, and practice."[12] As we see in this 1624 example, central to the Eurocentric viewpoint was the idea that every person must become a Christian in order to have any legal rights. Indeed, many apologists for the enslavement of African Americans, from the seventeenth century to the present day, have argued that one of the virtues of slavery was its bringing Christianity to those enslaved.

By the 1670s the lives of most people of African descent were severely restricted by the new laws legitimating and protecting slavery. The degradation of this slavery was clear. In one 1671 declaration Virginia's General Assembly put "sheep, horses, and cattle" in the same category as "negroes." Colonial laws early attempted to prevent black men and women from running away; there were barbaric laws encompassing the whipping, castration, or killing of rebellious slaves.[13] Slavery was much more than a system of coerced labor. Enslaved blacks were legally subjugated in or excluded from all societal institutions including the economic, legal, and political institutions. Slavery was a totalitarian system in which whites controlled the lives of black men, women, and children—a total racist society protecting white interests.

. . . In the 1770s and 1780s the white group interest in the slavery system was recognized in the defining political documents of the new nation. The Declaration of Independence, prepared mostly by the slaveholder Thomas Jefferson, originally contained language accusing the British king of pursuing slavery, of waging "cruel war against human nature itself, violating its most sacred rights of life and liberty in the persons of a distant people who never offended him, captivating them and carrying them into slavery in another hemisphere, or to incur miserable death in the transportation thither."[14] Such accusations against the king were hypocritical, since at least half the signatories to the Declaration, including Jefferson, were important slaveholders or involved in the slave trade. Moreover, because of pressure from slaveholding interests in the South and slave-trading interests in the North, this critique of slavery was omitted from the final version of the Declaration. Recall too that in 1787 the U.S. Constitution was made by elite white men, many of whom had strong ties to the entrenched system of black enslavement. . . .

Variations in Plantation Capitalism

. . . For most slaveholders in the South there was more to slavery than just profit making. As Jefferson and other leading slaveholders emphasized, an agricultural society was to be preferred to an urban society. In their view the gentleman's life necessitated owning black men, women, and children for social status as well as for profit.[15] One of the great ironies of the slavery system is the accent that these "gentlemen" and their "ladies" put on values such as chivalry and honor, even as they practiced barbarism.[16] The political economy of slavery was a blending of capitalism with persisting elements of feudalism.

In the decade preceding the Civil War, a quarter of the white families in southern and border states owned nearly four million black men, women, and children. Thus, a large number of white families were directly involved in slavery. It was these families, especially those who held the largest number of slaves on big farms and plantations, who were the most influential in controlling the regional economy and politics. An array of ordinary whites provided the infrastructure of the slavery system—providing transport, growing foodstuffs, policing slaves, running local government, and providing many of the skilled trades. The slaveholding oligarchy—all white men—maintained its hegemony over the nonslaveholding white majority not only by these critical economic ties but also by propagating an ideology of white supremacy and providing certain types of white privilege. Most whites accepted the reality of slavery because "it provided not only an escalator by which they might one day rise, but also a floor beneath which they could not fall." As long as this was the case, "a Southern white consensus in defense of the peculiar institution was more or less assured."[17]

What was the position of white women in this system? Whatever their class level, they were generally under the control of husbands and fathers. They clearly had far fewer rights than white men, and all suffered significantly from patriarchal oppression. Working-class women, the majority of southern white women, provided most of the household labor that supported male workers and farmers. Women in the affluent slaveholding families sometimes inherited slaves or controlled some of their husband's slaves. They played a direct role in maintaining the racist system. One prominent analysis notes that white "mistresses, even the kindest, commonly resorted to the whip to maintain order among people who were always supposed to be on call; among people who inevitably disappointed expectations; among people whose constant presence not merely as servants but as individuals with wills and passions of their own provided constant irritation along with constant, if indifferent, service."[18] There was some recorded discontent from these slaveholding women about their lives, but rarely did they oppose the slavery system that gave them their own version of white privilege.

Among social scientists there is some debate as to whether the southern system was capitalistic or just a unique enclave economy imbedded in a capitalistic market system.[19] However, both groups of scholars generally agree on two points that are important for our analysis: (1) the larger slaveholders were oriented to making profits off their enslaved laborers; and (2) these slaveholders oriented themselves to trading within a capitalistic world-market system. Whatever other social values they may have held, the larger plantation owners were also early capitalists. Slavery capitalism was a system of worker control no other capitalist system could match. Enslaved men and women had a larger share of the worth of their work taken from them than did wage workers because they were chattel property and at the mercy of their owners at all hours of the day.

The Structure of Slavery in the North

Many northern merchants and manufacturers were active in the slave trade or had economic ties to the slave plantations. At the time of the American Revolution, the slave trade was, in Lorenzo Greene's detailed analysis, the "very basis of the economic life of New England; about it revolved, and on it depended, most of [the region's] other industries."[20] Greene lists more than 160 prominent slaveholding families in the area. Slavery-linked businesses included those dealing in sugar, molasses, and rum, as well as those dealing with shipbuilding and shipping. Leading textile manufacturers were "active participants in the slave trade or active in commercial and industrial endeavors that were closely intertwined with the slave(ry) trade."[21] Indeed, some northern industrialists were strong supporters of southern slaveholders, and most others colluded in the slavery structure that buttressed their industries. In addition, northern manufactures, farmers, and professionals sometimes bought black laborers or servants for their families. Even some antislavery advocates, such as the respected Benjamin Franklin, had owned slaves at some point in their lives.

Significant numbers of black Americans were enslaved in some northern areas well into the 1800s. The colony of Massachusetts Bay had been the first to legalize slavery, and by the mid-1600s there were strict slavery laws throughout the northern colonies. By the 1720s more than a fifth of New York City's population was black, and most of these New Yorkers were enslaved. Indeed, New York City's famous Wall Street area was one of the first large colonial markets where whites bought and sold slaves. This savage business lasted in New York City until 1862, even after the Civil War had begun.[22]

White northerners sometimes responded to black attempts to break the bonds of slavery in the same way as white Southerners—with barbaric brutality. In New York there was great fear of slave revolts. In 1712 there was a major slave revolt in New York City; in retaliation whites hung, starved, or roasted to death fifteen African Americans. In New York state, where slaves made up 7 percent of the population in 1786, even a partial emancipation statute was not passed until 1799—and that statute only freed enslaved children born after July 4, 1799 and then only when they reached their mid-twenties. All enslaved black Americans there did not become free until the 1850s. In Massachusetts, famous for its antislavery abolitionists, one attempt to abolish slavery failed in the state House of Representatives in 1767. Not until the 1780s did pressures from the white populace force the abolition of slavery in New England. Even then, it was not a recognition of black civil rights but pressure from white workers, who objected to competing with enslaved laborers, that played the major role in forcing slavery's abolition.[23] Moreover, in northern states where black workers and their families were emancipated, they faced Jim Crow segregation and regular discrimination in jobs, housing, and public accommodations. They also faced much racist mocking in newspapers and in public entertainments such as blackface minstrelsy. The early enslavement of black Americans in the North was indeed a "deeply engrained coding" that facilitated later patterns of segregation and other institutional racism.[24]

Most white northerners, including most religious leaders, did not support the immediate emancipation of enslaved African Americans in the South until the first battles of the Civil War made this expedient.[25] Prior to the Civil War many whites in all regions felt that slavery could not be abolished because of its economic importance. Indeed, into the 1850s much of the merchant class of the North was allied politically with the southern planter class. Not only did northern merchants and traders buy products from southern plantations, they also made up a substantial part of the Democratic party in the

North, while southern elites dominated that party in the South.

The Barbarity of Slavery

Unjust enrichment for whites brought great immiseration for blacks. Considering the number of people killed or maimed in the process, and the scale and time involved, the enslavement of Africans is one of the most savage and barbaric aspects of European and American history. According to those enslaved, the slavery system was hellish and deadly beyond description and comprehension. Once captured, enslaved Africans were often taken to slave corrals or castles in Africa where they were chained, branded, and held for shipping abroad. Many died there in barbaric conditions. On the Atlantic voyage those enslaved were chained together in close quarters, again in death-dealing conditions. The horror of the Atlantic trade was summed up by one young African, who in his autobiography explained, "I was soon put down under the decks, and there I received such a salutation in my nostrils as I had never experienced in my life: so that with the loathsomeness of the stench, and crying together, I became so sick and low that I was not able to eat, nor had I the least desire to taste any thing. . . . On my refusing to eat, one of them held me fast by the hands, and laid me across, I think the windlass, and tied my feet, while the other flogged me severely. . . . One day, when we had a smooth sea and moderate wind, two of my wearied countrymen who were chained together (I was near them at the time), preferring death to such a life of misery, somehow made through the nettings and jumped into the sea."[26]

The conditions of those enslaved at the points of destination were also brutal and oppressive. William Wells Brown, the son of a white slaveowner and an enslaved black woman, reported on what happened to an assertive man named Randall. One day a white overseer, named Grove Cook, got three white friends to help him subdue Randall. As Brown explains, "He refused to go; whereupon he was attacked by the overseer and his companions, when he turned upon them, and laid them, one after another, prostrated on the ground. [One man] drew out his pistol, and fired at him, and brought him to the ground by a pistol ball. The others rushed upon him with their clubs, and beat him over the head and face, until they succeeded in tying him. He was taken to the barn, and tied to a beam. Cook gave him over one hundred lashes with a heavy cowhide, had him washed with salt and water, and left him tied during the day. The next day he was untied, and taken to a blacksmith's shop, and had a ball and chain attached to his leg."[27]

Brown recounts that this brave man was forced to work hard in the fields with the chain on him and that the slaveowner was pleased with the sadistic cruelty of his overseer. Brown observed numerous beatings and killings of black men and women by whites during years of enslavement. The extant narratives of those enslaved are replete with accounts of chains, mutilation, stocks, whippings, starvation, and imprisonment.[28]

The Rape of Enslaved Women

Once fully instituted, the arrangements of slavery became much more than a machine for generating economic wealth. They constituted a well-developed system for the social and sexual control of black men and women.[29] During slavery, and later under legal segregation, many African and African American women were raped by white men, including sailors, slavemasters, overseers, and employers. Under the American system of racism the children resulting from the coerced sexual relations were automatically classified as black, even though they had substantial European ancestry. Indeed, it is estimated today that at least three-quarters of "black" Americans have at least one white ancestor. No other racial or ethnic group's physical makeup has been so substantially determined by the sexual depredations of white men. Recently, Patricia Williams, a black law professor, has described the case of Austin Miller, the thirty-five-year-old white lawyer who bought her eleven-year-old great-great-grandmother,

Sophie. By the time Sophie was twelve, Miller had made her pregnant with the child who was Williams's great-grandmother Mary. Sophie's child was taken from her and became a house servant to Miller's white children. Williams's great-great-grandfather was thus one of a large number of white men who were rapists of black women or molesters of black children.[30]

Most of the surviving narratives of enslaved black women have accounts—sometimes quite numerous—of sexual exploitation by white men. Take the case of an enslaved black woman named Celia. In 1850 a prosperous Missouri farmer, Robert Newsom, bought Celia, then a fourteen-year-old, and soon thereafter raped her. Over the next five years, Newsom sexually attacked her numerous times, fathering two children by her. In the summer of 1855 Newsom came to Celia's cabin one last time to rape her, she hit him with a stick, and he died from the blows. In a travesty of justice, Celia was convicted in a Missouri court of the "crime" and hung in late December 1855.[31] Black women were doubly oppressed by the institution of slavery; they had no redress for the brutal crimes committed against them.

Like Miller and Newsom, many of these oppressors were respectable men in their communities. One of the most famous was Thomas Jefferson. In his forties he coerced the enslaved teenager Sally Hemings into his bed. That he fathered at least one child with her has now been confirmed by DNA testing, and it is presumed that he fathered several other children by her. Yet in his lifetime Jefferson never admitted to this coercive relationship.[32] Until the DNA evidence showed the reality of the relationship, most white historians and commentators denied that Jefferson could have had children with an enslaved woman. The reason for this denial doubtless lies in the fact that Jefferson is an American icon. As the first professional biographer of Jefferson, James Parton, put it in 1874, "If Jefferson was wrong, America is wrong. If America is right, Jefferson was right."[33]

One of the most oppressive aspects of American racism lies in this sexual thread, which weaves itself through various manifestations of racism to the present. White men have often raped African American women with impunity, especially during the nation's first three centuries. Many white men developed a contradictory set of attitudes that saw black women as human enough to be exotic objects of sexual desire, yet as less than human in their rights to protection from sexual attack. Given that most such men proclaimed themselves to be virtuous and religious, such sexual attitudes and actions contradicted their expressed morality. The tensions between this image of themselves as virtuous and their sexualized feelings and actions toward black women—often coupled with a denial at the conscious level of these feelings—seem to have led to a projection of many white men's sexual desires onto black men. As the historian Winthrop Jordan has argued, white men's passion for black women was "not fully acceptable to the society or the self and hence not readily admissible. Sexual desires could be effectively denied and the accompanying anxiety and guilt in some measure assuaged, however, by imputing them to others."[34]

Given this projection of white males' desires into black men, one can better understand certain aspects of U.S. racism—the obsession of many white men (and women) with the black man as a rapist . . . and the extraordinarily brutal and often sexualized attacks on black men in thousands of lynchings and other violent attacks. . . .

African Immiseration

Numerous African societies paid a heavy, often catastrophic, price for the Atlantic slave trade. For several centuries many of the African continent's young people were ripped from its shores, thereby damaging the future development of the continent. Millions of Africans were lost in the slave trade, so many that the use of the term *the black holocaust* seems appropriate for this savage process. An estimated ten million Africans survived the Atlantic crossings to the Americas, with many millions more killed or lost to deprivation and disease on the way, or back in Africa before embarkation. Estimates for the total number enslaved or killed in the attempt to enslave at all points in Africa and the Atlantic trade suggest a figure of at least twenty-eight million from the 1400s to slavery's abolition in most areas by the late 1800s.[35]

Over time, this Atlantic trade in human beings had serious negative effects on social institutions in parts of Africa, a destruction that greatly facilitated later European exploitation of that continent. Recall W. E. B. Du Bois's argument that African colonization is usually omitted or downplayed in mainstream histories of European development, wealth, and affluence. Yet any serious understanding of the development of European wealth must center on early and late African colonialism, for the labor and mineral resources of Africans were taken to help create that European prosperity. Similarly, much African immiseration is linked to the creation of white prosperity over the course of North American history.

A number of scholars and popular writers have accented the role of Africans in this Atlantic slave trade, sometimes in order to play down the European role.[36] Yet one must put the African participation in perspective. Europeans were not enslaved by Africans. And virtually all Africans enslaved in the Americas were taken from their continent by European traders or merchants and sold to Europeans in the Americas. This Atlantic trade in human beings began when European ships arrived seeking commerce with African societies whose economies were not centered in profit making from enslavement. As Europeans grew in power along the coast, African nations were played off against each other, just as European colonizers in the Americas played off one indigenous nation there against another. Significantly, the European intruders had some six hundred slave ports built for their bloody trade, and they themselves recorded at least three hundred battles with Africans as part of the enslavement process. Africans did not seek out this system. In some cases Africans were kidnapped directly by Europeans slavers. In numerous other cases African political leaders, who had often at first traded certain African goods for European goods, ran out of these items and, pressed by the European slavers, turned to trading people held in servitude.[37]

Certainly, some leaders at the top of the hierarchies of African societies worked with the European slavers to provide the human cargo the latter sought. Indeed, trading in slaves became addictive for some African leaders without other goods to trade to Europeans. Those who were traded as slaves often included temporary wards, such as children of the poor or widows (who were then in the care of African leaders), as well as those captured in battles with other societies. Apparently, most African leaders did not realize that those traded would become permanently enslaved as property without *any* human rights and would often be worked to death in just a few years. In numerous West African societies many of those held in involuntary servitude were treated more like wards or indentured servants than like the rights-less chattel property they became in the Americas. They were often part of a family unit, had some legal rights, and could marry, own property, and sometimes inherit from their masters.[38] It is also important to note that many Africans saw the Atlantic slave trade as a serious threat, even as a sickness, and local healing societies developed to fight it. There was also substantial violent resistance to the Atlantic slave trade by Africans.

A Distinctive Form of Slavery

The enslavement of Africans in the Americas was not only more extreme than slavery in most African societies but also more oppressive than slavery in ancient societies such as the Roman Empire. Unlike Roman slaves, American slaves were generally forbidden by law to read or write. In the Americas the Europeans applied slavery, as Du Bois reminds us, "on a scale and with an elaborateness of detail of which no former world ever dreamed. The imperial width of the thing—the heaven-defying audacity—makes its modern newness."[39] An essential feature of North American slavery was the denial of most human liberties. Slaves "could own nothing; they could make no contracts; they could hold no property; nor traffic in property; they could not hire out; they could not legally marry . . . they could not appeal from their master; they could be punished at will."[40] In North America human beings were reduced to the status of things to be bought and sold.

Even the English language was "made an instrument of domination and silencing; it was used to regulate and police access to authority and knowledge among colonized peoples."[41] Enslaved Africans were from many different societies, and they were forced to learn the language of their oppressors. This was probably the most forced of all adaptations to the English language. Voluntary immigrants to the United States have been allowed to retain much more of their home languages and have probably kept more of the home culture associated with those languages. In the destruction of African languages and their more or less complete replacement by a new language we see how extensive the system of antiblack racism is. Enforced adaptation to the English language not only marked the movement of early English colonizers across the lands of conquest, but also marks today—in attacks on black English and on Spanish—similar attempts to maintain white cultural dominance over those long subordinated.

ILL-GOTTEN GAINS: WEALTH AND PROSPERITY FROM SLAVERY

The enslavement of Africans was not just the work of slave traders and adventurers. Nor was it something marginal to the economic interests of the elites on both sides of the Atlantic. Instead, slavery was a system created, supported, and financed by a very large number of the leading political, business, and intellectual figures of the day. We can, as an example, take just one major enterprise of the early eighteenth century, the famous British South Sea Company. This was an official company set up to transport enslaved Africans overseas. Stockholders in this company included the leading physical scientist Sir Isaac Newton, major authors like Jonathan Swift and Daniel Defoe, and the founder of the Bank of England, the Earl of Halifax. They also included most members of the House of Lords and of the House of Commons. Many aristocrats also held stock in the company.[42] Clearly, the leading men of Britain were directly and financially involved in the slave trade. Similarly, many leading Americans, including George Washington, Thomas Jefferson, Patrick Henry, George Mason, and James Madison, profited greatly from slavery or the slave trade. These men saw slavery as an honorable business activity.

Building the Wealth of Britain and Continental Europe

The British merchants of the eighteenth century recognized the centrality of slavery in building the wealth of their nation. For example, in the 1740s one business pamphleteer wrote about Britain's wealth this way:

> The most approved judges of the Commercial Interests of these Kingdoms have ever been of the opinion that our West-India and African Trades are the most nationally beneficial of any we carry on. It is also allowed on all hands, that the trade to Africa is the Branch which renders our American Colonies and Plantations so advantageous to Great Britain: that Traffic only affording our Planters a constant supply of Negro Servants for the Culture, of their Lands in the Produce of Sugars, Tobacco, Rice, Rum, Cotton, Fustick, Pimento, and all other our Plantation Produce: so that the extensive Employment of our Shipping in, to, and from America, the great Brood of Seamen consequent thereupon, and the daily Bread of the most considerable Part of our British Manufactures, are owing primarily to the Labour of Negroes; who, as they were the first happy instruments of raising our Plantations: so their Labour only can support and preserve them, and render them still more and more profitable to their Mother-Kingdom. The Negroe-Trade therefore, and the natural consequences resulting from it, may be justly esteemed an inexhaustible Fund of Wealth and Naval Power to this Nation.[43]

This remarkable business summary accents the primary role of the "labour of Negroes" to British shipping and manufacturing, and thus to "inexhaustible fund of wealth" for that nation.

The economic trade generated by British and French plantations in the Americas was the source of much of the capital for the commercial and industrial revolutions of the two nations. British and French industry, shipping, naval and merchant marine development, banking, and insurance were significantly stimulated by or grounded in the labor of enslaved Africans in their respective colonies.[44] From the early 1700s to the mid-1800s a large proportion of the major agricultural exports in world trade were produced by enslaved Africans. British port cities became prosperous as centers for the trade in Africans and British industrial cities became prosperous because of the manufacturing of goods with cotton from slave plantations. Textiles manufacturing was the core industry of the Industrial Revolution, and most of the raw cotton was grown by enslaved laborers. Liverpool slave traders, Caribbean sugar planters, and Manchester manufacturers were major sources of circulating capital in the eighteenth and early nineteenth centuries. Circulating through banking and lending enterprises, the profits from international trade—much of it directly or indirectly related to the slave trade and the trade in slave-produced products—provided a substantial part of the large-scale investments in British industry in this period, growth that in turn led to many new technologies and products of the Industrial Revolution. These investments also spurred a rapid buildup of the financial and insurance industries.[45] Some of these powerful institutions have persisted to the present day. Barclay's Bank was founded with profits from the slave trade, and Lloyds of London prospered early on by insuring slave ships and their cargos.[46]

The most famous technological development of the period, James Watt's much-improved version of the steam engine developed during the 1760s, accelerated the industrial development of Europe and its far-flung colonies. Capital accumulated from the West Indies trade in slaves and slave-produced products directly bankrolled Watt's reworking of the steam engine. Numerous industries, such as the metallurgical industries—which made possible the manufacturing of chains for slaves as well as new machinery, bridges, and rails—and the important railroad industry, were significantly spurred by the profits generated from the trade in slaves, products of plantations, and food and manufacturing exports flowing from Britain back to the American plantations and to Africa. In turn, much additional economic activity was generated as these profits flowed into all forms of European and colonial consumption. Economic activity was stimulated even if the recipients of the income from the slave trade and plantations put it into land, coaches, or banks.[47]

Slaveholders were not the only beneficiaries of the slavery system; those who bought and sold products of plantations were also major beneficiaries. This latter group included merchants and consumers in many nations. In addition, many white workers in Britain and other parts of Europe owed their livelihoods directly or indirectly to the trade in slaves and plantation products.[48] It seems unlikely that British and other European economic development would have occurred when it did without the very substantial capital generated by the slavery system.

We should note some important political and cultural linkages to this burgeoning economic system. In the eighteenth and early nineteenth centuries the British parliament was dominated on many issues by those with economic interests in the slave trade, slave plantations, or commercial trade with the plantations.[49] In addition, in Britain and North America the revival of the arts—music, painting, sculptures, and essay writing—in this period was spurred in part by substantial funding from patrons made prosperous by various slavery enterprises. For example, some of George Friedrich Handel's oratorios and anthems were commissioned by an investor in slave plantations (the Duke of Chandos), and major libraries and art galleries were built by similar patrons.[50]

Slavery and Economic Development in the Americas

Coerced black laborers constituted the "founding stone of a new economic system . . . for the modern world."[51] It is unlikely that the American colonies and, later, the United States would have seen dramatic agricultural and industrial development in the eighteenth and nineteenth centuries without the blood and sweat of those enslaved. Much of the wealth generated between the early 1700s and the 1860s came from the slave trade and the labor of enslaved men, women, and children on plantations and in other profit-making enterprises. In the seventeenth century the famous triangular trade emerged between Europe, Africa, and the American colonies. Europe and America provided ships and some agricultural exports, while Africa provided the enslaved laborers. As Eric

Williams has noted, sugar plantations in the West Indies "became the hub of the British Empire, of immense importance to the grandeur and prosperity of England," and it was the African laborers who made the West Indies the "most precious colonies ever recorded in the whole annals of imperialism."[52] Recent reviews of the evidence have concluded that the main economic bridge between Europe and the overseas colonies in this period was the slave-sugar complex.[53] The Caribbean plantations also spurred mainland development. Much of the oats, corn, flour, fish, lumber, soap, candles, and livestock exported by the continental colonies went to the West Indies plantations. In 1770 no less than *three-quarters* of all New England exports of foodstuffs went to the West Indian plantations or to Africa.[54] A substantial proportion of the wealth of the New England and Middle Atlantic colonies came from the nefarious trade with slave plantations in the southern colonies and the Caribbean.

From the early 1700s to the mid-1800s much of the surplus capital and wealth of North America came directly, or by means of economic multiplier effects, from the slave trade and slave plantations.[55] With the growing demand for textiles, U.S. cotton production expanded greatly between the 1790s and the beginning of the Civil War. Cotton was shipped to British and New England textile mills, greatly spurring the wheels of British, U.S., and international commerce. By the mid-nineteenth century New England cotton mills were the industrial leaders in value added, and second in number of employees, in the United States. Without slave labor it seems likely that there would have been no successful textile industry, and without the cotton textile industry—the first major U.S. industry—it is unclear how or when the United States would have become a major industrial power.[56] In the first half of the nineteenth century many northern merchants, bankers, and shipping companies became, as Doulass North has noted, "closely tied to cotton. New York became both the center of the import trade and the financial center for the cotton trade."[57] Slave-grown cotton became ever more central to the U.S. economy and accounted for about half of all exports, and thus for a large share of the profits generated by exports.

In the North the profits from the cotton economy and from the sale of products to slave plantations stimulated the growth of investment in financial and insurance enterprises, other service industries, and various types of manufacturing concerns, as well as, by means of taxes, of investment in government infrastructure projects. Cotton-related activities were perhaps the most important source of economic expansion in the United States before the Civil War, and most of the cotton was grown by enslaved black Americans.[58] Their agricultural production undergirded national economic development. As Ronald Takaki has noted, "The income derived from the export of cotton set in motion the process of accelerated market and industrial development—the Market Revolution."[59]

Before the American revolution, trading in slaves was an honorable profession in northern ports, and after the revolution it was equally as honorable to trade in products made by slaves or in manufactured products traded to plantations. One biographer of the leading merchant, T. H. Perkins, concluded that there was not a New England "merchant of any prominence who was not then directly or indirectly involved in this trade."[60] As the nineteenth century progressed, the sons and grandsons of the earlier traders in slaves and slave-related products often became the captains of the textile and other major industries in the North. The business profits made off enslavement were thereby transmitted across generations.[61]

British and New England manufacturers' demand for cotton fueled the demand for more enslaved workers and for more Native American land. The leading cotton states—Mississippi, Alabama, and South Carolina—were carved out of Native American lands, and as the cotton system expanded westward, the lands of more indigenous societies were taken. Land was usually taken by force or threat of force.[62] By 1850 most of the nation's enslaved population was involved in cotton production. Labor was perhaps the most critical factor in American economic production in the eighteenth and nineteenth centuries, so any scarcity in workers slowed development. "Slave labor not only removed this scarcity, but also made possible the development of the industry that spurred economic growth."[63] In the decade before the Civil War the dollar value of those enslaved was estimated by one leading planter to be $2 billion—a figure then exceeding the total value of *all* northern factories.[64]

Not only did the southern agricultural system provide fiber for the textile mills of the North, but profits from the cotton trade also generated demand for western foodstuffs and northern manufactured products. And the coerced labor of black men, women, and children in southern agriculture built up profits that were used by many white slaveowners for luxurious living, for further investments in plantations and related enterprises, for deposits in banks, or for paying off bank loans. Such capital—and the related capital generated in the international trade in southern products—could be used or borrowed by merchants, shippers, railroad executives, and other industrialists in the North or South.[65]

The economic prosperity and industrial development of Western nations, including the United States, were grounded to a substantial degree in the slavery system. Ali Mazrui summarizes the point, saying that "one of the forces that fed into the industrial revolution was slave labor. Western production levels were transformed. But so were Western living standards, life expectancy, population growth, and the globalization of capitalism."[66] Indeed, even the educational system of the new nation was sometimes funded from profits off slavery or the slave trade. For example, the founders of Brown University in Rhode Island made some of their fortunes by building slave ships and investing in the slave trade.[67]

The Wealth of Powerful Slaveholders

In the century prior to the Civil War the slaveholding oligarchy of the southern and border states controlled a huge share of the resources and riches of the nation. By the early nineteenth century the slaveholders owned much of the nation's most productive land and much of the agricultural produce for export. They owned a large proportion of the nation's livestock, warehouses, plantation buildings, and processing mills, as well as large numbers of enslaved workers. As a result, the South was the most economically prosperous and politically powerful region from the mid-1700s to the 1850s.[68]

The theft of land and the enslavement of Africans became the foundation of prosperity for many white families. George Washington, the leading general, chair of the Constitutional Convention, and first president, was one of the wealthiest Americans. Owner of more than 36,000 acres in Virginia and Maryland, he held substantial securities in banks and land companies. By 1783 his own accounting showed 216 enslaved black Americans under his control, including those he held and those of his wife's estate; in their lifetimes he and his wife had enslaved many more. Reading Washington's careful records, one can see that Washington viewed black men, women, and children as "little more than economic units," like farm animals whose purpose was to bring him monetary profit.[69] Enslaved blacks made possible his luxurious lifestyle. As Fritz Hirchfeld has documented, "Slaves washed his linens, sewed his shirts, polished his boots, saddled his horse, chopped the wood for his fireplaces, powdered his wig, drove his carriage, cooked his meals, served his table, poured his wine, posted his letters, lit the lamps, swept the porch, looked after the guests, planted the flowers in his gardens, trimmed the hedges, dusted the furniture, cleaned the windows, made the beds, and performed the myriad domestic chores. . . ."[70] Though Washington said he was opposed to violent brutality against those enslaved, his actions contradicted his stated view. His overseers were allowed to use flogging, and he vigorously pursued runways. He could be severe in his punishment, as in the case of one black man sold to the West Indies plantations—unusually savage places known for enslaved laborers being worked to an early death. Exhibiting his inhumanity, Washington wrote to his broker that this black man, was a "rogue and a runaway" and should be kept handcuffed.[71]

Similarly, the principal author of the Declaration of Independence, Thomas Jefferson, was considered very wealthy because he owned 10,000 acres of land and because, by the early 1800s, he held 185 African Americans in bondage. He owned several hundred black

Americans over his lifetime. His often extravagant lifestyle was made possible by those he enslaved. While Jefferson was sometimes critical of slavery, he rarely freed any slaves. The man seen as a principal progenitor of American liberty, who penned the phrase "all men are created equal," was an unrepentant Virginia slaveholder. He fathered at least one child whom he kept as a slave, and he chased down his fugitive slaves and had them severely whipped.[72] Like many wealthy men in the South and the North, Washington and Jefferson gained their prosperity on the bloody backs of those black men, women, and children they enslaved.

SLAVEHOLDERS AND THE AMERICAN GOVERNMENT

Another Irony of the American Revolution

Without the capital and wealth generated by enslaved black Americans it is possible that there would not have been an American Revolution and, thus, a United States. One of history's great ironies is the fact that the Declaration of Independence's "all men are created equal" did not apply to African Americans, yet the American victory in the struggle against Great Britain was possible substantially because the wealth generated by the slavery system and its economic spinoffs was available to help finance and support the American Revolution. A significant proportion of the money amassed or borrowed to fight that revolution came, directly or indirectly, from capital generated by the plantations and the trade in slaves and slave-produced products.[73] Money borrowed from northern sources often had its ultimate origin in the slavery constellation, as did some of the money borrowed from overseas. France's involvement in the American Revolution was essential to its successful outcome, and, as Edmund Morgan has shown, the "single most valuable product with which to purchase assistance was tobacco, produced mainly by slave labor. . . . To a large degree it may be said that Americans bought their independence with slave labor."[74]

The political structure established after the revolution continued to reflect the elite interest in slavery and in controlling African Americans, whether enslaved or free. The mainstream view of the U.S. government sees it and its actions as set, from its first decades, in the context of democracy—as the result of competing group interests jockeying for position through democratic political mechanisms. From this viewpoint, there is often a denial of the highly elitist and racialized character of the U.S. government.

A contrasting view sees the early U.S. state as very undemocratic and as central to the creation of systemic racism and to the formation of racial groups.[75] Historically, white male elites have worked through local and federal governments to create social institutions serving their interests. In the early development of the U.S. state, white women, African Americans, and Native Americans had no representation. The white male ruling class created a racialized state, which played a central role in defining who was "black" and "white" and what the benefits of being in each racial class were. For African Americans—and Native Americans forced onto reservations—this took the form of a police state. The standard dictionary definition of *police state* is "a political unit characterized by repressive governmental control of political, economic, and social life usually by an arbitrary exercise of power by police."[76] While the usual example of this is a totalitarian exercise of European government such as that of Nazi Germany, for most blacks police-state repression of their lives lasted, under slavery and later segregation, until the 1960s. Indeed, certain elements of this police state can still be seen in contemporary policing practices that unjustly target black men and women.

Slavery dominated U.S. politics in many ways between the making of the Constitution and the beginning of Civil War. The first U.S. president was a leading slaveholder, as were the third and fourth presidents. For fifty of the first sixty-four years of the new nation the president of the United States was a slave owner. The Speaker of the House was a slave owner for twenty-eight of the first thirty-five years of the nation's history, and before the Civil War the president pro tem of the Senate was usually a slaveholder.[77] The Chief Justices of the Supreme Court for most of the period up to the Civil War, John Marshall and Roger B. Taney, were slaveholders, as were numerous other members of that high court.

In the decades after the U.S. Constitution was put into place, the slavery system continued to shape legal and political decision making in fundamental ways, including the building of constitutional law in a series of federal court decisions such as *Dred Scott*. . . . For decades few major decisions made by the federal legislative and judicial branches went against the interests of the nation's slaveholding oligarchy, and foreign and domestic policies generally did not conflict with the interests of those centrally involved with the slavery system. George Washington's presidential administration even lent money to French planters in Haiti to put down a major slave uprising there. John Adams, his successor and not a slaveholder, took action to support the rebels, with an eye to U.S. influence in the area. Thomas Jefferson, another slaveholder and the third president, reversed Adams's policy and moved to support France's attempt to reconquer Haiti. Moreover, in the first half of the nineteenth century much U.S. territorial expansion, such as into areas of Mexico, was undergirded by the slaveholders' interest in additional land for yet more slave plantations.[78]

The slaveholding oligarchy was not seriously challenged until the middle of the nineteenth century. By the decade of the 1850s a major schism in the ruling class, that between southern planters and northern industrialists who had little economic interest in slavery, was becoming clear in battles over such issues as the expansion of slavery into western lands and over tariffs. Southern planters opposed tariffs on imports and pressed for expansion of the slaveholding system into new western areas, while northern immigrant farmers and allied railroad interests increasingly pressed to keep those lands available for immigrant farmers. Fearful of its economic and political future, the South's slaveholding oligarchy eventually moved to secede. The victory of the North in the subsequent Civil War marked the arrival of northern industrialists and merchants as a dominant force in the U.S. economy and government.[79]

The grip of slavery on the nation could be seen even as the southern states were seceding and the nation was moving to war. Recall that President Abraham Lincoln was willing to make major concessions to slaveholding interests to preserve the union. Certain members of the Republican Party talked with representatives of the southern planters and proposed a thirteenth amendment to the Constitution that would guarantee slavery in the South. Lincoln was willing to accept this amendment, even though it perpetuated enslavement. Yet the southern oligarchy rejected this compromise proposal, apparently because they thought they could win a war.[80]. . .

Notes

1. United Nations, "Convention on the Prevention and Punishment of Genocide," *The United Nations and Human Rights: 1945–1995* (New York: United Nations Department of Public Information, 1995), p. 151.

2. Charles W. Mills, *The Racial Contract* (Ithaca, NY: Cornell University Press, 1997), pp. 98, 155; David E. Stannard, *The American Holocaust: Columbus and the Conquest of the New World* (New York: Oxford University Press, 1992).

3. William T. Hagan, *American Indians* (Chicago: University of Chicago Press, 1961), p. 14. The discussion of these wars is taken from pp. 12–15. An earlier, much less developed version of this discussion, as well as that in a few later paragraphs of this chapter, appears in Joe R. Feagin and Clairece B. Feagin, *Racial and Ethnic Relations*, 6th ed. (Upper Saddle River, NJ: Prentice-Hall, 1999), chapters 7 and 8.

4. Michael P. Rogin, *Fathers and Children: Andrew Jackson and the Subjugation of the American Indian* (New York: Knopf, 1975), p. 319.

5. Winthrop D. Jordan, *White over Black: American Attitudes toward the Negro, 1550–1812* (Chapel Hill: University of North Carolina Press, 1968), pp. 239–41.

6. Benjamin B. Ringer, *"We the People" and Others* (New York: Tavistock, 1983), pp. 134–38.

7. *Dred Scott v. John F. A. Sandford*, 60 U.S. 393, 403–404 (1857).

8. Ibid., 408.

9. Ringer, *"We the People" and Others*, p. 36.

10. Robin Blackburn, *The Making of New World Slavery: From the Baroque to the Modern, 1492–1800* (London: Verso, 1997), p. 10.

11. A. Leon Higginbotham, Jr., *Shades of Freedom: Racial Politics and the Presumptions of the American Legal Process* (New York: Oxford University Press, 1996), pp. 14–51.

12. Forrest G. Wood, *The Arrogance of Faith: Christianity and Race in America from the Colonial Era to the Twentieth Century* (New York: Knopf, 1990), p. xviii.

13. Higginbotham, *Shades of Freedom*, p. xxiii; Lawrence M. Friedman, *A History of American Law* (New York: Simon and Schuster, 1973), pp. 72–76, 192–200; Herbert Aptheker, *American Negro Slave Revolts* (New York: International Publishers, 1943), pp. 53–78.

14. Thomas Jefferson, quoted in Peter M. Bergman, *The Chronological History of the Negro in America* (New York: Harper & Row, 1969), p. 52.

15. Ronald Segal, *The Black Diaspora* (New York: Farrar, Straus and Giroux, 1995), pp. 58–59.

16. Kenneth S. Greenberg, *Honor and Slavery* (Princeton, NJ: Princeton University Press, 1996).

17. Peter J. Parish, *Slavery: History and Historians* (New York: Harper and Row, 1989), p. 129; see also pp. 126–32.

18. Elizabeth Fox-Genovese, *Within the Plantation Household: Black and White Women of the Old South* (Chapel Hill: University of North Carolina Press, 1988), p. 24.

19. See Kenneth Stampp, *The Peculiar Institution: Slavery in the Ante-Bellum South* (New York: Vintage Books, 1956); and Robert W. Roel and Stanley Engerman, *Time on the Cross: The Economics of American Negro Slavery* (Boston: Little, Brown, 1974). For a summary of the scholars and their views, see Fox-Genovese, *Within the Plantation Household*, pp. 56–86.

20. Lorenzo J. Greene, *The Negro in Colonial New England* (New York: Atheneum, 1969), pp. 56–69. This quote is on pp. 68–69.

21. Ronald Bailey, "The Other Side of Slavery," *Agricultural History* 68 (Spring 1994): 36.

22. James W. Loewen, *Lies My Teacher Told Me: Everything Your American History Textbook Got Wrong* (New York: The New Press, 1995), p. 135.

23. A. Leon Higginbotham, Jr., *In the Matter of Color* (New York: Oxford University Press, 1978), pp. 63–70, 144–49. An earlier discussion of some data in this section appeared in Joe R. Feagin, "Slavery Unwilling to Die: The Background of Black Oppression in the 1980s," *Journal of Black Studies* 17 (December 1986): 173–200.

24. Ringer, *"We the People" and Others*, p. 533.

25. John R. McKivigan, "The Northern Churches and the Moral Problem of Slavery." in *The Meaning of Slavery in the North*, eds. David Roediger and Martin H. Blatt (New York: Garland, 1998), pp. 77–94.

26. Olaudah Equiano, "The Interesting Narrative of the Life of Olaudah Equiano," in *Afro-American History*, ed. Thomas R. Frazier (New York: Harcourt, Brace & World, 1970), pp. 18–20.

27. William Wells Brown, *From Fugitive Slave to Free Man*, ed. William L. Andrews (New York: Mentor Books, 1993), p. 30.

28. See T. Lindsay Baker and Julie P. Baker, eds., *The WPA Oklahoma Slave Narratives* (Norman: University of Oklahoma Press, 1996).

29. See Patricia Morton, introduction to *Discovering the Women in Slavery*, ed. Patricia Morton (Athens: University of Georgia Press, 1996).

30. Patricia J. Williams, *The Alchemy of Race and Rights* (Cambridge, MA: Harvard University Press, 1991), pp. 154–56.

31. Melton A. McLaurin, *Celia: A Slave* (Athens: University of Georgia Press, 1991); see also Harriet A. Jacobs, *Incidents in the Life of a Slave Girl*, ed. Jean Fagan Yellin (Cambridge, MA: Harvard University Press, 1987).

32. The three-quarters-white Hemings was the half-sister of Jefferson's deceased wife. Jerry Fresia, *Toward an American Revolution: Exposing the Constitution and Other Illusions* (Boston: South End, 1988), pp. 1–2; Dinitia Smith and Nicholas Wade, "DNA Evidence Links Thomas Jefferson to Slave's Offspring," *Gainesville Sun*, November 1, 1998, 4A.

33. James Parton, quoted in Paul Finkelman, *Slavery and the Founders: Race and Liberty in the Age of Jefferson* (Armonk, NY: M. E. Sharpe, 1996), p. 143.

34. Jordan, *White over Black*, p. 153.

35. The lower estimates come from Philip D. Curtin, *The African Slave Trade: A Census* (University of Wisconsin Press, 1968). The higher and probably more accurate figures are calculated in Joseph E. Inikori, ed., *Forced Migration* (New York: Africana Publishing, 1982), pp. 19–33; and S. E. Anderson, *The Black Holocaust* (New York: Writers and Readers Press, 1995), pp. 156–58.

36. See Dinesh D'Souza, *The End of Racism: Principles for a Multiracial Society* (New York: Free Press, 1995), pp. 70–87.

37. I am partially indebted here to an interpretation of the literature suggested to me by Holly Hanson. See also John Thornton, *Africa and Africans in the Making of the Atlantic World, 1400–1680* (New York: Cambridge University Press, 1992), pp. 5–9; and Molefi Kete Asante, "The Wonders of Africa," post to Discussion List for African American Studies (H-Afro-Am), November, 1999.

38. Stanley M. Elkins, *A Problem in American Institutional and Intellectual Life* (New York: Grosset and Dunlap, 1963), pp. 96–97. This was true as well of the slave trade between sub-Saharan Africa and certain Islamic countries.

39. W. E. B. Du Bois, *Darkwater* (1920), as reprinted in *The Oxford W. E. B. Du Bois Reader*, ed. Eric J. Sundquist (New York: Oxford, 1996), p. 504.

40. W. E. B. Du Bois, *Black Reconstruction in America 1860–1880* (New York: Atheneum, 1992 [1935]), p. 10.

41. John Willinsky, *Learning to Divide the World: Education at Empire's End* (Minneapolis: University of Minnesota Press, 1998), p. 191.

42. Rafael Tammariello, "The Slave Trade," *Las Vegas Review-Journal*, February 8, 1998, 1E.

43. J. H. Parry and P. M. Sherlock, *A Short History of the West Indies*, 3rd ed. (New York: St. Martin's Press, 1971), p. 110–11. I am influenced here by William M. Wiecek, *The Sources of Antislavery Constitutionalism in America, 1760–1848* (Ithaca, NY: Cornell University Press, 1977), pp. 15–16.

44. William M. Wiecek, "The Origins of the Law of Slavery in British North America," *Cardozo Law Review* 17 (May, 1996): 1739.

45. Williams, *Capitalism and Slavery*, pp. 98–107; Douglass C. North, *The Economic Growth of the United States, 1790–1860* (Englewood Cliffs, NJ: Prentice-Hall, 1961), pp. 38–45; Bailey, "The Other Side of Slavery," p. 40; Blackburn, *The Making of New World Slavery*, chapter 12.

46. Anderson, *The Black Holocaust*, p. 19.

47. Barbara L. Solow and Stanley L. Engerman, "British Capitalism and Caribbean Slavery: The Legacy of Eric Williams: An Introduction," in *British Capitalism and Caribbean Slavery: The Legacy of Eric Williams* (Cambridge: Cambridge University Press, 1987), pp. 8–9.

48. Wilson E. Williams, *Africa and the Rise of Capitalism* (New York: AMS Press, 1975 [1938]), pp. 23–25.

49. Williams, *Capitalism and Slavery*, pp. 93–95, 102–107.

50. See the documentary *The Art of Darkness*, written by David Dabydeen and directed by David Maloney, Central Production, 1986. I am indebted to Joseph Rahme for suggesting this point.

51. Du Bois, *Black Reconstruction*, p. 15.

52. Williams, *Capitalism and Slavery*, p. 52.

53. Solow and Engerman, "British Capitalism and Caribbean Slavery," p. 4.

54. Ibid., pp. 5–7; Ronald Bailey, "'Those Valuable People, the Africans,'" in *The Meaning of Slavery in the North*, eds. Roediger and Blatt, p. 11.

55. See Fred Bateman and Thomas Weiss, *A Deplorable Scarcity: The Failure of Industrialization in the Slave Economy* (Chapel Hill: University of North Carolina Press, 1981); and Stanley Lebergott, *The Americans: An Economic Record* (New York: Norton, 1984).

56. Robert S. Browne, "Achieving Parity through Reparations," in *The Wealth of Races: The Present Value of Benefits from Past Injustices*, ed. Richard F. America (New York: Greenwood Press, 1990), pp. 201–202.

57. North, *The Economic Growth of the United States, 1790–1860*, p. 63.

58. Ibid., p. 68.

59. Ronald T. Takaki, *Iron Cages: Race and Culture in 19th-Century America* (New York: Oxford University Press, 1990), p. 78.

60. Bailey, "'Those Valuable People, the Africans,'" in *The Meaning of Slavery in the North*, eds. Roediger and Blatt, p. 14.

61. Ibid., p. 19.

62. North, *The Economic Growth of the United States, 1790–1860*, p. 41; Takaki, *Iron Cages*, p. 77.

63. Browne, "Achieving Parity through Reparations," p. 201.

64. Segal, *The Black Diaspora*, pp. 56–58.

65. North, *The Economic Growth of the United States, 1790–1860*, p. 122.

66. Ali A. Mazrui, "Who Should Pay for Slave Reparations to Africa," *World Press Review* (August 1993): 22.

67. Anderson, *The Black Holocaust*, p. 20.

68. Herbert Aptheker, *The Unfolding Drama: Studies in U.S. History*, ed. Bettina Aptheker (New York: International Publishers, 1978, p. 84.

Slavery was profitable for most slaveholders and the cost of maintaining slave labor was low. See Segal, *The Black Diaspora*.

69. Fritz Hirschfeld, *George Washington and Slavery: A Documentary Portrayal* (Columbia: University of Missouri Press, 1997), p. 49. See also pp. 16, 37.

70. Hirschfeld, *George Washington and Slavery*, p. 236.

71. Ibid., pp. 68–69.

72. Takaki, *Iron Cages*, pp. 43–54.

73. Derrick Bell, "White Supremacy in America: Its Legal Legacy, Its Economic Costs," in *Critical White Studies: Looking Behind the Mirror*, eds. Richard Delgado and Jean Stefancic (Philadelphia: Temple University Press, 1999, p. 596.

74. Edmund S. Morgan, *American Slavery, American Freedom: The Ordeal of Virginia* (New York: Norton, 1975), p. 5.

75. Jack Niemonen, "The Role of the State in the Sociology of Racial and Ethnic Relations: Some Theoretical Considerations," *Free Inquiry in Creative Sociology* 23 (May 1995).

76. *Merriam-Webster's Collegiate Dictionary*, 10th ed. (Springfield, MA: Merriam-Webster, 1999, p. 901.

77. William Lee Miller, *Arguing about Slavery: The Great Battle in the United States Congress* (New York: Knopf, 1996), p. 13.

78. Loewen, *Lies My Teacher Told Me*, pp. 143–144.

79. Aptheker, *The Unfolding Drama*, p. 83.

80. Herbert Aptheker, unpublished lectures on American History, Minneapolis, University of Minnesota, 1984. I draw here on tapes of the lectures.

DISCUSSION QUESTIONS

1. How was slavery in the United States different from slavery anywhere else? What sorts of human rights were limited for African Americans under slavery? What were some of the types of barbarities committed by slavemasters? Did they vary by gender (of whites and of blacks)?

2. What were some facts you learned about America's forefathers and slavery that you never knew before reading this essay? Why do you think such history is not taught in schools? Should it be? Why or why not?

3. Typically we think of only the South being involved in slavery. What are the ways Feagin outlines that white northerners, as well as other non-slaveholding whites, benefited from the institution of slavery? Was there any slavery in the North? Why does history teach us a more "spotless" version of the North and its leaders than the one that Feagin presents?

SOUTHERN WOMEN, SOUTHERN HOUSEHOLDS

Elizabeth Fox-Genovese

. . . Antebellum southern women, like all others, lived in a discrete social system and political economy within which gender, class, and race relations shaped their lives and identities. Thus, even a preliminary sketch of the history of southern women must attend scrupulously both to their immediate conditions and to the larger social system in which the immediate conditions were embedded and by which they were informed. We have, in a sense, two views: the view from within and the view from without— the view of the participants and the view of the historians. Women do not normally experience their lives as manifestations of the laws of political economy, although they may register sharply the vicissitudes of economic fortunes. The papers of southern women are accounts of troubles with servants and children, of struggles for faith, of friendships, and of turning hems. These intimate personal details and perceptions constitute a valuable record in themselves and suggest patterns of a larger social experience. We inevitably abstract from historical evidence in order to construct a narrative or an analysis. The most significant differences among historians occur at this stage of abstraction, which itself influences the ways in which we interpret and organize the specific evidence. Southern history abounds in these debates, which afford some of the most lively and theoretically informed writing in American history. But the debates have not yet taken adequate account of the history of southern women. Nor has the experience of southern women significantly penetrated the "larger" debates, which badly need closer attention to gender.

Southern women belonged to a slave society that differed decisively from the northern bourgeois society to which it was politically bound. Slavery as a social system shaped the experience of all its women, for slavery influenced the nature of the whole society, not least its persisting rural character. Southern slave society consisted largely of a network of households that contained within themselves the decisive relations of production and reproduction. In the South, in contrast to the North, the household retained a vigor that permitted southerners to ascribe many matters—notably labor relations, but also important aspects of gender relations—to the private sphere, whereas northerners would increasingly ascribe them to the public spheres of market and state. The household structure and social relations of southern society had multiple and far-reaching consequences for all spheres of southern life, including law, political economy, politics, and slaveholders' relations with yeomen and other nonslaveholding whites. And it had special consequences for gender relations in general and women's experience in particular.[1]

The persistence in the South of the household as the dominant unit of production and reproduction guaranteed the power of men in society, even as measured by nineteenth-century bourgeois standards. During the period in which northern society was undergoing a reconversion of household into home and ideologically ascribing it to the female sphere, southern society was reinforcing the centrality of plantation and farm households that provided continuities and discontinuities in the experience of women of different classes and races. Variations in the wealth of households significantly differentiated women's experience, but the common structure as a unit of production and reproduction under men's dominance provided some

basic similarity. Effectively, the practical and ideological importance of the household in southern society reinforced gender constraints by ascribing all women to the domination of the male heads of households and to the company of the women of their own households. In 1853 Mary Kendall, a transplanted New Englander, wrote to her sister of her special pleasure in receiving a letter from her, for "I seldom see any person aside from our own family, and those employed upon the plantation. For about three weeks I did not have the pleasure of seeing *one white female face*, there being no white family except our own upon the plantation." The experience of black slave women differed radically from that of all white women, for they belonged to households that were not governed by their own husbands, brothers, and fathers. But even black slave women shared with white women of different social classes some of the constraints of prevalent gender conventions.[2]

As members of a slave society, southern women differed in essential respects from other American women, although their experience has not figured prominently in the development of American women's history, much less influenced the theory that informs generalizations about the experience of American women.[3] Southern women's history should force us to think seriously about the relation between the experiences that unite women as members of a gender and those that divide them as members of specific communities, classes, and races. It should, in other words, challenge us to recognize class and race as central, rather than incidental, to women's identities and behavior—to their sense of themselves as women.

American women's history, notwithstanding its success in challenging the dominant interpretations of gender, has followed the road of the great American consensus with respect to race and class. Historians of the "American woman" have charted "her" experience and traced her blossoming consciousness from the farms and towns of New England through the abolitionist and women's rights movements of that New England diaspora traced by Frederick Jackson Turner, to the Sanitary Commission, the Women's Clubs, the Woman's Christian Temperance Movement, and access to higher education. From there, the modal history has progressed to the emergence of professional careers in social work or related occupations; growing participation in government through the Consumers' League, the Women's Bureau of the Department of Labor, and the activities of the New Deal; and on to the National Organization for Women (NOW), the vice-presidential candidacy of Geraldine Ferraro, and the fight for women's right to abortion.[4]

The tendency to generalize the experience of the women of one region to cover that of all American women has obscured essential differences of class and race. The generalization might be defended if it could be shown that structural similarities transcended regional variations, which could then appropriately be dismissed as little more than accidents of local color. But "New Englandization" cannot be reduced to local color, for the original New England model derives directly from dominant American attitudes toward class relations in history, and beyond them toward the prevailing mythology of who Americans are as a people.

The New England women whose experience has provided the dominant models for women's history belonged overwhelmingly to the emerging bourgeoisie. To be sure, industrial capitalism developed slowly and unevenly in New England as elsewhere; nonetheless, the market governed the development of social and gender relations even among people whose lives it touched indirectly. Some women's historians, notably Christine Stansell and Carroll Smith-Rosenberg, have challenged the simplicity of the New England model by insisting on the variations in women's experience by class. Stansell, for example, cogently argues that during the antebellum period the working-class women of New York City, who were less than impressed by the purported sisterliness of upper- and middle-class women, developed a distinct subculture, including particular attitudes toward work, family, sexuality, and self-presentation. And Smith-Rosenberg develops a welcome picture of women's special roles in an emerging bourgeois culture. Despite these promising new directions, we still lack a revised picture of the complex roles of different groups of women in the development of American life and political culture, much less a reassessment of the roles and values of southern women.[5]

Smith-Rosenberg's evocation of bourgeois culture, like Stansell's insistence on class conflict among women, should begin to move us beyond the uncritical acceptance of the cultural and political predominance of the fabled middle classes. Yet ultimately, we must also explain the persistence of that predominance and its abiding sway over our vision of our own identity as a people, for Americans have clung tenaciously to the view of themselves as a democratic, middle-class society. The very term *middle class* derives from a literature that sought to describe social stratification as an analytical alternative to class relations. Many southern women, like women throughout the country, can be said to have been "middle-class," broadly construed, but to have belonged to the middle class in a society in which some people owned others carried fateful consequences. To be a "middle-class" employer of free labor or of no labor at all was one thing. To be a "middle-class" owner of human flesh was—materially, ideologically, psychologically—quite another. Most societies, most systems of social relations, have a large middle, if only because most sociological analyses structure data in a manner that guarantees it. The question remains: Middle of what?

The model of womanhood that emerged in the northeastern part of the country rested upon a view of class relations that sought to deny the significance of class divisions—that sought to promote the illusion that all men were truly equal. This view claimed to embody universal rather than specifically middle-class values and, in the name of universalism, sought to impose middle-class values on the rest of the nation. That attempt, which began with evangelicalism, nativism, and an emphasis on the work ethic, ended with antislavery, the Republican party, and the war for the Union. Any attempt to apply such a model to women who—whatever else may be said about them—ended up on the other side of that confrontation requires some fancy footwork. Yet most historians who have considered the history of southern women at all have absorbed large doses of that model, even if they have also protested against simple assimilation of the experience of southern women with that of their northern "sisters."[6]

Joan Jensen has argued that the northeastern model of separate spheres does not adequately explain the experience of the small group of mid-Atlantic farm women whom she has carefully studied. For these women, the initial impact of capitalism resulted in a refiguration of their work within farm households, and only gradually in a loosening of the bonds that tied them to those households. Their religious convictions as Hicksite Quakers and their special experiences gradually led a small fraction of the wealthiest among them to espouse the cause of women's rights. But by that time they had reason to view their destinies as, in essential respects, separate from those of their household kin. Jensen's work offers a microcosm of the possible variations within the experience of different groups of women throughout the mid-Atlantic states and possibly the midwestern ones as well. But it also confirms that the logic of northern development, broadly interpreted, led toward women's growing engagement with the market, first as members of households and gradually as individuals. The development of southern slave society did not promote the same result. In this respect the experience of northern women, despite innumerable variations according to subregion and class, differed fundamentally from that of southern women, black and white.[7] The history of southern women does not constitute another regional variation on the main story; it constitutes another story.

Women's history, in part as a natural attempt to establish its own claims, has tended to emphasize what women shared across class and racial lines. It has, in short, tended toward an essentialist interpretation of women's experience—indeed, of women's "being." By "essentialist," I mean a transhistorical view of women that emphasizes the core biological aspects of women's identity, independent of time and place, class, nation, and race. From the perspective of many women's historians, to emphasize the class and racial determinants of women's experience and, especially, women's consciousness is to compromise the integrity of women's perception and to mute the pervasiveness of sexism and male dominance. Women's history has paid attention to the experience of women of different classes and is, increasingly if still inadequately, paying attention to the experience of women of different races. The problem is not that we have no history of working-class or

black women. It is that, with notable exceptions, the histories we do have are being written as if class and race did not shape women's experience and even their identities.[8]

Neither women's history nor women's identities can responsibly be abstracted from the social relations of class and race in the society and communities with which we are here concerned. The history of the women of the Old South illustrates what should be a general rule of women's history: The history of women cannot be written without attention to women's relations with men in general and with "their" men in particular, nor without attention to the other women of their society. If we try to work with a general, not to mention an essentialist, view of women's nature, we must end in banality. All women, like all men, are a product of social relations defined to include gender, class, nationality, and race. Their innermost identities, their ideals for themselves, and their views of the world all derive from their sense of themselves as a woman in relation to men and other women—their sense of themselves as the female members of specific societies.

Class and race deeply divided southern women, notwithstanding their shared experience of life in rural households under the domination of men. There is almost no evidence to suggest that slaveholding women envisioned themselves as the "sisters" of yeoman women, although there may have been some blurring at the margins when kin relations crossed class lines. In contrast, there is reason to believe that some slaveholding women felt minimal kinship with their female slaves, with whom they might have intimate, if tension-fraught, relations in everyday life. In general, but for women in particular, class relations in southern society remained essentially hierarchical. If anything, relations among women of different classes strengthened and reaffirmed class distance among free white families and served as an antidote to the elements of egalitarianism—or at least formal political democracy—that characterized relations among free white men. The relations among women also reaffirmed the special race relations of slave society, for the more established slaveholding women viewed their female slaves as somehow part of their effective universe in a way that they did not view yeoman women or even arrivistes. But they unavoidably viewed those slaves as social and racial inferiors whose station in life was that of perpetual servants. Thus, the arrivistes could in time "arrive," whereas the slaves had no prospects and the nonslave-holders could be perceived as having none.

Gender, race, and class relations constituted the grid that defined southern women's objective positions in their society, constituted the elements from which they fashioned their views of themselves and their world, constituted the relations of different groups of southern women to one another. The class relations that divided and interlocked southern women played a central role in their respective identities. Slaveholding, slave, yeoman, poor white, and middle-class town women, as members of a gender, shared the imposition of male dominance, but their experience of that dominance differed significantly according to class and race.

The forms of male prejudice and dominance differ among societies that assign specific purposes and forms to prejudice and domination. The distinctive forms of male dominance in the South developed in conjunction with the development of slavery as a social system and reflected the rural character that slavery reinforced in southern society. In the South, as in many other societies, church and state substantially reinforced the prevalent forms of male dominance, some of which were national and some regionally specific. Within the South, the forms varied considerably according to community. Like religion and the law, the rural character of southern slave society impinged upon women of all classes and races in innumerable, albeit different, ways. Above all, it circumscribed their mobility and the size of the communities to which they belonged or within which they developed their sense of themselves. For most women, male dominance appeared specifically as a direct manifestation of the social and gender relations of particular communities, however much accepted as a general law of life.[9]

Superficially, the experience of southern women paralleled that of their northern counterparts in many ways. Religious conviction lay at the heart of country women's struggle to know

themselves and to apply their knowledge so as to live and die as Christian women. The language of the Bible and sermons shaped country women's models of female excellence. The church offered one of their few social encounters outside the household, as well as their most immediate court for the enforcement of social relations and behavior. Christianity as a system of belief and the church as network and institution functioned analogously for southern and northern town and country women. Jean Friedman has convincingly argued that religion contributed to, rather than alleviated, southern women's sense of living in an "enclosed garden" under the domination of men. Yet most southern women probably experienced that enclosure within their purportedly ordained station as a natural manifestation of human and divine order rather than as arbitrary imprisonment.[10]

Southern religious values imperceptibly merged with the high culture and high politics of the slaveholders, which in turn permeated southern society. Religion, politics, and culture were rooted in and continually transformed the slaveholders' daily lives and attitudes. Women contributed to the hegemony of the slaveholding class, even though men normally figured as its premier spokesmen, and no claim to understand them can ignore those contributions. Slaveholding women, who never figured as mere passive victims of male dominance, benefited from their membership in a ruling class. Slave, yeoman, and poor white women experienced their own subordination as, in some way, legitimated by women as well as by men. Thus, the behavior and attitudes of slaveholding women in their daily lives simultaneously reflected and contributed to the ideology of the slaveholders and strengthened their cultural and political influence over society. The relations of slaveholding women with the other classes of society—notably the slaves, yeomen, and poor whites—articulated attributes of class and race as well as gender. As ladies, slaveholding women enacted the differences between social groups at least as much as they did the similarities among women. As ladies, they reinforced slaveholding ideology even as they reformulated it in feminine guise.

The slaveholders enunciated their ideology in a variety of published discourses—political, economic, religious, social, literary—but only a minority of those to whom they were directed, including women of the slaveholding class, read them. And yet broad dissemination ensured that the messages of this formal intellectual work ultimately touched the ordinary lives of slaveholding women and influenced their relations with the men and women of other classes. The private papers of slaveholding women reveal that many of them engaged with the high culture of their society through a wide variety of printed texts. Few followed Louisa McCord in her passion for political economy, but many concerned themselves with religion, literature, and history. The ways in which and the extent to which women shared in this literate culture varied considerably, but many had access through participation in the networks of institutions through which ideas were disseminated and class relations consolidated. The slaveholders, women and men, were bound together in a web of belief and behavior by schools, churches, watering places or resorts, and villages, and by lecture halls that supplemented the family gatherings around the fire, at which the head of the household read aloud the Bible or a printed sermon or some other elevating or suitable work.[11]

The schools and churches of southern society developed on the basis of available resources and choices about whom to instruct and whom to hold in church fellowship. The choices resulted, albeit unequally, from the beliefs and goals of the members of different classes and races. Thus, if a group of black slaves sought to establish a church or a school, they would either have to do so in secrecy and under adverse circumstances, or with white support and control. Even yeomen, not to mention poor whites, did not, with their scarce resources, enjoy wide choice in such matters. Within the various classes, the choices of women always partly reflected their class's view of proper gender relations and roles, in tension with women's independent views and access to resources. Some southern women of all classes and races found access to schooling and especially to church membership. Southern women may even have outnumbered southern men in church membership, although possibly not in church attendance. The figures here remain far from conclusive, and possibly one of the significant differences between northern and southern

society lay precisely in the greater proportion of men to women in southern church attendance, if not membership.

No southern woman shared equal access to schooling with the men of her own class, although by the 1850s increasing numbers of women were attending academies sponsored by the churches and the more reflective political leaders. And although slaveholders frequently expended considerable effort to provide their daughters with educations appropriate to their station, they firmly discouraged those daughters from becoming teachers. When the disruptions of the war finally made it possible for Elizabeth Grimball to take a position as a teacher, her mother, Meta Morris Grimball, reported that although "the old Mauma has acted throughout [defeat and emancipation] with perfect consideration, she was terribly mortified by Elizabeth being a teacher, & Gabriella, & Charlotte keeping a school." Teaching a Sunday-school class might be viewed as a social responsibility; teaching a favorite slave to read might even be tolerated; but earning a salary for regular teaching was viewed as an unfortunate necessity for widows or, even worse, wives who had fallen victim to their husbands' inadequacies. It was not a fit occupation for a lady.[12]

Education underscores the difference between southern women and women throughout the rest of the country. In the late eighteenth century, northern bourgeois and, in lesser measure, southern slaveholders discovered the virtues of educating women to meet their responsibilities as republican mothers. But whereas, in the South, that elite tradition long continued to dominate prevailing attitudes toward women's education, in the North it was rapidly supplemented by a practical commitment to educating young women for careers as teachers. Because the South lagged far behind the North in the development of common schools, it did not develop the same expanding demand for low-paid, female teachers and, accordingly, did not develop institutions to train them. The South had nothing that resembled Emma Willard's academy in Troy, New York, which especially trained teachers. When circumstances forced slaveholding women to turn to teaching as a means of supporting themselves, they invariably opened small, transitory private schools, not unlike the dame schools of late-colonial New England. In northern society, education emerged as an essential ingredient in training displaced rural children and immigrants to take their places in a capitalist economy. Young women who were marrying later, or perhaps not at all, and who were no longer essential to their parents' households, were ideal candidates for the task of basic instruction, especially since they could be paid less than men for the same work.[13]

The figure of the lady, especially the plantation mistress, dominated southern ideals of womanhood. That slaveholding ladies were massively outnumbered by nonslaveholding or small-slaveholding women challenges any easy assumptions about the relation between the ideal and reality but does not undermine the power of the ideal. The temptation to demystify the figure of the lady has proved almost irresistible. It has even been argued that the plantation mistress closely resembled slave women in being the victim of the double burden of patriarchy and slavery. According to this view, southern ladies, isolated on plantations and condemned to bear many children, endured husbands who whored in the slave quarters and slaves who combined sauciness with sloth and indifference. It has been, if anything, more seductive to reason that ladies, who themselves suffered male domination, were the primary, if secret, critics of their society—nothing less than closet feminists and abolitionists who saw slavery as a "monstrous system." "Poor women, poor slaves," in the widely quoted words of Mary Boykin Chesnut. But most ladies, like Mary Chestnut herself, were hardly prepared to do without slaves and enthusiastically supported secession. Above all, they did not advance an alternate model of womanhood. The North, too, had its ladies and fashionable women, but northern society preferred to celebrate the virtues of domesticity over those of privilege.[14]

This modern view of the southern woman as the leading opponent of southern institutions strikingly conforms to that espoused by northern abolitionist women, including those southern expatriates, the Grimké sisters, who loudly denounced the special toll that slavery exacted from white women: In their view, the condition of women in a slave society can only be compared to that of slaves; life in a slave society intensified both women's enslavement and their consciousness of it. These perceptions encourage the view that privileged southern women were alienated from their own society and were feminists in much the same sense as were the northern advocates of women's rights. Black slave women figure in this picture of southern women primarily as evidence of the society's sexual disarray and as burdens on already overburdened slaveholding women. Rather than living a life of ease and privilege, so this argument goes, the southern lady lived a life of ceaseless responsibility and toil, as "the slave of slaves."[15] In truth, she did neither.

Slave women did not see their mistresses as oppressed sisters. But recent work on Afro-American slave women has—notwithstanding its generally high quality and good intentions—also paid inadequate attention to the consequences of class and racial oppression for slave women's sense of themselves as women. Similarly, historians of the slave community have minimized the consequences of enslavement for the relations between slave women and men, and, in defending the strength and vitality of Afro-American culture, have too easily assumed that the slaves developed their own strong attachment to a "normal," nuclear family life—a remarkably egalitarian form of conjugal domesticity and companionship. The skewing of this picture derived primarily from assumptions about slave men and women as couples; assumptions about the most likely foundations for the demonstrably strong attachment of slaves to their families; and assumptions about the necessary underpinnings for male strength. These assumptions were accompanied by respectful attention to slave women as workers and as members of the slave community. Indeed, most of the male historians of slavery delighted in celebrating the strength of slave women, but they also did their best to make those women fit into their own preconceptions of what a strong woman should be—a cross between middle-class domesticity and the virtuous woman of Proverbs.[16]

The history of slave women, like that of the women of other oppressed groups, races, nations, and classes, demonstrates how dangerous it can be to study women in isolation from the interlocking systems of class, gender, and race relations that constitute any society. By modern feminist standards, slave women did escape some of the fetters of privilege that imprisoned white northern women. But surely they did not escape the larger constraints imposed by life in a slave society. Nor is there any reason to believe that they, any more than their men, escaped a heavy dose of cultural domination, even though they might appropriate, reinterpret, and turn to their own advantage those distinct elements of white culture that they could assimilate into an Afro-American culture of their own making. What can be the political and cultural moral of the story of slave women's purported independence? Did that independence materially free them from their own enslavement? From the perspective of Afro-Americans as a people, should the independence of women be interpreted as a collective gain, or merely as the confirmation of slave men's weakness relative to white men? Nothing can be gained by pretending that these complexities do not exist. Even the recognition of black women's "double" oppression and their uniquely creative solutions to the problems that confront all women cannot explain away the consequences of the enslavement of black men for black women's identities.

Gender constitutes an indispensable category of analysis because it imposes the recognition that to be a woman or a man is to participate in a set of social relations in a specific way. When white slaveholding women invoked their own sense of "honor," as many did, they were invoking an ideal of excellence that could not be divorced from their identification with their men and their reliance on their class position for a sense of who they were. The ideal of honor was related, however imprecisely, to the ability to command the bodies and labor of others, to a model of social hierarchy in which some were born and would die superior to others, whatever their personal failings and economic vicissitudes. The independence and strength of slave women were inscribed in a social system in which slaveholding women had the right to command the obedience and deference of slave men, in which slaveholding men had the right to exploit the bodies of slave women, and in which slave men did not have the right to resist either

form of assault, although they often did at the risk of their lives. Obviously, there were limits to the deference slave men could extract from slave women under these conditions. But how do we evaluate a female strength that may have derived less from African traditions than from an enslavement that stripped men of all the normal attributes of male power: legal and social fatherhood, the control of property, the ability to dominate households?

The ways in which various authors want the story to end impinges on every effort to write it. Either the power that some people exercise over others has consequences or it does not. If it does not, then the arguments for freedom and liberation lose much of their force. If it does, then those who have suffered the inescapable dependence of forcibly imposed power must face the consequences. Those who favor the essentialist view of women's history may find, in the abstraction of the effects of slavery on black men, an asset for the story they wish to tell. Others may find the perspective daunting. Stripping men of power may well encourage female autonomy, but black women, slave and free, lived in a world dominated by men, even if those men were not of their own race. Nothing can disguise the horrible economic and social consequences of slavery for black men and women, both separately and together.

Everyone agrees that slavery imposed special burdens upon women. W. E. B. Du Bois reserved his harshest indictment of the white South for the treatment suffered by black women, and feminists like Angela Davis have similarly insisted upon the "double burden" that afflicts Afro-American women. Even slavery itself, Du Bois wrote, he could forgive, "for slavery is a world-old habit." But one thing he could "never forgive, neither in this world nor the world to come: its wanton and continued and persistent insulting of the black womanhood to which it sought and seeks to prostitute its lust." Du Bois's moving and revealing remarks rest on an unquestioning acceptance of an ideal of womanhood and, in this respect, invite comparison with those of Sojourner Truth at the middle of the nineteenth century. For Sojourner Truth, speaking to a white, middle-class, women's rights audience, called into question the very notion of womanhood in the experience of slave women. Her frequently cited remarks bear reiteration:

> Dat man ober dar say dat woman need to be lifted ober ditches, and to have de best place every whar. Nobody eber helped me into carriages, or ober mud puddles, or gives me any best place and ar'n't I a woman? Look at me! Look at my arm! I have plowed, and planted, and gathered into barns, and no man could head me—and ar'n't I a woman? I could work as much and eat as much as a man (when I could get it), and bear de lash as well—and ar'n't I a woman? I have borne thirteen chilern and seen em mos' all sold off into slavery, and when I cried out with a mother's grief, none but Jesus heard—and ar'n't I a woman?[17]

Truth and Du Bois concur that slavery assaulted the womanhood of slave women, but tellingly they emphasize different aspects of that womanhood: Truth, work and motherhood; Du Bois, sexuality. Both implicitly acknowledge that slavery decisively shaped the experience of slave women—that masters in particular and whites in general enjoyed the power to use and abuse slave women. Both Truth and Du Bois also draw upon an ideal of womanhood, or the idea of being a woman, to provide a standard for that core identity of slave women which resisted the use and abuse. Slave women, both Truth and Du Bois asserted, remained women although they were denied the protections that the dominant white society claimed to offer women, remained women although they were denied the attributes assigned by the dominant white society to womanhood. Du Bois represents the culmination of the most generous version of an Afro-American cultural tradition extending back to the free black community of the antebellum period. For if Du Bois deeply appreciates the strengths and accomplishments of Afro-American women, he also implicitly supports the view that bourgeois domesticity offers the best model for the assimilation of Afro-Americans into their rightful place in American society. He assumes the desirability of stable nuclear families under the leadership of men while allowing plenty of space for women's strength.

The structures and conventions of the white world hedged in slave women almost as firmly as they did white women, albeit more erratically and violently. In this respect, the racist component of class oppression and the black-nationalist dimension of class consciousness and struggle emerge from the history of Afro-American slave women and dramatize problems inherent in all women's history. These racial and nationalist dimensions reinforce rather than negate the class dimension of women's experience. Afro-American slaves did not enjoy the freedom to preserve intact their African ancestors' view of the world. However determined their resistance and however resolute their spirit, forced transplantation to the New World deprived them of the material bases of West African culture, especially in the southern colonies, and later states, of North America, in which the ratio of white to black and the average size of plantations militated against their establishing potentially autonomous enclaves free of white influence. Afro-American culture owed more to the persistent struggle between slaves and masters than to passive acceptance, but recognition of the tenacity of the struggle should not obscure the inescapability of white influence. The interactions between slaveholders and slaves rested upon a prior history of a wide variety of informal interactions between slaveholding and nonslaveholding whites and slaves during the seventeenth and eighteenth centuries.

The evidence from slavery and from Reconstruction strongly suggests that black men espoused their own version of "white" views of male dominance within and without the family, and that they actively encouraged the domestic subordination of women as a necessary contribution to the survival and progress of "the race." James Horton has suggested that, at least among the free blacks of the North, this attitude imposed a terrible burden on women. Should women seek, however modestly, to assert their own rights, they were seen as guilty not merely of personal rebellion against one man, but of political rebellion against the interests of their people. Evelyn Brooks has demonstrated how firmly the black men of the National Baptist Convention USA, Incorporated, insisted on the domestic subordination of women as an essential weapon in the struggle for respectability for black people. She has also demonstrated how fiercely the women resisted the men's demands while finding their own ways to struggle against the oppression of black people and promote opportunities for black women.[18]

Women's historians, including Pan-African feminists, question the prevalence of these attitudes, although the evidence strongly suggests that antebellum northern free blacks and many postbellum freed men and women espoused them. Suzanne Lebsock, for example, argues that antebellum free black women, given the opportunity, chose to live without husbands. Other work on the free black women of New Orleans, Louisiana, and Mobile, Alabama, confirms that there was a strikingly high proportion of free black female heads of households. But census data do not reveal the reasons that free black women chose to avoid marriage, although they do reveal that, because many more free black women than free black men lived in the cities, opportunities for marriage were limited. Lebsock sees their behavior as the manifestation of a commitment to women's networks, but she does not determine whether these women preferred to live without men altogether nor explore all the possible reasons for their avoidance of marriage. At least in New Orleans and Mobile, many free black female heads of households had liaisons with white men, who provided them with property and resources but who could not marry them. In Charleston, many free black women were "married" to slave men. Free black women may have chosen to avoid the control that a husband could legally exercise over their lives, but this reading also suggests that these women expected black men to embrace the dominant white model of gender relations. Alternatively, free black women may have chosen to avoid marriage out of a reasonable concern that the white community would be more likely to view property held by men—as a married woman's property would be—as a potential threat to white dominance. Whatever the explanation, it must be assessed against the powerful evidence that freed men and women enthusiastically sought marriage after emancipation.[19]

The relation between African and Afro-American patterns remains unclear. Let us assume that West African traditions allowed women greater independence from the dominance of one man within a nuclear family than British traditions allowed white women; let us also assume that many of the West African societies from which most slaves came featured distinct matrilineal or matrifocal practices, or both. How should we assess the persistence of those traditions under slavery and their contribution to the slaves' struggles with their masters? And how do we assess the significance of West African practices of polygyny? West African societies did promote clear models of gender relations and, whatever the differences between those and Anglo-Saxon models, they rarely encouraged women's political and military leadership. Throughout the antebellum period, slave women resisted slavery in innumerable ways, but they did not figure among the leadership of the larger, organized revolts. This pattern suggests that the West African values favoring male political and military leadership received powerful support from Anglo-American social and gender relations. In other words, the amalgamation of West African and Anglo-Saxon customs imposed undeniable constraints on slave women, who, like other southern women, forged their lives and identities within the constraints of a specific slave society. . . .

NOTES

1. Fox-Genovese, Elizabeth. 1983. "Antebellum Southern Households: A New Perspective on a Familiar Question." *Review.* 7: pp. 215–253.

2. Mary Kendall to "Sister Lydia," 20 June 1853, *Hamilton-Kendall Family Papers*, Georgia Department of Archives and History, Atlanta, Georgia.

3. Fox-Genovese, Elizabeth. 1982. "Placing Women's History in History." *New Left Review.* 133: pp. 5–29

4. Bordin, Ruth. 1981. *Women and Temperance: The Quest for Power and Liberty, 1873–1900*. Philadelphia.

5. Stansell, Christine. 1986. City of Women: Sex and Class in New York, 1789–1860. New York. Smith-Rosenberg, Carroll. *Disorderly Conduct: Vision of Gender in Victorian America*. New York.

6. Turner, Fredrick Jackson. 1935. *The United States, 1830–1850: The Nation and Its Sections*. New York. Foner, Eric. 1970. *Free Soil, Free Labor, Free Men: The Ideology of the Republican Party Before the Civil War*. New York.

7. Jensen, Joan. 1986. *Loosening the Bonds: Mid-Atlantic Farm Women, 1750–1850.* New Haven, Conn.

8. Fox-Genovese, Elizabeth. 1987. "Culture and Consciousness in the Intellectual History of European Women." *Signs*: 12: pp. 529–547.

9. Bryant, Keith. 1980. "Role and Status of the Female Yeomanry in the Ante-Bellum South: The Literary View. *Southern Quarterly.* 18: pp. 73–88.

10. Boatwright, Eleanor. 1941. "The Political and Civil Status of Women in Georgia: 1783-1860." *Georgia Historical Quarterly.* 25:301–324.

11. Freidman, Jean. 1985 *The Enclosed Garden: Women and Community in the Evangelical South, 1830–1900.* Chapel Hill, NC.

12. Harding, Vincent. 1981. *There is A River: The Black Struggle for Freedom in America.* New York.

13. Kerber, Linda. 1974. "Daughters of Columbia: Educating Women for the Republic. 1787–1805. In Stanley Elkins and Eric McKitrick (eds.), *The Hofstader Aegis: A Memorial.* pp. 36–59. New York.

14. Scott, Anne. 1970. *The Southern Lady From Pedestal to Politics, 1830–1930.* Chicago.

15. Woodward, C. Vann. 1981. *Mary Chesnut's Civil War.* pp xlvii–liii. New Haven, Conn. Clinton, Catherine. 1982. *The Plantation Mistress: Woman's World in the Old South.* pp 16–35. New York.

16. White, Deborah. 1985. *Ar'n't I a Woman: Female Slaves in the Ante-Bellum South.* New York.

17. Du Bois, W. E. B. 1975. *Darkwater: Voices From the Veil.* p. 72. Millwood, N.Y.

18. Horton, James O. 1986. "Freedom's Yoke: Gender Conventions Among Ante-Bellum Free Blacks." *Feminist Studies.* 12: pp. 51–76.

19. Lebsock, Suzanne. 1982. "Free Black Women and The Question of Matriarchy: Petersburg, Va., 1754–1820." *Feminist Studies.* 8: pp. 271–292. DeBow, J. D. B. 1854. *Statistical View of the United States.* Washington, D.C.

DISCUSSION QUESTIONS

1. Why have New England women's experiences been generalized as American women's history? How does an incorporation of southern women's experiences change the story?

2. What did male domination look like during the 1800s, and how did northern and southern women experience it differently? How did black and white southern women experience it differently?

3. What are the different scholarly positions on the status of black women during slavery? Were black women "stronger" and more equal to men than white women were? What is the author's answer to this question? Do you agree or disagree with her, and why?

CURRENT DEBATES

HOW DID SLAVERY AFFECT THE ORIGINS OF AFRICAN AMERICAN CULTURE?

A debate over the impact of slavery on African American culture began in the 1960s and continues to the present day. Stanley Elkins, in his 1959 book, *Slavery: A Problem in American Institutional and Intellectual Life*, laid down the terms of the debate. Elkins argued that very few, if any, cultural elements survived the rigors of the voyage from Africa into slavery. Black culture in America, he concluded, was created in response to the repressive plantation system and in the context of brutalization, total control of the slaves by their owners, and dehumanization. He argued that black culture was "made in America," but in an abnormal, even pathological social setting. The plantation was a sick society that dominated and infantilized black slaves. The dominant reality for slaves—and the only significant other person in their lives—was the master. Elkins described the system as a "perverted patriarchy" that psychologically forced the slaves to identify with their oppressors and to absorb the racist values at the core of the structure. Perhaps the most provocative point of his analysis was his comparison of the slave plantations to Nazi concentration camps: brutally closed systems that dehumanized and infantilized their inmates by making them totally dependent on the "perverted father figures" of the camp guards.

Elkins's book has been called "a work of great intellectual audacity, based on a methodology which has little connection with conventional historical research and arriving at conclusions which were challenging or outrageous, according to one's point of view" (Parish, 1989, p. 7). The book stimulated an enormous amount of controversy and research on the impact of slavery and the origins of African American culture. Among the most significant rejoinders was a book by John Blassingame, *The Slave Community: Plantation Life in the Antebellum South* (1972), in which he argues that African American culture is a combination of elements, some from the traditional cultures of Africa and others fabricated on the plantation. Blassingame's work is significant for a number of reasons. It was the first major work on slavery by a black historian, but more important, it introduced a new perspective. Relying heavily on the autobiographies of former slaves and other previously neglected sources, Blassingame was able to focus on the institution of slavery from the perspective of the slave rather than that of the master.

A third view is presented in an excerpt from the writings of Deborah Gray White. She argues that Elkins, Blassingame, and others write from the perspective of the male slave only, to the point of excluding the female experience. In the passage from her 1985 book, *Ar'n't I a Woman? Female Slaves in the Plantation South*, she also addresses the problems of research in the area of minority group females and summarizes some of what has been learned from recent scholarship on the impact of slavery.

Although they differ dramatically in many ways, all three of these views are consistent with the conclusion that slavery created a powerless status for African Americans and a strong tradition of racism and prejudice in the white community. In many ways, black and white Americans today continue to struggle with these legacies of "the peculiar institution."

REFERENCE

Parish, Peter J. 1989. *Slavery: History and Historians*. New York: Harper & Row.

SLAVERY CREATED THE AFRICAN AMERICAN CULTURE

Stanley Elkins

American slavery was a "closed" system—one in which contacts [between slaves and] free society could occur only on the most narrowly circumscribed of terms. The next question is whether living in such a "closed system" might not have produced noticeable effects on upon the slave's very personality. . . .

[According to the lore of white Southerners,] the plantation slave was docile but irresponsible, loyal but lazy, humble but chronically given to lying and stealing: his behavior was full of infantile silliness and his talk inflated with childish exaggeration. His relationship with his master was one of utter dependence and child-like attachment: it was indeed this childlike quality that was the very key to his being. Although the merest hint of [his] "manhood" might fill the Southern breast with scorn, the child, "in his place," could be both exasperating and lovable. . . .

[To what extent were these stereotypical traits stamped on the personalities of the slaves? I assume] that there were elements in the very structure of the plantation system—its "closed" character—that could sustain infantalism as a normal feature of behavior. These elements . . . were effective and pervasive enough to require that such infantalism be characterized as something much more basic than mere "accommodation." It will be assumed that the sanctions of the system were in themselves sufficient to produce a recognizable personality type [that incorporated infantalism]. . . .

Both [the Nazi concentration camps and the American slave plantations] were closed systems from which all standards based on prior connections had been effectively detached. A working adjustment to either system required a childlike conformity, a limited choice of "significant other." Cruelty *per se* cannot be considered the primary key to this; of far greater importance was the simple "closedness" of the system, in which all lines of authority descended from the master and in which alternative social bases that might have supported alternative standards were systematically suppressed. The individual, consequently, for his very psychic security, had to picture his master in some way as the "good father," even when, as in the concentration camp, it made no sense at all.

For the Negro child, in particular, the plantation offered no really satisfactory father-image other than the master. The "real" father was virtually without authority over his child, since discipline, parental responsibility, and control of rewards and punishments all rested in other hands; the slave father could not even protect the mother of his children.

From the master's viewpoint, slaves had been defined in law as property, and the master's power over his property must be absolute. . . . Absolute power for him meant absolute dependency for the slave—the dependency not of the developing child but of the perpetual child. For the master, the role most aptly fitting such a relationship would naturally be that of father.

SOURCE: Elkins, Stanley. (1959). *Slavery: A Problem in American Institutional and Intellectual Life* (pp. 81–81, 86, 130–131). New York: Universal Library.

AFRICAN AMERICAN CULTURE WAS CREATED BY AN INTERPLAY OF ELEMENTS FROM AFRICA AND AMERICA

John Blassingame

Acculturation in the United States invoked the mutual interaction between two cultures, with Europeans and Africans borrowing from each other. When the African stepped on board a European ship he left all of the artifacts or physical objects of his culture behind him. In Africa, as in most societies, these objects were far less important than values, ideas, relationships, and behavioral patterns.

The similarities between many European and African cultural elements enabled the slave to continue to engage in many traditional activities or to create a synthesis of European and African cultures. In the process of acculturation the slave made European forms serve African functions. An example of this is religion. Most Africans believed in a Creator, or all-powerful God whom one addressed directly through prayers, sacrifices, rituals, songs, and dances. At the same time, they had a panoply of lesser gods, each of whom governed one aspect of life.

Christian forms were so similar to African religious patterns that it was relatively easy for the early slaves to incorporate them with their traditional practices and beliefs. In America, Jehovah replaced the Creator, and Jesus, the Holy Ghost, and the Saints replaced the lesser gods. The Africans preserved many of their sacred ceremonies in the conventional Christian rituals and ceremonies: songs, dances, feasts, festivals, funeral dirges, amulets, prayers, images, and priests. . . .

The Africans retained enough manhood to rebel because the southern plantation was not a rationally organized institution designed to crush every manifestation of individual will or for systematic extermination. Whatever the impact of slavery on their behavior and attitudes, it did not force them to concentrate all of their psychic energy on survival. Once they acquired the language of their master, the Africans learned that their labors, and therefore their lives, were of considerable value. As a result, they were assured of the bare minimum of food, shelter, and clothing. Although provisions were often inadequate and led to many complaints from slaves, they survived. . . .

The American slave was able to retain many African elements and an emotional contact with his motherland. The contact, however tenuous, enabled the slave to link European and African forms to create a distinctive culture.

SOURCE: Blassingame, John W. (1972). *The Slave Community: Plantation Life in the Antebellum South.* New York: Oxford University Press.

THE EXPERIENCES OF FEMALE SLAVES HAS BEEN UNDER-RESEARCHED AND UNDER-REPORTED

Deborah Gray White

Stanley Elkins began [the debate] by alleging that the American slave master had such absolute power and authority over the bondsman that the slave was reduced to childlike dependency. "Sambo," Elkins argued, was more than a product of Southern fantasy. He could not be dismissed as a "stereotype." . . .

Elkins' thesis had a profound effect upon the research and writing of the history of slavery. The direction that the research took, however, was in large part pre-determined because Elkins' *Slavery* defined the parameters of the debate. In a very subtle way these parameters had more to do with the nature of male slavery than with female slavery. . . .

John Blassingame's *The Slave Community* is a classic but much of it deals with male status. For instance, Blassingame stressed the fact that many masters recognized the male as the head of the family. He observed that during courtship, men flattered women and exaggerated their prowess. There was, however, little discussion of the reciprocal activities of slave women. Blassingame also described how slave men gained status in the family and slave community, but did not do the same for women. . . .

The reality of slave life gives us reason to suspect that we do black women a disservice when we rob them of a history that placed them at the side of their men in their race's struggle for freedom. The present study takes a look at slave women and argues that they were not submissive, subordinate, or prudish and they were not expected to be so. Women had

different roles from those of men and they also had a great deal in common with their African foremothers, who held positions not inferior but complementary to those of men. . . .

Source material on the general nature of slavery exists in abundance, but it is very difficult to find source material about slave women in particular. Slave women are everywhere, yet nowhere. . . .

The source problem is directly related to what was and still is the black woman's condition. Every economic and political index demonstrated the black woman's virtual powerlessness in American society. A consequence of the double jeopardy and powerlessness is the black woman's invisibility. . . .

The history of slavery has come a long way. We have learned that race relations were never so clear-cut as to be solely a matter of white over black, but that in the assimilation of culture, in the interaction of blacks and whites, there were gray areas and relationships more aptly described in terms of black over white. We have also begun to understand that despite the brutality and inhumanity, or perhaps because of it, a distinct African American culture based on close-knit kinship relationships grew and thrived, and that it was this culture that sustained black people through many trials before and after emancipation.

SOURCE: White, Deborah Gray. (1985). *Ar'n't I a Woman? Female Slaves in the Plantation South* (pp. 17–18, 21–25). New York: Norton, 21–25.

QUESTIONS TO CONSIDER

1. Why is the origin of African American culture an important issue? What difference does it make today? If you believe Elkins is correct, what are the implications for dealing with racial inequality in the present? Could a culture that was created under a pathological system and a sick society be an adequate basis for the pursuit of equality and justice today? Is Elkins's thesis a form of blaming the victim? Is it a way of blaming the present inequality of the black community on an "inadequate" culture, thus absolving the rest of society from blame?

2. If you agree with Blassingame's or White's viewpoints, what are the implications for how African Americans think about their history and about themselves? What difference does it make if your roots are in Africa or in colonial Virginia or, as Blassingame and White argue, in both?

3. What does White add to the debate? What are some of the challenges in researching the experiences of female slaves? How did the experiences of female slaves differ from those of male slaves?

4

INDUSTRIALIZATION AND DOMINANT-MINORITY RELATIONS:

From Slavery to Segregation and the Coming of Post-Industrial Society

American race relations entered a new era with the emancipation of the slaves at the end of the Civil War. After Reconstruction, a brief respite from racial oppression, whites in the South began building a system of racial segregation under which blacks were consigned to an inferior status by force of law. By the dawn of the twentieth century, de jure segregation was in full force. There were separate and unequal black school systems, job markets, and neighborhoods, and racial inequality was institutionalized in virtually every aspect of southern society, including public transportation, parks and playgrounds, and rest rooms and water fountains. Black southerners were disenfranchised and left politically powerless and without basic civil and political rights.

At the same time that racial segregation was evolving in the South, other minority groups were being victimized by systems of oppression and exploitation. Mexican Americans in the Southwest were used as a cheap labor force in agriculture, mining, railroad construction, and other areas of the economy. Native Americans were herded onto reservations where they were either forced to Americanize or were ignored and left to starve. Immigrants from Europe became a seemingly inexhaustible source of labor power for the industrializing east coast, while immigrants from Asia helped to build railroads, dig mines, and do menial farm work on the west coast.

Underlying the various dominant-minority relations was the powerful hand of industrialization, urbanization, and modernization. As the United States switched from the labor-intensive economies of an agricultural nation to the machine-dependent technologies of the industrial era, new minority groups were created and the situations of other minority groups were transformed. For example, black southerners responded to the injustices of de jure segregation by moving out of the South to areas–mostly in the urban, industrializing North and Midwest–that offered new opportunities for jobs and for freedom and dignity. Of course, life outside the South was hardly a racial utopia, and black migrants were forced to deal with new forms of discrimination and racism.

The selections in this chapter address this time of change and turmoil in various ways. The Narrative Portrait is a selection from Richard Wright that expresses the agonies and hopes of the black migrants from the South. The first reading, by Angela Davis, examines the situation of black women following emancipation and argues strongly that de jure segregation simply continued (and sometimes worsened) the exclusion and oppression of slavery. The second reading raises the issue of affirmative action and brings us more into the contemporary era. Although the structures of inequality of the past—slavery and de jure segregation, for example—have been dismantled, large, persistent gaps remain between virtually every minority group and the dominant group in income, education, occupational prestige, health care, and other measures of equality, life chances, and quality of life. These gaps are partly the legacy of the inequalities of the past and partly the result of continuing (but more subtle) discrimination in the present. Similar gaps and similar issues characterize gender relations in modern America.

Affirmative action refers to a number of different strategies for trying to close the remaining racial and gender gaps and bring the United States closer to the ideal of a truly equal society. David Oppenheimer identifies and analyzes five varieties of affirmative action and tries to clarify the terms of the debate over this policy. The chapter closes with a Current Debate on the topic. Thomas Sowell presents arguments against affirmative action and Orlando Patterson counters with arguments in support. Richard Kahlenberg brings a different perspective to the debate and argues that affirmative action should be based on class, not on race or ethnicity.

NARRATIVE PORTRAIT

THE KITCHENETTE

Richard Wright (1908–1960), one of the most powerful writers of the twentieth century, lived through and wrote about southern segregation and about the exodus of black people out of the South that was, on so many levels, a rejection of southern racism and racial oppression. Wright grew up in the South during the height of the Jim Crow system, and his passionate hatred for bigotry is expressed in his major works *Native Son* (1940) and the autobiographical *Black Boy* (1945).

In 1941, Wright helped to produce *Twelve Million Black Voices,* a folk history of African Americans. A combination of photos and brief essays, the work is a powerful commentary on three centuries of oppression. The following selection is adapted from "Death on the City Pavement," which expresses Wright's view of the black migration out of the South, a journey he himself experienced. This bittersweet migration often traded the harsh, rural repression of the South for the overcrowded, anonymous ghettoes of the North. Housing discrimination, both overt and covert, confined black migrants to the least desirable, most overcrowded areas of the city—in many cases, the neighborhoods that had first housed immigrants from Europe. Unscrupulous landlords subdivided buildings into the tiniest possible apartments ("kitchenettes"), and as impoverished newcomers who could afford no better, black migrants were forced to cope with overpriced, substandard housing as best they could. Much of the passage, incidentally, could have been written about any twentieth-century minority group.

DEATH ON THE CITY PAVEMENT

Richard Wright

A war sets up in our emotions: one part of our feelings tells us it is good to be in the city, that we have a chance at life here, that we need but turn a corner to become a stranger, that we need no longer bow and dodge at the sight of the Lords of the Land. Another part of our feelings tells us that, in terms of worry and strain, the cost of living in the kitchenettes is too high, that the city heaps too much responsibility on us and gives too little security in return. . . .

The kitchenette, with its filth and foul air, with its one toilet for thirty or more tenants, kills our black babies so fast that in many cities twice as many of them die as white babies. . . .

The kitchenette scatters death so widely among us that our death rate exceeds our birth rate, and if it were not for the trains and autos bringing us daily into the city from the plantations, we black folk who dwell in northern cities would die out entirely over the course of a few years. . . .

The kitchenette throws desperate and unhappy people into an unbearable closeness of association, thereby increasing latent friction, giving birth to never-ending quarrels of recrimination, accusation, and vindictiveness, producing warped personalities.

The kitchenette injects pressure and tension into our individual personalities, making many of us give up the struggle, walk off and leave wives, husbands, and even children behind to shift for themselves. . . .

The kitchenette reaches out with fingers of golden bribes to the officials of the city, persuading them to allow old firetraps to remain standing and occupied long after they should have been torn down.

The kitchenette is the funnel through which our pulverized lives flow to ruin and death on the city pavement, at a profit. . . .

SOURCE: Wright, Richard. (1988). *Twelve Million Black Voices* (pp. 105–111). New York: Thunder's Mouth Press.

READINGS

In this section, we explore the impact of industrial and post-industrial economies on dominant-minority relations in the United States. It is evident that the job opportunity structure at any given time has clear implications for minority group members, who often occupy the lowest-rung positions on the *stratification* ladder. The first reading by Angela Davis, "The Meaning of Emancipation for Black Women," is perhaps the most striking example of this reality, since black women occupy that lowest rung on both race and gender dimensions of inequality. Davis makes a crucial point not often acknowledged in modern discussions of

African Americans—that the deplorable, government-sanctioned mistreatment of blacks in the United States did not end with the cessation of slavery. In fact, the post-slavery jobs available to African Americans—in sharecropping, the convict lease system, and domestic work—were in some ways worse than their fate under slavery. We see that *de jure segregation,* or segregation by law, often referred to as Jim Crow, greatly curtailed any prospects of freedom for African Americans for another hundred years following the Emancipation Proclamation. Not unlike under slavery, black women who worked as domestics additionally faced the threat of sexual abuse at the hands of white men, who faced no repercussions for their actions.

Turning our attention to the post-industrial economy, where the less blatant process of racism continues in the form of *modern institutional discrimination,* author David Oppenheimer addresses the legal efforts to combat such discrimination in the form of affirmative action. When the *occupational segregation* of racial minorities and women described persisted despite laws to the contrary, Republican President Richard Nixon asserted that affirmative action was necessary to combat the centuries of legal economic exclusion of these groups. During a more prosperous economy, even a Republican president was able to interject such measures fairly easily. However, less than a decade later, beginning with the economic recession of the 1980s, white men began to file lawsuits challenging these programs, and the courts supported many of those challenges. Thus, the "quota model" that most Americans think of when they hear "affirmative action" has been all but eliminated, as Oppenheimer points out, since the U.S. Supreme Court has consistently found such policies to be in violation of the Fourteenth Amendment. Yet the mythical legend of the white male who could not get a job due to a likewise mythical "unqualified" minority persists despite these facts. As the author separates the different policies known as affirmative action into five different "models," tracing the legal precedents set around each one, it becomes evident how large the gap is between the public debate around affirmative action and the legal reality of how it is implemented. For example, in 2003, President George W. Bush spoke out against a University of Michigan admissions practice, calling it a "quota system," yet the school actually added 20 points (out of a possible total 150) to members of underrepresented groups' applications, making it not a quota system at all. Instead, it fits the "Preference" model as described by Oppenheimer, in which such points can be earned in many other ways, such as veteran status, economic status, or extracurricular activities. Indeed, Bush undoubtedly benefited from such a point structure himself when his family name helped his admission into Yale University. With such misunderstandings abounding, from the top leadership of our country on down, it is evident that by reading about the legal reality of affirmative action and the various forms it takes in actual practice, we can better inform our positions on the debate. As stratification continues to place minorities and women who are now equal under the law at the bottom rungs of the occupational structure, the challenge will be to find ways to combat this pattern that the majority of the American public can support and understand.

THE MEANING OF EMANCIPATION ACCORDING TO BLACK WOMEN

Angela Davis

After a quarter of a century of "freedom," vast numbers of Black women were still working in the fields. Those who had made it into the "big house" found the door toward new opportunities sealed shut—unless they preferred, for example, to wash clothes at home for a medley of white families as opposed to performing a medley of household jobs for a single white family. Only an infinitesimal number of Black women had managed to escape from the fields, from the kitchen or from the washroom. According to the 1890 census, there were 2.7 million Black girls and women over the age of ten. More than a million of them worked for wages: 38.7 percent in agriculture; 30.8 percent in household domestic service; 15.6 percent in laundry work; and a negligible 2.8 percent in manufacturing.[1] The few who found jobs in industry usually performed the dirtiest and lowest-paid work. And they had not really made a significant breakthrough, for their slave mothers had also worked in the Southern cotton mills, in the sugar refineries and even in the mines. For Black women in 1890, freedom must have appeared to be even more remote in the future than it had been at the end of the Civil War.

As during slavery, Black women who worked in agriculture—as sharecroppers, tenant farmers or farmworkers—were no less oppressed than the men alongside whom they labored the day long. They were often compelled to sign "contracts" with landowners who wanted to reduplicate the antebellum conditions. The contract's expiration date was frequently a mere formality, since landlords could claim that workers owed them more than the equivalent of the prescribed labor period. In the aftermath of emancipation the masses of Black people—men and women alike—found themselves in an indefinite state of peonage. Sharecroppers, who ostensibly owned the products of their labor, were no better off than the outright peons. Those who "rented" land immediately after emancipation rarely possessed money to meet the rent payments, or to purchase other necessities before they harvested their first crop. Demanding as much as 30 percent in interest, landowners and merchants alike held mortgages on the crops.

> Of course the farmers could pay no such interest and the end of the first year found them in debt—the second year they tried again, but there was the old debt and the new interest to pay, and in this way, the "mortgage system" has gotten a

hold on everything that it seems impossible to shake off.[2]

Through the convict lease system, Black people were forced to play the same old roles carved out for them by slavery. Men and women alike were arrested and imprisoned at the slightest pretext—in order to be leased out by the authorities as convict laborers. Whereas the slaveholders had recognized limits to the cruelty with which they exploited their "valuable" human property, no such cautions were necessary for the postwar planters who rented Black convicts for relatively short terms. "In many cases sick convicts are made to toil until they drop dead in their tracks."[3]

Using slavery as its model, the convict lease system did not discriminate between male and female labor. Men and women were frequently housed together in the same stockade and were yoked together during the workday. In a resolution passed by the 1883 Texas State Convention of Negroes, "the practice of yoking or chaining male and female convicts together" was "strongly condemned."[4] Likewise, at the Founding Convention of the Afro-American League in 1890, one of the seven reasons motivating the creation of this organization was "(t)he odious and demoralizing penitentiary system of the South, its chain gangs, convict leases and indiscriminate mixing of males and females."[5]

As W. E. B. DuBois observed, the profit potential of the convict lease system persuaded many Southern planters to rely exclusively on convict labor—some employing a labor force of hundreds of Black prisoners.[6] As a result, both employers and state authorities acquired a compelling economic interest in increasing the prison population. "Since 1876," DuBois points out, "Negroes have been arrested on the slightest provocation and given long sentences or fines which they were compelled to work out."[7]

This perversion of the criminal justice system was oppressive to the ex-slave population as a whole. But the women were especially susceptible to the brutal assaults of the judicial system. The sexual abuse they had routinely suffered during the era of slavery was not arrested by the advent of emancipation. As a matter of fact, it was still true that "colored women were looked upon as the legitimate prey of white men . . . "[8]—and if they resisted white men's sexual attacks, they were frequently thrown into prison to be further victimized by a system which was a "return to another form of slavery."[9]

During the post-slavery period, most Black women workers who did not toil in the fields were compelled to become domestic servants. Their predicament, no less than that of their sisters who were sharecroppers or convict laborers, bore the familiar stamp of slavery. Indeed, slavery itself had been euphemistically called the "domestic institution" and slaves had been designated as innocuous "domestic servants." In the eyes of the former slaveholders, "domestic service" must have been a courteous term for a contemptible occupation not a half-step away from slavery. While Black women worked as cooks, nursemaids, chambermaids and all-purpose domestics, white women in the South unanimously rejected this line of work. Outside the South, white women who worked as domestics were generally European immigrants who, like their ex-slave sisters, were compelled to take whatever employment they could find.

The occupational equation of Black women with domestic service was not, however, a simple vestige of slavery destined to disappear with the passage of time. For almost a century they would be unable to escape domestic work in any significant numbers. A Georgia domestic worker's story, recorded by a New York journalist in 1912,[10] reflected Black women's economic predicament of previous decades as well as for many years to come. More than two-thirds of the Black women in her town were forced to hire themselves out as cooks, nursemaids, washerwomen, chambermaids, hucksters and janitresses, and were caught up in conditions ". . . just as bad as, if not worse than, it was during slavery."[11]

For more than thirty years this Black woman had involuntarily lived in all the households where she was employed. Working as many as fourteen hours a day, she was generally allowed an afternoon visit with her own family only once every two weeks. She was, in her own words, "the slave, body and soul"[12] of her white employers. She was always called by her first name—never Mrs. . . .—and was not infrequently referred to as their "nigger," in other words, their slave.[13]

One of the most humiliating aspects of domestic service in the South—another affirmation of its affinity with slavery—was the temporary revocation of Jim Crow laws as long as the Black servant was in the presence of a white person.

> . . . I have gone on the streetcars or the railroad trains with the white children, and . . . I could sit anywhere I desired, front or back. If a white man happened to ask some other white man, "What is that nigger doing in here?" and was told, "Oh, she's the nurse of those white children in front of her" immediately there was the hush of peace. Everything was all right, as long as I was in the white man's part of the streetcar or in the white man's coach as a servant—a slave—but as soon as I did not present myself as a menial . . . by my not having the white children with me, I would be forthwith assigned to the "nigger" seats or the "colored people's coach."[14]

From Reconstruction to the present, Black women household workers have considered sexual abuse perpetrated by the "man of the house" as one of their major occupational hazards. Time after time they have been victims of extortion on the job, compelled to choose between sexual submission and absolute poverty for themselves and their families. The Georgia woman lost one of her live-in jobs because "I refused to let the madam's husband kiss me."[15]

> . . . (S)oon after I was installed as cook, he walked up to me, threw his arms around me, and was in the act of kissing me, when I demanded to know what he meant, and shoved him away. I was young then, and newly married, and didn't know then what has been a burden to my mind and heart ever since: that a colored woman's virtue in this part of the country has no protection.[16]

As during slavery times, the Black man who protested such treatment of his sister, daughter or wife could always expect to be punished for his efforts.

> When my husband went to the man who had insulted me, the man cursed him, and slapped

him, and—had him arrested! The police fined my husband $25.[17]

After she testified under oath in court, "(t)he old judge looked up and said: 'This court will never take the word of a nigger against the word of a white man.'"[18]

In 1919, when the Southern leaders of the National Association of Colored Women drew up their grievances, the conditions of domestic service were first on their list. It was with good reason that they protested what they politely termed, "exposure to moral temptations"[19] on the job. Undoubtedly, the domestic worker from Georgia would have expressed unqualified agreement with the Association's protests. In her words,

> I believe nearly all white men take, and expect to take, undue liberties with their colored female servants—not only the fathers, but in many cases the sons also. Those servants who rebel against such familiarity must either leave or expect a mighty hard time, if they stay.[20]

Since slavery, the vulnerable condition of the household worker has continued to nourish many of the lingering myths about the "immorality" of Black women. In this classic "catch-22" situation, household work is considered degrading because it has been disproportionately performed by Black women, who in turn are viewed as "inept" and "promiscuous." But their ostensible ineptness and promiscuity are myths which are repeatedly confirmed by the degrading work they are compelled to do. As W. E. B. DuBois said, any white man of "decency" would certainly cut his daughter's throat before he permitted her to accept domestic employment.[21]

When Black people began to migrate northward, men and women alike discovered that their white employers outside the South were not fundamentally different from their former owners in their attitudes about the occupational potentials of the newly freed slaves. They also believed, it seemed, that *"Negroes are servants, servants are Negroes."*[22] According to the 1890 census, Delaware was the only state outside the South where the majority of Black people were farmworkers and sharecroppers as opposed to

domestic servants.[23] In thirty-two out of forty-eight states, domestic service was the dominant occupation for men and women alike. In seven out of ten of these states, there were more Black people working as domestics than in all the other occupations combined.[24] The census report was proof that *Negroes are servants, servants are Negroes.*

Isabel Eaton's companion essay on domestic service, published in DuBois' 1899 study *The Philadelphia Negro,* reveals that 60 percent of all Black workers in the state of Pennsylvania were engaged in some form of domestic work.[25] The predicament of women was even worse, for all but nine percent—14,297 out of 15,704—of Black women workers were employed as domestics.[26] When they had traveled North seeking to escape the old slavery, they had discovered that there were simply no other occupations open to them. In researching her study, Eaton interviewed several women who had previously taught school, but had been fired because of "prejudice."[27] Expelled from the classroom, they were compelled to work in the washroom and the kitchen.

Of the fifty-five employers interviewed by Eaton, only one preferred white servants over Black ones.[28] In the words of one woman,

> I think the colored people are much maligned in regard to honesty, cleanliness and trustworthiness; my experience of them is that they are immaculate in every way, and they are perfectly honest; indeed I can't say enough about them.[29]

Racism works in convoluted ways. The employers who thought they were complimenting Black people by stating their preference for them over whites were arguing, in reality, that menial servants—slaves, to be frank—were what Black people were destined to be. Another employer described her cook as ". . . very industrious and careful—painstaking. She is a good, faithful creature, and very grateful."[30] Of course, the "good" servant is always faithful, trustworthy and grateful. U.S. literature and the popular media in this country furnish numerous stereotypes of the Black woman as faithful, enduring servant. The Dilseys (à la Faulkner), the Berenices (of *Member of the Wedding*) and the Aunt Jemimas of commercial fame have become stock characters of U.S. culture. Thus the one woman interviewed by Eaton who did prefer white servants confessed that she actually employed Black help ". . . because they look more like servants."[31] The tautological definition of Black people as servants is indeed one of the essential props of racist ideology.

Racism and sexism frequently converge—and the condition of white women workers is often tied to the oppressive predicament of women of color. Thus the wages received by white women domestics have always been fixed by the racist criteria used to calculate the wages of Black women servants. Immigrant women compelled to accept household employment earned little more than their Black counterparts. As far as their wage-earning potential was concerned, they were closer, by far, to their Black sisters than to their white brothers who worked for a living.[32]

If white women never resorted to domestic work unless they were certain of finding nothing better, Black women were trapped in these occupations until the advent of World War II. Even in the 1940s, there were street-corner markets in New York and other large cities—modern versions of slavery's auction block—inviting white women to take their pick from the crowds of Black women seeking work.

Every morning, rain or shine, groups of women with brown paper bags or cheap suitcases stand on streetcorners in the Bronx and Brooklyn waiting for a chance to get some work. . . . Once hired on the "slave market," the women often find after a day's back-breaking toil, that they worked longer than was arranged, got less than was promised, were forced to accept clothing instead of cash and were exploited beyond human endurance. Only the urgent need for money makes them submit to this routine daily.[33]

New York could claim about two hundred of these "slave markets," many of them located in the Bronx, where "almost any corner above 167th Street" was a gathering point for Black women seeking work.[34] In a 1938 article published in *The Nation,* "Our Feudal Housewives," as the piece was entitled, were said to work some seventy-two hours a week, receiving the lowest wages of all occupations.[35]

The least fulfilling of all employment, domestic work has also been the most difficult to unionize. As early as 1881, domestic workers were among the women who joined the locals of the Knights of Labor when it rescinded its ban on female membership.[36] But many decades later, union organizers seeking to unite domestic workers confronted the very same obstacles as their predecessors. Dora Jones founded and led the New York Domestic Workers Union during the 1930s.[37] By 1939—five years after the union was founded—only 350 out of 100,000 domestics in the state had been recruited. Given the enormous difficulties of organizing domestics, however, this was hardly a small accomplishment.

White women—feminists included—have revealed a historical reluctance to acknowledge the struggles of household workers. They have rarely been involved in the Sisyphean task of ameliorating the conditions of domestic service. The convenient omission of household workers' problems from the programs of "middle-class" feminists past and present has often turned out to be a veiled justification—at least on the part of the affluent women—of their own exploitative treatment of their maids. In 1902 the author of an article entitled "A Nine-Hour Day for Domestic Servants" described a conversation with a feminist friend who had asked her to sign a petition urging employers to furnish seats for women clerks.

"The girls," she said, "have to stand on their feet ten hours a day and it makes my heart ache to see their tired faces."

"Mrs. Jones," said I, "how many hours a day does your maid stand upon her feet?"

"Why, I don't know," she gasped, "five or six I suppose."

"At what time does she rise?"

"At six."

"And at what hour does she finish at night?"

"Oh, about eight, I think, generally."

"That makes fourteen hours. . . ."

". . . (S)he can often sit down at her work."

"At what work? Washing? Ironing? Sweeping? Making beds? Cooking? Washing dishes? . . . Perhaps she sits for two hours at her meals and preparing vegetables, and four days in the week she has an hour in the afternoon.

According to that, your maid is on her feet at least eleven hours a day with a score of stair-climbings included. It seems to me that her case is more pitiable than that of the store clerk."

My caller rose with red cheeks and flashing eyes. "My maid always has Sunday after dinner," she said.

"Yes, but the clerk has all day Sunday. Please don't go until I have signed that petition. No one would be more thankful than I to see the clerks have a chance to sit. . . ."[38]

This feminist activist was perpetrating the very oppression she protested. Yet her contradictory behavior and her inordinate insensitivity are not without explanation, for people who work as servants are generally viewed as less than human beings. Inherent in the dynamic of the master-servant (or mistress-maid) relationship, said the philosopher Hegel, is the constant striving to annihilate the consciousness of the servant. The clerk referred to in the conversation was a wage laborer—a human being possessing at least a modicum of independence from her employer and her work. The servant, on the other hand, labored solely for the purpose of satisfying her mistress' needs. Probably viewing her servant as a mere extension of herself, the feminist could hardly be conscious of her own active role as an oppressor.

As Angelina Grimke had declared in her *Appeal to the Christian Women of the South,* white women who did not challenge the institution of slavery bore a heavy responsibility for its inhumanity. In the same vein, the Domestic Workers Union exposed the role of middle-class housewives in the oppression of Black domestic workers.

The housewife stands condemned as the worst employer in the country. . . .
The housewives of the United States make their million and a half employees work an average of seventy-two hours a week and pay them . . . whatever they can squeeze out of their budget after the grocer, the butcher . . . (etc.) have been paid.[39]

Black women's desperate economic situation—they perform the worst of all jobs and are ignored to boot—did not show signs of change until the outbreak of World War II. On the eve of the war, according to the 1940 census, 59.5 percent of employed Black women were domestic workers and another 10.4 percent worked in non-domestic service occupations.[40] Since approximately 16 percent still worked in the fields, scarcely one out of ten Black women workers had really begun to escape the old grip of slavery. Even those who managed to enter industry and professional work had little to boast about, for they were consigned, as a rule, to the worst-paid jobs in these occupations. When the United States stepped into World War II and female labor kept the war economy rolling, more than four hundred thousand Black women said goodbye to their domestic jobs. At the war's peak, they had more than doubled their numbers in industry. But even so—and this qualification is inevitable—as late as 1960 at least one-third of Black women workers remained chained to the same old household jobs and an additional one-fifth were non-domestic service workers.[41]

In a fiercely critical essay entitled "The Servant in the House," W. E. B. DuBois argued that as long as domestic service was the rule for Black people, emancipation would always remain a conceptual abstraction. ". . . (T)he Negro," DuBois insisted, "will not approach freedom until this hateful badge of slavery and medievalism has been reduced to less than ten percent."[42] The changes prompted by the Second World War provided only a hint of progress. After eight long decades of "emancipation," the signs of freedom were shadows so vague and so distant that one strained and squinted to get a glimpse of them.

Notes

1. Wertheimer, *op. cit.*, p. 228.

2. Aptheker, *A Documentary History*, Vol. 2, p. 747. "Tenant Farming in Alabama, 1889" from *The Journal of Negro Education* XVII (1948), pp. 46ff.

3. Aptheker, *A Documentary History*, Vol. 2, p. 689. Texas State Convention of Negroes, 1883.

4. *Ibid.*, p. 690.

5. Aptheker, *A Documentary History*, Vol. 2, p. 704. Founding Convention of Afro-American League, 1890.

6. DuBois, *Black Reconstruction in America*, p. 698.

7. *Ibid.*

8. *Ibid.*, p. 699.

9. *Ibid.*, p. 698.

10. Aptheker, *A Documentary History of the Negro People in the United States*, Vol. 1 (Secaucus, N.J.: The Citadel Press, 1973), p. 46. "A Southern Domestic Worker Speaks," *The Independent*, Vol. LXXII (January 25, 1912).

11. *Ibid.*, p. 46.

12. *Ibid.*, p. 47.

13. *Ibid.*, p. 50.

14. *Ibid.*

15. *Ibid.*, p. 49.

16. *Ibid.*

17. *Ibid.*

18. *Ibid.*

19. Lerner, *Black Women in White America*, p. 462. "The Colored Women's Statement to the Women's Missionary Council, American Missionary Association."

20. Aptheker, *A Documentary History*, Vol. 1, p. 49.

21. DuBois, *Darkwater*, p. 116.

22. *Ibid.*, p. 115.

23. Isabel Eaton, "Special Report on Negro Domestic Service" in W. E. B. DuBois, *The Philadelphia Negro* (New York: Schocken Books, 1967. First edition: 1899), p. 427.

24. *Ibid.*

25. *Ibid.*, p. 428.

26. *Ibid.*

27. *Ibid.*, p. 465.

28. *Ibid.*, p. 484.

29. *Ibid.*, p. 485.

30. *Ibid.*

31. *Ibid.*, p. 484.

32. *Ibid.*, p. 449. Eaton presents evidence which ". . . points to the probability that among women in domestic service at least, there is no difference between 'white pay and black pay,' . . . "

33. Lerner, *Black Women in White America*, pp. 229–231. Louise Mitchell, "Slave Markets Typify Exploitation of Domestics," *The Daily Worker*, May 5, 1940.

34. Gerda Lerner, *The Female Experience: An American Documentary* (Indianapolis: Bobbs-Merrill, 1977), p. 269.

35. *Ibid.*, p. 268.

36. Wertheimer, *op. cit.*, pp. 182–183.

37. Lerner, *Black Women in White America*, p. 232.

38. Inez Goodman, "A Nine-Hour Day for Domestic Servants," *The Independent*, Vol. LIX (February 13, 1902). Quoted in Baxandall *et al.,* pp. 213–214.

39. Lerner, *The Female Experience*, p. 268.

40. Jacquelyne Johnson Jackson, "Black Women in a Racist Society," in Charles Willie et al., editors, *Racism and Mental Health* (Pittsburgh: University of Pittsburgh Press, 1973), p. 236.

41. *Ibid.*

42. DuBois, *Darkwater*, p. 115.

DISCUSSION QUESTIONS

1. Why does Davis liken both the convict lease system and domestic service work to slavery? What aspects of the work resemble slavery and why? Do you agree with her characterization?

2. Were conditions for blacks after slavery's official end any better in the North? What were the problems and difficulties that existed in the North in terms of black employment?

3. What does Davis mean when she describes a white feminist as "perpetrating the very oppression she protested"? Why was liberation of women narrowly defined so as not to include the liberation of black women from domestic servitude? Today, is feminism in general defined in such a way that it has limited appeal to women of color? Why or why not?

DISTINGUISHING FIVE MODELS OF AFFIRMATIVE ACTION

David B. Oppenheimer

I. INTRODUCTION

Over the last two decades few topics have been more controversial than affirmative action. To its critics, affirmative action is both a euphemism for discrimination against white men and a system that bureaucratizes the entire society at the cost of meritocratic decision making; it is a symbol for all that has gone wrong with American society since the sixties. To its supporters, it is a first step towards remedying the crime of slavery and eliminating the discriminatory preferences that have guaranteed white men the easiest paths to wealth and power; it is a symbol of justice, and a promise of a future of hope.

For all of the debate, all of the court decisions discussing affirmative action, and all of the articles and books on the subject, there is no consensus on what the term "affirmative action" means. The purpose of this essay is to clarify the issue by identifying and distinguishing five models of affirmative action, and to suggest that the debate focuses too much attention on the use of quotas. I herein propose that in discussing affirmative action we often confuse its many manifestations, which can be grouped into five models: strict quotas favoring women or minorities (Model I); preference systems in which women or minorities are given some preference over white men (Model II); self-examination plans in which the failure to reach expected goals within expected periods of time triggers self-study, to determine whether discrimination is interfering with a decision-making process (Model III); outreach plans in which attempts are made to include more women and minorities within the pool of persons from which selections are made (Model IV); and, affirmative commitments not to discriminate (Model V).

It is my premise that the broad differences between these five models, and the confusion over the meaning of affirmative action exacerbates the disagreement about its legitimacy. . . .

II. THE FIVE MODELS

Model I, the quota model, is probably the model which is most often viewed by the public as the "typical" affirmative action plan. In a true quota model a certain number of jobs, or promotions, or classroom seats, are set aside to be occupied only by women or minorities. The affirmative action plan described in the lead opinion in *Regents of the University of California v. Bakke*[1] is a Model I plan. In *Bakke,* a white candidate for medical school sued the University, complaining that he was rejected because the school set aside sixteen spots exclusively for minority students in each entering class of the medical school at its Davis campus. Minority students could be considered for admission either under the regular process or the affirmative action program, but white students, regardless of their qualifications, could only be considered under the regular admissions program.[2] The Court held that the University's plan constituted impermissible race discrimination in violation of the fourteenth amendment.[3]

The plan described in the majority opinion of the Court's recent decision in *City of Richmond v. J.A. Croson Co.* is another example of Model I affirmative action.[4] In that case, the city of Richmond, Virginia passed an ordinance requiring its contractors to set aside a minimum of 30% of their work on city contracts to subcontract out to minority-owned firms.[5] The effect was that minority-owned firms could compete for 100% of the available work, while white firms could compete for only 70% of the work.[6] Here too the Court ruled that the plan violated the fourteenth amendment.[7] In both *Bakke* and *City of Richmond* the Court's rejection of the plan was premised on the plan's contravention of the principle that racial preferences violate the fourteenth amendment,[8] but both recognized the possibility that plans linked to evidence of prior discrimination and limited in their scope to remedying that past discrimination could be permitted.[9]

Although they are scrutinized most closely by courts, Model I plans are not uniformly rejected as improper. The Supreme Court approved a Model I plan in *United Steelworkers v. Weber.*[10] There, a union and an employer agreed to create a program to train existing employees for skilled craft positions. Fifty percent of the positions in the training program were reserved for Black employees.[11] The Supreme Court rejected a challenge brought under the federal employment discrimination law[12] by a white worker who was denied participation in the program. The Court reasoned that the plan was limited in scope and duration, created new opportunities for white as well as Black workers, and was tied to prior discrimination.[13]

The affirmative action plans in *Weber, Bakke* and *City of Richmond* were voluntarily enacted, but Model I plans may also be imposed by a court. For example, in *United States v. Paradise,* the Court approved a United States District Court order imposing a 50% quota for promotions of Alabama state troopers from private to corporal.[14] The quota was imposed after the state had ignored prior court-imposed promotional goals for over a decade.[15]

Similarly, a Model I plan may be created by Congress. In *Fullilove v. Klutznik* the Court upheld a federal law requiring 10% of all federal funds used for local public works projects to be used for services or supplies from minority business enterprises.[16]

Model I plans are usually defended as remedial; they attempt to provide effective remedies for prior race or sex discrimination.[17] In *Paradise,* for example, the quota was imposed because the district court found that the state of Alabama had systematically excluded Blacks from any employment as state troopers for several decades and had ignored prior goals for hiring and promotion imposed by the court. The Court concluded that no other method would succeed in forcing the state of Alabama to promote Black troopers.[18] In *City of Richmond* the city imposed its quota after finding that less than 1% of its contractors and subcontractors were Black, although the city's population was over 50% Black. It concluded that the disparity was the result of discrimination.[19] The Court rejected the plan in part because it rejected the city's conclusion as insufficiently supported by the facts. The city had demonstrated a disparity between population and contracts, but had not established that there was any disparity between the number of available minority contractors and the number of contracts they received.[20]

Some Model I plans look to social needs as well as past discrimination for their justification. In *Bakke,* for example, the University claimed its plan was designed to respond to, among other things, the small number of minority physicians due to prior discrimination, and the need for physicians in medically underserved communities.[21] And in *Wygant v. Jackson Board of Education,* the Court reviewed (and rejected) a plan that required layoffs of school teachers to be determined by both race and seniority, rather than seniority alone, in order to retain more Black teachers to act as "role models" for their Black students.[22]

Model II, the preference model, is distinguished from Model I chiefly by a lack of rigidity; Model II plans are race- or gender-conscious but flexible. One example is the Harvard undergraduate admissions plan described approvingly by Justice Powell in his lead opinion in *Bakke.*[23] Harvard's plan considers race as a factor in reviewing two questions which are applied to all applicants, but from which minority applicants are more likely to benefit: whether the applicant has had to overcome greater barriers to success which should be considered in his or her evaluation, and whether the school's need for diversity in order to offer the richest possible education to its students would be promoted by the applicant's admission.[24] Race thus establishes a preference, but there are no absolute numerical quotas to be filled. The questions addressed in evaluating minority applicants also permit the admission, despite otherwise noncompetitive grades or test scores, of unusual white applicants.

Another common example of a Model II plan, although outside the context of affirmative action, is a veterans' bonus. An example of this is found in *Personnel Administrator of Massachusetts v. Feeney.*[25] There, Massachusetts established a hiring preference for veterans by granting them bonus points on a civil service examination. As a result, although there was no Model I quota, veterans had a significant advantage over non-veterans in competing for state jobs.[26]

A third example of a Model II preference plan is the plan originally agreed to by the city of Memphis[27] which became the focus of the court's decision in *Firefighters Local Union No. 1784 v. Stotts.*[28] There, in a consent decree settling a race discrimination claim against its fire department, the city agreed that women and minority city employees who worked outside the fire department could apply for fire department job openings before white male city employees, or any non-employees. Only if the jobs were not filled by existing women or minority employees would they be opened to others.[29] The issue the Supreme Court considered arose when the District Court later amended its order to protect the new minority employees from layoff. The Supreme Court rejected the amendment as beyond the scope of the parties' agreement.[30]

Model III, the self-examination model, describes a form of affirmative action which is prevalent in government and large private industries. The model typically involves utilizing goals and timetables for the inclusion of women and minorities in certain job categories. An employer begins the process by comparing its workforce with the community of persons qualified to fill its positions. This analysis will often reveal that in certain job categories the number of women or minorities is less than one would expect, given the number of qualified women and minorities in the local labor market. The underlying assumption is that, in the absence of discrimination, the percentage of qualified women and minorities in the local labor market would be approximately the same as those employed by any particular employer.

If an employer discovers a significant disparity between the number of women and minorities it employs and the number in the labor market, the employer attempts to determine the reason. If no apparent non-discriminatory reason is discovered through research, the employer adopts a goal of employing a workforce which, in time, will mirror the relevant labor market. The employer analyzes its turnover and schedules interim dates by which it expects specific progress toward its goal. These are expressed as "timetables" for progress toward the goal. The employer uses the timetables to determine whether it is meeting its goals. The operative assumption is that in the absence of discrimination the goals will be met. If they are not, there is a need for further self-examination, to determine whether discrimination is occurring somewhere in the selection system.

Most federal contractors are required to adopt affirmative action plans using the self-examination model.[31] This model is also used in the settlement of employment discrimination cases. For example, in *Local No. 93, Int'l Ass'n of Firefighters, AFL-CIO C.L.C. v. City of Cleveland,* the Court approved a consent decree which included an affirmative action plan using goals and timetables for the promotion of Black firefighters.[32]

A variation on a goals and timetables plan which also fits within the self-examination model is the voluntary adverse impact analysis. In *Griggs v. Duke Power Co.*[33] the Court ruled that practices which are neutral on their face, and even neutral in their intent, but have an adverse impact on a protected group, violate Title VII of the 1964 Civil Rights Act.[34] The practice at issue in *Griggs* was the requirement that new employees have high school degrees, and in some instances that they pass two standardized intelligence tests. These requirements adversely impacted Black job applicants.[35]

Attempts at voluntary compliance with the *Griggs* ruling may require self-examination of pre-employment or promotional tests, and other selection devices, to determine their impact. Where an adverse impact is discovered, the employer must either validate the selection device as "demonstrably a reasonable measure of job performance,"[36] or engage in an affirmative action process of finding another, less discriminatory, selection device.[37]

Model IV, the outreach model, is generally based on the assumption that a workforce or school enrollment which contains few minorities or women is the result of insufficient knowledge or communication. A Model IV affirmative action plan may be the result of a Model III-type self-examination, in which it is determined that more minorities or women would make themselves applicants if they were simply recruited, or recruited more vigorously. This assumption has its roots, in part, in recognition that past practices of the employer or school may have included recruiting or selection devices which were intended to screen out women or minorities, or which had that effect. Hiring based on nepotism or word of mouth, selecting from certain schools, neighborhoods or agencies, and favoring promotions from within, are all examples of such practices in the employment setting. Favoring the children of alumni or prominent community members in school admissions is another example.[38] As subjective selection decisions which screen out minorities have come under greater scrutiny,[39] Model IV outreach plans have become one obvious antidote.

Support programs for minorities or women are another form of Model IV affirmative action. An employer may offer special promotional classes for women or minorities to encourage them to move into jobs traditionally held by white males, or to move into management. The assumption behind such Model IV plans is that race and sex discrimination have created social barriers which make it harder for minorities and women to qualify for those positions without assistance. Similarly, schools may create special orientation and tutoring programs to support students admitted under Model I or Model II plans, or may offer such support as an inducement to attract women and minority applicants in a Model IV plan.

Model V, the non-discrimination model, has two distinct aspects.[40] The first is active non-discrimination. Affirmative decisions such as a decision to stop discriminating, to act to avoid discrimination, to prevent employees from discriminating, and to abandon practices which have a discriminatory effect may all be part of an affirmative action program. Although the law requires non-discrimination,[41] voluntary compliance takes place over a broad spectrum. Upon self-examination, or as a result of litigation, an employer, school or governmental agency may discover that its agents are engaging in discrimination, or that it has adopted policies with a discriminatory effect. It may choose to defend its conduct or may, as an affirmative action device, decide to alter it. It may elect to train its employees regarding the obligation to avoid discrimination, or may be required to train them as affirmative relief ordered by a court.

The second aspect of Model V is passive non-discrimination. Theoretically, mere passive non-discrimination, or the resolution by judgment or settlement of discrimination claims, are distinguishable from affirmative actions to prevent or avoid discrimination. They are logically excluded from a description of affirmative action. I believe, however, that affirmative action as generally discussed and understood includes passive non-discrimination and decisions to hire or admit complainants who have alleged a discriminatory exclusion. The public perceptions of non-discrimination and affirmative action are intertwined. When a court's decision that an individual was the victim of unlawful discrimination results in the payment of damages and an order of employment, admission or reinstatement, the remedy is likely to be perceived as a form of affirmative action. When an employer-defendant, or potential defendant, agrees to a remedy to settle or avoid a discrimination action, it is even more likely to be seen as affirmative action, by observers if not by the participants. The failure to recognize that at least some of the participants in a public debate about affirmative action are likely to use the term to include non-discrimination compounds the confusion which occurs when the subject is discussed.

Reduced to their simplest expressions, then, these are the five distinguishable models of affirmative action: 1) the quota model; 2) the preference, or special consideration, model; 3) the self-examination model; 4) the outreach model; and 5) the non-discrimination model.

The broad language of the Supreme Court decisions on affirmative action suggests that all race-based or gender-based preferences are suspect.[42] The decisions suggest that in order to be permissible, any plan must be narrow in scope, and tied to well-established prior discrimination.[43] But if the decisions are examined with regard to the different models of affirmative action, one realizes that only Model I plans are suspect. Model I plans must fall within strict limits or they are impermissible; Model II plans will be carefully scrutinized but are likely to be approved, and Models III, IV, and V are uniformly permitted.

NOTES

1. 438 U.S. 265, 272–75 (1978). The Court issued six separate opinions in *Bakke*. Justice Powell, who provided the swing vote, wrote the lead opinion for the Court.

2. *Id.* at 319–20. One issue that the University neglected to raise in its defense is that in 1974, the year that Allan Bakke was denied admission, only 15 students were admitted under the special admissions program. The sixteenth spot was returned to the regular admissions process. J. Dreyfuss & C. Lawrence, THE BAKKE CASE: THE POLITICS OF INEQUALITY 41 (1979). Given this fact of its apparent flexibility, the special admissions program was really a Model II plan, not a Model I plan.

Another interesting fact that Dreyfuss and Lawrence note is that at the time Bakke applied to Davis, the medical school had a third method of admitting students. The admissions committee had an understanding with the school's dean that the dean could select as many as five students for each entering class. This was not an uncommon practice at medical schools, and it acted as a sort of affirmative action program for the well-connected. Dreyfuss and Lawrence point out that Bakke could have almost as easily been bumped off the admissions list by one of these "privilege quota" students as by one of the special admissions students. This issue was not raised in the case. *Id.* at 24–25.

3. Bakke, 438 U.S at 320.

4. 109 S.Ct. 706 (1999). Like the *Bakke* decision, *City of Richmond* does not offer a clear-cut majority ruling. Justice O'Connor delivered the opinion of the Court, with Rehnquist, C.J., and White, Stevens, and Kennedy, JJ., joining in various Parts.

5. *Id.* at 712.

6. *Id.* at 723. The majority and dissent had a different view on how rigid, or absolute, the quota was. Richmond's plan had an escape clause in the form of a waiver procedure. The contractor could apply for a waiver of the 30% requirement on the grounds that after due diligence it found that it was not possible on a particular job to sub-contract 30% of the work to minority sub-contractors. *Id.* at 750. The dissent viewed the plan as failing within Model II, not Model I.

7. *Id.* at 723–28.

8. Bakke, 438 U.S. at 320; City of Richmond, 109 S.Ct. at 723–28.

9. Bakke, 438 U.S. at 307–08; City of Richmond, 109 S.Ct. at 728–29.

10. 443 U.S. 193 (1979).

11. *Id.* at 198.

12. Civil Rights Act of 1964, Title VII, 42 U.S.C. § 2000e-2000e-17.

13. 443 U.S. at 208–09.

14. 480 U.S. 149, 185 (1987).

15. *Id.* at 163–65.

16. 448 U.S. 448 (1980).

17. One recent article suggests that the defense and analysis or quota cases is overly concerned with proof of past discrimination, and thus too "sin"-based. See Sullivan, *The Supreme Court, 1985 Term —Sins of Discrimination: Last Term's Affirmative Action Cases,* 100 HARV. L. REV. 78 (1986). In this article, Kathleen Sullivan argues that the Court has erred in looking to the question of whether there was past discrimination to determine whether an affirmative action quota is permissible. Such an analysis focuses on the guilt or innocence of the sinner and the displaced white man, instead of looking to social needs. The result is a stifling sympathy for the white male "victim" as one blamelessly punished.

Sullivan proposes a forward-looking analysis that justifies affirmative action not as a remedy but as part of a design for a better society. She suggests that the justifications include: dispelling the notion that white supremacy governs our social institutions, improving services to minority constituencies, averting racial tension, and increasing diversity. Such preferences, when granted by a white majority and disfavoring whites, should not be constitutionally suspect under a *Carolene Products* analysis. See United States v. Carolene Products, 304 U.S. 144, 152 n.4 (1938).

In a similar vein, another recent paper suggests that the Court views Model I affirmative action plans as punitive, and permits their imposition only when prior discrimination is shown to have been malicious and thus worthy of punishment. Unpublished manuscript by Sheila Foster, associate attorney at Morrison & Foerster, San Francisco (Dec. 1987).

18. Paradise, 480 U.S. 149 at 171–77.

19. 109 S.Ct. at 714.

20. *Id.* at 725.

21. 438 U.S. 265, 306 (1978).

22. 106 S.Ct. 1842, 1847–48 (1986).

23. 438 U.S. at 306.

24. *Id.* at 317.

25. 442 U.S. 256 (1979).

26. *Id.* at 264. The Court held that hiring preference did not discriminate against women in violation of the fourteenth amendment. Even though virtually all Massachusetts veterans were men, the court found no discriminatory purpose, because the statute distinguished between veterans and non-veterans, not between men and women. *Id.* at 280–81.

27. *See* Stotts v. Memphis Fire Dep't, 679 F.2d 541, 571–73 (6th Cir. 1982), *rev'd* 467 U.S. 561 (1984).

28. 467 U.S. 561 (1984).

29. 679 F.2d at 572 (consent decree § 6).

30. Stotts, 467 U.S. at 573–75.

31. *See* 41 C.F.R. § 60–212 (1989).

32. 478 U.S. 501, 509, 530 (1986).

33. 401 U.S. 424 (1971).

34. *Id.* at 431.

35. *Id.*

36. *Id.* at 436.

37. *Id.*

38. *See* Dreyfuss & Lawrence, *supra* note 3.

39. *See, e.g.,* Watson v. Fort Worth Bank and Trust, 108 S.Ct. 2777 (1988) (subjective or discriminatory employment practices challenged as violating Title VII may, in appropriate cases, be analyzed under a disparate impact analysis).

40. In Strauss, *The Myth of Colorblindness,* 1986 Sup. Ct. Rev. 99, the author argues that nondiscrimination and affirmative action are indistinguishable in that discrimination and affirmative action cases are interchangeable in analysis. (He further argues that when so viewed affirmative action may, at times, be constitutionally compelled.) While I also conclude that affirmative action and discrimination cases can be interchangeable, Strauss comes to his argument from a different perspective from mine, which I believe to be incorrect.

Strauss argues that the principle of non-discrimination is based on ignoring essentially correct stereotypes and generalizations in deference to public policy. Thus, he believes, employers may have valid economic motives for discrimination which we insist on overriding in the interest of a greater public good. Thus is nondiscrimination indistinguishable from affirmatively promoting those same interests through affirmative action. His argument depends on his premise that the stereotypes and generalizations which lead to discrimination have some general validity.

The support Strauss provides for this premise undermines his argument. For example, he points to Palmore v. Sidoti, 466 U.S. 429 (1984) as an example of the operation of his argument. Strauss at 100–08. In *Palmore,* a family court denied a divorced white mother custody of her child because she had married a Black man. The court reasoned that it is not in the best interest of a child to be raised in an interracial home. The Supreme Count reversed on the ground that the family court impermissibly used race as a factor in deciding the custody issue. Strauss defers to the trial judge's assessment that the child would be subject to significant psychological damage if raised in an interracial home. Thus, he reasons, the decision was in the best interest of the child and the reversal, although defensible as good public policy, was race discrimination. The problem with this position is the acceptance of the unsupported (and probably insupportable) finding that a child is harmed by growing up in an interracial home.

41. *See,. e.g.,* Civil Rights Act of 1964, Title VII, 42 U.S.C. § 2000e-2000e-17.

42. *See, e.g.,* University of California Regents v. Bakke, 438 U.S. 265, 291 (1978) (opinion of Powell, J., joined by White, J.).

43. See City of Richmond v. J.A. Croson Co., 109 S.Ct. 706, 728 (1989).

DISCUSSION QUESTIONS

1. Why do you think the debate around affirmative action so often centers around the quota model, and not the other models that are more frequently approved and used? Does the public even think of the other models as forms of affirmative action? If affirmative action were reframed in the public debate as Models III, IV, and V, would there be more public support for it? Would you support it? Who stands to gain by keeping the more limited definition in the public eye?

2. As discussed with Model II, do you think if people have "had to overcome greater barriers to success" to get to the same point as another candidate, should this be a factor in considering them for a position, if it includes race and gender as well as other "unusual white applicants"? What might such information tell us about a candidate? Do you think it would be "reverse discrimination," as some would suggest?

3. Were you aware before reading this piece that affirmative action was both a race- and gender-conscious policy? If affirmative action is also aimed at protecting women from discrimination, why do you think the debates center more frequently upon race?

CURRENT DEBATES

AFFIRMATIVE ACTION

Should minorities be favored in the job market? Should colleges and graduate schools judge minority candidates differently than members of the dominant group? Programs that confer advantages on minorities at work and at school—attempts to take affirmative action in the struggle to achieve racial integration and equality—have been controversial since their inception in the 1960s. The arguments in favor of affirmative action usually cite the intractability of institutional discrimination, the pervasiveness of racism, and the continuing importance of race in American life. Without a strong program to force employers to balance their workforces and to require college admissions programs to seek out qualified minority candidates, the racial status quo will be perpetuated indefinitely.

Opponents often argue that affirmative action actually hurts the groups it is intended to help and that the "reverse discrimination" used by these programs is simply wrong. A familiar argument against affirmative action is that if racial discrimination was wrong when used to perpetuate the privileges of whites under slavery and segregation, then it is just as wrong as a technique to combat racial inequality. Discrimination is discrimination, and the United States should strive to be "color-blind," not color-conscious. A third view shifts the terms of the debate and argues that the real barriers to equality are based on class, not race, and that affirmative action programs need to be reformulated on this basis. These arguments are reprised in the selections following.

We should note that the controversy over affirmative action divides minority groups as well as the larger society and that this split is reflected in the writings below. Thomas Sowell, an economist, and Orlando Patterson, a sociologist, are both African Americans, while Richard Kahlenberg, a lawyer and scholar, is white.

AFFIRMATIVE ACTION CASTS SUSPICIONS ON LEGITIMATE BLACK ACHIEVEMENT AND DEPICTS AFRICAN AMERICANS AS INCAPABLE

Thomas Sowell

The Hippocratic Oath says: "First, do no harm." By that standard, affirmative action would have been gotten rid of years ago. There are many ways in which it hurts the very people it claims to help, as well as polarizing the society at large.

A couple of years ago, I met with the editorial staff of one of the leading publications in America. Among them was a black man who was by no means stupid—but he said many stupid things at that meeting. . . . Why? He was mismatched, out of his league, among people who were at the pinnacle of their profession. If he played it straight, he would have been nobody in this setting, though there are probably hundreds of other reputable publications on which he would have been a valuable and respected writer. Saying off-the-wall things was his only way of even seeming to be significant among the cream of the crop of his profession. . . .

Nor was this man unique. There is a whole class of such people teaching in the leading law schools, many of them promoting a convoluted set of doctrines known as critical race theory. Their counterparts can also be found in literature, among other fields. . . .

Affirmative action also amounts to a virtual moratorium on recognition of black achievement. Consider the case of [Supreme Court] Justice Clarence Thomas. His critics have repeatedly accused him of benefiting from affirmative action, when he went to college or to law school, and then wanting to deny its benefits to other blacks. In all the endless reiterations of this theme, no one has ever found it necessary to demonstrate that it was true.

It so happens that affirmative action had not yet begun when Clarence Thomas entered Holy Cross College. Nor has anyone even considered it necessary to try to show that Thomas was admitted under the Yale law school's affirmative action program, rather than by the regular admissions process. . . .

It so happens that the same law school class that included Clarence Thomas also included Bill Clinton and Hillary Rodham. Yet no one has ever questioned their credentials going in or coming out. Justice Thomas' credentials are questioned precisely because of affirmative action, even though his record may have been as good as—or better than—that of the [Clintons]. In short, blacks fall under a cloud of suspicion of being substandard, even when they match or surpass the performances of their white counterparts. Who gains from creating such awkward situations and the unnecessary problems that flow from them?

Guilty whites gain by salving their guilt through affirmative action. Black hustlers gain by either getting things for themselves or by leading movements which are able to dispense largess that they have talked or pressured guilty whites into providing.

Institutions, such as universities, that receive millions of federal dollars gain by having enough black body count around to avoid having the flow of that money jeopardized by claims of discrimination based on statistics.

Liberals who secretly believe that blacks are innately inferior . . . feel like they have done the best they can do by giving blacks or other minorities something that those minorities would otherwise be incapable of getting.

Do any of the people who claim to want to see blacks advance ever ask: Under what conditions have blacks in fact been most successful? Where have they advanced most? Blacks have done best in situations radically different from those of affirmative action. Blacks are overrepresented in sports and entertainment, especially among the highest-paid performers. In both fields, competition is merciless. You can be the top performer this year and yet they will drop you like a hot potato if your performance slacks off next year.

Nobody has given blacks anything in sports or entertainment. Blacks have had to shape up or ship out. Most shape up. It is where blacks are given double standards and coddled that they end up tarnished in their own eyes or in the eyes of others.

SOURCE: Sowell, Thomas. (1997). How "Affirmative Action" Hurts Blacks. *Forbes,* October 6, 160, p. 64.

WHY WE STILL NEED AFFIRMATIVE ACTION

Orlando Patterson

The most important way in which affirmative action helps those on the outside is to provide them access to circles and networks that they would otherwise never penetrate.

For Afro-Americans, one of the most egregious effects of past ethnic exclusion has been their isolation from cultural capital and personal networks that are essential for success in America. This important sociological fact is usually simply neglected by those who imagine capitalist America to be a perfectly competitive, meritocratic system in which people rise to their positions based solely on their training and motivation. There is some truth to this but it is at best a half-truth. . . .

My argument, in a nutshell, is that two features of American society make it impossible for Afro-Americans to achieve parity without some sustained, though not permanent, policy of affirmative action. These are, first, the ratio of Afro-Americans to Euro-Americans which, second, operates in conjunction with certain well-known characteristics of internal labor markets.

Let us assume that there is a firm with one hundred entry-level employees, exactly 13 of whom are Afro-Americans, and that all these employees have . . . equal . . . ability, educational attainment, and motivation. Let us assume further an . . . unbiased . . . organization [and staff]. . . . Even under these circumstances . . . it is almost certain that the Afro-American . . . employees will never make it to the top echelons of the organization if there is no account taken of ethnicity in promotion; indeed, they will hardly move beyond their entry-level jobs.

These claims seem counterintuitive because we assume that, in the normal course of events, each equally qualified entry-level Afro-American will have a 13% chance of being promoted, resulting eventually in a similar ratio of Afro-Americans moving up the firm's opportunity ladder. This is what misguided liberal and neo-conservatives have in mind when they speak naively about a "color-blind" system. The problem with this logic is that it disregards the fact that when firms promote workers they consider not simply the characteristics of the employees but organizational criteria, among the most important of which is the degree to which a candidate for promotion will fit into the upper echelon for which he or she is being considered. And it is precisely here that Afro-Americans lose out because of their small numbers, their ethnic differences, and the tendency of personnel officers to follow one well-established law of microsociology, first formally propounded by the sociologist George Casper Homans.

The very simple principle of human behavior—call it the principle of homophyly—is that people who share common attitudes tend to marry each other, tend to play more together, and in general tend to get along better and to form more effective work teams. Thus, a non-racist personnel officer, under no pressure to consider ethnic attributes—indeed, under strong misguided pressure to follow a "color-blind" policy—would always find it organizationally rational to choose a Euro-American person for promotion . . . in spite of the technical equality of the Afro-American candidates. The Euro-American person's organizational fit—which comes simply from being Euro-American—will so significantly reduce the cost to the organization of incorporation and training that it would be irresponsible of our ethnically unbiased personnel officer, under orders to select in a color-blind manner, ever to promote an Afro-American person.

Of course, when one introduces one well-known real-world feature of American society to this model of "color-blind" organizational behavior, the cards are even more heavily stacked against our thirteen entry-level Afro-American employees: This is the fact that Euro-Americans have a hard time taking orders from Afro-American supervisors. . . . This being so, the cost to our non-racist . . . personnel officer becomes even greater; and it gets worse the more real-world attitudes and behaviors we introduce.

SOURCE: Patterson, Orlando. (1997). *The Ordeal of Integration* (pp. 160–162). Washington, DC: Civitas.

AFFIRMATIVE ACTION SHOULD BE BASED ON CLASS RATHER THAN RACE

Richard Kahlenberg

Class-based affirmative action, a system of preferences for the economically disadvantaged . . . will achieve the legitimate goals of affirmative action while avoiding the major pitfalls associated with race and gender preferences. . . . The central and overriding argument for class-based affirmative action is that it will help move us from today's inadequate system of formal equal opportunity toward a more genuine system . . . under which individuals born into very different circumstances can flourish to their natural potential. . . . Equal opportunity exists when individuals have equal life chances to develop their natural talents to the fullest, should they choose to take the time and effort to do so.

[Equal opportunity] stresses equality to the extent that social factors should not be allowed to inhibit the chance to develop one's natural talents. It stresses liberty to the extent that it does not guarantee equal results: The naturally talented are allowed to do better than the untalented to the extent, and only to the extent, that individuals work hard to achieve what they are capable of achieving. . . . Equal opportunity is, as Gary Wills (the conservative newspaper columnist) notes, "The great agreed-on undebated premise of our politics. Left and right,

liberal and conservative, Democrat and Republican, all work from this basis."

As long as anti-discrimination laws work, race and gender are not impediments per se, but class differences . . . remain and civil rights legislation does nothing to address that inequality. Some are born poor and underprivileged, other wealthy and advantaged. In this sense, anti-discrimination laws may be seen as necessary but not sufficient for achieving equal opportunity. . . .

If we are trying to place the most talented in the most important positions, formal equal opportunity is not enough. Failing to correct for the social positions into which people are born runs the great risk of missing most of the latent talent of the poor. . . .

[If] we want to reward hard work, failing to provide an equal start is morally indefensible. To reward individuals born with advantages arising from their parents' effort makes no moral sense. Indeed, Theodore Roosevelt, in pushing for a heavily progressive income tax in 1906, argued that a commitment to rugged individualism required each generation to run its own race.

SOURCE: Kahlenberg, Richard. (1997). *The Remedy: Class, Race, and Affirmative Action (*pp. 83–86). New York: Basic Books.

QUESTIONS TO CONSIDER

1. What assumptions does Sowell make about the overall fairness of the American workplace? What are the implications of his argument that blacks have been most successful precisely in the areas where affirmative action has been irrelevant: entertainment and sports? In contrast, what assumptions does Patterson make about the ability of employers to make unbiased decisions about promotions? What assumptions are evident in Kahlenburg's argument?

2. What are the limitations of a "color-blind" approach? Why does Patterson call it "naïve"? How strong is his argument compared to Sowell's? Which would you choose? Why?

3. Based on Patterson's position, design a simple affirmative action program for your workplace or school. How would your program change if you incorporated Kahlenburg's ideas?

4. Which of these three positions is most appealing to you? If you agree with Sowell, what other programs could be used to combat institutional discrimination? If you agree with Patterson, how would you respond to the charge of "reverse discrimination"? If you choose Kalhenburg, how would you answer the criticism that class-based remedies ignore the realities of racism and prejudice?

Part III

Understanding Dominant-Minority Relations in the United States Today

5

AFRICAN AMERICANS

The system of de jure segregation that perpetuated the oppression and exploitation of African Americans following slavery came to an end in the 1960s, destroyed by a combination of court rulings, legislation, and the courageous activism of civil rights demonstrators. Since that time, the status of African Americans has improved in many ways. The black middle class has increased in size and affluence, average levels of education have risen, and the income gap between blacks and whites has diminished. At the dawn of the twenty-first century, African Americans can be found at all levels of society and include some of the wealthiest, most respected and prestigious people in the world.

At the same time, enormous problems of poverty and powerlessness, racism and exclusion remain. Black Americans are still three times more likely to live in poverty as whites and, even more distressing, one-third of black children (versus about 13 percent of white children) will be raised in poverty. The black urban underclass continues to grow, and black Americans are the victims of continuing, systematic discrimination in every societal institution, including, in particular, the criminal justice system. Antiblack prejudice and racism persist in American culture and in the minds of many, albeit in a somewhat muted and covert form.

The selections in this chapter address this mixture of racial progress and failure from a number of angles. The Narrative Portrait focuses on the loneliness and alienation that sometimes affects upwardly mobile black Americans and other peoples of color. The story of Leanita McClain raises questions about the meaning of success, the price of living in multiple worlds, and the persistence of prejudice at the highest levels of American society.

The Readings examine antiblack racism, discrimination, and exclusion across a broad spectrum of American life. Eduardo Bonilla-Silva and Tyrone Forman document the "modern" or symbolic form that racism has assumed in the United States. The overt, unapologetic prejudice of the past has evolved into a more subtle form that tends to hide just below the surface but continues to view African Americans as unworthy of full equality. Angela Davis explores the dynamics of racism and discrimination in the criminal justice system, an area in which race relations are particularly volatile and sensitive. She documents the racism, discrimination, and sexism that is built into the system, including the racist results of the so-called War on Drugs. She then examines the many ways in which the disproportionate imprisonment of blacks is blamed on the black community, blaming the victims and thereby insulating the institution from charges of racism.

In the third reading, Kathleen Korgen analyzes the ways in which racism affects close, cross-racial friendships. She finds that the members of these intimate relationships develop strategies for avoiding the topic of race and ignoring the "elephant in the living room." Racism remains so pervasive in American society, however, that it affects even close friendships, a fact that suggests how far we remain from the ideal of a truly "color-blind" society.

The Current Debate focuses on a proposal for narrowing the racial gaps in income and quality of life. The idea of paying reparations to blacks for the kidnapping of their ancestors from Africa, the centuries of slavery, and the continued exploitation under de jure segregation is controversial, to say the least. The black community is not unanimous in its support for reparations, as pointed out by John McWhorter, but there are some compelling reasons to consider the possibility, as argued by Manning Marable. Furthermore, as Joe Feagin and Eileen O'Brien point out, there are precedents for such repayments and the possibility of positive outcomes far exceed the mere transfer of cash.

NARRATIVE PORTRAIT

THE PRICE OF SUCCESS

The selection following raises questions about the cost of upward mobility for people of color in U.S. society. Success on white middle-class terms may well require the suppression of habits and patterns learned in earliest childhood and separation from relationships deeply rooted in one's biography. Of course, many make the transition without regret for what was left behind. Others find the price too high, the alienation from self and background too agonizing, the strain of navigating multiple social worlds too exhausting.

Leanita McClain was a highly successful journalist and an African American female. She won numerous awards and was the first African American to be named a member of the *Chicago Tribune*'s editorial board. She was also named one of the ten outstanding working women in America by *Glamour* magazine. She was born in Chicago's housing projects and survived gang warfare, poverty, and despair. As an adult, she lived in multiple social worlds. From the black to the white community and from the lower to the upper middle class, she navigated the perils of race, class, and gender in the United States. In 1984, at the age of 32, she took her own life. The following selection is excerpted from a magazine piece on professional black women that focused on her life and death.

TO BE BLACK, GIFTED, AND ALONE

Bebe Moore Campbell

Her success had netted her a posh address in the city's predominantly white, gentrified north side, but McClain wasn't entirely comfortable in her new setting. In October, 1980, in *Newsweek*'s "My Turn" column, she wrote, "It is impossible for me to forget where I come from as long as I am prey to the jive hustler who does not hesitate to exploit my childhood friendship. I am reminded, too, when I go back to my old neighborhood in fear—and have my purse snatched—and sit down to a business lunch and have an old classmate wait on my table. I recall the girl I played dolls with who now rears five children on welfare, the boy from church who is in prison for murder, the pal found dead of a drug overdose. . . . Sometimes when I wait at the bus stop, I meet my aunt getting off the bus with other cleaning ladies on their way to do my neighbor's floors."

McClain realized that she couldn't go home again. Yet, despite her fair skin and sandy hair, despite her credentials and awards, she didn't have access to her new world either. . . . "She got thrown into a white world and was expected to act the part," says a friend. "She was often fighting and grappling with her real self. She couldn't even write what she wanted. She had to bottle up her rage."

As her personal desires eluded her [her marriage to journalist Clarence Page had ended, as had several other relationships] and the values of her old and new worlds collided, close friends witnessed spells of hysterical crying, brooding silence, and mounting depression. . . . For all of her accoutrements of professional success, McClain was as full of despair as any ghetto dweller. On the night of what would have been her tenth wedding anniversary, McClain swallowed a huge overdose of amitriptyline and left both worlds behind. . . .

It is rare for a black woman to ascend to the professional heights that McClain attained. . . . Understandably, then, the loss of McClain's influence, power, and her ability to be a role model is perceived by some blacks as a group loss. . . . [Other professional black women interviewed for this article know] that a black woman's climb to corporate power is at least as arduous as survival in the ghetto: They see a part of themselves in Leanita McClain's life.

Stress is the common experience these women all share. . . . [This] stress is from the oppressive combination of racism, sexism, and professional competition that separates black women not only from their white colleagues, but also insidiously pits them against their black male professional counterparts. The overload on black executive women often results in their pulling away from a cultural identity that includes family and old friends. Corporate racism was expected. What was unexpected was the various degrees of culture shock, isolation, and alienation that black women experience as they attempt to . . . assimilate their culturally distinct selves into organizations that reward conformity. . . .

No one ever imagined the time when blacks would be insiders. . . . No one fully understood what overcoming the barriers of discrimination would mean for people who had been outsiders for centuries. Freedom, yes. But freedom to do what? To be whom? . . .

White women may chafe under corporate dress codes, behavioral constraints, and sexism, [but] they don't have the additional burden of compromising their cultural selves. If black women . . . relinquish their cultural selves, they are unable to function in the old world that still claims them. They learn to wear a mask.

"Each day, when I get into my car, I always begin the ride to work by turning on a black radio station so that it blares," says Karen [another professional black woman interviewed for the story]. "I boogey all the way down the highway. A few blocks from my job, I turn the music down and stop shaking my shoulders. When my building comes into view, I turn the music off, because I know the curtain is about to go up." . . .

Leanita McClain had felt guilty about moving away from her old friends; she felt awkward about fitting the militant blacks' stereotype of a "sell out." "I am not comfortably middle class," she wrote. "I am uncomfortably middle class." . . . Isolated from blacks, black executive women often are alienated from the whites with whom they are supposed to assimilate. . . . McClain wrote, "Some of my 'liberal' white acquaintances hint that I am a freak, that my success is less a matter of talent than of luck and affirmative action. I may live among them, but it is difficult to live with them."

Towards the end of her life, Leanita McClain's loneliness was perhaps a heavier burden than her professional struggles. The combination was, for her, unbearable. . . . [Monroe Anderson, a reporter for the *Tribune* said] "It's difficult for a black woman to make it without a personal relationship. Black women have to battle racism and sexism and then come home to loneliness, or again do battle. For the majority of professional black women, it's not good." . . .

Leanita McClain finally laid her burden down and escaped the narrow alley located between pain and desire to another place. Her unanswered question continues to haunt her sisters. "I have made it, but where?"

SOURCE: Campbell, Bebe Moore. (1993). To Be Black, Gifted, and Alone. In V. Cyrus (Ed.), *Experiencing Race, Class, and Gender in the United States.* Mountain View, CA: Mayfield.

In order to comprehend fully the situation of African Americans today, it is necessary to understand the dynamics of *modern racism* (also sometimes referred to as *laissez-faire racism, symbolic racism,* or *color-blind racism.*) The three readings for this section examine how modern racism manifests itself in the United States in the criminal justice system, in whites' attitudes about African Americans, and in even the more intimate settings of close black–white friendships. The first reading, "I Am Not a Racist But . . . ," reviews some of the literature on symbolic or laissez-faire racism, which shows that on traditional measures of prejudice, whites' abstract attitudes on race have become more egalitarian, yet whites also tend not to support concrete policy measures to ensure that equality. However, having done their own research study combining surveys and in-depth interviews, Eduardo Bonilla-Silva and Tyrone A. Forman demonstrate that even the idea that white prejudice has declined should be suspect, since the same whites that answer in non-prejudiced ways on surveys express more prejudiced views in an in-depth interview setting where they are able to qualify and clarify their opinions. In the interviews, respondents use what the authors call a "new 'racetalk,'" which presents prejudiced views in a more "sanitized" way. For example, in response to a question about whether blacks are lazy, one respondent says, "I don't want to say waiting for a handout, but [to] some extent, that's kind of what I am hinting at." We see that a large majority of the whites interviewed do not believe African Americans face discrimination to any significant extent, and in fact, more than a third of the sample described blacks as whining or lying about discrimination. Thus, rather than attributing the disadvantaged situation of blacks to *structural* sources such as institutionalized discrimination (as do only a few "progressive" interviewees), most of the whites see blacks' situation in the United States as a result of their supposed cultural inferiority (also known as the *culture of poverty* argument). Such misattribution, coupled with the new "racetalk" that seeks to avoid stating prejudice directly, is described as *color-blind racism*—the post-1960s way that racial inequality is maintained and reproduced.

Some of the policy implications of this modern form of racism are explored in the second reading, "Race and Criminalization," about African Americans and the prison industry. Like the authors of the first reading, Angela Davis describes race as being disguised in "encoded language" today, amounting to what she terms "camouflaged racism." An example is the "Three strikes, you're out" laws requiring life sentences for those convicted for a crime three times. Although this law appears race-neutral, it has a major disproportionate impact on African Americans, an effect people tend to blame on the "culture of poverty" of blacks rather than on structural racism embedded in the criminal justice system. Davis points out this is done by Republicans and Democrats alike, citing President Bill Clinton as an example of someone who spoke of racial inequality as a matter of the "heart" (or as traditional prejudice) rather than as institutional. The high statistics of black representation in prisons that have become familiar to many are often taken as evidence of "black criminality" rather than as a problem with the system. Davis also links the expansion of the prison industry to the globalization of capitalism, since corporations are now turning to the cheap labor of prisoners in the same way they exploit unorganized labor in Third World countries. Thus, now capitalist profit depends upon keeping the prisons full, and effectively disenfranchised African Americans serve as easy targets to this end. As the prison population increases dramatically, one of the fastest growing demographic group of prisoners has been women, and especially black women. Davis explores this gender and race connection as well, bringing our attention to how sexist and racist stereotypes converge upon black female drug users, whose only options become being criminalized as unfit mothers in order to get treatment for their addictions. Even though the majority of U.S. drug users are white, prisons continue to be filled with African

American women and men, most of whom are there for drug-related crimes. Again, the apparently race-neutral War on Drugs provides yet another example of modern racism (and sexism) in action.

The third reading provides a final look at how Americans seek to minimize overt references to race even in the context of their close interracial friendships. In her article, "The Elephant in the Living Room," Kathleen Korgen reveals that a majority of the forty black–white close friendship pairs she interviewed did not seriously discuss race at any point during their relationship. The color-blind strategy to ignore or avoid race, or else to relegate it to the non-serious realm of joking, is prevalent with her respondents, and further illustrates the color-blind racism discussed in the first reading. Korgen's research also returns us to how power shapes the meaning of interactions between dominant and minority group members, a topic we began exploring in Chapter 1. Specifically, when two friends joke about each other's race, whether someone has "crossed the line" really depends on who is saying what, because of the different racial histories of the two groups. Also, for the few friends who do discuss seriously issues of race, the teaching process does not become an even trade, since the black friends end up doing far more educating of their white friends than the reverse. Thus, even as the few progressives in Bonilla-Silva's and Forman's research are still struggling with their own stereotypes, so too are these few progressive cross-racial friendships dealing with the legacy of racism as they try to break down its barriers. These readings taken together show us just how much work still needs to be done to ensure full social and political equality for African Americans.

"I Am Not a Racist, But . . .": Mapping White College Students' Racial Ideology in the USA

Eduardo Bonilla-Silva and Tyrone A. Forman

Introduction

Since the civil rights period it has become common for Whites to use phrases such as "I am not a racist, but . . ." as shields to avoid being labeled as "racist" when expressing racial ideas' (Van Dijk, 1984: 120). These discursive maneuvers or *semantic moves* are usually followed by negative statements on the general character of minorities (e.g. "they are lazy," "they have too many babies") or on government-sponsored policies and programs that promote racial equality (e.g. "affirmative action is reverse discrimination," "no-one should be forced to integrate").[1] Qualitative work has captured these discursive maneuvers on issues as diverse as crime, welfare, affirmative action, government intervention, neighborhood and school integration (Blauner, 1989; Feagin and Sikes, 1994; Feagin and Vera, 1995; MacLeod, 1995; Rieder, 1985; Rubin, 1994; Terkel, 1993; Weis and Fine, 1996; Wellman, 1977). For example, Margaret Welch, angry about not getting a scholarship in college, told Studs Terkel: "I've never been prejudiced, but why the hell are you doing this to me?" (Terkel, 1993: 70). Doug Craigen, a 32-year-old White truck driver, declared to Lillian Rubin: "I am not a racist, but sometimes they [Asians] give me the creeps" (Rubin, 1994: 188). . . .

These prejudiced expressions clash with research that suggests that racial attitudes have improved dramatically in the USA. Beginning with Hyman and Sheatsley's widely cited paper in *Scientific American (1964)*, survey research has documented substantial change in Whites' racial views (e.g. Firebaugh and Davis, 1988; Lipset, 1996; Niemi, Mueller and Smith, 1989; Smith and Sheatsley, 1984; Schuman et al., 1988; Sniderman and Piazza, 1993). . . .

The conflicting findings regarding the character of Whites' racial views based on interviews and surveys as well as the differing interpretations of survey-based attitudinal research (see Bobo and Hutchings, 1996; Hochschild, 1995; Kinder and Sanders, 1996; Lipset, 1996; Schuman et al., 1988, 1997; Sniderman and Carmines, 1997; Sniderman and Piazza, 1993) have produced a new puzzle: *What is the meaning of contemporary Whites' racial views?* How can *Whites* claim to believe in racial equality and yet oppose programs to reduce racial inequality? Why is it that a large proportion of *Whites*, who claim in surveys that they agree with the principle of integration, do not mind their kids mixing with non-Whites, have no objection to interracial marriages, and do not mind people of color moving into their neighborhoods continue to live in all-White neighborhoods and send their kids to mostly White schools? Finally, why is it that interview-based research consistently reports higher levels of prejudice among Whites?

To explore the meaning of contemporary Whites' views, this article examines White racial attitudes from both a different conceptual perspective and with a different methodology. Conceptually, we situate the racial attitudes of Whites as part of a larger racial ideology that functions to preserve the contemporary racial order.[2] Here we build on the work of others who have argued that the complexity of contemporary White racial attitudes reflects changes occurring in the USA since the late 1940s (Bonilla-Silva and Lewis, 1999; Brooks, 1990; Smith, 1995). Specifically, they claim that the dramatic social, political, economic and demographic changes in the USA since the 1940s combined with the political mobilization of various minority groups in the 1950s and 1960s, forced a change in the US racial structure—the network of social, political, and economic racial relations that produces and reproduces racial positions. In general terms, White privilege since the 1960s is maintained in a new fashion, in covert, institutional, and apparently nonracial ways (Bobo et al., 1997; Bonilla-Silva and Lewis, 1999; Jackman, 1994, 1996; Kovel, 1984; Smith, 1995; Wellman, 1977).

In consonance with this new structure, various analysts have pointed out that a new racial ideology has emerged that, in contrast to the Jim Crow racism or the ideology of the color line (Johnson, 1943, 1946; Myrdal, 1944), avoids direct racial discourse but effectively safeguards racial privilege (Bobo et al., 1997; Bonilla-Silva and Lewis, 1999; Essed, 1996; Jackman, 1994; Kovel, 1984). That ideology also shapes the very nature and style of contemporary racial discussions. In fact, in the post civil rights era, overt discussions of racial issues have become so taboo that it has become extremely difficult to assess racial attitudes and behavior using conventional research strategies (Myers, 1993; Van Dijk, 1984, 1987, 1997). Although we agree with those who suggest that there has been a normative change in terms of what is appropriate racial discourse and even racial etiquette (Schuman et al., 1988), we disagree with their interpretation of its meaning. Whereas they suggest that there is a "mixture of progress and resistance, certainty and ambivalence, striking movement and mere surface change" (p. 212), we believe (1) that there has been a rearticulation of the dominant racial themes (less *overt* expression of racial resentment about issues anchored in the Jim Crow era such as strict racial segregation in schools, neighborhoods, and social life in general, and more resentment on new issues such as affirmative action, government intervention, and welfare) and (2) that a new way of talking about racial issues in public venues—a new *racetalk*—has emerged. Nonetheless, the new racial ideology continues to help in the reproduction of White supremacy.

. . . Our main concern in this article is tracking White college students' interpretive repertoires on racial matters as expressed during in-depth interviews and comparing them to their views as expressed in responses to survey items. We do this in order to demonstrate that the survey research paradox of contemporary White views on race is not a paradox after all.

RESEARCH DESIGN

The 1997 Social Attitudes of College Students Survey was a sample of undergraduate students at four universities. One school was located in the south, another in the midwest, and two were located in the west. Data collection occurred during the spring of 1997. All students surveyed were enrolled in social science courses. The questionnaire was administered during a class period. Students were informed that participation in the study was voluntary. Fewer than 10 percent declined to participate and a total of 732 students completed the survey. There were no significant differences on demographic characteristics between students who chose to participate and those that did not. All of the analyses reported in this article use only White respondents ($N = 541$). The sample sizes of other racial groups are too small for reliable statistical comparison. . . .

We conducted in-depth interviews with a random sample of the White college students that had completed the survey because prior research has found differences in Whites' racial attitudes depending on mode of data collection (Dovidio and Gaertner, 1986; Dovidio et al., 1989; Groves, Fultz et al., 1992; Krysan, 1998; Sigall and Page, 1971). . . . In order to facilitate our selection of respondents for the in-depth interviews, we asked each respondent surveyed to provide on the first page of the survey their name, telephone, and e-mail address. After the students were chosen the page was discarded. Over 80 percent of the . . . White college students who completed the survey . . . provided contact information. There were no significant differences between students that provided contact information and the 20 percent who did not on either several racial attitude items or demographic characteristics. We randomly selected 41 White college students (approximately 10%) who had completed the survey and provided contact information. Interviews were conducted during the spring of 1997. In order to minimize race of interviewer effects (see Anderson et al., 1988a, 1988b), the interviews were conducted by three White graduate students and two White advanced undergraduate students. Whenever possible, we also matched respondents by gender (Kane and Macaulay, 1993). The interviews were conducted using an interview guide that addressed several issues explored in the survey instrument. The time of interviews ranged from 1 to 2.5 hours. The present study draws more extensively on the in-depth interview data, addressing White college students' general and specific racial attitudes, social distance preferences, and reported interactions with racial minorities. . . .

TOWARD AN ANALYSIS OF CONTEMPORARY WHITE IDEOLOGY

White College Students' Views: Survey Results

Table 5.1 shows the responses of White students to questions on affirmative action. The table provides results on the total sample . . . as well as on the 41 students selected for the interviews. A number of things are clear from these data. First, the interview sample mirrors the total sample, something that holds for all the tables.[3] If anything, the interview respondents are slightly more likely to support affirmative action measures. Second, Whites seem to openly oppose or have serious reservations about these programs, regardless of how the question is worded. These findings are quite consistent with previous research on Whites' attitudes toward affirmative action (Kluegel, 1990; Kluegel and Smith, 1986; Lipset, 1996; Schuman and Steeh, 1996; Steeh and Krysan, 1996). . . . Third, most of the respondents fear the effects of affirmative action programs on their life chances. This fear is evident in the large proportion of respondents (70% or higher) who believe that it is "somewhat likely" or "very likely" that they will lose out on a job, promotion, or admission to a college due to affirmative action (see questions G1, G2, and G3). This finding is interesting because it goes against other research on affirmative action that shows that these programs have had little impact on Whites (Glass Ceiling Commission, 1995; Edley, 1996; Herring and Collins, 1995; Hochschild, 1995; Wicker, 1996). More significantly, the results are intriguing because these college students are from mostly middle-class backgrounds and are not in a vulnerable social position.

In Table 5.2 we show the results on social distance items. Our results in Table 5.2 are consistent with those of previous research. A very high proportion of Whites claim to approve of interracial marriage, friendship with Blacks, and with people of color moving into predominantly

Table 5.1   White Students' Views on Affirmative Action Items

Affirmative Action Questions	*Survey sample (%) (N = 410)*	*Interview sample (%) (N = 41)*
B21. An anti-affirmative action proposition passed by a substantial margin in California in 1996. If a similar proposition was put on the ballot in your locality, would you support it, oppose it, or would you neither oppose nor support it?		
1. Support	25.8	37.5
2. Neither Support Nor Oppose	38.3	25.0
3. Oppose	35.9	37.5
χ^2		n.s.
C18. Sometimes Black job seekers should be given special consideration in hiring.		
1. Agree	13.3	17.9
2. Neither Agree Nor Disagree	21.6	17.9
3. Disagree	65.2	64.1
χ^2		n.s.
G1. Affirmative Action programs for Blacks have reduced Whites' chances for jobs, promotions, and admissions to schools and training programs.		
1. Agree	50.8	36.6
2. Neither Agree Nor Disagree	26.2	17.1
3. Disagree	23.0	46.3
χ^2		**
G2. What do you think are the chances these days that a White person won't get a job or a promotion while an equally or less qualified Black person gets one instead?		
1. Very Likely	11.1	17.9
2. Somewhat Likely	60.3	46.2
3. Not Very Likely	28.7	35.9
χ^2		n.s.
G3. What do you think are the chances these days that a White person won't get admitted to a school while an equally or less qualified Black gets admitted instead?		
1. Very Likely	26.3	15.0
2. Somewhat Likely	52.9	60.0
3. Not Very Likely	20.8	25.0
χ^2		n.s.
G4. Some people say that because of past discrimination it is sometimes necessary for colleges and universities to reserve openings for Black students.Others oppose quotas because they say quotas discriminate against Whites. What about your opinion: Are you for or against quotas to admit Black students?		
1. For	12.4	22.5
2. Not Sure	36.7	27.5
3. Against	50.9	50.0
χ^2		n.s.

SOURCE: Social Attitudes of College Students Survey. 1997.

$*p < .05$, $**p < .01$, n.s. = not significant.

Table 5.2   White Students' Views on Social Distance Items

Social Distance Questions	*Survey sample (%) (N = 410)*	*Interview sample (%) (N = 41)*
Traditional Items		
B2. If a Black family with about the same income and education as you moved next door, would you mind it a lot, a little, or not at all?		
1. Not at all	92.1	95.1
χ^2		n.s.
B12. Do you approve or disapprove of marriage between Whites and Blacks?		
1. Approve	79.4	90.2
2. Not Sure	13.7	4.9
3. Disapprove	6.9	4.9
χ^2		n.s.
B7. How strongly would you object if a member of your family had a friendship with a Black person?		
1. No objection	91.9	95.1
χ^2		n.s.
Nontraditional Items		
A13. Think of the five people with whom you interact the most on an almost daily basis. Of these five, how many of them are Black?		
1. None	67.7	68.3
2. One	19.6	24.4
3. Two or more	12.7	7.3
χ^2		n.s.
A15. Have you invited a Black person for lunch or dinner recently?		
1. No	67.8	75.0
2. Yes	32.2	25.0
χ^2		n.s.

SOURCE: Social Attitudes of College Students Survey, 1997.

*$p < .05$, **$p < .01$, n.s. = not significant.

White neighborhoods (Firebaugh and Davis, 1988; Niemi et al., 1989; Schuman et al., 1988; Sniderman and Piazza, 1993). However, results based on two non-traditional measures of social distance from Blacks indicate something different. A majority of Whites (68%) state that they do not interact with any Black person on a daily basis and that they have not recently invited a Black person for lunch or dinner. Although suggestive, this finding is somewhat inconclusive since it is possible that Whites have changed their attitudes on social distance but do not have the opportunity to interact meaningfully with Blacks because of residential and school

segregation (Massey and Denton, 1993; Orfield and Eaton, 1996; Wilson, 1987).

Finally, in Table 5.3 we display our results on Whites' beliefs about the significance of discrimination for Blacks' life chances. Interestingly, most Whites (87%) believe that discrimination affects the life chances of Blacks and approximately a third (30%) agree with the statement that "Blacks are in the position that they are because of contemporary discrimination" (for similar findings, see Lipset and Schneider, 1978). In contrast, a slight majority of White college students believe that preferences should not be used as a criterion for hiring (53.4% were

Table 5.3   White Students' Views on Significance of Discrimination on Blacks' Life Chances

Significance of Discrimination Questions	*Survey sample (%) (N = 410)*	*Interview sample (%) (N = 41)*
B13. Do you agree or disagree with the following statement? Discrimination against Blacks is no longer a problem in the United States		
1. Agree	8.1	7.3
2. Neither Agree Nor Disagree	4.9	4.9
3. Disagree	87.0	87.8
χ^2		n.s.
B17. On the whole, do you think that most Whites in the USA want to see Blacks get a better break, do they want to keep Blacks down, or don't care one way or the other?		
1. Better Break	20.1	17.5
2. Don't Care One Way or the Other	62.9	65.0
3. Keep Blacks Down	17.0	17.5
χ^2		n.s.
E6. Some people say that because of past discrimination against Blacks, preference in hiring and promotion should be given to Blacks. Others say preferential hiring and promotion of Blacks is wrong because it gives Blacks advantages that they haven't earned. Are you for or against preferences in hiring and promotion to Blacks?		
1. Against	54.1	47.5
2. Not Sure	38.6	47.5
3. For	7.1	5.0
χ^2		n.s.
F5. Blacks are in the position that they are as a group because of contemporary discrimination.		
1. Agree	30.6	48.7
2. Neither Agree Nor Disagree	39.3	20.5
3. Disagree	30.1	30.8
χ^2		*

SOURCE: Social Attitudes of College Students Survey, 1997.

*$p < .05$, **$p < .01$, n.s. = not significant.

"against") and 83 per cent of the White respondents also believe that Whites either want to give Blacks a "better break" or at least "don't care one way or the other". Again, these results are somewhat contradictory (Schuman et al., 1988).

Although most White college students believe that Blacks experience discrimination and that this explains in part their contemporary status; at the same time, they believe that most Whites want to give Blacks a "better break" or "don't care one way or another" and that preferences should not play any part in hiring and promotion decisions.

Accordingly, based on these survey results, we could construct a variety of interpretations of White college students' racial attitudes. If we based our analysis on the respondents' answers to traditional questions, we would conclude, as most social scientist do, that Whites are racially tolerant. If we use all of our survey findings, we could conclude, as Schuman and his colleagues do (1988), that Whites have contradictory racial views. Finally, if we give more credence to our respondents' answers to the modern racism questions (B17, C18, E6, G1, G2, G3, and G4) and some of the new questions (A13, A15, B21) than

Table 5.4　　　Views on Interracial Marriage (Total sample, N = 40)[1]

	Respondents % (N)
Support Interracial Marriage/Integrated Life	12.5 (5)
Support Interracial Marriage/Segregated Life	17.5 (7)
Reservations toward Interracial Marriage/Integrated Life	10.0 (4)
Reservations toward Interracial Marriage/Segregated Life	52.5 (21)
Oppose Interracial Marriage/Integrated Life	0 (0)
Oppose Interracial Marriage/Segregated Life	7.5 (3)

[1]The question was not asked of one of the students in the sample.

to their answers to traditional items, we could conclude that Whites are significantly more racially prejudiced in their views than previous research has concluded. In the next section we use the 41 in-depth interviews with White students to make sense of our conflicting survey findings.

WHITE COLLEGE STUDENTS' VIEWS—IN-DEPTH INTERVIEWS

"If Two People Love Each Other . . .": Whites' Views on Interracial Marriages

Our strategy for interpreting our interview data on intermarriage was as follows. First, we read carefully the respondents' answers to a specific question about whether or not they approved of interracial marriages. Then we examined their romantic history and what kind of friends they had throughout their lives. In some cases, we examined their views on other matters because they contained information relevant to interracial marriage. Based on the composite picture of the respondents that we obtained using this strategy, we classified them into six categories (see Table 5.4).

Five of the respondents (category 1) had lifestyles consistent with their views on inter-marriages, 28 had reservations from serious to outright opposition (categories 3–6), and 7 claimed to approve of intermarriage but had lifestyles inconsistent with the interracial perspective that they presumably endorsed (category 2). For presentation purposes, we will provide one example of respondents in category 2 (since this was the hardest group to make sense of) and one of the respondents in categories 4 (the modal category) and 6.

The first case is Ray, a student at a large midwestern university, an example of students in category 2. Ray answered the question about interracial marriage by stating that:

I think that there's . . . *I think that interracial marriage is totally legitimate. I think if two people love each other* and *they* want to spend the rest of their lives together, I think *they* should definitely get married. And race should in no way be an inhibitive factor. . . . (Interview # 150: 13)

Although Ray supports interracial marriages (despite using some *indirectness*), his life prior to college and during college was racially segregated. He grew up in a large city in the midwest, in an upper middle-class neighborhood that he characterized as "all *White*" (Interview # 150: 2) and described his friends as "what the average suburban kid is like nowadays" (Interview # 150: 3). More significantly, Ray, who was extremely articulate in the interview, stuttered remarkably in the question (asked *before* the one on intermarriage) dealing with whether or not he had ever been attracted to Blacks. His response was as follows:

. . . Um, so, to answer that question, no. Um, but I would not . . . I mean, *I would not . . . I mean, I would not ever preclude, uh, a Black woman from being my girlfriend on the basis that she was Black*. Ya know, I mean . . . ya know what I mean? If you're looking from the standpoint of attraction, I mean, I think that, ya know . . . I think, ya know, I think, ya know, I think, ya know, all women are, I mean, all women have a sort of different type of beauty if you will. And I think that for Black women it's somewhat different than *White* women. Um, but I don't think it's, ya know,

I mean, it's, it's . . . it's nothing that would ever stop me from like, uh . . . I mean, I don't know, I mean, I don't [know] if that's . . . I mean, that's just sort of been my impression. I mean, it's not like I would ever say, "no, I'll never have a Black girlfriend," *but it just seems to me like I'm not as attracted to Black women as I am to White women for whatever reason. It's not about prejudice, it's just sort of like, ya know, whatever. Just sort of the way . . . way . . . like, I see White women as compared to Black women, ya know?* (Interview # 150: 12)

As is evident from Ray's statement, he is not attracted to Black women, something that clashes with his self-proclaimed color-blind approach to love and his support for interracial marriages. More significantly, he seemed aware of how problematic that sounded and used all sorts of rhetorical strategies to save face.

The next case is an example of students who had reservations about interracial marriages who lived a primarily segregated life (category 4), the modal group in our sample. We found regularities (Brown and Yule, 1983) in the structure of their answers similar to the ones we found among those who responded "yes and no" to the affirmative action question. Their answers usually included the rhetorical moves of *apparent agreement* and *apparent admission*—a formal statement of support for interracial marriages followed or preceded by statements qualifying the support in terms of what might happen to the kids, how the relationship might affect the families, or references to how their parents would never approve of such relationships.

The next example is Sally, a student at a large midwestern university. She replied to the interracial marriage question as follows:

I certainly don't oppose the marriage, not at all. Um . . .depending on where I am, if I had to have a concern, yes, it would be for the children. . . . Ya know, it can be nasty and then other kids wouldn't even notice. I think . . . *I could care less what anyone else does with their lives, as long as they are really happy.* And if the parents can set a really strong foundation at home, it can be conquered, *but I'm sure, in some places, it could cause a problem.* (Interview # 221: 5)

Sally's answer included displacement (concerns for the children and the certainty that interracial marriages would be problematic in some places) and indirectness ("I could care less what *anyone else* does . . . as long as *they* are really happy") alongside her initial apparent admission semantic move ("I certainly don't oppose the marriage"). Sally's apprehension on this subject matched the nature of her life and her specific views on Blacks. Sally's life was, in terms of interactions, relationships, and residence, almost entirely racially segregated. When questioned about her romantic life, Sally said that she had never dated a person of color and recognized that "I've never been attracted to a Black person" and that "I never look at what they look like . . . it just hasn't occurred in my life" (Interview # 221: 5).

The final case is Eric, a student at a large midwestern university, an example of the students who openly expressed serious reservations about interracial marriages (category 6). It is significant to point out that even the three students who stated that they would not enter into these relationships, claimed that there was nothing wrong with interracial relationships per se. . . .

Eric used the *apparent admission* semantic move ("I would say that I agree with that") in his reply but could not camouflage very well his true feelings ("If I were to ask if I had a daughter or something like that, or even one of my sisters, um . . . were [sic] to going to get married to a minority or a Black, I . . . I would probably . . . it would probably bother me a little bit"). Interestingly, Eric claimed in the interview that he had been romantically interested in an Asian-Indian woman his first year in college. However, that interest "never turned out to be a real big [deal]" (Interview # 248: 9). Despite Eric's fleeting attraction to a person of color, his life was racially segregated: no minority friends and no meaningful interaction with any Black person.

The results in this section clash with our survey results. Whereas in the survey the students seemed to favor interracial contacts of all kinds with Blacks, the interview data suggest otherwise. Whites' serious reservations if not opposition to interracial marriages are expressed as "concerns" for the welfare of the offspring of those relationships, upsetting the family, or the reaction of the larger community to the marriage. All these statements—a number of the respondents themselves classified these arguments as excuses—seem to be rationalizations to *discursively* avoid stating opposition to interracial marriages. This is quite significant since they could easily *state* that they have no problems with intermarriage. The fact that very few do so in an unequivocal manner, gives credence to the argument that Whites' racial aversion for Blacks is deeply ingrained into their unconscious (Fanon, 1967; Hernton, 1988; Jordan, 1977; Kovel, 1984). Finally, the respondents' comments about their romantic lives and friendships clearly indicate that rather than being color-blind, they are very color conscious.

"I KIND OF SUPPORT AND OPPOSE . . .": WHITES' VIEWS ON AFFIRMATIVE ACTION

Intentionally, we did not define affirmative action in our interview protocol. We were particularly interested in how the respondents themselves defined the various programs that have emerged since the 1970s to enhance the chances of minorities getting jobs, promotions, access to institutions of higher learning, etc.[4] Although some of the students hesitated and asked for a definition of the program, to which our interviewers replied "what do you think it is?", most answered based on what they thought affirmative action meant.

Content analysis of the responses of the 41 students interviewed shows that most (85%) oppose affirmative action. This degree of opposition was somewhat higher than the results obtained in the survey. However, unlike in the survey, only a quarter (10 out of 41) came out and opposed affirmative action in a straightforward manner. In part, this may be the result of a general belief that if they express their views too openly on affirmative action, diversity, or any other race-related issue, they are going to be labeled as "racist."[5] Although we were able to detect some of this reticence through discursive analysis, many respondents expressed their concern explicitly. For instance, Bob, a student at a large southern university and who openly opposed affirmative action, said, "I oppose

them [affirmative action programs], mainly because, *I am not a racist but* because I think you should have the best person for the job" (Interview # 6: 13). Mark, a student, at a large midwestern university, who said that he couldn't give a "definite answer" on affirmative action, later mentioned that companies need to diversify because "we need diversity, and if you don't have diversity, *then people call you a racist and you have to deal with all of those accusations*" (Interview # 6: 24).

Since respondents were very sensitive to not appearing "racist," most (26 out of 41) expressed their opposition to affirmative action indirectly. Brian, a student at a large southern university, responded to the affirmative action questions by saying: "Man . . . that's another one where [laughs] . . . *I kind of support and oppose it*" (Interview # 10:8). If we had based our analysis only on the students' responses to this one question, we would have had to conclude that most Whites are truly torn apart about affirmative action, that they have "non attitudes" (see Converse, 1964, 1970, 1974), or are "ambivalent" (Katz et al., 1986). However, we included several questions in the interview schedule that dealt either directly or indirectly with affirmative action. Therefore we were able to make sense of respondents' vacillations concerning affirmative action.

In many cases, a thorough reading of the complete response to the primary affirmative action question helped us to understand that the "yes and no" responses really meant "no." For example, Brian, the student cited earlier who was seemingly ambivalent about affirmative action, went on to say, "Pretty much the same thing I said before . . . I don't know, *if I come,* I don't know, *somebody underqualified shouldn't get chosen,* you know?" (Interview # 6: 8). After being probed about whether he thought that what he had just described was an example of reverse discrimination, Brian replied, "Um, pretty much, I mean, yeah."

Furthermore, Brian's response to a specific question asking if he supported a program to give minorities unique opportunities in education suggests that his hesitations and his *topic avoidance by claiming ignorance* and *ambivalence* ("I don't know" and "I am not sure") in the earlier quote were just semantic moves that allowed him to voice safely his opposition to affirmative action ("somebody underqualified shouldn't get chosen") (see Van Dijk, 1984: 109, 131–2). Brian's response to a question about providing unique educational opportunities to minorities was the following:

Brian: Um . . . mmm, that's a tough one. *I don't, you mean, unique opportunities, as far as, just because you are, they are that race, like quotas type of thing or . . .*

Int.: Well, why don't you stipulate the kind of program that you would support and where your limits might be for that.

Brian: All right. . . . Um . . .mmm, let's see, uh . . . I, I don't know (laughs), *I am not sure about like, the problem is like, I don't know, like, 'cause I don't think race should come into like the picture at all, like I don't think they should be given unique opportunities.* . . . (Interview # 10: 8)

In Brian's case as well as in many of the other cases where students apparently wavered on affirmative action, we looked at their responses to questions dealing with job-related cases at the fictitious ABZ company.[6] Brian's answers to these questions clearly indicate that he believes that programs that give *any* additional opportunities to minorities to compensate for past and present discrimination amount to reverse discrimination. For instance, Brian's response to the first scenario included the displacement semantic move, "It seems like *the White guy* might be a little upset," although at the end of his statement he resorted to apparent admission by saying, "I guess I don't have a problem with it." Moments later, when probed about how he would respond to someone who characterized the company's decision as reverse racism, Brian said that "I would say, *yeah, it is*" (Interview # 6: 9). . . .

The student's comments on affirmative action in interviews suggest that there is even more opposition to affirmative action than our survey results indicate. Also, the opposition to affirmative action of our respondents seems to be related to racial prejudice. However, we recognize that many survey analysts doubt this interpretation and suggest that Whites' opposition to these programs is "political," "ideological," or that it expresses "value duality"

(Katz et al., 1986; Kluegel and Smith, 1986; Lipset, 1996; Sniderman and Piazza, 1993). Thus, to strengthen our case, we add another piece of information. In the elaboration of their arguments against affirmative action, 27 of the 41 respondents used spontaneously one of two story-lines or argumentation schemata (Van Dijk, 1984, 1987). The fact that so many of the respondents used the same "stories" underscores the fact that Whites seem to have a shared cognition and that these stories have become part of the ideological racial repertoire about how the world is and ought to be. The two stories were "The past is the past" and "Present generations cannot be blamed for the mistakes of past generations" and were mobilized as justification for not doing anything about the effects of past and contemporary discrimination.

We present one example to illustrate how these stories were mobilized. The example is Sally, a student at a large midwestern university, who answered the question about whether or not Blacks should be compensated for the history of oppression that they have endured by saying:

Absolutely no. How long are you gonna rely on it? I had nothing to do with it. . . . I think it's turning into a crutch that they're getting to fall back on their histories. . . . I just think that every individual should do it for themselves and achieve for themselves. (Interview # 221: 10)

Sally's angry tone in this answer saturated all her responses to the affirmative action questions. For instance, she stated in her response to another question that minorities feel like "supervictims" and asked rhetorically, inspired by the arguments from Shelby Steele that she learned in her sociology course, "For how long are you gonna be able to rely on an oppressed history of your ancestors?" (Interview # 221: 11–12).

"I Believe That They Believe . . .": White Beliefs about Contemporary Discrimination against Blacks

We asked the subjects to define racism for us and then followed up with five related questions.[7] The students that we interviewed defined racism as "prejudice based on race," "a feeling of racial superiority," "very stupid . . . lots of ignorance," "psychological war," "hating people because of their skin color," and "the belief that one race is superior to the other." Only five of the subjects mentioned or implied that racism was societal, institutional, or structural, and of these only two truly believed that racism is part and parcel of American society. More importantly, very few of the subjects described this country as "racist" or suggested that minorities face systemic disadvantages, in this or in any other part of the interviews. Thus, Whites primarily think that racism is a belief that a few individuals hold and which might lead them to discriminate against some people.

Notwithstanding these findings, it is important to explore Whites' beliefs about the prevalence of discrimination against minorities and about how much it affects the life chances of minorities in the USA. Our analysis revealed that most of the subjects (35 out of 41) expressed serious doubts about whether discrimination affects minorities in a significant way. As in the cases of their responses to the affirmation action and intermarriage questions, very few respondents (14%) who expressed doubts about the significance of discrimination did so consistently in all the questions. . . .

The students provided several examples, suggesting that minorities use racism as an excuse, that discrimination works against Whites nowadays, that discrimination is not such an important factor in the USA, and that other factors such as motivation, values, or credentials may account for Blacks' lack of mobility. . . .

If Whites . . . do not understand or appreciate how race matters for minorities in the USA and yet hear them complaining about discrimination, then the obvious next step is to regard minorities' complaints as whining, excuses, or untrue (Hochschild, 1995). This specific charge was made directly by 14 of the respondents. For example, Kara, a student at a large midwestern university, denied explicitly and without discursive reservations that discrimination affects significantly the life chances of minorities, in her answer to the first question on discrimination:

Int.: Some Black people claim that they face a great deal of racism in their daily lives, and a lot of other people claim that that's not the case. What do you think?

Kara: I would think, presently speaking, like people in my generation, I don't think it's . . . as much that there is racism that, *but Black people almost go into their experiences feeling like they should be discriminated against and I think that makes them hypersensitive.* (Interview # 251: 13)

Kara went on to say that she believes that Blacks receive preferential treatment in admissions or, in her words "being Black, if you just look at applying to graduate schools or things, that's a big part." To the question of why she thinks Blacks have worse jobs, income, and housing than Whites she replied:

. . . part of me wants to say like work ethic, but I don't know if that is being fair. . . . I just don't know, I think that if you look at the inner city, you can definitely see they're just stuck, like those people cannot really get out . . . like in the suburbs . . . I don't know why that would be. I mean, I am sure they are discriminated against but . . . (Interview # 251: 13)

Immediately after, Kara answered the question about whether or not Blacks are lazy by saying that:

I think, to some extent, that's true. Just from like looking at the Black people that I've met in my classes and the few I knew before college that . . . not like they're—*I don't want to say waiting for a handout, but [to] some extent, that's kind of what I am hinting at.* Like almost like they feel like they were discriminated against hundreds of years ago, now what are you gonna give me? Ya know, or maybe even it's just their background, that they've never, like maybe they're first generation to be in college so they feel like, just that is enough for them. (Interview # 251: 14)

Although some Whites acknowledge that minorities experience discrimination or racism, they still complain about reverse racism, affirmative action, and a number of other racially perceived policies. This occurs in part because in their view, racism is a phenomenon that affects few minorities or affects them in minor ways, and thus has little impact on the life chances of minorities, in particular, and American society more generally. For many Whites, racism is a matter of a few rotten apples such as David Duke, Mark Fuhrman, and the policemen who beat Rodney King rather than a "system of social relations in which Whites typically have more access to the means of power, wealth, and esteem than Blacks [and other minorities]" (Hartman and Husband, 1974: 48). Furthermore, Whites either do not understand or do not believe the new institutional, subtle, and apparently non-racial character of the American racial structure (Bonilla-Silva and Lewis, 1999; Carmichael and Hamilton, 1967; Hochschild, 1995; Jackman, 1994; Smith, 1995). These two factors combined may explain why Whites regard the complaints of minorities about discrimination as exaggerations or excuses. If Whites "don't see" discrimination and do not understand the systemic racial character of our society (Kluegel and Smith, 1982, 1986), then they must interpret minorities' claims of discrimination as false (Essed, 1996) and blame minorities for their lower socio-economic status (Kluegel, 1990).

COLOR-BLIND RACISM:
TOWARD AN ANALYSIS OF WHITE COLLEGE STUDENTS' COLLECTIVE REPRESENTATIONS IN THE USA

In the previous sections we demonstrated that White students use a number of rhetorical strategies that allow them to safely voice racial views that might be otherwise interpreted as racist. In this section, we examine whether or not what students were saying through the rhetorical maze of "I don't know," "I am not sure," and "I am not a racist, but" fits the themes of color blind racism, the dominant racial ideology in the post-civil rights era (Bonilla-Silva, 1998). . . .

The Central Themes of Color-Blind Racism

In recent work, Bobo and his coauthors (Bobo and Kluegel, 1997, Bobo et al., 1997)

have labeled post civil rights racial ideology as "laissez faire racism." Laissez faire racism, unlike Jim Crow racism, is "an ideology that blames Blacks themselves for their poorer relative economic standing, seeing it as a function of perceived cultural inferiority" (Bobo and Kluegel, 1997: 95). Other social analysts have pointed out that post civil rights racial hostility is "muted" (Jackman, 1994) or is expressed as "resentment" (Kinder and Sanders, 1996). We argue that post civil rights racial ideology should be called *color-blind racism* since the notion of color blindness is the global justification Whites use to defend the racial status quo. Table 5.5 presents the central elements of color-blind racism and of alternative racial ideologies (Bonilla-Silva, 1998; Crenshaw, 1996; Essed, 1996; Jackman, 1994; Kovel, 1984). . . .

"They Are" and "We Are":
Otherizing Talk among Students

If the USA had truly achieved the color blind dream of Martin Luther King, Whites would not see Blackness as otherness, as difference that entails inferiority. However, in interview after interview, White students constructed a 'we-they' dichotomy of Blacks and Whites.

For instance, Bob, a student at a southern university from a working-class background, argued that Blacks have a different culture than Whites. He states:

> I think it's true. Um, I think that Blacks have a lot stronger sense of family. Well at least from my own um I always hear about my friends going to family picnics and going to the park and stuff and church, um. My parents, um, I know I have over thirty cousins, and I know like three of them. So I, I think, I think it has to do with family values. (Interview # 6: 8)

Although Bob seems to have positive valuation of Blacks' culture, his next comment suggests otherwise. Bob's answer to the questions, "Do you think the origins of these differences, are they natural, cultural, environmental?" was the following:

> I think it's cultural, they way they were raised, the way their parents were raised. My parents worked,

Table 5.5   Central Elements of Dominant and Alternative Contemporary Racial Interpretive Repertories in the USA.

Dominant Framework (Color-Blind Ideology)	*Alternative Frameworks (Cultural Pluralism, Nationalism, & Others)*
1. *Abstract and decontextualized* notions of liberalism (e.g. "Race should not be a factor when judging people")	*Concrete and contextualized* notions of liberalism or more radical egalitarian theories for distributing social goods
2. *Cultural* rationale for explaining the status of racial subjects in society (e.g. "Blacks are lazy" or "Blacks lack the proper work ethic")	*Political* rationale for explaining the status of racial subjects in society (e.g. "Blacks have been left behind by the system")
3. Avoidance of racist language and direct racial references in explaining racially based or racially perceived issues such as affirmative action, school busing, or interracial dating (Note: Color-blinders utilize indirect subtle and racially coded words to talk about racial matters)	
4. *Naturalization* of matters that reflect the effects arguments (e.g. explaining segregation or limited interracial marriage as a natural outcome)	Explanation of race-related issues with race-related of White supremacy (e.g. segregation as the product of the racialized actions of the state, realtors, and individual Whites
5. Denial of *structural* character of "racism" and discrimination viewed as limited, sporadic, and declining in significance	Understanding racism as "societal" and recognition of new forms of discrimination
6. Invoke the *free-market* or *laissez faire* ideology thus to justify contemporary racial inequality (e.g. "Kids should be exposed to all kinds of cultures but it cannot be imposed on them through busing")	Recognition that "market" outcomes have a racial bent and support of special programs to ameliorate racial inequities

my grandparents worked, so they didn't have a lot of strong family outings and gatherings, like Easter, stuff like that, that's about it, um . . . that's what I think. (Interview # 6: 8)

As evident from this statement, Bob's apparently positive evaluation of the family life of Blacks is tied to his belief that Blacks do not work. Hence, he believes that, unlike Whites, Blacks have time to concentrate on family matters. This interpretation of Bob's views was confirmed by Bob himself later on in the interview in his response to a question dealing with why Blacks have worse jobs, income, and housing than Whites. After pointing out that discrimination "may play a factor," Bob added that there were other factors. We cite him at length because his answer clearly illustrates his negative views on Blacks' culture.

Like . . . motivation, uh, family values. . . . Here I, I know I argued a minute ago that they have

stronger family values but I know a lot of my [minority] friends didn't have fathers, and they don't have . . . Their mothers were gone all the time, so they'd stay out and play all day. If they wanted something, they'd go out and steal it. Um, they don't have the money to have a lawn mower, so they can't mow yards like I did. And granted, I didn't even have to do that. I mean, my parents wouldn't give me things I asked, but if I really needed something, I'd get it. Um, if I, they'd let me work it off but these kids, they couldn't do that, so they'd get stuck in a rut, they'd start making minimum wage, they get a girlfriend, get her pregnant and they get stuck stuck in a big ongoing cycle, a big circle, and their kids, and their kids, like that. Um whereas like immigrants, like say . . . Jewish people, came over this country and had, you know, they, it was like in their heads that they were going to do better. And that's why I think nowadays they own a lot of things. People who were persecuted against in other countries come here and do *real* well, but it you're here all along, well, for a long time, you get used to how you are. . . . (Interview # 6:9)

Here Bob clearly states his belief that Blacks' family values are *inferior* to those of Whites. Black families are described as pathological, Black children as out of control, and Blacks in general as lacking the work ethic. In contrast, Bob views Whites as people who are entrepreneurial (mow yards even though they don't really need that extra money), can control their impulses (Blacks get their girlfriends "pregnant" and "get stuck in a rut"), and fight against all odds to overcome life's obstacles (White immigrants struggled but were able to overcome).

Although based on our analysis of the students' responses to the interview questions on affirmative action, interracial marriage, and the significance of discrimination for Blacks' life chances, most students were not racially tolerant (36 out of 41), we classified five of them as racial progressives. These racial progressives did not subscribe to the 'we-they' dichotomy, were more likely to find problems with the way in which Whites see Blacks, and were more understanding of the significance of discrimination in society. These students formulated their positions from alternative racial ideological frameworks (see Table 5.5). For instance, Lynn, a student at a large midwestern university from a lower middle-class background who grew up in a small town, began her interview by acknowledging that her community was very racist. She said that her village was a "hick town" and that "there was a lot of stereotypes" (Interview # 196: 1). Whereas most White students felt quite comfortable with their segregated neighborhoods and did not even realize that they were segregated, racial progressives such as Lynn disliked the lack of diversity in their communities. In Lynn's words:

Um, I actually disliked it a lot because there was a lot of . . . um a lot of racist people and it was nothing for my friends to make very racist remarks . . . especially because they didn't know anybody of any other race, so it didn't bother them. And they were feeding off the stereotypes . . . that were really negative. (Interview # 196: 2)

Lynn also recognized that discrimination is central in explaining Blacks' status in the USA. For example, Lynn's response to a question on why there are so few minorities at the top of the occupational structure was the following:

Uh, discrimination. Um . . . just cuz they've had to come back from slavery and everything and . . . they're not fully integrated into . . . ya know . . . they just still aren't accepted. A lot of the old views are there. (Interview # 196: 10)

More significantly, although most Whites recognized that there are "racists out there," racial progressives such as Lynn were more likely to acknowledge that they themselves had problems. Lynn's response to a question on dealing with Blacks' claim that they face a great deal of racism in their daily lives elicited the following response:

I would say . . . I'd say yeah, they do, probably. Um . . . just, um, like I know . . . I do this, I've been trained to do this. Like, when I walk down the street at night . . . by myself, and I meet a White guy on the street, I'm not as scared as if I meet a Black guy on the street. I keep telling myself that's stupid, but . . . that's how I've been trained. I mean just little things like that, I mean, I don't think they're like discriminating, I guess, on a large scale every single day, but . . . yeah, in little ways like that. (Interview # 196: 9)

Although we believe that White progressives *tended* to formulate their views from an alternative racial ideology, they were not totally free from the influence of the dominant racial ideology. For instance, Lynn, who had agreed with the decision of a hypothetical ABZ company to hire an equally qualified Black applicant over a White to increase diversity "because obviously if they're 97 percent White . . . they've probably been discriminating in the past" (Interview # 196: 12), opposed hiring the Black candidate when the justification was that the ABZ company had discriminated in the past. Using a variety of semantic moves to shield her from being perceived as prejudiced, she stated:

I think I'd disagree because, I mean, even though it's kinda what affirmative action . . . well, it's not really, because . . . um . . . I don't think like . . . my generation should have to . . . I mean, in a way, we should, but we shouldn't be . . . punished really harshly for the things that our ancestors did, on the one hand. But on the other hand, I think that . . . how we should try and change the way we do things. So we aren't doing the same things that our ancestors did. (Interview # 196: 14)

Furthermore, although Lynn had stated that she supported affirmative action because "the White male is pretty instilled . . . very much still represses . . . um, people and other minorities" (Interview # 196: 12), she vented anger toward the program and even said that if she was involved in an affirmative action type of situation, "it would anger me. . . . I mean, because, ya know, *I* as an individual got . . . ya know, ripped off and, ya know, getting a job . . . even though, even if I thought I was more qualified" (Interview # 196: 14–15). Finally, although she expressed concern about the lack of diversity in the village where she grew up, had taken classes with racial minorities while at university, and had even reported having had Black acquaintances in her first year in college, all her primary associations at the time of the interview were with Whites. . . .

Mandy, a student at a large western university from a working-class background, . . . unlike most White students, believed that discrimination is a central reason why Blacks are worse off than Whites in the USA today. She even narrated a case of racial discrimination that she witnessed. Mandy said that while she was shopping in a store, the clerk totally ignored her as soon as a Black man entered the store and pointed out that she "could've stuck anything in my backpack if I wanted to" (Interview # 504: 10). Mandy narrated what happened after as follows:

[The clerk] went over to the guns, picking out a gun, and I am standing there with money in my hand, and this guy goes "Can I help you?" to the guy. He says, "Do you need something, sir? Is there anything you need?" and just keep looking at him. And so I said, you know, "Here's my money (laughs) if you want to take it." And he's all "Sorry" and he is taking my money, but he's still keeping an eye on this guy, and I looked at the guy, and he had this look on his face that just broke my heart because you could tell . . . that he has to deal with this, and I had never had to deal with that. (Interview # 504: 10)

Whereas the typical White student interpreted Blacks' status as Blacks' own fault, Mandy acknowledged the role of discrimination and even understood the significance of White privilege. She states:

Oh, definitely [the overall inferior status of Black is] due to discrimination. It's not a coincidence . . . that a large population in this country lives in substandard housing, and, and, substandard jobs and schools . . . but I went to middle school in a richer neighborhood because my mom lied about where we lived, but I think that if you were Black in the community and tried to go over to a White school that was more wealthy . . . you wouldn't be able to do that because people would know exactly were you came from . . . and I just think that there is something at work keeping people in their spot. (Interview # 504: 11)

Finally, Mandy's answers concerning a hypothetical company's hiring practices, exemplifies how racial progressives framed racially perceived issues differently than reasonable racists. For example, Mandy supported the company's decision in the second case (White applicant scored 85 and Black applicant 80) and pointed out that "I thought that five percentage points wasn't enough of a difference in terms of a score" (Interview # 504: 18). When she was probed about whether these decisions could be construed as reverse racism, she said that "if the country [has] a history of hiring White people over Black people, then it's about damn time they hired a Black person, and if it's discriminatory toward the White person, too bad. They need a little dose of what it feels like" (Interview # 504: 17).

DISCUSSION

Four points emerged from our examination of White college students' views on fundamental racial issues—affirmative action, interracial marriage, and the significance of discrimination. *First*, White students exhibited more prejudiced views in the interview than in their survey responses. . . .

Second, although, based on the interview data, the respondents were more prejudiced than in the survey, they used a variety of semantic moves to save face. Interview respondents consistently used phrases such as "I don't know," "I am not sure," "I am not prejudiced," or "I agree and disagree," rather than explicitly expressing their racial views. . . . The large degree to which respondents used semantic moves was astounding. Our respondents used these moves from 68 percent of the time on the affirmative action question to 85 percent on the direct intermarriage and significance of discrimination questions. This amounts to a new *racetalk*. Unlike during the Jim Crow period, when Whites openly expressed their racial views (Dollard, 1938; Johnson, 1943, 1946; Myrdal, 1944), today Whites express their racial views in a sanitized way. . . .

Third, we showed how useful a discursive approach is for deciphering the meaning of Whites' racial views. . . . As we showed, our respondents were not truly ambivalent about crucial racial issues. Their hesitations were part of a strategic talk to avoid appearing racist. Our respondents did not seem to experience cognitive dissonance (Festinger, 1957) because their opposition to affirmative action and other racially coded programs was couched *within* the discourse of liberalism. Thus, the apparent discursive contradictions and hesitations ("Yes and no" or "I am not sure about that one") were *resolved* by turning liberalism into an *abstract* matter. This strategy allowed them to feel that it is the government and Blacks who are being unfair. Moreover, the students' strong principled position collapsed when issues of past discrimination were raised. That is, students moved from the philosophical principles of liberalism into practical rationality (Billig et al., 1988; Wetherell and Potter, 1992). Virtually no policy alternatives were envisioned as feasible for addressing the profound inequality existing between Blacks and Whites. This casts serious doubt on arguments that suggest that class-based or color-blind policies can unite Whites and racial minorities (Sniderman and Carmines,

1997; Wilson, 1987). Finally, 27 of the respondents used either "The past is the past" or "Present generations cannot be blamed for the mistakes of past generations" anti-egalitarian story lines in their responses to the question, "Do you believe that the history of oppression endured by minorities merits the intervention of the government on their behalf?". . . This discursive flexibility in moving from strict liberalism to practical matters is central to racial ideology. In order to work, all ideologies must allow some "room" to handle contradictions, exceptions, and change. Rather than being eternally fixed, ideologies should be conceived as processes or as ideological practices (Jackman, 1994; Wetherell and Potter, 1992).

Fourth, based on the analysis of our data, we found that the students' defense of White supremacy is no longer based on the parameters of Jim Crow racism but is instead based on a new racial ideology. As many analysts have pointed out (Bobo et al., 1997; Bonilla-Silva and Lewis, 1999; Essed, 1996; Prager, 1982), the crux of the post civil rights racial ideology is twofold. First, Whites resolutely deny that racial inequality is structural and, second, they explain it as the result of Blacks' "cultural deficiency" (e.g. they are lazy, their families are in shambles, their communities are bursting with crime). . . . Thus, not surprisingly, most of our White respondents blamed Blacks themselves for their lower status. At best, the students felt pity for Blacks, at worst many openly expressed contempt and hostility toward Blacks. . . .

We want to conclude this article with a comment on the politics of color-blind racism. The interview data reveal that the liberal, free market, and pragmatic rhetoric of color-blind racism allows Whites to defend White supremacy in an apparently nonracial manner (Bobo and Hutchings, 1996; Bobo and Smith, 1994; Carmines and Merriman, 1993; Kluegel and Bobo, 1993; Jackman, 1994). Color-blind racism allows Whites to appear "not racist" ("I believe in equality"), preserve their privileged status ("Discrimination ended in the sixties!"), blame Blacks for their lower status ("If you guys just work hard!"), and criticize any institutional approach—such as affirmative action—that attempts to ameliorate racial inequality ("Reverse discrimination!"). Hence, the task of progressive social analysts is to blow the whistle on color-blind racism. We must unmask color-blind racists by showing how their views, arguments, and lifestyles are (White) color-coded. We must also show how their color-blind rationales defend systemic White privilege. Analytically this implies developing new questions for our surveys and using new strategies for the analysis of contemporary racial attitudes. Politically it implies that we must concentrate our efforts in fighting the new racists, all the nice Whites who tell us "I am not a racist but . . ."

NOTES

1. Semantic moves are "strategically managed relations between propositions" (Van Dijk, 1987: 86). They are called *semantic* because the strategic function of a proposition is determined by the "content of speech act sequences," that is, by the link between a proposition and a preceding or subsequent proposition. The overall goal of these moves, the *semantic strategy*, is to save face, that is, to avoid appearing "racist."

2. By racial ideology we mean the *changing* dogma that provides "the rationalization for social, political, and economic interactions between the races" (Bonilla-Silva, 1997: 474). The central function of racial ideology is explaining and, ultimately, justifying racial inequality (Prager, 1982). Unlike the notion of attitudes, which is bounded by methodological individualism, the notion of racial ideology regards the beliefs of actors as fundamentally shaped by their group interests. Whereas attitudes ultimately represent degrees of affect toward non-Whites, racial ideology signifies the collective views and interests of Whites. Thus it is possible for Whites to have non-prejudiced attitudes and still subscribe to the central themes of the dominant racial ideology (Hartman and Husband, 1974: 54–5; Pettigrew, 1985).

3. This approach is congruent with the symbolic interaction tradition in sociology. As symbolic interactionists, we believe that "the meanings that things have for human beings are central in their own right," that those meanings "are socially produced through interaction with one's fellows, and that in the process of interaction, the meanings of things are interpreted and reinterpreted" (Blumer, 1969: 2–5). However, unlike many followers of this tradition, we pay attention to how the larger social system produces the themes and boundaries of the meanings produced through interaction.

4. Although we recognize that all people engage in what social psychologists label as *self-presentation,* it is clear that our subjects primarily resorted to *ideal* and *tactical* rather than *authentic* self-presentation (Baumeister, 1982; Swann, 1987).

5. The specific wording of the three questions was the following:

(a) Suppose that two candidates apply for a job at the ABZ company, a company that has a workforce that is 97 percent White. They take an examination and both applicants score 80 (70 was the minimum score required to pass the test). The company decides to hire the Black applicant over the White applicant because the company is concerned with the lack of diversity of its workforce. Under these conditions, do you agree or disagree with the decision of the ABZ company?

(b) Suppose that the Black applicant in the above case scored 80 on the exam and the White candidate scored 85 (70 was the minimum score required to pass the test). The company, despite the fact that the White applicant did slightly better than the Black applicant, decided to hire the Black applicant because of its concern with the lack of diversity of its workforce. Under these conditions, do you agree with the decision of the ABZ company?

(c) Suppose that the decision of hiring the Black applicant over the White applicant in the previous two cases was justified by the ABZ company not in terms of the need to diversify its workforce but because the company had discriminated in the past against Blacks in terms of hiring. Under these conditions, would you agree or disagree with the decision of the ABZ company?

6. The specific wording of the questions was:

(1) Some Blacks claim that they face a great deal of racism in their daily lives. Many people claim that this is not the case. What do you think?

(2) Many Blacks and other minorities claim that they do not get access to good jobs because of discrimination and that, when they get the jobs, they are not promoted at the same speed and to the same jobs as their White peers. What do you think?

(3) On average, Blacks have worse jobs, income, and housing than Whites. Do you think that this is due to discrimination or something else?

(4) Many Whites explain the status of Blacks in this country today as a result of Blacks lacking motivation, not having the proper work ethic, or being lazy. What do you think?

(5) How do you explain the fact that very few minorities are at the top of the occupational structure in this country?

7. The specific wording of the questions was:

(1) Some Blacks claim that they face a great deal of racism in their daily lives. Many people claim this is not the case. What do you think?

(2) Many Blacks and other minorities claim that they do not get access to good jobs because of discrimination and that, when they get the jobs, they are not promoted at the same speed and to the same jobs as their White peers. What do you think?

(3) On average, Blacks have worse jobs, income, and housing than Whites. Do you think that this is due to discrimination or something else?

(4) Many Whites explain the status of Blacks in this country today as a result of Blacks lacking motivation, not having the proper work ethic, or being lazy. What do you think?

(5) How do you explain the fact that very few minorities are at the top of the occupational structure in this country?

References

Anderson, Barbara, Silver, Brian and Abramson, Paul (1988a) 'The Effects of Race of the Interviewer on Measures of Electoral Participation by Blacks in SRC National Election Studies,' *Public Opinion Quarterly* 52(1): 53–83.

Anderson, Barbara, Silver, Brian and Abramson, Paul (1988b) 'The Effects of the Race of Interviewer on Race-Related Attitudes of Black Respondents in SCR/CPS National Election Studies,' *Public Opinion Quarterly* 52(3): 289–324.

Baumeister, R. F. (1982) 'A Self-Presentational View of Social Phenomena,' *Psychological Bulletin* 91(1): 3–26.

Billig, Michael, Condor, Susan, Edwards, Derek, Gane, Mike, Middleton, David and Radley, Alan (1988) *Ideological Dilemmas: A Social Psychology of Everyday Thinking*. London: Sage.

Blauner, Bob (1989) *Black Lives, White Lives: Three Decades of Race Relations in America*. Berkeley and Los Angeles: University of California Press.

Blumer, Herbert (1967) *Symbolic Interactionism: Perspective and Method*. Englewood Cliffs, NJ: Prentice Hall.

Bobo, Lawrence, and Hutchings, Vincent (1996) 'Perceptions of Racial Competition in a Multiracial Setting,' *American Sociological Review* 61(6), December: 951–72.

Bobo, Lawrence and Kluegel, James R. (1993) 'Opposition to Race-Targeting: Self-Interest, Stratification Ideology, or Racial Attitudes?,' *American Sociological Review* 58:443–64.

Bobo, Lawrence and Kluegel, James R. (1997) 'Status, Ideology, and Dimensions of Whites' Racial Beliefs and Attitudes; Progress and Stagnation,' in Steven A. Tuch and Jack Martin (eds) *Racial Attitudes in the 1990s: Continuity and Change*, pp. 93–120. Westport, CT: Praeger.

Bobo, Lawrence, Kluegel, James and Smith, Ryan (1997) 'Laissez faire Racism: The Crystallization of a Kinder, Gentler, Antiblack Ideology,' in Steven A. Tuch and Jack Martin (eds) *Racial Attitudes in the 1990s: Continuity and Change*, pp. 15–42. Westport, CT: Praeger.

Bonilla-Silva, Eduardo (1997) 'Rethinking Racism: Toward a Structural Interpretation,' *American Sociological Review*, Vol. 62(3), June: 465–80.

Bonilla-Silva, Eduardo (1998) 'Racial Attitudes or Racial Ideology: Toward a New Paradigm for Examining Whites' Racial Views,' unpublished manuscript, Texas A&M University.

Bonilla-Silva, Eduardo and Lewis, Amanda E. (1999) 'The New Racism: Racial Structure in the United States, 1960s–1990s,' in Paul Wong (ed.) *Race, Ethnicity, and Nationality in the United States: Toward the Twenty-First Century*, pp. 55–101, Boulder, CO: Westview Press.

Brooks, Roy L. (1990) *Rethinking the American Race Problem*. Berkeley: University of California Press.

Brown, Gillian, and Yule, George (1983) *Discourse Analysis*. Cambridge: Cambridge University Press.

Carmichael, Stokely and Hamilton, Charles V. (1967) *Black Power: The Politics of Liberation in America*. New York: Vintage Books.

Carmines, Edward G. and Merriman, W. Richard, Jr. (1993) 'The Changing American Dilemma: Liberal Values and Racial Polices,' in Paul M. Sniderman, Philip E. Tetlock and Edward G. Carmines (eds) *Prejudice, Politics, and the American Dilemma*, pp. 237–55. Stanford, CA: Stanford University Press.

Converse, Phillip E. (1964) 'The Nature of Belief Systems in Mass Publics,' in David E. Apter (ed.) *Ideology and Discontent,* pp. 206–61, London: Free Press of Glencoe.

Converse, Phillip E. (1970) 'Attitudes and Non-attitudes: Continuation of a Dialogue,' in E.R. Tufte (ed.) *The Quantitative Analysis of Social Problems,* pp. 168–89. Reading, MA: Addison-Wesley.

Converse, Phillip E. (1997) 'Comment: The Status of Nonattitudes.' *American Political Science Review* 68: 650–66.

Crenshaw, Kimberlé Williams (1997) 'Color-blind Dreams and Racial Nightmares: Reconfiguring Racism in the Post-Civil Rights Era,' in Toni Morrison and Claudia Brodsky Lacour (eds) *Birth of a Nation'hood,* pp. 97–68. New York: Pantheon.

Dollard, John (1937) *Caste and Class in a Southern Town.* London: Yale University Press.

Dovidio, John F. and Gaertner, Samuel L. (1986) 'How Do Attitudes Guide Behavior?' in R.M. Sorrentino and E.T. Higgins (eds) *The Handbook of Motivation and Cognition: Foundations of Social Behavior,* pp. 204–43. New York: Guilford Press.

Dovidio, John F., Mann, J. F. and Gaertner, Samuel L. (1989) 'Resistance to Affirmative Action: The Implications of Aversive Racism,' in F. Blanchard and F. Crosby (eds) *Affirmative Action in Perspective,* pp. 81–102. New York: Springer-Verlag.

Edley, Christopher Jr. (1996) *Not All Black and White: Affirmative Action and American Values.* New York: Hill and Wang.

Essed, Philomena (1996) *Diversity: Gender, Color, and Culture.* Amherst, MA: University of Massachusetts Press.

Fanon, Frantz (1967) *Black Skins, White Masks.* New York: Grove Press.

Feagin, Joe and Sikes, Melvin (1994) *Living With Racism: The Black Middle Class Experience.* Boston, MA: Beacon Press.

Feagin, Joe and Vera, Hernan (1995) *White Racism: The Basics.* New York: Routledge.

Festinger, Leon (1957) *A Theory of Cognitive Dissonance.* Evanston, IL: Row, Peterson, and Company.

Firebaugh, Glen and Davis, Kenneth E. (1988) 'Trends in Anti-Black Prejudice, 1972–1984: Region and Cohort Effects,' *American Journal of Sociology* 94: 251–72.

Glass Ceiling Commission (1995) *Good for Business: Making Full Use of the Nation's Human Capital.* Washington, DC: Government Printing Office.

Groves, Robert, Fultz, Nancy H. and Martin, Elizabeth (1992) 'Direct Questioning About Comprehension in a Survey Setting,' in Judith M. Tanur (ed.) *Questions About Questions: Inquiries Into the 4 Cognitive Bases of Surveys,* pp. 49–61. New York: Russell Sage Foundation.

Hartman, Paul and Husband, Charles (1974) *Racism and the Mass Media: A Study of the Role of the Mass Media in the Formation of White Beliefs and Attitudes in Britain.* London: David Porter.

Herring, Cedric, and Collins, Sharon (1995) 'Retreat from Equal Opportunity? The Case of Affirmative Action,' in Michael Peter Smith and Joe Feagin (eds) *The Bubbling Cauldron,* pp. 163–81. Minneapolis: University of Minnesota Press.

Hernton, Calvin C. (1988) *Sex and Racism in America.* New York: Anchor Books/Doubleday.

Hochschild, Jennifer (1995) *Facing Up to the American Dream: Race, Class, and the Soul of the Nation,* Princeton. NJ: Princeton University Press.

Hyman, Herbert H. and Sheatsley, Paul B. (1964) 'Attitudes Toward Desegregation' *Scientific American* 195 (Dec): 85–9.

Jackman, Mary R. (1994) *Velvet Glove: Paternalism and Conflict in Gender, Class, and Race Relations.* Berkeley: University of California Press.

Jackman, Mary R. (1996) 'Individualism self-interest, and White Racism', *Social Science Quarterly 77* (4): 760–7.

Johnson, Charles S. (1943) *Patterns of Negro Segregation.* New York: Harper and Brothers.

Johnson, Charles S. (1946) *Racial Attitudes: Interviews Revealing Attitudes of Northern and Southern White Persons of a Wide Range of Occupational and Educational Levels, Toward Negroes.* Nashville, TN: Social Science Institute, Fisk University.

Jordan, Withrop D. (1977) *White Over Black: American Attitudes Toward the Negro, 1550–1812.* New York: W.W. Norton.

Kane, Emily and Macaulay, Laura (1993) 'Interviewer Gender and Gender Attitudes,' *Public Opinion Quarterly* 57(1): 1–28.

Katz, Irwin, Wackenhut, Joyce and Hass, R. Glen (1986) 'Racial Ambivalence, Value Duality, and Behavior,' in John Dovidio and Samuel L. Gaertner (eds) *Prejudice, Discrimination, and Racism,* pp. 35–60. Orlando, FL: Academic Press.

Kinder, Donald and Sanders, Lynn M. (1996) *Divided by Color: Racial Politics and Democratic Ideals.* Chicago and London: University of Chicago Press.

Kluegel, James R. (1990). 'Trends in Whites' Explanations of the Gap Black-White

Socioeconomic Status, 1977–1989,' *American Sociological Review* 55(4), August: 512–25.

Kluegel, James R. and Smith, Eliot R. (1982) 'Whites' Beliefs about Blacks' Opportunity,' *American Sociological Review* 47: 518–32.

Kluegel, James R. and Smith, Eliot R. (1986) *Beliefs About Inequality: Americans' Views of What Is and What Ought to Be.* New York: Aldine de Gruyter.

Kovel, Joel (1984) *White Racism: A Psychohistory.* New York: Columbia University Press.

Krysan, Maria (1998) 'Privacy and the Expression of White Racial Attitudes,' *Public Opinion Quarterly* 62(4): 506–44.

Lipset, Seymour M. (1996) *American Exceptionalism: A Double-Edged Sword.* New York and London: W. W. Norton.

Lipset, Seymour and Schneider, William (1978) 'The Bakke Case: How Would It Be Decided at the Bar of Public Opinion,' *Public Opinion* 1(1): 38–44.

MacLeod, Jay (1995) *Ain't No Makin' It: Aspirations and Attainment in a Low-Income Neighborhood.* Boulder, CO: Westview Press.

Massey, Douglas S. and Denton, Nancy A. (1993) *Segregation and the Making of the Underclass.* Cambridge, MA: Harvard University Press.

Myers, Samuel L. (1993) 'Measuring and Detecting Discrimination in the Post-Civil Rights Era,' *in John H. Stanfield II and Rutledge M. Dennis (eds) Race and Ethnicity in Research,* pp. 172–97. Newbury Park, CA: Sage.

Myrdal, Gunnar (1944) *An American Dilemma: The Negro Problem and Modern Democracy I.* New York and London: Harper and Brothers Publishers.

Nieme, Richard G, Mueller, John and Smith, Tom W. (1989) *Trends in Public Opinion: A Compendium of Survey Data.* New York: Greenwood Press.

Orfield, Gary and Eaton, Susan, E. (1996) *Dismantling Desegregation: The Quiet Reversal of Brown v. Board of Education.* New York: New York Press.

Pettigrew, Thomas F. (1985) 'New Black–White Patterns: How Best to Conceptualize Them?,' *Annual Review of Sociology* 11: 329–46.

Prager, Jeffrey (1982) 'American Racial Ideology as Collective Representation,' *Ethnic and Racial Studies* 5(1), January: 99–119.

Rieder, Jonathan (1985) *Carnasarie: The Jews and Italians of Brooklyn against Liberalism.* Cambridge, MA: Harvard University Press.

Rubin, Lillian (1994) *Families on the Fault Line: America's Working Class Speaks about the Family, the Economy, Race, and Ethnicity.* New York: HarperCollins.

Schuman, Howard and Steeh, Charlotte (1996) 'The Complexity of Racial Attitudes in America,' in Silvia Pedraza and Ruben Rumbaut (eds) *Origins and Destinies,* pp. 455–69. Belmont, CA: Wadsworth.

Schuman, Howard, Steeh, Charlotte and Bobo, Lawrence (1988) *Racial Attitudes in America: Trends and Interpretations.* Boston, MA: Harvard University Press.

Schuman, Howard, Steeh, Charlotte, Bobo, Lawrence and Krysan, Maria (1997) *Racial Attitudes in America: Trends and Interpretations,* rev edn, Boston, MA: Harvard University Press.

Sigall, Harold and Page, Richard (1971) 'Current Stereotypes: A Little Fading, A Little Faking,' *Journal of Personality and Social Psychology* 18(2), January: 247–55.

Smith, Robert C. (1995) *Racism in the Post Civil Rights Period: Now You See It, Now You Don't.* Albany: State University of New York Press.

Smith, Tom W. and Sheatsley, Paul B. (1984) 'American Attitudes toward Race Relations,' *Public Opinion* 7(5): 14–15, 50–3.

Sniderman, Paul M. and Piazza, Thomas (1993) *The Scare of Race.* Boston, MA: Harvard University Press.

Sniderman, Paul M. and Carmines, Edward G. (1997) *Reaching Beyond Race.* Cambridge, MA: Harvard University Press.

Steeh, Charlotte and Krysan, Maria (1996) 'Affirmative Action and the Public, 1970–1995,' *Public Opinion Quarterly* 60: 128–58.

Swann, W. B., Jr. (1987) 'Identity Negotiation: Where Two Roads Meet,' *Journal of Personality and Social Psychology* 53(6): 1038–51.

Terkel, Studs (1993) *Race: How Black and Whites Think and Feel About The American Obsession.* New York: Doubleday.

Van Dijk, Teun A. (1977) *Text and Context Explorations in the Semantics and Pragmatics of Discourse.* London and New York: Longman.

Van Dijk, Teun A. (1984) *Prejudice in Discourse: An Analysis of Ethnic Prejudice in Cognition and Conversation.* Amsterdam and Philadelphia, PA: John Benjamins Publishing Co.

Van Dijk, Teun A. (1987) *Communicating Racism: Ethnic Prejudice in Thought and Talk.* Beverly Hills, CA: Sage.

Van Dijk, Teun A. (1997) 'Political Discourse and Racism: Describing Others in Western Parliaments,' in Stephen Harold Riggins (ed.) *The Language and Politics of Exclusion: Others in Discourse,* pp. 31–64. Thousands Oaks, CA: Sage.

Weis, Lois, and Fine, Michelle (1996) 'Narrating the 1980s and 1990s: Voices of Poor and Working-Class White and African American Men,' *Anthropology and Education Quarterly* 27(4): 493–516.

Wellman, David (1977) *Portraits of White Racism*. Berkeley, CA: University of California Press.

Wetherell, Margaret and Jonathan Potter (1992) *Mapping the Language of Racism: Discourse and the Legitimation of Exploitation*. New York: Columbia University Press.

Wicker, Tom (1996) *Tragic Failure: Racial Integration in America*. New York: William Morrow and Company.

Wilson, William Julius (1987) *The Truly Disadvantaged*. Chicago, IL: University of Chicago Press.

DISCUSSION QUESTIONS

1. What is the "new racetalk" that the authors' analysis reveals in this essay? Do these results indicate that prejudice has reduced or has merely taken a new form that is equally, or even more, harmful?

2. Why do you think a sizeable group of whites say they support interracial marriages but lead segregated lives? Of the different possibilities in Table 5.4 for views on interracial marriage and type of life (integrated/segregated) where would you place yourself and why?

3. What is meant by "color-blind racism"? How can one be racist if one is "color-blind"? What are the alternatives?

4. Why do you think so many whites do not believe racial discrimination exists? What are the policy implications of this pattern?

RACE AND CRIMINALIZATION: BLACK AMERICANS AND THE PUNISHMENT INDUSTRY

Angela Davis

In this post-civil-rights era, as racial barriers in high economic and political realms are apparently shattered with predictable regularity, race itself becomes an increasingly proscribed subject. In the dominant political discourse it is no longer acknowledged as a pervasive structural phenomenon, requiring the continuation of such strategies as affirmative action, but rather is represented primarily as a complex of prejudicial attitudes, which carry equal weight across all racial boundaries. Black leadership is thus often discredited and the identification of race as a public, political issue itself called into question through the invocation of, and application of the epithet "black racist" to such figures as Louis Farrakhan and Khalid Abdul Muhammad. Public debates about the role of the state that once focused very sharply and openly on issues of "race" and racism are now expected to unfold in the absence of any direct acknowledgment of the persistence—and indeed further entrenchment—of racially structured power relationships. Because race is ostracized from some of the most impassioned debates of this period, their racialized character becomes increasingly difficult to identify by those who are unable—or do not want—to decipher the encoded language. This means that hidden racist arguments can be mobilized readily across racial boundaries and political alignments. Political positions once easily defined as conservative, liberal, and sometimes even radical therefore have a tendency to lose their distinctiveness in the face of the seductions of this camouflaged racism.

President Clinton chose the date of the Million Man March, convened by Minister Louis Farrakhan of the Nation of Islam, to issue a call for a "national conversation on race," borrowing ironically the exact words Lani Guinier (whose nomination for Assistant Attorney

General in charge of civil rights he had previously withdrawn because her writings focused too sharply on issues of race).[1] Guinier's ideas had been so easily dismissed because of the prevailing ideological equation of the "end of racism" with the removal of all allusions to race. If conservative positions argue that race consciousness itself impedes the process of solving the problem of race—i.e., achieving race blindness—then Clinton's speech indicated an attempt to reconcile the two, positing race consciousness as a means of moving toward race blindness. "'There are too many today, white and black, on the left and the right, on the street comers and radio waves, who seek to sow division for their own purposes. To them I say: 'No more. We must be one.'"

While Clinton did acknowledge "the awful history and stubborn persistence of racism," his remarks foregrounded those reasons for the "racial divide" that "are rooted in the fact that we still haven't learned to talk frankly, to listen carefully and to work together across racial lines." Race, he insisted, is not about government, but about the hearts of people. Of course, it would be absurd to deny the degree to which racism infects deep and multiple ways the national psyche. However, the relegation of race to matters of the heart tends to render it increasingly difficult to identify the deep structural entrenchment of contemporary racism.

When the structural character of racism is ignored in discussions about crime and the rising population of incarcerated people, the racial imbalance in jails and prisons is treated as a contingency, at best as a product of the "culture of poverty," and at worst as proof of an assumed black monopoly on criminality. The high proportion of black people in the criminal justice system is thus normalized and neither the state nor the general public is required to talk about and act on the meaning of that racial imbalance. Thus Republican and Democratic elected officials alike have successfully called for laws mandating life sentences for three-time "criminals," without having to answer for the racial implications of these laws. By relying on the alleged "race-blindness" of such laws, black people are surreptitiously constructed as racial subjects, thus manipulated, exploited, and abused, while the structural persistence of racism—albeit in changed forms—in social and economic institutions, and in the national culture as a whole, is adamantly denied.

Crime is thus one of the masquerades behind which "race," with all its menacing ideological complexity, mobilizes old public fears and creates new ones. The current anti-crime debate takes place within a reified mathematical realm—a strategy reminiscent of Malthus's notion of the geometrical increase in population and the arithmetical increase in food sources, thus the inevitability of poverty and the means of suppressing it: war, disease, famine, and natural disasters. As a matter of fact, the persisting neo-Malthusian approach to population control, which, instead of seeking to solve those pressing social problems that result in real pain and suffering in people's lives, calls for the elimination of those suffering lives—finds strong resonances in the public discussion about expurgating the "nation" of crime. These discussions include arguments deployed by those who are leading the call for more prisons and employ statistics in the same fetishistic and misleading way as Malthus did more than two centuries ago. Take for example James Wooten's comments in the *Heritage Foundation State Backgrounder:*

> If the 55 percent of the estimated 800,000 current state and federal prisoners who are violent offenders were subject to serving 85 percent of their sentence, and assuming that those violent offenders would have committed 10 violent crimes a year while on the street, then the number of crimes prevented each year by truth in sentencing would be 4,000,000. That would be over 2/3 of the 6,000,000 violent crimes reported.[2]

In *Reader's Digest,* Senior Editor Eugene H. Methvin writes:

> If we again double the present federal and state prison population—to somewhere between 1 million and 1.5 million and leave our city and country jail population at the present 400,000, we will break the back of America's thirty-year crime wave.[3]

The real human beings—a vastly disproportionate number of whom are black and Latino/a men and women—designated by these numbers in a seemingly race-neutral way are deemed fetishistically exchangeable with the crimes they have already committed or will allegedly commit in the future. The real impact of imprisonment on their lives never need be examined. The inevitable part played by the punishment industry in the reproduction of crime never need be discussed. The dangerous and indeed fascistic trend toward progressively greater numbers of hidden, incarcerated human populations is itself rendered invisible. All that matters is the elimination of crime—and you get rid of crime by getting rid of people who, according to the prevailing racial common sense, are the most likely people to whom criminal acts will be attributed. Never mind that if this strategy is seriously and consistently pursued, the majority of young black men and a fast-growing proportion of young black women will spend a good portion of their lives behind walls and bars in order to serve as a reminder that the state is aggressively confronting its enemy.[4]

While I do not want to locate a response to these arguments on the same level of mathematical abstraction and fetishism I have been problematizing, it is helpful, I think, to consider how many people are presently incarcerated or whose lives are subject to the direct surveillance of the criminal justice system. There are already approximately 1 million people in state and federal prisons in the United States, not counting the 500,000 in city and county jails or the 600,000 on parole or the 3 million people on probation or the 60,000 young people in juvenile facilities. Which is to say that there are presently over 5.1 million people either incarcerated, on parole, or on probation. Many of those presently on probation or parole would be behind bars under the conditions of the recently passed crime bill. According to the Sentencing Project, even before the passage of the crime bill, black people were 7.8 times more likely to be imprisoned than whites.[5] The Sentencing Project's most recent report[6] indicates that 32.2 percent of young black men and 12.3 percent of young Latino men between the ages of twenty and twenty-nine are either in prison, in jail, or on probation or parole. This is in comparison with 6.7 percent of young white men. A total of 827,440 young African-American males are

under the supervision of the criminal justice system, at a cost of $6 billion per year. A major strength of the 1995 report, as compared to its predecessor, is its acknowledgment that the racialized impact of the criminal justice system is also gendered and that the relatively smaller number of African-American women drawn into the system should not relieve us of the responsibility of understanding the encounter of gender and race in arrest and incarceration practices. Moreover, the increases in women's contact with the criminal justice system have been even more dramatic than those of men.

> The 78 percent increase in criminal justice control rates for black women was more than double the increase for black men and for white women, and more than nine times the increase for white men. . . . Although research on women of color in the criminal justice system is limited, existing data and research suggest that it is the combination of race and sex effects that is at the root of the trends which appear in our data. For example, while the number of blacks and Hispanics in prison is growing at an alarming rate, the rate of increase for women is even greater. Between 1980 and 1992 the female prison population increased 276 percent, compared to 163 percent for men. Unlike men of color, women of color thus belong to two groups that are experiencing particular dramatic growth in their contact with the criminal justice system.[7]

It has been estimated that by the year 2000 the number of people imprisoned will surpass 2 million, a grossly disproportionate number of whom will be black people, and that the cost will be over $40 billion a year,[8] a figure that is reminiscent of the way the military budget devoured—and, continues to devour—the country's resources. This out-of-control punishment industry is an extremely effective criminalization industry, for the racial imbalance in incarcerated populations is not recognized as evidence of structural racism, but rather is invoked as a consequence of the assumed criminality of black people. In other words, the criminalization process works so well precisely because of the hidden logic of racism. Racist logic is deeply entrenched in the nation's material and psychic structures. It is something with which we all are very familiar. The logic, in fact, can persist, even when direct allusions to "race" are removed.

Even those communities that are most deeply injured by this racist logic have learned how to rely upon it, particularly when open allusions to race are not necessary. Thus, in the absence of broad, radical grassroots movements in poor black communities so devastated by new forms of youth-perpetrated violence, the ideological options are extremely sparse. Often there are no other ways to express collective rage and despair but to demand that police sweep the community clean of crack and Uzis, and of people who use and sell drugs and wield weapons. Ironically, Carol Moseley-Braun, the first black woman senator in our nation's history, was an enthusiastic sponsor of the Senate Anticrime Bill, whose passage in November 1993 paved the way for the August 25, 1994, passage of the bill by the House. Or perhaps there is little irony here. It may be precisely because there is a Carol Moseley-Braun in the Senate and a Clarence Thomas in the Supreme Court—and concomitant class differentiations and other factors responsible for far more heterogeneity in black communities than at any other time in this country's history—that implicit consent to antiblack racist logic (not to speak of racism toward other groups) becomes far more widespread among black people. Wahneema Lubiano's explorations of the complexities of state domination as it operates within and through the subjectivities of those who are the targets of this domination facilitates an understanding of this dilemma.[9]

Borrowing the title of Cornel West's recent work, race *matters*. Moreover, it matters in ways that are far more threatening and simultaneously less discernible than those to which we have grown accustomed. Race matters inform, more than ever, the ideological and material structures of US society. And, as the current discourses on crime, welfare, and immigration reveal, race, gender, and class matter enormously in the continuing elaboration of public policy and its impact on the real lives of human beings.

And how does race matter? Fear has always been an integral component of racism. The ideological reproduction of a fear of black people, whether economically or sexually grounded, is rapidly gravitating toward and being grounded in a fear of crime. A question to be raised in this context is whether and how the increasing fear of crime—this ideologically produced fear of crime—serves to render racism simultaneously more invisible and more virulent. Perhaps one way to approach an answer to this question is to consider how this fear of crime effectively summons black people to imagine black people as the enemy. How many black people present at this conference have successfully extricated ourselves from the ideological power of the figure of the young black male as criminal—or at least seriously confronted it? The lack of a significant black presence in the rather feeble opposition to the "three strikes, you're out" bills, which have been proposed and/or passed in forty states already, evidences the disarming effect of this ideology.

California is one of the states that has passed the "three strikes, you're out" bill. Immediately after the passage of that bill, Governor Pete Wilson began to argue for a "two strikes, you're out" bill. Three, he said, is too many. Soon we will hear calls for "one strike, you're out." Following this mathematical regression, we can imagine that at some point the hardcore anticrime advocates will be arguing that to stop the crime wave, we can't wait until even one crime is committed. Their slogan will be: "Get them before the first strike!" And because certain populations have already been criminalized, there will be those who say, "We know who the real criminals are—let's get them before they have a chance to act out their criminality."

The fear of crime has attained a status that bears a sinister similarity to the fear of communism as it came to restructure social perceptions during the fifties and sixties. The figure of the "criminal"—the racialized figure of the criminal—has come to represent the most menacing enemy of "American society." Virtually anything is acceptable—torture, brutality, vast expenditures of public funds—as long as it is done in the name of public safety. Racism has always found an easy route from its embeddedness in social structures to the psyches of collectives and individuals precisely because it mobilizes deep fears. While explicit, old-style racism may be increasingly socially unacceptable—precisely as a result of antiracist movements over the last forty years—this does not mean that US society has been purged of racism. In fact, racism is more deeply embedded in socio-economic structures, and the vast populations of incarcerated people of color is dramatic evidence of the way racism systematically structures economic relations. At the same time, this structural racism is rarely recognized as "racism." What we have come to recognize as open, explicit racism has in many ways begun to be replaced by a secluded, camouflaged kind of racism, whose influence on people's daily lives is as pervasive and systematic as the explicit forms of racism associated with the era of the struggle for civil rights.

The ideological space for the proliferations of this racialized fear of crime has been opened by the transformations in international politics created by the fall of the European socialist countries. Communism is no longer the quintessential enemy against which the nation imagines its identity. This space is now inhabited by ideological constructions of crime, drugs, immigration, and welfare. Of course, the enemy within is far more dangerous than the enemy without, and a black enemy within is the most dangerous of all.

Because of the tendency to view it as an abstract site into which all manner of undesirables are deposited, the prison is the perfect site for the simultaneous production and concealment of racism. The abstract character of the public perception of prisons militates against an engagement with the real issues afflicting the communities from which prisoners are drawn in such disproportionate numbers. This is the ideological work that the prison performs—it relieves us of the responsibility of seriously engaging with the problems of late capitalism, of transnational capitalism. The naturalization of black people as criminals thus also erects ideological barriers to an understanding of the connections between late twentieth-century structural racism and the globalization of capital.

The vast expansion of the power of capitalist corporations over the lives of people of color and poor people in general has been accompanied by a waning anticapitalist consciousness. As capital moves with ease across national borders, legitimized by recent trade agreements

such as NAFTA [North American Free Trade Agreement] and GATT [General Agreement on Tariffs and Trade], corporations are allowed to close shop in the United States and transfer manufacturing operations to nations providing cheap labor pools. In fleeing organized labor in the US to avoid paying higher wages and benefits, they leave entire communities in shambles, consigning huge numbers of people to joblessness, leaving them prey to the drug trade, destroying the economic base of these communities, thus affecting the education system, social welfare—and turning the people who live in those communities into perfect candidates for prison. At the same time, they create an economic demand for prisons, which stimulates the economy, providing jobs in the correctional industry for people who often come from the very populations that are criminalized by this process. It is a horrifying and self-reproducing cycle.

Ironically, prisons themselves are becoming a source of cheap labor that attracts corporate capitalism—as yet on a relatively small scale—in a way that parallels the attraction unorganized labor in Third World countries exerts. A statement by Michael Lamar Powell, a prisoner in Capshaw, Alabama, dramatically reveals this new development:

> I cannot go on strike, nor can I unionize. I am not covered by workers' compensation of the Fair Labor Standards Act. I agree to work late-night and weekend shifts. I do just what I am told, no matter what it is. I am hired and fired at will, and I am not even paid minimum wage: I earn one dollar a month. I cannot even voice grievances or complaints, except at the risk of incurring arbitrary discipline or some covert retaliation.
>
> You need not worry about NAFTA and your jobs going to Mexico and other Third World countries. I will have at least five percent of your jobs by the end of this decade.
>
> I am called prison labor. I am the New American Worker.[10]

This "new American worker" will be drawn from the ranks of a racialized population whose historical superexploitation—from the era of slavery to the present—has been legitimized by racism. At the same time, the expansion of convict labor is accompanied in some states by the old paraphernalia of ankle chains that symbolically links convict labor with slave labor. At least three states—Alabama, Florida, and Arizona—have reinstituted the chain gang. Moreover, as Michael Powell so incisively reveals, there is a new dimension to the racism inherent in this process, which structurally links the superexploitation of prison labor to the globalization of capital.

In California, whose prison system is the largest in the country and one of the largest in the world, the passage of an inmate labor initiative in 1990 has presented businesses seeking cheap labor with opportunities uncannily similar to those in Third World countries. As of June 1994, a range of companies were employing prison labor in nine California prisons. Under the auspices of the Joint Venture Program, work now being performed on prison grounds includes computerized telephone messaging, dental apparatus assembly, computer data entry, plastic parts fabrication, electronic component manufacturing at the Central California Women's facility at Chowchilla, security glass manufacturing, swine production, oak furniture manufacturing, and the production of stainless steel tanks and equipment. In a California Corrections Department brochure designed to promote the program, it is described as "an innovative public-private partnership that makes good business sense."[11] According to the owner of Tower Communications, whom the brochure quotes,

> The operation is cost effective, dependable and trouble free. . . . Tower Communications has successfully operated a message center utilizing inmates on the grounds of a California state prison. If you're a business leader planning expansion, considering relocation because of a deficient labor pool, starting a new enterprise, look into the benefits of using inmate labor.

The employer benefits listed by the brochure include

> federal and state tax incentives; no benefit package (retirement pay, vacation pay, sick leave, medical benefits); long-term lease agreements at far below market value costs; discount rates on

Workers Compensation; build a consistent, qualified work force; on call labor pool (no car breakdowns, no babysitting problems); option of hiring job-ready ex-offenders and minimizing costs; becoming a partner in public safety.

There is a major, yet invisible, racial supposition in such claims about the profitability of a convict labor force. The acceptability of the superexploitation of convict labor is largely based on the historical conjuncture of racism and incarceration practices. The already disproportionately black convict labor force will become increasingly black if the racially imbalanced incarceration practices continue.

The complicated yet unacknowledged structural presence of racism in the US punishment industry also includes the fact that the punishment industry which sequesters ever larger sectors of the black population attracts vast amounts of capital. Ideologically, as I have argued, the racialized fear of crime has begun to succeed the fear of communism. This corresponds to a structural tendency for capital that previously flowed toward the military industry to now move toward the punishment industry. The ease with which suggestions are made for prison construction costing in the multibillions of dollars is reminiscent of the military buildup: economic mobilization to defeat communism has turned into economic mobilization to defeat crime. The ideological construction of crime is thus complemented and bolstered by the material construction of jails and prisons. The more jails and prisons are constructed, the greater the fear of crime, and the greater the fear of crime, the stronger the cry for more jails and prisons, ad infinitum. The law enforcement industry bears remarkable parallels to the military industry (just as there are anti-communist resonances in the anti-crime campaign). This connection between the military industry and the punishment industry is revealed in a May 1994 *Wall Street Journal* article entitled "Making Crime Pay: The Cold War of the '90s":

> Parts of the defense establishment are cashing in, too, scenting a logical new line of business to help them offset military cutbacks. Westinghouse Electric Corp., Minnesota Mining and

Manufacturing Co., GDE Systems (a division of the old General Dynamics) and Alliant Techsystems Inc., for instance, are pushing crimefighting equipment and have created special divisions to retool their defense technology for America's streets.

According to the article, a conference sponsored by the National Institute of Justice, the research arm of the justice Department, was organized around the theme "Law Enforcement Technology in the Twenty-first Century." The Secretary of Defense was a major presenter at this conference, which explored topics like "the role of the defense industry, particularly for dual use and conversion":

Hot topics: defense-industry technology that could lower the level of violence involved in crime fighting. Sandia National Laboratories, for instance, is experimenting with a dense foam that can be sprayed at suspects, temporarily blinding and deafening them under breathable bubbles. Stinger Corporation is working on "smart guns," which will fire only for the owner, and retractable spiked barrier strips to unfurl in front of fleeing vehicles. Westinghouse is promoting the "smart car," in which minicomputers could be linked up with big mainframes at the police department, allowing for speedy booking of prisoners, as well as quick exchanges of information.[12]

Again, race provides a silent justification for the technological expansion of law enforcement, which, in turn, intensifies racist arrest and incarceration practices. This skyrocketing punishment industry, whose growth is silently but powerfully sustained by the persistence of racism, creates an economic demand for more jails and prisons and thus for similarly spiraling criminalization practices, which, in turn, fuels the fear of crime.

Most debates addressing the crisis resulting from overcrowding in prisons and jails focus on male institutions. Meanwhile, women's institutions and jail space for women are proportionately proliferating at an even more astounding rate than men's. If race is largely an absent factor in the discussions about crime and punishment, gender seems not even to merit a place carved out by its absence. Historically, the imprisonment of women has served to criminalize women in a way that is more complicated than is the case with men. This female criminalization process has had more to do with the marking of certain groups of women as undomesticated and hypersexual, as women who refuse to embrace the nuclear family as paradigm. The current liberal-conservative discourse around welfare criminalizes black single mothers, who are represented as deficient, manless, drug-using breeders of children, and as reproducers of an attendant culture of poverty. The woman who does drugs is criminalized both because she is a drug user and because, as a consequence, she cannot be a good mother. In some states, pregnant women are being imprisoned for using crack because of possible damage to the fetus.

According to the US Department of Justice, women are far more likely than men to be imprisoned for a drug conviction.[13] However, if women wish to receive treatment for their drug problems, often their only option, if they cannot pay for a drug program, is to be arrested and sentenced to a drug program via the criminal justice system. Yet when US Surgeon General Joycelyn Elders alluded to the importance of opening discussion on the decriminalization of drugs, the Clinton administration immediately disassociated itself from her remarks. Decriminalization of drugs would greatly reduce the numbers of incarcerated women, for the 278 percent increase in the numbers of black women in state and federal prisons (as compared with the 186 percent increase in the numbers of black men) can be largely attributed to the phenomenal rise in drug-related and specifically crack-related imprisonment. According to the Sentencing Project's 1995 report, the increase amounted to 828 percent.[14]

Official refusals to even consider decriminalization of drugs as a possible strategy that might begin to reverse present incarceration practices further bolsters the ideological staying power of the prison. In his well-known study of the history of the prison and its related technologies of discipline, Michel Foucault pointed out that an evolving contradiction is at the very heart of the historical project of imprisonment.

For a century and a half, the prison has always been offered as its own remedy: . . . the realization of the corrective project as the only method of overcoming the impossibility of implementing it.[15]

As I have attempted to argue, within the US historical context, racism plays a pivotal role in sustaining this contradiction. In fact, Foucault's theory regarding the prison's tendency to serve as its own enduring justification becomes even more compelling if the role of race is also acknowledged. Moreover, moving beyond the parameters of what I consider the double impasse implied by his theory—the discursive impasse his theory discovers and that of the theory itself—I want to conclude by suggesting the possibility of radical race-conscious strategies designed to disrupt the stranglehold of criminalization and incarceration practices.

In the course of a recent collaborative research project with UC Santa Barbara sociologist Kum-Kum Bhavnani, in which we interviewed thirty-five women at the San Francisco County jail, the complex ways in which race and gender help to produce a punishment industry that reproduces the very problems it purports to solve became dramatically apparent. Our interviews focused on the women's ideas about imprisonment and how they themselves imagine alternatives to incarceration. Their various critiques of the prison system and of the existing "alternatives," all of which are tied to reimprisonment as a last resort, led us to reflect more deeply about the importance of retrieving, retheorizing, and reactivating the radical abolitionist strategy first proposed in connection with the prison reform movements of the sixties and seventies.

We are presently attempting to theorize women's imprisonment in ways that allow us to formulate a radical abolitionist strategy departing from, but not restricted in its conclusions to, women's jails and prisons. Our goal is to formulate alternatives to incarceration that substantively reflect the voices and agency of a variety of imprisoned women. We wish to open up channels for their involvement in the current debates around alternatives to incarceration,

while not denying our own role as mediators and interpreters and our own political positioning in these debates. We also want to distinguish explorations of alternatives from the spate of "alternative punishments" or what are now called "intermediate sanctions" presently being proposed and/or implemented by and through state and local correctional systems.

This is a long-range project that has three dimensions: academic research, public policy, and community organizing. In other words, for this project to be successful, it must build bridges between academic work, legislative and other policy interventions, and grassroots campaigns calling, for example, for the decriminalization of drugs and prostitution—and for the reversal of the present proliferation of jails and prisons.

Raising the possibility of abolishing jails and prisons as the institutionalized and normalized means of addressing social problems in an era of migrating corporations, unemployment and homelessness, and collapsing public services, from health care to education, can hopefully help to interrupt the current law-and-order discourse that has such a grip on the collective imagination, facilitated as it is by deep and hidden influences of racism. This late twentieth-century "abolitionism," with its nineteenth-century resonances, may also lead to a historical recontextualization of the practice of imprisonment. With the passage of the Thirteenth Amendment, slavery was abolished for all except convicts—and in a sense the exclusion from citizenship accomplished by the slave system has persisted within the US prison system. Only three states allow prisoners to vote, and approximately 4 million people are denied the right to vote because of their present or past incarceration. A radical strategy to abolish jails and prisons as the normal way of dealing with the social problems of late capitalism is not a strategy for abstract abolition. It is designed to force a rethinking of the increasingly repressive role of the state during this era of late capitalism and to carve out a space for resistance.

NOTES

1. See coverage by the *Austin-American Statesman,* October 17, 1995.

2. Quoted in Charles S. Clark, "Prison Overcrowding," *Congressional Quartet Researcher,* 4, no. 5 (February 4, 1994), 97–119.

3. Ibid.

4. Marc Mauer, *Young Black Men and the Criminal Justice System: A Growing National Problem* (Washington, DC: The Sentencing Project, February 1990).

5. Reported in an Alexander Cockburn article, *Philadelphia Inquirer,* August 29, 1994.

6. Marc Mauer and Tracy Huling, *Young Black Americans and the Criminal Justice System: Five Years Later* (Washington, DC: The Sentencing Project, October 1995).

7. Ibid., 18.

8. See Cockburn, *Philadelphia Inquirer,* August 29, 1994.

9. See Wahneema Lubiano, "Black Ladies, Welfare Queens, and State Minstrels: Ideological War by Narrative Means," in *Race-ing Justice, En-gendering Power: Essays on Anita Hill, Clarence Thomas, and the Construction of Social Reality,* ed. Toni Morrison (New York: Pantheon, 1992).

10. Michael Powell, "Modern Slavery American Style," 1995, unpublished essay (author's papers).

11. I wish to acknowledge Julie Brown, who acquired this brochure from the Califomia Department of Correction in the course of researching the role of convict labor.

12. "Making Crime Pay: The Cold War of the '90s," *Wall Street Journal,* May 12, 1994.

13. Lawrence Rence, A. Greenfield, Stephanie Minor-Harper, *Women in Prison* (Washington DC: US Dept. of Justice, Office of Justice Programs, Bureau of Statistics, 1991) '

14. Mauer and Huling, *Young Black Americans and the Criminal Justice System: Five Years Later,* 19.

15. Michel Foucault, *Discipline and Punish: The Birth of the Prison,* trans. Alan Sheridan (New York: Vintage, 1979), 395.

Discussion Questions

1. How is it possible that bills like "Three strikes, you're out" that do not mention race are evidence of antiblack racism, as the author suggests? What is meant by an ideology, and how does the role of ideology help explain why blacks such as Carol Moseley-Braun can also support such racist measures?

2. What is the relationship between the international expansion of capitalism and the proliferation of prisons in the United States, according to Davis? How have prisons-for-profit affected the rising numbers of blacks in prison?

3. What is the "female criminalization" process and how does it work? In solution to some of these problems, Davis suggests decriminalization of drugs. What would this look like, and how would treating drug use as an illness to be cured rather than a felony for which one is imprisoned change women's lives?

4. At the end of this essay, Davis suggests the abolition of the prison system. What would this look like, and how would it help the problems of racism and sexism she discusses?

The Elephant in the Living Room: The Issue of Race in Close Black/White Friendships

Kathleen Odell Korgen

I can't even think of any one thing that we've talked about in terms of race. Because it's just . . . You know, we're friends. That's where it is. That's the way it is. (Kofi, black, 35)

[Race does not come up] at all. Except for when we're like, ripping on each other. (Paul, white, 18)

I think race died down a long time ago in Vinnie's and my relationship. Now, it's personal [laughs]. It's just personal. . . . It just doesn't come up anymore except when talking about others and their deal with race. (Rod, black, 45)

There is no escaping the fact that we live in a race-conscious and divided society. All blacks and whites in close interracial friendships must somehow deal with this reality of race as they interact with their close friend. Consciously or not, the pair must agree upon and carry out a strategy to somehow "demilitarize" the topic of race and discuss it with defenses down or somehow find a way to sidestep the subject while still remaining close to one another.

An examination of forty pairs of close black/white friends reveals that cross-racial friends tend to handle the issue of race in one of three primary ways. In each case, the friends actively constructed a means to "disarm" the topic, so that it would not come between them and harm their friendship. Each pair developed its own means of handling this delicate task. However, it is possible to discern three basic behavioral patterns by which the friends dealt with the issue of race in their relationships:

1. Ignoring/avoiding the topic of race.

2. Joking about race.

3. Seriously discussing racial issues.

While some pairs exhibited traits from more than one category, one of the three strategies was clearly dominant in each of the dyads.

IGNORING/AVOIDING RACE

Just as race does not play a major role in the development of cross-racial friendships, it is not usually a topic of serious discussion in most close black/white friendships. As Walid Afifi and Laura Guerrero suggest, in their article "Some Things Are Better Left Unsaid II: Topic Avoidance in Friendships,"[1] the discussion of racial issues in cross-racial friendships is not necessarily an indication of the closeness of these relationships. Topic avoidance is not uncommon in close friendships. While self-disclosure is an integral part of these relationships,[2] researchers also now note that people consider some topics to be "taboo" and avoid discussing them even with close friends.[3]

Similar to platonic, cross-sex close friendships in which dating and sexual experiences

are rarely discussed,[4] many close interracial friends do not talk to one another about racial issues. Afifi and Guerrero maintain that individuals in cross-sex friendships avoid discussing such topics as dating and sex at the "heart" of the tension in many such relationships. Friends in platonic, cross-sex relationships deal with what communication scholars Samter and Cupach describe as "the need to 'de-emphasize' sexuality."[5] The majority of these interracial friends deal with their racial differences by avoiding or ignoring the issue of race in their relationships. Whether consciously or not, the majority of these pairs have managed to avoid the volatile topic of race just as platonic, cross-sex friends stay away from the issue of sex.

Twenty of the forty pairs rarely discuss the issue of race. While there is no overt attempt to ignore or sidestep the topic, it seldom arises. When race does become a focus of conversation, the discussion usually consists of

a. discussions of what seem, at least to the white friend, seemingly isolated experiences of discrimination the black friend has faced,
b. brief debates about unavoidable, national, race-related incidents (e.g. O.J. Simpson's guilt or innocence), or
c. the topic of "light" conversation (e.g. importance of considering skin tones when purchasing clothes and makeup).

Kyle and Patrick provide a good example of how the first type of pair deals with the issue of race. As Kyle, a white, middle class, college student from a primarily white suburb in the Northeast puts it, race is "never" something that "enters into our relationship."

It's not even like something that comes up in like conversation. Even now, it's like me and him, and just, and all my friends and stuff. We just, you know, Pat is Pat. We don't look at him as being black or whoever, you know. I never. I mean, obviously we know he is. But it just never, it never like enters into our relationship. (Kyle, white, 23)

One of the few times that Kyle remembers discussing race occurred when he, with Pat and some white friends, were pulled over by the police in a car.

> They'd [the police] pull him over and they, you know, they pulled me and my friends and he'd be in the car and they'd think we'd be up to you know . . . [We'd] say it's ridiculous. [We'd] say and Pat would say "the reason they're doing this and that, you know, [is] because I'm black." It's a typical, you know, stereotype that if you're black, you're some kind of criminal. You know, and I know he's encountered that, stuff like that. And it offends him, you know, it's ridiculous. It offends, you know, it offends me, it offends my friends. (Kyle, white, 23)

Those conversations, though, did not occur either outside such incidents or current news events.

Elizabeth and Louise, both middle class professionals and natives of Southern California, only discuss race during national news events such as the O.J. Simpson murder trial. As Louise describes,

> The only time we really got into something about race was during the O.J. Simpson trial and I thought he was not guilty and she thought he was guilty. . . . So, you know, we kind of. We discussed it for a while. And I told her my side, she told me her side. And ah, forget it. Let's go on to something else, and then we talked about something else. (Louise, black, 45)

While Louise and Elizabeth are very comfortable with one another, the O.J. Simpson trial provided one of the very few occasions where race entered into their friendship. When asked, individually, if race is ever an issue in their friendship, both brought up their discussion of O.J.'s guilt or innocence. Neither Louise nor Elizabeth agreed with the other's view and both realized that their disagreement was race-based. Like most white Americans, Elizabeth believed that he was guilty and like the majority of black Americans, Louise maintained that he was innocent.[6] However, they simply chose to agree to disagree and talk "about something else," rather than continue it and highlight the racial division that existed between them.

Dave and Kofi, two middle class professionals in their mid-thirties who have been best friends since meeting at their New England college, never discuss race. When asked if the topic of race comes up much between he and his friend Dave, Kofi, a native of Africa who came to the United States as a boy, said,

> No, it doesn't. . . . Hey, I know he's a Caucasian man. I know that. And I'm sure that he sees me as an African American person. But we don't. There are no issues. I mean, we don't talk about race per se. I can't even think of any one thing that we've talked about in terms of race. Because it's just . . . You know, we're friends. That's where it is. That's the way it is. (Kofi, black, 36)

Dave, who grew up in a predominantly white, New England neighborhood, echoed Kofi's statement when he tried to explain why he and Kofi do not discuss racial issues.

> Certainly it's not anything that I consciously avoided. I think we. I don't know, we're just two shallow guys. I don't know [laughs]. I don't know. Again, certainly, it's not anything that was consciously not brought up on my part. It's just ah, never been an issue with us. (Dave, white, 35)

The responses that both Kofi and Dave give to the question about whether they discuss race in their friendship reveals their unease with the topic. While Dave jokes that they just must be "two shallow guys" for not talking about race, Kofi describes him as the opposite of shallow, "not the kind of person that says a lot but . . . does things." Best friends since college, both men take their friendship very seriously and are clearly committed to one another. They have discussed extremely personal issues with each other and, as Kofi says, Dave is "not the type to open up [but] he opened up [to me]." Somehow, though, without conscious effort, the two have never discussed the issue that divides so many black and white Americans from one another— race. Just as platonic cross-sex friends "de-emphasize" sexuality when they're together, Kofi and Dave, like the majority of the interracial friends, have "de-emphasized race" in their relationship.

JOKING ABOUT RACE

Ignoring or limiting discussions of race is one means of dealing with the "elephant in the living room." However, there are some pairs of friends who turn to their racial differences with humor as a means of cementing their relationship. The first time one makes fun of the other with a racial joke or slur and receives a good humored, similarly racist and abusive response, they know their friendship is on solid ground. These pairs of friends trade incessant racial barbs, yet rarely have a serious discussion about race or racial issues. Communication experts would not be surprised to learn that this is most common among young, male pairs of friends.

Nine of the forty pairs of friends fall chiefly into this category of black/white friends. Instead of generally ignoring the topic, this group deals with the issue of race by hurling racial insults at one another. Six of these pairs of friends consist of young men now in college. Three pairs of women also bring up race primarily through joking, though they also discuss individual incidents of racism that they have either faced or noticed.

Joe and Devin represent this second way close, black/white friends may deal with the issue of race. Joe, raised in a primarily white, upper-middle class, New York suburb, aptly sums up the role race plays in these friendships by saying,

> You know, when I look at friendships in general or specifically my friendship with Joe, it's amazing how much race plays a role, but doesn't play a role. How much we joke about it, but we never talk about it seriously. (Joe, black, 18)

To them, racial stereotypes can be used as "in" jokes that bring them closer together. In many ways, their interactions are similar to those of the interracial buddy/partner characters Mel Gibson and Danny Glover play in the series of *Lethal Action* movies. As Devin, who grew up in a middle class, predominantly white, New England town describes it,

> We make a weird fun of each other's ethnic backgrounds so much; it's incredible. . . . Like we found each other's stereotypes—I'm Irish and

German—so we're, we're pretty bad with it. . . . Like I saw him at lunch, we were eating, and I saw him come back from one of the meal booths . . . and I was like 'What you got there—some fried chicken and Koolade?'" [He, in turn, might say something like] "Why don't you build a new gas chamber?" (Devin, white, 18)

Aware that people overhearing them are often aghast, Joe and Devin joke with each other in ways that they would never joke with others. They also readily admit that they would never permit others, outside their close circle of friends, to joke either with themselves or their close friend in a similar manner. Each expressed a strong willingness to defend their friend from any racial insults that others might deliver.

Vern and James, college students who both grew up in lower middle class, New Jersey neighborhoods areas, with increasing numbers of blacks, also use the topic of race as fodder for put-downs of one another. When asked if race has ever come up or been an issue in their friendship, Vern's succinct response was

> No, not at all. Except for when we're, like, ripping on each other. (Vern, white, 18)

When asked the same question, separately, James's response was almost identical to Vern's:

> Just like joking. We always joke about people's races all the time. (James, black, 18)

Like Joe and Devin, and the majority of the young male interracial friends, Vern and James use racial jokes as a means of both bonding and acknowledging the "elephant in the living room" without having to address, with any depth, the fact that race affects them both in different ways.

While in some friendship pairs the line may seem very far off, there is a line that the friends know to avoid crossing when joking with one another. As Steven describes it,

> Well, you know, we talk about stuff, mostly joking. And, you know, it's a really open kind of friendship. You know, I'll say things and, you know, he'll say things and whenever those lines

are crossed we know, you know, all you have to do is say "I'm not comfortable with that." And he backs off and I back off. . . .

When asked who crosses the line more often, Steven said,

On the issue of race? It's probably him crossing the line and me telling him that that's not something I'm comfortable with. But, I mean, it doesn't happen often. But, on the other hand, I don't think I've ever crossed a racial line with him, you know. And that just goes with the whole, you know, I think it's more serious . . . saying things that are offensive towards black people than it is saying things that are offensive towards white people. I guess it's just kind of society today. (Steven, black, 19)

The differing positions of the white and black "no crossing" line when it comes to racial jokes has nothing to do with political correctness. Young men who insult each other with as much wit and effort to disgust one another as these young men are not bound by current "adult" rules of verbal etiquette in their exchanges with one another. In some ways, they are carrying on the time-honored tradition of disparaging one another that male youths have acted out with each other for decades. Those who manage to deliver the most outrageous insults, while avoiding hitting a spot that is a little too sensitive and starting a fight, gain in stature among their friends.[7]

The reason that blacks are more sensitive than whites to racial jokes is intimately connected with the fact that blacks have been the butt of racial slurs and jokes associated with their devaluation, dehumanization, and lynching,[8] throughout the history of the United States. Today, as a group, blacks are still socially, politically, and economically in lower standing than whites. Whites, as a racial group, on the other hand, have not faced such abuse and still hold disproportionate economic, political, and social power in the United States. Just as it is easier to bear a "you are so ugly" joke when you are relatively good looking, it is much easier to take a racial insult when your race is in a position of power relative to those hurling the insults.

The fact that both friends feel comfortable, on the whole, trading race-based insults with one another is a sign of their closeness, despite their racial differences. Trading jokes and insults can also give the surface impression that the two friends are on an equal playing field. The only indication that the field is still slanted is the fact that racial insults are more likely to injure the black friend than the white one.

Seriously Discussing Race

The friends who openly discuss the different positions of blacks and whites in society are those who represent the third category of responses of close, interracial friends to the issue of race. These friends directly comment, with great seriousness, on the "elephant in the living room." Eleven of the friendship pairs have discussed race at length. They were deeply interested, usually near the beginning of their friendship, to discover all that they could about their friend's different racial background and perspective. Typically, the discussions would begin with the white friend asking the black friend questions. However, the conversations would almost always include multiple exchanges of opinions and information.

With each pair, however, the topic of race arose less frequently as time went by.[9] In all friendships, the differences in the friends that first seemed novel become normal, and less of a conversation maker as the friendship develops. The black/white friends who spent hours learning from each other's experiences and opinions on racial issues towards the beginning of their friendship, gradually turned to other topics as their friendship developed. After many years of friendship, the friends tended to talk about race only when discussing a news item or dealing with the racial issues of "others." Their lengthy talks about the subject earlier in their friendship often enable them to now feel confident that they know the other's thoughts on a current racial event or issue without having to ask.

Evan and Bob, friends now for many years, illustrate the third way in which many black/white friends deal with issues of race over time. While they eagerly discussed issues concerning race when they first became friends, their conversations now tend to focus on other topics. As Evan states,

> Well, I can tell you, Bob and I [spent] a lot of time just talking about race. Differences and attitudes, you know, things like that.... So, we've done a lot of exploring, he and I. Just questioning each other and talking in general. [But] we have a tendency now to focus on the similarities, instead of the differences.... We don't talk about it too much anymore now because we're past that. We've asked all the questions we want to ask. Or, we've covered that ground and we know the answer.
>
> [However], I would still not hesitate at all if a question came up about race or something like that. In fact, I've often thought to myself, if I ever have a problem, with an African American employee, I'll call Bob first and run it by him to get his view on it before I took any action. (Evan, white, 41)

So, while, they have already "covered that ground," Evan and Bob have not decided to now simply ignore race. Instead, it has become just one of the many reasons, like guidance on work issues, jogging, marital issues, etc., for which they might turn to each other for advice. Evan and Bob value each other on multiple levels, and embrace the many identities, including racial, of each.

In some ways similar to Evan and Bob, Caroline turned to Janet for a sounding board when she dealt with issues of race in her work life. When Caroline a white, upper-middle class, mid-western professor and professional consultant, first started work at a company that, aside from her, was virtually all black, she was grateful to find her assistant, Janet, very willing to guide her through what for her was a new cultural environment. When asked how often she and Janet had discussions about racial issues, Caroline said,

> I think early on, a lot. You know, like typically every day something would be coming up.... Because I was surrounded, for the first time in my life, with African American women, working in [this] setting. And I truly wanted to understand their point of view. And I would say that Janet

was sort of a, um, a critical person in helping me to understand a world that I had never experienced before. She was much more savvy in that world of employees that we had to work with that had problems and our clients, our residents and their families.... I mean, she was absolutely indispensable in helping me learn cultural ins and outs. (Caroline, white, 53)

Through the trust and rapport they developed through working together, Janet and Caroline have become very close friends and "part of one another's family" over the ten years they have known each other. Their relationship is markedly different than the hierarchical workplace relationships between whites and blacks that Hudson and Hines-Hudson described. While Caroline was, in reality, Janet's superior in the hierarchical structure of their company, Caroline repeatedly described their working relationship in terms that stressed their collaborative efforts. In the workplace Caroline depended upon Janet's willingness to share her knowledge of black culture. The fact that Caroline treated Janet as an equal at work in some ways balanced the playing field and most likely contributed to the ease with which their close friendship developed.

Caroline's and Janet's experience was rare. Approximately four-fifths of the friendship pairs in this sample are comprised of two people with similar educational and economic backgrounds. However, more than most other pairs of friends in this sample, the support Caroline and Janet gave each other dealing with issues of race was mutual. Because Janet was Caroline's assistant when they first met, and Caroline was educationally and financially in a superior situation, she was able to provide Janet much guidance and support in attaining further degrees in higher education and negotiating the predominantly white corporate world.

Typically among the friendship pairs, the teaching about culture was primarily one-sided. Black people, living in a white dominated society, are usually much more knowledgeable about white culture than whites are of black culture and therefore have less need of a tutorial about the other race. They, in many ways, must be bicultural, able to live in both black and white worlds. W. E. B. DuBois described this as having a "double consciousness" in *The Souls of Black Folk.*[10] Whites, on the other hand, while they may be fans of Michael Jordan and the Wayans brothers, do not often look into everyday black America. In the pairs in which race was an open topic, the white interviewees spoke appreciatively of their friend's assistance in their efforts to learn and understand the cultural differences that exist between many black and white Americans.

Given the American obsession with race, one might think that the vast majority of close black/white friends would discuss racial issues often. Yet, the overwhelming majority of friendship pairs (97.5%) did not make race the centerpiece of their friendship. Even pairs who have serious discussions about racism in US society concentrate on other aspects of their friendship. Rod describes this phenomenon within his friendship with Vinnie.

I think race died down a long time ago in Vinnie's and my relationship. Now, it's personal [laughs]. It's just personal. You know, this is so corny. I know he's a white guy, you know, and he knows I'm a black guy. But that's not a part of it. It's just the blood we've shed. You know, and the tears we've cried. I don't think it's. It just doesn't come up anymore except when talking about others and their deal with race. And how we see some people

just doing some stupid things. And that's when, you know, they'll get our hair up. . . . Like we won't tolerate racial insensitivity or anything like that on our team. But it wouldn't manifest itself because, cause we're there. You know. So, I think, in response to, does race come up?, it comes up when dealing with others but not when dealing with each other. (Rod, black, 45)

Having grown completely comfortable with the racial differences between them, their attention towards race now focuses outward. Through the example of their friendship, and the way they coach together, Rod and Vinnie show their players and those around them that close friendships can be formed across the racial divide.

In their own ways, interracial friends develop strategies to keep race from consuming their friendship. The typical means, topic avoidance, is successful through the efforts of both the white and the black individuals in each of the pairs. The existence of these cross-racial friendships makes it clear that close friendships are possible across the racial divide. However, the fact that the majority of close black/white friends do not seriously discuss issues of race is a testimony to the still painful and volatile separation that exists between black and white Americans.

Notes

1. See Afifi, Walid and Laura Guerrero (1998). "Some Things Are Better Left Unsaid II: Topic Avoidance in Friendships" *Communication Quarterly,* 46, 3, pp. 231–249.

2. See Monsour, M., Harris, B., Kurzweil, N. & Beard C. (1994). "Challenges Confronting Cross-Sex Friendships: 'Much Ado About Nothing?'" *Sex Roles,* 31, pp. 55–77.; Parks, M. R. and Floyd, K. (1996). "Meanings for Closeness and Intimacy in Friendship." *Journal of Social and Personal Relationships,* 13, pp. 85–107; Derlega, V. J., Metts, S. Petronio, S. and Margulis, S. T. (1993). *Self-Disclosure.* Newbury Park, CA: Sage.

3. See Afifi, Walid and Laura Guerrero (1998). "Some Things Are Better Left Unsaid II: Topic Avoidance in Friendships" *Communication Quarterly,*

46, 3, pp. 231–249; Guerrero, Laura and Walid Affifi. (1995) "Some Things Are Better Left Unsaid: Topic Avoidance in Family Relationships*." Communication Quarterly,* 43, pp. 276–296.

4. See Afifi, Walid and Laura Guerrero (1998). "Some Things Are Better Left Unsaid II: Topic Avoidance in Friendships" *Communication Quarterly,* 46, 3, pp. 231–249.

5. See Samter, Wendy and William Cupach (1998). "Friendly Fire: Topical Variations in Conflict among Same and Cross-Sex Friends." *Communication Studies,* 49, 42, pp. 121–138.

6. Newport, Frank and Lydia Saad (1997). "Civil Trial Didn't Alter Public's View of Simpson Case." *Gallup News Service,* February 7, 1997. [http://www. gallup.com/poll/releases/pr970207.asp]

7. One of the anonymous reviewers pointed out that "this ritual is referred to in the black community

as 'playing the dozens.' Hitting the hot spot usually means saying something derogatory about someone's mother."

8. The fact that these types of jokes are still told is evident in the fact that one white, twenty-four year old interviewee related a joke her boyfriend recently heard as follows: "This one guy goes, 'I have no problem with black people. I've got one in my family tree.' And, and then someone goes 'Oh really' and he goes, 'Yah, he's hanging in my backyard.' She was appalled both by the joke and that people could still be so "stupid" and "ignorant."

9. One pair, who met in grade school and are now in their late twenties, did not seriously discuss their different thoughts and experiences concerning race until they were in college. Since that time, they have followed the trend of the other pairs in this category and have talked about racial issues less often as time passes.

10. DuBois, W. E. B. (1961). *The Souls of Black Folk: Essays and Sketches.* Greenwich: Fawcett.

Discussion Questions

1. Why do you think certain close black–white friends use racial joking as part of their communication processes? Do you feel such joking is appropriate, and if so, under what conditions? What reasons does the author give for blacks being more sensitive to racial joking than whites? What does this tell us about the social nature of prejudice and its relationship to power?

2. Why did serious discussions of race tend to involve black people teaching whites about their culture, and not vice versa? Is it fair that blacks end up bearing the burden of being "teacher" in interracial settings? What are the alternatives to whites expecting blacks to teach them about race?

3. Does the fact that most black–white friends do not seriously discuss race indicate that they have "gotten past" race, and thus indicate progress, or does it indicate a "painful and volatile" separation, as the author suggests? Do whites and blacks discuss race more honestly and openly in the presence of those who share their racial identity? What would need to change in society in order for people to feel comfortable discussing race with those unlike themselves?

CURRENT DEBATES

REPARATIONS

Should African Americans be compensated for the losses they suffered as a result of their kidnapping from Africa, their centuries of slavery, and their continuing oppression under de jure segregation? What, if anything, does American society owe for the centuries of uncompensated labor performed by African Americans and the oppression and coerced inequality of the Jim Crow era? Should present-day Americans be held accountable for the actions of their ancestors? What about the families and businesses that grew rich from the labor of blacks (and other minorities) in the past? To what extent are they responsible for the continuing racial gaps in income and wealth documented in this chapter?

The idea that America owes reparations to African Americans is not new but has been gaining momentum in recent years (Smith, 2001), spurred in part by a best-selling book (Robinson, 2001) and a lawsuit filed in 2002. Also, the issue may receive a great deal of attention on college campuses in the future, in part as a serious issue worthy of discussion in its own right and in part as a focus of activism, as students question the relationship between their school's endowment and slavery.

In the excerpts below, Joe Feagin and Eileen O'Brien, while arguing for reparations, place the debate in a comparative and historical context. Manning Marable and John McWhorter present some of the central arguments for and against reparations.

REFERENCES

Robinson, Randall. 2001. *The Debt: What America Owes to Blacks*. New York: Plume.

Smith, Vern. 2001. Debating the Wages of Slavery. *Newsweek,* August 27, pp. 20–25.

REPARATIONS FOR AFRICAN AMERICANS IN HISTORICAL CONTEXT

Joe R. Feagin and Eileen O'Brien

Many discussions of reparations for African Americans seem to suggest that such compensation is a wild idea well beyond conventional U.S. practice or policy. This is not, however, the case. The principle of individual and group compensation for damages done by others is accepted by the federal government and the larger society in regard to some claims, but only grudgingly and incompletely for others, such as those by African Americans who have been harmed by racial oppression. For example, recent anti-crime legislation, in the form of the Victims of Crime Act, codifies the principle of compensation for victims of crimes. In addition, as a nation, we now expect corporations to compensate the deformed children of mothers who took drugs without knowing their consequences. . . . The fact that those who ran the corporation in the initial period of damage are deceased does not relieve the corporation from having to pay compensation to those damaged later on from the earlier actions. Injured children can sue for redress many years later. Clearly, in some cases monetary compensation for past injustices is accepted and expected.

Long after the Nazi party had been out of power and most of its leaders had grown old or died, the U.S. government continued to press the German government to make tens of billions of dollars in reparations to the families of those killed in the Holocaust and to the state of Israel. In recent years, the federal government has grudgingly agreed to (modest) reparations for those Japanese Americans who were interned during World War II. Federal courts have also awarded nearly a billion dollars in compensatory damages to Native American groups whose lands were stolen in violation of treaties. Significantly, however, these slow moves to compensate some victims of racial oppression have not yet been extended, even modestly, to African Americans. . . .

In his 1946 book *The World and Africa,* W. E. B. Du Bois argued that the poverty in Europe's African colonies was "a main cause of wealth and luxury in Europe" (1965, p. 37). . . . Du Bois argued that the history of African colonization is omitted from mainstream histories of European development and wealth. A serious understanding of European wealth must *center* on the history of exploitation and oppression in Africa, for the resources of Africans were taken to help create Europe's wealth. To a substantial degree, Europeans were rich because Africans were poor. Africa's economic development—its resources, land, and labor—had been and was being sacrificed to spur European economic progress.

In our view, a similar argument is applicable to the development of the wealth and affluence of the white population in the United States. From its first decades, white-settler colonialism in North America involved the extreme exploitation of enslaved African Americans. European colonists built up much wealth by stealing the labor of African Americans and the land of Native Americans.

Racial oppression carried out by white Americans has lasted for nearly four centuries, and has done great damage to the lives, opportunities, communities, and futures of African Americans. The actions of white Americans over many generations sharply reduced the income of African Americans, and thus their economic and cultural capital. Legal segregation in the South, where most African Americans resided until recent decades, forced black men and women into lower-paying jobs or into unemployment, where they could not earn incomes sufficient to support their families adequately, much less to save. In the 1930s, two-thirds of African Americans still lived in the South, and most were descendants of recently enslaved Americans. They were still firmly entrenched in the semi-slavery of legal segregation, which did not allow the accumulation of wealth. Significant property holding was not even available as a possibility to a majority of African Americans until the late 1960s. . . .

Most whites do not understand the extent to which the racial oppression of the past continues to fuel inequalities in the present. Although affirmative action programs (where they still exist) attempt to redress discrimination by increasing job or educational opportunities for African Americans in a few organizations, such programs do little to address the large-scale wealth inequality between black and white Americans. All the "equal opportunity" programs and policies one could envisage would not touch the assets of whites who long ago reaped the benefits of not being subjected to legal segregation during the United States' most

prosperous economic times in the nineteenth and twentieth centuries. . . .

Wealth transmission is a critical factor in the reproduction of racial oppression. Given the nature of whites' disproportionate share of America's wealth and the historical conditions under which it was acquired—often at the expense of African Americans—it is of little significance that legal discrimination and segregation exist today. The argument that "Jim Crow is a thing of the past" misses the point, because the huge racial disparities in wealth today are a *direct* outgrowth of the economic and social privileges one group secured unfairly, if not brutally, at the expense of another group.

SOURCE: Feagin, Joe and O'Brien, Eileen. (1999). Reparations for African Americans in Historical Context. In *When Sorry Isn't Enough: The ontroversy over Apologies and Reparations for Human Injustice.* Roy L. Brooks (ed.). New York: New York University Press.

REPARATIONS ARE AN IDEA WHOSE TIME HAS COME

Manning Marable

In 1854 my great-grandfather, Morris Marable, was sold on an auction block in Georgia for $500. For his white slave master, the sale was just "business as usual." But to Morris Marable and his heirs, slavery was a crime against our humanity. This pattern of human-rights violations against enslaved African Americans continued under Jim Crow segregation for nearly another century.

The fundamental problem of American democracy in the 21st century is the problem of "structural racism": the deep patterns of socio-economic inequality and accumulated disadvantage that are coded by race, and constantly justified in public discourse by both racist stereotypes and white indifference. Do Americans have the capacity and vision to dismantle these structural barriers that deny democratic rights and opportunities to millions of their fellow citizens?

This country has previously witnessed two great struggles to achieve a truly multicultural democracy. The First Reconstruction

(1865–1877) ended slavery and briefly gave black men voting rights, but gave no meaningful compensation for two centuries of unpaid labor. The promise of "40 acres and a mule" was for most blacks a dream deferred.

The Second Reconstruction (1954–1968), or the modern civil-rights movement, outlawed legal segregation in public accommodations and gave blacks voting rights. But these successes paradoxically obscure the tremendous human costs of historically accumulated disadvantage that remain central to black Americans' lives.

The disproportionate wealth that most whites enjoy today was first constructed from centuries of unpaid black labor. Many white institutions, including Ivy League universities, insurance companies and banks, profited from slavery. This pattern of white privilege and black inequality continues today.

Demanding reparations is not just about compensation for slavery and segregation. It is, more important, an educational campaign to highlight the contemporary reality of "racial deficits" of all kinds, the unequal conditions that impact blacks regardless of class. Structural racism's barriers include "equity inequity," the absence of black capital formation that is a direct consequence of America's history. One third of all black households actually have negative net wealth. In 1998 the typical black family's net wealth was $16,400, less than one fifth that of white families. Black families are denied home loans at twice the rate of whites.

Blacks remain the last hired and first fired during recessions. During the 1990–91 recession, African Americans suffered disproportionately. At Coca-Cola, 42 percent of employees who lost their jobs were black. At Sears, 54 percent were black. Blacks have significantly shorter life expectancies, in part due to racism in the health establishment. Blacks are statistically less likely than whites to be referred for kidney transplants or early-stage cancer surgery.

In criminal justice, African Americans constitute only one seventh of all drug users. Yet we account for 35 percent of all drug arrests, 55 percent of drug convictions and 75 percent of prison admissions for drug offenses. . . .

White Americans today aren't guilty of carrying out slavery and segregation. But whites have a moral and political responsibility to acknowledge the continuing burden of history's structural racism.

A reparations trust fund could be established, with the goal of closing the socioeconomic gaps between blacks and whites. Funds would be targeted specifically toward poor, disadvantaged communities with the greatest need, not to individuals.

Let's eliminate the racial unfairness in capital markets that perpetuates black poverty. A national commitment to expand black homeownership, full employment and quality health care would benefit all Americans, regardless of race.

Reparations could begin America's Third Reconstruction, the final chapter in the 400-year struggle to abolish slavery and its destructive consequences. As Malcolm X said in 1961, hundreds of years of racism and labor exploitation are "worth more than a cup of coffee at a white cafe. We are here to collect back wages."

SOURCE: Marable, Manning. (2001). An Idea Whose Time Has Come . . . Whites Have an Obligation to Recognize Slavery's Legacy. *Newsweek,* August 27, p. 22.

WHY I DON'T WANT REPARATIONS FOR SLAVERY

John McWhorter

My childhood was a typical one for a black American in his mid-thirties. I grew up middle class in a quiet, safe neighborhood in Philadelphia. [My] mother taught social work at Temple University and my father was a student activities administrator there. My parents were far from wealthy, . . . but I had everything I needed plus some extras. . . .

Contrary to popular belief, I was by no means extraordinarily "lucky" or "unusual" among black Americans of the post-Civil Rights era. . . . [T]oday, there are legions of black adults in the United States who grew up as I did. As a child, I never had trouble finding black peers, and as an adult, meeting black people with life histories like mine requires no searching. In short, in our

moment, black success is a norm. Less than one in four black families now live below the poverty line, and the black underclass is at most one out of five blacks. This is what the Civil Rights revolution helped make possible, and I grew up exhilarated at belonging to a race that had made such progress in the face of many obstacles.

Yet today, numerous black officials tell the public that lives like mine are statistical noise, that the overriding situation for blacks is one of penury, dismissal, and spiritual desperation. Under this analysis, the blood of slavery remains on the hands of mainstream America until it allocates a large sum of money to "repair" the unsurmounted damage done to our race over four centuries. . . .

The shorthand version of the reparations idea is that living blacks are "owed" the money that our slave ancestors were denied for their unpaid servitude. But few black Americans even know the names or life stories of their slave ancestors; almost none of us have pictures or keepsakes from that far back. . . . Yes, my slave ancestors were "blood" to me; yes, what was done to them was unthinkable. But the 150 years between me and them has rendered our tie little more than biological. Paying anyone for the suffering of long-dead strangers . . . would be more a matter of blood money than "reparation." . . .

Perhaps recognizing this, the reparations movement is now drifting away from the "back salary" argument to justifications emphasizing the effects of slavery since Emancipation. It is said blacks deserve payment for residual echoes of their earlier disenfranchisement and segregation. This justification, however, is predicated upon the misconception that in 2001, most blacks are "struggling."

This view denies the stunning success that the race has achieved over the past 40 years. It persists because many Americans, black and white, have accepted the leftist notion which arose in the mid-1960s that blacks are primarily victims in this country, that racism and structural injustice hobble all but a few individual blacks. Based on emotion, victimologist thought ignores the facts of contemporary black success and progress, because they do not square with the "blame game."

Reparations cannot logically rely on a depiction of black Americans as a race still reeling from the brutal experience of slavery and its aftereffects. The reality is that, by any estimation, in the year 2001 there are more middle-class blacks than poor ones. The large majority of black Americans, while surely not immune to the slings and arrows of the eternal injustices of life on earth, are now leading dignified lives as new variations on what it means to be American. . . .

Any effort to repair problems in black America must focus on helping people to help themselves. Funds must be devoted to ushering welfare mothers into working for a living, so that their children do not grow up learning that employment is something "other people" do. Inner city communities should be helped to rebuild themselves, in part through making it easier for residents to buy their homes. Police forces ought to be trained to avoid brutality, which turns young blacks against the mainstream today, and to work with, rather than against, the communities they serve.

Finally, this country must support all possible efforts to liberate black children from the soul-extinguishing influence of ossified urban public schools, and to move them into experimental or all-minority schools where a culture of competition is fostered. This will help undo the sense that intellectual excellence is a "white" endeavor. Surely we must improve the public schools as well, including increasing the exposure of young black children to standardized tests. But we also must make sure another generation of black children are not lost during the years it will take for these schools to get their acts together. . . .

Ultimately, a race shows its worth not by how much charity it can extract from others, but in how well it can do in the absence of charity. Black America has elicited more charity from its former oppressors than any race in human history—justifiably in my view. However, this can only serve as a spark—the real work is now ours.

SOURCE: McWhorter, John. (2001). Blood Money, An Analysis of Slavery Reparations. *The American Enterprise*, July 12:5, p. 18.

QUESTIONS TO CONSIDER

1. Feagin and O'Brien justify reparations for African Americans, in part, by making comparisons to other situations in which victimized groups have been compensated. Are the situations they cite truly comparable to slavery and segregation? If so, what are the similarities that make that make the situations comparable? If not, explain the differences that make the comparison invalid.

2. Feagin and O'Brien agree with Marable that whites share responsibility for the "continuing burden of history's structural racism." Evaluate

this argument in light of the continuing racial gaps in income and education. (Data on race differences are available from the U.S. Bureau of the Census at www.census.gov.) Does McWhorter's assessment of black success make sense in terms of these gaps? Is the difference between Marable and McWhorter merely one of emphasis? Is Marable seeing the glass "half-empty" and McWhorter seeing it "half-full"? Or, is there a deeper division between the two points of view? If so, what is it?

3. People often think of reparations for slavery in terms of cash payments to individuals. What other forms could reparations take? McWhorter advocates programs of improvement (workfare, schools, and so on) for black communities. How are these different from "reparations"?

4. Consider Marable's point that the reparations issue can be used as an educational tool. Could the campaign for reparations be used to counteract white racism and indifference? How?

6

NATIVE AMERICANS

While African Americans lost their freedom under slavery, Native Americans lost their land, their resources, and their lives. Hostilities between Anglo-Americans and the Native tribes began shortly after the first white settlements were established, and continued for nearly 300 years. The tribes resisted the advances of white civilization as best they could, but eventually they succumbed to the superior power and larger size of the growing American society. At the end of armed hostilities, the tribes were forced into federally controlled reservations, often hundreds of miles from their traditional homelands. The reservations were typically on the least desirable, least productive land, and, for much of the past 100 years, Indians have had to struggle mightily to wrest from them even a meager subsistence.

Since the end of the Indian wars, federal policy toward the tribes has fluctuated between neglect and coerced acculturation. The federally controlled Indian school system exemplifies the latter. Indian children on the reservation were required to attend boarding schools where they were made to learn English, adopt Christianity, and follow other Anglo cultural practices. Mary Crow Dog, in the first Narrative Portrait, paints a grim picture of everyday life at the Indian schools. However, the efforts to Americanize Indians and exterminate their cultures was, at best, only partly successful. As illustrated in the second Narrative Portrait by John Lame Deer, Native American cultures and values survive into the present.

The three Readings for this chapter document the persistence of Native American cultures and the continuing discrimination and racism they face. Russell Thornton provides an overview of the situation of Native Americans and some background on present-day issues, including a summary of the effects of changing federal policy. Leonard Peltier examines the issues from a very personal point of view: he is currently in prison for his protest activities in support of Native American causes. Paula Gunn Allen addresses some of the problems that Indians face as a result of their conquest by white society and also examines the gender issues faced by Native American women as a result of their subordinate positions both within the larger society and within their tribes.

The Current Debate raises an issue that, to members of the dominant group, might seem excessively "politically correct": Should Columbus Day be celebrated? However, the arguments presented here not only raise a legitimate historical question (Was Columbus's "discovery" the first step in a bloody campaign of genocide or the dawning of a new age of cultural advancement for the Americas?), they also demonstrate the persistence of an Indian point of view, separate from and critical of the Anglo world, and the persistence of issues unique to Indians that are directly traceable to the military conquest that began that fateful day in 1492.

NARRATIVE PORTRAITS

NATIVE AMERICAN EXPERIENCE AND PERSPECTIVE

By the end of the nineteenth century, Native Americans had been defeated militarily, and those that survived the vicious conflicts were herded onto reservations where they remained isolated, impoverished, and powerless. Sometimes, in the nineteenth and twentieth centuries, the tribes were subjected to various forms of coercive acculturation and attempts to "civilize" and Americanize them, experiences that left them bitter, resentful, and contemptuous of the cruel paternalism of the larger society. At other times, Native Americans were simply ignored and left to their own devices, experiences that permitted them to preserve some of their languages and many aspects of their traditional culture. The selection by Mary Crow Dog—a member of the Sioux tribe who became deeply involved in the Red Power movement that began in the 1960s—recounts one experience with coercive acculturation in the form of Indian boarding schools, and the selection by John Lame Deer—also a Sioux—illustrates the reality of a continuing, unassimilated Native American view of white society.

The boarding schools remembered so vividly by Mary Crow Dog have been much improved in recent decades. Facilities have been modernized and the faculty upgraded. The curriculum has been revised and often includes elements of Native American culture and language. Still, it was not that long ago that coercive acculturation at its worst was the daily routine, and she vividly recalls some of the horrors of her experiences at a reservation boarding school. As you read her words, keep in mind that she was born in 1955 and started school in the early 1960s, only a generation or two ago.

In the 1972 interview summarized, John Lame Deer gives his view of the technologically advanced society that surrounds him. Through his words, we can hear the voices of the Indian cultures that have survived and the strong suggestion that Native Americans are, in many ways, more advanced than the dazzling sophisticates of urban America.

LAKOTA WOMAN

Mary Crow Dog

It is almost impossible to explain to a sympathetic white person what a typical old Indian boarding school was like; how it affected the Indian child suddenly dumped into it like a small creature from another world, helpless, defenseless, bewildered, trying desperately to survive and sometimes not surviving at all. Even now, when these schools are so much improved, when . . . the teachers [are] well-intentioned, even trained in child psychology—unfortunately the psychology of white children, which is different from ours—the shock to the child upon arrival is still tremendous. . . .

In the traditional Sioux family, the child is never left alone. It is always surrounded by relatives, carried around, enveloped in warmth. It is treated with the respect due to any human being, even a small one. It is seldom forced to do anything against its will, seldom screamed at, and never beaten. . . . And then suddenly a bus or car arrives full of strangers, who yank the child out of the arms of those who love it, taking it screaming to the boarding school. The only word I can think of for what is done to these children is kidnapping. . . .

The mission school at St. Francis was a curse for our family for generations. My grandmother went there, then my mother, then my sisters and I. At one time or another, every one of us tried to run away. Grandma told me about the bad times she experienced at St. Francis. In those days they let students go home only for one week every year. Two days were used up for transportation, which meant spending just five days out of every 365 with her family. . . . My mother had much the same experiences but never wanted to talk about them, and then there was I, in the same place. . . . Nothing had changed since my grandmother's days. I have been told that even in the '70s they were still beating children at that school. All I got out of school was being taught how to pray. I learned quickly that I would be beaten if I failed in my devotions or, God forbid, prayed the wrong way, especially prayed in Indian to Wakan Tanka, the Indian creator. . . .

My classroom was right next to the principal's office and almost every day I could hear him swatting the boys. Beating was the common punishment for not doing one's homework, or for being late to school. It had such a bad effect upon me that I hated and mistrusted every white person on sight, because I met only one kind. It was not until much later that I met sincere white people I could relate to and be friends with. Racism breeds racism in reverse.

SOURCE: Crow Dog, Mary, & Erdoes, Richard. (1990). *Lakota Woman* (pp. 28–34). New York: HarperCollins.

LISTENING TO THE AIR

John Lame Deer

You have made it hard for us to experience nature in the good way by being part of it. Even here (a Sioux reservation in South Dakota) we are conscious that somewhere out in those hills there are missile silos and radar stations. White men always pick the few unspoiled, beautiful, awesome spots for these abominations. You have raped and violated these lands, always saying, "gimme, gimme, gimme," and never giving anything back. . . . You have not only despoiled the earth, the rocks, the minerals, all of which you call "dead" but which are very much alive; you have even changed the animals, . . . changed them in a horrible way, so no one can recognize them. There is power in a buffalo—spiritual, magic power—but there is no power in an Angus, in a Hereford.

There is power in an antelope, but not in a goat or a sheep, which holds still while you butcher it, which will eat your newspaper if you let it. There was great power in a wolf, even in a coyote. You made him into a freak—a toy poodle, a Pekinese, a lap dog. You can't do much with a cat, which is like an Indian, unchangeable. So you fix it, alter it, declaw it, even cut its vocal cords so you can experiment on it in a laboratory without being disturbed by its cries. . . .

You have not only altered, declawed, and malformed your winged and four-legged cousins; you have done it to yourselves. You have changed men into chairmen of boards, into office workers, into time-clock punchers. You have changed women into housewives, truly fearful creatures. . . . You live in prisons which you have built for yourselves, calling them "homes," offices, factories. We have a new joke on the reservations: "What is cultural deprivation?" Answer: "Being an upper-middle-class white kid living in a split-level suburban home with a color TV.". . .

I think white people are so afraid of the world they created that they don't want to see, feel, smell, or hear it. The feeling of rain or snow on your face, being numbed by an icy wind and thawing out before a smoking fire, coming out of a hot sweat bath and plunging into a cold stream, these things make you feel alive, but you don't want them anymore. Living in boxes that shut out the heat of the summer and the chill of winter, living inside a body that no longer has a scent, hearing the noise of the hi-fi rather than listening to the sounds of nature, watching some actor on TV have a make-believe experience when you no longer experience anything for yourself, eating food without taste—that's your way. It's no good.

SOURCE: Lame Deer, John (Fire), & Erdoes, Richard. (1972). Listening to the Air. In *Lame Deer, Seeker of Visions* (pp. 119–121). New York: Simon and Schuster.

READINGS

Native Americans are yet another minority group whose experiences have been profoundly shaped by whites as the dominant majority group. Once white settlers arrived on Native land, their stance toward Native Americans was based on a view that this group was a military threat that needed to be contained or eliminated. Whites' individualistic orientation and their exploitative approach toward the land contrasted sharply with Native Americans' collectivist orientation and deep respect for the connection between nature and humanity. Whites' devaluation of Native American values, combined with their stance of conquest and greater power over Native Americans, resulted in a situation of colonization and conquest whose effects are still being felt today. The first Reading, "Trends Among American Indians in the United States," examines some of these contemporary issues. After giving some background on estimated numbers of Native Americans and where they are located in the United States, author Russell Thornton discusses some of the U.S. government's policies toward them. We see that since 1976, Native Americans have had to assemble many documents to prove that they are a tribe before they can receive any kind of government recognition. Additionally, the government has had a long history of forcing Native Americans into federally run schools intended to "civilize" and to Christianize them. This view that Native Americans need to be civilized stems directly from the "savage" stereotype created by whites to rationalize their policies of termination and extermination of individual Native Americans and entire tribes. The legacy of this paternalistic relationship with the government can be seen today in the small number of educational institutions that are truly run by and for Native Americans. By the end of this Reading, however, Thornton seems to describe a more optimistic future by focusing on the Repatriation Movement and the successes they have had in reclaiming Native American artifacts and skeletal remains back from museums to their proper descendents and communities.

A key organizer of the American Indian Movement (AIM), Leonard Peltier is the author of the second Reading. The Reading is an excerpt from his book, *Prison Writings,* which is written in diary-like vignettes reflecting back upon his life. Peltier is currently in a federal prison as a result of his role in a political protest organized by AIM. Although he is charged with the murder of a federal officer, the key witnesses used by the government to convict him have now confessed that they were coerced by federal officials into providing false testimony. However, this evidence has not been allowed to grant him a pardon or retrial, and he has been imprisoned for decades. This Reading begins with Peltier explaining why he sees himself as an Indian, and not an American, and continues to assert how prison has been just one way the government has sought to contain the Native American population. Peltier's reflections on his early years demonstrate the persistent poverty, dehumanizing "civilizing" education, and violent discrimination and prejudice that Native Americans faced, including Eisenhower's "termination and relocation" policy of the 1950s, which directly impacted the young Peltier. Peltier's writing shows the struggle Native Americans face just to speak their own language and practice their own religion—actions he describes as his "first crimes" in the eyes of authorities. We see how Indian culture and customs are a healing comfort to Peltier, and simultaneously we see how difficult it is just to be able to know and practice one's culture due to the dominant group's extermination efforts toward Native Americans.

Paula Gunn Allen focuses distinctly on these struggles in the third Reading, "Angry Women Are Building." From a Native American woman's perspective, Allen concurs with Peltier that the key issue facing Native Americans is survival. However, Allen defines survival as not only cultural but "biological" or physical as well. The high rates of poverty, alcoholism, infant mortality, and sterilization without consent are just some of the problems faced by Native

American women and can often be linked back to the policies of conquest and colonization by whites. In particular, Allen makes the argument that the rape and physical violence against women perpetrated by Native American men is a direct result of them internalizing the negative, savage-like media imagery about Native Americans created by the dominant group. In fact, gender relations were reported to be more egalitarian among Native Americans before their contact with white society. The violence against women (and also alcoholism) that is so predominant for Native Americans today is not a part of indigenous Native culture, yet this violence now threatens to destroy it. Allen writes with a passion and urgency that both documents the issues and shows how anger quite understandably results from being an enduring target of oppression.

TRENDS AMONG AMERICAN INDIANS IN THE UNITED STATES[1]

Russell Thornton

Scholars debate the size of the aboriginal population north of present-day Mexico, and the magnitude of population decline beginning sometime after A.D. 1500 and continuing to about 1900. Early in the twentieth century, for the region north of the Rio Grande, James Mooney estimated individual indigenous tribal population sizes at first European contact, summed them by regions, then totaled them, arriving at an estimate of 1,152,950 aboriginal people in that region of what would become North America (Mooney, 1910, 1928). Subsequent scholars generally accepted Mooney's estimate, although one—Alfred L. Kroeber—suggested the number was excessive and lowered it.

In 1966, however, Henry Dobyns used depopulation ratios to assert an aboriginal population size, for this area, of between 9 and 12 million people (Dobyns, 1966). In 1983, Dobyns used depopulation ratios from epidemics along with possible carrying capacities to assert some 18 million native Americans for North America—i.e., northern Mexico as well as the present-day United States, Canada, and Greenland (Dobyns, 1983).

Most scholars now agree that Mooney's population estimate significantly underestimated aboriginal population size for the area north of the Rio Grande and, thus, the baseline from which the area's aboriginal population decline may be assessed.[2] By the same token, most scholars consider Dobyns's estimates to be

excessive.[3] Other contemporary estimates, some of which are shown in Table 6.1, have varied from around 2 million to somewhat more than 7 million. The 7+ million estimate for north of present-day Mexico (Thornton, 1987) includes more than 5 million people in the present-day United States area and more than 2 million for present-day Canada, Alaska, and Greenland. Despite dissension about earlier population levels, there is no argument that substantial depopulation did occur after European arrival. The native population of the United States, Canada, and Greenland reached a nadir of perhaps 375,000 by 1900 (Thornton, 1987), although a somewhat larger nadir population has been argued (Ubelaker, 1988).

Trends in demographics, as well as in tribal sovereignty, economic development, education, and repatriation will be discussed here, with emphasis on change since the 1950s.

DEMOGRAPHIC AND RELATED TRENDS

Population Recovery

At the beginning of the twentieth century, the American Indian population of the United States and Canada began to increase. For the United States, census enumerations suggest almost continuous increase since 1900 (Table 6.1), a result of both decreases in mortality rates and increases in fertility rates. In fact, fertility has

Table 6.1   Twentieth Century Estimates of the Aboriginal Population of North America

North America[a]	United States	Research (Date)
1,148,000	846,000	Mooney (1910)
1.148,000	—	Rivet (1924)
2–3,000,000	—	Sapper (1924)
1,153,000	849,000	Mooney (1928)
1,002,000	—	Wilcox (1931)
900,000	720,000	Kroeber (1939)
1,000,000	—	Rosenblatt (1945)
1,000,000	—	Steward (1949)
2–2,500,000	—	Ashburn (1947)
1,001,000	—	Steward (1949)
2,240,000	—	Aschmann (1959)
1–2,000,000	—	Driver (1961)
9.8–12,500,000	—	Dobyns (1966)
3,500,000	2,500,000	Driver (1969)
2,171,000	—	Ubelaker (1976)
4,400,000	—	Denevan (1976)
—	1,845,000	Thornton (1981)
18,000,000	—	Dobyns (1983)
5-10,000,000	—	Hughes (1983)
12,000,000	—	Ramenofsky (1987)
7,000,000	5,000,000	Thornton (1987)
1,894,000	—	Ubelaker (1988)
2-8,000,000	—	Zambardino (1989)

[a]North of Mesoamerica.

Table 6.2   American Indian and Alaska Native[a] Population in the United States, 1900-1990

Year	Population
1900	237,000
1910	291,000
1920	261,000
1930	362,000
1940	366,000
1950	377,000
1960	552,000
1970	827,000
1980	1,420,000
1990	1,959,000

Note: [a]American Indian, Inuit, and Aleut.

SOURCE: U.S. Bureau of the Census (1993).

remained higher for American Indians than for the U.S. population as a whole (see Thornton et al., 1991). The increase has also been a result of changes in the number of individuals self-identifying as "Indian" on recent U.S. censuses. Not including Inuits (Eskimo) and Aleuts, the American Indian population increased from 524,000 in 1960, to 793,000 in 1970, to 1.4 million in 1980, to more than 1.8 million in 1990, largely because of changing racial definitions from one census to another. It has been estimated that about 25 percent of the change from 1960 to 1970, about 60 percent of the change from 1970 to 1980, and about 35 percent of the change from 1980 to 1990 resulted from these changing identifications (Passel, 1976; Passel and Berman, 1986; Harris, 1994). Changing self-identification has generally been attributed to racial and ethnic consciousness-raising during the 1960s and 1970s, as well as

American Indian political mobilization during the period.[4]

If Inuits and Aleuts are added to the more than 1.8 million American Indians enumerated in the 1990 Census, there was a total of more than 1.9 million native Americans in the United States in 1990 (U.S. Bureau of the Census, 1994). Adding in natives of Canada, the total in 1990 was approximately 2.75 million native Americans. This is obviously a significant increase over the 375,000 estimated for 1900 (Thornton, 1987); however, it is far less than the 7+ million in 1492. It is also only a very small fraction of the total population of the United States (more than 250 million in 1990) and Canada (more than 25 million in 1990).

U.S. census enumerations also provide self-reported tribal affiliations and ancestries. According to the 1990 Census, the 10 largest tribal affiliations in the United States are Cherokee, 308,000; Navajo, 219,000; Chippewa (Ojibwe), 104,000; Sioux, 103,000; Choctaw, 82,000; Pueblo, 53,000; Apache, 50,000; Iroquois, 49,000; Lumbee, 48,000; and Creek, 44,000 (U.S. Bureau of the Census, 1993: Figure 6.1).[5]

Tribal Enrollment

There are 317 American Indian tribes in the United States that are "recognized" by the federal government and receive services from the

Figure 6.1. Native American Populations According to the 1990 Census.

SOURCE: U.S. Bureau of the Census (2000). URL: http://tiger.census.gov/cgi-bin/mapbrowse.tbl.

U.S. Bureau of Indian Affairs (BIA). There are also some 217 Alaska Native Village Areas identified in the 1990 Census, with populations of 9,807 American Indians, 32,502 Inuits, and 4,935 Aleuts (U.S. Bureau of the Census, 1992), some 125 to 150 tribes that are seeking federal recognition, and dozens of other groups who might do so in the future.

In 1990, some 437,079 American Indians, 182 Inuits, and 97 Aleuts lived on 314 reservations and trust lands; half of these—218,290 American Indians, 25 Inuits, and 5 Aleuts—lived on the 10 largest reservations and trust lands (Table 6.3; U.S. Bureau of the Census, 1993).

BIA has, generally, required a one-fourth degree of American Indian "ancestry" (blood quantum) and/or tribal membership to recognize an individual as American Indian.

Tribal membership requirements are typically set forth in tribal constitutions, approved by BIA. Each tribe also has a set of requirements for membership (enrollment) of individuals, generally including a blood-quantum requirement, and requirements vary widely (Table 6.4). The Walker River Paiute require at least a one-half Indian (or tribal) blood quantum, while many tribes—e.g., Navajo—require a one-fourth blood quantum. Some tribes, generally in Oklahoma or California, require a one-eighth or one-sixteenth or one-thirty-second blood quantum. Many tribes have no minimum blood-quantum requirement, but do require some degree of American Indian lineage (Thornton, 1997). American Indian tribes on reservations tend to have higher blood-quantum requirements for membership than those not on reservations, as indicated in Table 6.4; and those with higher blood-quantum requirements tend to be slightly smaller than tribes with lower blood-quantum requirements.

The total membership of the more than 300 federally recognized tribes in the late 1980s was slightly more than 1 million; hence, only about 60 percent of the more than 1.8 million individuals self-identified as American Indian on the 1990 Census were actually enrolled in a federally recognized tribe (Thornton, 1997). Differences in self-identification and tribal enrollment varied considerably from tribe to tribe. For example, most of the more than 219,000 Navajo in the 1990 Census were

Table 6.3   The 10 Largest Reservations and Trust Lands

Navajo Reservations and Trust Lands	143,405
Pine Ridge Reservation and Trust Lands	11,182
Fort Apache Reservation	9,825
Gila River Reservation	9,116
Papago Reservation	8,480
Rosebud Reservation and Trust Lands	8,043
San Carlos Reservation	7,110
Zuni Pueblo	7,073
Hopi Pueblo and Trust Lands	7,061
Blackfeet Reservation	7,025

SOURCE: U.S. Bureau of the Census (1993).

Table 6.4   Blood-Quantum Requirements by Reservation Basis and Membership Size

	More than ¼	¼ or Less	No Minimum Requirement
Number of tribes	21	183	98
Reservation based	85.7%	83.1%	63.9%
Median number of individual members	1,022	1,096	1,185

NOTE: Information not available for 15 tribes.

SOURCES: Thornton (1987); U.S. Bureau of Indian Affairs (unpublished tribal constitutions and tribal enrollment data obtained by the author).

enrolled in the Navajo Nation, but only about one-third of the more than 300,000 Cherokee were enrolled in one of the three Cherokee tribes—Cherokee Nation of Oklahoma, Eastern Band of Cherokee Indians, and United Keetoowah Band of Cherokee Indians.[6]

Redistribution and Urbanization

By the beginning of the twentieth century, American Indian groups that survived European contact had been redistributed (Figure 6.1). Much of this redistribution occurred during the nineteenth century with American Indian "removals," the establishment of the reservation system, and the subsequent elimination and allotment of some reservations. According to the 1990 Census, the 10 states with the largest American Indian populations were: Oklahoma, 252,000; California, 242,000; Arizona, 204,000; New Mexico, 134,000; Alaska, 86,000; Washington, 81,000; North Carolina, 80,000; Texas, 66,000;

New York, 63,000; and Michigan, 56,000 (U.S. Bureau of the Census, 1993).

A redistribution of American Indians also occurred through urbanization in the United States and Canada. As shown in Table 6.5, only 0.4 percent of the American Indians in the United States lived in urban areas in 1900. By 1950, the number had increased to 13.4 percent; in 1990, 56.2 percent of American Indians lived in urban areas (U.S. Bureau of the Census, 1992; Thornton, 1997).

Important in this urbanization was the migration to cities and towns, some of which occurred under the BIA relocation program, which began in 1950 to assist American Indians in moving from reservations and rural areas to selected urban areas (Thornton, 1994). U.S. cities with the largest American Indian populations are New York City, Oklahoma City, Phoenix, Tulsa, Los Angeles, Minneapolis-St. Paul, Anchorage, and Albuquerque (Thornton, 1994).[7]

Table 6.5   Percentage Urban of American
Indian Population of the United
States, 1900 to 1990

Year	Percentage Urban
1900	0.4
1910	4.5
1920	6.1
1930	9.9
1940	7.2
1950	13.4
1960	27.9
1970	44.5
1980	49.0
1990	56.2

Issues in the Twenty-First Century

New demographic threats will be faced by American Indians in the twenty-first century because of urbanization and its partner, inter-marriage. As populations of American Indians declined, and as they came into increased contact with Whites, Blacks, and others, American Indians increasingly married non-Indians, and this pattern has accelerated with the recent increase in urbanization. In the United States today, almost 60 percent of all American Indians (as defined by the Office of Management and Budget) are married to non-Indians (Sandefur and McKinnell, 1985; Eschbach, 1995). It has also been argued that those "Native Americans" by way of self-identification—or "'new' Native Americans" (Thornton, 1997)—are more likely to be inter-married (Eschbach, 1995; Nagel, 1995).

Urbanization has also created some decreased sense of tribal identity. In the 1970 Census, about 20 percent of American Indians overall reported no tribal affiliation. Only about 10 percent of those on reservations reported no affiliation, whereas 30 percent of those in urban areas reported no affiliation (Thornton, 1987). The 1980 and 1990 Censuses report no comparable urban/reservation data; however, 25 percent of the American Indians in the 1980 Census and 15 percent of those in the 1990 Census reported no tribal affiliation (Thornton, 1994; U.S. Bureau of the Census, 1994). The 1990 Census also indicates that only about one-fourth of all American Indians speak an Indian language at home (U.S. Bureau of the Census, 1992); census enumerations indicate also that urban residents are far less likely than reservation residents to speak an Indian language or participate in cultural activities (Thornton, 1987).

If these trends continue, both the genetic and tribal distinctiveness of the total American Indian population will be greatly lessened. An American Indian population comprised primarily of "'old' Native Americans" strongly attached to their tribes will change to a population with a predominance of "'new' Native Americans" who may or may not have tribal attachments or even tribal identities. It may even make sense at some point in the future to speak mainly of Native American ancestry or ethnicity (Thornton, 1997).

SOVEREIGNTY AND POLITICAL PARTICIPATION

The idea of American Indian tribal sovereignty within the United States and the related issue of political participation within the larger American society have long been important issues for American Indians. They have, however, achieved new prominence in recent decades.

Sovereignty: Myth or Reality?

Chief Justice John Marshall described American Indian tribes as "domestic dependent nations" with "aspects of sovereignty" (Strickland, 1998). As Strickland pointed out (Strickland, 1998):

[F]rom the beginning of the Republic, the courts have acknowledged that Native American government is rooted in an established legal and historical relationship between the United States and Native American tribes or nations. This is at the heart of Native American constitutionalism and grows from precontact tribal sovereignty. [Moreover] the rights and obligations of Native Americans, unique to Indian law, derive from a legal status as members or descendants of a sovereign Indian tribe, not from race. [Nevertheless] for the Native American, law and the courts have been seen alternatively as shields of protection and swords of extermination, examples of balanced justice and instruments of a conquering empire (p. 248).

The federal government has a long history of defining, and thereby determining, the tribal status of both American Indian groups and American Indian individuals (Thornton, 1987). In 1871, Congress enacted legislation that basically destroyed tribal sovereignty, by ending the rights of American Indian groups to negotiate treaties with the United States. It said, "Hereafter no Indian Nation or Tribe within the Territory of the United States shall be acknowledged or recognized as an independent nation, tribe, or power with whom the United States may contract by treaty" (Blackwell and Mehaffey, 1983:53). Between then and 1934, American Indian tribes "became increasingly disorganized, in part because of other legislation passed in the late 1800s calling for the allotment of tribal lands" (Thornton, 1987:195). In 1934, the Indian Reorganization Act was passed, allowing that an American Indian group had "rights to organize for its common welfare," and delineated steps whereby this might occur (Cohen, 1982). Subsequently, though, "the U.S. government adopted policies more or less aimed at ending the special legal status of American Indian tribes, and in fact, 61 tribes were officially terminated" (Thornton, 1987:195)—i.e., no longer recognized by the federal government for the purposes of having relations.

Self-Determination Since Nixon

President Richard Nixon rejected the idea of terminating American Indian tribes, and in 1976 the Federal Acknowledgment was created, specifying seven mandatory criteria for an American Indian group to achieve federal recognition. It also placed the "burden of proof" on the American Indian group itself (Thornton, 1987). The seven criteria are:

1. A statement of facts establishing that the petitioner has been identified from historical times until the present on a substantially continuous basis, as "American Indian," or "aboriginal."

2. Evidence that a substantial portion of the petitioning group inhabits a specific area or lives in a community viewed as American Indian and distinct from other populations in the area, and that its members are descendants of an Indian tribe which historically inhabited a specific area.

3. A statement of facts which establishes that the petitioner has maintained tribal political influence or other authority over its members as an autonomous entity throughout history until the present.

4. A copy of the group's present governing document, or in the absence of a written document, a statement describing in full the membership criteria and the procedures through which the group currently governs its affairs and its members.

5. A list of all known current members of the group and a copy of each available former list of members based on the tribe's own defined criteria.

6. The membership of the petitioning group is composed principally of persons who are not members of any other North American tribe.

7. The petitioner is not, nor are its members, the subject of congressional legislation which has expressly terminated or forbidden the federal relationship (U.S. Bureau of Indian Affairs, 1978).

Given that a tribe is federally recognized, however, "the courts have consistently recognized that one of an Indian tribe's most basic powers is the authority to determine questions of its own membership. A tribe has power to grant, revoke, and qualify membership" (Cohen, 1982).

Legal Status Today

Today, American Indian tribes as entities are healthy, if not thriving. Both tribes and individuals, however, are dominated by a maze of laws and their interpretation. Strickland (1998) notes:

Much contemporary confusion results from the duality of traditional tribal law and federally enforced regulations. . . . The courts have powers of life-and-death proportion over tribal existence. The nature of U.S. constitutional law and public policy is such that legal issues loom large in even the smallest details of Native American cultural, economic, and political life. More than four thousand statutes and treaties controlling relations with Native Americans have been enacted and approved by Congress. Federal regulations and guidelines implementing these are even more numerous. The tribe's own laws, and some state statutes dealing with Indians, further complicate this legal maze (p. 252).

Importantly, American Indian tribes and individuals are unique in American society—they are the only segment of the U.S. population with a separate legal status, both as groups and as individuals.

As Native American peoples prepare to move into the twenty-first century, the issues facing tribes are not substantially different from those faced over the last five centuries. . . . The miracle of the past 500 years is that Native American people and their values have survived in the face of the most unbelievable onslaughts. There is little question that the law and the courts have been, and will continue to be, a major battlefield in the struggle for sovereign survival (Strickland, 1998:255).

Increased Political Participation

Until the late nineteenth century, American Indians were the dominant "minority group" the U.S. government had to deal with on the national, political scene. From the Civil War until the 1980s, however, American Indians were a "moral" but not "powerful" minority political group.

With the reaffirmation and reestablishment of American Indian tribes as legal entities since the 1970s, and the accompanying economic well-being of some of these tribes, however, American Indian tribes are becoming increasingly important and increasingly sophisticated political actors, something we have not seen since the subjugation of the great Sioux Nations around 1890.

ECONOMIC DEVELOPMENT AND ECONOMIC WELL-BEING

One of the most intriguing developments since the 1970s is the increased economic development of American Indian tribes and the increased control of American Indian tribes over this development. As Snipp (1988) noted,

Historically, American Indians have been one of the most economically deprived segments of American society. Joblessness and the accouterments of poverty, such as high infant-mortality rates and alcoholism, have been a traditional plague among Indian people (p. 1). . . . [A]s internal colonies, Indian lands are being developed primarily for the benefit of the outside, non-Indian economy (p. 3). [Thus] the tribes have been relatively unsuccessful in capturing the material benefits of development, and some observers claim that Indians are now exposed to subtle forms of economic exploitation, in addition to the political dominance they have experienced as captive nations.

Since Snipp made his arguments, the situation has changed partially; certainly not totally.

What Is Tribal Economic Development? Does It Translate to Tribal and Individual Well-Being?

Tribal economic development is generally conceived of as an increase in economic activities, particularly successful ones, on the part of the tribe itself as an entity, rather than increased economic well-being of tribal members per se. Individual economic well-being, nevertheless, is an important objective of tribal economic development; and American Indian tribes and individuals engage in virtually the entire spectrum of economic activities available in modern society, ranging from small service industries to manufacturing to extraction of natural resources—fishing, logging, hunting, etc. In some instances, the ability to exploit such resources has involved extensive legal issues engendered by American Indians' unique legal status in American society (Olson, 1988).

Tribes are also engaged in activities more specifically related to American Indian culture and themselves as American Indian peoples or peoples in rural areas. As is the case with many indigenous peoples worldwide, American Indian tribes are often involved in tourism, as objects of tourism or providers of facilities for tourists in tribal areas or both. Activities related to tourism on tribal lands include running museums, gift shops, gas stations, hotels, and restaurants; providing transportation and other direct services; and performing cultural plays, pow wows, dances, and, sometimes, ceremonies.

American Indian tribes have also engaged in economic activities available to them because of (rather than in spite of) their unique legal status in American society. First and foremost is legal gambling. In some instances, tribes have built and/or operate large, successful casinos that have brought some degree of prosperity to them and their members. Some of the more successful ones are operated by the Mississippi Choctaw in Philadelphia and Mississippi and by the Pequot in Connecticut.

Generally, tribal and individual economic well-being go hand in hand. It is not, however, always a simple, straightforward matter. For example, it is typically an issue of some discussion—and often dissension—as to how much of the "profits" from economic activities are to be either turned back into the business in question; used for tribal activities involving health, education, and welfare programs; distributed to tribal members individually; or used to fund other tribal activities. "Other activities" might include buying sacred tribal sites back from state governments (the Mississippi Choctaw considered buying their sacred mound from Mississippi), or giving donations to the National Museum of the American Indian (as did the Pequot), or making direct political campaign contributions (as was the case with the Southern Cheyenne of Oklahoma).

Conflicting Values and Traditions

Important in the decision to engage in economic activities is the issue of the type of activity to engage in and how chosen activities may or, typically, may not fit into the traditional cultural values of the tribe. Nowhere does more conflict occur than in considering the issue of gambling. Some tribes have explicitly decided not to engage in such activities—as profitable as they might be—because they conflict with important values. Wilma Mankiller, the former principal chief of the Cherokee Nation of Oklahoma, said that one of the most difficult decisions she made as principal chief was the decision that the Nation would not engage in gaming. "I literally cried when I made the decision," she said (personal conversation with the author). Gaming could have been very profitable for the Cherokee Nation and could have improved the economic well-being of tribal members, but it is also against Cherokee values.

There are American Indian communities who see economic development either as a return to old subsistence practices or as simply a reaffirmation of such practices. The attempt by the Makah Nation of Neah Bay, Washington, to return to traditional whaling practices is a case in point. Similarly, there are Inuit communities in Alaska who still cherish their traditional, subsistence lifestyles and are determined to preserve them.

EDUCATION OF AMERICAN INDIANS

Europeans sought to convert to Christianity and educate ("civilize," as they defined it) the native peoples of this hemisphere since, virtually, their first arrival. . . .

The efforts were very much a part of European colonization: "Indians could not be Christians until they first abandoned native habits and accepted 'civilized' customs. . . . 'Civilization and salvation' was the credo of nearly every North American missionary, which often proved to be a euphemism for cultural invasion and tribal decline" (Ronda and Axtell, 1978:30). Europeans' plans for the education of American Indians included not only mission schools but also colleges. The objectives were basically the same—train an elite group of natives who would then teach their own people "civilization and salvation." . . .

Government Schools

As Whites struggled with the idea of the new country they were creating, they sought to place American Indians within it. It became important

Table 6.6 Schools Under the Auspices of the Five Tribes

	Schools		Orphan Homes/	
	Day	*Boarding*	*Academies*	*Others*
Cherokee Nation	140	1	1	1 colored high school 2 seminaries
Creek Nation	52	6 (2 colored)	1 (1 colored)	
Choctaw Nation	190		5	
Chicksaw Nation	16	3	1	
Seminole Nation	Unknown number of schools			

NOTE: "Colored" denotes schools for former slaves of the Cherokee and Creek nations.

SOURCE: U.S. Bureau of Indian Affairs (1903).

for enlightened thinkers, like the revolutionary founding fathers, to believe that American Indians could attain equality with Whites through proper training. . . .

Thomas Jefferson advocated intermarriage as well as the adoption of White lifestyles through training. After telling a gathering of Indians to adopt farming and private property, he predicted to them, "you will become one people with us; your blood will mix with ours, and will spread with ours over this great island" (Jefferson). Thus, intermarriage with Whites would "uplift" the entire American Indian race. The problem was those American Indians who insisted on being "Indians" and living un-"White" lifestyles. The solution became mandatory training and education for all American Indians. . . .

Boarding and Other Schools

When one thinks of the history of the education of American Indians, one thinks first of the American Indian boarding and day schools provided by the U.S. government primarily for elementary and secondary education and vocational and technical training. The schools began generally after the Civil War, with many established in the 1870s through 1890s. Several were on reservations.

In 1878, a group of American Indian students were sent to Hampton Normal and Agricultural Institute (now Hampton University) in Virginia, established in 1868 for former slaves. The Indians were some of the Kiowa, Comanche, and Cheyenne former prisoners, members of southern plains tribes, involved in the "Outbreak of 1874" during the winter of 1874–1875. They had been imprisoned at Fort Marion, Florida.[8] Other American Indian students soon followed, and American Indians continued to attend Hampton until 1923.

Carlisle Indian School, of football and Jim Thorpe fame, established at Carlisle, Pennsylvania, in 1879, under Richard H. Pratt, was the first American Indian off-reservation boarding school. It restricted students' access to their families and gave them half a day of education and half a day of work. It also had an outing system, whereby students were placed with a White family to work for three years. Other boarding schools included Chilocco Industrial School in Oklahoma (1884), Albuquerque Indian School (1886), Santa Fe School (1890), Phoenix School (1892), Pipestone Indian Training School in Minnesota (1893), Chamberlain School in South Dakota (1898), and Riverside School in California (1902).

A 1903 report (U.S. Bureau of Indian Affairs, 1903) describes 221 government schools on reservations, 93 boarding schools, and 128 day schools, in addition to schools provided by states and schools in Indian Territory under the auspices of the Five Tribes (Table 6.6). Also listed are 26 off-reservation boarding schools and five off-reservation day schools.

A quarter-century later, it was realized that such schools were not providing the appropriate type of education. The Meriam Report of 1928 noted "that the whole Indian problem is essentially an educational one" (Meriam, 1928:348), and called for the redirection of the education of American Indians. As a result, the 1930s became a turning point, with educational objectives becoming more sympathetic to American Indians. Slowly, schools established for American Indians began to incorporate aspects of American Indian history and culture into their curricula. Following the Meriam Report, the number of boarding schools decreased, as students were increasingly channeled to day schools and, especially, public schools.

By the 1950s, public school education for American Indians had become more prevalent, following legislation terminating federal relationships with tribes and the relocation of American Indians to urban areas, "thus dumping many thousands of additional Indian students into the *public* school system" (Noriega, 1992:386). There were still, however, well over 200 American Indian schools run by the U.S. government. By 1968, the education of American Indians in the United States was, in the words of the U.S. Senate Special Subcommittee on Indian Education, "a national tragedy" (Prucha, 1975). The solution was greater involvement of American Indians in their own schools. Specific federal legislation was passed—the Indian Education Act of 1972 and the Indian Self-Determination and Educational Assistance Act of 1975. Also "survival schools" were established by the American Indian Movement, in urban areas primarily (Heart of the Earth in Minneapolis and The Red Schoolhouse in St. Paul, Minnesota), but also on reservations.

In 1999, there were almost 100 American Indian day and boarding schools.

Colleges

The first all-American Indian college in North America was Bacone College in Muskogee, Oklahoma, founded in 1880 by the Baptist Home Mission Board. Several academies were then established to provide students for Bacone—the Cherokee Academy, the Choctaw Academy, the Seminole Female Academy, the Waco Baptist Academy for the Wichita (at Anadarko), and The Lone Wolf Mission among the Kiowa (Prucha, 1975).

Pembroke State University was established in 1887 at Lumberton, North Carolina, it, too, solely for the education of American Indians. Originally an elementary and secondary school, Pembroke became a two-year, then four-year college, then a university in 1969, and was the only four-year, state-supported university in the United States exclusively for American Indians. Both Bacone and Pembroke State eventually expanded their mandate to include non-American Indians.

Haskell Indian Nations University (formerly Haskell Institute) in Lawrence, Kansas, was first established as the U.S. Indian Industrial Training School in 1884 as a boarding school focused on agricultural education. A decade later it changed its name to Haskell Institute as it expanded its training. In 1970, it became Haskell Indian Junior College; its current name was taken in 1993, after receiving accreditation to offer a bachelor's degree in education. It is still only for American Indians, and provides higher education to federally recognized tribal members. In 1995, it had the full-time equivalent of 890 students, representing some 147 tribes.

Since 1969, 29 tribal colleges have been established, either solely or primarily for American Indians. The first was the Navajo Community College in Tsaile, Arizona (1969). Typically, these schools are two-year community colleges offering associate degrees in academic, vocational, and technical areas; they also have programs in American Indian studies, frequently focused on their own tribe. As of 1996, there were three four-year colleges and one offering a master's degree (National Research Council, 1996:56). There are also other two-year community colleges, not wholly tribally run, that offer instruction in American Indian studies.

American Indian Studies

The Civil Rights Movement emerged fully in the 1960s. Accompanying it was heightened ethnic consciousness; not only Black became beautiful, any shade became beautiful and any ethnic origin became meaningful. Against these forces, the American academic system was changed. Students became important decision makers in their own education and educational institutions. Formerly all-male colleges became co-ed; and colleges and universities became more racially and ethnically integrated. As increasing numbers of minority students entered higher education, ethnic studies developed organizationally, if not intellectually. Ethnic studies courses found their way into curricula; and ethnic studies programs, departments, and degrees were created. A main driving force was the increased number of Black students calling for Black studies programs. Other groups followed their lead.

The impetus for the development of "Native American" studies was increased numbers of American Indian students. They formed organizations and associations and lobbied university faculties and administrators for academic programs to accompany the student support programs that were developing, and to receive their share of the ethnic studies impetus.

By the mid-1970s, 76 of 100 colleges and universities surveyed had courses dealing with American Indian concerns (Locke, 1974). When American Indian studies entered the academic system, however, it did so primarily as a reaction to the way American Indians were usually studied, rather than as a positive, worthy body of knowledge in its own right. Of particular concern, and inciting particular opposition, was the type of research conducted under the aegis of anthropology, and the "all inclusiveness" of anthropology as the discipline encompassing American Indian studies. An important problem had been anthropology's focus on American Indians at the point of the "ethnographic present," as if frozen in time with little prior history—and certainly no significant subsequent history—as "real" American Indians. In no small way, American Indian studies were also a protest against the technique of researchers establishing "friendships" with American Indians solely for research purposes.

American Indian studies also reacted against the history curriculum's lack of inclusion of American Indians as part of mainstream American history. What American Indian history was included, focused all too frequently on wars, battles, and American Indian warriors, and too little on American Indian views, philosophies, or the oral record. American Indian history was virtually limited to literature

covering American Indian-White relationships, as though American Indians had no other history as a group or individually as nations. And, finally, American Indian studies reacted against the almost total lack of study of American Indian societies and cultures by other disciplines, such as sociology, political science, psychology, art, music, literature, religion, or philosophy. The main emphasis of the new area became American Indian history, a topic seemingly present in every American Indian studies program. Focusing on ethnic history was a means of going beyond the traditional anthropological approach, recognizing that American Indians were real people with significant pasts and futures. . . .

There was interest in presenting and describing native cultures, religions, art, music, customs, and practices; and a consideration of contemporary issues was ever-present. Other subjects included federal Indian law (typically not "Native American law," as traditionally practiced), the education of American Indians, and American Indian languages and linguistics.

There is the same mix of topics 30 years later, although some have been added—e.g., economic development. "Native American" literature is at the forefront of the humanities facet of American Indian studies. American Indian history in the form of "ethnohistory" remains at the forefront of the social science component.[9] . . .

Despite all the activity, American Indian studies as a separate intellectual entity in higher education is underdeveloped. This does not mean that acceptable courses are not offered (though little innovation may be shown in the courses), that important community service and applied activities are not performed, that students are not adequately advised, or even that important research and writings have not been accomplished. All have, to one degree or another.[10] However, the full potential of American Indian studies is unrealized in most American Indian studies programs, in whatever fashion they are organized.

REPATRIATION . . .

The repatriation of American Indian human remains as well as the repatriation of funerary objects and other cultural objects, identified as "objects of patrimony"—i.e., something owned by the entire people—such as wampum belts, or sacred objects such as medicine bundles, is occurring today because of determined efforts by American Indians to achieve legal changes in American society.

Collecting Human Remains as Objects of Study

It has been estimated that objects obtained from graves and other sacred sites, and skeletal remains of "hundreds of thousands" of American Indians are held in various universities, museums, historical societies, and even private collections in the United States and in other countries (Price, 1991). Whatever the actual figure, the estimates indicate a sizeable problem. It is also estimated that the skeletons, or more typically pieces of them, of several hundred American Indians and countless objects buried with them are uncovered every year in highway, housing, and other types of construction (Price, 1991).

American Indian remains and artifacts have been objects of study and intrigue to non-American Indians for centuries. Reported excavations of American Indian burial sites and mounds date from the eighteenth century. American Indian crania have been objects of particular scientific interest since the early nineteenth century. Various scholars actively collected American Indian remains, seeking to explain possible migration from Asia by comparing American Indians with Asians (Bieder, 1986). They also sought to explain physical and cultural differences between and among native peoples and others; often cultural differences were seen as a result of racial ones. In 1839, Morton published *Crania Americana,* reporting that Caucasians had larger brain capacities and therefore higher intelligence than American Indians, and the "science" of phrenology soon developed. Collecting crania became more widespread, as scholars attempted to relate intelligence, personality, and character to skulls and brains. . . .

Some of the human remains and objects subject to legal repatriation were obtained appropriately, with the permission if not actual support of American Indians at the time. Many, however, were not. The fact that many of the human remains and objects were obtained by grave robbing, theft, and fraudulent acts adds to American Indian discomfort and further legitimates claims for repatriation. . . .

Important Research Findings

Research on American Indians' skeletal remains has generated much important knowledge about such diverse topics as population size and composition, cultural patterns of tooth mutilation, diseases among populations and customs of treatments for the diseases, life expectancies, growth patterns, population affinities, origins and migrations, and diets, including dates when corn was introduced into the diets of the native peoples of North America (Buikstra, 1992). From studying human remains of American Indians we now know, for example, that tuberculosis was present in this hemisphere prior to European contact, as were some other infectious diseases, especially treponema infections; that certain native groups had serious iron deficiencies from a diet heavily dependent on corn;[11] and that among some groups, males with more social prestige—as reflected by burial objects—were physically larger than males with less social prestige (perhaps because they had better diets, perhaps because bigger men were simply given more prestige). . . .

Some scholars and others assert that the scientific knowledge to be gained from the remains and cultural objects outweigh claims American Indians may have on them. They argue that the scientific value is important not only to native peoples themselves but to the public at large as scholars attempt to reconstruct histories of American Indians. A related view is that the remains and objects now housed in museums and educational institutions belong not only to American Indians, but to all Americans, even to all peoples of the world, as part of the heritage of all humanity. Yet another view is that scholars are keeping and studying the remains because American Indians do not know what they are doing when requesting repatriation. Perhaps they think that someday American Indians will want this knowledge, and it is up to science to preserve it for them.

The Repatriation Movement

Many American Indians believe repatriation must occur despite any scholarly or general public good that may be derived from the study or display of the remains and objects. They assert that cultural and spiritual factors outweigh science and education. Furthermore, they point out that society and the government have already placed all sorts of restrictions on research deemed inappropriate. Particularly important, American Indians contend, is that Americans have been resolute in regard to returning to the United States the remains of American soldiers who died on foreign shores defending this country. American Indian skeletons obtained from battlefields, as many of those in the Army Medical Museum were, are remains of American Indians who died defending their homelands. It is felt that refusal to return the remains of American Indian warriors killed in battle implies that these fighters—and civilians killed in battles and massacres—are less deserving of an honorable burial than American servicemen and -women who died for the United States.

American Indians have attempted to legally prevent the collection of their human remains and cultural objects for more than a century (Cole, 1985). In the 1970s and 1980s, they increasingly demanded that ancestral remains and sacred objects be returned to them for proper disposal or care. . . .

The private sector also became involved in the repatriation movement, just as it did in the Civil Rights Movement. A major turning point was when Elizabeth Sackler purchased for $39,050 three Hopi and Navajo ceremonial masks in 1991. Her intent was to return them to the tribes. She then established the American Indian Ritual Object Repatriation Foundation to assist native groups in retrieving important cultural objects from private individuals and organizations.[12] The Foundation continues to be active in repatriation.

During the 1980s, the Pan-Indian Repatriation Movement began to experience some success through the passage of federal and state laws not only calling for the repatriation of human remains and objects to descendants, but also preventing the further disenfranchisement of

remains and objects. Not only has the success of the repatriation movement revitalized Native America by providing new-found self-esteem, the task of actually repatriating human remains and cultural objects has also revitalized communities by bringing members together in the struggle as well as reaffirming important knowledge about many cultural and sacred objects. It is not always an easy undertaking, however; but the end result is worth it. . . .

The repatriation process has great potential for bridging the gap between native worlds and larger society. As it developed, repatriation of human remains polarized advocates of reburial and advocates of study and preservation in repositories. Little compromise occurred between American Indian repatriation activists and researchers; yet, some degree of compromise is not only desirable, it is necessary. Science and scholarship have much to offer to American Indians, as American Indians attempt to recapture their lost histories. American Indians are no longer powerless in American society, but are important actors in shaping their own destinies. American Indian values, wishes, and perspectives must be respected by scholars. Although some disciplines such as anthropology have histories of applied work with American Indians, the repatriation process is providing new challenges for the application of scholarly disciplines to real-life concerns of American Indians. . . .

SUMMARY AND CONCLUSIONS

Trends in demographics, tribal sovereignty, economic development, education, and repatriation are extremely important for American Indians in American society. Demographically, American Indians are now not only surviving in society, but also increasing in numbers. However, the ways American Indians define themselves, and are defined by our society, are changing; and this may have far-reaching implications for American Indians in the twenty-first century.

American Indian tribal sovereignty is alive if not well, and numerous court cases will continue to emerge as the legal relationships between American Indians and society continue to be debated, refined, and changed. Important, however, is the fact that American Indians may once again emerge as powerful political players on the national scene—not just as moral entities, but also as significant economic entities. This is in part because of the newly possible economic development of American Indian tribes. The twenty-first century holds much promise for American Indians in this regard.

Educationally, American Indians have gained some measure of control over the education of their youth, a trend unlikely to reverse itself in the new century. Also important, educationally, is the emergence of American Indian studies. It has the potential to fundamentally alter American conceptions about American Indians and bring important new knowledge bases within the realm of academe; unfortunately, that potential is largely unfilled.

Finally, the legally mandated repatriation of American Indian human remains and objects back to the native communities from which they came—and to which many would say they belong—is fundamentally altering the relationships of American Indians with society and academe. Important in this is the movement toward alleviating the traumas of history many American Indians experienced with colonialism and still find unresolved.

NOTES

1. The sections of this paper on demography, education, and repatriation were drawn freely from my chapters on the same topics in Thornton (1998).

2. Dates for Mooney's regional estimates, from which his overall estimate was derived, varied from A.D. 1600 to A.D. 1845, depending on the region in question. A reason for his underestimate, scholars now realize, was Mooney's assumption that little population decline had occurred prior to his dates for the beginning of an extended European presence in a region. In fact, it seems that prior depopulation had occurred in most, if not all, regions.

3. There have been various criticisms of Dobyns's methodologies, particularly those in his 1983 book but also those in his 1966 paper.

4. Changing self-identification was perhaps also a result of individuals of mixed ancestry who formerly did not identify as American Indian because of the stigma attached to such an identity by the larger society. Clearly, however, some individuals with minimal, or no, Native American ancestry may have identified as American Indian because of the desire to affirm a marginal, or establish a nonexistent, ethnic identity.

5. It should be noted that about 11 percent of those individuals identifying as Native American in the 1990 Census did not report a tribal affiliation.

6. The situation in Canada is somewhat different. In Canada one must be registered under the Indian Act of Canada to be an "official" Indian. Categories of Canadian Indians include: (1) status (or registered) Indians, those recognized under the Act; and (2) nonstatus (or nonregistered) Indians, those never registered under the Act or those who gave up their registration (and became "enfranchised"). Status Indians are subdivided into treaty and nontreaty Indians, depending on whether the group ever entered into a treaty relationship with the Canadian government. There are also the Métis—individuals of Indian and White ancestry not legally recognized as Indians. Some 500,000 of the 575,000 Canadian Indians in the mid-1980s were registered. About 70 percent of Canadian Indians live on one of the 2,272 reserves. There were 578 bands of Canadian Indians in the early 1980s, most containing fewer than 500 members. Only three bands had more than 5,000 members: Six Nations of the Grand River, 11,172; Blood, 6,083; and Kahnawake, 5,226.

7. Canadian provinces with the largest number of Native Americans are Ontario, British Columbia, Saskatchewan, and Manitoba. Approximately 40 percent of Canadian Native Americans lived in cities in the mid-1980s, particularly Vancouver, Edmonton, Regina, Winnipeg, Toronto, and Montreal. This was an increase from the 30 percent who lived in cities in the early 1970s, and the mere 13 percent who lived in cities in 1961. However, still only about 20 percent of Canadian Inuits live in cities, while only about 30 percent of the status Indians do.

8. This event is represented in the Dohasan Kiowa Winter Count with a picture of Big Meat, who was killed by soldiers. Above his head is a drawing of Fort Sill, Indian Territory (I.T., now Oklahoma), where some Kiowa were also imprisoned. (See A Chronicle of the Kiowa Indians (1832–1892).

Berkeley: R. H. Lowie Museum of Anthropology, University of California, Berkeley, pp. 10, 18, footnote O.)

9. The repatriation of American Indian human remains, grave goods, sacred objects, and objects of cultural patrimony from museums, colleges, universities, and elsewhere as mandated by the Native American Graves Protection and Repatriation Act (NAGPRA) of 1990 as well as the National Museum of the American Indian (NMAI) Act of 1989 (which limited its provisions to the Smithsonian Institution) has greatly expanded the importance of ethnohistory, particularly to native peoples but also to museums and educational institutions. Critical to the repatriation process under both NAGPRA and the NMAI Act is the establishment of cultural affiliation between contemporary groups and historic groups represented by the remains or objects. Thus, American Indian groups may, and often must, present different types of evidence to establish cultural affiliation—archaeological evidence, including physical anthropology, written history, oral traditions, ethnography, etc. For repatriation, archaeology and physical anthropology are important components of ethnohistory, along with anthropology and history. The archaeological record and the written record may be eventually reconciled with American Indian memories, in oral traditions, or otherwise.

10. There are journals devoted to Native American studies—e.g., American Indian Quarterly, Northeast Indian Studies, American Indian Culture and Research Journal, and Wicazo Sa Review.

11. These and other topics are discussed in Verano and Ubelaker (1992).

12. The Foundation has recently published Mending the Circle to assist native groups with their repatriation efforts; it is distributed free of charge to them.

REFERENCES

Bieder, R. 1986. *Science Encounters the Indian, 1820–1880: The Early Years of American Ethnology*. Norman: University of Oklahoma Press.

Blackwell, C., and J. Mehaffey. 1983. American Indians, trust and recognition. In *Nonrecognized American Indian Tribes: An Historical and Legal Perspective*, F. Porter, III, ed. Occasional Papers Series, no. 7. Chicago: The Newberry Library.

Buikstra, J. 1992. Diet and disease in late prehistory. Pp. 87–101 in *Disease and Demography in the Americas*, J. Verano and D. Ubelaker, eds. Washington, D.C.: Smithsonian Institution Press.

Cohen, F. 1982 [1942]. *Handbook of Federal Indian Law* (reprint). New York: AMS Press.

Cole, D. 1985. *Captured Heritage: The Scramble for Northwest Coast Artifacts*. Seattle: University of Washington Press.

Dobyns, H. 1966. Estimating Aboriginal American population: An appraisal of techniques with a new hemispheric estimate. *Current Anthropology* 7:395–416.

———.1983. *Their Number Become Thinned: Native American Population Dynamics in Eastern North America*. Knoxville: University of Tennessee Press.

Eschbach, K. 1995. The enduring and vanishing American Indian. *Ethnic and Racial Studies* 18:95.

Harris, D. 1994. The 1990 Census count of American Indians: What do the numbers really mean? *Social Science Quarterly* 15:583.

Jefferson, T. n.d. Thomas Jefferson address, War Department, National Archives.

Locke, P. 1974. *A Survey of College and University Programs for American Indians*. Boulder, CO: Western Interstate Commission for Higher Education.

Meriam, L. 1928. *The Problem of Indian* Administration. Baltimore: The Johns Hopkins Press.

Mooney, J. 1910. Population. In *Handbook of American Indians North of Mexico*, F. Hodge, ed. Washington, D.C.: U.S. Government Printing Office.

———. 1928. The aboriginal population of America north of Mexico. In *Smithsonian Miscellaneous Collections*, Vol. 80, J. Swanton, ed. Washington, D.C.: U.S. Government Printing Office.

Nagel, J. 1995. *Politics and the resurgence of American Indian ethnic identity*. American Sociological Review 60:953.

National Research Council. 1996. *Colleges of Agriculture at the Land Grant Universities: Public Service and Public Policy*. Washington, D.C.: National Academy Press.

Noriega, J. 1992. American Indian education in the United States: Indoctrination for subordination to colonialism. In *The State of Native America: Genocide, Colonization, and Resistance*, M. Jaimes, ed. Boston: South End Press.

Olson, M. 1988. The legal road to economic development: Fishing rights in western Washington. Pp. 77–112 in *Public Policy Impacts on American Indian Economic Development*, C. Snipp, ed. Albuquerque: Institute for Native American Development, Development Series No. 4, University of New Mexico.

Passel, J. 1976. Provisional evaluation of the 1970 Census count of American Indians. *Demography* 13:397–409.

Passel, J., and P. Berman. 1986. Quality of 1980 Census data for American Indians. *Social Biology* 33:986.

Price, H., III. 1991. *Disputing the Dead: U.S. Law on Aboriginal Remains and Grave Goods*. Columbia: University of Missouri Press.

Prucha, F., ed. 1975. *Documents of United States Indian Policy*. Lincoln: University of Nebraska Press.

Ronda, J., and J. Axtell 1978. *Indian Missions: A Critical Bibliography*. Bloomington: Indiana University Press.

Sandefur, G., and T. McKinnell. 1985. *Intermarriage Among Blacks, Whites and American Indians*. Paper presented at the meetings of the American Sociological Association, Washington, D.C.

Snipp, C. 1988. Public policy impacts and American Indian economic development. In *Public Policy Impacts on American Indian Economic Development*, C. Snipp, ed. Albuquerque: Institute for Native American Development, Development Series No. 4, University of New Mexico.

Strickland, R. 1998. The eagle's empire. In *Studying Native America: Prospects and Problems*, R. Thornton, ed. Madison: University of Wisconsin Press.

Thornton, R. 1987. *American Indian Holocaust and Survival: A Population History since 1492*. Norman: University of Oklahoma Press.

———. 1994. Urbanization. Pp. 670–671 in *Native Americans in the Twentieth Century: An Encyclopedia*, M. Davis, ed. New York: Garland.

———. 1997. Tribal membership requirements and the demography of "old" and "new" Native Americans. *Population Research and Policy Review* 7:9.

———. 1998. *Studying Native America: Problems and Prospects*. Thornton, R. ed. Madison: University of Wisconsin Press.

Thornton, R., G. Sandefur, and C. Snipp. 1991. American Indian fertility history. American Indian Quarterly 15:359–367.

U.S. Bureau of the Census. 1992. *1990 Census of Population: General Population Characteristics: American Indian and Alaska Native Areas*. Washington, D.C.: U.S. Government Printing Office.

———. 1993. *We the. . . First Americans*. Washington, D.C.: U.S. Government Printing Office.

———. 1994. *1990 Census of the Population: Characteristics of American Indians by Tribe and Language*. Washington, D.C.: U.S. Government Printing Office.

U.S. Bureau of Indian Affairs 1903. *Statistics of Indian Tribes, Agencies, and Schools, 1903*. Washington, D.C.: U.S. Government Printing Office.

———. 1978. Guidelines for Preparing a Petition for Federal Acknowledgment as an Indian Tribe. Washington, D.C., photocopy:3, 8–11, 17.

Ubelaker, D. 1988. North American Indian population size, A.D. 1500 to 1985. *American Journal of Physical Anthropology* 77:289–294.

Verano, J., and Ubelaker, D., eds. 1992. *Disease and Demography in the Americas*. Washington, D.C.: Smithsonian Institution Press.

DISCUSSION QUESTIONS

1. Why do American Indian tribes have to meet a long list of criteria before they can be recognized as a tribe by the federal government? Why is this the only U.S. racial group that has to "prove" its identity for the purposes of federal recognition?

2. On the issue of gambling to bring economic development to Native Americans, what are the different views surrounding this activity? What do these differences tell us about the diversity within the category of "American Indian"?

3. The author suggests that repatriation should involve a fair compromise between the scientific community and American Indian communities in terms of how skeletal remains and artifacts should be used. Do you agree or disagree with this position? If other non-Indian families have to give permission for their families' remains and possessions to be used for science, why haven't Native Americans been accorded these same rights? Can the term "paternalism" be applied here, and if so, how?

Growing Up Indian

Leonard Peltier

Like most Indian people, I have several names. In Indian Way, names come to you in the course of your life, not just when you're born. Some come during childhood ceremonies; others are given on special occasions throughout your life. Each name gives you a new sense of yourself and your own possibilities. And each name gives you something to live up to. It points out the direction you're supposed to take in this life. One of my names is Tate Wikuwa, which means "Wind Chases the Sun" in the Dakota language. That name was my great-grandfather's. Another name, bestowed on me by my Native Canadian brethren, is Gwarth-ee-lass, meaning "He Leads the People."

I find special inspiration in both of those names. The first, to me, represents total freedom—a goal even most of those outside prison walls never achieve. When I think that name to myself—Wind Chases the Sun—I feel free in my heart, able to melt through stone walls and steel bars and ride the wind through pure sunlight to the Sky World. No walls or bars or rolls of razor wire can stop me from doing that. And the second name—He Leads the People—to me, represents total commitment, a goal I strive for even within these walls, reaching out as best I can to help my people.

Maybe it seems presumptuous, even absurd—a man like me, in prison for two lifetimes, speaking of leading his people. But, like Nelson Mandela, you never know when you will suddenly and unexpectedly be called upon. He, too, knows what it's like to sit here in prison, year after year, decade after decade. I try to keep myself ready if ever I'm needed. I work at it within these walls, with my fellow inmates, with my supporters around the world, with people of good will everywhere. A strong leader shows mercy. He compromises for the good of all. He listens to every side and never makes hasty decisions that could hurt the people. I'm trying very hard to be the kind of leader I myself could respect.

So, in our way, my names tell me and others who I am. Each of my names should be an inspiration to me. Here at Leavenworth—in fact anywhere in the U.S. prison system—my official name is #89637–132. Not much imagination, or inspiration, *there.*

My Christian name, though I don't consider myself to be a Christian, is Leonard Peltier. The last name's French, from the French fur hunters and voyageurs who came through our country more than a century ago, and I take genuine pride in that holy blood, too. The name is a shortening of Pelletier, but has come to be pronounced, in the American fashion, Pel-teer. My first name was given to me by my grandmother, who said I cried so hard as a baby that I sounded like a "little lion." She named me Leonard, she said, because it sounded like "lion-hearted." I don't know how she figured that out, but years later I looked it up in a dictionary of names and found that Leonard literally means "lion-hearted."

Though my bloodline is predominantly Ojibway and Dakota Sioux, I have also married into, and been adopted in the traditional way by, the Lakota Sioux people. All the Lakota/Dakota/Nakota people—also known as Sioux—are one great nation of nations. We Indians are many nations, but one People. I myself was brought up on both Sioux and Ojibway (Chippewa) reservations in the land known to you as America.

I would like to say with all sincerity—and with no disrespect—that I don't consider myself an American citizen. I am a native of Great Turtle Island. I am of the Ikce Wicasa—the Common People, the Original People. Our sacred land is under occupation, and we are now *all* prisoners, not just me.

Even so, I love being an Indian, for all of its burdens and all of its responsibilities. Being an Indian is my greatest pride. I thank Wakan Tanka, the Great Mystery, for making me Indian. I love my people. If you must accuse me of something, accuse me of that—being an Indian. To that crime—and to that crime alone—I plead guilty.

My crime's being an Indian.
What's yours?. . .

When you grow up Indian you quickly learn that the so-called American Dream isn't for you. For you that dream's a nightmare. Ask any Indian kid: you're out just walking across the street of some little off-reservation town and there's this white cop suddenly comes up to you, grabs you by your long hair, pushes you up against a car, frisks you, gives you a couple good jabs in the ribs with his nightstick, then sends you off with a warning sneer: "Watch yourself, Tonto!" He doesn't do that to white kids, just Indians. You can hear him chuckling with delight as you limp off, clutching your bruised ribs. If you talk smart when they hassle you, off to the slammer you go. Keep these Injuns in their place, you know.

Truth is, they actually need us. Who else would they fill up their jails and prisons with in places like the Dakotas and New Mexico if they didn't have Indians? Think of all the cops and judges and guards and lawyers who'd be out of work if they didn't have Indians to oppress! We keep the system going. We help give the American system of injustice the criminals it needs. At least being prison fodder is *some* kind of reason for being. Prison's the only university, the only finishing school many young Indian brothers ever see. Same for blacks and Latinos. So-called Latinos, of course, are what white man calls Indians who live south of the Rio Grande. White man's books will tell you there are only 2.5 million or so of us Indians here in America. But there are more than 200 million of us right here in this Western Hemisphere, in the Americas, and hundreds of millions more indigenous peoples around this Mother Earth. We are the Original People. We are one of the fingers on the hand of humankind. Why is it we are unrepresented in our own lands, and without a seat—or many seats—in the United Nations? Why is it we're allowed to send our delegates only to prisons and to cemeteries?

Oddly enough, oppressed by the same people, we Indians often wind up fighting each other for what few perks are left to us in prison or society at large. "Set'm against each other and let'm fight it out while we rip them off!"

That's been white man's strategy for five hundred years, and, hey, it's worked damned well for them! So, when you grow up Indian, you don't have to become a criminal, you already *are* a criminal. You never know innocence.

I was brought up into a world like that. It's a world most white people never see and will never know. When they do happen to drive by an Indian "rez" while out on vacation to see the four white presidential faces that desecrate the face of the holy mountain they call Mt. Rushmore, they gawk at us. They don't stop and say hello. They don't wave. They don't smile. They gawk. "Look!" the parents tell the kids as they pass by in their shiny car, pointing their finger at us—"There's an Indian!" . . . People drive through a reservation and see half a dozen junk cars in some Indian family's front yard and they shake their heads, saying, "These dirty Indians, how can they live like that? Why don't they get rid of those junkers?"

Maybe these people, so quick to judge, don't understand the higher mathematics of being poor. They don't realize that, when you can't afford to buy or commercially repair a car, it may take six or eight junkers out in the yard to keep one junker going on the road. Those yard junkers take on a special value in Indian eyes: they're the source of that hard-to-come-by and almost sacred commodity in Indian country—transportation. Without wheels out in the empty distances of the rez, you're utterly isolated. When the family's one working car breaks down, one of those yard junkers may provide precisely the part that's needed so that Pop can drive seventy miles to town each day to his menial job and help feed his often-hungry family. To such a family, those junkers out in the yard represent survival.

Besides, there's often some old auntie who sleeps, even lives, in those old wrecks. And, if you open the trunk or the glove compartment, you'll often see lovingly stacked rows of Indian corn and beans, sage, and sweetgrass, arranged in there like fine jewels. There's a poetry in those junkyards. Those old junkers can hold holy things in their rusted innards. Sort of like us Indians. Remember that next time you drive through a rez and see those junkers in the yard. They're holy, too. . . .

I was born on September 12, 1944, in Grand Forks, North Dakota. My father, Leo, was three-fourths Chippewa (Ojibway) and—he always told us—one-fourth French. My mother, Alvina Showers, had a Dakota Sioux mother and a Chippewa father. When I was four my parents separated, then divorced, and my sister Betty Ann and I went to live with my father's parents, Alex and Mary Dubois-Peltier, on the Turtle Mountain Reservation, about four miles north of Belcourt, North Dakota. In Indian Way, the grandparents often bring up the kids; the old knowledge passes down not so much from parent to child as from grandparent to grandchild. That's in part why we honor our Elders. In our way, when you grow old, you *become* an Elder—and that's something to look forward to your whole life. So being raised by my grandparents—"Gramps" and "Gamma" we little kids called them—was one of the truly beautiful things in my life. Gamma taught me the old songs and stories, and even a little medicine. Gramps would take me out hunting, show me how to make things, how to survive all on your own out in the wild.

As a child, I became fluent in *métis*—a French-Indian mixture—as well as English, and I also spoke some Sioux, Ojibway, and French words. Since every language gives you a different view of reality, I soon saw that there were many realities you had to cope with in this life, most of them unpleasant.

At the time, our family used to work in the potato fields, migrating during harvest season from the reservation to the Red River Valley. You picked the spuds by hand, getting only 8 to 10 cents for a bushel. My job when I was small was to run up ahead and shake the spuds loose from the vines so the others could come along and pick them up more quickly. We lived at that time in a small log house, about twenty feet by fifteen feet. No water or electricity. We carried water from a distant spring or well. We cut and hauled wood for heat and cooking. I worked long hours, grew big and strong, and had no particular complaints about life, hard as it was. From my earliest years, living through each day was a matter of survival. That's just the way it

was. It seemed natural. It made a survivor of me, that hard life. I've been a survivor ever since.

I was brought up with both Christian religion and Indian traditional religion. My grandmother believed in Indian traditional religion and also was a Catholic. Everyone knew that if you were Catholic, or at least Christian, you got more government assistance. I attended both kinds of services. Gamma didn't really get the spiritual relief she was seeking out of the Catholic's religion, so she never stopped going to Indian ceremonies. For medical problems she often went to a medicine man. That's how I was introduced to Indian religion. I was also introduced to Catholic religion, but that was something I lost faith in at an early age. I must have been about nine years old, I remember thinking to myself that I could never be a good, believing Catholic; it all seemed so harsh and far removed and devoid of human caring, at least where Indians were concerned. I don't want to criticize Catholics; that's just the way a child saw it. Maybe they were a lot harsher in my time than today. I understand there have been changes over the years, I don't know. For the sake of Indian children still in parochial care, I hope so.

In any case, I always felt more at home, more at ease, with Indian religion; it made me feel like I belonged, like I was wanted *as* an Indian and it also seemed loving and caring and wonderfully mystical and bound to our Mother the Earth and our Grandfather the Sky and to Wakan Tanka, the Great Mystery. And, in the sweat lodge and the Sun Dance, it taught you to deal with pain—something white man would always see that you as an Indian would have plenty of in this life. Our Elders spoke of the Original Instructions given to us by Wakan Tanka, and how the very first Instruction of all is to *survive*! Those same Elders taught us that we're not here to *preserve* our tradition, but to *live* it. Those lessons of the Elders have held me in good stead throughout my life. I've needed them often, and will no doubt continue needing them. . . .

Around 1950, during particularly hard times on the rez, my grandfather took the family out to Montana, hoping to make some money working in the mines or logging camps there. We lived awhile in Butte, where, at age six, I got everyone in trouble by refusing to run away when three white kids started flinging rocks at me. "Go on home, you dirty Indian!" they laughed, using me for what they thought was a defenseless target. I got hit several times before I picked up a small rock, really just a large pebble, and sent it whistling back at them in defense. Damned if it didn't hit one of them smack on the temple. You could see the blood running down his face and he was screaming like he was about to die. I was terrified.

I ran home, hid under the bed, and prayed and prayed that that white boy wouldn't die. "Oh, let him live!" I remember crying. "Let him live!" A while later a big shiny automobile came pulling up in front of our little rented house. Big shiny automobiles always spelled trouble for Indians. A white woman got out. She was yelling and screaming and carrying on, warning she was going to have to put me away in the reformatory and calling Gamma dirty names like "stupid bitch" and "filthy squaw," things like that. When she left she shouted she was going right to the police, have the whole "dirty bunch" of us thrown in jail.

I listened to it all from under the bed, shivering the whole while. When Gamma came in and demanded to know what had happened, I was too scared to even talk. I just held my hand to my mouth. That was one of the few times Gramps ever spanked me; words and a hard look were usually all that was necessary to keep discipline in our family. But that time Gramps really gave it to me with a horse strap. I kept my hand over my mouth the whole spanking so I wouldn't cry, and he really laid into me. Finally I told him what happened. He shook his head with tears welling up in the wrinkled corners of his eyes, and then he smiled the saddest smile and patted me on the head. He said I wasn't wrong, but that I still shouldn't have done it, throw that stone back at them. I should have thought of the family. Now we'd all have to pack up quick and get right out of there before the law came and made big trouble. "You're not s'posed to rile these white folks, boy," Gramps said. "They'll come back and get you every time. That's just the way they are." We packed up and headed back to North Dakota

that very evening. Nobody chided me about it again. In fact, my sister clapped her hands and declared me a hero. "Not a hero," Gramps said, "he's a warrior!" I took tremendous pride in that.

After Gramps died of pneumonia when I was eight, life became really hard for us. My grandmother was left alone. She spoke hardly any English, had almost no income, and was trying to raise three small kids—me, my sister, and our cousin Pauline. I tried stocking the table with my slingshot, coming up with an occasional squirrel or maybe a small bird; mostly Gamma used them to flavor the otherwise vegetarian soup. I never could seem to catch a rabbit with my slingshot, like the big fat ones Gramps had gotten now and then with his single-shot-22 for Gamma's beloved rabbit stew. Given the cold North Dakota winters, hunger became a really big problem for us. We had no bread, no milk, hardly anything else. I thought that gnawing ache in my belly was just the way I was supposed to feel.

One day in the fall of 1953, a big black government car came and took us kids away to the Bureau of Indian Affairs boarding school in Wahpeton, North Dakota. I remember Gamma weeping in the doorway as she watched them take us off. We had no suitcases, just bundles. First thing after we got there, they cut off our long hair, stripped us naked, then doused us with powdered DDT. I thought I was going to die. That place, I can tell you, was very, very strict. It was more like a reformatory than a school. You were whacked on the butt with a yardstick for the smallest infraction, even if you so much as looked someone in the eye. That was considered insubordination, trying to relate to another person as a human being.

I consider my years at Wahpeton my first imprisonment, and it was for the same crime as all the others: being an Indian. We had to speak English. We were beaten if we were caught speaking our own language. Still, we did. We'd sneak behind the buildings, the way kids today sneak out to smoke behind the school, and we'd talk Indian to each other. I guess that's where I first became a "hardened criminal," as the FBI calls me. And you could say that the first infraction in my criminal career was speaking my own language. There's an act of violence for you! . . .

After graduating from Wahpeton in 1957, I went to Flandreau, down in South Dakota, where I finished ninth grade. Then I went back home to Turtle Mountain Reservation, where my father had returned to live. I guess I was growing up to be a pretty normal teenager. I wanted a car, and built one out of spare parts. I got so good at it that later on, in Seattle, I would get into the body-and-fender shop business.

Living on the rez as a young teen, I attended lots of powwows and religious ceremonies, but I also went to the largely white school dances and listened to a lot of rock radio: Elvis, the Everly Brothers, Buddy Holly were some of my favorites. I was drawn to both cultures. I found myself spread-eagled between them, really, and, like many of my Indian brothers and sisters, I was nearly torn apart by the contradictions and conflicts between the two that I both saw in the outside world and felt within myself.

This was during the last years of the Eisenhower administration, when a resolution was passed by Congress and signed by President Eisenhower to "terminate" all Indian reservations and to "relocate" us off our lands and into the cities. Those suddenly became the most important, the most feared, words in our vocabulary: "termination" and "relocation." I can think of few words more sinister in the English language, at least to Indian people. I guess the Jews of Europe must have felt that way about Nazi words like "final solution" and "resettlement in the East." To us, those words were an assault on our very existence as a people, an attempt to eradicate us.

We were given two choices: either relocate or starve. Later, court decisions would declare this compulsory policy totally illegal, which it was, but that was no comfort to us at the time. We pleaded with the government to let us stay on our land and to create some employment on the reservation, as they had promised to do, but all that was in vain. The ones we went to for help, the Bureau of Indian Affairs, were the last ones, it seemed, with any intention of helping us. It's no accident that the BIA started off back in the 1800s as part of the Department of War. They're still waging war on us today.

To implement their inhuman policy, the federal government in the late 1950s cut off the reservations' already meager supply of food and commodities—the pitiful little "payment" they'd promised us in those treaties to recompense us for all the vast and holy continent they'd stolen. Hunger was the only thing we had plenty of; yeah, there was plenty of that to go around, enough for everybody. When frantic mothers took their bloated-bellied children to the clinic, the nurses smiled and told them the children just had "gas." A little girl who lived right near us on the reservation died of malnutrition. Sounds like "termination" to me.

"Termination" was nothing new in red-white relations, really. They'd been trying to terminate us since 1492. They've always wanted to get rid of us, and I suppose they'll never stop trying. Indian people were offered money to get off the rez and move to cities like Minneapolis, Milwaukee, Cleveland, Los Angeles, and Chicago, where all those wonderful inner-city slums and mean streets were waiting for us. With the reservation under threat of termination, housing was severely limited. Our lands were being leased right out from under us by white ranchers and mining interests, or annexed by the U.S. government. My family, like many others, wound up with nowhere to stay. We were being all but forced off the rez to go to the newly sprouting urban "red ghettos" the government was so keen on sending us to. Sometimes we shuttled between relatives, sometimes we slept in the car. . . .

I was about fourteen at the time. My dad, who'd returned to live with us, had started attending community meetings on the reservation to discuss the government's decision to terminate Turtle Mountain. I went along with him to those meetings, more to eat the few little snacks they served on such occasions than to hear the political arguments. But at one of those meetings I chanced to do a little listening for a change, and something started stirring deep inside me—even deeper than the hunger in my belly. Some women were weeping aloud about having starving children at home. One Ojibway lady, a cousin of mine—I'll always remember it—stood up angrily and asked in a loud, emotional, tear-filled voice, "Where are our warriors? Why don't they stand up and fight for their starving people?"

That sent electric vibrations from my scalp all the way down my spine to the soles of my feet. It was like a revelation to me—that there was actually something worthwhile you could *do* with your life, something more important than living your own selfish little life day by day. Yes, there was something more important than your poor miserable self—your *People.* You could actually stand up and fight for them! Now *that* was something I had never learned in school or heard about on the radio. I'd only learned in school and from society at large that being Indian was something I was supposed to be ashamed of, something I was supposed to cast aside for my own well-being. "Kill the Indian to save the man!" was their official motto! Now here was this woman challenging me to the roots of my being with the notion of the *People.* Yes, the People, the Tiospaye as the Lakota call the extended family, and by extension, as I would come to see in later years, *all* Indian people, all indigenous people, all human beings of good heart. I vowed right then and there that I would become a warrior and that I'd always work to help my people. It's a vow I've done my best to keep.

About that same time, I renewed my interest in Indian religion and Indian Way, taking part in ceremonies and sensing something echoing deep inside myself. One night in 1958, a few friends and I sneaked out to watch the Sun Dance at Turtle Mountain, which was held secretly because piercing went on, which was illegal at the time. We got a few close-up glimpses of the Sun Dancers, with the rivulets of blood running down their chests. I was impressed that no one was screaming or hollering or whimpering. Those guys looked fiercely proud; I envied them and vowed that someday I would be a Sun Dancer. Then, my friends and I were actually arrested by BIA police as we came out of the Sun Dance grounds. They claimed we were drunk—a total lie—and jailed us overnight. They were afraid to arrest the Sun Dancers, who would surely have put up a fight, but we young teenagers were there, and we were Indian, so why not arrest us? They did. Here I was, not yet fifteen, and already I was getting firsthand experience in government-fabricated criminal charges and false imprisonment. I began to realize that my real crime was simply being who I was—an Indian.

So speaking my language was my first crime, and practicing my religion was the second. When I was also arrested that winter for siphoning some diesel fuel from an army reserve truck to heat my grandmother's freezing house, I was arrested again and spent a couple of weeks in jail. That was my first stretch of hard time. So trying to keep my family from freezing was my third crime, the third strike against me. Henceforth, I would be considered "incorrigible." My career as a "hardened criminal" was already well on its way. . . .

DISCUSSION QUESTIONS

1. Why does Peltier say he does not consider himself an American? When your people grow up for centuries on certain land, and then it is overtaken by people who rename it "America" and treat you as a foreigner in your own land, what kinds of emotions might you experience?

2. What do you think was the rationale behind converting American Indians to Catholicism and sending children to prison-like boarding school? How might this treatment make a young child feel about his or her heritage? When, as a child, Peltier's family had to pick up and move because he fought back against racial slurs, what messages might this have communicated to him about the differences between whites and Indians in American society?

3. What are some of the cultural values and traditions that warm Peltier's heart despite society's disparagement of them? What might be the effect on a group of people for the dominant group to strip away such sources of pride and dignity? Are there ways to annihilate a people without killing them directly? If so, what are some ways to do this, according to Peltier? Are the underestimated counts of Native Americans' population in the United States a part of this process?

ANGRY WOMEN ARE BUILDING: ISSUES AND STRUGGLES FACING AMERICAN INDIAN WOMEN TODAY

Paula Gunn Allen

The central issue that confronts American Indian women throughout the hemisphere is survival, *literal survival,* both on a cultural and biological level. According to the 1980 census, population of American Indians is just over one million. This figure, which is disputed by some American Indians, is probably a fair estimate, and it carries certain implications. [Editors' note: The 1995 population is over two million.]

Some researchers put our pre-contact population at more than 45 million, while others put it at around 20 million. The U.S. government long put it at 450,000—a comforting if imaginary figure, though at one point it was put at around 270,000. If our current population is around one million; if, as some researchers estimate, around 25 percent of Indian women and 10 percent of Indian men in the United States have been sterilized without informed consent; if our average life expectancy is, as the best-informed research presently says, 55 years; if our infant mortality rate continues at well above national standards; if our average unemployment for all segments of our population—male, female, young, adult, and middle-aged—is between 60 and 90 percent; if the U.S. government continues its policy of termination, relocation, removal, and assimilation along with the destruction of wilderness, reservation land, and its resources, and severe curtailment of hunting, fishing, timber harvesting and water-use rights—then existing tribes are facing the threat of extinction which for several hundred tribal groups has already become fact in the past five hundred years.

In this nation of more than 200 million, the Indian people constitute less than one-half of one percent of the population. [Editors' note: In 1995, this figure was one percent.] In a nation that offers refuge, sympathy, and billions of dollars in aid from federal and private sources in the form of food to the hungry, medicine to the sick, and comfort to the dying, the indigenous subject population goes hungry, homeless, impoverished, cut out of the American deal, new, old, and in between. Americans are daily made aware of the worldwide slaughter of native peoples such as the Cambodians, the Palestinians, the Armenians, the Jews—who constitute only a few groups faced with genocide in this century. . . . The American Indian people are in a situation comparable to the imminent genocide in many parts of the world today. The plight of our people north and south of us is no better; to the south it is considerably worse. Consciously or unconsciously, deliberately, as a matter of national policy, or accidentally as a matter of "fate," *every single government,* right, left, or centrist in the western hemisphere is consciously or subconsciously dedicated to the extinction of those tribal people who live within its borders.

Within this geopolitical charnel house, American Indian women struggle on every front for the survival of our children, our people, our self-respect, our value systems, and our way of life. The past five hundred years testify to our skill at waging this struggle: for all the varied weapons of extinction pointed at our heads, we endure.

We survive war and conquest; we survive colonization, acculturation, assimilation: we survive beating, rape, starvation, mutilation, sterilization, abandonment, neglect, death of our children, our loved ones, destruction of our land, our homes, our past, and our future. We survive, and we do more than just survive. We bond, we care, we fight, we teach, we nurse, we bear, we feed, we earn, we laugh, we love, we hang in there, no matter what.

Of course, some, many of us, just give up. Many are alcoholics, many are addicts. Many abandon the children, the old ones. Many commit suicide. Many become violent, go insane. Many go "white" and are never seen or heard from again. But enough hold on to their traditions and their ways so that even after almost five hundred brutal years, we endure. And we even write songs and poems, make paintings and drawings that say "We walk in beauty. Let us continue."

Currently our struggles are on two fronts: physical survival and cultural survival. For women this means fighting alcoholism and drug abuse (our own and that of our husbands, lovers, parents, children);[1] poverty; affluence— a destroyer of people who are not traditionally socialized to deal with large sums of money; rape, incest, battering by Indian men; assaults on fertility and other health matters by the Indian Health Service and the Public Health Service; high infant mortality due to substandard medical care, nutrition, and health information; poor educational opportunities or education that takes us away from our traditions, language, and communities; suicide, homicide, or similar expressions of self-hatred; lack of economic opportunities; substandard housing; sometimes violent and always virulent racist attitudes and behaviors directed against us by an entertainment and educational system that wants only one thing from Indians: our silence, our invisibility, and our collective death.

A headline in the *Navajo Times* . . . reported that rape was the number one crime on the Navajo reservation. In a professional mental health journal of the Indian Health Services, Phyllis Old Dog Cross reported that incest and rape are common among Indian women seeking services and that their incidence is increasing. "It is believed that at least 80 percent of the Native Women seen at the regional psychiatric service center (five state area) have experienced some sort of sexual assault."[2] Among the forms of abuse being suffered by Native American women, Old Dog Cross cites a recent phenomenon, something called "training." This form of gang rape is "a punitive act of a group of males who band together and get even or take revenge on a selected woman."[3]

These and other cases of violence against women are powerful evidence that the status of women within the tribes has suffered grievous decline since contact, and the decline has increased in intensity in recent years. The amount of violence against women, alcoholism, and violence, abuse, and neglect by women against their children and their aged relatives have all increased. These social ills were virtually unheard of among most tribes fifty years ago, popular American opinion to the contrary. As Old Dog Cross remarks:

> Rapid, unstable and irrational change was required of the Indian people if they were to survive. Incredible loss of all that had meaning was the norm. Inhuman treatment, murder, death, and punishment was a typical experience for all the tribal groups and some didn't survive.
>
> The dominant society devoted its efforts to the attempt to change the Indian into a white-Indian. No inhuman pressure to effect this change was overlooked. These pressures included starvation, incarceration and enforced education. Religious and healing customs were banished.
>
> In spite of the years of oppression, the Indian and the Indian spirit survived. Not, however, without adverse effect. One of the major effects was the loss of cultured values and the concomitant loss of personal identity. . . The Indian was taught to be ashamed of being Indian and to emulate the non-Indian. In short, "white was right." For the Indian male, the only route to be successful, to be good, to be right, and to have an identity was to be as much like the white man as he could.[4]

Often it is said that the increase of violence against women is a result of various sociological factors such as oppression, racism, poverty, hopelessness, emasculation of men, and loss of male self-esteem as their own place within traditional society has been systematically destroyed by increasing urbanization, industrialization, and institutionalization, but seldom do we notice that for the past forty to fifty years, American popular media have depicted American Indian men as bloodthirsty savages devoted to treating women cruelly. While traditional Indian men seldom did any such thing— and in fact among most tribes abuse of women was simply unthinkable, as was abuse of children or the aged—the lie about "usual" male Indian behavior seems to have taken root and now bears its brutal and bitter fruit.

Image casting and image control constitute the central process that American Indian women must come to terms with, for on that control rests our sense of self, our claim to a past and to a future that we define and that we build. Images of Indians in media and educational materials profoundly influence how we act, how we relate to the world and to each other, and how we value ourselves. They also determine to a large extent how our men act toward us, toward our children, and toward each other. The popular American media image of Indian people as savages with no conscience, no compassion, and no sense of the value of human life and human dignity was hardly true of the tribes—however true it was of the invaders. But as Adolf Hitler noted a little over fifty years ago, if you tell a lie big enough and often enough, it will be believed. Evidently, while Americans and people all over the world have been led into a deep and unquestioned belief that American Indians are cruel savages, a number of American Indian men have been equally deluded into internalizing that image and acting on it. Media images, literary images, and artistic images, particularly those embedded in popular culture, must be changed before Indian women will see much relief from the violence that destroys so many lives.

To survive culturally, American Indian women must often fight the United States government, the tribal governments, women and men of their tribe or their urban community who are virulently misogynist or who are threatened by attempts to change the images foisted on us over the centuries by whites. The colonizers' revisions of our lives, values, and histories have devastated us at the most critical level of all—that of our own minds, our own sense of who we are.

Many women express strong opposition to those who would alter our life supports, steal our tribal lands, colonize our cultures and cultural expressions, and revise our very identities. We must strive to maintain tribal status; we must make certain that the tribes continue to be legally recognized entities, sovereign nations within the larger United States, and we must wage this struggle in many ways—political, educational, literary, artistic, individual, and communal. We are doing all we can: as mothers and grandmothers; as family members and tribal members; as professionals, workers, artists, shamans, leaders, chiefs, speakers, writers, and organizers, we daily demonstrate that we have no intention of disappearing, of being silent, or of quietly acquiescing in our extinction.

NOTES

1. It is likely, say some researchers, that fetal alcohol syndrome, which is serious among many Indian groups, will be so serious among the White Mountain Apache and the Pine Ridge Sioux that if present trends continue, by the year 2000 some people estimate that almost one-half of all children born on those reservations will in some way be affected by FAS. (Michael Dorris, Native American Studies, Dartmouth College, private conversation. Dorris has done extensive research into the syndrome as it affects native populations in the United States as well as in New Zealand.)

2. Phyllis Old Dog Cross, "Sexual Abuse, a New Threat to the Native American Woman: An Overview," Listening Post. A Periodical of the Mental Health Programs of Indian Health Services, vol. 6, no. 2 (April 1982), p. 18.

3. Old Dog Cross, p. 18.

4. Old Dog Cross, p. 20.

DISCUSSION QUESTIONS

1. What are some of the conditions that threaten American Indians' survival today? According to this assessment, are things any different for Native Americans today than they were, say, 50 or 100 years ago?

2. Is cultural genocide just as damaging as physical genocide? When members of a tribe "go 'white' and are never seen or heard from again," how does this affect American Indians as a people? Could it be true that governments everywhere are either "consciously or subconsciously" aiding in this process, as Allen suggests? If so, in what ways?

3. If various forms of abuse and neglect existing in Native American communities today "were virtually

unheard of among most tribes fifty years ago," why do you think they exist at such a high rate today? What is it about colonization and conquest of a people that causes such negative consequences among them? How do negative media images of oneself create negative consequences, such as violence against women, discussed by Allen?

CURRENT DEBATES

SHOULD COLUMBUS DAY BE CELEBRATED?

Most issues that separate Native Americans and the larger society concern the control or ownership of tangible resources such as water supplies, fishing or mineral rights, and land. Other issues focus on more symbolic matters: nicknames for sports teams (Redskins, Braves, Seminoles), cheers at football and baseball games that feature mock Indian gestures (tomahawk chops), music, and dance, and the commercial use of Indian symbols and historical figures. Non-Indians often dismiss these symbolic issues as trivial, silly, or the result of an exaggerated concern for political correctness. To Native Americans, however, they may be deeply felt, touch many nerves, and connect (if only symbolically) to many other issues.

One such issue centers on the fall holiday designated to honor the arrival of Christopher Columbus in the New World. Did this day mark the beginnings of a great new civilization in the Western Hemisphere or did it foreshadow the bloody, savage end of the ancient civilizations that had occupied these lands for thousands of years? Should this day be used to celebrate the arrival of European traditions or to mourn the cultures, languages, lifestyles, and people that would be lost in the centuries following 1492?

The selections that follow outline this debate. Christopher Hitchens, while acknowledging the brutality of the conquest, argues that the benefits of development and modernity the resulted from the European conquest makes 1492, all in all, a "very good year." Glenn Morris and Russel Means take the opposite point of view and argue strongly that Columbus Day should be seen as a day of mourning, while N. Scott Momaday attempts to find a middle ground between these two positions.

COLUMBUS DAY SHOULD BE CELEBRATED

Christopher Hitchens

My old comrade David Dellinger, hero of the anti-imperialist movement, telephoned the other day to tell me of the fast he was undertaking to protest the celebration of racism, conquest and plunder that impended on Columbus Day. I am as respectful of my elders as any ancestor-worshiping Iroquois, and David has been to prison for his beliefs more times than I have had hot dinners, but a hot dinner—with steak frites, cheese and salad and a decent half bottle of something, all complete—was what I urged him to go and have. Break your fast, old thing, I beseeched; 1492 was a very good year.

I can never quite decide whether the anti-Columbus movement is merely risible or faintly sinister. It is risible in the same way that all movements of conservative anachronism are risible, and reminds me of Evelyn Waugh's complaint that he could never find a politician who would promise to put the clock back. It is sinister, though, because it is an ignorant celebration of stasis and backwardness, with an unpleasant tinge of self-hatred.

Not long ago, another good man, Ted Solotaroff, sent me a book he had helped edit called *Black Hills/White Justice,* by Edward Lazarus. This details the long courtroom battle fought by various factions of the Sioux to reclaim their rights in the mountains of South Dakota. You can guess the story: treaties broken, lands filched, settlements put to the torch, women and children vilely abused. And all of it done by the Sioux to the Kiowa Indians, who had controlled the Black Hills before the Sioux got there in 1814. Actually, the book deals mainly with the greed and depredation of the palefaces, which is no doubt as it should be. But it is honest enough to say that the Sioux did drive off the Kiowa, and it quotes Chief Black Hawk saying candidly, "These lands once belonged to the Kiowas and the Crows, but we whipped these nations out of them, and in this we did what the white men do when they want the lands of the Indians."

This is only a micro-illustration of the absurdity of rounding a claim of right or justice on the idea of the indigenous. The Arawaks who were done in by Columbus's sailors, the Inca, the Comanche and the rest were not the original but only the most recent inhabitants. (Arizona Indians refer cryptically to the Hohokam—"the people before"—who populated that valley in advance of them.) Some advocates now take nonsense and place it on stilts, referring to "Native Americans" and thus employing (a) the most condescending colonial adjective for indigenes, namely "native"; and (b) the one term the description is expressly designed to repudiate, namely "American."

Even if the matter of who came "first" could be decided, it would be pointless except as a means to devalue the claims of those—some millions of Irish, English, German, Italian, Jewish and other refugee workers—who migrated across the Atlantic many years after at least some of the "natives" migrated across the Aleutian Island chain. How can a sensibility that represents mass emigration and immigration as mere conquest and settler colonialism dare to call itself "progressive"? But those who view the history of North America as a narrative of genocide and slavery are, it seems to me,

hopelessly stuck on this reactionary position. They can think of the Western expansion of the United States only in terms of plague blankets, bootleg booze and dead buffalo, never in terms of the medicine chest, the wheel and the railway.

One need not be an automatic positivist about this. But it does happen to be the way that history is made, and to complain about it is as empty as complaint about climatic, geological or tectonic shift. Not all changes and victories are "progress"? The Roman conquest and subjugation of Britain was, I think, a huge advance because it brought the savage English tribes within reach of Mediterranean (including Ptolemaic and Phoenician as well as Greek and Latin) civilization, whereas the Norman Conquest looks like just another random triumph of might.

The very dynasty that funded Columbus put an end to Andalusia in the same year, and thus blew up the cultural bridge between the high attainments of Islamic North Africa and Mesopotamia and the relative backwardness of Castilian Christendom. Still, for that synthesis to have occurred in the first place, creating the marvels of Cordoba and Granada, wars of expansion and conversion and displacement had to be won and lost. Reapportioning Andalusia according to "precedent" would be as futile an idea as restoring Sioux rights that are only "ancestral" as far back as 1814. The Sioux should be able to claim the same rights and titles as any other citizen, and should be compensated for past injury. That goes without saying. But the anti-Columbus movement is bored by concepts of this kind, preferring to flagellate about original sin and therefore, inevitably, to brood about the illusory counterpart to that exploded concept—the Garden of Eden.

Forget it. As Marx wrote about India, the impact of a more developed society upon a culture (or a series of warring cultures, since there was no such nation as India before the British Empire) can spread aspects of modernity and enlightenment that outlive and transcend the conqueror. This isn't always true; the British probably left Africa worse off than they found it, and they certainly retarded the whole life of Ireland. But it is sometimes unambiguously the case that a certain coincidence of ideas, technologies, population movements and politico-military victories leaves humanity on a slightly higher plane than it knew before. The transformation of part of the northern part of this continent into "America" inaugurated a nearly boundless epoch of opportunity and innovation, and thus deserves to be celebrated with great vim and gusto, with or without the participation of those who wish they had never been born.

SOURCE: *The Nation,* Oct 19, 1992, vol. 255 no. 12.

WHY COLUMBUS DAY CELEBRATIONS AND PARADES SHOULD BE OPPOSED

Glenn Morris and Russell Means

When Taino Indians saved Christopher Columbus from certain death on the fateful morning of Oct. 12, 1492, a glorious opportunity presented itself. The cultures of Europe and the Americas could have merged and the beauty of both races could have flourished. Unfortunately, what occurred was neither beautiful nor heroic. Just as Columbus could not, and did not, "discover" a hemisphere that was already inhabited by nearly 100 million people, his arrival cannot, and will not, be recognized as a heroic and celebratory event by indigenous peoples. . . .

From an indigenous vantage point, Columbus' arrival was a disaster from the beginning. Although his own diaries indicated that he was greeted by the Taino Indians with the most generous hospitality he had ever known, he immediately began the enslavement and slaughter of the Indian peoples of the Caribbean islands. . . . Columbus was personally responsible for enslavement and murder of indigenous peoples [and for] the design and operation of the encomienda system that tied Indians as slaves to the lands stolen from them by the European invaders.

. . . Columbus personally oversaw the genocide of the Taino Indian nation of what is now Haiti and the Dominican Republic. Consequently, this murderer, despite his historical notoriety, deserves no recognition or accolades as a hero; he deserves no respect as a visionary; and he is not worthy of a state or national holiday in his honor.

Defenders of Columbus and his holiday argue that indigenous peoples unfairly judge Columbus, a 15th century actor, by the moral and legal standards of the late 20th century. Such a defense implies that no moral or legal constraints applied to individuals such as Columbus, or countries, in 1492. [However], not only were there European moral and legal principles in 1492, but they largely favored the rights of indigenous peoples to be free from unjustified invasion and pillage by Europeans.

Unfortunately, the issue of Columbus and Columbus Day is not easily resolvable with a disposition of Columbus, the man. Columbus Day as a national, and international, phenomenon reflects a much larger dynamic that promotes myriad myths and historical lies that have been used through the ages to dehumanize Indians, justifying the theft of our lands, the attempted destruction of our nations, and the genocide against our people.

Since the 15th Century, the myth of Columbus' discovery has been used in the development of laws and policies that reek of Orwell's doublespeak: theft equals the righteous spread of civilization, genocide is God's deliverance of the wilderness from the savages, and the destruction of Indian societies implies the superiority of European values and institutions over indigenous ones.

Columbus Day is a perpetuation of racist assumptions that the Western Hemisphere was a wasteland cluttered with savages awaiting the blessings of Western "civilization." Throughout the hemisphere, educational systems perpetuate these myths—suggesting that indigenous peoples have contributed nothing to the world, and, consequently, should be grateful for their colonization and their microwave ovens.

... [N]ot only was the Western Hemisphere a virtual ecological and health paradise prior to 1492, but the Indians of the Americas have been responsible for such revolutionary global contributions as the model for U.S. constitutional government, agricultural advances that currently provide 60 percent of the world's daily diet, and hundreds of medical and medicinal techniques still in use today.

If you find it difficult to believe that Indians had developed highly complex and sophisticated societies, then you have been victimized by an educational and social system that has given you a retarded, distorted view of history. The operation of this view has also enabled every country in this hemisphere, including the U.S., to continue its destruction of Indian peoples. From the jungles of Brazil to the highlands of Guatemala, from the Chaco of Paraguay to the Supreme Court of the United States, Indian people remain in a perpetual state of danger from the systems that Christopher Columbus began in 1492.

Throughout the Americas, Indian people remain at the bottom of every socioeconomic indicator, we are under continuing physical attack, and are afforded the least access to economic, political, or legal redress. Despite these constant and unbridled assaults, we have resisted, we have survived, and we refuse to surrender any more of our homeland or to disappear into the romantic sunset.

To dignify Columbus and his legacy with parades, holidays and other celebrations is intolerable to us. As the original peoples of this land, we cannot, and will not, countenance social and political festivities that celebrate our genocide. We are embarking on a two-pronged campaign in the quincentenary year to confront the continuing racism against Indian people.

First, we are advocating that the divisive Columbus Day holiday should be replaced by a celebration that is much more inclusive and more accurately reflective of the cultural and racial richness of the Americas. Such a holiday will provide respect and acknowledgement to every group and individual of the importance and value of their heritage, and will allow a more honest and accurate portrayal of the evolution of the hemisphere. It will also provide an opportunity for greater understanding and respect as our societies move ahead into the next 500 years. . . .

Second, and related to the first, is the advancement of an active militant campaign to demand that federal, state, and local authorities begin the removal of anti-Indian icons throughout the country. Beginning with Columbus, we are insisting on the removal of statues, street names, public parks, and any other public object that seeks to celebrate or honor devastators of Indian peoples. We will take an active role of opposition to public displays, parades, and celebrations that champion Indian haters. We encourage others, in every community in the land, to educate themselves and to take responsibility for the removal of anti-Indian vestiges among them.

For people of goodwill, there is no better time for the re-examination of the past, and a rectification of the historical record for future generations, than the 500th anniversary of Columbus' arrival. There is no better place for this re-examination to begin than in Colorado, the birthplace of the Columbus Day holiday.

SOURCE: http://www.dickshovel.com/colum.html.

THE VALUE OF NATIVE AMERICAN CULTURE AND INDIAN IDENTITY

N. Scott Momaday

I've done some thinking on Columbus. . . . I think [the anniversary] is a wonderfully important time to reflect over the meaning of Columbus's voyages to America, and the following establishment of colonial settlements in the New World. The whole history of Indian/white relationships from 1492 to the present is a large subject to get at, but it is eminently worth thinking about. I would hope that the question would produce greater awareness of Native cultures, the importance of those cultures, and indeed the indispensable importance of them in the light of the twenty-first century.

I think we are on the brink of disaster on many fronts. I believe that the Native people can help us out of that, help push us back from the brink. . . . [I think] that it is possible to reverse this march towards annihilation that we have begun on the nuclear front and on the ecological front. I think that the Native American broad experience of the environment in the Americas is an important research resource for us.

I have just returned from Europe, and [they] seem more keenly aware of ecological problems that we are here. We're very comfortable. We have committed ourselves to a technological society in such a way that it is hard for us to see anything outside that context. So, it's very hard for us to understand that we are polluting the atmosphere. We know we are, but we have the tendency to think that we are so intelligent as a people and we have achieved such a high degree of civilization that the solutions will come about in the course of time. That's a dangerous attitude. . . .

Native people seem to live harmoniously with the physical world as it is [and they] need to be as informed as the rest of us, because they probably have more solutions. . . .

I was thinking about what [Columbus's] discovery meant finally, in the long run. Of course, it is hard to say, but certainly one valid aspect is the complete revolution in the Americas. . . .

I have mixed feelings about celebrating the event which was certainly, in some perspectives, tragic. . . . I had similar feelings in 1976 at the Bicentennial of the Constitution. I had a hard time with that, as a Native American, knowing that there was no reason whatsoever to celebrate the 200th anniversary but, on the other hand, I felt that was a fairly narrow attitude. . . . If Indians exclude themselves from [these celebrations], that's a negative thing. If they can find a way to celebrate it on a real basis, that's positive. . . .

The major issues we (Native Americans) face now are survival—how to live in the modern world. Part of that is how to remain Indian, how to assimilate without ceasing to be an Indian. I think some important strides have been made. Indians remain Indians, and against some pretty good odds. They remain Indians and, in some cases, by a thread. Their languages are being lost at a tremendous rate, poverty is rampant, as is alcoholism. But still there are Indians, and the traditional world is intact.

It's a matter of identity. It's thinking about who I am. I grew up on Indian reservations, and then I went away from the Indian world and entered a different context. But I continue to think of myself as Indian. . . . I think this is what most Indian people are doing today. They go off the reservation, but they keep an idea of themselves as Indians. That's the trick.

I've been asked, how do you define an Indian, is it a matter of blood content? I say no, an Indian is someone who thinks of themselves as Indian. But that's not so easy to do and one has to earn the entitlement somehow. You have to have a certain experience of the world in order to formulate this idea. I know how my father saw the world, and his father before him. That's how I see the world.

SOURCE: Nabakov, Peter. (Ed.). (1999). *Native American Testimony* (rev. ed., pp. 437–440). New York: Penguin.

QUESTIONS TO CONSIDER

1. Hitchens argues that, ultimately, European culture spread "modernity and enlightenment" to the Western Hemisphere. Is his argument an example of what Morris and Means call the "Orwellian doublespeak" that equates the "destruction of Indian societies" with the "superiority of European values and institutions"? Do you detect ethnocentrism, subtle racism, or arrogance in Hitchens' argument? How convincing is Hitchens' point that "Native" Americans are merely the most recent of a long series of inhabitants of the North American continent and have no particular claims on the title of "indigenous"?

2. Morris and Means argue that people that have trouble believing that Indians could develop complex civilizations have been victimized by a educational system that perpetuates distorted views. Does this point hold true for your education? What (if anything) did you learn about Indians during your elementary and high school experiences? How does this compare to what you learned about other groups (including the dominant group)?

3. Should Columbus Day be celebrated? Is it racist to celebrate the arrival of European culture in the Western Hemisphere? Which arguments from Hitchens and Morris and Means were most persuasive? Why? What about the implications for other minority groups? Do those who oppose Columbus Day thereby insult Italian Americans? Are they rejecting the Western European tradition that is at the core of American culture?

4. What does Momaday add to the argument? How does he try to reconcile the opposing points of view? What does he mean when he says that it would be positive for Indians to find a way to celebrate events like Columbus Day on a "real basis"? What kinds of positive outcomes does he have in mind? In his view, is it possible to retain an Indian identity and still celebrate Columbus Day? How?

7

HISPANIC AMERICANS

Hispanic Americans are an extremely diverse group. They trace their origins to scores of different nations and vary from each other in racial characteristics, dialect, and other ways. Mexicans living in the Southwest and West in the early 1800s were the first to become a Hispanic American minority group as a result of the U.S. expansion and the military defeat of Mexico. Since that time, the group has been augmented by immigrants from Mexico, especially during the past several decades, and, today, Mexican Americans are the largest Hispanic American group.

Puerto Ricans, the second largest Hispanic American group, began migrating in large numbers in the 1940s and 1950s and settled predominantly in the urban Northeast. Although both Puerto Ricans and Mexican Americans can be found at all levels of U.S. class structure, they average well below national standards in education, income, and poverty.

Cuban Americans are the third largest Hispanic group. They began immigrating just 40 years ago, fleeing the socialist revolution of Fidel Castro. They settled in southern Florida and especially in the Miami area, where a thriving Cuban American local economy has raised their average social class position relative to Mexican Americans and Puerto Ricans.

Other sizeable Hispanic American groups come from Colombia, the Dominican Republic, El Salvador, Nicaragua, Peru, and several other nations. Immigration has been particularly heavy since the mid-1960s, and Hispanic Americans, taken as a single entity, are now the largest U.S. minority group.

Many Hispanic Americans face the same kinds of problems as African Americans: urban poverty, racism and discrimination, crime, failing school systems, and the prospect of a continuing disconnection from the mainstream economy. In addition, a large percentage of Hispanic Americans are recent immigrants or the children of immigrants and must cope with language barriers and lack of familiarity with U.S. customs. Taken together, these problems create formidable challenges for Hispanic Americans.

This chapter begins with a look at the concept of "macho," a term that changed its meaning from positive to negative as it moved from the Hispanic to the Anglo community. The focus on stereotypes and prejudice continues in the Reading by Jane Hill. She analyzes "Mock Spanish" and shows how this seemingly innocent and playful language pattern sustains negative images and expresses disdain and contempt, although in an indirect and "socially acceptable" way. The Reading by Elizabeth Martinez argues for a shift in the U.S. racial paradigm away from the "black/white" dichotomy to a more encompassing (and realistic) vision that explicitly incorporates Hispanic Americans and other groups. This expanded view of American group relations is particularly necessary as the number and percentage of peoples who are both nonwhite and nonblack increases.

The chapter ends with a look at one of the more controversial issues faced by the United States: immigration. How many immigrants should be admitted? What criteria should be used to decide admissions? Peter Brimelow argues that the number should be lowered because contemporary immigrants are becoming more and more an economic burden on the larger society. Reynolds Farley takes the opposite point of view, and George Borjas argues for a different way of approaching the question. Immigration is an issue not only for Hispanics but for many other fast-growing American minority groups, including Asian Americans, the subjects of the next chapter.

NARRATIVE PORTRAIT

THE MEANING OF MACHO

Words as well as people can immigrate, and in both cases, the process can be transforming. In the following passage, Rose Guilbault, a newspaper editor and columnist, reflects on the meaning of one term that has become central to the dominant group's view of Hispanic males. The image evoked by the term *macho* changed from positive to negative as it found its way into American English, a process that reflects dominant-minority relations and partly defines them.

AMERICANIZATION IS TOUGH ON MACHO

Rose Del Castillo Guilbault

What is *macho?* That depends on which side of the border you come from. . . . The negative connotations of *macho* in this country are troublesome to Hispanics.

The Hispanic *macho* is manly, responsible, hardworking, a man in charge, a patriarch. A man who expresses strength through silence. . . .

The American *macho* is chauvinist, a brute, uncouth, loud, abrasive, capable of inflicting pain, and sexually promiscuous.

Quintessential macho models in this country are Sylvester Stallone, Arnold Schwarzenegger, and Charles Bronson. . . . They exude toughness, independence, masculinity. But a closer look reveals their machismo is really violence masquerading as courage, sullenness disguised as silence and irresponsibility camouflaged as independence. . . .

In Spanish, macho ennobles Latin males. In English it devalues them. This pattern seems consistent with the conflicts ethnic minority males experience in this country. Typically the cultural traits other societies value don't translate as desirable characteristics in America.

I watched my own father struggle with these cultural ambiguities. He worked on a farm for 20 years. He laid down miles of irrigation pipe, carefully plowed long, neat rows in fields, . . . stoically worked 20-hour days during the harvest season, accepting the long hours as part of agricultural work. When the boss complained or upbraided him for minor mistakes, he kept quiet, even when it was obvious that the boss had erred.

He handled the most menial tasks with pride. At home he was a good provider. . . . Americans regarded my father as decidedly un-*macho*. His character was interpreted as non-assertive, his loyalty non-ambition, and his quietness, ignorance. I once overheard the boss's son blame him for plowing crooked rows. . . . My father merely smiled at the lie, knowing the boy had done it, . . . confident his good work was well-known. . . . Seeing my embarrassment, my father dismissed the incident, saying "They're the dumb ones. Imagine me fighting with a kid."

I tried not to look at him with American eyes because sometimes the reflection hurt. . . .

In the United States, I believe it was the feminist movement of the early '70s that changed *macho*'s meaning. Perhaps my generation of Latin women was in part responsible. I recall Chicanas complaining about the chauvinistic nature of Latin men and the notion they wanted their women barefoot, pregnant, and in the kitchen. The generalization that Latin men embodied chauvinistic traits led to this . . . twist of semantics. Suddenly a word that represented something positive in one culture became a negative stereotype in another. . . .

The impact of language in our society is undeniable. And the misuse of *macho* hints at a deeper cultural misunderstanding that extends beyond mere word definitions.

SOURCE: Guilbault, Rose Del Castillo. (1989, Aug. 20). Americanization Is Tough on "Macho." "This World," *San Francisco Chronicle*. Reprinted in Doloros La Guardia & Hans Guth (Eds.), *American Voices* (pp. 163–165). Mountain View, CA: Mayfield.

READINGS

The two Readings for this section both explore the meaning of prejudice and racism for Latinos in U.S. society today. The first reading, "Mock Spanish," demonstrates how butchered uses of the Spanish language function to reproduce negative stereotypes about Hispanic Americans, especially Mexicans. From advertisements and greeting cards to movies and political campaigns, author Jane Hill provides numerous examples of how Mock Spanish is used to conjure up these stereotypical images of Latinos as sneaky, untrustworthy, and cheap. Hill uses the term *dual indexicality* to refer to the two meanings behind the mock Spanish utterances. The first meaning is the conscious intent of the speaker to convey humor and even warmth toward Hispanic people and culture, while the second meaning is the negative racial stereotypes unacknowledged by the speaker. The Reading raises important questions about racial humor and the process by which we assess whether or not a joke is racist, because our criteria for assessment often tend to privilege the intent of the (white) speaker rather than the effect on the (nonwhite) targets of the joke, and Hill presents a strong critique of this power dynamic. That is, even when the speaker claims not to be prejudiced and even has Latino friends, the joke he or she tells can still be racist in its effects, by perpetuating negative ideas about Hispanic culture unknowingly. Hill characterizes Mock Spanish as *elite racist discourse*, since the speakers are not overt in expressing prejudice, but communicate racist stereotypes in more subtle ways, especially through the mass media, which normalizes the images. The evidence presented here is yet another reminder of the *modern racism* we have been reviewing throughout this volume. Additionally, Hill points to negative stereotypical depictions of Latinos such as the caricatures of "Mexicans hidden under huge sombreros" and others as seen in the film *Encino Man,* and asks why comparable images of African Americans (like Mammy in a kerchief or Sambo with a slice of watermelon) elicit more outrage today than these similar anti-Hispanic images. These parallels between the racism faced by Hispanic Americans and African Americans that often seem to go literally unseen in the United States raise questions that are explored further in the second reading.

Elizabeth Martinez's "Seeing More Than Black and White" poses a direct challenge to the *black/white model* of racism from a Latina woman's perspective. She points out that the media focuses almost exclusively on the racism faced by African Americans rather than comparable atrocities that are also directed at Hispanic Americans. This amounts to a divide-and-conquer or "Oppression Olympics" dynamic, which Martinez argues keeps minorities competing with each other rather than uniting together into one stronger force against white racism. Expanding the black/white model will become increasingly important as the United States becomes a majority nonwhite nation, and the largest percentage of that nonwhite majority will be Latinos of various ethnicities, rather than blacks. Martinez also refutes the claim that Latinos face "national minority" oppression (or discrimination based on *ethnicity*) rather than oppression based on *race*, citing numerous examples of race-based anti-Latino discrimination. Often times African Americans are not aware that they share such common historical experiences with Hispanic Americans, such as lynchings and police brutality. Moreover, Martinez critiques the dualistic thinking that limits racism to a black/white issue as the same limited frame of mind that perpetuates racism in general. Latinos' mixed racial heritage (*mestizaje*) that combines Native American, European, and African ancestry is a striking piece of evidence for the limits of such dualistic frameworks. This Reading takes the stance that as long as racism is conceived as solely a black/white issue, it will never be fully conquered or eliminated. Multiple racial realities are the wave of the future, and Latinos stand in the forefront of that optimistic complexity.

MOCK SPANISH: A SITE FOR THE INDEXICAL REPRODUCTION OF RACISM IN AMERICAN ENGLISH

Jane H. Hill

INTRODUCTION

I was first drawn to the study of "Mock Spanish"[1] by a puzzle. In the southwestern United States, English speakers of "Anglo"[2] ethnic affiliation make considerable use of Spanish in casual speech, in spite of the fact that the great majority of them are utterly monolingual in English under most definitions. However, these monolinguals both produce Spanish and consume it, especially in the form of Mock Spanish humor. Mock Spanish has, I believe, intensified during precisely the same period when opposition to the use of Spanish by its native speakers has grown, reaching its peak in the passage of "Official English" statutes in several states during the last decade.[3]

As I began to explore this question, I realized that I had also engaged a larger one: In a society where for at least the last 20 years to be called a "racist" is a dire insult, and where opinion leaders almost universally concur that "racism" is unacceptable, how is racism continually reproduced? For virulent racism unquestionably persists in the United States. People of color feel it intensely in almost every dimension of their lives. Studies by researchers of every political persuasion continue to show substantial gaps between the several racialized groups and so-called "whites" on every quantifiable dimension

of economic prosperity, educational success, and health (including both infant mortality and life expectancy). I argue here that everyday talk, of a type that is almost never characterized (at least by Anglos) as "racist," is one of the most important sites for the covert reproduction of this racism. "Mock Spanish," the topic of this paper, is one example of such a site.

"Mock Spanish" exemplifies a strategy of dominant groups that I . . . call . . . "incorporation" (Hill, 1995). By incorporation, members of dominant groups expropriate desirable resources, both material and symbolic, from subordinate groups. Through incorporation, . . . "whiteness" is elevated. Qualities taken from the system of "color" are reshaped within whiteness into valued properties of mind and culture. This process leaves a residue that is assigned to the system of color, consisting of undesirable qualities of body and nature. These justify the low position of people of color in the hierarchy of races, and this low rank in turn legitimates their exclusion from resources that are reserved to whiteness. By using Mock Spanish, "Anglos" signal that they possess desirable qualities: a sense of humor, a playful skill with a foreign language, authentic regional roots, an easy-going attitude toward life. The semiotic function by which Mock Spanish assigns these qualities to its Anglo speakers has been called "direct indexicality" by Ochs (1990). "Direct indexicality" is visible to discursive consciousness. When asked about a specific instance of Mock Spanish, speakers will often volunteer that it is humorous, or shows that they lived among Spanish speakers and picked up some of the language, or is intended to convey warmth and hospitality appropriate to the Southwestern region. They also easily accept such interpretations when I volunteer them.

The racist and racializing residue of Mock Spanish is assigned to members of historically Spanish-speaking populations by indirect indexicality (Ochs 1990). Through this process, such people are endowed with gross sexual appetites, political corruption, laziness, disorders of language, and mental incapacity [and this identity] restricts Mexican-Americans and Puerto Ricans largely to the lowest sectors of the regional and national economies. This indexicality is "indirect" because it is not acknowledged, and in fact is actively denied as a possible function of their usage, by speakers of Mock Spanish. . . .

The purpose of this paper is to argue for this semiotic analysis of "dual indexicality." The argument, in summary, is that speakers and hearers can only interpret utterances in Mock Spanish insofar as they have access to the negative residue of meaning. Those who hear Mock Spanish jokes, for instance, cannot possibly "get" them—that is, the jokes will not be funny—unless the hearer has instant, unreflecting access to a cultural model of "Spanish speakers" that includes the negative residue.

Furthermore, I suggest that Mock Spanish usages actively produce this residue.

They carry with them, of course, a debris of racist history that is known to most speakers: they presuppose . . . a racist and racialized image. But insofar as speakers laugh at Mock Spanish jokes, or, indeed, interpret Mock Spanish expressions in any of the several appropriate ways, such imagery is also entailed, locally re-produced in the interaction, and thus made available in turn as a presupposition of ensuing interactions.

I suggest that Mock Spanish is a new (at least to the theory of racist discourse) type of what van Dijk (1993) has called "elite racist discourse." . . . [T]he most productive usage of the system is, I have found, among middle-and

upper-income, college-educated whites. Mock Spanish is not heard, nor are printed tokens of it usually encountered, at truck stops, country-music bars, or in the "Employees Only" section of gas stations. Instead, the domain of Mock Spanish is the graduate seminar, the boardroom, the country-club reception. It is found issuing from the mouths of working-class whites only in the mass media, and is placed there by writers who come from elite backgrounds.

I am, myself, a "native speaker" of Mock Spanish. I grew up in West Los Angeles, in a neighborhood where the notoriously wealthy districts of Westwood, Brentwood, and Belair come together. On school playgrounds populated by the children of film directors, real estate magnates, and university professors I learned to say "Adios" and "el cheapo" and "Hasty banana." The explosion of Mock Spanish that can be heard today in mass media is produced by the highly-paid Ivy-Leaguers who write "The Simpsons," "Roseanne," "Northern Exposure," and "Terminator Two: Judgment Day," and by the more modest literati who compose greeting-card texts and coffee-cup slogans. This suggests an extremely important property of the large structure of racism—that it is "distributed" within the social system of whiteness.

Racist practice in its crudest forms—the obscene insult, the lynching—is assigned within this larger structure to the trailing edge of the upwardly-mobile social continuum of "whiteness." People who overtly manifest such practices are often defined by opinion makers as a minority of "white trash" or "thugs" (even when many surface signs suggest that they are members of the social and economic mainstream). Those who aspire to advancement within whiteness practice instead what is often called "New Racism," the various forms of exclusion and pejoration that are deniable, or justifiable as "fair" or "realistic." The covert practices of Mock Spanish can even be contributed to the system of whiteness by people who are not, personally, racist in any of the usual senses. However, by using Mock Spanish they play their part in a larger racist system, and contribute to its pernicious and lethal effects. I first review the history of Mock Spanish. I then illustrate contemporary Mock Spanish usage, emphasizing that it constitutes a linguistic system of substantial regularity. In the course of exemplifying this system, I argue for the semiotic interpretation of Mock Spanish as manifesting "dual indexicality" by which desirable qualities are assigned to Anglos, and undesirable qualities are assigned to members of historically Spanish-speaking populations. . . . I conclude with a brief discussion of additional evidence, beyond the semiotic analysis, that Mock Spanish constitutes a racist discourse.

A BRIEF HISTORY OF MOCK SPANISH

Mock Spanish is quite old in American English. The earliest attestation I have found is from the *Dictionary of American Regional English* (Cassidy 1985:508; henceforth, DARE), where we are told that the jail in the city of Mobile was called, in 1792, the "calaboose." This word is from Spanish *calabozo* "prison" (especially, a subterranean cell, or an isolation cell within a prison). . . . DARE (p. 411) [also] attests . . . awareness of what I call Mock Spanish as a pejorating and vulgar register at an early period, in a citation for "buckaroo" from Hart's Vigilante Girl, set in Northern California: "I can talk what they call 'buckayro' Spanish. It ain't got but thirteen words in it, and twelve of them are cuss words. . . ."

Today, I think it would be fair to speak of an "explosion" of Mock Spanish. I hear it constantly, and it is especially common at what I call "sites of mass reproduction": films, television shows, including the Saturday morning cartoons watched religiously by most children, greeting cards, video games, political cartoons, coffee-cup slogans intended for display on the office desk, bumper stickers, refrigerator magnets, and the like. These items are marketed far beyond the Southwest. . . .

MOCK SPANISH AS A SYSTEM
OF STRATEGIES FOR BORROWING

. . . Mock Spanish is only one of at least three registers of "Anglo Spanish." . . . "Cowboy" Spanish is a register of loan words for plants (mesquite), animals (coyote), land forms (mesa), food (tamale), architecture (patio), legal

institutions (vigilante), and (the source of my name for it), an extensive terminology associated with the technology of managing range cattle from horseback, among which the words "lariat" and "bronco" are among the best known. "Cowboy" Spanish is largely restricted to the U.S. Southwest, but has some overlap, in both lexicon and usage patterns, with Mock Spanish.

The second register is "Nouvelle" Spanish.[4] This is used in marketing the Southwest as "the land of mañana," a place for a relaxing vacation or a peaceful retirement. It produces luxury hotels named "La Paloma," street names in upscale Anglo neighborhoods like "Calle Sin Envidia," and restaurant placemats that wish the diner "Buenas Dias." . . . [B]oth Cowboy Spanish and Nouvelle Spanish share with Mock Spanish a more or less complete disregard for the grammatical niceties of any dialect of Spanish itself. . . .

Mock Spanish itself is a system of four major strategies for the "incorporation" of Spanish-language materials into English. These strategies yield expressions that belong to a pragmatic zone bounded on one end by the merely jocular, and on the other by the obscene insult. They include . . . (1) "Semantic derogation": the borrowing of neutral or positive Spanish loan words which function in Mock Spanish in a jocular and/or pejorative sense and (2) "Euphemism": the borrowing of negative, including scatological and obscene, Spanish words, as euphemisms for English words, or for use in their own right as jocular and/or pejorative expressions, . . . and (3) "Hyperanglicization": absurd mispronunciations, that endow commonplace Spanish words or expressions with a jocular and/or pejorative sense and can create vulgar puns.

STRATEGY I: MOCK
SPANISH SEMANTIC DEROGATION

In "semantic derogation"[5] a positive or neutral Spanish word is borrowed as a Mock Spanish expression and given a humorous or negative meaning. [Consider two examples using] the Spanish greeting *Adios*. In Spanish *Adios* is an entirely neutral farewell. While it includes the root *Dios*, "God;" it has about as much to do with "God" for most Spanish speakers as the English "goodbye," a contraction of "God be with ye," does for English speakers. But it is at the very least polite, and, like "Goodbye," it is not in the least slangy. [The first example] is a greeting card. . . . On the front of the card a small figure, coded as "Mexican" by his big sombrero and striped serape, says, "Adiós."[6] Turning to the inside of the card we find [not a standard "Best of luck in your new job/ house/etc." message but, instead,] "That's Spanish for, Sure, go ahead and leave your friends, the only people who really care about you, the ones who would loan you their last thin dime, give you the shirts of their backs, sure. Just take off."

The second, even more obvious, [example] of the semantic pejoration of "Adios" is [the expression] "Adios, cucaracha" with a picture of a fleeing roach, is a bus-bench advertisement for a Tucson exterminating company. The bench is . . . in one of the most exclusive Anglo neighborhoods, so it is highly unlikely that the ad is addressed to a Spanish-speaking audience. Note that Spanish cucaracha is chosen over English "cockroach," to convey heightened contempt.

The final example of "Adios" appears in . . . "Terminator 2: Judgment Day," a film which made heavy use of Mock Spanish. In the film . . . the child John Connor must live, because thirty years into the future he will successfully lead a bedraggled band of human survivors in the final war against machines. The machines have twice sent an evil cyborg, a "Terminator," into the past to kill him. But the humans of the future send a good terminator, played by Arnold Schwarzenegger, into the past to protect the boy. The "Adios" scene is at the end of the film. . . . The Good Terminator has finally destroyed his evil opponent. . . . The Good Terminator, John Connor, and Connor's heroic mother Sarah have stolen the arm of the first Terminator. . . [and] the arm must be destroyed, so that the Terminator technology can never threaten humanity. As young Connor [destroys] the evil artifact. . . , he says "Adios." Then we realize that the Good Terminator, whom the humans have come to love and admire, must also destroy himself—his

futuristic metal body is as dangerous as those of his evil opponents. Sarah must lower him into the steel. As he descends, he looks one last time at his human friends and says, "Goodbye." The contrast could not be more clear: "Adios" for evil, "Goodbye" for good.

These uses of "Adios" cannot be understood except under the "dual indexicality" analysis. By direct indexicality they project variously humor, a streetwise acquaintance with Spanish, a sense of Southwestern regional identity (especially for the greeting card and the advertising sign), and, for the "Terminator 2" screenwriters, a representation of what they take to be the appropriate speech for a white street kid from Los Angeles.[7] Finally, they are all obviously intended as insults. Neither the humor nor the insult is available as a meaning unless a second, indirect, set of indexicals is present. By indirect indexicality these instances of "Adios" evoke . . . a greeting that would be uttered by an untrustworthy and insincere person, the kind of person who might stab you in the back, the kind of person who would use a word to mean its opposite. The person thus conjured up is, clearly, a speaker of Spanish. And of course this stereotype, of the sneaky and untrustworthy "Latin lover" or the sneering "Mexican bandit," is undeniably available to American English speakers. Only this presence makes possible the humorous and/or insulting quality of "Adios" in these usages.[8]

A second derogated Spanish greeting, "Hasta la vista, baby" also appears in "Terminator 2," from which origin it became an immensely popular slogan that continues to circulate in American usage, in a variety of variants including "Hasta la bye-bye," "Hasta la pasta," and "Hasta la baby, vista."[9] [There are] two occurrences in the film. In the first scene, the Good Terminator is driving John Connor and his mother to a desert hideout. The dialogue is as follows:

Mother:	Keep it under sixty-five, we don't want to be pulled over.
Terminator:	Affirmative. (in a clipped, machine-like tone)
John Connor:	No no no no no no. You gotta listen to the way people talk. You don't

say "Affirmative," or some shit like that, you say "No problemo." And if someone comes off to you with an attitude, you say "Eat me." And if you want to shine them on, you say, "Hasta la vista, baby."

Terminator: Hasta la vista, baby. (still in a machine-like voice)

John Connor: Yeah, "Later, dickwad." And if someone gets upset, you say, "Chill out," or, you can do combinations.

Terminator: Chill out, dickwad. (in a machine-like voice)

John Connor: That's great! See, you're gettin' it.

Terminator: No problemo. (in a somewhat more natural voice)

This fascinating scene clearly locates Mock Spanish in the same register with extremely vulgar English expressions. But notice that this register, and its Mock Spanish component, is "the way people talk." If the Terminator is to become human, to be redeemed from his machine nature, he must learn to talk this way too. By learning Mock Spanish, the Terminator becomes more like the witty, resourceful young John Connor, and gains the boy's approval. This is a superb demonstration of the direct indexicality of Mock Spanish: it recruits positive qualities to whiteness. However, the indirect indexicality is also made vivid in this passage. [In] associating "Hasta la vista" with "Eat me" and "Dickwad," . . . Spanish speakers [are associated with] filth and obscenity, [as is] their language. . . . In the next scene we see the most famous token of "Hasta la vista, baby," when Schwarzenegger utters his newly-acquired line as he destroys the evil terminator with a powerful gun.[10] During the 1992 presidential campaign Schwarzenegger, a Republican stalwart, appeared on many occasions in support of President George Bush, uttering the famous line as a threat against Bush's opponents. Bush himself also used the line occasionally. . . . Thus it was clearly judged by campaign managers and consultants as highly effective, resonating deeply with public sentiment.[11] This suggests that the simultaneous pleasures of feeling

oneself streetwise and witty, while accessing an extremely negative image of Spanish and its speakers, are widely available to American politicians and voters.

[Several] further examples illustrate the strategy of semantic derogation. [One] is a political cartoon from the *Arizona Daily Star,* caricaturing Ross Perot, running for President in 1992 against George Bush and Bill Clinton on a third-party ticket. Perot, who is much given to speaking from charts, holds a list that urges support for him because (among other reasons), there are "Bucks flyin' into my 'Perot for El Presidente' treasure trove." Here, the direct indexicality is humorous, and permits the comprehending reader to feel cosmopolitan and streetwise. However, the expression is clearly intended to criticize Perot, to suggest that he is pompous and absurd. In order to interpret the insult, the reader must have access to a highly negative image of the sort of person who might be called "El Presidente." This is, of course, the classic tin-horn Latin American dictator, dripping with undeserved medals and presiding in a corrupt and ineffectual manner over a backwater banana republic. Through indirect indexicality, the Mock Spanish expression reproduces this stereotype.

[Another example, from] a "Calvin and Hobbes" comic strip, shows Calvin and his tiger friend Hobbes in one of their endless silly debates about who will be the highest officer in their tree-house club. Hobbes proclaims himself "El Tigre Numero Uno." This is not, however, mere self-aggrandizement: mainly, the locution satirizes the grandiose titles that Calvin makes up for himself, like "Supreme Dictator for Life." Again, by direct indexicality, "El Tigre Numero Uno" is funny, and is also part of Hobbes' cool and witty persona. But to capture the absurdity and the insult, we must also have access to indirect indexicality, which picks out, again, the stereotype of the tinhorn Latin American dictator.

[A third example] illustrates a very common Mock Spanish usage, of Spanish nada "nothing." In Mock Spanish the word has been pejorated from this merely neutral meaning into a more extreme sense, meaning "absolutely nothing." One formulaic usage, "Zip, zero, nada" (and minor variants) has become wildly popular; I have seen it in television commercials for free drinks with hamburgers, in newspaper announcements for no-fee checking accounts, and, most recently, in an editorial piece in the *Arizona Daily Star* (August 20, 1995) in which an urban planner chastises the Pima County Board of Supervisors for spending "zero dollars—*nada*, zip" on improving a dangerous street intersection. . . .

Finally, [to] illustrate a common use of semantic derogation, the use of Mock Spanish to express "cheapness" [I have a] newspaper advertisement for a sale at Contents, an exclusive furniture store in Tucson. The deep price cuts are announced under the headline "Contemporary and Southwestern Dining, For Pesos." Here, the direct indexicality is not only "light" and jocular; it is almost certainly also invoking regional ambiance. The store flatters its clientele by suggesting that they are "of the Southwest," able to interpret these Spanish expressions. However, in order to understand how these customers could interpret "For Pesos" (which is surely not intended literally), we must assume that the indirect indexicality presupposed and/or entailed here is that the peso is a currency of very low value. "For Deutschemarks" or "For Yen" would hardly serve the same purpose! This advertisement is dense with Mock Spanish, driving home the message about bargains with, "Si our menu of fine southwestern and contemporary dining tables and chairs at prices that are muy bueno, now during our Winter Sale . . . Plus, caramba, there's Masterplan, our interior design service that helps you avoid costly decorating errors. . . . Hurry in today before we say adios to these sale savings, amigo."

The strategy of semantic derogation is highly productive, and includes such well-known expressions as "macho," "the big enchilada," and "No way, José," in addition to the examples above. For every one of these usages, in order to understand how the expression can be properly interpreted, we must assume the division between a set of direct indexes (such as "humorous," "streetwise" "light-hearted," and "regional identity") and a set of indirect indexes which presuppose or entail a highly negative image of the Spanish language, its speakers, and the culture and institutions associated with them.

STRATEGY II: MOCK SPANISH EUPHEMISM

The second strategy borrows Spanish words that have highly negative connotations even in the original language, including scatological and obscene expressions. The Mock Spanish form serves as a euphemism for the corresponding rude English word, or creates anew, especially negative semantic space. The first [example] illustrating this strategy is of a coffee cup [which] was purchased . . . in a card and gift shop only a few doors from the University of Arizona campus (the source of many of the items discussed here; the store is, of course, targeting its merchandise at the campus community, thus supporting my claim that Mock Spanish is part of elite usage). The cup bears the slogan, "Caca de Toro," obviously a euphemism for the English expression, "Bullshit." There exist, of course, coffee cups that say "Bullshit," but it seems clear that the "Caca de toro" coffee cup would be more widely acceptable, seen as less vulgar and insulting, than a cup with the English expression. Again, the direct indexicality of this cup is that its owner is a person with a sense of humor, the independence of mind to express a negative attitude, and enough sophistication to understand the Spanish expression (although this expression is not formulaic in Spanish; it is a translation from English). The indirect indexicality required for understanding why the slogan is in Spanish, however, must be that this language is particularly suited to scatology, and that its speakers are perhaps especially given to its use, failing to make the fine distinctions between the polite and the vulgar that might be made by an English speaker.[12]

The second illustration of the strategy of borrowing negative Spanish words is of a gift coffee cup bearing the expression "Peon." Unlike "Caca de Toro," which does not exist as an idiom in Spanish, *peón* is well-established in that language in a negative meaning . . . and referring . . . to people in low occupations. . . . In Latin America it came to designate a person held in debt servitude in a low occupation. . . . It is highly unlikely that the anticipated owner of the cup would be "an unskilled laborer." Instead, the owner could even be a manager, but would be expressing an ironic complaint about being exploited and maltreated. . . .

[The next example] . . . of the . . . strategy . . . is not at all humorous. [It appeared on] the cover of the *Tucson Weekly,* a weekly free newspaper (paid for by advertising) known for its outspoken, even radical, point of view. The cover shows a young Mexican-American man along with the title of the feature article: *Gang-Bangers: La Muerte y la Sangre en el Barrio Centro* ("Death and Blood in the *Barrio Centro*"). What is curious here is the unusual choice of Spanish for the language of the subtitle; I cannot remember another case where the *Tucson Weekly* used such a long expression in Spanish. Unfortunately, the Spanish title . . . suggests a stereotyped association between gang membership and Chicano ethnicity that is not borne out by the facts; many young people in gangs in Tucson are Anglos (and there are also a few African-American gangs). I believe that the Spanish title intends to convey the special direness of the gang threat: "La Muerte y la Sangre" has a sort of Hemingwayesque ring, suggesting that the author of the essay will plumb the most profound depths of the human condition.

However, at the same time, the Spanish title has a softening effect—just as "Caca de Toro" is less offensive than "bullshit," "La Muerte y la Sangre" is somehow more distant, less immediate for the English-speaking reader than "Blood and Death." "La Muerte y la Sangre," in short, is something that happens to "Mexican" kids. Here, the direct indexicality thus is probably the sophistication, the ethnographic depth, enjoyed by the author and, in turn, by the reader of the essay. The indirect indexicality is that "muerte" and "sangre" are at the same time more horrible, and yet less serious, than "death" and "blood"— they are, in short, a peculiarly "Spanish" condition capturing some quality of existence in the lower depths that is not available to Anglos in their own language.

The final example of the strategy of euphemism is illustrated by . . . the 1992 film *Encino Man.* This film was obviously aimed at young people, and carried, astonishingly, a "PG" rating. The hip (white) teenage subculture of Southern California is apparently viewed by young people across the country as highly attractive, and the film features the actor Pauly Shore, a former MTV announcer, who exemplifies it. Shore is famous for using the variety of English that is closely associated with this subculture, a variety that makes heavy use of Mock Spanish.[13] Indeed, there are far more instances of Mock Spanish in the film than I have space to include. The example that I have chosen is an elaborate and extraordinarily vulgar and obscene joke at the expense of a Chicana character that is acceptable in a film aimed at children because it is uttered in Spanish. It is an especially clear and dramatic attestation of the Mock Spanish strategy of euphemism.

The plot of *Encino Man* is that two teenage boys who live in Encino (a wealthy suburb of Los Angeles) dig a swimming pool in their backyard and find a Cro-Magnon man encased in a block of ice. They thaw him out, name him "Linc" (as in "Missing"), and take him to high school. The clip opens as "Stoney," Pauly Shore's character, escorts "Linc" to his Spanish class. "Spanish," explains Stoney, "is guacamole, chips, and salsa." Stoney then raises his leg and makes a farting noise. The stereotyped and racist vision of Spanish-speaking culture thus conveyed needs no further comment. Stoney continues in "Spanish": "The dia es mi hermanos, the day is beautiful." (The stereotype reproduced here is that Spanish is a language studied by the dimmest scholars.) . . .

[Later in the film,] Stoney and his friend have taken Linc to a bar frequented by cholos, stereotyped as absurd in dress and manner. As the scene opens, the lead cholo threatens Stoney and Dave, warning them not to bother his "muchacha, " or he will make sure that they are "no longer recognizable as a man." Linc does not hear the threat, because he is already approaching the cholo's girlfriend, shown as a ridiculous Latin sexpot, writhing hotly in time to the salsa beat of the dance music. Linc grabs the girl and carries her off-screen in classic cave-man style. The cholo finds them dancing together and pulls a knife on Linc, saying, (with subtitles), "Te dije, si yo veo a alguién con mi mujer, lo mato." ("I told you, if I see anybody with my woman, I kill him"). Linc extricates himself from the situation by using the two lines from the morning's Spanish class: "El queso está viejo y podrido. Donde está el sanitario?" ("The cheese is old and moldy. Where is the bathroom?").

The astounded cholo gapes at him and then begins to laugh. "You're right, *ese*," he chuckles. "She's not worth it!" The girl slaps the cholo, who collapses, weeping, into the arms of his supporters. Just as when, in "Terminator 2: Judgment Day," the Good Terminator becomes fully human when he learns Mock Spanish, Linc the cave-man is at his most clever and resourceful when he uses the language. While the direct indexicality of Linc's vulgar joke is positive, enhancing his image, the indirect indexicality . . . is almost entirely negative. Indeed, here the indirect indexicality is really not indirect, but fully expressed in the visual images that accompany the talk. The film is trivial and deeply sexist.

But what is especially striking about the film is its casual racism: Here, the indirect indexicality . . . is amply reinforced by the grossly racist depictions of the cholo and his girlfriend. If similar depictions of African-American characters were to appear in a release from a major studio, there would almost certainly be public outcry. However, as far as I know, "Encino Man" passed quite unnoticed. The implications of this fact for the socialization of white youth are quite horrifying.

There are, of course, innumerable examples of this second strategy. . . . Like semantic pejoration, Mock Spanish euphemism is highly productive, and every case of it I have ever encountered requires the dual-indexicality analysis: Speakers express their sense of humor and cosmopolitanism by direct indexicality, while pejorating and denigrating Spanish language and culture by indirect indexicality, the latter being absolutely required for successful interpretation and appreciation of the humor.

HYPERANGLICIZATION AND BOLD MISPRONUNCIATION

For those readers of this paper who have never heard Mock Spanish, it is important to know that it is almost always pronounced in entirely English-language phonology; Mock Spanish cannot be understood as "code-switching" in the usual sense. However, Mock Spanish forms are often more than merely Anglicized. Instead, they undergo what I call (Hill 1993a) "hyperanglicization," yielding pronunciations that are widely known to be ludicrous departures from their Spanish originals. These absurd mispronunciations provide a rich source of vulgar puns, some of them best rendered in writing, as in the following examples.

[The first example is] a Christmas card, the front of [which] says "Pablo, the Christmas Chihuahua, has a holiday wish for you" over a drawing of a ludicrously ugly little dog wearing a huge sombrero and scratching frantically at the many fleas visibly jumping around on his hairless body. The greeting inside the card . . . is "Fleas Navidad," a pun on the Spanish Christmas salutation, *Feliz Navidad*. The second example . . . is of a thank-you card, [the front of which] shows . . . a tiny mouse crouching in a sea of grass, and the word "Muchas" ("Many"). Opening the card, we find more grass and the word "Grass-ias," a hyperanglicized version of Spanish *gracias* "Thanks" that yields the pun.[14] . . .

[Another example consists] of a menu from a Mexican restaurant in Tucson. . . . Baja Bennie's, the source for this menu, is . . . in an area that is notoriously almost exclusively Anglo. It is a favorite place for young Anglo professionals. The Baja Bennie's menu parodies the menus in legitimate Mexican-food venues with silly Mock Spanish section headings like "El Figuro Trimmo." This section is explained as "Bennie's answer to the Border Patrol, sort of our Mex-er-size area . . . ," a note that would be interpreted as the grossest sort of insult by almost any Chicano. . . .

FURTHER EVIDENCE FOR RACISM IN MOCK SPANISH

Thus far, I have argued that Mock Spanish is ineluctably racist because it can only be understood by speakers insofar as they have access to its indirect indexical force, of relentless denigration of the Spanish language, culture, and people. However, there is additional evidence that Mock Spanish is a racist discourse.

Occasionally Mock Spanish usage reveals its fundamental character by being embedded in grossly racist texts. I owe one example to Jodi

Goldman, who found an article from *The Koala,* the University of California at San Diego student satirical newspaper, from April 6, 1994. This satirical piece requires contextualization: college students from institutions along the border often choose to spend "Spring Break" at beach resorts in Mexico, a dislocation which many take as an excuse to go on an alcohol-fueled orgy of misbehavior that is a source of exasperation to Mexicans and enormous concern to college officials and parents in the United States (serious injuries and even deaths are unfortunately not rare).

The article in *The Koala* is a fantasy about being arrested on a beer-sodden Spring Break at Rosarita Beach in Baja California, and is entitled "Que pasa en tus pantalones?" The author provides a parodic "pronunciation guide" to her name: "By Pamela Benjamin (pronounced: Pahm-eh-lah Ben-haam-een)." The article features many elaborate instances of Mock Spanish, but I will restrict myself to one revealing paragraph, which the author introduces by noting that "I have no knowledge of Spanish." She continues:

> "My brother taught me a few phrases: 'Cuanto cuesta es tu Madre?' (How much does your mother cost?), 'Que pasa en tus pantalones?' (What's happening in your pants?), and the answer for that question, 'Una fiesta en mi pantalones, y tu invito,' (There's a party in my pants, and you're invited.)

> "These phrases were of no help to me when captured by Mr. Hideous, Huge-sweat-rings-on-his-uniform, Body-oder[sic]-of-a-rotting-mule, Must-eat-at-least-10-tortas-a-day, Mexican Federale guy. I thought I was going to die, not only from his smell, but from the killer cockroaches the size of hamsters in the back seat. I thought to myself, "No problem, Pam. You can deal with this. Stay calm, don't scream, and say something in Spanish. He'll notice your amazing brilliance and let you go." Unfortunately, the first thing that popped out was, "Cuanto Cuesta es tu Madre?" My doom was sealed.

Here, one hardly needs the "dual indexical-ity" analysis: Mexico is clearly depicted as a corrupt and filthy country, where the only Spanish one needs are the few phrases necessary to buy the services of a prostitute.

Mock Spanish in print is very frequently associated with patently racist imagery, [including "bean jokes," images of stereotyped "Mexicans" shown barefoot and wearing huge sombreros, etc.]. Many Mexican-Americans find caricatures of Mexicans hidden under huge sombreros to be grossly offensive. They have precisely the force for them that the picture of a grinning black boy with a slice of watermelon, or a fat-cheeked mammy with her head done up in a kerchief, have for African Americans. Following many years of effort by Latino citizens' groups, this image has been largely eliminated from mainstream advertising and mass media (an important example was the agreement by the Frito-Lay Corporation to give up its trademark caricature of the "Frito Bandido"). However, it survives vigorously in a variety of minor media such as on . . . greeting cards.[15]

Teun van Dijk, in *Elite Discourse and Racism,* argues that in a theory of racist discourse it is essential to take into account what he calls "minority competence," the assessment of a situation, as racist or non-racist, by "those who experience racism as such, that is, the competent or 'conscious' members of minority groups"(van Dijk 1993:18). This is a fundamental departure from the tradition that regards the views of the targets of racism as unreliable, because biased. Instead, it suggests that we view competent members of minority communities as especially likely to be able to make nuanced discriminations between racist and non-racist or anti-racist practice, because it is precisely they who have the most at stake in making such distinctions.

Van Dijk recognizes that there may be wide variation among minority-group members in general. I have never addressed an audience on this topic without having an Anglo member of the audience tell me that my analysis is incorrect, because a Mexican-American or Puerto Rican friend of theirs once sent them a card, or told them a joke, with Mock Spanish content. I have no doubt that they are telling the truth about their experiences. Certainly some Mexican-Americans find the tokens of Mock Spanish that I have shown them (including many of the items described above) to be entertaining. However, I find that those Mexican-Americans who laugh at Mock Spanish are generally very young (many of them have been college freshmen or sophomores) or relatively naive and uneducated. Older people are almost unanimous in immediately reacting negatively to these tokens. Many of them recognize the Mock Spanish genre immediately, and volunteer stories about times that Anglos have offended them by using Mock Spanish to them, such as calling them "Amigo" or asking them "Comprende?" . . . In summary, thoughtful people among the Latino and Chicano population in the Southwest usually define Mock Spanish as a racist practice.[16]

Conclusion: Mock Spanish Is a New Kind of Elite Racist Discourse

I have shown that Mock Spanish usages cannot be interpreted unless interlocutors reproduce, through indirect indexicality, very negative images of Spanish and its speakers. It functions, therefore, as a racist discourse in itself. I have also shown that uses of Mock Spanish often occur with grossly racist imagery. . . . Furthermore, I have shown that many Mexican-Americans . . . concur that it is racist, and I have argued, following van Dijk (1993), that their views must be taken very seriously. However, I have found in discussing this work that many Anglos find my conclusions implausible. How, they argue, can Mock Spanish be racist? They use it, and they are not racist. . . . How could anyone call "Calvin and Hobbes" a racist comic strip, or "Terminator 2: Judgment Day" a racist film?

I would argue, along with many contemporary theorists of racism . . . that to find that an action or utterance is "racist," one does not have to demonstrate that the racism is consciously intended. Racism is judged, instead, by its effects: of successful discrimination and exclusion of members of the racialized group from goods and resources enjoyed by members of the racializing group. It is easy to demonstrate that such discrimination and exclusion not only has existed in the past against Mexican Americans

and other members of historically Spanish-speaking populations in the United States, but continues today.

Furthermore, the semiotic analysis that I have proposed above demonstrates that Mock Spanish is discriminatory and denigrating in its indexical meaning, that it cannot be understood without knowing about the stereotypes that such indexes presuppose and entail, even if speakers believe that what they are doing is inoffensive joking. Mock Spanish is effective precisely because of its relative deniability, because people are not aware of "being racist," even in a mild way, let alone in a vulgar way. Through its use, the "upwardly mobile system of whiteness" is created covertly, through the indirect indexicality of hundreds of taken-for-granted commonplace utterances that function to "racialize" their targets, constructing them as members of a human group represented as essentially inferior. . . . [I]t is through these covert indexes that the deepest structures of the self, those that are least accessible to inquiry and modification, are laid down. Indeed, . . . covert semiosis is at least as, if not more, powerful than overt meaning in the construction of the world through linguistic practice. . . .

A second argument that is often used against my analysis is that there are in American English many expressions that mock other languages besides Spanish. This is, of course, correct. . . . It seems to me obvious, however, that these other "mock" usages are today scattered and relatively unproductive, in stark comparison with Mock Spanish. . . .

Finally, I suggest that "Mock Spanish" constitutes a new type of racist discourse.

The kinds of examples that van Dijk (1993) treats as illustrations of "elite racist discourse" are nearly all far more overt, addressing directly whether privileges and rights (such as immigration, or access to public housing) should be extended to members of racialized populations. For instance, van Dijk points out that elite racist discourse can be identified when it is accompanied by qualifying expressions. Someone might say: "Of course I don't dislike foreigners, some of them are fine people, but our country has already admitted too many immigrants." Even though such a speaker would deny that the statement "Our country already has too many immigrants" was racist, the qualifying statement shows that the speaker knows that it could be heard in that way, rather than only an absolutely neutral scientific judgment that shows that the speaker is in control of statistical evidence about what percentage of immigrants is optimal for national development.

People who use Mock Spanish do not use such qualifying expressions. Nobody would say, "Of course Arnold Schwarzenegger has many Mexican-American friends, but he said 'Hasta la vista, baby' at the rally for Bush," or, "I have the highest respect for the Mexican people, but no problemo." . . . These facts enlarge our understanding of the continuum of racist discourse. A picket sign that says "Wetbacks go home!" is obvious vulgar racism. Van Dijk has demonstrated that expressions like, "I don't have anything against Mexicans as such. But we can't pay to deliver the baby of every pregnant lady in Mexico who wants her kid to be an American citizen" constitute clear cases of "elite racist discourse." To these two types we need to add a third, at the most covert end of the continuum, reproducing racism almost entirely through indirect indexicality. This type is exemplified by cases like "Hasta la vista, baby." The first is easily identifiable as racist and is almost always avoided by the powerful; indeed, public vulgar racism precisely indexes powerlessness. The second sounds sleazy and weasely to many thoughtful Anglos. But the last seems to most Anglos to be utterly innocent, even delightful and clever. I would argue, however, that this last is the most powerful of the three. Because of its seeming innocence, it can find its way into a film seen by literally hundreds of millions of people, and can become a clever new casual expression, functioning in that useful range of meanings that range between light talk and insult, that is used by everyone from six-year-olds to senatorial candidates. And each time that it is used, it inexorably reproduces a highly negative stereotype of speakers of Spanish.

American racism almost certainly includes other, similar strategic systems that might be identified by careful research. Especially, similar devices that function to pejorate and racialize African Americans and Asian Americans should be sought and analyzed. Furthermore, many questions remain about Mock Spanish itself. For instance, its history needs more careful investigation. We need to develop techniques by which to show when it has been more, and when less, intense and productive, and whether this ebb and flow of productivity coincides with economic cycles or other possibly related phenomena. More information is needed about who uses Mock Spanish. I have concluded, on the basis of limited and informal observation, that it is largely an elite usage, but it may be extending its reach across the social organization of the system of Whiteness. What are its functions in parts of the English-speaking world like Canada and Ireland . . . , where Spanish-speaking populations are minuscule and largely irrelevant to the local racist system?

Furthermore, Mock Spanish raises a whole range of fascinating questions about the role of humor in discrimination. One of the most compelling arguments of conservative foes of what is called "Political Correctness" is that the "politically correct" have no sense of humor. It strikes me that vulgar racism, for those who practice it, also seems to be fun, full of shared humor. Signs saying "No Mexicans or Dogs served here" were obviously intended to be hilarious. The Good Old Boys at a recent weekend retreat of "law enforcement officers" featured on the national news probably found the "Nigger Check Point" sign (assuming that it was really there, and not faked by their enemies) to be a real thigh-slapper. The drunken laughter of the lynch mob is a stereotype of American history. Unlike the deadly serious, careful register of "elite racist discourse" that van Dijk has identified, systems like Mock Spanish share humor uncomfortably with the cackling of the mob, in the snickering of the corner boys as one of their number sticks out a foot and trips up a black man. How important is humor and joking in the reproduction of racism? (And, of course, of sexism, anti-Semitism, and other systems of discrimination and exclusion.)

In summary, much remains to be done. I believe that linguistic anthropologists are especially well-qualified by the power and subtlety of the analytical tools that are available to us today, to make progress in these matters that are so important to the health of our society.

NOTES

1. In some previous papers on this phenomenon . . . , and in several lectures, I referred to this system as "Junk Spanish." I found that this term was very frequently misunderstood as a reference to so-called "Border Spanish," the code-switching, somewhat Anglicized forms of Spanish that can be heard from some speakers in the U.S. Southwest. I am indebted to James Fernandez for a very convincing explanation of why this misunderstanding was so pervasive, and for the suggestion of "Mock Spanish." Fernandez points out that for English speakers the association between "junk"—ruin and decline—and the Mediterranean areas of Europe (and their colonial offshoots) is hundreds of years old. The use of "junk" plays into this system. "Mock" both avoids this metaphorical system and makes clearer the central function and social location of the register of English that I address here.

2. The term "Anglo" is widely used in the Southwest for "white people." It is an all-encompassing term that includes Italians, Greeks, Irish, etc. Its existence (it is a short, monomorphemic element) is eloquent testimony to the social reality of this group, the members of which often like to argue that they are too diverse internally for such a single label. I will use this term for this social unit in the remainder of the paper.

3. In Arizona, "Official English" legislation, pushed by the national organization U.S. English, took the form of an amendment to the state constitution that included particularly restrictive language, that in the business of "the state and all its dependencies" (which include the University of Arizona), officers of the state (which includes me), "shall act in English and in no other language." The only exclusions were for the criminal courts, the teaching of foreign languages, and health and safety emergencies. Both the federal district court and the Ninth Circuit Court of Appeals have held this amendment to be in violation of the first and fourteenth amendments of the U.S. Constitution. . . .

4. This name borrows from "Nouvelle Southwest Cuisine." . . .

5. I take this expression from the work of Muriel Schulz (1975) on the historical semantic trajectory of words with female referents, such as "queen" (which has acquired the sense of "transvestite," in contrast to "king") and "housewife" (which has the contracted offshoot "hussy," in contrast to "husband," which has no such derogated relative).

6. The correct use of the accent mark on the *o* here is nothing short of astonishing. Written Mock Spanish is usually orthographically absurd.

7. "John Connor" has been "raised up rough" by an aunt and uncle, since his mother is locked in a lunatic asylum because she keeps talking about the first terminator. He is represented at the beginning of the film as running wild in the streets. I have no idea whether working-class white kids in Los Angeles today actually talk like John Connor. I do know, however, that the exposure of the screenwriters of such a film to the talk of kids is far more likely to be at the catered birthday party in Bel Air or in the parking lot of the Montessori School than on the actual mean streets of L.A.

8. There is no doubt that "Adios" is also used, at least in the Southwest, when speakers wish merely to be "warm" rather than funny and insulting. In this case, the stereotype of "Mexicans" (or perhaps the stereotype is of some gruff old Anglo rancher from the 1860's who has helped you fight off the Apaches) is that of generosity and hospitality. This usage does not, of course, cancel out the force of the very common use of "Adios" to convey insult.

9. I owe the "Hasta la baby, vista" example to Jodi Goldman, who found it in *The Koala* a satirical newspaper published by UCSD students, in the March 8, 1993 Edition. The phrase appears in an ad parodying the advertising for "Terminator 2: Judgment Day." I thank Kathryn Woolard for sending me the work of Ms. Goldman and other students.

10. In the film, the miraculous properties of the terminator metal permit the pieces of the evil terminator's shattered body to flow together and reconstitute him; he comes after Schwarzenegger and his charges again! This detail is neglected by politicians who use "Hasta la vista, baby" as an expression for final dismissal.

11. In Texas, the Democratic candidate Robert Krueger used "Hasta la vista, baby" in a television commercial where he dressed in a peculiar black suit apparently intended to allude to "Zorro," a . . . Mexican bandit from 1950's television. . . .

12. Spanish is, of course, by no means the only European language that is used as a source of "softened" scatological and obscene expressions for English speakers; one thinks immediately of Yiddish *dreck* and French *merde*. But Mock Spanish is a far more productive source. Another example along the

same lines is a Mock Spanish version of the widely-distributed slogan "Shit Happens," seen on bumper stickers and other paraphernalia. Bumper stickers are available that read "Caca Pasa."

13. I am indebted to Jay Sanders for drawing my attention to the use of Mock Spanish by Southern California teens; he contributed to a course in Discourse Analysis tapes of young female friends of his (who were from Thousand Oaks, not Encino), chatting casually on the phone using unusually high frequencies of Mock Spanish. Pauly Shore has made several films since "Encino Man" that probably deserve attention as well.

14. There is another, more vulgar version of this greeting that I have not seen. I owe the description of it to Barbara Babcock, who received a card where the front showed Hawaiian hula dancers, face forward, and the word "Muchas." Opening the card revealed a rear view of the dancers, buttocks clearly visible through their grass skirts, and the word "Grassy-ass."

15. Dominique Louisor-White and Dolores Valencia Tanno (1994), of the Communications department at California State University at San Bernardino, found that Mexican-American television newscasters in the Los Angeles area were increasingly likely to choose fully Spanish pronunciations of names when reading the news, starting with the pronunciation of their own names, since they regarded the usual Anglicized pronunciations as disrespectful. (They often encountered opposition to their pronunciation from Anglo station managers.)

16. I do make a claim to a sense of humor. But I have stopped using Mock Spanish, and I urge others to avoid it as well. As soon as Spanish is used within English in such a way that *de lujo* is as common as *de luxe*, that *camarones en mojo de ajo* are as prestigious a dish as *truite a la muniére*, and that *señorita*, like *mademoiselle*, can allude to good breeding as much as to erotic possibility, I'll go back to being as funny as possible with Spanish loan materials. Given the present context, I think that Mock Spanish is harmful—it is humor at the expense of people who don't need any more problems.

REFERENCES

Cassidy, Frederic G. 1985. *Dictionary of American Regional English.* Harvard University Press: Cambridge, Mass.

Hill, Jane H. 1993a. Hasta la vista, baby: Anglo Spanish in the American Southwest. *Critique of Anthropology* 13:145–176.

Hill, Jane. 1995. "Language, History, and Identity: Ethnolinguistic Studies of the Arizona Tewa." *American Indian Culture and Research Journal,* 19:205–210.

Louisor-White, Dominique and Dolores Valencia Tanno. 1994. Code-switching in the public forum: New expressions of cultural identity and persuasion. Paper presented at the Conference on Hispanic Language and Social Identity, University of New Mexico, Albuquerque NM, February 10–12, 1994.

Ochs, E. 1990. "Indexicality and Socialization." In J. W. Stigler, R. A. Shweder, & G. Herdt (Eds.). *Cultural Psychology* (pp. 287–308). Cambridge: Cambridge University Press.

Schulz, Muriel. 1975. The semantic derogation of women. In B. Thorne and N. Henley (eds)., *Language and Sex: Difference and Dominance,* pp. 64–73. Rowley, MA: Newbury.

Van Dijk, Teun Adreianus. 1993. *Elite Discourse and Racism.* Sage Publications: Newbury Park, Calif.

DISCUSSION QUESTIONS

1. If racism is covert and unintended, is it still racism? How does Hill make the case that Mock Spanish helps to reproduce and sustain racism in the larger society? Is her case convincing? What evidence does cite? If she is correct, under what conditions would it not be racist to tell an "ethnic" joke? Is ethnic or racial humor always racist?

2. What is "dual indexicality" and how does it work? What's the difference between direct and indirect indexicality? Cite and explore an example from your own discourse, the conversations of others, or from the mass media (TV, movies, and so on).

SEEING MORE THAN BLACK AND WHITE:
LATINOS, RACISM, AND THE CULTURAL DIVIDES

Elizabeth Martinez

. . .

When [Henry] Kissinger [Secretary of State under President Nixon] said years ago "nothing important ever happens in the south," he articulated a contemptuous indifference toward Latin America, its people, and their culture which has long dominated U.S. institutions and attitudes. Mexico may be great for a vacation, and some people like burritos but the usual image of Latin America combines incompetence with absurdity in loud colors. My parents, both Spanish teachers, endured decades of being told kids were better off learning French.

U.S. political culture is not only Anglo-dominated but also embraces an exceptionally stubborn national self-centeredness, with no global vision other than relations of domination. The U.S. refuses to see itself as one nation sitting on a continent with 20 others all speaking languages other than English and having the right not to be dominated.

Such arrogant indifference extends to Latinos within the U.S. The mass media complain, "people can't relate to Hispanics"—or Asians, they say. Such arrogant indifference has played an important role in invisibilizing La Raza (except where we become a serious nuisance or a handy scapegoat). It is one reason the U.S. harbors an exclusively white-on-Black concept of racism. It is one barrier to new thinking about racism which is crucial today. There are others.

GOOD-BYE WHITE MAJORITY

In a society as thoroughly and violently racialized as the United States, white-Black relations have defined racism for centuries. Today the composition and culture of the U.S. are changing rapidly. We need to consider seriously whether we can afford to maintain an exclusively white/Black model of racism when the population will be 32 percent Latin/Asian/Pacific American and Native American—in short, neither Black nor white—by the year 2050. We are challenged to recognize that multi-colored racism is mushrooming, and then strategize how to resist it. We are challenged to move beyond a dualism comprised of two white supremacist inventions: Blackness and Whiteness.

At stake in those challenges is building a united anti-racist force strong enough to resist contemporary racist strategies of divide-and-conquer. Strong enough in the long run, to help defeat racism itself. Doesn't an exclusively Black/white model of racism discourage the perception of common interests among people of color and thus impede a solidarity that can challenge white supremacy? Doesn't it encourage the isolation of African Americans from potential allies? Doesn't it advise all people of color to spend too much energy understanding our lives in relation to Whiteness, and thus freeze us in a defensive, often self-destructive mode?

NO "OPPRESSION OLYMPICS"

For a Latina to talk about recognizing the multi-colored varieties of racism is not, and should not be, yet another round in the Oppression Olympics. We don't need more competition among different social groupings for that "Most Oppressed" gold. We don't need more comparisons of suffering between women and Blacks, the disabled and the gay, Latino teenagers and white seniors, or whatever. We don't need more surveys like the recent much publicized Harris Poll showing that different peoples of color are prejudiced toward each other—a poll patently designed to demonstrate that us coloreds are no better than white folk. (The survey never asked people about positive attitudes.)

Rather, we need greater knowledge, understanding, and openness to learning about each other's histories and present needs as a basis for working together. Nothing could seem more urgent in an era when increasing impoverishment encourages a self-imposed separatism among people of color as a desperate attempt at community survival. Nothing could seem more important as we search for new social change strategies in a time of ideological confusion.

My call to rethink concepts of racism in the U.S. today is being sounded elsewhere. Among academics, liberal foundation administrators, and activist-intellectuals, you can hear talk of the need for a new "racial paradigm" or model. But new thinking seems to proceed in fits and starts, as if dogged by a fear of stepping on toes, of feeling threatened, or of losing one's base. With a few notable exceptions, even our progressive scholars of color do not make the leap from perfunctorily saluting a vague multiculturalism to serious analysis. We seem to have made little progress, if any, since Bob Blauner's 1972 book *Racial Oppression in America.* Recognizing the limits of the white-Black axis, Blauner critiqued White America's ignorance of and indifference to the Chicano/a experience with racism.

Real opposition to new paradigms also exists. There are academics scrambling for one flavor of ethnic studies funds versus another. There are politicians who cultivate distrust of others to keep their own communities loyal. When we hear, for example, of Black/Latino friction, dismay should be quickly followed by investigation. In cities like Los Angeles and New York, it may turn out that political figures scrapping for patronage and payola have played a narrow nationalist game, whipping up economic anxiety and generating resentment that sets communities against each other.

So the goal here, in speaking about moving beyond a bipolar concept of racism is to build stronger unity against white supremacy. The goal is to see our similarities of experience and needs. If that goal sounds naive, think about the hundreds of organizations formed by grassroots women of different colors coming together in recent years. Their growth is one of today's most energetic motions and it spans all ages. Think about the multicultural environmental justice movement. Think about the coalitions to save schools. Small rainbows of our own making are there, to brighten a long road through hellish times.

It is in such practice, through daily struggle together, that we are most likely to find the road to greater solidarity against a common enemy. But we also need a will to find it and ideas about where, including some new theory.

THE WEST GOES EAST

Until very recently, Latino invisibility—like that of Native Americans and Asian/Pacific Americans—has been close to absolute in U.S. seats of power, major institutions, and the non-Latino public mind. Having lived on both the East and West Coasts for long periods, I feel qualified to pronounce: an especially myopic view of Latinos prevails in the East. This, despite such data as a 24.4 percent Latino population of New York City alone in 1991, or the fact that in 1990 more Puerto Ricans were killed by New York police under suspicious circumstances than any other ethnic group. Latino populations are growing rapidly in many eastern cities and the rural South, yet remain invisible or stigmatized—usually both.

Eastern blinders persist. I've even heard that the need for a new racial paradigm is dismissed in New York as a California hang-up. A black Puerto Rican friend in New York, when we talked about experiences of racism common to Black and brown, said "People here don't see Border Patrol brutality against Mexicans as a form of police repression," despite the fact that the Border Patrol is the largest and most uncontrolled police force in the U.S. It would seem that an old ignorance has combined with new immigrant bashing to sustain divisions today.

While the East (and most of the Midwest) usually remains myopic, the West Coast has barely begun to move away from its own denial. Less than two years ago in San Francisco, a city almost half Latino or Asian/Pacific American, a leading daily newspaper could publish a major series on contemporary racial issues and follow the exclusively Black-white paradigm. Although millions of TV viewers saw massive Latino participation in the April 1992 Los

Angeles uprising, which included 18 out of 50 deaths and the majority of arrests, the mass media and most people labeled that event "a Black riot."

If the West Coast has more recognition of those who are neither Black nor white, it is mostly out of fear about the proximate demise of its white majority. A second, closely related reason is the relentless campaign by California Governor Pete Wilson to scapegoat immigrants for economic problems and pass racist, unconstitutional laws attacking their health, education, and children's future. Wilson has almost single-handedly made the word "immigrant" mean Mexican or other Latino (and sometimes Asian). Who thinks of all the people coming from the former Soviet Union and other countries? The absolute racism of this has too often been successfully masked by reactionary anti-immigrant groups like FAIR [the Federation for American Immigration Reform] blaming immigrants for the staggering African-American unemployment rate. . . .

As this suggests, what has been a regional issue mostly limited to western states is becoming a national issue. If you thought Latinos were just "Messicans" down at the border, wake up—they are all over North Carolina, Pennsylvania and 8th Avenue Manhattan now. A qualitative change is taking place. With the broader geographic spread of Latinos and Asian/Pacific Islanders has come a nationalization of racist practices and attitudes that were once regional. The west goes east, we could say.

Like the monster Hydra, racism is growing some ugly new heads. We will have to look at them closely.

The Roots of Racism and Latinos

A bipolar model of racism—racism as white on Black—has never really been accurate. Looking for the roots of racism in the U.S. we can begin with the genocide against American Indians which made possible the U.S. land base, crucial to white settlement and early capitalist growth. Soon came the massive enslavement of African people which facilitated that growth. As slave labor became economically critical, "blackness" became ideologically critical; it provided the

very source of "whiteness" and the heart of racism. Franz Fanon would write, "colour is the most outward manifestation of race."

If Native Americans had been a crucial labor force during those same centuries, living and working in the white man's sphere, our racist ideology might have evolved differently. "The tawny," as Ben Franklin dubbed them, might have defined the opposite of what he called "the lovely white." But with Indians decimated and survivors moved to distant concentration camps they became unlikely candidates for this function. Similarly, Mexicans were concentrated in the distant West; elsewhere Anglo fear of them or need to control was rare. They also did not provide the foundation for a definition of whiteness.

Some anti-racist left activists have put forth the idea that only African Americans experience racism as such and that the suffering of other people of color results from national minority rather than racial oppression. From this viewpoint, the exclusively white/Black model for racism is correct. Latinos then, experience exploitation and repression for reasons of culture and nationality—not for their "race." (It should go without saying . . . that while racism is an all-too-real social fact, race has no scientific basis.)

Does the distinction hold? This and other theoretical questions call for more analysis and more expertise than one article can offer. In the meantime let's try on the idea that Latinos do suffer for their nationality and culture, especially language. They became part of the U.S. through the 1846–48 war on Mexico and thus a foreign population to be colonized. But as they were reduced to cheap or semi-slave labor, they quickly came to suffer for their "race"—meaning, as non-whites. In the Southwest of a super-racialized nation the broad parallelism of race and class embrace Mexicans ferociously.

The bridge here might be a definition of racism as "the reduction of the cultural to the biological," in the words of French scholar Christian Delacampagne now working in Egypt. Or: "racism exists wherever it is claimed that a given social status is explained by a given natural characteristic." We know that line: Mexicans are just naturally lazy and have too many children so they're poor and exploited.

The discrimination, oppression and hatred experienced by Native Americans, Mexicans, Asian/Pacific Islanders, and Arab Americans are forms of racism. Speaking only of Latinos, we have seen in California and the Southwest especially along the border, almost 150 years of relentless repression which today includes Central Americans among its targets. That history reveals hundreds of lynchings between 1847 and 1935, the use of counter-insurgency armed forces beginning with the Texas Rangers, random torture and murder by Anglo ranchers, forced labor, rape by border lawmen, and the prevailing Anglo belief that a Mexican life doesn't equal a dog's in value.

But wait. If color is so key to racial definition, as Fanon and others say, perhaps people of Mexican background experience racism less than national minority oppression because they are not dark enough as a group. For White America, shades of skin color are crucial to defining worth. The influence of those shades has also been internalized by communities of color. Many Latinos can and often want to pass for whites; therefore, White America may see them as less threatening than darker sisters and brothers.

Here we confront more of the complexity around us today, with questions like: What about the usually poor, very dark Mexican or Central American of strong Indian or African heritage? (Yes, folks, 200,000–300,000 Africans were brought to Mexico as slaves, which is far, far more than the Spaniards who came.) And what about the effects of accented speech or foreign name, characteristics that may instantly subvert "passing"?

What about those cases where a Mexican-American is never accepted, no matter how light-skinned, well-dressed or well-spoken? A Chicano lawyer friend coming home from a professional conference in suit, tie and briefcase found himself on a bus near San Diego that was suddenly stopped by the Border Patrol. An agent came on board and made a beeline through the all-white rows of passengers direct to my friend. "Your papers." The agent didn't believe Jose was coming from a U.S. conference and took him off the bus to await proof. Jose was lucky; too many Chicanos and Mexicans end up killed.

In a land where the national identity is white, having the "wrong" nationality becomes grounds for racist abuse. Who would draw a sharp line between today's national minority oppression in the form of immigrant-bashing, and racism?

None of this aims to equate the African American and Latino experiences; that isn't necessary even if it were accurate. Many reasons exist for the persistence of the white/Black paradigm of racism; they include numbers, history, and the psychology of whiteness. In particular they include centuries of slave revolts, a Civil War, and an ongoing resistance to racism that cracked this society wide open while the world watched. Nor has the misery imposed on Black people lessened in recent years. New thinking about racism can and should keep this experience at the center.

A DEADLY DUALISM

The exclusively white/Black concept of race and racism in the U.S. rests on a western, Protestant form of dualism woven into both race and gender relations from earliest times. In the dualist universe there is only black and white. A disdain, indeed fear, of mixture haunts the Yankee soul; there is no room for any kind of multi-faceted identity, any hybridism.

As a people, La Raza combines three sets of roots—indigenous, European, and African—all in widely varying degrees. In short, we represent a profoundly un-American concept: *mestizaje* (pronounced mess-tee-zah-hey), the mixing of peoples and emergence of new peoples. A highly racialized society like this one cannot deal with or allow room for *mestizaje*. It has never learned to do much more than hiss "miscegenation!" Or, like that Alabama high school principal who recently denied the right of a mixed-blood pupil to attend the prom, to say: "your parents made a mistake." Apparently we, all the millions of La Raza, are just that—a mistake.

Mexicans in the U.S. also defy the either-or, dualistic mind in that, on the one hand, we are a colonized people displaced from the ancestral homeland with roots in the present-day U.S. that go back centuries. Those ancestors didn't cross the border; the border crossed them. At the same time many of us have come to the U.S. more recently as "immigrants" seeking work. The complexity of Raza baffles and frustrates most Anglos; they want to put one neat label on us. It baffles many Latinos too, who often end up categorizing themselves racially as "Other" for lack of anything better. For that matter, the term "Latino" which I use here is a monumental simplification; it refers to 20-plus nationalities and a wide range of classes.

But we need to grapple with the complexity, for there is more to come. If anything, this nation will see more *mestizaje* in future, embracing innumerable ethnic combinations. What will be its effects? Only one thing seems certain: "white" shall cease to be the national identity.

A glimpse at the next century tells us how much we need to look beyond the white/Black model of race relations and racism. White/Black are real poles, central to the history of U.S. racism. We can neither ignore them nor stop there. But our effectiveness in fighting racism depends on seeing the changes taking place, trying to perceive the contours of the future. From the time of the Greeks to the present, racism around the world has had certain commonalties but no permanently fixed character. It is evolving again today, and we'd best labor to read the new faces of this Hydra-headed monster. Remember, for every head that Hydra lost it grew two more.

Sometimes the problem seems so clear. Last year I showed slides of Chicano history to a Oakland high school class with 47 African Americans and three Latino students. The images included lynchings and police beatings of Mexicans and other Latinos, and many years of resistance. At the end one Black student asked, "Seems like we have had a lot of experiences in common—so why can't Blacks and Mexicans get along better?" No answers, but there was the first step: asking the question. . . .

DISCUSSION QUESTIONS

1. What does Martinez mean by the "Oppression Olympics"? Why is it destructive, from her point of view, to compete for the "most oppressed" gold? What should nonwhites be pursuing instead? What can minority groups learn from each other? How would (white) America change if nonwhite groups learned to "get along better"?

2. Martinez argues that the dualistic white/black model of racism encourages people of color "to spend too much energy understanding our lives in relation to Whiteness." What does she mean by this? What is "whiteness" and how does it relate to nonwhite groups? Is Martinez addressing a psychological process only, or are there political or economic (or other) dimensions?

3. Martinez discusses the struggle of nonwhite and dispossessed groups against "a common enemy." Who is that enemy? White people? Whiteness?

4. What are some specific ways discussed by Martinez in which nonwhites and Hispanic Americans in general are "invisibilized" and scapegoated?

5. Is the oppression and discrimination faced by Latinos mainly based on race or ethnicity, culture, and language? How would Martinez answer this question? What difference does it make? How?

CURRENT DEBATES

IS IMMIGRATION HARMFUL OR HELPFUL TO THE UNITED STATES?

Immigration is once again a topic of public concern and debate in the United States: How many immigrants should be admitted? What skills and education levels should immigrants bring? What economic impact does immigration have on the larger society? How long will it take (if ever) for the present wave of immigrants to assimilate?

Several aspects of this broad debate are addressed in the debate that follows. Peter Brimelow, a journalist and an immigrant himself, presented a passionate argument against current immigration policy in his best selling book *Alien Nation* (1995). In this excerpt, Brimelow argues that recent immigrants are swelling the welfare rolls and placing more demands on already strained local, state, and national budgets. He is particularly concerned about the effects of a new immigration policy instituted in 1965. The newer policy replaced a system that was overtly racist (for example, it gave strong preference to immigrants from Northern and Western Europe and provided little or no room for immigrants from Africa or Asia, regardless of their potential to contribute to U.S. society). The policy instituted in 1965 raised the numerical limit on the number of immigrants and emphasized family reunification (that is, immigrants with close relatives in the United States were given a high priority). Brimelow argues that the result has been a dangerous decline in educational and skill levels of the immigrant stream.

A rejoinder is presented by sociologist Reynolds Farley (1996), whose analysis is generally pro-immigration. He argues that the negative effects of post-1965 immigration have generally been modest and that even the least skilled immigrants can find niches in the American economy that do not greatly disturb the status of native-born workers.

Thirdly, George Borjas (1999) looks at the way in which immigration issues are typically raised in the United States and argues for a new approach. He argues that the debate over immigration should be not so much about numbers but what kind of society the United States is and would like to become. Borjas also broadens the debate and places it in a more global context.

IMMIGRATION IS HARMFUL

Peter Brimelow

Today, immigration . . . is not determined by economics; it is determined—or at least profoundly distorted—by public policy. . . . [The] effect of the 1965 reform [in immigration policy] has been to uncouple legal immigration from the needs of the U.S. economy. A low point was reached in 1986, when less than 8 percent of over 600,000 legal immigrants were admitted on the basis of skills. [Most of the remainder were admitted under family reunification provisions.] Of course, some of the family-reunification immigrants will have skills. But it is purely an accident whether their skills are wanted in the U.S. economy.

The family-reunification policy inevitably contributes to two striking characteristics of the post-1965 flow:

- Firstly: The post-1965 immigrants are, on average, less skilled than earlier immigrants. And getting even less so. As George Borjas

[a leading immigration researcher] put it: "The skill level of successive immigrant waves admitted to the U.S. has declined precipitously in the last two or three decades."

- Secondly: The post-1965 immigrants unmistakably display more mis-matching between what they can do and what America needs. They seem not to be fitting as well into the economy as did earlier immigrants. Instead, they are showing a greater tendency to become what used to be called a "public charge."

[In] 1970 the average recent immigrant had 0.35 less years of schooling than native-born Americans. By 1990, the average recent immigrant had 1.32 years less schooling. . . . [Economists] view education as a proxy for skills. And the relative decline in immigrant education seems to be confirmed by the relative decline in their earnings that has occurred in the same period.

In 1970, immigrants on average actually earned some 3 percent more than native-born Americans. . . . But in 1990, the immigrant achievement had disappeared: immigrants on average earned 16.2 percent less than native-born Americans.

The second striking characteristic of the post-1965 immigrant flow: increased mismatching with the U.S. labor market. This shows up in the immigrants' increasing tendency to go on welfare.

In the early 1980s, immigration researchers were generally pretty complacent about immigration's impact on the United States. It became an article of faith . . . that immigrants earned more, and went on welfare less, than native-born Americans.

The reason for this complacency, of course: The researchers were looking at old data. It still substantially reflected pre-1965 immigrants.

By the early 1990s, the scene had changed completely. It was becoming clear that, among the post-1965 immigrants, welfare participation rates were sharply higher. Immigrant welfare participation was, on average, higher than native-born Americans (9.1 vs. 7.4 percent). And what's more, immigrant households on welfare tended to consume more, and increasingly more, than native-born households on welfare. (In 1970, 6.7 percent of all welfare cash benefits went to immigrants; in 1990, 13.1 percent.)

(And note that "welfare" means just cash programs like Aid to Families with Dependent Children, Supplementary Security Income, and general assistance—not non-cash programs like Food Stamps and Medicaid, for which there are no good numbers.) . . .

Examining the group of immigrants arriving in the five years before 1970 reveals even more depressing news: Welfare participation actually increased the longer they stayed in the United States. Originally, their rate was 5.5 percent; the 1990 census reported it at 9.8 percent. All waves of immigrants show a similar drift. The conclusion is unavoidable: Immigrants are assimilating into the welfare system.

SOURCE: Brimelow, Peter. (1995). *Alien Nation* (pp. 141–149). New York: Random House.

IMMIGRATION IS NOT HARMFUL

Reynolds Farley

During the 1980s, the native-born labor force with a high school education or less fell from 55 million to 48 million, reflecting the shift toward greater educational attainment and the retirement of older workers who had less schooling. But 3 million immigrants who arrived in the 1980s had high school educations or less. Isn't it obvious that this high volume of immigration depresses employment opportunities and lowers wages for native-born Americans who lack college training? Wouldn't wages rise if we immediately terminated the flow of immigrants? Can't we blame the high level of immigration for the declining wages [of American workers]?

Because of the importance of immigration, this issue receives a great deal of attention. While there are still disagreements about the details, there is consensus that the effects of immigration on the employment prospects and wages of natives are modest. Summarizing several dozen studies based on the 1970 and 1980 census, Fix and Pascal (Fix, Michael, and Pascal, Jeffrey. 1994. *Immigration and Immigrants: Setting the Record Straight.* Washington, D.C.: Urban Institute, p. 49) conclude that if immigrants as a share of the labor force in a metropolis went up from 10 percent . . . to 20 percent, the labor force participation rate of natives would drop only 1 percent, net of all other factors. . . .

This seems counterintuitive. How can the presence of many immigrants not depress employment opportunities and lower wages for natives? The economists who model these processes report that four factors explain this puzzle. First, immigration is concentrated in metropolises that are growing rapidly, most of them in the South and Southwest. Booming populations and economic growth in these places create thousands of jobs each year, and a fraction are filled by immigrants. Migrants, to a large degree, are fitting into occupational slots created by economic and demographic growth. Second, the presence of immigrants . . . may permit industries [that would otherwise move offshore] to thrive. . . . In recent years, the garment industry has prospered in New York, Los Angeles, and Miami largely because immigrants from China and the Caribbean are willing to work long hours for small paychecks, producing the costly dresses and suits that highly educated women need as they pursue careers. . . . And it is clear that quite a few new arrivals set up their own businesses, thereby hiring workers. . . .

Third, many immigrants fill jobs that native-born Americans are reluctant to accept—for example, the stoop labor traditionally needed in agriculture [or the jobs as nannies created] as women increasingly devote themselves to full-time jobs. . . .

There may be a fourth reason: employers may prefer illegals to citizens. Recent immigrants may, perhaps, be easily exploited and are unlikely to file suits about violations of minimum wage laws [or health] violations.

[Opposition to immigration will continue despite the evidence that immigration does little harm to the employment and wage prospects of natives.] Opposition . . . will come from those states and cities whose budgets are greatly impacted by the high volume of recent immigration. Several studies have investigated the financial consequences of undocumented immigration, especially in the seven states most affected. There were approximately three million illegals in those states in 1992 who paid an estimated $1.9 billion annually in state sales taxes, state and local property taxes, and state income taxes (Clark, Rebecca; Passel, Jeffrey; Zimmerman, Wendy; Fix, Michael. 1994. *Fiscal Impacts of Undocumented Aliens: Selected Estimates for Seven States.* Washington, D.C.: Urban Institute Press).

The investigators considered the three most expensive state programs used by illegal aliens: the costs of emergency medical care, public schools, and prisons. These charges came to about $4 billion, implying that illegals imposed a burden of $2 billion upon taxpayers in these seven states. Although $2 billion is a very large sum and gives a clear indication of the substantial cost illegals place on local governments, the total expenditure of the governments in these seven states in 1992 was approximately $245 billion, so the termination of all undocumented immigrants would produce only a very modest reduction in state spending.

SOURCE: Farley, Reynolds. (1996). *The New American Reality* (pp. 199–207). New York: Russell Sage Foundation.

We Need to Reframe the Immigration Debate

George Borjas

As the 21st century begins, the United States is about to embark once again upon a historic debate about the type of immigration policy that the country should pursue. As in the past, the cost-benefit calculus frames the terms of the debate: Who loses from immigration, and by how much? Who wins from immigration, and by how much? . . .

[These costs and benefits] are also symptoms of pursuing particular immigration policies. By arguing over . . . these symptoms—whether immigrants use a lot of welfare, whether consumer prices are lowered by immigration—the immigration debate is, in a sense, worrying about the height of trees in the forest, rather than the shape of the forest.

Typically, those who argue over . . . a particular social policy takes sides by grasping onto a specific fact, and from that fact they immediately infer some policy reform that the country should pursue. In my view, this [approach] is just plain wrong.

To see why, single out a particular symptom of immigration over which there is little disagreement: Immigrant use of welfare is high. The policy implications of this fact depend crucially on what the U.S. is trying to accomplish. If the goal of immigration policy is to ensure that immigration did not place a fiscal burden on the native population, this symptom [implies] that U.S. should take steps to restrict the entry of potential welfare recipients. If, in contrast, the goal of immigration policy is to help the poorest people in the world, this symptom has no relevance—it is the price that the country must pay to achieve a particular humanitarian objective.

In the end, a debate over the policy implications of . . . immigration cannot be based on the evidence alone. *Any policy discussion requires explicitly stated assumptions about what constitutes the national interest.* [Emphasis in the original.] It is the combination of the evidence with an assumption about what Americans desire that permits an informed debate. . . . [First, the American people must] answer the bigger question: What should immigration policy accomplish?

Of course, answering this question is very difficult, even when the debate is restricted purely to . . . economic issues. To see why, divide the world into three distinct constituencies: the current population of the U.S., the immigrants themselves, and those who remain in the source countries. To draw policy conclusions from the symptoms of immigration, one has to know whose economic welfare the United States should try to improve when setting policy—that of natives, immigrants, the rest of the world, or some mix thereof. The policy implications implied by the symptoms depend crucially on whose interests the United States cares most about.

By framing the issue in this fashion, the trade-offs implicit in immigration policy are made crystal clear. The native population probably benefits a great deal when the United States admits high-quality scientific manpower, but the people left behind in the source countries probably lose a lot. Similarly, immigrants benefit when immigration policy favors the entry of their relatives, but natives may lose because this policy does not screen the new entrants and might let in many persons who qualify for social services. . . .

How many and which types of immigrants should the country then admit? The evidence [leads me to conclude that] the United States would be better off by adopting an immigration policy that favored skilled workers. And a plausible argument can also be made that the country would be better off with a slight reduction in the number of immigrants. . . .

In theory, the United States should admit an immigrant as long as the contribution made by the immigrant exceeds the costs imposed by the immigrant. It is difficult to come up with the "magic number" unless one becomes much more specific about how to balance the facts that immigration increases the size of the economic pie *and* changes how the pie is split. Those who care about economic efficiency will typically want to see more immigrants: The greater the number of immigrants, the greater the gains to employers (through lower wages) and consumers (through lower prices). Those who care about distributional issues [and income inequality] will typically want to see fewer immigrants: The greater the number of immigrants, the greater the dislocation in labor markets, and the greater the losses suffered by those who compete with immigrant workers [typically, native workers who are already low wage]. . . .

In the end, the objective of immigration policy will reflect a political consensus that inevitably incorporates the conflicting social and economic interests of various demographic, socioeconomic, and ethnic groups, as well as political and humanitarian concerns. Perhaps after debating these issues, the American people will place the economic concerns aside, and choose an immigration policy that stresses the humanitarian or political consequences of immigration.

Such a resolution of the debate does not diminish the value of entering a discussion that informs the country about the economic consequences of immigration. A wise decision requires that the American people be fully aware of the price they will have to pay if the United States chooses to adopt an immigration policy that minimizes or ignores economic considerations.

SOURCE: Borjas, George. (1999). *Heaven's Door: Immigration Policy and the American Economy* (pp. 4, 15–16). Princeton, NJ: Princeton University Press.

QUESTIONS TO CONSIDER

1. Consider the nature of the arguments presented by Brimelow and Farley. To what extent do the appeal to emotion? To what extent do they base their arguments on evidence and logic? What specific disagreements over "facts" can you identify? What information would you need to resolve these disagreements?

2. What does Borjas add to the debate? Does his approach offer a way to resolve the disagreements between the other two authors? In Borjas's terms, what constituencies do Brimelow and Farley have in mind (native population, immigrants, or those left behind)? How might their arguments change if they considered a different constituency?

3. These authors focus on economic consequences. What arguments for and against immigration can be developed on moral, political, cultural, or social principles? How does the debate change when the focus shifts away from economic costs and benefits?

4. What opinions about immigration would you expect to find in the different constituencies of U.S. society? Among African Americans? Among blue-collar workers? Among third- and fourth-generation Latinos? From undergraduate social science majors? Find some relevant opinions from members of these groups in your library. Check public opinion research and recent newspapers (especially those published in California, Texas, Florida, and New York) and news magazines.

8

Asian Americans
and Pacific Islanders

The term "Asian Americans and Pacific Islanders" imposes a label on a variety of groups that in reality have very little in common. These groups differ from each other in language, religion, cuisines, physical appearance, and in countless other ways. The category includes people who trace their origins to countries as diverse as China, Japan, the Philippines, Pakistan, Samoa, Vietnam, India, and scores of others. Some members of the group have American roots going back nearly 200 years, while others are the newest of newcomers.

Even considered as a whole, Asian Americans and Pacific Islanders are few in number and comprise about 4 percent of the national population. Because of high rates of immigration, however, these groups are growing rapidly, as is their impact on American society, and they are projected to make up 10 percent of the population by 2050.

Of all the groups in this category, Chinese Americans and Japanese Americans have the longest histories in the United States. Immigrants from China began arriving in the early 1800s to fill jobs in the burgeoning economy of the west coast, and immigrants from Japan began arriving in significant numbers at the end of the 1800s. Both groups faced intense, bitter campaigns of discrimination and racism and, as a result, formed ethnic enclaves or separate, largely self-contained sub-economies (for example, Chinatowns).

Other groups of Asian Americans and Pacific Islanders began immigrating in large numbers after the 1965 change in U.S. immigration laws. This immigration stream is extremely diverse and includes highly educated professionals, refugees fleeing warfare or persecution, laborers, and large numbers of illegal immigrants. Some of these immigrants are attracted by jobs at the highest levels of American society and are medical practitioners, engineers, college faculty, and scientists. Others provide a cheap workforce for the ethnic enclaves and take jobs that are poorly paid, have few if any benefits, and little security. Although Asian Americans and Pacific Islanders can be found at every level of the economy, there is a tendency for these groups to be "bipolar" and occupy positions at the very top and the very bottom of the job market.

Some of the diversity within these groups is suggested by the two Narrative Portraits. The first is from Ho Yang, who immigrated decades ago and entered an ethnic enclave. The second, by Vo Thi Tam, recounts the experiences of a refugee who arrived much more recently and with very few resources or connections to assist her adjustment to American life.

One thing that Asian Americans and Pacific Islanders do share is the widespread perception that they are successful and well-behaved: a "model minority." This stereotype is, of course, greatly exaggerated and certainly does not apply to many recent immigrants, especially the refugee groups and those who find themselves at the bottom of the ethnic enclave economies.

Nevertheless, the stereotype is reinforced by the fact that, on the average, many Asian American and Pacific Islander groups are at or above national norms for income, years of education, and poverty rates.

How much truth is there to the stereotype of the model minority? The Reading by Won Moo Hurh and Kwang Chung Kim exposes some of the problems and limitations of the image of Asian "success." Victor Hwang, in the second Reading, analyzes hate crimes against the group and explores some of the problems that Asian Americans and Pacific Islanders share with other minority groups of color.

Although the model minority image is clearly a stereotype and greatly exaggerated, the fact that at least some Asian American and Pacific Islander groups compare favorably with national averages (and rank much higher than other racial minority groups) demands exploration. The Current Debate section presents several distinct views on the sources of Asian success. Harry Kitano argues that the key to success lies in the value systems Asian immigrants bring with them, while Alejandro Portes and Min Zhou attribute the relative success to the enclave economies. Finally, Ronald Takaki, like Hurh and Kim, explores some of the not-so-hidden political agendas that underlie the attribution of success to Asian Americans

NARRATIVE PORTRAITS

TWO STORIES OF IMMIGRATION

The following accounts illustrate some of the variety of Asian Americans. The first recounts the experiences of Ho Yang, who immigrated to San Francisco's Chinatown as a young boy in 1920. He describes some of the dynamics of the enclave community he grew to be a part of. At the time of the interview (1980), he was an officer in one of the family associations that helped to organize and structure the Chinese American community.

The second account is from Vo Thi Tam, a Vietnamese refugee whose husband had been an officer in the South Vietnamese Air Force. She describes a harrowing passage to America during which she became separated from her husband, was attacked by pirates, and gave birth in a refugee camp. These two Asian immigrants arrived in the United States under vastly different circumstances. What consequences would such differences have for their experiences in U.S. society?

HO YANG

My village in Kwantung Province is very small, only about a hundred people, and it was really poor. . . . We used cows for plows, you know, because buffaloes were expensive. A whole life would depend on a cow. In fact, when a cow died there, I think the family wept more than when a relative died. . . .

My father went to Canton and worked there, and after a while, he saved up enough money and he came to the United States. And when I

was 13, he came back to China and got me. He couldn't bring my mother for some legal reason, and my sister wanted to stay with her, so I was the only one he brought back. . . .

Later, I went back to China to get married. I had a friend over here who said, "You want to get married? Maybe I'll write a letter to my niece in China." And I said, "Well, all right, you can try. It won't hurt." And it turned out to be all right with her . . . and we've been together for more than 40 years now. . . .

There's really two reasons people like to live in Chinatown. One is the language. Some Chinese have been here for thirty years and they've never been out of Chinatown and they can't speak English. The other reason is the work here. People own little shops. There must be over 200 shops in Chinatown. Little butcher shops, little curio shops, noodle shops, all those kinds of shops. It's usually just a husband and wife, and the kids work in there. And the small restaurants are family style. Everybody helps; washing dishes, waiters and waitresses, and all that. The money isn't too good but it's all in the family.

Many of the Chinese ladies, they go to the garment factory. . . . My wife did that. . . .

[The] main reason ladies go in them is this: If you don't understand English, you can't go to work in an American place. Also, Americans pay you by the hour and you can't go too slow. Too slow and they fire you, you know. But in Chinatown, they go by piecework—so much a dozen. . . . And ladies with children, it's good for them, too, because they can bring their little kids with them and can run around there. And if the ladies need to leave, they're free to go to take their kids to school, because by the piece, the less time you spend there, the less money you get. Sometimes they call those companies sweatshops, because the pay is so low, but they're better now than they were before.

VO THI TAM

[To escape] we got together with some other families and bought a big fishing boat. . . . Altogether there were about 37 of us that were to leave. I was five months pregnant.

[On the day of the escape, they were to rendezvous with her husband and another man outside the harbor] but there was no one there. [A patrol boat was approaching] and there was a discussion aboard the boat and the end of it was the people on our boat decided to leave without my husband and the other man. (Long pause)

When we reached the high seas, we discovered that the water container was leaking and only a little was left. So we had to ration the water from then on. We had brought some rice and some other food . . . but the sea was so wavy that we could not cook anything at all. So all we had was raw rice and a few lemons and very little water. After seven days we ran out of water, so all we had to drink was the sea water. . . . Everyone was sick and, at one point, my mother and my little boy, four years old, were in agony, about to die. And the other people on the boat said that if they were agonizing like that, it would be better to throw them overboard so as to save them pain. . . .

[While we] were discussing throwing my mother and son overboard, we could see [a] ship coming and we were very happy. . . . When the boats came together, the people came on board . . . and made all of us go aboard the bigger boat. They began to search us—cutting off our blouses, our bras, searching everywhere. . . . Finally, they pried up the planks of our boat, trying to see if there was any gold or jewelry hidden there. And when they had taken everything, they put us back on our boat and pushed us away.

[The group was attacked twice more by pirates before finally reaching land in Malaysia. Once ashore, yet another group attacked them and one of the women was raped. They were finally rescued by Malaysian police and taken to a refugee camp on Bidong Island.] Perhaps in the beginning it was all right there, maybe for ten thousand people or so, but when we arrived, there were already fifteen to seventeen thousand crowded onto thirty acres. There was no facilities, no housing, nothing. . . .

The Malaysian authorities did what they could but . . . there were no sanitary installations, and many people had diarrhea. It was very hard to stop sickness under those conditions. . . . When the monsoons came, the floor of our shelter was all mud. We had one blanket and a board to lie on, and that was all. . . . After four months, it was time for my baby to come. Fortunately, we had many doctors among us, because many . . . had escaped from Vietnam, so we had medical care but no equipment. There was no bed, no hospital, no nothing, just a wooden plank to lie down on and let the baby be born. . . . After the delivery I had to get up and . . . make room for the next one to be born.

[After seven months in the camp, they finally came to the United States.] It was like waking up after a bad nightmare. Like coming out of hell into paradise. [Shortly after her arrival, Vo Thi Tam learned that her husband had been recaptured and was a prisoner in Vietnam.]

SOURCE: Morrison, Joan, & Zabusky, Charlotte Fox Zabusky. (1980). *American Mosaic: The Immigrant Experience in the Words of Those Who Lived It* (pp. 79–80, 446–450). New York: Dutton.

READINGS

Like Hispanic Americans, Asian Americans belong to a racial category within the United States that lumps together many diverse peoples with vastly differing experiences. Yet unlike Latinos, Asian Americans and Pacific Islanders cannot even point to a single language or common religion that binds them. What this group does have in common is a shared experience of how the dominant group (whites) in the United States perceives them. Their coming together under one *pan-ethnic* racial rubric is a clear example of how race is a *social construction,* often created using the definition of those in power. Although their national origins may place them as foreigners, even enemies to each other, Asian Americans face certain common prejudices in the eyes of whites, particularly the "model minority" stereotype. This is often seen as a "positive stereotype," but our first Reading, "The 'Success' Image of Asian Americans," raises some questions, both about the validity of the stereotype and the negative consequences it may have for Asian Americans as a group. As to the validity of Asian American "success" relative to other minority groups, the authors point out that the use of family income as an indicator of success may mask several issues of racial discrimination still faced by Asian Americans. By not taking into account the hours worked or the number of wage earners in the home, it may appear that Asian Americans are on a par with whites in terms of income, yet they are working many more hours or combining more household wage earners to get to that figure than whites do. Further, by not taking into account levels of education, we are unaware that Asian Americans at every level have to have higher degrees than whites for the same earning power. That is, they are getting lower levels of return on their education. The authors argue that this over-exaggeration of how well Asian Americans are doing means that much-needed social programs are not extended to them as a result. Also, this so-called positive stigma has some severely negative and even deadly consequences, as it has made Asian Americans the target of hate crimes, usually committed by whites who are angry about and envious of their supposed success.

The second Reading explores this issue of hate crimes against Asian Americans in more depth. In "The Interrelationship Between Anti-Asian Violence and Asian America," Victor Hwang discusses two different incidents, each highlighting different aspects of hate crimes and the multiple layers of injury that they cause. In the first incident, a 63-year-old Korean American woman is brutally beaten just because of her race, and Hwang argues that this woman's injuries are not only physical but emotional as well. The way people react to her after the attack only adds insult to injury in various ways, since certain well-meaning individuals may not have harmed her physically, but they still assaulted her humanity. The beating and its aftermath cause a transformation in the victim, who had heretofore internalized the model minority stereotype and developed a *false consciousness* as a result. She abandons her antagonistic views toward blacks, fueled by this model-minority idea, and for the first time realizes the common experiences they share as racial minorities. In the second incident, swastikas are painted on Asian-owned and Asian-related businesses, signed by the "Sunset White Boys." Again, the author finds exploring the aftermath of the incident to be just as meaningful as the incident itself. From institutions to individuals, the initial desire to minimize the significance of the racist attacks, and the delay in efforts to respond to the crime is clear. Further, although the town seems to give lip service to condemning the actual attacks, the sentiment behind them is shared by many, as evidenced in a town meeting where venting about people of color "taking over" the area becomes more important than expressing concern for the business owners who were attacked. Hwang asks us to consider anti-Asian prejudice not just as isolated violent acts of bigotry but as social products for which we are collectively responsible. In doing so, he takes a decisively different turn than most popular media representations of hate crimes and ultimately shows us how a seemingly positive stereotype can have severely harmful consequences.

The "Success" Image of Asian Americans:
Its Validity, and Its Practical and Theoretical Implications

Won Moo Hurh and Kwang Chung Kim

Introduction

In an effort to lessen the spectre of the "Yellow Peril," the U.S. Congress passed the Chinese Exclusion Act and President Chester A. Arthur signed the bill on 6 May 1882. This law, which prohibited Chinese immigration to the United States until 1943, was an actual consequence of the negative Chinese image held by a majority of Americans (Isaacs 1962). These negative images, such as "Chinese deceit, cunning, idolatry, despotism, xenophobia, cruelty, infanticide, and intellectual and sexual perversity," were already reflected in the public media prior to the arrival of the first wave of Chinese labourers to California in 1848 (Miller 1969, p. 201). The early Chinese immigrants were initially received as "exotic curiosities" but this soon changed to "unassimilable, immoral, treacherous heathens" who would take away whites' jobs and possibly also their women (Lyman 1970; Sue and Kitano 1973). This unfavourable perception of Chinese immigrants was later extended to Japanese, Korean, and Filipino immigrants and then persisted for a century with little modification.

However, in 1982, the centennial year of the Chinese Exclusion Act of 1882, *Newsweek*

published an article entitled, "Asian-Americans: A Model Minority," conveying a positive image of Chinese, Japanese, Koreans, and Vietnamese in the United States:

> Despite years of discrimination—much of it enforced by the federal government—the difficulties of acculturation and a recent backlash against their burgeoning numbers, Asian-Americans now enjoy the nation's highest median family income. ... The Chinese have a term for it—"gung-ho"— and the industrious Asians believe they are contributing a needed shot of some vanishing American values: thrift, strong family ties, sacrifice for the children. *(Newsweek,* 6 December 1982, p. 39)

The dominant group's perception of racial and ethnic minorities usually fluctuates over time depending on the vicissitudes of international relations, the national socio-economic structure, the dominant group's cultural values, and the minority's adaptive capacities. However, the amplitude of recent changes in majority American's perception of Asian Americans has certainly been dramatic.

What factors would account for this change? To what extent is the success image of Asian

Americans true? How would such a model-minority image affect Asian Americans, the other minorities (black and Mexican Americans), and majority Americans themselves?

The debate on the success image of Asian Americans is certainly not a new issue. Since the mid-1960s a considerable number of scholarly works have been published, either supporting or rejecting the validity of the success image (for details on this polemic issue, see Chun 1980; Kim and Hurh 1983). Beyond the question of the validity, however, this article purports to explore practical and theoretical implications of the dominant group's positive labelling of a racial/ethnic minority.

MAJORITY AMERICANS' IMAGE OF ASIAN AMERICANS: AN HISTORICAL OVERVIEW

. . . Asian Americans have . . . been a target for severe prejudice and discrimination. Ironically, much of the past discriminatory practices have been legitimized by the U.S. Congress and federal government (institutional racism). Anti-Asian legislation was, however, largely a consequence of majority Americans' negative stereotypes of Asians. For example, the Immigration Act of 1924 grew out of the anti-Oriental image held by whites, especially by those who resided on the west coast. This law has thus been commonly known as the Oriental Exclusion Act. In other words, Anglo-Americans' negative images (stereotypes) of Chinese and Japanese were largely confirmed by national and state institutions.

In general, ethnic stereotypes are exaggerated images of the characteristics of particular ethnic group. . . . In Walter Lippmann's terms, stereotypes are "pictures in our heads" which may be either negative or positive, or relatively true or false (Lippmann 1922). They are simplified, time-saving, and convenient devices often used by the dominant group to sort out "bad guys" from "good guys" or vice versa, and in so doing one can label, isolate, confine, or exclude a particular defenseless minority group. In this respect, verbalized stereotypes anticipate and often bring actual consequences: a typical case of self-fulfilling prophecy. . . .

The majority of Americans' image of "Orientals" has fluctuated over time, reflecting the changes in international relations and in socioeconomic and political conditions of the United States. As Sue and Kitano (1973) observe, the early negative image of Chinese reflects America's economic problems and unemployment in the late 1800s. The negative image which was extended later to Japanese became worse in 1940, reflecting the U.S. involvement in World War II. During that war the Chinese image was somewhat improved as China was an American ally, but soon after the war the image became ambivalent due to the establishment of the Peoples' Republic of China in 1949 (Lyman 1974, pp. 119–133). . . . American perception of Chinese fluctuated back and forth; but generally, the past negative image of the Asian population in the United States has been transformed into a positive one, especially in the 1960s.

The change in the majority Americans' image of Asian Americans may largely be attributed to the professionalization and upward social mobility of young Chinese and Japanese Americans who were generally American-born and college-educated (Lyman 1974, p. 119). Moreover, the influx of college-educated immigrants from Korea, the Philippines, Taiwan, Hong Kong and India since the revision of the U.S. immigration law in 1965 reinforced the positive image of Asian Americans. Another significant factor in accentuating the success image of Asian Americans was the Civil Rights movement in the 1960s. As Chun (1980, p. 2) correctly observes, "at that time [in the sixties], when the nation was still groping for solutions to its racial unrest, the portrayal of Asian Americans as a successful minority seemed to serve a need": the need to blame blacks and other disadvantaged minorities for their own failure and the nation's "race problems." In 1966, the success image of Japanese and Chinese Americans was conveyed to the American public by *New York Times Magazine* (1966) and *U.S. News & World Report* (1966). Nowadays, the success image is extended to other Asians, such as Koreans, Filipinos, Vietnamese and Asian Indians *(Newsweek* 1982; *Time* 1985). Thus "unassimilable heathens" became "successful model minorities" in about 100 years. . . . The validity and implications of the success image of Asian Americans will be examined next.

VALIDITY OF THE ASIAN-AMERICAN "SUCCESS" IMAGE

As mentioned earlier, Asian Americans' success stories began to appear in the American popular press in the mid-1960s. . . . Although the success theme includes a stereotype about the Asian American problem-free family and community life, most of the past studies on Asian Americans focused their attention on the socio-economic status that Asian Americans achieved in comparison with that of the dominant group (particularly white males). In such a conceptual framework, Asian Americans would be considered "successful," if the level of their socio-economic achievement reached or exceeded that of whites. The socio-economic achievement is then empirically measured by the following indices: (1) education (the mean or median years of schooling or the proportion of those who completed high school or college education); (2) occupation (the mean occupational prestige or the proportion of those who are employed in technical or professional occupations or in white collar occupations as a whole); and (3) earnings (family or individual).

By the above measures, Asian Americans are generally found to have been successful. Japanese Americans have achieved a level of education similar to that of whites since the early 1940s (Fogel 1966). Since 1960, both native- and foreign-born Chinese Americans have achieved a level of education equal to, or even higher than, that of whites (Hirschman and Wong 1981). According to the 1980 census data, both native- and foreign-born Filipinos and the immigrants from Korea and India also exhibit a high level of education. . . .

In terms of economic achievement, prior to World War II, a high proportion of Japanese and Chinese Americans were in small business. The small business tradition had changed little during the war, although the wartime relocation reduced the number of Japanese small businesses.

In the post-war period, a high proportion of young Japanese and Chinese Americans gained access to technical or professional occupations through their higher education. Due to such an increased access to technical or professional occupations and continued participation in small business, a higher proportion of Japanese and Chinese Americans have been employed in white collar occupations than have whites (Hirschman and Wong 1981). Today, Koreans and other Asian immigrants tend to show a similar occupational distribution. In these conditions, our sample estimation from the 1980 census reveals that the occupational prestige scores of many Asian male groups are on the average higher than those of white males (cf. Stevens and Cho 1985).

The high proportion of Asian Americans in white collar occupations and their high rate of labour-force participation resulted in a relatively high family income in the past (Urban Associates, 1974; Wu 1980). The 1980 census confirms this point again . . . . [F]our of the six largest Asian ethnic groups (Japanese, Chinese, Filipinos and Asian Indians) maintain a higher mean annual family income than white families. Another Asian group (Koreans) is very close to whites in their family income. Even in their annual mean individual earnings, three Asian ethnic groups (Japanese, Chinese and Asian Indians) exceed those of whites. . . .

[However,] minority members may pay a higher price than whites for achieving a given level of status. It is, therefore, necessary to examine additionally the relative amount of investment made or price paid by minority members, when the nature of their socio-economic achievement is empirically tested.

Family income eloquently illustrates this point. As already reviewed, many Asian Americans have higher family incomes than whites; however, the Asian families are likely to pay a disproportionately higher price for it. Chun (1980, p. 4) states this issue as follows:

> [Asian Americans'] high income may be the result of longer work hours or sacrificed weekends. It follows that for the household income to be a usable index for purposes of group comparison, one has to make adjustments for the number of

wage earners and the number of hours worked. In addition, since education is known to be a substantial contributor to occupational mobility as well as higher income, the level of wage income should be adjusted at least for wage earner's education.

. . . Asian Americans cannot be considered "successful" under the following conditions: . . . (a) the level of Asian achievement is equal to that of whites, but Asians pay a higher price than whites; (b) whites and Asians are equal in the price paid, but Asians achieve less than whites; (c) Asians achieve a higher level of status, but Asians pay disproportionately a higher price than whites; and (d) Asians achieve less than whites, but Asians pay a higher price than whites. In all of these cases the reward (achievement) rate per unit of cost (investment) is smaller for Asian Americans than for whites. The existence of such a differential rate of reward would demonstrate that Asian Americans experience disadvantaged discrimination or inequality in the achievement of socio-economic status. As long as they are disadvantaged or discriminated against, they cannot be considered successful regardless of the level of their achievement. . . .

. . . [When adjusted for variations in education, occupational prestige, weeks worked, etc.,] the earnings ratio of foreign-born Asian males in general (except Japanese) ranges from .68 to .89, revealing the fact that they earn less than white males under the equivalent condition of investment. Moreover, the earnings ratio of foreign-born Asian males is not generally better than that of non-Asian minorities, such as black and Mexican Americans. At this point we must also emphasize the fact that foreign-born Asian males are found to be placed in the American labour market quite differently from other minority (non-Asian) males—the former's original earnings are greater than their adjusted earnings, whereas the reverse is true for the latter. This means, for foreign-born Asian males, their earnings inequity problems largely derive from the discriminatory mechanism of the American labour market; whereas for non-Asian minority males, their earnings problems involve both labour market barriers and a relative lack of human capital.

A surprisingly high earnings ratio of foreign-born Japanese males may indicate that they are occupationally more associated with the export-oriented Japanese economy than the U.S. economy (Nee and Sanders 1985). . . . The investment factors important to American workers do not seem to explain effectively the earnings of these Japanese foreign-born workers.

The earnings ratio of native-born Japanese, Chinese and Filipino males is higher than that of foreign-born males in their own ethnic groups; however, these native-born Asian males still earn less than white males under the equivalent condition of investment. This finding concurs with the observation made by Hirschman and Wong (1981, p. 507).

. . . native-born Japanese, Chinese and Filipino men . . . have average earnings roughly equivalent to or higher than white men. However, since the backgrounds of Asian American men (education and occupation) are generally higher than that of whites, parity of earnings does not indicate similarity of the earnings determination process.

Regardless of their racial or ethnic status, the earnings ratio of female workers is uniformly lower than that of their male counterparts in their respective racial or ethnic group. This pattern suggests that female workers' problems of severe earnings inequity derive from their gender status rather than from their racial or ethnic status. No wonder the earnings ratio of white females is no better than that of other females. Therefore these facts do not support the contention that minority female workers are doubly disadvantaged.

The preceding findings concerning Asian Americans are hardly surprising, when their labour market experiences are reviewed. In spite of their high education, Asian Americans are repeatedly found to have experienced a great deal of difficulty in getting jobs commensurate with their education. . . . Under these circumstances, overqualification for their jobs or underutilization of their education (underemployment) has been the most persistent and serious occupational problem for both native- and foreign-born Asian Americans (Kim 1982; Li 1980). We thus observe from the 1980 census data that Asian Americans still earn less than whites despite an additional year of schooling.

Due to such problems of underemployment and other labour market barriers, Asian Americans are generally employed in relatively unfavourable conditions. Our study of Korean immigrants in the Los Angeles area (Hurh and Kim 1984) shows that Korean immigrants are clustered into the following three types of occupations: (1) self-employed small business; (2) other white-collar occupations; and (3) low-skilled manual or service occupations. Korean small businesses are heavily concentrated in their own ethnic community or in the difficult markets of other minority communities (Bonacich and Jung 1982). In this situation, the owner-operators of small business and their family members work for unusually long hours under an intensive competitive pressure (Hurh and Kim 1984; Kim and Hurh 1985). For business survival, they are also forced to take a variety of physical and economic risks.

Those Koreans in the other two types of occupations indicate that the majority of their work colleagues are minority workers, including Koreans or a combination of minority and white workers. The Korean workers employed in such a situation are found to be paid less than those who work mainly with white workers. What this study reveals is that the majority of Korean immigrants either hold inferior occupations and/or work in unfavourable conditions. . . .

Chinese Americans are highly polarized into two types of occupations: (1) those in low-skilled manual or service occupations and (2) those in technical or professional occupations (Ng 1977; Tsai 1980; Wu 1980). Workers in the first type suffer from a variety of severe labour market disadvantages. Even those in the second type are found to face serious career problems as stated below:

> That is to say, although education may have enabled Chinese Americans to enter certain professional and technical occupations that require special and often lengthy training, they tend to be paid less once in these occupations. Because the ceiling of their potential attainment seems to be fixed at a lower level over their entire careers, they are on the whole underutilized. One might

say that they run less risk of "rising to their level of incompetence." (Wu 1980, p. 54)

Such career problems are not unique to Chinese Americans. In general, Asian Americans are excluded from positions of power and influence, and are thus concentrated in low-ranked positions (Kuo 1979). . . .

Three important conclusions may be drawn from the preceding analysis of the labour market experiences of Asian Americans. First, the common measurement of the Asian Americans' "success" which does not test the investment aspect of Asian American's socioeconomic status is conceptually too simplistic and thus distorts the complex reality of Asian Americans' labour market experiences. As a result, this simplistic approach remains blind to Asians' experience of disadvantage, discrimination or inequity, while it promotes the Asian success image.

Second, the success theme has been indiscriminately applied to both native- and foreign-born Asian Americans. It has been observed, however, that the two groups of Asians are subject to different processes of earnings allocation. They should therefore be separately treated in future research, especially when the majority of certain Asian groups are foreign born, such as Koreans . . . and Asian Indians. Third, regardless of their ethnic status, the native-born Asian males are still relatively more disadvantaged than white males. . . .

IMPLICATION OF THE SUCCESS STEREOTYPE

Practical Consequence

. . . In contrast to the rosy picture portrayed in the success literature, the cost of being a model minority seems to be higher than the benefit for the following reasons. First, Asian Americans are considered by the dominant group as "successful" and "problem free" and not in need of social programmes designed to benefit disadvantaged minorities such as black and Mexican Americans. As the U.S. Commission on Civil Rights (1980, p. 19) aptly put it: "If a minority group is viewed as successful, it is unlikely that its members will be included in programmes designed to alleviate problems they encounter as minorities." A number of cases of official inattention to the problems and needs of Asian Americans have already been reported in public documents and scholarly publications (U.S. Commission on Civil Rights 1977, 1979, and 1980; Kim, Bok-Lim 1973, 1978; Kim, E. H. 1975; Kitano and Sue 1973). . . .

Suffice to say that the success image serves a negative function which is to ignore the real problems and needs of Asian Americans, such as unemployment, poverty and mental illness among the elderly, and increasing rates of divorce and juvenile delinquency (Kim, Bok-Lim 1973, 1978). . . .

Another negative function of the success image deals with disguised underemployment and the development of a "false consciousness" among Asian Americans. We have already discussed the problem of disguised underemployment which gives not only a false image of Asian Americans' success to the dominant group but also develops an illusion of status attainment among Asian Americans themselves. Despite underemployment, Asian Americans tend to accept the dominant group's definition of success in order to minimize their feelings of relative deprivation and discontentment. As the feminine stereotype "normalizes" women's underemployment in the American society (institutional sexism), the "hardwork/success" image about Asian Americans has routinized their underemployment (institutional racism). In other words, underemployment is a "normal" or "usual" price Asian Americans have been paying for their "success"—the attainment of the middle-class status. . . . For example, our study of the Korean immigrants in the Los Angeles area reveals that the general level of Korean immigrants' life satisfaction is rather high in spite of their pervasive underemployment (Hurh and Kim 1984). The American social structure of ethnic confinement (social and occupational) limits the range of the immigrants' socio-economic opportunities, and the immigrants' perception of such structural limitations (including their own cultural handicap) would tend to lower the levels of their aspirations. As a consequence, they may feel relatively satisfied with their immigrant life in spite of an objectively apparent status inconsistency in the new country (Hurh and Kim 1980, 1984: 138–55). . . .

The dominant group's stereotype of Asian Americans as a model minority also affects negatively other minorities. Since the Asian Americans' "success" may be considered by the dominant group as a proof of openness in the American opportunity structure, there is a constant danger that other less successful minorities could be regarded as "inferior" and/or "lazy." These less achieving minorities may be blamed for their own failure and become victims of scapegoating ("Japanese have made it. Why can't they?"). Such effects of the Asian American success image on other minorities have not been studied empirically. The probable effects may be summarized as follows: (1) incorrect perception of Asian Americans' upward mobility; (2) an increased sense of relative deprivation; and (3) a feeling of *ressentiment* against Asian Americans (Yu 1980). The last aspect has recently become increasingly problematic since a large number of Asian Americans, especially Korean immigrants, are engaged in small businesses in black and Mexican American communities. . . . Moreover, there seems to be a resurgence in anti-Asian sentiment and activities among whites—across the nation in the form of violence, vandalism, harassment and intimidation. The evidence collected by the U.S. Commission on Civil Rights (1986, p. 58) suggests that "one factor contributing to anti-Asian activity is economic competition between recent refugees and immigrants and other persons in the same community."

Finally, the practical consequences of the Asian success image on the dominant group encompass all the afore-mentioned functions of the stereotype: (1) exclusion of Asian Americans from social programmes supported by public and private agencies (benefit-denying/fund-saving function); (2) disguise of Asian Americans' underemployment (institutional racism promoting function); (3) justification of the American open social system (system preserving function); (4) displacement of the system's fault to less-achieving minorities (victim blaming function); and (5) anti-Asian sentiment and activities (*ressentiment* reinforcing function). Most of these functions may not have been intended . . . nevertheless the consequences are real. . . .

REFERENCES

Bonacich, Edna, and Tae Hwan Jung. 1982. "A portrait of Korean small business in Los Angeles, 1977," in Eui-Young Yu, Earl H. Phillip and Eun Sik Yang (eds.), *Koreans in Los Angeles: Prospects and Promises,* Los Angeles: Koryo Research Institute and Center for Korean-American and Korean Studies, California State University, pp. 75–98.

Chun, Ki-Taek. 1980. "The myth of Asian American success and its educational ramifications." *IRCD Bulletin* (A Publication of the Institute for Urban and Minority Education, Teachers College, Columbia University), vol. 15, no. 1, pp. 1–12.

Fogel, Walter. 1966. "The effects of low educational attainment on income: A comparative study of selected ethnic groups," *Journal of Human Resources,* vol. 1, no. 2, pp. 22–40.

Hirschman, Charles, and Morrison G. Wong. 1981. "Trends in socio-economic achievement among immigrant and native-born Asian Americans," *Sociological Quarterly,* vol. 22, no. 4, pp. 495–514.

Hurh, Won Moo, and Kwang Chung Kim. 1980. "The process of Korean immigrants' adaptation in the U.S.: Length of residence and life satisfaction," a paper presented at the annual meeting, American Sociological Association, New York, August 27–31.

———. 1984. *Korean Immigrants in America: A Structural Analysis of Ethnic Confinement and Adhesive Adaptation,* Madison, NJ: Fairleigh Dickinson University Press.

Isaacs, Harold R. 1962. *Images of Asia: American view of China and India,* New York: Capricorn Books.

Kim, Bok-Lim. 1973. "Asian Americans: no model minority," *Social Work,* vol. 18, no. 2, pp. 44–53.

———. 1978. *The Asian Americans: Changing Patterns, Changing Needs,* Montclair, NJ: Association for Korean Christian Scholars in North America.

Kim, Elaine H. 1975. "The myth of Asian American success," *Asian American Review,* vol. 2, no. 1, pp. 122–49.

Kim, Kwang Chung, and Won Moo Hurh. 1983. "Korean Americans and the 'success' image: a critique," *Amerasia,* vol. 10, no. 2, pp. 3–21.

———. 1985. "Ethnic resources utilization of Korean immigrant entrepreneurs in the Chicago minority area." *International Migration Review, 19*(1), 82–111.

Kim, Sukja Paik. 1982. "Underemployment of recent Asian immigrants: Koreans in Los Angeles," unpublished Ph.D. dissertation, Virginia Commonwealth University, Richmond, Virginia.

Kitano, Harry H. L., and Stanley Sue. 1973. "The model minorities," *Journal of Social Issues,* vol. 29, no. 2, pp. 1–9.

Kuo, Wen H. 1979. "On the study of Asian Americans: Its current state and agenda," *Sociological Quarterly,* vol. 20, no. 2, pp. 279–90.

Li, Angelina H. 1980. *Labor Utilization and the Assimilation of Asian Americans,* Springfield, VA: National Technical Information Service, U.S. Department of Commerce.

Lippmann, Walter. 1922. *Public Opinion,* New York: Harcourt, Brace.

Lyman, Stanford M. 1970. *The Asians in the West,* Reno, NV: Desert Research Institute.

———. 1974. *Chinese Americans,* New York: Random House.

Miller, Stuart C. 1969. *The Unwelcome Immigrant: The American Image of the Chinese, 1885–1982,* Berkeley, California: University of California Press.

Nee, Victor, and Jimy Sanders. 1985. "The road to parity: determinants of the socio-economic achievements of Asian Americans," *Ethnic and Racial Studies,* vol. 8, no. 1, pp. 75–93.

New York Times Magazine. 1966. "Success story, Japanese American style," January 9: 38.

Newsweek. 1982. "Asian-Americans: A 'model minority,'" December 6, pp. 39–51.

Ng, Wing-Cheung. 1977. "An evaluation of the labor market status of Chinese Americans," *Amerasia,* vol. 4, no. 1, pp. 101–22.

Stevens, Gillian, and Joo Hyun Cho. 1985. "Socioeconomic indexes and the new 1980 census occupational classification scheme," *Social Science Research,* vol. 14, no. 2, pp. 142–68.

Sue, Stanley and Harry H. Kitano. 1973. "Stereotypes as a measure of success," *Journal of Social Issues,* vol. 29, no. 2, pp. 83–98.

Time. 1985. "To America with skills: a wave of arrivals from the Far East enriches the country's talent pool," July 8, pp. 43–6.

Tsai, Frank Wen-Hui. 1980. "Diversity and conflict between old and new Chinese immigrants in the United States," in Roy Simon Bryce-Laporte (ed.) *Sourcebook on the New Immigration,* New Brunswick, NJ: Transaction Books, pp. 329–37.

Urban Associates, Inc. 1974. A *Study of Selected Socio-Economic Characteristics of Ethnic Minorities Based on the 1970 Census, vol. 11. Asian Americans,* Arlington, VA: Urban Associates, Inc.

U.S. Commission On Civil Rights. 1977. *The Forgotten Minority: Asian Americans in New York City,* Washington, DC: U.S. Government Printing Office.

U.S. Commission On Civil Rights. 1979. *Civil Rights Issues of Asian and Pacific Americans: Myths and Realities,* Washington, DC: U.S. Government Printing Office.

———. 1980. *Success of Asian Americans: Fact or Fiction?* Washington, DC: U.S. Government Printing Office.

———. 1986. *Recent Activities Against Citizens Residents of Asian Descent.* Washington, D.C.: U.S. Government Printing Office.

U S. News & World Report. 1966. "Success Stories of one minority group in U.S.," December, p. 73. York: Basic Books.

Wu, Yuan-li and John Ma. 1980. *The Economic Condition of Chinese Americans.* Chicago: Pacific/Asian Mental Health Research Center, 1980. 208p. (Monograph Series, No. 3).

Yu, Jin H. 1980. *The Korean Merchants in the Black Community,* Elkin's Park, PA: Philip Jaisohn Foundation.

DISCUSSION QUESTIONS

1. Of the two stereotypes of Asian Americans mentioned in this article ("unassimilable heathen" and "successful model minorities"), which, if either, has been more common in your personal experience? Why do you suppose this might be so?

2. Studies that support the "success" image generally use socioeconomic criteria (education, occupation, and earnings) to measure success. What other criteria might be used as a definition of "success"? How do you suppose Asian American groups would compare on these criteria?

3. What do authors mean when they say that Asian Americans are overqualified for their jobs and underutilized for their education? What evidence do they cite to support this conclusion? Is this the most "persistent and serious" problem for Asian Americans? Why or why not?

4. What effect does the idea of Asian American success have on other minority groups? Why would other groups feel resentment? What could Asian Americans do to address these problems? What could other minority groups and the dominant group do?

THE INTERRELATIONSHIP BETWEEN ANTI-ASIAN VIOLENCE AND ASIAN AMERICA

Victor M. Hwang

INTRODUCTION

The concept of the Asian Pacific American community is unique in the field of American race relations. Our community is neither united by a common experience such as slavery or by a common language such as Spanish. We are individually Vietnamese Amerasians, second generation South Asian Americans, kibei, third generation Sansei, . . . 1.5 generation Korean Americans, . . . Pilipino seniors, Taiwanese nationalists, and more. . . . Our community encompasses differences in ethnicity, religion, language, culture, class, color, immigration history, politics and even race.

What we obviously do have most in common is the way that we look to those outside our community and the way we are treated in America based upon the way we look. Our commonality begins with a recognition that . . . you are constantly at risk of being killed without warning or provocation based upon the belief that you are a foreign "Jap." Whether you are second generation South Asian American or a fifth generation Chinatown native, we are faced constantly with the implicit and explicit question, "No, really, where are you from?"

Yet, while anti-Asian violence forces individuals to band together at times for physical or political protection, it plays a much greater role in shaping the Asian Pacific American [APA] community than simply acting as the outside threat which drives the flock together. It is not the action of anti-Asian violence which is so important to the development of our community as much as it is the reaction to the incident. For "Asian America" lives not in the Chinatowns or the Little Tokyos, but in the hearts of those who recognize that incidents of anti-Asian violence are not isolated attacks, but are part of the historical treatment of Asians in America for the past two hundred years.

. . . [T]he pattern of anti-Asian violence dictates the role and character of our community and its relationship to mainstream society. . . . [T]he unspoken policy and history of America has been to erase the experience of Asians in America and to silence the voice of the community. Thus, we have been displaced from our role in American history, from our place in America, and more than two hundred years after the first Asians came to America, we are still being collectively told to go back to where we came from.

It is in our struggle against this pattern of violence and its underlying message of physical, political, and historical exclusion that we find ourselves as Asian Pacific Americans. Not every Asian in America is a member of the Asian Pacific American community. . . . [W]e become Asian Americans as we begin to recognize that we share a common bond and experience with all other Asians in America based upon our history, our treatment and our status as a racial minority in the United States. The formation of the community begins not when ten Asian families happen to live in the same neighborhood, but when one family has been attacked and the other nine rally to their assistance.

The Asian American community is based on an understanding and appreciation of the fact that we have struggled for nearly two centuries against this violence and exclusion. . . . From the early organizing efforts of the Chinese Six Companies in San Francisco to protect the Chinese workers from nativist attacks to the more recent campaign to bring justice to the killers of Vincent Chin and Kao Kuan Chung, Asian Americans have not always been the silent victims of hate crimes, but have strived to defend and empower our communities in the American tradition.

This paper will discuss the role of anti-Asian violence as a foil and as a catalyst in the development of an Asian American identity and a community. Our community lives in the contradiction, in the friction between competing notions of ethnicity and nationality, in the margins and as a wedge between black and white in American society. It is not a physical community, but one that exists in flashes, in movements, in speeches, in hearts and minds, and in struggle. It is within the heat of the response to these incidents of extreme racial violence that we continue to forge our identity and our sense of community. We build our community in times of crisis by speaking out against the incidents of anti-Asian violence and claiming our piece of history.

However, in times of racial tension, it is sometimes difficult to process the elements of the hate crime to craft a . . . response which serves both the needs of the individual victim as well as empowering the community. In this paper, I will explore two recent incidents of anti-Asian violence as a framework to discussing the crafting and mis-crafting of a progressive community response. I believe we should approach hate crimes in the same way a doctor would approach a medical problem. Prior to making a diagnosis, we need to understand the nature of the injury as well as who has been hurt. Further, without an understanding of the history of anti-Asian violence, hate crimes, and the community, we can do little for either the protection of the individual or the development of Asian America.

ANTI-ASIAN VIOLENCE AND THE INDIVIDUAL: WHAT IS THE INJURY?

Individual victims of hate crimes and their families often suffer injuries far beyond the physical wounds inflicted upon them. It is both the sticks and stones which break our bones and the accompanying words and hateful intent which hurt us. Like a snake's bite, the venomous injuries of anti-Asian violence go far deeper than the physical injury because they are intended to inject a poison to strike at the core of our being. As advocates, we must recognize the injury to the internal psyche as well as the physical injury in crafting a remedy for the individual and the community. Just as you cannot treat a snake bite with a Band-Aid, you cannot treat the hate crime as either a simple crime or an accident.

The Incident

Sylvia is a 63 year old Korean American who came to the United States as a teenager. She grew up in Washington, D.C., the daughter of a Korean minister and attended an all-white segregated high school. She spent most of her adult years in Arizona . . . where, as she describes it, she never thought she experienced much racism. . . . "Oh, every once in a while, my kids would tell me that someone had called them a Chinaman in school or had tried to put them down on account of their race," she said. "But I always told them just to work harder and prove to every one else that they were superior. I knew that we were descendants of a proud people with many centuries of culture and civilization. I never worried much about what the other people thought. I knew we were better."

She never had much contact with African Americans, but says that she always sort of looked down her nose at them since she felt that they tended to complain too much about racism and did not adopt the Asian work ethic to work twice as hard when confronted with racist behavior.

Sylvia moved to California a number of years ago and ironically it was in San Francisco that she experienced her first taste of anti-Asian violence. She was coming out of the Borders Bookstore in Union Square when a 6-foot tall "Timothy McVeigh"-looking Caucasian man ran up to her and said "My mother is not Chinese but yours is." Sylvia was somewhat taken aback, but tried to ignore him while she passed him.

He repeated the remark from behind her and when she did not react, he picked her up from behind and threw her against a nearby concrete wall, shattering her hip. Her assailant then ran away. As she lay there in shock, she was assaulted again in a much more painful and personal way as two Caucasian tourists walked by and in an attempt to be helpful, asked her if she spoke English.

Sylvia noted afterwards that even in an emergency situation, the first thought that crossed the minds of these Caucasians upon seeing an injured Asian woman was not the injury, but the race. "I was so outraged then, I couldn't even respond. Here I lay, on the ground, I was beaten, my hip was shattered, and the first thing they asked me was if I spoke English, not if I was ok, if I needed help, or if they should call an ambulance. The first thing they asked me was if I spoke English. . . . I was so shocked, I couldn't even say anything."

Sylvia was eventually taken to the hospital and underwent extensive surgery to have her entire hip replaced. But as her physical injuries were treated by the doctors, her psychological injuries remained unattended, festering as she fell into a deep depression. "My co-workers, who were mostly Caucasian, came by to see me and I guess that they were trying to be funny. One of them said something like 'Well, at least you got a new hip.' At that moment, I just felt so angry because they couldn't understand that I was almost killed because of my race. I just didn't think I could ever see them in the same light again."

. . . Her friends felt that she was obsessed with the racial nature of the attack and that she should not dwell on the incident. Sylvia, on the other hand, felt like she was unable to talk with them anymore.

The police . . . were unable to develop any substantive leads and, in the opinion of the family, discouraged them from pursuing an active criminal investigation. Time and time again, Sylvia was told by the officer in charge of the investigation it was not worth her while to pursue the assailant, suggesting it was better to forget the incident and simply let old wounds heal. . . .

But as time progressed, Sylvia did not just "get over" the racial attack. Her mental health continued to deteriorate. . . . [Her family was] frustrated over the lack of police response, angry over the racist nature of the attack, and distressed over Sylvia's deepening depression. . . .

The Response: What Is the Injury?

In treating only her physical injuries, the doctors . . . were able to replace her shattered hip, [but] they were unable to give her a replacement for her shattered frame of reference which had helped her in life to interpret, deflect, and respond to racism. . . . In failing to address the underlying cause of the injury, the doctors failed to treat the most serious injury of all—the one to her psyche. As such, Sylvia was left feeling confused and powerless, without the ability to either explain or prevent another unprovoked attack.

The isolated hate crime is particularly venomous because of its seemingly random nature and the inability of the victim to rationalize its occurrence. Even as children, we learn to create mental defenses and white lies to guard against the mental attacks from others. Rationalization is an important defense in our logical world and, as thinking beings, it is important for us to believe that the world is controlled by rationality. . . . The inability to explain the incident subjects the victim to further trauma because if you can't explain it, there's nothing you can do to prevent it from happening again. . . .

Victims of burglary may rationalize that they did not take enough safety precautions and install a better alarm system. Someone who is involved in an automobile accident will try to remember to look both ways next time before crossing the street. But there is nothing you can do to hide your race, skin color, gender, or sexual orientation. There is simply no escape or change in behavior possible for victims of hate crimes and they understand that they have to live with the possibility of reoccurrence without warning. In Sylvia's case and in other similar cases, this helplessness may be exacerbated by the fact that the actual perpetrators are rarely caught.

Moreover, this may be compounded by the fact that victims of hate crimes may have never even viewed themselves as representatives of the community, but in the hate crime they are subject to attack, not as individuals, but as symbols. They are stripped of their individuality and reduced to their race. . . . Sylvia was not attacked for anything about her, anything she stood for, but on the basis of her birth. Her "crime" in the eyes of the attacker was . . . the crime of her ancestors . . . being born "Chinese." The message was direct and terrifying—you are different from me and so you must be hurt.

This is the poison of hate crimes which distinguishes it from other types of victimization. The consistent message of [Anti-Asian] violence . . . is that you . . . do not belong here, you are not an American. This message was one that Sylvia was not prepared to receive. . . . Like many immigrants, Sylvia always believed in the ideal of America as the land of equality and opportunity. If you worked hard, you could get ahead, blend in, and be considered an equal. In the instances where she or her family were confronted with racist attitudes, her external response was to work twice as hard to go around the wall of racism, to work harder to prove her worth as an American.

In coming to America, Asians accept the unspoken racial hierarchy which will allow them to succeed up to the point where they hit the glass ceiling. They do not even carry the expectations of parity with whites. As such, they are identified as the "model minority," willing to accept a second-class standard of living as opposed to the African Americans whose civil rights paradigm has demanded an equal playing field. As in Sylvia's case, it is precisely due to this reason that many immigrants look down upon African Americans, because they themselves have made the difficult choice to swallow their pride and accept their status to provide their children with a better future. Sylvia believed that African Americans chose to complain too much and did not work hard enough to fight their way through the wall of racism.

The attack shook Sylvia to the core not only due to the extreme violence, but because it forced her to confront the fact that . . . the years of work that she put into proving herself . . . offered little protection . . . from either the attacker or the tourists who did not view her as an equal American. In an incident lasting less than a minute, one man stripped her of her veneer, her status as an honorary white, and reduced her to her race. Despite years of sacrifice and hard work to form a protective layer of class, assimilation, and privilege, she understood now that she was still as vulnerable as the newly-arrived Asian immigrant or the African American. . . . [Y]ou could not just turn your back and try to ignore the racism because it would just follow you and haunt you. The advice that she had given herself and her children for years simply did not work and failed to protect her from the brutal assault.

The attack also undermined Sylvia's second learned form of psychological defense of internally strengthening herself against racist attacks by relying upon her heritage as a Korean immigrant. . . . [I]n America, as a guest or sojourner, she could accept second class citizenship . . . [by] saying, "I don't deserve to be treated like a regular American and I don't need to respond to these demeaning attitudes because I have another home in Korea where they treat me like an equal." This is a standard form of mental gamesmanship that we all engage in to protect our sense of pride when denied a certain goal; we always create a lie that we didn't really want it anyway.

However, [after the attack] . . . she was no longer able to ignore the fact that her rights had been violated and that she was not respected as an equal in the country where she had spent the majority of her life. . . . [S]he was viewed as a foreigner, as an outsider, told physically and orally that she did not belong.

The inability to use her birthplace heritage as a source of comfort was a first step towards establishing an identity as an Asian American. . . . Lost and feeling abandoned, Sylvia fell into a depression over the realization that she was homeless, neither Korean nor American. In this nether world, she could no longer claim the protection of her cultural heritage or the promises of American equality.

Sylvia's Response: Knocking Down Walls

Metaphorically speaking, Sylvia was thrown against the concrete wall of racial reality, which forced her to re-examine her internal and external defenses which were previously erected to deny or mitigate the existence of racism in her life. . . . The life-threatening nature of her injuries forced her to take a second look not only at racism, but her own responses and attitudes in the past.

Sylvia's response . . . was to build an entirely new frame of reference in relating to American society incorporating elements of Asian American and cross-cultural studies. Ironically, at the time that she was subject to this hate violence, Sylvia had been taking a class in cross-cultural studies to become a certified ESL [English as a Second Language] instructor. . . . She tells me that initially she . . . found many of the African American attitudes to be tiresome. "Why couldn't they just work harder?" I thought, "Why do they always complain so much?"

. . . [T]he attack prompted Sylvia to re-examine her beliefs and attitudes towards all of race relations with a particular emphasis on African Americans. By turning to the theories she acquired through cross-racial studies courses, she found a framework for recovery, a new structure for re-evaluating her own life and experiences through the lens of race. After her attack, that which had been theoretical and incomprehensible found form and substance. What had previously existed outside her reality now became her point of view. She read books on Martin Luther King Jr. and other African American leaders, looking to them for answers.

As she began to understand the broader context of racism and race relations in the United States, her incident of hate violence began to seem less a random occurrence. At the same time, it became less painful as she read about the history of African Americans in the U.S. "I just stopped feeling sorry for myself. After all, it had just happened to me for a few times. But this sort of thing was happening to African Americans all the time."

Talking with her children and others about her experiences and newfound framework, she eagerly embraced learning about new cultures and ideas. It was as if she were born again at the age of 63. . . .

"In a way, my biggest regret is that this beating I suffered didn't happen to me 60 years earlier," she laughs. "I now look back on my life and think how blind I was. I now spend time reflecting on my whole life and I think what I might have done different if only my eyes had been opened sooner to the racism in our society. I wish I had been able to do more; to do something about it."

Sylvia credits her exploration and increased understanding of the African American struggle with providing her with the strength and context to fight her way out of her pit of depression. "I don't hate white people. I still don't know that much about black people, but I know more now about where I fit in than I did before."

Sylvia has recovered both physically and psychologically and now continues to attend classes in exploring race relations and cultural studies. After the release of the 1996 National Asian Pacific American Legal Consortium report on violence against Asian Pacific Americans, Sylvia was profiled widely by the media including an appearance on the Lehrer News Hour. She hopes to be certified as an ESL instructor soon and intends to teach new immigrants not only about English, but about America.

SWASTIKAS IN THE SUNSET: WHO IS THE VICTIM?

The Incident

The Sunset District of San Francisco is an affordable, residential and small business community located in the western section of the city.... It is a culturally diverse and middle-class neighborhood with a long-established Irish, Jewish and Russian community and a rapidly growing Asian American immigrant population. The Asian American population of the Sunset District has doubled in recent years and many now refer to the area as the "New Chinatown." The area has historically prided itself on its neighborhood "mom and pop" stores and has been highly resistant to the influx of chain stores and fast food franchises.

In 1996, a Chinese American business owner opened a Burger King franchise in the area, which was immediately met with community resistance, both reasoned and racist. While some residents protested the change in the neighborhood character, others posted flyers calling for "Chinks and Burger King Out of the Sunset." The Burger King was subject to a barrage of vandalism, graffiti, and protests through the following months, continuing to this day.

In February of 1997, . . . the "SWB" or "Sunset White Boys" carved swastikas into the glass storefronts of nearly two dozen Asian American businesses [located in the Sunset District]. The placement and selectivity of the swastikas was particularly ominous in

that primarily Asian-owned businesses were targeted and non-Asian businesses were passed over.... The clinical precision exercised in the choice of the targets indicated a familiarity with the community, leading people to suspect that this was an "inside" job. There were also the biblical overtones of genocide and divine retribution.

The vandalism ranged from small, red spray-painted swastikas accompanied by the initials "SWB" to three-foot high swastikas carved with some sharp instrument into the glass storefronts of several Asian-owned businesses....

Surprisingly, many of the store owners were immigrants from China and Vietnam who confessed ignorance at the significance of the swastikas. All they knew was that they were vandalized once again, and due to the indifferent or hostile treatment that they had received at the hands of the police in previous cases . . . , most failed to even report the occurrence. Many did not even realize that other Asian businesses along the street had suffered similar etchings and more than a week went by without any action being taken. During this time, the swastikas remained prominently displayed to the public.

The swastikas were finally brought to the attention of a Chinese American officer in another jurisdiction who decided to look into it on his own. The Asian Law Caucus was notified . . . and immediately responded to the location to document the hate vandalism, interview the targeted merchants and offer assistance....

Even after I spoke with them, some of the store owners indicated that they did not intend to replace the glass panes defaced with swastikas since vandalism was rampant and they would just be hit again after spending the money.... In fact, many were surprised that what they viewed as another routine round of vandalism had attracted outside attention. After speaking with the merchants and documenting the incidents, we alerted the mainstream press. Both print and broadcast media ran widespread coverage on the swastikas even though the vandalism had taken place a week earlier. In response to the media coverage and subsequent public outcry, police and elected officials flocked to the community.

The Response: Who Is the Victim?

The response to a hate crime must be carefully tailored to address both the needs and concerns of the primary victim and also that of the community. A directed and strategic response works to counter the hateful message of exclusion and intimidation. However, in many cases it is unclear at the outset who the primary victim is and towards whom the communal remedy should be directed. Was the true victim of the hate crime the more established Jewish community at large which was forced to confront the painful reminder of the Holocaust? Or was the victim the potential APA . . . store owner, resident, or customer considering coming into the Sunset District but who was then scared away by the prospect of being racially targeted because of his/her ethnicity? Or was it the San Francisco community at large? The responses of various authorities in this case differed depending upon their determinations on the identity of the victim. While all were successful in achieving some measure of combating hate crimes, no one fully addressed the underlying tensions which created the hate-filled environment.

The Police Response

Typically, the police are focused solely on the apprehension of the criminal and exhibit little sympathy or understanding of the needs of the victim or community. Generally, they are reluctant to categorize any case as a hate crime, perhaps out of an unwillingness to invest the extra time into conducting additional investigation, or perhaps due to a resistance to taint their jurisdiction with an insinuation of racism.

In this case, the police responded exceptionally poorly, which was surprising given the fact that San Francisco Police Department Chief Fred Lau is Chinese American and for years the department maintained a separate investigative unit specifically trained and devoted to working on hate crimes. In response to press inquiries, the police captain incredulously countered that these carvings were not hate crimes since swastikas are anti-Semitic in nature and not anti-Asian. While this initial statement was quickly retracted, the captain then adopted the position that these acts of vandalism were the acts of juveniles and therefore, should not be taken seriously. The acts were dismissed and somehow excused as childish pranks and therefore, not worthy of community discussion and intervention.

Under increasing scrutiny and public pressure, Chief Fred Lau intervened. Several bilingual officers were re-assigned to patrol the Sunset District, the case was turned over to the special hate crimes unit, and general police presence in the area was increased over the short term in an attempt to apprehend the perpetrator(s).

Several juveniles were soon arrested and the newspaper headlines reported that the responsible parties had been found. Conveniently, one of the youths was Filipino and so the police took the opportunity to declare that this was clearly not a hate crime since one of the suspects was Asian. Weeks later, with smaller fanfare, it was reported that the youths who were arrested—while admitting to general tagging in the neighborhood—did not actually have anything to do with the swastikas. After a few weeks when community and media pressure died down, nothing further was heard from the police regarding their efforts to find the perpetrators.

Asian American Merchants as Victims?

One Asian American San Francisco county supervisor organized a highly successful volunteer clean-up day and recruited elected officials, union labor, community members and donations of materials to clean up all of the graffiti, sweep the streets, and replace the glass at no charge to the merchants. Volunteers turned out from all parts of the city and the media flocked. The event removed the obvious signs of hate and arguably sent a message to the perpetrators and the community that such hate violence would not be tolerated and that San Francisco was united in stamping out the signs of racism. The clean-up day was successful in removing the swastikas from public view, in giving the community a chance to directly demonstrate its commitment to fighting hate crimes, and bringing together diverse communities for a day to take a joint stand against hate crimes.

However, . . . it is questionable as to how successful [the clean-up day] was in addressing the underlying attitudes that lead to acts of hate.

In addressing the problem as one of vandalism, the effort failed to acknowledge that the swastikas were reflective of ideas and beliefs held much closer to heart of the community. The focus upon the physical element of the hate crime overlooked the intangible factors of prejudice and racial tensions which had created an environment conducive to the racist expression of the swastikas.

On the other hand, one may argue the lesson learned in bringing together diverse communities to tackle a common goal was that the volunteer physical labor itself served as a symbol of the community coming together to fight anti-Asian violence. Undoubtedly, a major part of this effort was intended to impart upon the individual merchants that they were a part of the community and to demonstrate that in times of crisis they could rely upon the community to come to their assistance.

The focus upon these individual merchants was perhaps misplaced in that many of them were unaware of the historical and genocidal significance of the swastikas. Given their political naiveté, it is debatable as to whether or not they were truly the victims of a hate crime and whether or not they could appreciate the reasons for the volunteer response. . . .

Certainly, the store owners were economically and physically the victims of vandalism, but can they also be considered the victims of a hate crime if some failed to understand the intended message of the perpetrator(s)? Given that several did not understand the importance of the symbols, was it critical for the people and politicians to rally behind them in a show of community support?

According to the traditional principles of criminal law and specifically the law around hate crimes, these store owners are the victims of a hate crime. Generally, the definition of a hate crime turns on the intent of the perpetrator and not the understanding of the victim. For example, many jurisdictions hold that a man who is attacked because he is perceived to be gay—even if he is not—would be the victim of a hate crime and the perpetrator could be subject to enhanced penalties. On the other hand, a person who fights with a gay person motivated solely by a dispute over a parking space, would not be subject to a hate crime even if the gay person was subjectively afraid that the dispute was over his sexual orientation. This follows the general principles of criminal law that focuses on the intent of the perpetrator.

However, what makes hate crimes punishable above and beyond the physical act of criminality is the recognition that hate violence carries levels of psychological and emotional impact well beyond the simple commission of the crime. The penalties for hate crimes are more severe because we recognize that based upon a history of racial intolerance, the victims are particularly vulnerable and suffer levels of injuries far beyond the physical and objective damages. A cross-burning on an African American lawn is much more than an act of arson or vandalism. It carries with it the clear threat of further escalation of violence when considered in the context of historical precedent. Thus, when the victim does not understand or is unaware of the message of hate, much of the psychological trauma and venom of the crime is not present and from the individual victim's viewpoint, it becomes indistinguishable from a simple act of vandalism. . . .

Therefore, should some of the merchants who did understand the message of intimidation and racial hatred and suffered the psychological consequences be considered hate violence victims while the other merchants are not? . . . Clearly, the focus on the individual level makes little sense because the bottom line is that property-based hate crimes such as these are clearly an attack upon the community. Common sense dictates that the use of a swastika defines the incident as one of hate violence given its symbolism for racial hatred and violence regardless of the understanding of the owner of the property. But if the merchants were not particularly intimidated by this act, then was the clean-up perhaps for the benefit of the community as opposed to assisting these particular individuals? After all, the older neighborhood is predominantly Jewish and was certainly put on notice . . . once the swastikas were carved into their community stores. A more cynical and jaded viewpoint would be that the clean-up was not directed at helping the Asian American merchants at all but rather at the larger Jewish community which had to be confronted with these symbols every day.

The Neighborhood/Geographic Community as Victim?

A second Asian American county supervisor organized two town hall meetings to facilitate discussions on the placement of swastikas in the community. The events were advertised in several languages to both the Asian merchants and the Sunset community at large. Myself and several other volunteers conducted outreach to the merchants along the Irving corridor in an attempt to encourage their participation in the hearings. A non-Asian leader in hate crimes coalition work was selected to lead the discussions and hate crimes "experts," police, elected officials, media, and community groups were invited to attend.

Nearly two hundred people attended the first town hall meeting, but virtually none of the Asian merchants attended either of the sessions. The discussions were mostly dominated by a number of neighborhood conservation and watch groups from the Sunset community—many of whom were involved and continued to be involved in the efforts to drive the Burger King out of the Sunset District.

The first forum was opened with statements of support from local elected officials and presentations by the hate crimes experts. However, as the discussions progressed and the floor was opened up to those in attendance, the talk quickly turned to combating vandalism generally in the community and the changing character of the neighborhood. The changing character of the neighborhood, of course, was a euphemism for the rapid growth of the Asian American community in the Sunset district. . . . More neighborhood watch groups and closer cooperation with the police were proposed, a vandalism task force and hotline were discussed, and after the opening few minutes, the discussion of "hate" had been dropped and the audience spoke only of the "crimes."

In a more disturbing segment of the town hall meeting, audience members testified that the real problem contributing to the rise in crime was the fact that the community had changed so much that they did not feel that this was their community anymore. Some attendees remarked that Asian-language signs dominated the streets and you no longer heard English being spoken.

Others commented that these "new" residents packed too many family members in a house, did not try to assimilate, hung out only with their own, did not participate in the civic affairs of the community, and generally did not fit into the Sunset character.

It is important to note that this was as much a case of ethnic conflict as it was a dispute between long time residents and newcomers. Some of those who spoke out against the transformation of the neighborhood included established Japanese Americans who could not read the Chinese language signs or understand the foreign languages being spoken on the street.

In an ironic twist, several residents complained that the merchants were at fault for not acting quickly to eradicate the swastikas once they appeared. These residents stated that they were offended that the stores did not act responsibly and rapidly to remove these signs of hate once they were carved on their front window-panes. The residents who appeared at this public forum indicated that the problem was that the Asians did not participate in the neighborhood watches and other civic duties of the "community" and thus, hate crimes and vandalism were allowed to flourish. In a loosely-controlled forum, the audience had come full circle in scape-goating the victims as the perpetrators, and these were the voices and faces heard that night on the eleven o'clock news. . . .

In earlier discussions, the Asian American merchants expressed a general disinterest in attending such a forum and noted that the scheduled times conflicted with their business hours. . . . I think the true reason why many failed to attend was a premonition that their issues, concern and needs were not going to be addressed in this public setting. Perhaps the merchants thought they would not be able to communicate the depth of their hopes and fears through an interpreter. Many expressed a fear in becoming involved and subjecting themselves to potential future retaliation. And maybe they already knew who their neighbors were and did not want to walk into a hostile trap.

In trying to open up discussions with the community, the officials had allowed the content of the discourse to shift without moderation and granted legitimacy and press to a particular viewpoint of the community. In empowering a certain segment of the community which was hostile to the "Asian invasion," the town hall meetings served to further divide and separate the community. . . .

All of a sudden, it became clear "who killed Vincent Chin,"[1] these community leaders who had turned out to ostensibly combat hate crimes were in fact perpetuating much of the hate crimes messages in their own homes. No doubt, it was some juvenile that had committed the physical act of vandalism, but the hate was something being taught at home. The town hall meetings ended with the second forum. Nothing ever came of those meetings. . . .

The Asian Pacific American Community as Victim?

The swastikas were only a symptom of a more deeply rooted problem. The vandalism was neither a juvenile prank, nor a simple act of vandalism, but rather a powerful symbol of communities in conflict and a visible mark of the underlying tensions around a changing demographic in the Sunset District.

. . . [T]he intent behind the swastikas was not a childish thought, but one shared by a large segment of the community. Asian Americans in the Sunset district were being told both by symbol and by comments made in community forums that they were threatening the integrity and character of the neighborhood. . . . And, in the town hall discussions, while many residents repudiated the specific action taken in this case, no one spoke against the underlying message of racial intolerance and disharmony.

Anti-Asian violence is the friction generated from two communities beginning to rub up against each other where there is no discussion or relationship between the communities. Viewing this situation in a historical context, what happened in the Sunset District was identical to what happened in countless other cities . . . where a fast-growing Asian American immigrant population began to threaten the character of an "older" neighborhood. . . . Because we are perceived as new, because we are seen as foreign, we are interpreted as a threat. . . . As our community continues to grow, we can only expect to see a greater incidence of hate violence directed against us.

CONCLUSION

. . . The Asian American identity is based upon an understanding that anti-Asian violence has played an integral part in the history of both America and Asian America and that it has always served to exclude and deny us our rightful place. . . . [I]n combating anti-Asian violence, we fight the message that we do not belong. It is a recognition that the attack upon the individual is an attempt to silence us all and therefore, to break our silence, we must speak up for the individual. Thus, while the community may be defined by the isolation and exclusion by the mainstream, it is also created from the response to anti-Asian violence.

But more than exclusion, it is a recognition that Asian America lives in the hearts of those in our community. The history of Asian Americans reflects the struggle for recognition and equality. Our forefathers planted seeds in the cracks of mountains and they planted dynamite high above the railroads, in concentration camps located in the deserts of Wyoming and Arizona, across the oceans on flotsam and refugee boats, parachuted in from modem jets and seared in the fires of Koreatown. The acres of history that we have tilled have not been welcoming or fertile, but we have persevered and out of the desert we have taken seed and we have grown. The promise of America is not happiness or equality, but the pursuit of happiness and the opportunity to advocate for equality. In order for us to be recognized as equals, we must struggle to assert our right to sit at the table.

NOTE

1. "Who killed Vincent Chin?," is a question raised in the documentary by the same name directed by Renee Tajima-Pena and Christine Choy. Vincent Chin was killed by two unemployed autoworkers on June 19, 1982, a week before he was to be wed. The two murderers yelled at Chin "It's because of

motherf***ers like you that we are out of work," chased him down the street and one held him while the other beat his head in with a baseball bat. His murderers never served a day in jail and were sentenced to three years probation and a $3000 fine. The case became a symbol for anti-Asian violence in America and the filmmakers raised in their documentary the question of societal responsibility for Chin's death. The high level of Japan-bashing and Asian-bashing promulgated by the auto manufacturers, especially in this period, created an environment conducive to violence and anti-Asian American violence.

DISCUSSION QUESTIONS

1. What, role according to Hwang, does violence play in creating an Asian Pacific community? What does he mean when he says that violence is a "foil and catalyst" in the development of community?

2. How does Sylvia illustrate the "false consciousness" of Asian Americans mentioned by Hurh? How does the attack change the way she thinks about herself, her place in American society, and her view of African Americans?

3. How does the image of APA communities presented by Hwang differ from the image of the "model minority" analyzed in the article by Hurh?

4. How did the various responses to the vandalism in the Sunset District illustrate anti-Asian prejudice? Did the strength of the Asian community increase as a result of these attacks? Did the larger society develop a deeper understanding of Asian Americans? Why or why not?

CURRENT DEBATES

ASIAN AMERICAN "SUCCESS": WHAT ARE THE DIMENSIONS, CAUSES, AND IMPLICATIONS FOR OTHER MINORITY GROUPS?

When considered as a group and judged by the usual American criteria (for example, income, prestige, or educational levels), Asian Americans are remarkably successful. They not only rank higher than other minority groups of color, they often rank higher than the dominant group. What accounts for this high status? Are there problems among Asian Americans that are obscured by the glittering statistics of success? Asian Americans are so successful that they are sometimes referred to as "America's model minority." Are there some hidden moral or political agendas in this label?

The debate over Asian American success generally falls into three camps, each reflected in the selections below. Some analysts focus on cultural explanations and stress the "good values" (hard work, respect for elders, and so on) that are said to characterize Asian American communities. This viewpoint is presented here in the writings of sociologist Harry Kitano (1980). He argues that the success of the Japanese in America is due in part to their culture and in part to their strength of character, resiliency, and flexibility.

A second line of argument is presented by sociologists Alejandro Portes and Min Zhou (1992). They use a structural perspective that links the success of Chinese Americans to their enclave economy. They also draw some provocative comparisons between Chinese Americans and African Americans, suggesting that the "thorough acculturation" of the African American community has weakened its economic vitality.

The third point of view is represented by sociologist Ronald Takaki, who sharply questions the whole notion of Asian American success and points out the limits and qualifications that need to be observed when comparing Asian Americans with other groups. Takaki also points to a hidden agenda of those who single out Asian Americans as a "model minority": the chastisement of other minority groups, particularly African Americans.

THE SUCCESS OF JAPANESE AMERICANS IS CULTURAL

Harry Kitano

Social interaction among Japanese Americans is governed by behavioral norms such as enryo and amae. These derive from Confucian ideas about human relationships and define the dimensions of interaction and exchange between superior and inferior members of a social group. Although these forms of behavior were brought over by Issei (first generation) immigrants, they still survive in attenuated form among the Nisei (second generation) and even the Sansei (third generation).

Enryo prescribes the way in which a social inferior must show deference and self-abnegation before a superior. Hesitancy to speak out at meetings, the automatic refusal of a second helping, and selecting a less desired object are all manifestations of enryo. . . .

Amae behavior softens a power relationship through the acting out of dependency and weakness, and expresses the need for attention, recognition, acceptance, and nurture. A child displays amae to gain the sympathy and indulgence of a parent. A young, anxious-to-please employee in a business firm will act with exaggerated meekness and confusion to give his superior an opportunity to provide paternal advice and treat him as a protégé. Through the ritual display of weakness and dependency, reciprocal bonds of loyalty, devotion, and trust are formed. In this way amae creates strong emotional ties that strengthen cohesion within the family, business organization, and community.

Japanese Americans inherit an almost reverential attitude toward work. Their ancestors struggled for survival in a crowded island country with limited natural resources and they placed great value on industry and self-discipline. Certain traditional attitudes encourage resilient behavior in the face of setbacks and complement the moral imperative to work hard. Many Japanese Americans are familiar with the common expressions gaman and gambotte which mean "don't let it bother you," "don't give up." These dicta, derived from Buddhist teachings, encourage Japanese people to

conceal frustration or disappointment and to carry on. A tradition that places great value on work and persistence has helped many Japanese Americans to acquire good jobs and to get ahead.

The submerging of the individual to the interest of the group is another basic Japanese tradition, and one that produces strong social cohesion and an oblique style of behavior, one manifestation of which is the indirection or allusiveness of much communication between Japanese; another is the polite, consensual behavior expected in all social contacts. Both are common in Japan and visible among Japanese Americans. Today, even third- and fourth-generation Japanese Americans are apt to be seen by others as agreeable, unaggressive, willing to accept subordinate roles, and reluctant to put themselves forward. . . .

The history of the Japanese Americans in the United States is one of both resilience and adaptation. Suffering from discriminatory laws and racial hostility in the first half of the 20th century, Japanese Americans were nonetheless able to create stable ethnic communities and separate, but vital, social organizations. Since the end of World War II, with the disappearance of legal discrimination and the weakening of social restrictions, they have assimilated more readily into American society and shown rapid economic progress. Scholars have searched for the key to their remarkable record of adaptation. Some have pointed to the Japanese family, others to a strong group orientation, and still others to Japanese moral training; all of these theories often tend to overemphasize the degree to which Japanese traditions have been maintained. Japanese Americans have displayed a pragmatic attitude toward American life. [Rather] than rigidly maintaining their traditions, Japanese Americans have woven American values and behavior into the fabric of their culture and have seized new social, cultural, and economic avenues as they have become available, extending the limits of ethnicity by striking a workable balance between ethnic cohesion and accommodation.

SOURCE: Kitano, H. (1980). Japanese. In Stephen Thornstrom et al. (Eds.), *Harvard Encyclopedia of Ethnic Groups* (pp. 570–571). Cambridge, MA: Harvard University Press.

THE "SUCCESS" OF CHINESE AMERICANS IS STRUCTURAL

Alejandro Portes and Min Zhou

[What lessons for ethnic poverty can we find in the experiences of Chinese Americans and other groups that have constructed ethnic enclaves?] A tempting option—and one to which many experts have not been averse—is to resort to culturalistic explanations. According to these interpretations, certain groups do better because they possess the "right" kind of values. This view is, of course, not too different from assimilation theory except that, instead of learning the proper values after arrival, immigrants bring them ready made. A moment's reflection suffices to demonstrate the untenability of this explanation. . . .

The very diversity of [the] groups [which have constructed enclave economies] conspires against explanations that find the roots of economic mobility in the unique values associated with a particular culture. If we had to invoke a particular "ethic" to account for the business achievements of Chinese and Jews, Koreans and Cubans, Lebanese and Dominicans, we would wind up with a very messy theory. In terms of professed religions alone, we would have to identify those unique values leading Confucianists and Buddhists, Greek Orthodox and Roman Catholics into successful business ventures. In addition, culturalistic explanations have little predictive power since they are invoked only after a particular group has demonstrated its economic prowess. . . .

There is no alternative but to search for the relevant causal process in the social structure of the ethnic community. [Several] common aspects in the economic experience of the immigrant communities [are] relevant. . . .

[First is] the "bounded solidarity" created among immigrants by virtue of their foreignness and being treated as [different]. As consumers, immigrants manifest a consistent preference for items associated with the country of origin, both for their intrinsic utility and as symbolic representations of a distinct identity. As workers, they often prefer to work among "their own," interacting in their native language even if this means sacrificing some material benefits. As investors, they commonly opt for firms in the country of origin or in the ethnic community rather than trusting their money to impersonal outside organizations.

Bounded solidarity [is accompanied by] "enforceable trust" against malfeasance among prospective ethnic entrepreneurs. Confidence that business associates will not resort to double-dealing is cemented in something more tangible than generalized cultural loyalty since it also relies on the ostracism of violators, cutting them off from sources of credit and opportunity. [Enforceable trust] is the key mechanism underlying the smooth operation of rotating credit associations among Asian immigrant communities.

Bounded solidarity and enforceable trust as sources of social capital do not inhere in the moral convictions of individuals or in the value orientations in which they were socialized. [These benefits] accrue by virtue of [the group's] minority [status] in the host country and as a result of being subjected to mainstream pressure to accept their low place in the ethnic hierarchy. Such pressures prompt the revalorization of the symbols of a common nationality and the privileging of the ethnic community as the place where the status of underprivileged menial labor can be avoided. . . .

Black Americans, Mexican Americans, and mainland Puerto Ricans today lag significantly behind the immigrant groups in their entrepreneurial orientation. [This] lack of entrepreneurial presence is even more remarkable because of the large size of these minorities and the significant consumer market that they represent. . . .

We believe that the dearth of entrepreneurship among these groups is related to the dissolution of the structural underpinnings of the social capital resources noted above: bounded solidarity and enforceable trust. A thorough process of acculturation among U.S.-born members of each of these groups has led to a gradual weakening of their sense of community and to a re-orientation towards the values, expectations, and preferences of the cultural mainstream. [Complete] assimilation among domestic minorities leads to identification with the mainstream views, including a disparaging evaluation of their own group. . . .

[Even] groups with a modest level of human capital have managed to create an entrepreneurial presence when the necessary social capital, created by specific historical conditions, was present. This was certainly the case among turn-of-the-century Chinese. [It] was also true of segregated black communities during the same time period. The current desperate conditions in many inner-city neighborhoods have led some black leaders to recall wistfully the period of segregation. [As one black leader said]:

[T]he same kind of business enclave that exists in the Cuban community or in the Jewish community existed in the black community when the consumer base was contained [i.e., segregated from the larger society] and needed goods and services that had to be provided by someone in the neighborhood. Today, blacks will not buy within their neighborhood if they can help it; they want to go to the malls and blend with mainstream consumers.

Hence, thorough acculturation and the formal end of segregation led to the dissipation of the social capital formerly present in restricted black enclaves and the consequent weakening of minority entrepreneurship. As blacks attempted to join the mainstream, they found that lingering discrimination barred or slowed down their progress in the labor market, while consumption of outside goods and services undermined their own community business base.

SOURCE: Portes, A., & Zhou, M. (1992). Gaining the Upper Hand: Economic Mobility Among Immigrant and Domestic Minorities. *Ethnic and Racial Studies,* 15:513–518.

THE SUCCESS OF ASIAN AMERICANS HAS BEEN EXAGGERATED, IN PART TO CRITICIZE OTHER MINORITY GROUPS

Ronald Takaki

African American "failure" has been contrasted with Asian American "success." In 1984, William Raspberry of the *Washington Post* noted that Asian Americans on the West Coast had "in fact" "outstripped" whites in income. Blacks should stop blaming racism for their plight, he argued, and follow the example of the self-reliant Asian Americans. In 1986, *NBC Nightly News* and *McNeil/Lehrer Report* aired special segments on Asian Americans and their achievements. *U.S. News and World Report* featured Asian American advances in a cover story, and *Newsweek* focused a lead article on "Asian Americans: A 'Model Minority'" while *Fortune* applauded them as "America's super minority."

But in their celebration of this model minority, these media pundits have exaggerated Asian American "success." Their comparisons of income between Asians and whites fail to recognize the regional location of the Asian American population. Concentrated in California, Hawaii, and New York, most Asian Americans reside in states with higher incomes but also higher costs of living than the national average. . . .

Asian American families have more persons working per family than white families. Thus, the family incomes of Asian Americans indicate the presence of more workers in each family rather than higher individual incomes. Actually, in terms of personal incomes, Asian Americans have not reached equality.

While many Asian Americans are doing well, others find themselves mired in poverty: they include Southeast-Asian refugees such as the Hmong . . . as well as immigrant workers trapped in Chinatowns. Eighty percent of the people in New York Chinatown, 74% of San Francisco Chinatown, and 88% of Los Angeles Chinatown are foreign born. Like the nineteenth century Chinese immigrants in search of gold mountain, they came here to seek a better life. But what they found instead was work in Chinatown's low wage service and garment industries. . . .

The myth of the Asian American "model minority" has been challenged, yet it continues to be widely believed. One reason for this is its instructional value. For whom are Asian Americans supposed to be a "model"? . . .

Asian Americans are being used to discipline blacks. If the failure of blacks on welfare warns Americans in general how they should not behave, the triumph of Asian Americans affirms the deeply rooted values of the Protestant ethic and self-reliance. Our society needs an Asian American "model minority" in an era anxious about a growing black underclass. If Asian Americans can make it on their own, why can't other groups? . . .

Betraying a certain nervousness over the seeming end of the American dream's boundlessness, praise for this "super minority" has become society's most recent jeremiad—a call for a renewed commitment to the traditional values of hard work, thrift, and industry. After all, it has been argued, the war on poverty and affirmative action were not really necessary. Look at the Asian Americans! They did it by pulling themselves up by their bootstraps. For blacks shut out of the labor market, the Asian American model provides the standards for acceptable behavior: blacks should not depend on welfare or affirmative action. While congratulating Asian Americans for their family values, hard work, and high incomes, President Ronald Reagan chastised blacks for their dependency on the "spider's web of welfare" and their failure to recognize that the "only barrier" to success was "within" them.

SOURCE: Takaki, R. (1993). *A Different Mirror: A History of Multicultural America* (pp. 414–417). Boston: Little, Brown.

QUESTIONS TO CONSIDER

1. If Kitano's analysis is correct, what could other minority groups learn from the Japanese experience? If Portes and Zhou are correct, what could other minority groups learn from the Chinese experience? Do Portes and Zhou use cultural factors as part of their explanation? How? Are Portes and Zhou advocating segregation? Pluralism? Assimilation?

2. Why would the United States "need" a model minority? How would you answer Takaki's question: "for whom are Asian Americans supposed to be a model?" Whose interests are being served by these comparisons? Do Asian Americans gain anything from these labels and comparisons? Do they lose anything?

9

WHITE ETHNIC GROUPS

During the century between the 1820s and 1920s, nearly 40 million people immigrated to the United States from Europe. This mass migration, the largest in human history, began in the nations of Northern and Western Europe (including Ireland, Norway, and Germany) and spread to the nations of Southern and Eastern Europe (including Italy, Poland, and Russia). The immigrants came from every nook and cranny of European society and included people from every conceivable background: aristocrats, paupers, criminals, peasants, artisans, skilled professionals, and everything in between. Some looked on the United States as the Promised Land and vowed never to leave. Some wanted only the chance to work and save money and return to their home villages as quickly as possible. Their impact on the young nation was vast: they swelled the population, helped farm the Midwest, made uncountable contributions to American art, music, literature, and architecture, and supplied a massive labor force for the industrialization of the United States. When this immigration stream began, the United States was a small, agricultural nation on the periphery of world events. When the period of mass immigration ended, the United States was industrialized and one of the strongest, most robust nations in the world, a transformation that is linked to the contributions of these immigrants in countless ways.

Although each immigrant had his or her own unique reasons for coming to the United States, most were motivated by the simple desire to find work that could sustain them and their families. They entered the economy in a variety of roles, but most took jobs in factories, mills, and mines and became the workforce for the Industrial Revolution that propelled the United States to world preeminence. These immigrant laborers carved out a place for themselves in the American economy—even though at the bottom rung of the job structure—from which their children and grandchildren were able to climb higher and, over the course of generations, eventually be assimilated into the great suburban middle class. Today, the descendants of the European immigrants are generally equal to national norms in terms of education, income, and other measure of equality.

As assimilation progressed over the generations, ethnic identity and the sense of a connection with "old country" traditions weakened and faded. For present-day descendants of the immigrants, ethnicity is largely symbolic and optional. That is, their ethnicity is a minor part of their self-image (if that) and has little effect on their values, voting habits, diet, friendships, place of residence, or job prospects. They may acknowledge their ethnicity on occasion (for example, St. Patrick's Day for the Irish), but, otherwise, are free to ignore it or celebrate it, as they choose. Increasingly, it seems that the sense of ethnicity for these groups has been merged into a broad, generalized white identity—not specific to any particular white ethnic group—that follows the racial contours that run through so much of our society.

The Narrative Portrait that begins this chapter is part of a sociological memoir of growing up in the 1930s, at a time when ethnic identity was still strong. David Gray discusses how he gradually became aware of the dividing lines that ran through the community of his boyhood and how he came to understand the difference between "us" and "the others." He also discusses how the Irish in his hometown used the local machinery of government to protect their own during the Great Depression. The Irish, and virtually every other white ethnic group, found ways to use the city government, labor unions, private businesses, the church, and other institutions—including organized crime and sports—to abet their rise to acceptance and equality.

The Readings in this chapter view the process of assimilation from a variety of perspectives. Karen Brodkin looks at some of the factors that helped Jewish Americans (but not African Americans and other minority groups of color) achieve acceptance in the larger society. Peggy McIntosh examines the dynamics of white privilege, the advantaged position now shared by the descendants of the European immigrants, and Lillian Rubin explores the intersection of race and class identities. The Current Debate extends the examination of white racial identity and discusses the meaning of whiteness in contemporary society.

NARRATIVE PORTRAIT

ETHNICITY, PREJUDICE, AND THE IRISH POLITICAL MACHINE

David Gray grew up a Welsh Protestant in the city of Scranton, Pennsylvania, during the 1930s and 1940s. At that time, this coal-mining town was split along ethnic lines and, in this memoir, Gray (1991) recounts his gradual socialization into the realities of in-groups and out-groups. He also describes how Scranton's Irish Catholic community responded to the Great Depression and how they used the local political machine to protect their own. Gray reflects on the consequences of these experiences for his own personal prejudices and sense of social distance.

Gray eventually left Scranton and earned a Ph.D. in sociology. He became a college professor and an accomplished and respected sociologist. His many admiring students included one of the editors of this book, who grew up in Scranton's Irish Catholic community a generation after Dr. Gray.

SHADOW OF THE PAST

David Gray

C. Wright Mills (an American sociologist) [stressed] the intimate relationship of "history, social structure, and biography." . . . Though he did not say so directly, the logic of Mills' position would surely indicate that, for self-knowledge, no biography is more important than one's own. Born within a social context not of our own making, subject to social forces we did not create, in retrospect, we attempt to understand. . . .

Personally, then, I did not ask to be born Welsh Protestant in Scranton, Pennsylvania. No more than Eddie Gilroy, with whom I attended . . . school, asked to be born Irish Catholic. But there we both were in the heart of the anthracite coal region . . . during the years of the Great Depression. . . . We were friends, good friends. During recess and after 3:00 P.M., he played second base and I played shortstop in the shrunken, dirt diamond in the schoolyard. . . . We thought we made a good double-play combination and, beyond the baseball field, we respected and liked each other as well.

But, there was something wrong with Eddie Gilroy. At age ten I didn't know exactly what it was. He didn't make many errors and we often shared whatever pennies we had . . . at the corner candy store. Still, there was something wrong with him—vague, general, apart from real experience, but true all the same.

His fundamental defect came into sharper focus at the age of twelve. Sunday movies had just arrived in Scranton and . . . I wanted to go with Eddie and Johnny Pesavento [but] I couldn't.

"Why?"

"Because Protestants don't go to the movies on Sunday—nor play cards, football, or baseball."

"How come Eddie and Johnny can go?"

"They're Catholic."

No one quite used the word "immoral" but . . . anyone who attended Sunday movies was certainly close to sinful. And the implication was clear: If Catholics did such bad things on Sunday, they surely did a lot of bad things on other days as well.

No matter, then, that Gilroy might sacrifice for even a Protestant runner to go to second, or let you borrow his glove, or share his candy. . . . His Catholicism permeated his being, . . . muting his individual qualities. Eddie wasn't the point, his Catholicism was.

[The] deeply held beliefs . . . of the adult world were visited upon the young. Most often subtly . . . but persistently and effectively, little Welsh Protestant boys and girls learned that Catholics were somehow the enemy. . . .

Unfortunately, from their vantage point, the Welsh of Scranton were not the only ones in town. While they had come to the coal regions in large numbers, others, in even larger numbers, had come also. Irish, Italian, Polish, German, many from eastern European countries, fewer who were Jewish—all constituted Scranton's ethnic portion of broader 19th century immigrant waves. With [some] obvious exceptions, most were Catholic.

In this communal setting—a very ethnically and religiously distinct one—the Great Depression arrived with particular force. [The region suffered from massive unemployment and began to lose population as people left in search of work elsewhere.] The coal industry, upon which the economy of Northeastern Pennsylvania essentially rested, was gone. The private sector, initially hard-hit, did not recover

[until after the 1960s]. The public sector consequently became the primary possibility for often meager, by no means high-paying jobs.

And the Irish, their political talents augmented by the fact that they were the largest single ethnic group in town, controlled political power. Allied with others of Catholic faith, the Irish did their best to take care of their religiously affiliated, politically important, own.

In Scranton's political life, the intimate relationship of religion, politics, and economics was clear for all to see. The mayor was Jimmy Hanlon, . . . the political boss, Mickey Lawlor, . . . McNulty ran the post office, and Judge Hoban the courts. From the mayor's office to trash collectors, with policemen, foremen, school teachers, truant officers, and dog catchers in between, the public payroll included the names of O'Neill, Hennigan, Lydon, Kennedy, Walsh, Gerrity, and O'Hoolihan. As the depression persisted, Welsh Protestants came to know (with reason but also as an act of faith) that Lewis, Griffiths, and Williams need not apply.

Pale shades of contemporary Northern Ireland, but with political power reversed. No shots were fired, perhaps because American democratic traditions compel accommodation and compromise. Nonetheless, among the Welsh, the general feeling of resentment on more than one occasion was punctuated with: "Those goddam Irish Catholics."

Whatever may have been true in pre-depression years, however tolerant or intolerant individuals may have been, . . . that Welsh sentiment was not at all limited to individuals guilty of irrational prejudice. It was communally shared. Jobs, homes, and lives were at stake, and religious affiliation was relevant to them all. Irish Catholic political power was a fact from which Welsh Protestant resentment followed. Prejudice there certainly was—deeply felt, poignantly articulated, subjectively often going beyond what facts would justify and, unfortunately, communicated to the young. . . .

The public sector was vulnerable to Irish Catholic control. The Welsh knew that. The private sector (banks, small businesses) simultaneously retained a diminished but tightened, now more consciously Protestant, ownership and/or control. Though the musically inclined Welsh never composed it, their regional battle hymn surely was: If Irish politicians were using their political power to control what they could, it was essential for Protestants to protect what they privately had.

SOURCE: Gray, David J. (1991). Shadow of the Past: The Rise and Fall of Prejudice in an American City. *The American Journal of Economics and Sociology,* 50:33–39.

READINGS

An examination of the experiences of white Americans from their initial immigration to the United States to modern times provides a good illustration of the difference between *ethnicity* and *race*. While ethnicity refers to a shared national origin and/or cultural heritage, race is a social construction denoting boundaries between the powerful and less powerful and thus often defined by the dominant group. Thus, there are many different ethnicities that make up the racial group of "white Americans," "Hispanic Americans," "Asian Americans," and so forth. When we investigate the situation of white Americans, it is evident that various ethnicities have gradually been incorporated into the dominant racial category of white over time, provided they met certain cultural, physical, and socioeconomic criteria. Our first Reading, "How Jews Became White," presents a case study of how one white ethnic group, Jewish Americans, succeeded in this process. For nearly two centuries of United States history, author Karen Brodkin documents the court rulings and laws that restricted the status of "white," and the rights of full citizenship that went along with it, to only Northwestern Europeans. This excluded Jews and many other ethnic groups. However, the achievement of a certain degree of socioeconomic success, thanks to the postwar economic boom of the late 1940s and early 1950s, allowed Jewish Americans like Brodkin (who was growing up right around this time) to be considered white Americans for the first time. What is useful about Brodkin's essay is her detailed analysis of the U.S. government's economic and social programs during this time period—policies she calls "affirmative action" for white males—which demonstrates how certain groups, particularly African Americans, were legally excluded from these unparalleled generous government subsidies of education and housing. In this way, she challenges the argument (typified by her parents' explanations) that Jews' *cultural* work ethic is responsible for their *assimilation* success story, pointing instead to these *structural* factors that allowed them to "become white" where other groups were not permitted to do so.

In an individualistic society such as the United States, we want to believe that factors such as hard work and motivation are responsible for certain groups' relative success. It is this "myth of meritocracy" that Peggy McIntosh seeks to challenge in our second Reading, "White Privilege and Male Privilege." Recall that in Part I of this book, we reviewed the concepts of *privilege* and *stigma,* and noted that members of minority groups are usually much more aware of their stigma than members of dominant groups are of their privilege. McIntosh illustrates this point writing from the perspective of a white woman who is quite aware of male privilege, being female and knowing all too well the limits she faces that her male counterparts do not have to face, yet utterly ignorant about her racial privilege as a white person until she challenged herself to study it. Upon doing so, she comes up with a now widely cited list of 46 white privileges covering many areas of life, from housing and employment to shopping and media representation. By definition, these privileges are *unearned.* People of color, compared to similarly situated whites in terms of class, gender, or age, cannot count on receiving such advantages even if they work just as hard or even harder than their white counterparts. Another crucial point McIntosh makes about privilege is that members of dominant groups are kept *oblivious* about its existence. No matter how obvious it is to members of minority groups, these advantages are something that whites have often never stopped to consider. Every time throughout history that the government has somehow limited nonwhites in the ways we have read about in this text, whites receive a corresponding privilege as a result. Even whites who are not discriminatory or prejudice benefit from these privileges. This reading sheds additional light upon why the socially constructed boundaries of whiteness are so closely guarded— because those who permeate them become the beneficiaries of all these privileges that McIntosh describes.

It is difficult to accept the idea of white privilege, especially for members of the white working class, who are struggling to make ends meet themselves. In our third Reading, Lillian Rubin explores the racial identities of men and women of white working-class backgrounds, who due to increased racial diversity in their communities now are having to consider their own racial identification with whiteness for the first time. As immigrants to the United States have become increasingly people of color, it is as if whites now have a visible scapegoat in times of economic difficulty. The men and women interviewed by Rubin make comments like "nobody speaks English anymore" and feel like "strangers in their own land." Even though they were once immigrants themselves, we see that it is not so much the foreignness of the new immigrants that they object to, but it is rather the color of their skin that leads these whites to reason that the new immigrants don't belong. Whereas previously whites had only sporadically identified ethnically (*symbolic ethnicity*) in times of Irish or Scottish festivals, for example, now they feel an investment in whiteness as they stake out in-group versus out-group territory, as if defending their privileged status. Yet it is important to keep in mind that an oppositional white identity such as this is not the only way to be white. As we move into Part IV of this book, we will consider other antiracist ways of being white that affirm and celebrate the advent of a multiracial society.

How Jews Became White

Karen Brodkin

> *The American nation was founded and developed by the Nordic race, but if a few more million members of the Alpine, Mediterranean and Semitic races are poured among us, the result must inevitably be a hybrid race of people as worthless and futile as the good-for-nothing mongrels of Central America and Southeastern Europe.*
>
> —Kenneth Roberts, qtd. in Carlson & Colburn (1972:312)

It is clear that Kenneth Roberts did not think of my ancestors as white like him. The late nineteenth and early decades of the twentieth centuries saw a steady stream of warnings by scientists, policymakers, and the popular press that "mongrelization" of the Nordic or Anglo-Saxon race—the real Americans—by inferior European races (as well as inferior non-European ones) was destroying the fabric of the nation. I continue to be surprised to read that America did not always regard its immigrant European workers as white, that they thought people from different nations were biologically

different. My parents, who are first-generation U.S.-born eastern European Jews, are not surprised. They expect anti-Semitism to be a part of the fabric of daily life, much as I expect racism to be part of it. They came of age in a Jewish world in the 1920s and 1930s at the peak of anti-Semitism in the United States (Gerber 1986). They are proud of their upward mobility and think of themselves as pulling themselves up by their own bootstraps. I grew up during the 1950s in the Euroethnic New York suburb of Valley Stream where Jews were simply one kind of white folks and where ethnicity meant little more to my generation than food and family heritage. Part of my familized ethnic heritage was the belief that Jews were smart and that our success was the result of our own efforts and abilities, reinforced by a culture that valued sticking together, hard work, education, and deferred gratification. Today, this belief in a Jewish version of Horatio Alger has become an entry point for racism by some mainstream Jewish organizations against African Americans especially, and for their opposition to affirmative action for people of color (Gordon 1964; Sowell 1981; Steinberg 1989: chap. 3).

It is certainly true that the United States has a history of anti-Semitism and of beliefs that Jews were members of an inferior race. But Jews were hardly alone. American anti-Semitism was part of a broader pattern of late-nineteenth-century racism against all southern and eastern European immigrants, as well as against Asian immigrants. These views justified all sorts of discriminatory treatment including closing the doors to immigration from Europe and Asia in the 1920s.[1] This picture changed radically after World War II. Suddenly the same folks who promoted nativism and xenophobia were eager to believe that the Euro-origin people whom they had deported, reviled as members of inferior races, and prevented from immigrating only a few years earlier were now model middle-class white suburban citizens.

It was not an educational epiphany that made those in power change their hearts, their minds, and our race. Instead, it was the biggest and best affirmative action program in the history of our nation, and it was for Euromales. There are similarities and differences in the ways each of the European immigrant groups became "whitened." I want to tell the story in a way that links anti-Semitism to other varieties of anti-European racism, because this foregrounds what Jews shared with other Euroimmigrants and shows changing notions of whiteness to be part of America's larger system of institutional racism.

EURORACES

The U.S. "discovery" that Europe had inferior and superior races came in response to the great waves of immigration from southern and eastern Europe in the late nineteenth century. Before that time, European immigrants—including Jews—had been largely assimilated into the white population. The twenty-three million European immigrants who came to work in U.S. cities after 1880 were too many and too concentrated to disperse and blend. Instead, they piled up in the country's most dilapidated urban areas, where they built new kinds of working-class ethnic communities. Since immigrants and their children made up more than 70 percent of the population of most of the country's largest cities, urban America came to take on a distinctly immigrant flavor. The golden age of industrialization in the United States was also the golden age of class struggle between the captains of the new industrial empires and the masses of manual workers whose labor made them rich. As the majority of mining and manufacturing workers, immigrants were visibly major players in these struggles (Higham 1955:226; Steinberg 1989:36).[2]

The Red Scare of 1919 clearly linked anti-immigrant to anti-working-class sentiment—to the extent that the Seattle general strike of native-born workers was blamed on foreign agitators. The Red Scare was fueled by economic depression, a massive postwar strike wave, the Russian revolution, and a new wave of postwar immigration. . . .

Not surprisingly, the belief in European races took root most deeply among the wealthy U.S.-born Protestant elite, who feared a hostile and seemingly unassimilable working class. By the end of the nineteenth century, Senator Henry Cabot Lodge pressed Congress to cut off immigration to the United States; Teddy Roosevelt raised the alarm of "race suicide" and took Anglo-Saxon women to task for allowing "native" stock to be outbred by inferior immigrants. In the twentieth century, these fears gained a great deal of social legitimacy thanks to the efforts of an influential network of aristocrats and scientists who developed theories of eugenics—breeding for a "better" humanity—and scientific racism. Key to these efforts was Madison Grant's influential *Passing of the Great Race,* in which he shared his discovery that there were three or four major European races ranging from the superior Nordics of northwestern Europe to the inferior southern and eastern races of Alpines, Mediterraneans, and, worst of all, Jews, who seemed to be everywhere in his native New York City. Grant's nightmare was race mixing among Europeans. For him, "the cross between any of the three European races and a Jew is a Jew" (qtd. in Higham 1955:156). He didn't have good things to say about Alpine or Mediterranean "races" either. For Grant, race and class were interwoven: the upper class was racially pure Nordic, and the lower classes came from the lower races.

Far from being on the fringe, Grant's views resonated with those of the nonimmigrant middle class. A *New York Times* reporter wrote of his visit to the Lower East Side:

> This neighborhood, peopled almost entirely by the people who claim to have been driven from Poland and Russia, is the eyesore of New York and perhaps the filthiest place on the western Continent. It is impossible for a Christian to live there because he will be driven out, either by blows or the dirt and stench. Cleanliness is an unknown quantity to these people. They cannot be lifted up to a higher plane because they do not want to be. If the cholera should ever get among these people, they would scatter its germs as a sower does grain. (qtd. in Schoener 1967:58)[3]

Such views were well within the mainstream of the early-twentieth-century scientific community. Grant and eugenicist Charles B. Davenport organized the Galton Society in 1918 in order to foster research and to otherwise promote eugenics and immigration restriction.[4] . . .

By the 1920s, scientific racism sanctified the notion that real Americans were white and real whites came from northwest Europe. Racism animated laws excluding and expelling Chinese in 1882, and then closing the door to immigration by virtually all Asians and most Europeans in 1924 (Saxton 1971, 1990). Northwestern European ancestry as a requisite for whiteness was set in legal concrete when the Supreme Court denied Bhagat Singh Thind the right to become a naturalized citizen under a 1790 federal law that allowed whites the right to become naturalized citizens. Thind argued that East Indians were the real Aryans and Caucasians, and therefore white. The Court countered that

the United States only wanted blond Aryans and Caucasians, "that the blond Scandinavian and the brown Hindu have a common ancestor in the dim reaches of antiquity, but the average man knows perfectly well that there are unmistakable and profound differences between them today" (Takaki 1989:298–299). A narrowly defined white, Christian race was also built into the 1705 Virginia "Act concerning servants and slaves." This statute stated "that no negroes, mulattos and Indians or other infidels or jews, Moors, Mahometans or other infidels shall, at any time, purchase any christian servant, nor any other except of their own complexion" (Martyn 1979:111).[5]

The 1930 census added its voice, distinguishing not only immigrant from "native" whites, but also native whites of native white parentage, and native whites of immigrant (or mixed) parentage. In distinguishing immigrant (southern and eastern Europeans) from "native" (northwestern Europeans), the census reflected the racial distinctions of the eugenicist-inspired intelligence tests.[6]

Racism and anti-immigrant sentiment in general and anti-Semitism in particular flourished in higher education. Jews were the first of the Euroimmigrant groups to enter colleges in significant numbers, so it wasn't surprising that they faced the brunt of discrimination there.[7] The Protestant elite complained that Jews were unwashed, uncouth, unrefined, loud, and pushy. Harvard University President A. Lawrence Lowell, who was also a vice president of the Immigration Restriction League, was openly opposed to Jews at Harvard. The Seven Sisters schools had a reputation for "flagrant discrimination." . . .

Anti-Semitic patterns set by these elite schools influenced standards of other schools, made anti-Semitism acceptable, and "made the aura of exclusivity a desirable commodity for the college-seeking clientele" (Synott 1986:250; and see Karabel 1984; Silberman 1985; Steinberg 1989: chaps. 5, 9). Fears that colleges "might soon be overrun by Jews" were publicly expressed at a 1918 meeting of the Association of New England Deans. In 1919 Columbia University took steps to decrease the number of entering Jews by a set of practices that soon came to be widely adopted. . . .

Columbia's quota against Jews was well known in my parents' community. My father is very proud of having beaten it and of being admitted to Columbia Dental School on the basis of his sculpting skill. In addition to demonstrating academic qualifications, he was asked to carve a soap ball, which he did so well and fast that his Protestant interviewer was willing to accept him. Although he became a teacher instead because the dental school tuition was too high, he took me to the dentist every week of my childhood and prolonged the agony by discussing the finer points of tooth filling and dental care. My father also almost failed the speech test required for his teaching license because he didn't speak "standard"—that is, nonimmigrant, nonaccented—English. For my parents and most of their friends, English was a second language learned when they went to school, since their home language was Yiddish. They saw the speech test as designed to keep all ethnics, not just Jews, out of teaching. . . .

My parents' conclusion is that Jewish success, like their own, was the result of hard work and of placing a high value on education. They went to Brooklyn College during the Depression. My mother worked days and started school at night, and my father went during the day. Both their families encouraged them. More accurately, their families expected this effort from them. Everyone they knew was in the same boat, and their world was made up of Jews who advanced as they did. The picture of New York—where most Jews lived—seems to back them up. In 1920, Jews made up 80 percent of the students at New York's City College, 90 percent of Hunter College, and before World War I, 40 percent of private Columbia University. By 1934, Jews made up almost 24 percent of all law students nationally, and 56 percent of those in New York City. Still, more Jews became public school teachers, like my parents and their friends, than doctors or lawyers (Steinberg 1989:137, 227). Steinberg has debunked the myth that Jews advanced because of the cultural value placed on education. This is not to say that Jews did not advance. They did. "Jewish success in America was a matter of historical timing. . . . [T]here was a fortuitous match between the experience and skills of Jewish immigrants, on the one

hand, and the manpower needs and opportunity structures, on the other" (1989:103). Jews were the only ones among the southern and eastern European immigrants who came from urban, commercial, craft, and manufacturing backgrounds, not least of which was garment manufacturing. They entered the United States in New York, center of the nation's booming garment industry, soon came to dominate its skilled (male) and "unskilled" (female) jobs, and found it an industry amenable to low-capital entrepreneurship. As a result, Jews were the first of the new European immigrants to create a middle class of small businesspersons early in the twentieth century. Jewish educational advances followed this business success and depended upon it, rather than creating it (see also Bodnar 1985 for a similar argument about mobility).

In the early twentieth century, Jewish college students entered a contested terrain in which the elite social mission was under challenge by a newer professional training mission. Pressure for change had begun to transform the curriculum and reorient college from a gentleman's bastion to a training ground for the middle-class professionals needed by an industrial economy. "The curriculum was overhauled to prepare students for careers in business, engineering, scientific farming, and the arts, and a variety of new professions such as accounting and pharmacy that were making their appearance in American colleges for the first time" (Steinberg 1989:229). Occupational training was precisely what drew Jews to college. In a setting where disparagement of intellectual pursuits and the gentleman's C were badges of distinction, it was not hard for Jews to excel.

How we interpret Jewish social mobility in this milieu depends on whom we compare Jews to. Compared with other immigrants, Jews were upwardly mobile. But compared with that of nonimmigrant whites, their mobility was very limited and circumscribed. Anti-immigrant racist and anti-Semitic barriers kept the Jewish middle class confined to a small number of occupations. Jews were excluded from mainstream corporate management and corporately employed professions, except in the garment and movie industries, which they built. Jews were almost totally excluded from university faculties (and the few that made it had powerful patrons). Jews were concentrated in small businesses, and in professions where they served a largely Jewish clientele (Davis 1990:146 n. 25; Silberman 1985:88–117; Sklare 1971:63–67). . . .

My parents' generation believed that Jews overcame anti-Semitic barriers because Jews are special. My belief is that the Jews who were upwardly mobile were special among Jews (and were also well placed to write the story). My generation might well counter our parents' story of pulling themselves up by their own bootstraps with, "But think what you might have been without the racism and with some affirmative action!" And that is precisely what the postwar boom, the decline of systematic public anti-immigrant racism and anti-Semitism, and governmental affirmative action extended to white males.

EUROETHNICS INTO WHITES

By the time I was an adolescent, Jews were just as white as the next white person. Until I was eight, I was a Jew in a world of Jews. Everyone on Avenue Z in Sheepshead Bay was Jewish. I spent my days playing and going to school on three blocks of Avenue Z, and visiting my grandparents in the nearby Jewish neighborhoods of Brighton Beach and Coney Island. There were plenty of Italians in my neighborhood, but they lived around the corner. They were a kind of Jew, but on the margins of my social horizons. Portuguese were even more distant, at the end of the bus ride, at Sheepshead Bay. . . . We left that world in 1949 when we moved to Valley Stream, Long Island, which was Protestant, Republican, and even had farms until Irish, Italian, and Jewish exurbanites like us gave it a more suburban and Democratic flavor. Neither religion nor ethnicity separated us at school or in the neighborhood. Except temporarily. In elementary school years, I remember a fair number of dirt-bomb (a good suburban weapon) wars on the block. Periodically one of the Catholic boys would accuse me or my brother of killing his God, to which we would reply, "Did not" and start lobbing dirt-bombs. Sometimes he would get his friends from Catholic school, and I would get mine from

public school kids on the block, some of whom were Catholic. Hostilities lasted no more than a couple of hours and punctuated an otherwise friendly relationship. They ended by junior high years, when other things became more important. Jews, Catholics, and Protestants, Italians, Irish, Poles, and "English" (I don't remember hearing WASP as a kid) were mixed up on the block and in school. We thought of ourselves as middle class and very enlightened because our ethnic backgrounds seemed so irrelevant to high school culture. We didn't see race (we thought), and racism was not part of our peer consciousness, nor were the immigrant or working-class histories of our families.

Like most chicken and egg problems, it's hard to know which came first. Did Jews and other Euroethnics become white because they became middle class? That is, did money whiten? Or did being incorporated in an expanded version of whiteness open up the economic doors to a middle-class status? Clearly, both tendencies were at work. Some of the changes set in motion during the war against fascism led to a more inclusive version of whiteness. Anti-Semitism and anti-European racism lost respectability. The 1940 census no longer distinguished native whites of native parentage from those, like my parents, of immigrant parentage, so that Euroimmigrants and their children were more securely white by submersion in an expanded notion of whiteness. (This census also changed the race of Mexicans to white [U.S. Bureau of the Census, 1940:4].) Theories of nurture and culture replaced theories of nature and biology. Instead of dirty and dangerous races who would destroy U.S. democracy, immigrants became ethnic groups whose children had successfully assimilated into the mainstream and risen to the middle class. In this new myth, Euroethnic suburbs like mine became the measure of U.S. democracy's victory over racism. Jewish mobility became a new Horatio Alger story. In time and with hard work, every ethnic group would get a piece of the pie, and the United States would be a nation with equal opportunity for all its people to become part of a prosperous middle-class majority. And it seemed that Euroethnic immigrants and their children were delighted to join middle America. [8]

This is not to say that anti-Semitism disappeared after World War II, only that it fell from fashion and was driven underground. . . .

Although changing views on who was white made it easier for Euroethnics to become middle class, it was also the case that economic prosperity played a very powerful role in the whitening process. Economic mobility of Jews and other Euroethnics rested ultimately on U.S. postwar economic prosperity with its enormously expanded need for professional, technical, and managerial labor, and on government assistance in providing it. The United States emerged from the war with the strongest economy in the world. . . . The postwar period was a historic moment for real class mobility and for the affluence we have erroneously come to believe was the U.S. norm. It was a time when the old white and the newly white masses became middle class.

The GI Bill of Rights, as the 1944 Serviceman's Readjustment Act was known, was arguably the most massive affirmative action program in U.S. history. It was created to develop needed labor-force skills, and to provide those who had them with a life-style that reflected their value to the economy. The GI benefits ultimately extended to sixteen million GIs (veterans of the Korean War as well) included priority in jobs—that is, preferential hiring, but no one objected to it then; financial support during the job search; small loans for starting up businesses; and, most important, low-interest home loans and educational benefits, which included tuition and living expenses (Brown 1946; Hurd 1946; Mosch 1975; *Postwar Jobs for Veterans* 1945; Willenz 1983). This legislation was rightly regarded as one of the most revolutionary postwar programs. I call it affirmative action because it was aimed at and disproportionately helped male, Euro-origin GIs. . . .

EDUCATION AND OCCUPATION

It is important to remember that prior to the war, a college degree was still very much a "mark of the upper class" (Willenz 1983:165). Colleges were largely finishing schools for Protestant elites. Before the postwar boom, schools could not begin to accommodate the American masses. Even in New York City before the 1930s, neither the public schools nor City College had room for more than a tiny fraction of potential immigrant students.

Not so after the war. The almost eight million GIs who took advantage of their educational benefits under the GI Bill caused "the greatest wave of college building in American history" (Nash et al. 1986:885). White male GIs were able to take advantage of their educational benefits for college and technical training, so they were particularly well positioned to seize the opportunities provided by the new demands for professional, managerial, and technical labor. "It has been well documented that the GI educational benefits transformed American higher education and raised the educational level of that generation and generations to come. With many provisions for assistance in upgrading their educational attainments veterans pulled ahead of nonveterans in earning capacity. In the long run it was the nonveterans who had fewer opportunities" (Willenz 1983:165).[9] . . .

Even more significantly, the postwar boom transformed the U.S. class structure—or at least its status structure—so that the middle class expanded to encompass most of the population. Before the war, most Jews, like most other Americans, were working class. Already upwardly mobile before the war relative to other immigrants, Jews floated high on this rising economic tide, and most of them entered the middle class. Still, even the high tide missed some Jews. As late as 1973, some 15 percent of New York's Jews were poor or near-poor, and in the 1960s, almost 25 percent of employed Jewish men remained manual workers (Steinberg 1989:89–90).

Educational and occupational GI benefits really constituted affirmative action programs for white males because they were decidedly not extended to African Americans or to women of any race. White male privilege was shaped against the backdrop of wartime racism and postwar sexism. During and after the war, there was an upsurge in white racist violence against black servicemen in public schools, and in the KKK, which spread to California and New York (Dalfiume 1969:133–134). The number of lynchings rose during the war, and in 1943 there were antiblack race riots in several large northern cities. Although there was a wartime labor shortage, black people were discriminated against in access to well-paid defense industry jobs and in housing. In 1946 there were white riots against African Americans across the South, and in Chicago and Philadelphia as well. Gains made as a result of the wartime Civil Rights movement, especially employment in defense-related industries, were lost with peacetime conversion as black workers were the first fired, often in violation of seniority (Wynn 1976:114, 116). White women were also laid off, ostensibly to make jobs for demobilized servicemen, and in the long run women lost most of the gains they had made in wartime (Kessler-Harris 1982). We now know that women did not leave the labor force in any significant numbers but instead were forced to find inferior jobs, largely nonunion, parttime, and clerical.

Theoretically available to all veterans, in practice women and black veterans did not get anywhere near their share of GI benefits. Because women's units were not treated as part of the military, women in them were not considered veterans and were ineligible for Veterans' Administration (VA) benefits (Willenz 1983:168). The barriers that almost completely shut African-American GIs out of their benefits were more complex. In Wynn's portrait (1976:115), black GIs anticipated starting new lives, just like their white counterparts. Over 43 percent hoped to return to school and most expected to relocate, to find better jobs in new lines of work. The exodus from the South toward the North and far West was particularly large. So it wasn't a question of any lack of ambition on the part of African-American GIs.

Rather, the military, the Veterans' Administration, the U.S. Employment Service, and the Federal Housing Administration (FHA) effectively denied African-American GIs access to their benefits and to the new educational, occupational, and residential opportunities. Black GIs who served in the thoroughly segregated armed forces during World War II served under white officers, usually Southerners (Binkin and Eitelberg 1982: Dalfiume 1969; Foner 1974; Johnson 1967; Nalty and MacGregor 1981). African-American soldiers were disproportionately

given dishonorable discharges, which denied them veterans' rights under the GI Bill. Thus between August and November 1946, 21 percent of white soldiers and 39 percent of black soldiers were dishonorably discharged. Those who did get an honorable discharge then faced the Veterans' Administration and the U.S. Employment Service. The latter, which was responsible for job placements, employed very few African Americans, especially in the South. This meant that black veterans did not receive much employment information, and that the offers they did receive were for low-paid and menial jobs. "In one survey of 50 cities, the movement of blacks into peacetime employment was found to be lagging far behind that of white veterans: in Arkansas 95 percent of the placements made by the USES for Afro-Americans were in service or unskilled jobs" (Nalty and MacGregor 1981:218, and see 60–61). African Americans were also less likely than whites, regardless of GI status, to gain new jobs commensurate with their wartime jobs, and they suffered more heavily. For example, in San Francisco by 1948, black Americans "had dropped back halfway to their pre-war employment status" (Wynn 1976:114, 116).[10]

Black GIs faced discrimination in the educational system as well. Despite the end of restrictions on Jews and other Euroethnics, African Americans were not welcome in white colleges. Black colleges were overcrowded, and the combination of segregation and prejudice made for few alternatives. About twenty thousand black veterans attended college by 1947, most in black colleges, but almost as many, fifteen thousand, could not gain entry. Predictably, the disproportionately few African Americans who did gain access to their educational benefits were able, like their white counterparts, to become doctors and engineers, and to enter the black middle class (Walker 1970).

SUBURBANIZATION

In 1949, ensconced at Valley Stream, I watched potato farms turn into Levittown and into Idlewild (later Kennedy) Airport. This was a major spectator sport in our first years on suburban Long Island. A typical weekend would bring various aunts, uncles, and cousins out from the city. After a huge meal we would pile in the car—itself a novelty—to look at the bull-dozed acres and comment on the matchbox con-struction. During the week, my mother and I would look at the houses going up within walk-ing distance.

Bill Levitt built a basic 900–1,000-square-foot, somewhat expandable house for a lower-middle-class and working-class market on Long Island, and later in Pennsylvania and New Jersey (Gans 1967). Levittown started out as two thousand units of rental housing at sixty dollars a month, designed to meet the low-income housing needs of returning war vets, many of whom, like my Aunt Evie and Uncle Julie, were living in quonset huts. By May 1947, Levitt and Sons had acquired enough land in Hempstead Township on Long Island to build four thousand houses, and by the next February, he'd built six thousand units and named the development after himself. After 1948, federal financing for the construction of rental housing tightened, and Levitt switched to building houses for sale. By 1951 Levittown was a devel-opment of some fifteen thousand families. . . .

At the beginning of World War II, about 33 percent of all U.S. families owned their houses. That percentage doubled in twenty years. Most Levittowners looked just like my family. They came from New York City or Long Island; about 17 percent were military, from nearby Mitchell Field; Levittown was their first house; and almost everyone was married. The 1947 inhabitants were over 75 percent white collar, but by 1950 more blue-collar families moved in, so that by 1951, "barely half" of the new residents were white collar, and by 1960 their occupational profile was somewhat more working class than for Nassau County as a whole. By this time too, almost one-third of Levittown's people were either foreign-born or, like my parents, first-generation U.S. born (Dobriner 1963:91, 100).

The FHA was key to buyers and builders alike. Thanks to it, suburbia was open to more than GIs. People like us would never have been in the market for houses without FHA and VA low-down-payment, low-interest, long-term loans to young buyers.[11] . . .

The FHA believed in racial segregation. Throughout its history, it publicly and actively promoted restrictive covenants. Before the war, these forbade sale to Jews and Catholics as well as to African Americans. The deed to my house in Detroit had such a covenant, which theoreti-cally prevented it from being sold to Jews or African Americans. Even after the Supreme Court ended legal enforcement of restrictive covenants in 1948, the FHA continued to encourage builders to write them against African Americans. FHA underwriting manuals openly insisted on racially homogeneous neigh-borhoods, and their loans were made only in white neighborhoods. I bought my Detroit house in 1972 from Jews who were leaving a largely African-American neighborhood. By that time, after the 1968 Fair Housing Act, restrictive covenants were a dead letter (although blockbusting by realtors was rapidly replacing it).

With the federal government behind them, virtually all developers refused to sell to African Americans. Palo Alto and Levittown, like most suburbs as late as 1960, were virtually all white. Out of 15,741 houses and 65,276 people, averaging 4.2 people per house, only 220 Levittowners, or 52 households, were "non-white." In 1958 Levitt announced publicly at a press conference to open his New Jersey devel-opment that he would not sell to black buyers. This caused a furor, since the state of New Jersey (but not the U.S. government) prohibited discrimination in federally subsidized housing. Levitt was sued and fought it, although he was ultimately persuaded by township ministers to integrate. . . .

The result of these policies was that African Americans were totally shut out of the suburban boom. An article in *Harper's* described the housing available to black GIs. "On his way to the base each morning, Sergeant Smith passes an attractive air-conditioned, FHA-financed housing project. It was built for service families. Its rents are little more than the Smiths pay for their shack. And there are half-a-dozen vacan-cies, but none for Negroes" (qtd. in Foner 1974:195).

Where my family felt the seductive pull of suburbia, Marshall Berman's experienced the brutal push of urban renewal. In the Bronx in the 1950s, Robert Moses's Cross-Bronx Expressway erased "a dozen solid, settled, densely populated neighborhoods like our own; ... something like 60,000 working- and lower-middle-class people, mostly Jews, but with many Italians, Irish and Blacks thrown in, would be thrown out of their homes. ... For ten years, through the late 1950s and early 1960s, the center of the Bronx was pounded and blasted and smashed" (1982:292).

Urban renewal made postwar cities into bad places to live. At a physical level, urban renewal reshaped them, and federal programs brought private developers and public officials together to create downtown central business districts where there had formerly been a mix of manufacturing, commerce, and working-class neighborhoods. Manufacturing was scattered to the peripheries of the city, which were ringed and bisected by a national system of highways. Some working-class neighborhoods were bulldozed, but others remained (Greer 1965; Hartman 1975; Squires 1989). In Los Angeles as in New York's Bronx, the postwar period saw massive freeway construction right through the heart of old working-class neighborhoods. In East Los Angeles and Santa Monica, Chicano and African-American communities were divided in half or blasted to smithereens by the highways bringing Angelenos to the new white suburbs, or to make way for civic monuments like Dodger Stadium (Pardo 1990; Social and Public Arts Resource Center 1990:80, 1983:12–13).

Urban renewal was the other side of the process by which Jewish and other working-class Euroimmigrants became middle class. It was the push to suburbia's seductive pull. The fortunate white survivors of urban renewal headed disproportionately for suburbia, where they could partake of prosperity and the good life. ...

If the federal stick of urban renewal joined the FHA carrot of cheap mortgages to send masses of Euros to the suburbs, the FHA had a different kind of one-two punch for African Americans. Segregation kept them out the suburbs, and redlining made sure they could not buy or repair their homes in the neighborhoods where they were allowed to live. The FHA practiced systematic redlining. This was a system developed by its predecessor, the Home Owners Loan Corporation (HOLC), which in the 1930s

developed an elaborate neighborhood rating system that placed the highest (green) value on all-white, middle-class neighborhoods, and the lowest (red) on racially nonwhite or mixed and working-class neighborhoods. High ratings meant high property values. The idea was that low property values in redlined neighborhoods made them bad investments. The FHA was, after all, created by and for banks and the housing industry. Redlining warned banks not to lend there, and the FHA would not insure mortgages in such neighborhoods. Redlining created a self-fulfilling prophecy. "With the assistance of local realtors and banks, it assigned one of the four ratings to every block in every city. The resulting information was then translated into the appropriate color [green, blue, yellow, and red] and duly recorded on secret 'Residential Security Maps' in local HOLC offices. The maps themselves were placed in elaborate 'City Survey Files,' which consisted of reports, questionnaires, and workpapers relating to current and future values of real estate" (Jackson 1985:197).[12]

FHA's and VA's refusal to guarantee loans in redlined neighborhoods made it virtually impossible for African Americans to borrow money for home improvement or purchase. Because these maps and surveys were quite secret, it took the 1960s Civil Rights movement to make these practices and their devastating consequences public. As a result, those who fought urban renewal or who sought to make a home in the urban ruins found themselves locked out of the middle class. They also faced an ideological assault that labeled their neighborhoods slums and called those who lived in them slum dwellers (Gans 1962).

The record is very clear that instead of seizing the opportunity to end institutionalized racism, the federal government did its best to shut and double seal the post-war window of opportunity in African Americans' faces. It consistently refused to combat segregation in the social institutions that were key for upward mobility: education, housing, and employment. Moreover, federal programs that were themselves designed to assist demobilized GIs and young families systematically discriminated against African Americans. Such programs reinforced white/nonwhite racial distinctions even as intrawhite racialization was falling out of fashion. This other side of the coin, that white men of northwestern or southeastern European ancestry were treated equally in theory and in practice with regard to the benefits they received, was part of the larger postwar whitening of Jews and other eastern and southern Europeans.

The myth that Jews pulled themselves up by their own bootstraps ignores the fact that it took federal programs to create the conditions whereby the abilities of Jews and other European immigrants could be recognized and rewarded rather than denigrated and denied. The GI Bill and FHA and VA mortgages were forms of affirmative action that allowed male Jews and other Euro-American men to become suburban homeowners and to get the training that allowed them—but not women vets or war workers—to become professionals, technicians, salesmen, and managers in a growing economy. Jews' and other white ethnics' upward mobility was the result of programs that allowed us to float on a rising economic tide. To African Americans, the government offered the cement boots of segregation, redlining, urban renewal, and discrimination.

Those racially skewed gains have been passed across the generations, so that racial inequality seems to maintain itself "naturally," even after legal segregation ended. Today, in a shrinking economy where downward mobility is the norm, the children and grandchildren of the postwar beneficiaries of the economic boom have some precious advantages. For example, having parents who own their own homes or who have decent retirement benefits can make a real difference in young people's ability to take on huge college loans or to come up with a down payment for a house. Even this simple inheritance helps perpetuate the gap between whites and nonwhites. Sure Jews needed ability, but ability was not enough to make it. The same applies even more in today's long recession.

NOTES

This is a revised and expanded version of a paper published in *Jewish Currents* in June 1992 and delivered at the 1992 meetings of the American Anthropological Association in the session *Blacks and Jews, 1992: Reaching across the Cultural Boundaries* organized by Angela Gilliam. I would like to thank Emily Abel, Katya Gibel Azoulay, Edna Bonacich, Angela Gilliam, Isabelle Gunning, Valerie Matsumoto, Regina Morantz-Sanchez, Roger Sanjek, Rabbi Chaim Seidler-Feller, Janet Silverstein, and Eloise Klein Healy's writing group for uncovering wonderful sources and for critical readings along the way.

1. Indeed, Boasian and Du Boisian anthropology developed in active political opposition to this nativism; on Du Bois, see Harrison and Nonini 1992.

2. On immigrants as part of the industrial work force, see Steinberg 1989:36.

3. I thank Roger Sanjek for providing me with this source.

4. It was intended, as Davenport wrote to the president of the American Museum of Natural History, Henry Fairfield Osborne, as "an anthropological society . . . with a central governing body, self-elected and self-perpetuating, and very limited in members, and also confined to native Americans who are anthropologically, socially and politically sound, no Bolsheviki need apply" (Barkan 1991:67–68).

4. I thank Valerie Matsumoto for telling me about the Third case and Katya Gibel Azoulay for providing this information to me on the Virginia statute.

6. "The distinction between white and colored" has been "the only racial classification which has been carried through all the 15 censuses." "Colored" consisted of "Negroes" and "other races": Mexican, Indian, Chinese, Japanese, Filipino, Hindu, Korean, Hawaiian, Malay, Siamese, and Samoan. (U.S. Bureau of the Census, 1930:25, 26).

7. For why Jews entered colleges earlier than other immigrants, and for a challenge to views that attribute it to Jewish culture, see Steinberg 1989.

8. Indeed, Jewish social scientists were prominent in creating this ideology of the United States as a meritocracy. Most prominent of course was Nathan Glazer, but among them also were Charles Silberman and Marshall Sklare.

9. The belief was widespread that "the GI Bill . . . helped millions of families move into the middle class" (Nash et al. 1986:885). A study that compares mobility among veterans and nonveterans

provides a kind of confirmation. In an unnamed small city in Illinois, Havighurst and his colleagues (1951) found no significant difference between veterans and nonveterans, but this was because apparently very few veterans used any of their GI benefits.

10. African Americans and Japanese Americans were the main target of wartime racism (see Murray 1992). By contrast, there were virtually no anti-German American or anti-Italian American policies in World War II (see Takaki 1989:357–406).

11. See Eichler 1982:5 for homeowning percentages; Jackson (1985:205) found an increase in families living in owner-occupied buildings, rising from 44 percent in 1934 to 63 percent in 1972; see Monkkonen 1988 on scarcity of mortgages; and Gelfand 1975, esp. chap. 6, on federal programs.

12. These ideas from the real estate industry were "codified and legitimated in 1930s work by University of Chicago sociologist Robert Park and real estate professor Homer Hoyt" (Jackson 1985:198–199).

REFERENCES

Binkin, Martin, and Mark J. Eitelberg. 1982. *Blacks and the Military.* Washington, D.C.: Brookings.

Bodnar, John. 1985. *The Transplanted: A History of Immigrants in Urban America.* Bloomington: Indiana University Press.

Brody, David. 1980. *Workers in Industrial America: Essays of the Twentieth Century Struggle.* New York: Oxford University Press.

Brown, Francis J. 1946. *Educational Opportunities for Veterans.* Washington, D.C.: Public Affairs Press, American Council on Public Affairs.

Carlson, Lewis H., and George A. Colburn. 1972. *In Their Place: White America Defines Her Minorities, 1850–1950.* New York: Wiley.

Dalfiume, Richard M. 1969. *Desegregation of the U.S. Armed Forces: Fighting on Two Fronts, 1939–1953.* Columbia: University of Missouri Press.

Davis, Mike. 1990. *City of Quartz.* London: Verso.

Dobriner, William M. 1963. *Class in Suburbia.* Englewood Cliffs, N.J.: Prentice-Hall.

Eichler, Ned. 1982. *The Merchant Builders.* Cambridge, Mass.: MIT Press.

Fields, Barbara Jeanne. 1990. Slavery, Race, and Ideology in the United States of America. *New Left Review* 181:95–118.

Foner, Jack. 1974. *Blacks and the Military in American History: A New Perspective.* New York: Praeger.

Gans, Herbert. 1962. *The Urban Villagers.* New York: Free Press.

———. 1967. *The Levittowners.* New York: Pantheon.

Gordon, Milton. 1964. *Assimilation in American Life.* New York: Oxford University Press.

Hartman, Chester. 1975. *Housing and Social Policy.* Englewood Cliffs, N.J.: Prentice-Hall.

Higham, John. 1955. *Strangers in the Land.* New Brunswick, N.J.: Rutgers University Press.

Hurd, Charles. 1946. *The Veterans' Program: A Complete Guide to Its Benefits, Rights, and Options.* New York: McGraw-Hill.

Jackson, Kenneth T. 1985. *Crabgrass Frontier: The Suburbanization of the United States.* New York: Oxford University Press.

Johnson, Jesse J. 1967. *Ebony Brass: An Autobiography of Negro Frustration amid Aspiration.* New York: Frederick.

Karabel, Jerome. 1984. Status-Group Struggle, Organizational Interests, and the Limits of Institutional Autonomy. *Theory and Society* 13:1–40.

Kessler-Harris, Alice. 1982. *Out to Work: A History of Wage-Earning Women in the United States.* New York: Oxford University Press.

Martyn, Byron Curti. 1979. Racism in the U.S.: A History of Anti-Miscegenation Legislation and Litigation. .Ph.D. diss., University of Southern California.

Mosch, Theodore R. 1975. *The GI Bill: A Breakthrough in Educational and Social Policy in the United States.* Hicksville, N.Y.: Exposition.

Nalty, Bernard C., and Morris J. MacGregor, eds. 1981. *Blacks in the Military: Essential Documents.* Wilmington, Del.: Scholarly Resources.

Nash, Gary B., Julie Roy Jeffrey, John R. Howe, Allen F. Davis, Peter J. Frederick, and Allen M. Winkler. 1986. *The American People: Creating a Nation and a Society.* New York: Harper and Row.

Pardo, Mary. 1990. Mexican-American Women Grassroots Community Activists: "Mothers of East Los Angeles." *Frontiers* 11: 1–7.

Postwar Jobs for Veterans. 1945. *Annals of the American Academy of Political and Social Science* 238 (March).

Saxton, Alexander. 1971. *The Indispensable Enemy.* Berkeley and Los Angeles: University of California Press.

Saxton, Alexander. 1990. *The Rise and Fall of the White Republic*. London: Verso.

Silberman, Charles. 1985. A *Certain People: American Jews and Their Lives Today*. New York: Summit.

Sklare, Marshall. 1971. *America's Jews*. New York: Random House.

Sowell, Thomas. 1981. *Ethnic America: A History*. New York: Basic.

Steinberg, Stephen. 1989. *The Ethnic Myth: Race, Ethnicity, and Class in America*. 2nd ed. Boston: Beacon.

Synott, Marcia Graham. 1986. Anti-Semitism and American Universities: Did Quotas Follow the Jews? In *Anti-Semitism in American History*, ed. David A. Gerber. Urbana: University of Illinois Press, 233–274.

Takaki, Ronald. 1989. *Strangers from a Different Shore*. Boston: Little, Brown.

Tobin, Gary A., ed. 1987. *Divided Neighborhoods: Changing Patterns of Racial Segregation*. Beverly Hills: Sage.

U.S. Bureau of the Census. 1930. *Fifteenth Census of the United* States. Vol. 2. Washington, D.C.: U.S Government Printing Office.

———. 1940. *Sixteenth Census of the United States*. Vol. 2. Washington, D.C.: U.S. Government Printing Office.

Walker, Olive. 1970. The Windsor Hills School Story. *Integrated Education: Race and Schools* 8(3): 4–9.

Willenz, June A. 1983. *Women Veterans: America's Forgotten Heroines*. New York: Continuum.

Wynn, Neil A. 1976. *The Afro-American and the Second World War*. London: Elek.

DISCUSSION QUESTIONS

1. How was it that in just a few decades, Jews in America went from being excluded from the full privileges of whiteness to being included? How do ethnicity and class combine to define who is "white" in the United States? What role does the government play in solidifying this definition?

2. Why weren't women and blacks able to take full advantage of their GI benefits, when they too had served their country in war? What were the processes by which blacks were excluded from post–World War II suburbanization? Why don't we learn about these more recent acts of black exclusion in our history lessons?

3. How are these exclusions of blacks from economic opportunities related to how Jews became white? What is meant by the author's calling these opportunities an "affirmative action" program for white males? How does this information affect what we take into account when comparing the experiences of white immigrant and other immigrant groups?

WHITE PRIVILEGE AND MALE PRIVILEGE: A PERSONAL ACCOUNT OF COMING TO SEE CORRESPONDENCES THROUGH WORK IN WOMEN'S STUDIES (1988)

Peggy McIntosh

Through work to bring materials and perspectives from Women Studies to the rest of the curriculum, I have often noticed men's unwillingness to grant that they are overprivileged in the curriculum, even though they may grant that women are disadvantaged. Denials that amount to taboos surround the subject of advantages that men gain from women's disadvantages. These denials protect male privilege from being fully recognized, acknowledged, lessened, or ended.

Thinking through unacknowledged male privilege as a phenomenon with a life of its own, I realized that since hierarchies in our society are interlocking, there was most likely a phenomenon of white privilege that was similarly denied and protected, but alive and real in its effects. As a white person, I realized I had been taught about racism as something that puts others at a disadvantage, but had been taught not to see one of its corollary aspects, white privilege, which puts me at an advantage.

I think whites are carefully taught not to recognize white privilege, as males are taught not to recognize male privilege. So I have begun in an untutored way to ask what it is like to have white privilege. This paper is a partial record of my personal observations and not a scholarly analysis. It is based on my daily experiences within my particular circumstances.

I have come to see white privilege as an invisible package of unearned assets that I can count on cashing in each day, but about which I was "meant' to remain oblivious. White privilege is like an invisible weightless knapsack of special provisions, assurances, tools, maps, guides, codebooks, passports, visas, clothes, compass, emergency gear, and blank checks.

Since I have had trouble facing white privilege, and describing its results in my life, I saw parallels here with men's reluctance to acknowledge male privilege. Only rarely will a man go beyond acknowledging that women are disadvantaged to acknowledging that men have unearned advantage, or that unearned privilege has not been good for men's development as human beings, or for society's development, or that privilege systems might ever be challenged and *changed.*

I will review here several types or layers of denial that I see at work protecting, and preventing awareness about, entrenched male privilege. Then I will draw parallels, from my own experience, with the denials that veil the facts of white privilege. Finally, I will list forty-six ordinary and daily ways in which I experience having white privilege, by contrast with my African American colleagues in the same building. This list is not intended to be generalizable. Others can make their own lists from within their own life circumstances.

Writing this paper has been difficult, despite warm receptions for the talks on which it is based.[1] For describing white privilege makes one newly accountable. As we in Women's Studies work reveal male privilege and ask men to give up some of their power, so one who writes about having white privilege must ask, "Having described it, what will I do to lessen or end it?"

The denial of men's overprivileged state takes many forms in discussions of curriculum change work. Some claim that men must be central in the curriculum because they have done most of what is important or distinctive in life or in civilization. Some recognize sexism in the curriculum but deny that it makes male students seem unduly important in life. Others agree that certain *individual* thinkers are male oriented but deny that there is any *systemic* tendency in disciplinary frameworks or epistemology to overempower men as a group. Those men who do grant that male privilege takes institutionalized and embedded forms are still likely to deny that male hegemony has opened doors for them personally. Virtually all men deny that male overreward alone can explain men's centrality in all the inner sanctums of our most powerful institutions. Moreover, those few who will acknowledge that male privilege systems have overempowered them usually end up doubting that we could dismantle these privilege systems. They may say they will work to improve women's status, in the society or in the university, but they can't or won't support the idea of lessening men's. In curricular terms, this is the point at which they say that they regret they cannot use any of the interesting new scholarship on women because the syllabus is full. When the talk turns to giving men less cultural room, even the most thoughtful and fair-minded of the men I know will tend to reflect, or fall back on, conservative assumptions about the inevitability of present gender relations and distributions of power, calling on precedent or sociobiology and psychobiology to demonstrate that male domination is natural and follows inevitably from evolutionary pressures. Others resort to arguments from "experience" or religion or social responsibility or wishing and dreaming.

After I realized, through faculty development work in Women's Studies, the extent to which men work from a base of unacknowledged privilege, I understood that much of their oppressiveness was unconscious. Then I remembered the frequent charges from women of color that white women whom they encounter are oppressive. I began to understand why we are justly seen as oppressive, even when we don't see ourselves that way. At the very least, obliviousness of one's privileged state can make a person or group irritating to be with. I began to count the ways in which I enjoy unearned skin privilege and have been conditioned into oblivion about its existence, unable to see that it put me "ahead" in any way, or put my people ahead, overrewarding us and yet also paradoxically damaging us, or that it could or should be changed.

My schooling gave me no training in seeing myself as an oppressor, as an unfairly advantaged person, or as a participant in a damaged culture. I was taught to see myself as an individual whose moral state depended on her individual moral will. At school, we were not taught about slavery in any depth; we were not taught to see slaveholders as damaged people. Slaves were seen as the only group at risk of being dehumanized. My schooling followed the pattern which Elizabeth Minnich has pointed out: whites are taught to think of their lives as morally neutral, normative, and average, and also ideal, so that when we work to benefit others, this is seen as work that will allow "them" to be more like "us." I think many of us know how obnoxious this attitude can be in men.

After frustration with men who would not recognize male privilege, I decided to try to work on myself at least by identifying some of the daily effects of white privilege in my life. It is crude work, at this stage, but I will give here a list of special circumstances and conditions I experience that I did not earn but that I have been made to feel are mine by birth, by citizenship, and by virtue of being a conscientious law-abiding "normal" person of goodwill. I have chosen those conditions that I think in my case *attach somewhat more to skin-color privilege* than to class, religion, ethnic status, or geographical location, though these other privileging factors are intricately intertwined. As far as I can see, my Afro-American co-workers, friends, and acquaintances with whom I come into daily or frequent contact in this particular time, place, and line of work cannot count on most of these conditions.

1. I can, if I wish, arrange to be in the company of people of my race most of the time.

2. I can avoid spending time with people whom I was trained to mistrust and who have learned to mistrust my kind or me.

3. If I should need to move, I can be pretty sure of renting or purchasing housing in an area which I can afford and in which I would want to live.

4. I can be reasonably sure that my neighbors in such a location will be neutral or pleasant to me.

5. I can go shopping alone most of the time, fairly well assured that I will not be followed or harassed by store detectives.

6. I can turn on the television or open to the front page of the paper and see people of my race widely and positively represented.

7. When I am told about our national heritage or about "civilization," I am shown that people of my color made it what it is.

8. I can be sure that my children will be given curricular materials that testify to the existence of their race.

9. If I want to, I can be pretty sure of finding a publisher for this piece on white privilege.

10. I can be fairly sure of having my voice heard in a group in which I am the only member of my race.

11. I can be casual about whether or not to listen to another woman's voice in a group in which she is the only member of her race.

12. I can go into a book shop and count on finding the writing of my race represented, into a supermarket and find the staple foods that fit with my cultural traditions, into a hairdresser's shop and find someone who can deal with my hair.

13. Whether I use checks, credit cards, or cash, I can count on my skin color not to work against the appearance that I am financially reliable.

14. I could arrange to protect our young children most of the time from people who might not like them.

15. I did not have to educate our children to be aware of systemic racism for their own daily physical protection.

16. I can be pretty sure that my children's teachers and employers will tolerate them if they fit school and workplace norms; my chief worries about them do not concern others' attitudes toward their race.

17. I can talk with my mouth full and not have people put this down to my color.

18. I can swear, or dress in secondhand clothes, or not answer letters, without having people attribute these choices to the bad morals, the poverty, or the illiteracy of my race.

19. I can speak in public to a powerful male group without putting my race on trial.

20. I can do well in a challenging situation without being called a credit to my race.

21. I am never asked to speak for all the people of my racial group.

22. I can remain oblivious to the language and customs of persons of color who constitute the world's majority without feeling in my culture any penalty for such oblivion.

23. I can criticize our government and talk about how much I fear its policies and behavior without being seen as a cultural outsider.

24. I can be reasonably sure that if I ask to talk to "the person in charge," I will be facing a person of my race.

25. If a traffic cop pulls me over or if the IRS audits my tax return, I can be sure I haven't been singled out because of my race.

26. I can easily buy posters, postcards, picture books, greeting cards, dolls, toys, and children's magazines featuring people of my race.

27. I can go home from most meetings of organizations I belong to feeling somewhat tied in, rather than isolated, out of place, outnumbered, unheard, held at a distance, or feared.

28. I can be pretty sure that an argument with a colleague of another race is more likely to jeopardize her chances for advancement than to jeopardize mine.

29. I can be fairly sure that if I argue for the promotion of a person of another race, or a program centering on race, this is not likely to cost me heavily within my present setting, even if my colleagues disagree with me.

30. If I declare there is a racial issue at hand, or there isn't a racial issue at hand, my race will lend me more credibility for either position than a person of color will have.

31. I can choose to ignore developments in minority writing and minority activist programs, or disparage them, or learn from them, but in any case, I can find ways to be more or less protected from negative consequences of any of these choices.

32. My culture gives me little fear about ignoring the perspectives and powers of people of other races.

33. I am not made acutely aware that my shape, bearing, or body odor will be taken as a reflection on my race.

34. I can worry about racism without being seen as self-interested or self-seeking.

35. I can take a job with an affirmative action employer without having co-workers on the job suspect that I got it because of my race.

36. If my day, week, or year is going badly, I need not ask of each negative episode or situation whether it has racial overtones.

37. I can be pretty sure of finding people who would be willing to talk to with me and advise me about my next steps, professionally.

38. I can think over many options, social, political, imaginative, or professional, without asking whether a person of my race would be accepted or allowed to do what I want to do.

39. I can be late to a meeting without having the lateness reflect on my race.

40. I can choose public accommodation without fearing that people of my race cannot get in or will be mistreated in the places I have chosen.

41. I can be sure that if I need legal or medical help, my race will not work against me.

42. I can arrange my activities so that I will never have to experience feelings of rejection owing to my race.

43. If I have low credibility as a leader, I can be sure that my race is not the problem.

44. I can easily find academic courses and institutions that give attention only to people of my race.

45. I can expect figurative language and imagery in all of the arts to testify to experiences of my race.

46. I can choose blemish cover or bandages in "flesh" color and have them more or less match my skin.

I repeatedly forgot each of the realizations on this list until I wrote it down. For me, white privilege has turned out to be an elusive and fugitive subject. The pressure to avoid it is great, for in facing it I must give up the myth of meritocracy. If these things are true, this is not such a free country, one's life is not what one makes it; many doors open for certain people through no virtues of their own. These perceptions mean also that my moral condition is not what I had been led to believe. The appearance of being a good citizen rather than a troublemaker comes in large part from having all sorts of doors open automatically because of my color.

A further paralysis of nerve comes from literary silence protecting privilege. My clearest memories of finding such analysis are in Lillian Smith's unparalleled *Killers of the Dream* and Margaret Andersen's review of Karen and Mamie Fields' *Lemon Swamp.* Smith, for example, wrote about walking toward black children on the street and knowing they would step into the gutter. Andersen contrasted the pleasure that she, as a white child, took on summer driving trips to the south with Karen Fields' memories of driving in a closed car stocked with all necessities lest, in stopping, her black family should suffer "insult, or worse." Adrienne Rich also recognizes and writes about daily experiences of privilege, but in my observation, white women's writing in this area is far more often on systemic racism than on our daily lives as light-skinned women.[2]

In unpacking this invisible knapsack of white privilege, I have listed conditions of daily experience that I once took for granted, as neutral, normal, and universally available to everybody, just as I once thought of a male-focused curriculum as the neutral or accurate account that can speak for all. Nor did I think of any of these perquisites as bad for the holder. I now think that we need a more finely differentiated taxonomy of privilege, for some of these varieties are only what one would want for everyone in a just society, and others give license to be ignorant, oblivious, arrogant, and destructive. Before proposing some more finely tuned categorization, I will make some observations about the general effects of these conditions on my life and expectations.

In this potpourri of examples, some privileges make me feel at home in the world. Others allow me to escape penalties or dangers that others suffer. Through some, I escape fear, anxiety, insult, injury, or a sense of not being welcome, not being real. Some keep me from having to hide, to be in disguise, to feel sick or crazy, to negotiate each transaction from the position of being an outsider or, within my group, a person who is suspected of having too close links with a dominant culture. Most keep me from having to be angry.

I see a pattern running through the matrix of white privilege, a pattern of assumptions that were passed on to me as a white person. There was one main piece of cultural turf; it was my own turf, and I was among those who could control the turf. I could measure up to the cultural standards and take advantage of the many options I saw around me to make what the culture would call a success of my life. *My skin color was an asset for any move I was educated to want to make.* I could think of myself as "belonging" in major ways and of making social systems work for me. I could freely disparage, fear, neglect, or be oblivious to anything outside of the dominant cultural forms. Being of the main culture, I could also criticize it fairly freely. My life was reflected back to me frequently enough so that I felt, with regard to my race, if not to my sex, like one of the real people.

Whether through the curriculum or in the newspaper, the television, the economic system, or the general look of people in the streets, I received daily signals and indications that my people counted and that others *either didn't exist or must be trying, not very successfully, to be like people of my race.* I was given cultural permission not to hear voices of people of other races or a tepid cultural tolerance for hearing or acting on such voices. I was also raised not to suffer seriously from anything that darker-skinned people might say about my group, "protected," though perhaps I should more accurately say *prohibited,* through the habits of my economic class and social group, from living in racially mixed groups or being reflective about interactions between people of differing races.

In proportion as my racial group was being made confident, comfortable, and oblivious, other groups were likely being made unconfident, uncomfortable, and alienated. Whiteness protected me from many kinds of hostility, distress, and violence, which I was being subtly trained to visit in turn upon people of color.

For this reason, the word "privilege" now seems to me misleading. Its connotations are too positive to fit the conditions and behaviors which "privilege systems" produce. We usually think of privilege as being a favored state, whether earned, or conferred by birth or luck. School graduates are reminded they are privileged and urged to use their (enviable) assets well. The word "privilege" carries the connotation of being something everyone must want. Yet some of the conditions I have described here work to systemically overempower certain groups. Such privilege simply *confers dominance,* gives permission to control, because of one's race or sex. The kind of privilege that gives license to some people to be, at best, thoughtless and, at worst, murderous should not continue to be referred to as a desirable attribute. Such "privilege" may be widely desired without being in any way beneficial to the whole society.

Moreover, though "privilege" may confer power, it does not confer moral strength. Those who do not depend on conferred dominance have traits and qualities that may never develop in those who do. Just as Women's Studies courses indicate that women survive their political circumstances to lead lives that hold the human race together, so "underprivileged" people of color who are the world's majority have survived their oppression and lived survivors' lives from which the white global minority can and must learn. In some groups, those dominated have actually become strong through *not* having all of these unearned advantages, and

this gives them a great deal to teach the others. Members of so-called privileged groups can seem foolish, ridiculous, infantile, or dangerous by contrast.

I want, then, to distinguish between earned strength and unearned power conferred systemically. Power from unearned privilege can look like strength when it is, in fact, permission to escape or to dominate. But not all of the privileges on my list are inevitably damaging. Some, like the expectation that neighbors will be decent to you, or that your race will not count against you in court, should be the norm in a just society and should be considered as the entitlement of everyone. Others, like the privilege not to listen to less powerful people, distort the humanity of the holders as well as the ignored groups. Still others, like finding one's staple foods everywhere, may be a function of being a member of a numerical majority in the population. Others have to do with not having to labor under pervasive negative stereotyping and mythology.

We might at least start by distinguishing between positive advantages that we can work to spread, to the point where they are not advantages at all but simply part of the normal civic and social fabric, and negative types of advantage that unless rejected will always reinforce our present hierarchies. For example, the positive "privilege" of belonging, the feeling that one belongs within the human circle, as Native Americans say, fosters development and should not be seen as privilege for a few. It is, let us say, an entitlement that none of us should have to earn; ideally it is an *unearned entitlement.* At present, since only a few have it, it is an *unearned advantage* for them. The negative "privilege" that gave me cultural permission not to take darker-skinned Others seriously can be seen as arbitrarily conferred dominance and should not be desirable for anyone. This paper results from a process of coming to see that some of the power that I originally saw as attendant on being a human being in the United States consisted in *unearned advantage* and *conferred dominance,* as well as other kinds of special circumstance not universally taken for granted.

In writing this paper I have also realized that white identity and status (as well as class identity and status) give me considerable power to choose whether to broach this subject and its trouble. I can pretty well decide whether to disappear and avoid and not listen and escape the dislike I may engender in other people through this essay, or interrupt, answer, interpret, preach, correct, criticize, and control to some extent what goes on in reaction to it. Being white, I am given considerable power to escape many kinds of danger or penalty as well as to choose which risks I want to take.

There is an analogy here, once again, with Women's Studies. Our male colleagues do not have a great deal to lose in supporting Women's Studies, but they do not have a great deal to lose if they oppose it either. They simply have the power to decide whether to commit themselves to more equitable distributions of power. They will probably feel few penalties whatever choice they make; they do not seem, in any obvious short-term sense, the ones at risk, though they and we are all at risk because of the behaviors that have been rewarded in them.

Through Women's Studies work I have met very few men who are truly distressed about systemic, unearned male advantage and conferred dominance. And so one question for me and others like me is whether we will be like them, or whether we will get truly distressed, even outraged, about unearned race advantage and conferred dominance and if so, what we will do to lessen them. In any case, we need to do more work in identifying how they actually affect our daily lives. We need more down-to-earth writing by people about these taboo subjects. We need more understanding of the ways in which white "privilege" damages white people, for these are not the same ways in which it damages the victimized. Skewed white psyches are an inseparable part of the picture, though I do not want to confuse the kinds of damage done to the holders of special assets and to those who suffer the deficits. Many, perhaps most, of our white students in the United States think that racism doesn't affect them because they are not people of color; they do not see "whiteness" as a racial identity. Many men likewise think that Women's Studies does not bear on their own existences because they are not female; they do not see themselves as having gendered identities. Insisting on the universal "effects" of "privilege" systems, then, becomes one of our chief tasks, and being more explicit about the

particular effects in particular contexts is another. Men need to join us in this work.

. . .

One factor seems clear about all of the interlocking oppressions. They take both active forms that we can see and embedded forms that members of the dominant group are taught not to see. In my class and place, I did not see myself as racist because I was taught to recognize racism only in individual acts of meanness by members of my group, never in invisible systems conferring racial dominance on my group from birth. Likewise, we are taught to think that sexism . . . is carried on only through intentional, individual acts of discrimination, meanness, or cruelty, rather than in invisible systems conferring unsought dominance on certain groups. Disapproving of the systems won't be enough to change them. I was taught to think that racism could end if white individuals changed their attitudes; many men think sexism can be ended by individual changes in daily behavior toward women. But a man's sex provides advantage for him whether or not he approves of the way in which dominance has been conferred on his group. A "white" skin in the United States opens many doors for whites whether or not we approve of the way dominance has been conferred on us. Individual acts can palliate, but cannot end, these problems. To redesign social systems, we need first to acknowledge their colossal unseen dimensions. The silences and denials surrounding privilege are the key political tool here. They keep the thinking about equality or equity incomplete, protecting unearned advantage and conferred dominance by making these taboo subjects. Most talk by whites about equal opportunity seems to me now to be about equal opportunity to try to get into a position of dominance while denying that *systems* of dominance exist.

Obliviousness about white advantage, like obliviousness about male advantage, is kept strongly inculturated in the United States so as to maintain the myth of meritocracy, the myth that democratic choice is equally available to all. Keeping most people unaware that freedom of confident action is there for just a small number of people props up those in power and serves to keep power in the hands of the same groups that have most of it already. Though systemic change takes many decades, there are pressing questions for me and I imagine for some others like me if we raise our daily consciousness on the perquisites of being light-skinned. What will we do with such knowledge? As we know from watching men, it is an open question whether we will choose to use unearned advantage to weaken invisible privilege systems and whether we will use any of our arbitrarily awarded power to try to reconstruct power systems on a broader base.

NOTES

1. This paper was presented at the Virginia Women's Studies Association conference in Richmond in April, 1986, and the American Educational Research Association conference in Boston in October, 1986, and discussed with two groups of participants in the Dodge seminars for Secondary School Teachers in New York and Boston in the spring of 1987.

2. Andersen, Margaret, "Race and the Social Science Curriculum: A Teaching and Learning Discussion." *Radical Teacher,* November, 1984, pp. 17–20. Smith, Lillian, *Killers of the Dream,* New York: W. W. Norton, 1949.

DISCUSSION QUESTIONS

1. Why do we tend to conceptualize racism and sexism as systems of disadvantage rather than as systems of advantage? Who stands to gain, and how, by this ideological framework? When you signed up to take a course in race and ethnicity, did you ever think that one of the groups you would learn about would be whites? Why or why not?

2. Examining McIntosh's list of 46 privileges, how many had you considered before? How many had you not considered before? Do any stand out to you in particular? Can you add more? Can you construct a similar list for male privileges?

3. What are the options the author suggests that someone can do once she or he recognizes the unearned privilege she or he receives? If people work to end negative privileges and make positive privilege exist for all, will this be enough to end inequality? Can inequality be ended through policies aimed at rectifying disadvantage, but not advantage? Why or why not?

"IS THIS A WHITE COUNTRY, OR WHAT?"

Lillian B. Rubin

"They're letting all these coloreds come in and soon there won't be any place left for white people," broods Tim Walsh, a 33-year-old white construction worker. "It makes you wonder. Is this a white country, or what?"

It's a question that nags at white America, one perhaps that's articulated most often and most clearly by the men and women of the working class. For it's they who feel most vulnerable, who have suffered the economic contractions of recent decades most keenly, who see the new immigrants most clearly as direct competitors for their jobs.

It's not whites alone who stew about immigrants. Native-born blacks, too, fear the newcomers nearly as much as whites—and for the same economic reasons. But for whites the issue is compounded by race, by the fact that the newcomers are primarily people of color. For them, therefore, their economic anxieties have combined with the changing face of America to create a profound uneasiness about immigration—a theme that was sounded by nearly 90 percent of the whites I met, even by those who are themselves first-generation, albeit well-assimilated, immigrants.

Sometimes they spoke about this in response to my questions; equally often the subject of immigration arose spontaneously as people gave voice to their concerns. But because the new immigrants are predominantly people of color, the discourse was almost always cast in terms of race as well as immigration, with the talk slipping from immigration to race and back again as if these are not two separate phenomena. "If we keep letting all them foreigners in, pretty soon there'll be more of them than us and then what will this country be like?" Tim's wife, Mary Anne, frets. "I mean, this is *our* country, but the way things are going, white people will be the minority in our own country. Now does that make any sense?"

Such fears are not new. Americans have always worried about the strangers who came to our shores, fearing that they would corrupt our society, dilute our culture, debase our values. So I remind Mary Anne, "When your ancestors came here, people also thought we were allowing too many foreigners into the country. Yet those earlier immigrants were successfully integrated into the American society. What's different now?"

"Oh, it's different, all right," she replies without hesitation. "When my people came, the immigrants were all white. That makes a big difference."

"Why do you think that's so?"

"I don't know; it just is, that's all. Look at the black people; they've been here a long time, and they still don't live like us—stealing and drugs and having all those babies."

"But you were talking about immigrants. Now you're talking about blacks, and they're not immigrants."

"Yeah, I know," she replies with a shrug. "But they're different, and there's enough problems with them, so we don't need any more. With all these other people coming here now, we just have more trouble. They don't talk English; and they think different from us, things like that."

Listening to Mary Anne's words I was reminded again how little we Americans look to history for its lessons, how impoverished is our historical memory. For, in fact, being white didn't make "a big difference" for many of those earlier immigrants. The dark-skinned Italians and the eastern European Jews who came in the late nineteenth and early twentieth centuries didn't look very white to the fair-skinned Americans who were here then. Indeed, the same people we now call white—Italians, Jews, Irish—were seen as another race at that time. Not black or Asian, it's true, but an alien other, a race apart, although one that didn't have a clearly defined name. Moreover, the racist fears and fantasies of native-born Americans were far less contained then than they are now, largely because there were few social constraints on their expression.

When, during the nineteenth century, for example, some Italians were taken for blacks and lynched in the South, the incidents passed virtually unnoticed. And if Mary Anne and Tim Walsh, both of Irish ancestry, had come to this country during the great Irish immigration of that period, they would have found themselves defined as an inferior race and described with the same language that was used to characterize blacks: "low-browed and savage, grovelling and bestial, lazy and wild, simian and sensual."[1] Not only during that period but for a long time afterward as well, the U.S. Census Bureau counted Irish as a distinct and separate group, much as it does today with the category it labels "Hispanic."

But there are two important differences between then and now, differences that can be summed up in a few words: the economy and race. Then, a growing industrial economy meant that there were plenty of jobs for both immigrant and native workers, something that can't be said for the contracting economy in which we live today. True, the arrival of the immigrants, who were more readily exploitable than native workers, put Americans at a disadvantage and created discord between the two groups. Nevertheless, work was available for both.

Then, too, the immigrants—no matter how they were labeled, no matter how reviled they may have been—were ultimately assimilable, if for no other reason than that they were white. As they began to lose their alien ways, it become possible for native Americans to see in the white ethnics of yesteryear a reflection of themselves. Once this shift in perception occurred, it was possible for the nation to incorporate them, to take them in, chew them up, digest them, and spit them out as Americans—with subcultural variations not always to the liking of those who hoped to control the manners and mores of the day, to be sure, but still recognizably white Americans.

Today's immigrants, however, are the racial other in a deep and profound way. It's true that race is not a fixed category, that it's no less an *idea* today than it was yesterday. And it's also possible, as I have already suggested, that we may be witness to social transformation from race to ethnicity among some of the most assimilated—read: middle-class—Asians and Latinos. But even if so, there's a long way to go before that metamorphosis is realized. Meanwhile, the immigrants of this era not only bring their own language and culture, they are also people of color—men, women, and children whose skin tones are different and whose characteristic features set them apart and justify the racial categories we lock them into.[2] And integrating masses of people of color into a society where race consciousness lies at the very heart of our central nervous system raises a whole new set of anxieties and tensions.

It's not surprising, therefore, that racial dissension has increased so sharply in recent years. What is surprising, however, is the passion for ethnicity and the preoccupation with ethnic identification among whites that seems suddenly to have burst upon the public scene. . . .

. . .

What does being German, Irish, French, Russian, Polish mean to someone who is an American? It's undoubtedly different for recent immigrants than for those who have been here for generations. But even for a relative newcomer, the inexorable process of becoming an American changes the meaning of ethnic identification and its hold on the internal life of the individual.

Nowhere have I seen this shift more eloquently described than in a recent opt-ed piece published in the *New York Times*. The author, a Vietnamese refugee writing on the day when Vietnamese either celebrate or mourn the fall of Saigon, depending on which side of the conflict they were on, writes:

> Although I sometimes mourn the loss of home and land, it's the American landscape and what it offers that solidify my hyphenated identity . . . Assimilation, education, the English language, the Amaerican 'I'—these things have carried me and many others further from that beloved tropical country than the C-130 ever could. . . . When did this happen? Who knows? One night, America quietly seeps in and takes hold of one's mind and body, and the Vietnamese soul of sorrows slowly fades away. In the morning, the Vietnamese American speaks a new language of materialism: his vocabulary includes terms like career choices, down payment, escrow, overtime.[3]

A new language emerges, but it lives at least for another generation, alongside the old one, Vietnamese, yes, but also American, with a newly developed sense of self and possibility—an identity that continues to grow stronger with each succeeding generation.

It's a process we have seen repeated throughout the history of American immigration. The American world reaches into the immigrant communities and shapes and changes the people who live in them.[4] By the second generation, ethnic identity already is attenuated; by the third, it usually has receded as a deeply meaningful part of life.

Residential segregation, occupational concentration, and a common language and culture—these historically have been the basis for ethnic solidarity and identification. As strangers in a new land, immigrants banded together, bound by their native tongue and shared culture. The sense of affinity they felt in these urban communities was natural; they were a touch of home, of the old country, of ways they understood: Once within their boundaries, they could feel whole again, sheltered from the ridicule and revulsion with which they were greeted by those who came before them. For whatever the myth about America's welcoming arms, nativist sentiment has nearly always been high and the anti-immigrant segment of the population large and noisy.

Ethnic solidarity and identity in America, then, was the consequence of the shared history each group brought with it, combined with the social and psychological experience of establishing themselves in the new land. But powerful as these were, the connections among the members of the group were heightened and sustained by the occupational concentration that followed—the Irish in the police departments of cities like Boston and San Francisco, for example, the Jews in New York City's garment industry, the east central Europeans in the mills and mines of western Pennsylvania.[5]

As each ethnic group moved into the labor force, its members often became concentrated in a particular occupation, largely because they were helped to find jobs there by those who went before them. For employers, this ethnic homogeneity made sense. They didn't have to cope with a babel of different languages, and they could count on the older workers to train the newcomers and keep them in line. For workers, there were advantages as well. It meant that they not only had compatible workmates, but that they weren't alone as they faced the jeers and contempt of their American-born counterparts. And perhaps most important, as more and more ethnic peers filled the available jobs, they began to develop some small measure of control in the workplace.

The same pattern of occupational concentration that was characteristic of yesterday's immigrant groups exists among the new immigrants today, and for the same reasons. The Cubans in Florida and the Dominicans in New York,[6] the various Asian groups in San Francisco, the Koreans in Los Angeles and New York—all continue to live in ethnic neighborhoods; all use the networks established there to find their way into the American labor force.[7]

For the white working-class ethnics whose immigrant past is little more than part of family lore, the occupational, residential, and linguistic chain has been broken. This is not to say that white ethnicity has ceased to be an observable phenomenon in American life. Cities like New York, Chicago, and San Francisco still have white ethnic districts that influence their culture, especially around food preferences and eating habits. But as in San Francisco's North Beach or New York's Little Italy, the people who once created vibrant neighborhoods, where a distinct subculture and language remained vividly alive, long ago moved out and left behind only the remnants of the commercial life of the old community. As such transformations took place, ethnicity became largely a private matter, a distant part of the family heritage that had little to do with the ongoing life of the family or community.

What, then, are we to make of the claims to ethnic identity that have become so prominent in recent years? Herbert Gans has called this identification "symbolic ethnicity"—that is, ethnicity that's invoked or not as the individual chooses.[8] Symbolic ethnicity, according to Gans, has little impact on a person's daily life and, because it is not connected to ethnic structures or activities—except for something like the wearing of the green on St. Patrick's Day—it makes no real contribution to ethnic solidarity or community.

The description is accurate. But it's a mistake to dismiss ethnic identification, even if only symbolic, as relatively meaningless. Symbols, after all, become symbolic precisely because they have meaning. In this case, the symbol has meaning at two levels: One is the personal and psychological, the other is the social and political.

At the personal level, in a nation as large and diverse as ours—a nation that defines itself by its immigrant past, where the metaphor for our national identity has been the melting pot—defining oneself in the context of an ethnic group is comforting. It provides a sense of belonging to some recognizable and manageable collectivity—an affiliation that has meaning because it's connected to the family where, when we were small children, we first learned about our relationship to the group. As Vilma Janowski, a 24-year-old first-generation Polish-American who came here as a child put it: "Knowing there's other people like you is really nice. It's like having a big family, even if you don't ever really see them. It's just nice to know they're there. Besides, if I said I was American, what would it mean? Nobody's just American."

Which is true. Being an American is different from being French or Dutch or any number of other nationalities because, except for Native Americans, there's no such thing as an American without a hyphen somewhere in the past. To identify with the front end of that hyphen is to maintain a connection—however tenuous, illusory, or sentimentalized—with our roots. It sets us apart from others, allows us the fantasy of uniqueness—a quest given particular urgency by a psychological culture that increasingly emphasizes the development of the self and personal history. Paradoxically, however, it also gives us a sense of belonging—of being one with others like ourselves—that helps to overcome some of the isolation of modern life.

But these psychological meanings have developed renewed force in recent years because of two significant sociopolitical events. The first was the civil rights movement with its call for racial equality. The second was the change in the immigration laws, which, for the first time in nearly half a century, allowed masses of immigrants to enter the country.

It was easy for northern whites to support the early demands of the civil rights movement when blacks were asking for the desegregation of buses and drinking fountains in the South. But supporting the black drive to end discrimination in jobs, housing, and education in the urban North was quite another matter—especially among those white ethnics whose hold on the ladder of mobility was tenuous at best and with whom blacks would be most likely to compete, whether in the job market, the neighborhood, or the classroom. As the courts and legislatures around the country began to honor some black claims for redress of past injustices, white hackles began to rise.

It wasn't black demands alone that fed the apprehensions of whites, however. In the background of the black civil rights drive, there stood a growing chorus of voices, as other racial groups—Asian Americans, Latinos, and Native Americans—joined the public fray to seek remedy for their own grievances. At the same time that these home-grown groups were making their voices heard and, not incidentally, affirming their distinctive cultural heritages and calling for public acknowledgment of them, the second great wave of immigration in this century washed across our shores.

After having closed the gates to mass immigration with the National Origins Act of 1924, Congress opened them again when it passed the Immigration Act of 1965.[9] This act, which was a series of amendments to the McCarran-Walter Act of 1952, essentially jettisoned the national origins provisions of earlier law and substituted overall hemisphere caps. The bill, according to immigration historian Roger Daniels, "changed the whole course of American immigration history" and left the door open for a vast increase in the numbers of immigrants.[10]

More striking than the increase in numbers has been the character of the new immigrants. Instead of the large numbers of western Europeans whom the sponsors had expected to take advantage of the new policy, it has been the people of Asia, Latin America, and the Caribbean who rushed to the boats. "It is doubtful if any drafter or supporter of the 1965 act envisaged this result," writes Daniels.[11] In fact, when members of Lyndon Johnson's administration, under whose tenure the bill became law, testified before Congress, they assured the legislators and the nation that few Asians would come in under the new law.[12]

This is a fascinating example of the unintended consequences of a political act. The change in the law was sponsored by northern Democrats who sought to appeal to their white ethnic constituencies by opening the gates to their countrymen once again—that is, to the people of eastern and southern Europe whom the 1924 law had kept out for nearly half a century. But those same white ethnics punished the Democratic Party by defecting to the Republicans during the Reagan-Bush years, a defection that was at least partly related to their anger about the new immigrants and the changing social balance of urban America.

During the decade of the 1980s, 2.5 million immigrants from Asian countries were admitted to the United States, an increase of more than 450 percent over the years between 1961 and 1970, when the number was slightly less than half a million. In 1990 alone, nearly as many Asian immigrants—one-third of a million—entered the country as came during the entire decade of the 1960s. Other groups show similarly noteworthy increases. Close to three-quarters of a million documented Mexicans crossed the border in the single year of 1990, compared to less than half a million during all of the 1960s. Central American immigration, too, climbed from just under one hundred thousand between 1961 and 1970 to more than triple that number during the 1980s. And immigrants from the Caribbean, who numbered a little more than half a million during the 1960s, increased to over three-quarters of a million in the years between 1981 and 1989.[13]

Despite these large increases and the perception that we are awash with new immigrants, it's worth noting that they are a much smaller proportion of the total population today, 6.2 percent, than they were in 1920, when they were a hefty 13.2 percent of all U.S. residents.[14] But the fact that most immigrants today are people of color gives them greater visibility than ever before.

Suddenly, the nation's urban landscape has been colored in ways unknown before. In 1970, the California cities that were the site of the original research for *Worlds of Pain* were almost exclusively white. Twenty years later, the 1990 census reports that their minority populations range from 54 to 69 percent. In the nation at large, the same census shows nearly one in four Americans with African, Asian, Latino, or Native American ancestry, up from one in five in 1980.[15] So dramatic is this shift that whites of European descent now make up just over two-thirds of the population in New York State, while in California they number only 57 percent. In cities like New York, San Francisco, and Los Angeles whites are a minority—accounting for 38, 47, and 37 percent of residents, respectively.

Twenty years ago the white population in all these cities was over 75 percent.[16]

The increased visibility of other racial groups has focused whites more self-consciously than ever on their own racial identification. Until the new immigration shifted the complexion of the land so perceptibly, whites didn't think of themselves as white in the same way that Chinese know they're Chinese and African Americans know they're black. Being white was simply a fact of life, one that didn't require any public statement, since it was the definitive social value against which all others were measured. "It's like everything's changed and I don't know what happened," complains Marianne Bardolino. "All of a sudden you have to be thinking all the time about these race things. I don't remember growing up thinking about being white like I think about it now. I'm not saying I didn't know there was coloreds and whites; it's just that I didn't go along thinking, *Gee, I'm a white person.* I never thought about it at all. But now with all the different colored people around, you have to think about it because they're thinking about it all the time."

"You say you feel pushed now to think about being white, but I'm not sure I understand why. What's changed?" I ask.

"I told you," she replies quickly, a small smile covering her impatience with my question. "It's because they think about what they are, and they want things their way, so now I have to think about what I am and what's good for me and my kids." She pauses briefly to let her thoughts catch up with her tongue, then continues. "I mean, if somebody's always yelling at you about being black or Asian or something, then it makes you think about being white. Like, they want the kids in school to learn about their culture, so then I think about being white and being Italian and say: What about my culture? If they're going to teach about theirs, what about mine?"

To which America's racial minorities respond with bewilderment. "I don't understand what white people want," says Gwen Tomalson. "They say if black kids are going to learn about black culture in school, then white people want their kids to learn about white culture. I don't get it. What do they think kids have been learning about all these years? It's all about white people and how they live and what they

accomplished. When I was in school you wouldn't have thought black people existed for all our books ever said about us."

As for the charge that they're "thinking about race all the time," as Marianne Bardolino complains, people of color insist that they're forced into it by a white world that never lets them forget. "If you're Chinese, you can't forget it, even if you want to, because there's always something that reminds you," Carol Kwan's husband, Andrew, remarks tartly. "I mean, if Chinese kids get good grades and get into the university, everybody's worried and you read about it in the papers."

While there's little doubt that racial anxieties are at the center of white concerns, our historic nativism also plays a part in escalating white alarm. The new immigrants bring with them a language and an ethnic culture that's vividly expressed wherever they congregate. And it's this also, the constant reminder of an alien presence from which whites are excluded, that's so troublesome to them.

The nativist impulse isn't, of course, given to the white working class alone. But for those in the upper reaches of the class and status hierarchy—those whose children go to private schools, whose closest contact with public transportation is the taxicab—the immigrant population supplies a source of cheap labor, whether as nannies for their children, maids in their households, or workers in their businesses. They may grouse and complain that "nobody speaks English anymore," just as working-class people do. But for the people who use immigrant labor, legal or illegal, there's a pay-off for the inconvenience—a payoff that doesn't exist for the families in this study but that sometimes costs them dearly.[17] For while it may be true that American workers aren't eager for many of the jobs immigrants are willing to take, it's also true that the presence of a large immigrant population—especially those who come from developing countries where living standards are far below our own—helps to make these jobs undesirable by keeping wages depressed well below what most American workers are willing to accept.[18]

Indeed, the economic basis of our immigration policies too often gets lost in the lore that we are a land that says to the world, "Give me your tired, your poor, your huddled masses, yearning to breathe free."[19] I don't mean to suggest that our humane impulses are a fiction, only that the reality is far more complex than Emma Lazarus' poem suggests. The massive immigration of the nineteenth and early twentieth centuries didn't just happen spontaneously. America may have been known as the land of opportunity to the Europeans who dreamed of coming here—a country where, as my parents once believed, the streets were lined with gold. But they believed these things because that's how America was sold by the agents who spread out across the face of Europe to recruit workers—men and women who were needed to keep the machines of our developing industrial society running and who, at the same time, gave the new industries a steady supply of hungry workers willing to work for wages far below those of native-born Americans.

The enormous number of immigrants who arrived during that period accomplished both those ends. In doing so, they set the stage for a long history of antipathy to foreign workers. For today, also, one function of the new immigrants is to keep our industries competitive in a global economy. Which simply is another way of saying that they serve to depress the wages of native American workers.

It's not surprising, therefore, that working-class women and men speak so angrily about the recent influx of immigrants. They not only see their jobs and their way of life threatened, they feel bruised and assaulted by an environment that seems suddenly to have turned color and in which they feel like strangers in their own land. So they chafe and complain: "They come here to take advantage of us, but they don't really want to learn our ways," Beverly Sowell, a 33-year-old white electronics assembler, grumbles irritably. "They live different than us; it's like another world how they live. And they're so clannish. They keep to themselves, and they don't even *try* to learn English. You go on the bus these days and you might as well be in a foreign country; everybody's talking some other language, you know, Chinese or Spanish or something. Lots of them have been here a long time, too, but they don't care; they just want to take what they can get."

But their complaints reveal an interesting paradox, an illuminating glimpse into the contradictions that beset native-born Americans in their relations with those who seek refuge here. On the one hand, they scorn the immigrants; on the other, they protest because they "keep to themselves." It's the same contradiction that dominates black-white relations. Whites refuse to integrate with blacks but are outraged when they stop knocking at the door, when they move to sustain the separation on their own terms—in black theme houses on campuses, for example, or in the newly developed black middle-class suburbs.

I wondered, as I listened to Beverly Sowell and others like her, why the same people who find the lifeways and languages of our foreign-born population offensive also care whether they "keep to themselves."

"Because like I said, they just shouldn't, that's all," Beverly says stubbornly. "If they're going to come here, they should be willing to learn our ways—you know what I mean, be real Americans. That's what my grandparents did, and that's what they should do."

"But your grandparents probably lived in an immigrant neighborhood when they first came here, too," I remind her.

"It was different," she insists. "I don't know why; it was. They wanted to be Americans; these here people now, I don't think they do. They just want to take advantage of this country."

She stops, thinks for a moment, then continues, "Right now it's awful in this country. Their kids come into the schools, and it's a big mess. There's not enough money for our kids to get a decent education, and we have to spend money to teach their kids English. It makes me mad. I went to public school, but I have to send my kids to Catholic school because now on top of the black kids, there's all these foreign kids who don't speak English. What kind of an education can kids get in a school like that? Something's wrong when plain old American kids can't go to their own schools.

"Everything's changed, and it doesn't make sense. Maybe you get it, but I don't. We can't take care of our own people and we keep bringing more and more foreigners in. Look at all the homeless. Why do we need more people here when our own people haven't got a place to sleep?"

"Why do we need more people here?"—a question Americans have asked for two centuries now. Historically, efforts to curb immigration have come during economic downturns, which suggests that when times are good, when American workers feel confident about their future, they're likely to be more generous in sharing their good fortune with foreigners. But when the economy falters, as it did in the 1990s, and workers worry about having to compete for jobs with people whose standard of living is well below their own, resistance to immigration rises. "Don't get me wrong; I've got nothing against these people," Tim Walsh demurs. "But they don't talk English, and they're used to a lot less, so they can work for less money than guys like me can. I see it all the time; they get hired and some white guy gets left out."

It's this confluence of forces—the racial and cultural diversity of our new immigrant population; the claims on the resources of the nation now being made by those minorities who, for generations, have called America their home; the failure of some of our basic institutions to serve the needs of our people; the contracting economy, which threatens the mobility aspirations of working-class families—all these have come together to leave white workers feeling as if everyone else is getting a piece of the action while they get nothing. "I feel like white people

are left out in the cold," protests Diane Johnson, a 28-year-old white single mother who believes she lost a job as a bus driver to a black woman. "First it's the blacks; now it's all those other colored people, and it's like everything always goes their way. It seems like a white person doesn't have a chance anymore. It's like the squeaky wheel gets the grease, and they've been squeaking and we haven't," she concludes angrily.

Until recently, whites didn't need to think about having to "squeak"—at least not specifically as whites. They have, of course, organized and squeaked at various times in the past—sometimes as ethnic groups, sometimes as workers. But not as whites. As whites they have been the dominant group, the favored ones, the ones who could count on getting the job when people of color could not. Now suddenly there are others—not just individual others but identifiable groups, people who share a history, a language, a culture, even a color—who lay claim to some of the rights and privileges that formerly had been labeled "for whites only." And whites react as if they've been betrayed, as if a sacred promise has been broken. They're white, aren't they? They're *real* Americans, aren't they? This is their country, isn't it?

NOTES

1. David R. Roediger, *The Wages of Whiteness* (New York: Verso, 1991), 133.

2. I'm aware that many Americans who have none of the characteristic features associated with their African heritage are still defined as black. This is one reason why I characterize race as an idea, not a fact. Nevertheless, the main point I am making here still holds—that is, the visible racial character of a people makes a difference in whether white Americans see them as assimilable or not.

3. *New York Times*, 30 April 1993.

4. For an excellent historical portrayal of the formation of ethnic communities among the east central European immigrants in Pennsylvania, the development of ethnic identity, and the process of Americanization, see Ewa Morawska, *For Bread with Butter* (New York: Cambridge University Press, 1985).

5. Ibid.

6. Alejandro Portes and Ruben G. Rumbaut, *Immigrant America* (Berkeley: University of California Press, 1990).

7. One need only walk the streets of New York to see the concentration of Koreans in the corner markets and the nail care salons that dot the city's landscape.

In San Francisco the Cambodians now own most of the donut shops in the city. It all started when, after working in such a shop, an enterprising young Cambodian combined the family resources and opened his own store and bakery. He now has 20 shops and has been instrumental in helping his countrymen open more, all of them buying their donuts from his bakery.

8. Herbert Gans, "Symbolic Ethnicity: The Future of Ethnic Groups and Cultures in America," *Ethnic and Racial Studies* 2 (1979):1–18.

9. Despite nativist protests, immigration had proceeded unchecked by government regulation until the

end of the nineteenth century. The first serious attempt to restrict immigration came in 1882 when, responding to the clamor about the growing immigration of Chinese laborers to California and other western states, Congress passed the Chinese Exclusion Act. But European immigration remained unimpeded. In the years between 1880 and 1924, twenty-four million newcomers arrived on these shores, most of them eastern and southern Europeans, all bringing their own language and culture, and all the target of pervasive bigotry and exploitation by native-born Americans. By the early part of the twentieth century, anti-immigration sentiments grew strong enough to gain congressional attention once again. The result was the National Origins Act of 1924, which established the quota system that sharply limited immigration, especially from the countries of southern and eastern Europe.

10. Roger Daniels, *Coming to America: A History of Immigration and Ethnicity in American Life* (New York: HarperCollins, 1990), 338–44.

11. Daniels, *Coming to America,* 341, writes further, "In his Liberty Island speech Lyndon Johnson stressed the fact that he was redressing the wrong done [by the McCarran-Walter Act] to those 'from southern or eastern Europe,' and although he did mention 'developing continents,' there was no other reference to Asian or Third World immigration."

12. For a further review of the Immigration Act of 1965, see chapter 13 (pp. 328–49) of *Coming to America.*

13. *Statistical Abstract,* U.S. Bureau of the Census (1992), Table 8, p. 11.

14. Ibid, Table 45, p. 42.

15. Ibid., Table 18, p. 18, and Table 26, p. 24.

16. U.S. Bureau of the Census, *Population Reports,* 1970 and 1990. Cited in Mike Davis, "The Body Count," *Crossroads* (June 1993). The difference in the racial composition of New York and San Francisco explains, at least in part, why black-white tensions are so much higher in New York City than they are in San Francisco. In New York, 38 percent of the population is now white, 30 percent black, 25 percent Hispanic, and 7 percent Asian. In San Francisco, whites make up 47 percent of the residents, blacks 11 percent, Hispanics 14 percent, and Asians 29 percent. Thus, blacks in New York reflect the kind of critical mass that generally sparks racial prejudices, fears, and conflicts. True, San Francisco's Asian population—three in ten of the city's residents—also form that kind of critical and noticeable mass. But whatever the American prejudice against Asians, and however much it has been acted out in the past, Asians do not stir the same kind of fear and hatred in white hearts as do blacks.

17. Zoë Baird, the first woman ever to be nominated to be attorney general of the United States, was forced to withdraw when it became known that she and her husband had hired an illegal immigrant as a nanny for their three-year-old child. The public indignation that followed the revelation came largely from people who were furious that, in a time of high unemployment, American workers were bypassed in favor of cheaper foreign labor.

18. This is now beginning to happen in more skilled jobs as well. In California's Silicon Valley, for example, software programmers and others are being displaced by Indian workers, people who are trained in India and recruited to work here because they are willing to do so for lower wages than similarly skilled Americans (*San Francisco Examiner,* 14 February 1993).

19. From Emma Lazarus' "The New Colossus," inscribed at the base of the Statue of Liberty in New York's harbor, the gateway through which most of the immigrants from Europe passed as they came in search of a new life.

DISCUSSION QUESTIONS

1. What does the white working-class respondent mean when he says this is a "white country"? How reflective of historical reality is this statement? Where does this perception come from? Do you think it is a commonly held belief among U.S. citizens today?

2. Rubin points out a paradox in the respondents' views on ethnic immigrants. On the one hand, immigrants are criticized for "keeping to themselves," yet at the same time the whites' contempt for the immigrants does not suggest they would be interested in congregating with other ethnicities in the first place. Why do you think immigrants are seen as "keeping to themselves"? Again, is this reflective of reality? Thinking back to the "Divided Fates" Reading from Chapter 2, what labor market

advantages might be available to those immigrants who maintain the ethnic networks that "keeping to themselves" suggests?

3. Gans's concept of "symbolic ethnicity" is discussed in this Reading. What is meant by this concept? Does it fit with or contradict the data presented by Rubin? Have you observed symbolic ethnicity in your own life or in the lives of others? What purpose do you think it serves, and how does it differ from "ethnicity" and "race" in general?

4. What do class and economics have to do with people's racial views and ideologies? How does perceived economic downturn and difficulty affect the degree of racial prejudice and animosity in a society? Compare and contrast the racial views expressed by college-educated whites in the "I Am Not a Racist But . . ." Reading in Chapter 5 with those expressed by the working-class whites in Rubin's article. Include both the content of the views and the way they are expressed in your analysis.

CURRENT DEBATES

THE RACIAL IDENTITIES OF WHITES AND BLACKS

Earlier, we referred to the merging of the separate white ethnic identities (Irish American, Polish American, Italian American, and so on) into a single, all-encompassing, generalized "European American" identity. In the selections following, we go beyond this assimilative process to consider some broader issues of racial identity in the United States today. A growing number of scholars have been exploring contemporary white racial identity, examining its nature and analyzing how it differs from the racial identity of nonwhites. In the first selection, Richard Dyer (2002) argues that whites see themselves in nonracial terms, as the norm against which all other groups are compared. The perception of whiteness as "normal" distances all other groups and reinforces the power relationships that have dominated American society virtually since its inception.

Mary Waters (1996) points out that "symbolic ethnicity," the ability to choose the extent to which one identifies with one's ancestral groups, is a luxury available only to whites. Members of racial and colonized groups are not free to excuse themselves from their groups, and those memberships continue to shape and limit their lives. Furthermore, argues Waters, the way in which whites think about their own ethnicity limits their ability to understand the situation and reactions of nonwhites, even when they are motivated by genuine acceptance of and interest in members of other groups.

Unlike other Current Debates, these selections are not opposed to each other. Rather, both challenge some "taken-for-granted" assumptions that are deeply embedded in the consciousness of white Americans, including, increasingly, the descendents of the white ethnic groups.

THE NEED TO UNDERSTAND WHITENESS

Richard Dyer

Racial imagery is central to the organization of the modern world. . . . Whose voices are listened to at international gatherings, who bombs and who is bombed, who gets what jobs, housing, access to health care and education . . . these are all largely inextricable from racial imagery. . . . Race is not the only factor governing these things . . . but it is never not a factor, never not in play. . . .

There has been an enormous amount of analysis of racial imagery in the past decades. . . . Yet, until recently, a notable absence from such work has been the study of images of white people. Indeed, to say that one is interested in race has come to mean that one is interested in any racial imagery other than that of white people.

This essay is about the racial imagery of white people. . . . This is not done merely to fill a gap in the analytical literature, but because there is something at stake in looking at . . . white racial imagery. As long as race is something only applied to non-white peoples, as long as white people are not racially seen and named, they/we function as a human norm. Other people are raced, we are just people.

There is no more powerful position that that of being "just" human. The claim to power is the claim to speak for the commonality of humanity. Raced people can't do that—they only speak for their own race.

The sense of white as non-raced is most evident in the absence of reference to whiteness in the habitual speech and writing of white people. . . . Whites will speak of, say, the black-ness or Chineseness of friends, neighbors, colleagues . . . and it may be in the most genuinely friendly and accepting manner, but we don't mention the whiteness of white people we know. An old style white comedian will often start a joke: "There's this bloke walking down the street and he meets a black geezer," never think-ing to race the bloke as well as the geezer. . . .

The assumption that white people are just people, which is not far off from saying that whites are people whereas other colors are something else, is endemic to white cul-ture. . . . The invisibility of whiteness as a racial position in white (which is to say dominant) discourse is of a piece with its ubiquity. . . . Whites are everywhere in representation. Yet precisely because of this and their placing as the norm they seem not to be represented to themselves *as* whites but as people who are variously gendered, classed, sexualized, and abled. At the level of racial representation, in other words, whites are not of a certain race, they're just the human race. . . .

This is why it is important to come to see whiteness. . . . [As] long as whiteness is felt to be the human condition, then it alone defines normality. . . . [The] equation of being white with being human secures a position or power. White people have power and believe that they think, feel, and act like and for all people; white people, unable to see their particularity, cannot take account of other people's [particularity]. . . . White power . . . reproduces itself . . . over-whelmingly because it is not seen as whiteness but as normal. White people need to learn to see themselves as white, to see their particularity. In other words, whiteness needs to be made strange.

SOURCE: Dyer, R. (1997). *White: Essays on Race and Culture*. New York: Routledge.

SYMBOLIC AND INVOLUNTARY ETHNICITY

Mary Waters

[Symbolic ethnicity is] confined to White Americans of European origin. Black Americans, Hispanic Americans, Asian Americans, and American Indians do not have the option of a symbolic ethnicity at pre-sent. . . . For all of the ways in which ethnicity does not matter for White Americans, it does matter for non-Whites. Who your ancestors are does affect your choice of spouse, where you live, what job you have, who your friends are, and what your chances are for success in American society, if those ancestors happen not to be from Europe. The reality is that White ethnics have a lot more choice and room to maneuver than they themselves think they do. The situation is very different for members of racial minorities, whose lives are strongly influ-enced by their race or national origin regardless of how much they choose to identify themselves in terms of their ancestries.

When white Americans learn the stories of how their [ancestors] triumphed . . . over adversity, they are usually told in terms of their individual efforts. . . . The important role of labor unions and other organized political and economic actors in their social and economic success are left out of the story in favor of a story of individual Americans rising up against . . . Old World intolerance and New World resistance. As a result, the "individualized" voluntary, cultural view of ethnicity for Whites is what is remembered. . . .

The symbolic ethnic tends to think that all groups are equal: everyone has a background that is their right to celebrate and pass on to their children. This leads to the conclusion that all identities are equal. . . . The important thing is to treat people as individuals and all equally. However, this assumption ignores the very big difference between an individualistic symbolic identity and a socially enforced and imposed racial identity. . . . When White Americans equate their own symbolic ethnicities with the socially enforced identities of non-White Americans, they obscure the fact that the experiences of Whites and non-Whites have been qualitatively different . . . and that the current identities of individuals partly reflect their unequal history. . . .

An example of the kind of misunderstanding that can arise because of the different understandings of the meaning and implications of symbolic versus [involuntary] identities concerns questions [college] students ask one another . . . in the dorms about personal appearance and customs. A very common type of interaction in the dorms concerns questions Whites ask Blacks about their hair. . . . Whites are generally quite curious about Black student's hair [and] wonder to themselves whether they should ask . . . questions. One thought experiment Whites perform is to ask themselves whether a particular question would upset them. Adopting a "do unto others" rule,

they ask themselves, "If a Black person was curious about my hair would I get upset?" The answer is usually "No, I would be happy to tell them." [So, assuming that everyone would be equally open, they proceed to ask their questions and are surprised when their] innocent questions . . . lead to resentment. The . . . stereotypes about Black Americans and the assumption that all Blacks are alike . . . has . . . power to hurt and offend a Black person. The innocent questions about Black hair also bring up the asymmetries between Black and White experience. Because Blacks tend to have more knowledge about Whites than vice versa, there is not an even exchange going on. . . . Because of the [historical] differences [between the groups], there are some connotations to Black hair that don't exist about White hair. (For instance, is straightening your hair a form of assimilation, . . . How is this related to looking "White"?) Finally, even a Black student who cheerfully disregards . . . these asymmetries will soon slam into another asymmetry if she willingly answers every innocent question asked of her. In a situation where Blacks make up only 10 percent of the student body, if every non-Black needs to be educated about hair, she will have to explain it to nine other students. As one Black student explained to me, after you've been asked a couple of times about something so personal you begin to feel like you are an attraction in a zoo, that you are at the university for the education of White students.

SOURCE: Waters, M. (1996). Optional Ethnicities: For Whites Only? In Pedraza, Sylvia, & Rumbaut, Rueben (Eds.), *Origins and Destinies* (pp. 449–452). Belmont, CA: Wadsworth.

Questions to Consider

1. Is Dyer right about the tendency to "race" only nonwhites? Can you detect this pattern in the everyday conversations of people around you? What are the implications of this tendency for people's perceptions of each other and the possibilities for honest, clear communication across group lines? What does he mean when he says that we need to make whiteness strange?

2. Can you extend Dyer's point to gender relations? Do only females have gender? How?

3. Is Waters saying that it's wrong to treat people equally and as individuals? How can it be wrong to be "color-blind"? What does she mean by her distinction between an "individualistic symbolic identity" and an "imposed racial identity"? Can you find examples in your experience of how these realities have hampered communication across group lines?

Part IV

Conclusions

10

ANTIRACIST SOLUTIONS

INTRODUCTION

Courses about inequality often leave students feeling depressed about the state of dominant-minority relations. Often the problems have been going on for much longer, and are much more widespread, than many students have considered or believed. In this final chapter, we present a diversity of writings that consider possible solution strategies for the problems of discrimination and racism that we have encountered throughout this book. Obviously, there is no single answer, and scholars and activists alike have struggled with different approaches to ending inequality. In introducing just a few key perspectives here, we hope to invite you as the reader to consider where you fit into the struggle to end oppression and what measures you might be willing to support to this end. In this way, we can end on a positive, proactive note rather than one of despair and inaction.

The first Reading comes from legal scholar Patricia Williams. Williams makes it clear that any strategy of colorblindness is a "childish" fiction. Using various examples from her life as an African American woman living in U.S. society, she demonstrates how colorblindness is a myth that we prop up to pretend we do not see differences. Although she agrees that colorblindness is an eventual ideal, she argues that we must first start where we are by acknowledging our different histories and the reality of the power that separates us. In other words, we must begin with looking at color in order to get to the point where color no longer matters. Williams concludes by reviewing some common excuses people use to assert that racism is permanent and therefore unsolvable. She challenges these positions and suggests some ways to begin approaching solutions.

Although he is also an African American legal scholar, Derrick Bell, author of the second reading, takes a different position by asserting the permanence of racism in U.S. society. Bell uses a writing style from the "critical race studies" approach that appears in law journals, in which legal points are laid out in dialogue between fictional characters. In this selection, the narrator is questioning "Geneva" about a policy proposal she has created called the "Racial Preference Licensing Act," and the rationale behind it. Through the discussion, Bell points out that racism is maintained not only through overt acts of exclusion, but through whites' "racial nepotism," whereby they hire and promote individuals with whom they feel more comfortable—namely, other whites. Rather than assuming whites are predominantly non-discriminating and structuring the law to punish the occasional aberration of discrimination, Bell suggests a different approach, which acknowledges that racial nepotism is the norm. With the racial preference licensing act, individual places of business purchase a license that will allow them to maintain racially segregated workplaces, hiring people only like themselves, for a fee that will be put toward educational and economic opportunities for people of color. Bell's innovative approach comes out of recognizing that through these several decades of civil rights legislation, rampant discrimination has continued to occur, only now under the guise of "equal opportunity for all." He echoes the sentiment of many people of color that overt racism is sometimes preferable to the subtle modern racism of today, because at least people of color know whom to avoid. With the racial preference license, that would be very clear. Rather than wasting any more time changing white hearts, from a realist position Bell deals solely with actions—actions he argues will help people of color directly, unlike the poorly enforced civil rights legislation currently in use.

Following this attention to differences between overt and covert racism, white sociologist Eileen O'Brien compares two antiracist organizations—one that focuses on fighting blatant racists like the KKK and one that focuses on less blatant, "good intentioned" forms of racism that the activists themselves might unknowingly perpetuate within their own workplaces, schools, or churches. This contrast comes out of O'Brien's study of the kinds of activities whites do to confront racism, or white *antiracism*. Antiracism is defined as a commitment in "thought, action, and practice to dismantling racism" and is thus distinguished from non-racism, in which racism is simply not mentioned, believed, or acknowledged. In studying white antiracists, O'Brien came across two organizations that were multiracial but had many white members, and contrast between the two groups provides an excellent illustration of how one's definition of racism directly affects the solutions that are developed for it. Using the analogy of picture frames, O'Brien proposes a broader definition of racism within which various groups could work on different aspects of the problem. At the end of this Reading, she offers three suggestions for what whites can do about racism, based directly upon the experiences of the activists she studied for her research.

The next Reading is by two white historians, Noel Ignatiev and John Garvey, editors of the journal *Race Traitor,* who disagree with "antiracism" and have a different proposal for what whites can do to end racism. They have called their strategy "new abolitionism," since they argue that the "white race" as a social construction must be abolished, and this can be done if whites become "race traitors." The way they can do this is by refusing to accept the privileges that come with whiteness, or the "white club." One example they touch upon is the polite warnings whites often receive from traffic cops who pull them over, as opposed to the often hostile treatment people of color encounter in the same scenario. It would obviously take a bold commitment on the part of those who appear white to the police officer to refuse to accept any privileges by letting the officer know, "I'm not really 'white.'" This new abolitionist strategy is based on the premise that race has no biological basis and is completely socially created. Thus, abolishing the white race means destroying the social meanings attached to it, not the physical bodies that seem to represent it. This conceptualization alerts us to why so many solution strategies for racism focus upon what whites can do: because whites' actions and inactions are so often what keeps the system of racism in motion.

Following this attention to whites, white educator Paul Kivel takes a different tack, arguing that the task for a white person is to be an *ally* to people of color. Kivel writes that being an ally includes listening to people of color, avoiding the tendency to be defensive, and examining one's own actions that may perpetuate power and privilege. He also lists 13 "basic tactics" that an ally can use, then presents a hypothetical conversation between Roberto and a teacher, demonstrating how an ally validates a person of color's report of discrimination and offers to help rather than second-guessing or minimizing the incident. This Reading ends by pointing out that allies must be committed for the long haul, requiring patience and humility as eventual interracial trust is established.

Our final selection is Judith Katz's checklist of different ways people can get involved in their personal, work, and school lives to help combat racism. She lists very specific suggestions, particularly geared toward college students but also appropriate to any age group. Whether you are an optimist, a realist, an antiracist, a race traitor, or an ally, there is undoubtedly someplace on this list where you can begin in the struggle to end oppression. As Margaret Mead once said, "Never doubt that a group of thoughtful committed citizens can change the world; indeed, it is the only thing that ever has."

THE EMPEROR'S NEW CLOTHES

Patricia J. Williams

My son used to attend a small nursery school. Over the course of one year, three different teachers in his school assured me that he was color-blind. Resigned to this diagnosis, I took my son to an ophthalmologist who tested him and pronounced his vision perfect. I could not figure out what was going on until I began to listen carefully to what he was saying about color.

As it turned out, my son did not misidentify color. He resisted identifying color at all. "I don't know," he would say when asked what color the grass was; or, most peculiarly, "It makes no difference." This latter remark, this assertion of the greenness of grass making no difference, was such a precociously cynical retort, that I began to suspect some social complication in which he was somehow invested.

The long and the short of it is that the well-meaning teachers at his predominantly white school had valiantly and repeatedly assured their charges that color makes no difference. "It doesn't matter," they told the children, "whether you're black or white or red or green or blue." Yet upon further investigation, the very reason that the teachers had felt it necessary to impart this lesson in the first place was that it *did* matter, and in predictably cruel ways: some of the children had been fighting about whether black people could play "good guys."

My son's anxious response was redefined by his teachers as physical deficiency. This anxiety redefined as deficiency suggests to me that it may be illustrative of the way in which the liberal ideal of color-blindness is too often confounded. That is to say, the very notion of blindness about color constitutes an ideological confusion at best, and denial at its very worst. I recognize, certainly, that the teachers were inspired by a desire to make whole a division in the ranks. But much is overlooked in the move to undo that which clearly and unfortunately matters just by labeling it that which "makes no difference." The dismissiveness, however unintentional, leaves those in my son's position pulled between the clarity of their own experience and the often alienating terms in which they must seek social acceptance.

There's a lot of that in the world right now: someone has just announced in no uncertain terms that he or she hates you because you're dark, let's say, or Catholic or a woman or the wrong height, and the panicked authority figures try to patch things up by reassuring you that race or gender or stature or your heartfelt religion doesn't matter; means nothing in the calculation of your humanity; is the most insignificant little puddle of beans in the world.

While I do want to underscore that I embrace colorblindness as a legitimate hope for the future, I worry that we tend to enshrine the notion with a kind of utopianism whose naïveté will ensure its elusiveness. In the material world ranging from playgrounds to politics, our ideals perhaps need more thoughtful, albeit more complicated, guardianship. By this I mean something more than the "I think therefore it is" school of idealism. "I don't think about color, therefore your problems don't exist." If only it were so easy.

But if indeed it's not that easy then the application of such quick fixes becomes not just a shortcut but a short-circuiting of the process of resolution. In the example of my son's experience at school, the collective aversion to confronting the social tensions he faced resulted in their being pathologized as his individual physical limitation. This is a phenomenon that happens all too frequently to children of color in a variety of contexts. In both the United States and the United Kingdom, the disproportionate numbers of black children who end up in special education or who are written off as failures attest to the degree to which this is a profound source of social anxiety.

In addition, the failure to deal straightforwardly with the pervasive practices of exclusion that infect even the very young allowed my son's white schoolmates to indulge in the false luxury of a prematurely imagined community. By this I mean that we can all be lulled rather too easily into a self-congratulatory stance of preached universalism—"We are the world! We are the children!" was the evocative, full-throated harmony of a few years ago. Yet nowhere has that been invoked more passionately than in the face of tidal waves of dissension, and even as "the" children learn that "we" children are not like "those," the benighted creatures on the other side of the pale.

This tension between material conditions and what one is cultured to see or not see—the dilemma of the emperor's new clothes, we might call it—is a tension faced by any society driven by bitter histories of imposed hierarchy. I don't mean to suggest that we need always go about feeling guilty or responsible or perpetually burdened by original sin or notions of political correctness. I do wish, however, to counsel against the facile innocence of those three notorious monkeys, Hear No Evil, See No Evil, and Speak No Evil. Theirs is a purity achieved through ignorance. Ours must be a world in which we know each other better.

To put it another way, it is a dangerous if comprehensible temptation to imagine inclusiveness by imagining away any obstacles. It is in this way that the moral high ground of good intentions knows its limits. We must be careful not to allow our intentions to verge into outright projection by substituting a fantasy of global seamlessness that is blinding rather than just color-blind.

This is a dilemma—being colored, so to speak, in a world of normative whiteness, whiteness being defined as the absence of color. The drive to conform our surroundings to whatever we know as "normal" is a powerful force—convention in many ways is more powerful than reason, and customs in some instances are more powerful than law. While surely most customs and conventions encode the insights of ancient wisdom, the habits of racial thought in Western society just as surely encapsulate some of the greatest mistakes in human history. So how do we rethink this most troubled of divisions, the fault line in our body politic, the fault line in ourselves? The ability to remain true to *one* self, it seems to me, must begin with the ethical project of considering how we can align a sense of ourselves with a sense of the world. This is the essence of integrity, is it not, never having to

split into a well-maintained "front" and a closely guarded "inside."

Creating community, in other words, involves this most difficult work of negotiating real divisions, of considering boundaries before we go crashing through, and of pondering our differences before we can ever agree on the terms of our sameness. For the discounted vision of the emperor's new clothes (or a little boy's color) is already the description of corrupted community.

Perhaps one reason that conversations about race are so often doomed to frustration is that the notion of whiteness as "race" is almost never implicated. One of the more difficult legacies of slavery and of colonialism is the degree to which racism's tenacious hold is manifested not merely in the divided demographics of neighborhood or education or class but also in the process of what media expert John Fiske calls the "exnomination" of whiteness as racial identity. Whiteness is unnamed, suppressed, beyond the realm of race. Exnomination permits whites to entertain the notion that race lives "over there" on the other side of the tracks, in black bodies and inner-city neighborhoods, in a dark netherworld where whites are not involved.

At this level, the creation of a sense of community is a lifelong negotiation of endless subtlety. One morning when my son was three, I took him to his preschool. He ran straight to a pile of Lego and proceeded to work. I crossed the room and put his lunchbox in the refrigerator, where I encountered a little girl sitting at a table, beating a mound of clay into submission with a plastic rolling pin. "I see a Mommy," she said to me cheerfully. "That must mean that your little boy is here somewhere, too."

"Yes, he's here," I answered, thinking how sweetly precocious she was. "There, he's over by the Lego."

She strained to see around the bookcases. "Oh yes," she said. "Now I see that black face of his."

I walked away without responding, enraged—how can one be so enraged at an innocent child—yet not knowing what to say just then, rushing to get the jaggedly dangerous broken glass of my emotions out of the room.

I remember being three years old so well. Three was the age when I learned that I was black, the colored kid, monkeychild, different.

What made me so angry and wordless in this encounter forty years later was the realization that none of the little white children who taught me to see my blackness as a mark probably ever learned to see themselves as white. In our culture, whiteness is rarely marked in the indicative there! there! sense of my bracketed blackness. And the majoritarian privilege of never noticing themselves was the beginning of an imbalance from which so much, so much else flowed.

But that is hard to talk about, even now, this insight acquired before I had the words to sort it out. Yet it is imperative to think about this phenomenon of closeting race, which I believe is a good deal more widespread than these small examples. In a sense, race matters are resented and repressed in much the same way as matters of sex and scandal: the subject is considered a rude and transgressive one in mixed company, a matter whose observation is sometimes inevitable, but about which, once seen, little should be heard nonetheless. Race thus tends to be treated as though it were an especially delicate category of social infirmity—so-called—like extreme obesity or disfigurement.

Every parent knows a little of this dynamic, if in other contexts: "Why doesn't that lady have any teeth?" comes the child's piping voice. "Why doesn't that gentleman have any hair?" And "Why is that little boy so black?" *Sssshhhh!* comes the anxious parental remonstrance. The poor thing can't help it. We must all pretend that nothing's wrong.

And thus we are coached upon pain of punishment not to see a thing.

Now, to be sure, the parent faces an ethical dilemma in that moment of childish vision unrestrained by social nicety. On the one hand, we rush to place a limit on what can be said to strangers and what must be withheld for fear of imposition or of hurting someone's feelings. As members of a broad society, we respect one another by learning not to inflict every last intimate, prying curiosity we may harbor upon everyone we meet.

That said, there remains the problem of how or whether we ever answer the question, and that is the dimension of this dynamic that is considerably more troubling.

"Why is that man wearing no clothes?" pipes the childish voice once more. And the parent panics at the complication of trying to explain. The naked man may be a nudist or a psychotic or perhaps the emperor of the realm, but the silencing that is passed from parent to child is not only about the teaching of restraint; it is calculated to circumnavigate the question as though it had never been asked. *"Stop asking such silly questions."*

A wall begins to grow around the forbidden gaze; for we all know, and children best of all, when someone wants to change the subject, forever. And so the child is left to the monstrous creativity of ignorance and wild imagination.

Again, I do believe that this unfortunate negotiation of social difference has much in common with discussions about race. Race is treated as though it were some sort of genetic leprosy or a biological train wreck. Those who privilege themselves as Un-raced—usually but not always those who are white—are always anxiously maintaining that it doesn't matter, even as they are quite busy feeling pity, no less, and thankful to God for their great good luck in having been spared so intolerable an affliction.

Meanwhile, those marked as Having Race are ground down by the pendular stresses of having to explain what it feels like to be You— why are you black, why are you black, why are you black, over and over again; or, alternatively, placed in a kind of conversational quarantine of muteness in which any mention of racial circumstance reduces all sides to tears, fears, fisticuffs, and other paroxysms of unseemly anguish.

This sad, habitual paralysis in the face of the foreign and the anxiety-producing. It is as though we are all skating across a pond that is not quite thoroughly frozen. Two centuries ago, or perhaps only a few decades ago, the lake was solidly frozen, and if for those skating across the surface things seemed much more secure, it was a much more dismal lot for those whose fates were frozen at the bottom of the pond. Over time, the weather of race relations has warmed somewhat, and a few of those at the bottom have found their way to the surface; we no longer hold our breath, and we have even learned to skate. The noisy, racial chasm still yawns darkly beneath us all, but we few brave souls glide gingerly above, upon a skim of hope, our bodies made light with denial, the black pond so dangerously and thinly iced with the conviction that talking about it will only make things worse.

And so the racial divide is exacerbated further by a welter of little lies that propel us foolishly around the edges of our most demanding social stresses: Black people are a happy people and if they would just stop complaining so much, they would see how happy they are. Black people who say they're unhappy are leftist agitators whose time would be better spent looking for a real job. White people are victims. Poor Bangladeshis are poor because they want to be. Poor white people are poor because rich Indians stole all the jobs under the ruse of affirmative action. There is no racism in the marketplace—"each according to his merit" goes the cant, even as the EEOC has a backlog of 70,000 cases by the most conservative estimates; even as top executives funnel the jobs to school chums and their next of kin, or chief executives at major corporations are captured on tape destroying subpoenaed records of ongoing discriminatory practices. Immigrants are taking over the whole world, but race makes no difference. If sixty percent of young black men are unemployed in the industrialized world, well, let them watch Oprah. If some people are determined to be homeless, well then let them have it, if homelessness is what they like so much. . . .

Anthropologist Michael Taussig has written about the phenomenon of public secrets. He writes of a ritual in Tierra del Fuego in which the men come out of the men's hut wearing masks. The women hail them by singing "Here come the spirits!" On some level, everyone must know that these are not spirits but husbands and brothers and fathers and sons, but so powerful is the ritual to the sense of community that it is upon pain of death that the women fail to greet them as spirits.

In our culture, I think that the power of race resembles just such a public secret. I understand the civic ritual that requires us to say in the face of all our differences, We are all one, we are the world. I understand the need for the publicly reiterated faith in public ideals as binding and sustaining community. Such beliefs are the very foundation of institutional legitimacy and no society can hold itself together without them.

Yet such binding force comes from a citizenry willing to suspend disbelief for the sake of honoring the spiritual power of our appointed ideals. And where suspicion, cynicism, and betrayal have eaten away at a community to the degree that the folk parading from the men's hut look like just a bunch of muggers wearing masks—or badges, as the case may be—then hailing the spirit will sound like a hollow incantation, empty theater, the weary habit of the dispossessed.

There is a crisis of community in the United States no less than in the rest of the world, of specific and complicated origin perhaps, but in this moment of global upheaval, worth studying for possibilities both won and lost. Whites fear blacks, blacks fear whites. Each is the enemy against whom the authorities will not act.

If racial and ethnic experience constitutes a divide that cannot be spoken, an even greater paradox is the degree to which a sense of commonality may be simultaneously created as well as threatened by notions of ethnicity and race. It is no wonder we end up deadlocked with so many of our most profound political problems. The "O. J. divide" (as it's come to be known in America) is merely a convenient metaphor for everything else we disagree about. Are you one of "us" or one of "them"? When I say "we," am I heard as referring only to other black people? When I employ the first person, will it only be heard as an exercise of what might be called the "royal I"—me as representative stand-in for all those of my kind. . . .

Certainly the great, philosophically inspiring quandary of my life is that despite the multiculturalism of my heritage and the profundity of my commitment to the notion of the "usness" of us all, I have little room but to negotiate most of my daily lived encounters as one of "them." How alien this sounds. This split without, the split within.

Yet in this way the public secret of human fallibility, whose silence we keep to honor our symbolic civic unity, is vastly complicated by the counter-secret of palpitating civil discord. Hail the spirit of our infallibly peaceful coexistence. Hail our common fate (even as young white men are forming their own private militias complete with grenade launchers and one in three young black men are in jail or on probation. . . .But shush, don't stare. . . .)

Such is the legacy of racism in the modern world. Perhaps it is less and less fashionable these days to consider too explicitly the kinds of costs that slavery and colonialism exacted, even as those historical disruptions have continued to scar contemporary social arrangements with the transcendent urgency of their hand-me-down grief.

I realize therefore that it might be considered impertinent to keep raising the ghost of slavery's triangle trade and waving it around; there is a pronounced preference in polite society for just letting bygones be bygones. And I concede that a more optimistic enterprise might be to begin any contemporary analysis of race with the Civil Rights Movement in the United States, or the Notting Hill riots in the United Kingdom. Beginning at those points is a way of focusing one's view and confining one's reference to the legitimately inspiring ideals that coalesced those movements: the aims of color-blindness, the equality of all people, and the possibility of peaceful coexistence.

Yet if that well-chosen temporal slice allows us to be optimistic about the possibility of progress, there are nonetheless limitations to such a frame. First, it is the conceptual prehistory of those movements that explains the toll of racism and its lingering effects. There can be no adequate explanation without reference to it. Second, the diasporic complexity of today's social problems requires an analysis that moves those ideals of the social movements of the 1960s and 1970s beyond themselves, into the present, into the future—to a more complex, practical grappling with such phenomena as the hybridizing of racial stereotypes with the fundamentalisms of gender, class, ethnicity, religion. Third, the problem of race is overlaid with crises in environmental and resource management that have triggered unparalleled migrations from rural to urban locations within national boundaries, and that have impassioned debates about immigration across national boundaries. Finally, not a few aspects of our New Age global economics, much like the commercial profiteering of colonialisms past, threaten to displace not just the very laws to which we persistently make such grand appeal

but the nation-state itself. I believe that a genuine, long-term optimism about the future of race relations depends on a thorough excavation of the same.

A memory slips into my mind. I was riding the train from New York to Washington, D.C., some years ago on my way to some lawyers' conference or other; I was accompanied by two black colleagues. An hour into the trip, the train stopped in the city of Philadelphia. A young white woman got on whom my colleagues knew. She was also a lawyer, headed to the same conference. She joined us, sitting among us in a double row of seats that faced each other. A little while later, the conductor came along. The new woman held up her ticket, but the conductor did not seem to see her. He saw four of us seated and only three ticket stubs.

"One of you hasn't paid," he said, staring at me, then at each of my two black friends. I remember pointing to the white woman, and someone else said, "Over there." But the conductor was resolute.

"Which one of you hasn't paid?" he asked again. Two of us kept saying, "Our receipts, see?" and the white woman, speaking *very* clearly said, "Here. I am trying to give you my ticket."

The conductor was scowling. He still did not hear. "I am not moving till one of you pays up."

It was the longest time before the conductor stopped staring in all the wrong directions. It was the longest time before he heard the new woman, pressing her ticket upon him, her voice reaching him finally as though from a great distance, passing through light-years of understanding as if from another universe. The realization that finally lit his face was like the dawning of a great surprise.

How precisely does the issue of color remain so powerfully determinative of everything from life circumstance to manner of death, in a world that is, by and large, officially "color-blind"? What metaphors mask the hierarchies that make racial domination frequently seem so "natural," so invisible, indeed so attractive? How does racism continue to evolve, post-slavery and post-equality legislation, across such geographic, temporal, and political distance?

No, I am not saying that this is the worst of times. But neither will I concede that this is the best of all possible worlds. And what a *good* thing, is it not, to try to imagine how much better we could be. . . .

"I had a dream," said my son the other morning. Then he paused. "No," he said, "it was more of a miracle. Do you know what a miracle is?"

"Tell me," I said, thunderstruck, and breathless with maternal awe.

"A miracle is when you have a dream and you open your eyes in it. It's when you wake up and your dream is all around you."

It was a pretty good definition, I thought. And even though my son's little miracle had something to do with pirates meeting dinosaurs, I do think that to a very great extent we dream our worlds into being. For better or worse, our customs and laws, our culture and society are sustained by the myths we embrace, the stories we recirculate to explain what we behold. I believe that racism's hardy persistence and immense adaptability are sustained by a habit of human imagination, deflective rhetoric, and hidden license. I believe no less that an optimistic course might be charted, if only we could imagine it. What a world it would be if we could all wake up and see all of ourselves reflected in the world, not merely in a territorial sense but with a kind of nonexclusive entitlement that grants not so much possession as investment. A peculiarly anachronistic notion of investment, I suppose, at once both ancient and futuristic. An investment that envisions each of us in each other.

. . .

Finally, I would like to return to what I think is one of the greatest obstacles to progress at this moment—the paralyzing claim that racism *has* no solution. Resembling often the schoolyard game of bullies tormenting those deemed wimps, this argument takes a number of forms:

Racism is not a problem, because racism is "universal"; all cultures are racist and xenophobic. Circling the wagons around one's own is just a "human thing."

Or: *Racism is not a problem because even if it is a problem, it's a social problem, and law, politics, and economic regulation have no place in the social realm. "People" will just have to deal with it "by themselves." Let them intermarry.* Not quite let them eat cake, but rather a romantic resolution to palpable political disparity.

Or: *Racism isn't a problem, because while white people* used *to hate black people, now it's black people who hate white people, so it's only fair for white people to hate black people in return.* And so the argument sloshes back and forth, forth and back, like a pendulum, like a lullaby, like the tolling of a knell.

Or: *Racism is a problem, but it's not* our *problem. Black people ought to help themselves before they lay claim to the sympathies of good white people.* I must say, I always wonder at this sifting out of the presumed responsibility of black people for their own fate that so casually overlooks the long history of self-help and intracommunity networks that do exist. Such self-help structures— churches, for example—are neither wealthy nor philanthropic in a way that matches those of some other groups, but much political rhetoric treats them as nonexistent. And while no one can argue that black self-help is not a fine thing, I wonder about its meaning when it is used as an injunction that black concerns be severed from the ethical question of how we as a society operate. These debates make me suspicious when they are raised so as to be at the core of arguments about black people overreaching, even as black people earn only two-thirds of what similarly educated and qualified white people do. These arguments fuel characterizations of antidiscrimination remedies as only having helped those who were already overprivileged to begin with; they feed images of those who speak publicly of racial discrimination as those who are merely "shaking down" the establishment, exploiting white guilt for personal profit.

With regard to all these configurations, let me just say that I am certain that the solution to racism lies in our ability to see its ubiquity but not to concede its inevitability. It lies in the collective and institutional power to make change, at least as much as with the individual will to change. It also lies in the absolute moral imperative to break the childish, deadly circularity of centuries of blindness to the shimmering brilliance of our common, ordinary humanity. . . .

THE RACIAL PREFERENCE LICENSING ACT

Derrick Bell

Racial nepotism rather than racial animus is the major motivation for much of the discrimination blacks experience.

—*Matthew S. Goldberg*

It was enacted as the Racial Preference Licensing Act. At an elaborate, nationally televised signing ceremony, the President—elected as a "racial moderate"—assured the nation that the new statute represented a realistic advance in race relations. "It is," he insisted, "certainly not a return to the segregation policies granted constitutional protection under the stigma-inflicting 'separate but equal' standard of *Plessy* v. *Ferguson* established roughly a century ago.[1]

"Far from being a retreat into our unhappy racial past," he explained, "the new law embodies a daring attempt to create a brighter racial future for all our citizens. Racial realism is the key to understanding this new law. It does not assume a nonexistent racial tolerance, but boldly proclaims its commitment to racial justice through the working of a marketplace that recognizes and seeks to balance the rights of our black citizens to fair treatment and the no less important right of some whites to an unfettered choice of customers, employees, and contractees."

Under the new act, all employers, proprietors of public facilities, and owners and managers of dwelling places, homes, and apartments could, on application to the federal government, obtain a license authorizing the holders, their managers, agents, and employees to exclude or separate persons on the basis of race and color. The license itself was expensive, though not prohibitively so. Once obtained, it required payment to a government commission of a tax of 3 percent of the income derived from whites employed, whites served, or products sold to whites during each quarter in which a policy of "racial preference" was in effect. Congress based its authority for the act on the commerce clause, the taxing power, and the general welfare clause of the Constitution.

License holders were required both to display their licenses prominently in a public place and to operate their businesses in accordance with the racially selective policies set out on their license. Specifically, discrimination had to be practiced in accordance with the license on a nonselective basis. Licenses were not available to those who, for example, might hire or rent to one token black and then discriminate against other applicants, using the license as a shield against discrimination suits. Persons of color wishing to charge discrimination against a facility not holding a license would carry the burden of proof, but such burden might be met with statistical and circumstantial as well as with direct evidence provided by white "testers." *Under the act, successful complainants would be entitled to damages set at ten thousand dollars per instance of unlicensed discrimination, including attorneys' fees.

License fees and commissions paid by license holders would be placed in an "equality fund" used to underwrite black businesses, to offer no-interest mortgage loans for black home buyers, and to provide scholarships for black students seeking college and vocational education. To counter charges that black people, as under *Plessy*, would be both segregated and never gain any significant benefit from the

---

* Testing is an effective, but too little utilized, technique to ferret out bias in the sale and rental of housing or in employment practices. Generally, in testing, people who are alike in virtually every way except race or ethnicity are sent to apply for jobs, housing, or mortgages. The results are then analyzed for how differently whites are treated compared with black or Hispanic people. In 1982, the Supreme Court found that testers in a housing discrimination suit, and the housing association to which they were attached, had standing to sue in their own right as injured parties.[2]

equality fund, the act provided that five major civil rights organizations (each named in the statute) would submit the name of a representative who would serve on the commission for one, nonrenewable three-year term.

The President committed himself and his administration to the effective enforcement of the Racial Preference Licensing Act. "It is time," he declared, "to bring hard-headed realism rather than well-intentioned idealism to bear on our long-standing racial problems. Policies adopted because they seemed right have usually failed. Actions taken to promote justice for blacks have brought injustice to whites without appreciably improving the status or standards of living for blacks, particularly for those who most need the protection those actions were intended to provide.

"Within the memories of many of our citizens, this nation has both affirmed policies of racial segregation and advocated polices of racial integration. Neither approach has been either satisfactory or effective in furthering harmony and domestic tranquillity." Recalling the Civil Rights Act of 1964[3] and its 1991 amendments,[4] the President pointed out that while the once-controversial public-accommodation provisions in the original 1964 act received unanimous judicial approval in the year of its adoption,[5] even three decades later the act's protective function, particularly in the employment area, had been undermined by both unenthusiastic enforcement and judicial decisions construing its provisions ever more narrowly.

"As we all know," the President continued "the Supreme Court has now raised grave questions about the continued validity of the 1964 Act and the Fair Housing Act of 1968[6]—along with their various predecessors and supplemental amendments as applied to racial discrimination. The Court stopped just short of declaring unconstitutional all laws prohibiting racial discrimination, and found that the existing civil rights acts were inconsistent with what it viewed as the essential 'racial forgiveness' principle in the landmark decision of *Brown* v. *Board of Education* of 1954.[7] The Court announced further that nothing in its decision was intended to affect the validity of the statutes' protection against discrimination based on sex, national origin, or religion.

"This is, of course, not an occasion for a legal seminar, but it is important that all citizens understand the background of the new racial preference statute we sign this evening. The Supreme Court expressed its concern that existing civil rights statutes created racial categories that failed to meet the heavy burden of justification placed on any governmental policy that seeks to classify persons on the basis of race. In 1989, the Court held that this heavy burden, called the 'strict scrutiny' standard, applied to remedial as well as to invidious racial classifications.[8] Our highest court reasoned that its 1954 decision in the landmark case of *Brown* v. *Board of Education* did not seek to identify and punish wrongdoers, and the implementation order in *Brown II*[9] a year later did not require immediate enforcement. Rather, *Brown II* asserted that delay was required, not only to permit time for the major changes required in Southern school policies, but also—and this is important—to enable accommodation to school integration which ran counter to the views and strong emotions of most Southern whites.

"In line with this reasoning," the President continued, "the Court referred with approval to the views of the late Yale law professor Alexander Bickel, who contended that any effort to enforce *Brown* as a criminal law would have failed, as have alcohol prohibition, antigambling, most sex laws, and other laws policing morals. Bickel said, 'It follows that in achieving integration, the task of the law . . . was not to punish law breakers but to diminish their number.'[10]

"Now the Court has found Professor Bickel's argument compelling. Viewed from the perspective provided by four decades, the Court says now that *Brown* was basically a call for a higher morality rather than a judicial decree authorizing Congress to coerce behavior allegedly unjust to blacks because that behavior recognized generally acknowledged differences in racial groups. This characterization of *Brown* explains why *Brown* was no more effective as an enforcement tool than were other 'morals-policing' laws such as alcohol prohibition, anti-gambling, and sex laws, all of which are hard to enforce precisely because they seek to protect our citizens' health and welfare against what a legislature deems self-abuse.

"Relying on this reasoning, the Court determined that laws requiring cessation of white conduct deemed harmful to blacks are hard to enforce because they seek to 'police morality.' While conceding both the states' and the federal government's broad powers to protect the health, safety, and welfare of its citizens, the Court found nothing in the Constitution authorizing regulation of what government at any particular time might deem appropriate 'moral' behavior. The exercise of such authority, the Court feared, could lead Congress to control the perceptions of what some whites believe about the humanity of some blacks. On this point," the President said, "I want to quote the opinion the Supreme Court has just handed down: 'Whatever the good intentions of such an undertaking, it clearly aimed for a spiritual result that might be urged by a religion but is beyond the reach of government coercion.'

"Many of us, of both political persuasions," the President went on, "were emboldened by the Court to seek racial harmony and justice along the route of mutual respect as suggested in its decision. This bill I now sign into law is the result of long debate and good-faith compromise. It is, as its opponents charge and its proponents concede, a radical new approach to the nation's continuing tensions over racial status. It maximizes freedom of racial choice for all our citizens while guaranteeing that people of color will benefit either directly from equal access or indirectly from the fruits of the license taxes paid by those who choose policies of racial exclusion.

"A few, final words. I respect the views of those who vigorously opposed this new law. And yet the course we take today was determined by many forces too powerful to ignore, too popular to resist, and too pregnant with potential to deny. We have vacillated long enough. We must move on toward what I predict will be a new and more candid and collaborative relationship among all our citizens. May God help us all as we seek with His help to pioneer a new path in our continuing crusade to bring justice and harmony to all races in America."

* * *

Well, Geneva, you've done it again, I thought to myself as I finished this second story well after midnight. After all our battles, I thought I'd finally pulled myself up to your advanced level of racial thinking—but the Racial Preference Licensing Act is too much.

"You still don't get it, do you?"

I looked up. There she was—the ultimate African queen—sitting on the small couch in my study. The mass of gray dreadlocks framing Geneva's strong features made a beautiful contrast with her smooth blue-black skin. She greeted me with her old smile, warm yet authoritative.

"Welcome," I said, trying to mask my shock with a bit of savoir-faire. "Do you always visit folks at two o'clock in the morning?"

She smiled. "I decided I could not leave it to you to figure out the real significance of my story."

"Well," I said, "I'm delighted to see you!" As indeed I was. It had been almost five years since Geneva disappeared at the close of the climatic civil rights conference that ended my book *And We Are Not Saved*. Seeing her now made me realize how much I had missed her, and I slipped back easily into our old relationship.

"Tell me, Geneva, how can you justify this law? After all, if the Fourteenth Amendment's equal protection clause retains any viability, it is to bar government-sponsored racial segregation. Even if—as is likely—you convince me of your law's potential, what are civil rights advocates going to say when I present it to them? As you know, it has taken me years to regain some acceptance within the civil rights community—since I suggested in print that civil rights lawyers who urge racial-balance remedies in all school desegregation cases were giving priority to their integration ideals over their clients' educational needs.[11] Much as I respect your insight on racial issues, Geneva, I think your story's going to turn the civil rights community against us at a time when our goal is to persuade them to broaden their thinking beyond traditional, integration-oriented goals."

"Oh ye of little faith!" she responded. "Even after all these years, you remain as suspicious of my truths as you are faithful to the civil rights ideals that events long ago rendered obsolete. Whatever its cost to relationships with your civil rights friends, accept the inevitability of my Racial Preference Licensing Act. And believe—if not me—yourself.

"Although you maintain your faith in the viability of the Fourteenth Amendment, in your writings you have acknowledged, albeit reluctantly, that whatever the civil rights law or constitutional provision, blacks gain little protection against one or another form of racial discrimination unless granting blacks a measure of relief will serve some interest of importance to whites.[12] Virtually every piece of civil rights legislation beginning with the Emancipation Proclamation supports your position.[13] Your beloved Fourteenth Amendment is a key illustration of this white self-interest principle. Enacted in 1868 to provide citizenship to the former slaves and their offspring, support for the amendment reflected Republicans' concern after the Civil War that the Southern Democrats, having lost the war, might win the peace. This was not a groundless fear. If the Southern states could rejoin the union, bar blacks from voting, and regain control of state government, they might soon become the dominant power in the federal government as well.[14]

"Of course, within a decade, when Republican interests changed and the society grew weary of racial remedies and was ready to sacrifice black rights to political expediency, both the Supreme Court and the nation simply ignored the original stated purpose of the Fourteenth Amendment's equal protection guarantee. In 1896, the *Plessy* v. *Ferguson* precedent gave legal validity to this distortion and then to a torrent of Jim Crow statutes. 'Separate but equal' was the judicial promise. Racial subordination became the legally enforceable fact."

"Well, sure," I mustered a response, "the Fourteenth Amendment's history is a definitive example of white self-interest lawmaking, but what is its relevance to your Racial Preference Licensing Act? It seems to me—and certainly will seem to most civil rights advocates—like a new, more subtle, but hardly less pernicious 'separate but equal' law. Is there something I'm missing?"

"You are—which is precisely why I am here."

"I could certainly," I said, "use more of an explanation for a law that entrusts our rights to free-market forces. The law and economics experts might welcome civil rights protections in this form,* but virtually all civil rights professionals will view legalizing racist practices as nothing less than a particularly vicious means of setting the struggle for racial justice back a century. I doubt I could communicate them effectively to most black people."

"Of course you can't! Neither they nor you really want to come to grips with the real role of racism in this country."

"And that is?"

---

*These law and economics experts, especially Richard Posner and John J. Donohue, accept Gary Becker's theory that markets drive out discriminatory employers because discrimination tends to minimize profits.[15] The essence of Posner and Donohue's debate on Title VII (the Equal Employment Opportunity Act) is whether "[l]egislation that prohibits employment discrimination . . . actually enhance[s] rather than impair[s] economic efficiency."[16] Donohue argues that the effects of the Title VII statutory scheme are to increase the rate at which discriminators are driven out of the market from the base rate, which many economists steeped in the neoclassical tradition would argue is the optimal rate. Posner questions whether this effect (the increased rate) occurs; and, significantly, also raises questions about whether the regulatory scheme, designed to decrease discrimination against blacks in employment decisions and thereby increase the net welfare of blacks, actually succeeds in doing so. If neither assumption is accurate, he states that the costs of enforcement and all other costs associated with administering Title VII "are a dead weight social loss that cannot be justified on grounds [not only of efficiency but] of social equity."[17]

Posner and David A. Strauss both make statements that would seem to indicate openness to such measures as the Racial Preference Licensing Act. Posner writes that "it might be that a tax on those whites [who discriminate because of an aversion to blacks and therefore would seek a license] for the benefit of blacks would be justifiable on the grounds of social equity [although this is not an *efficiency* justification in the wealth maximization sense]."[18] And Strauss asks, "Why would the objectives of compensatory justice and avoiding racial stratification not be better served, at less cost, if the legal system permitted statistical discrimination; captured the efficiency gains (and the gains for reduced administrative costs) through taxation, and transferred the proceeds to African Americans?"[19]

"My friend, know it! Racism is more than a group of bad white folks whose discriminatory predilections can be controlled by well-formed laws, vigorously enforced. Traditional civil rights laws tend to be ineffective because they are built on a law enforcement model. They assume that most citizens will obey the law; and when law breakers are held liable, a strong warning goes out that will discourage violators and encourage compliance. But the law enforcement model for civil rights breaks down when a great number of whites are willing—because of convenience, habit, distaste, fear, or simple preference—to violate the law. It then becomes almost impossible to enforce, because so many whites, though not discriminating themselves, identify more easily with those who do than with their victims."

"That much I understand," I replied. "Managers of hotels, restaurants, and other places of public accommodation have complied with antidiscrimination laws because they have discovered that, for the most part, it is far more profitable to serve blacks than to exclude or segregate them. On the other hand, these same establishments regularly discriminate against blacks seeking jobs."

"Precisely right, friend. A single establishment, often a single individual, can be inconsistent for any number of reasons, including the desire not to upset or inconvenience white customers or white employees. More often, management would prefer to hire the white than the black applicant. As one economist has argued, 'racial nepotism' rather than 'racial animus' is the major motivation for much of the discrimination blacks experience."[20]

"But nepotism," I objected, "is a preference for family members or relatives. What does it have to do with racial discrimination?"

Geneva gave me her "you are not serious" smile.

Then it hit me. "Of course! You're right, Geneva, it is hard to get out of the law enforcement model. You're suggesting that whites tend to treat one another like family, at least when there's a choice between them and us. So that terms like 'merit' and 'best qualified' are infinitely manipulable if and when whites must explain why they reject blacks to hire 'relatives'—even when the only relationship is that of race. So, unless there's some pressing reason for hiring, renting to, or otherwise dealing with a black, many whites will prefer to hire, rent to, sell to, or otherwise deal with a white—including one less qualified by objective measures and certainly one who is by any measure better qualified."

"Lord, I knew the man could figure it out! He just needed my presence."

"Well, since a little sarcasm is the usual price of gaining face-to-face access to your insight, Geneva, I am willing to pay. Actually, as I think about it, racial licensing is like that approach adopted some years ago by environmentalists who felt that licensing undesirable conduct was the best means of dealing with industry's arguments that it could not immediately comply with laws to protect the environment. The idea is, as I recall, that a sufficiently high licensing fee would make it profitable for industry to take steps to control the emissions (or whatever), and that thereby it would be possible to reduce damage to health and property much more cheaply than an attempt to control the entire polluting activity.[21]*

"Come to think of it, Geneva, there's even a precedent, of sorts, for the Equality Fund. College football's Fiesta Bowl authorities no doubt had a similar principle in mind when they announced in 1990 that they would create a minority scholarship fund of one hundred thousand dollars or endow an academic chair for minority students at each competing university;

---

*A similar economically based principle underlay the action of the Connecticut Legislature when in 1973 it enacted a statute mandating penalties equal to the capital and operating costs saved by not installing and operating equipment to meet applicable regulatory limits.[22] In 1977, Congress added "noncompliance penalties" patterned after the Connecticut compliance program to section 120 of the Clean Air Act. As of 1988, section 173(1)(A) of the Clean Air Act in effect permits the introduction of new pollution sources if "total allowable emissions" from existing and new sources are "sufficiently less than total emissions from existing sources allowed under the applicable implementation plan."[24]

the aim was to induce colleges to participate in the Fiesta Bowl in Arizona, a state whose populace has refused to recognize the Martin Luther King, Jr., holiday.[25] Sunkist Growers, Inc., the event's sponsor, agreed to match the amount. Further 'sweetening the pot,' one university president promised to donate all net proceeds to university programs benefiting minority students."[26]

"Both examples," remarked Geneva, "illustrate how pocketbook issues are always near the top of the list of motives for racial behavior. That's why compliance with traditional civil rights laws is particularly tough during a period of great economic uncertainty, white nepotism becoming most prevalent when jobs and reasonably priced housing are in short supply. During such times, racial tolerance dissolves into hostility."

"Just as during the 1890s," I interjected, "when economic conditions for the working classes were at another low point, and there was intense labor and racial strife.[27] Today, whites have concluded, as they did a century ago, that the country has done enough for black people despite the flood of evidence to the contrary. The Supreme Court's civil rights decisions reflect the public's lack of interest. In the meantime, enforcement of civil rights laws, never vigorous, has dawdled into the doldrums, and this inertia encourages open violation and discourages victims from filing complaints they fear will only add futility and possible retaliation to their misery."

"All true," Geneva agreed.

"But given the already strong anti-civil rights trends," I argued, "wouldn't the Racial Preference Licensing Act simply encourage them?"

"You are resistant," Geneva replied. "Don't you see? For the very reasons you offer, urging stronger civil rights laws barring discrimination in this period is not simply foolhardy; it's the waste of a valuable opportunity."

"Well," I acknowledged, "I have no doubt that a great many white people would prefer the Racial Preference Licensing Act to traditional civil rights laws. The licensing feature provides legal protection for their racially discriminatory policies—particularly in employment and housing—which whites have practiced covertly, despite the presence on the books of civil rights laws and Court decisions declaring those practices unlawful."

"It is even more attractive," Geneva said, "in that thoughtful whites will view the new law as a means of giving moral legitimacy to their discriminatory preferences by adopting the theory[28] that whites have a right of non-association (with blacks), and that this right should be recognized in law."

"On those grounds," I put in, "the act could expect support from white civil libertarians who think racial discrimination abhorrent but are troubled by the need to coerce correct behavior. Whites will not be happy about the Equality Fund, though these provisions might attract the support of black separatists who would see the fund as a fair trade for the integration they always distrusted.[29] But, believe me, Geneva, no such benefits will assuage the absolute opposition of most civil rights professionals—black and white. They remain committed—to the point of obsession—with integration notions that, however widely held in the 1960s, are woefully beyond reach today."

"Don't start again!" Geneva threw up her hands. "I understand and sympathize with your civil rights friends' unwillingness to accept the legalized reincarnation of Jim Crow. They remember all too well how many of our people suffered and sacrificed to bury those obnoxious signs 'Colored' and 'White.' I think that even if I could prove that the Racial Preference Licensing Act would usher in the racial millennium, civil rights professionals would be unwilling to—as they might put it—'squander our high principles in return for a mess of segregation-tainted pottage.' Victory on such grounds is, they would conclude, no victory at all."

"You mock them, Geneva, but integration advocates would see themselves as standing by their principles."

"Principles, hell! What I do not understand—and this is what I really want to get clear—is what principle is so compelling as to justify continued allegiance to obsolete civil rights strategies that have done little to prevent—and may have contributed to—the contemporary statistics regarding black crime, broken families, devastated neighborhoods, alcohol and drug abuse, out-of-wedlock births, illiteracy, unemployment, and welfare dependency?"

She stopped to take a deep breath, then went on. "Racial segregation was surely hateful, but let me tell you, friend, that if I knew that its return would restore our black communities to what they were before desegregation, I would think such a trade entitled to serious thought. I would not dismiss it self-righteously, as you tell me many black leaders would do. Black people simply cannot afford the luxury of rigidity on racial issues. This story is not intended to urge actual adoption of a racial preference licensing law, but to provoke blacks and their white allies to look beyond traditional civil rights views. We must learn to examine every racial policy, including those that seem most hostile to blacks, and determine whether there is unintended potential African Americans can exploit.

"Think about it! Given the way things have gone historically, if all existing civil rights laws were invalidated, legislation like the Racial Preference Licensing Act might be all African Americans could expect. And it could prove no less—and perhaps more—effective than those laws that now provide us the promise of protection without either the will or the resources to honor that promise."

"Most civil rights advocates," I replied, "would, on hearing that argument, likely respond by linking arms and singing three choruses of 'We Shall Overcome,'"

"You're probably right, friend—but it is your job, is it not, to make them see that racist opposition has polluted the dream that phrase once inspired? However comforting, the dream distracts us from the harsh racial reality closing in around you and ours."

As I did not respond, Geneva continued. "You have to make people *see*. Just as parents used to tell children stories about the stork to avoid telling them about sex, so for similarly evasive reasons many black people hold to dreams about a truly integrated society that is brought into being by the enforcement of laws barring discriminatory conduct. History and— one would hope—common sense tells us that dream is never coming true."

"Dreams and ideals are not evil, Geneva."

"Of course, they aren't, but we need to be realistic about our present and future civil rights activities. The question is whether the activity reflects and is intended to challenge the actual barriers we face rather than those that seem a threat to the integration ideology."

"That's all very high-sounding, Geneva, and I agree that we need a more realistic perspective, but how can I bring others to recognize that need?"

"We might begin by considering the advantages of such a radical measure as the Racial Preference Licensing Act. First, by authorizing racial discrimination, such a law would, as I suggested earlier, remove the long-argued concern that civil rights laws deny anyone the right of non-association.* With the compulsive element removed, people who discriminate against blacks without getting the license authorized by law, may not retain the unspoken but real public sympathy they now enjoy. They may be viewed as what they are: law breakers who deserve punishment.

"Second, by requiring the discriminator both to publicize and to pay all blacks a price for that 'right,' the law may dilute both the financial and the psychological benefits of racism. Today even the worst racist denies being a racist. Most whites pay a tremendous price for their reflexive and often unconscious racism, but few are ready to post their racial preferences on a public license and even less ready to make direct payments for the privilege of practicing discrimination. Paradoxically, gaining the right to practice openly what people now enthusiastically practice covertly, will take a lot of the joy out of discrimination and replace that joy with some costly pain.

"Third, black people will no longer have to divine—as we have regularly to do in this antidiscrimination era—whether an employer, a realtor, or a proprietor wants to exclude them. The license will give them—and the world— ample notice. Those who seek to discriminate without a license will place their businesses at risk of serious, even ruinous, penalties."

"It seems crazy," I began.

"Racism is hardly based on logic. We need to fight racism the way a forest ranger fights fire with fire." . . .

---

*Herbert Wechsler, for example, has suggested the decision in *Brown* v. *Board of Education* might be criticized as requiring "integration [that] forces an association upon those for whom it is unpleasant or repugnant."[30]

NOTES

The epigraph is from Matthew S. Goldberg, "Discrimination, Nepotism, and Long-Run Wage Differentials," *Quarterly Journal of Economics* 97 (1982): 307.

1. *Plessy* v. *Ferguson*, 163 U.S. 537 (1896) (upholding statute requiring segregated railway coaches).

2. *Havens Realty Co.* v. *Coleman*, 455 U.S. 363 (1982).

3. Civil Rights Act of 1964, 42 U.S.C. Secs. 1971, 1975a–1975d, 2000a–2000h-6 (1988).

4. Civil Rights Act of 1991, Public Law No. 102–166, 105 Stat. 1071 (1991).

5. See, for example, *Heart of Atlanta Motel, Inc.* v. *United States*, 379 U.S. 241 (1964), and *Katzenbach* v. *McClung*, 379 U.S. 294 (1964) (both cases upholding the public facilities provisions of Title II).

6. Fair Housing Act of 1968, Pub. L. 90–284, Title VIII, sections 801–19, 42 U.S.C. SS 3601–19 (1970) (as amended 1988, Section 13(a) of Pub. L. 100–430, short title "Fair Housing Amendments Act of 1988").

7. *Brown* v. *Board of Education*, 347 U.S. 483 (1954).

8. See *City of Richmond* v. *J. A. Croson Co.*, 488 U.S. 469 (1989).

9. *Brown v. Board of Education II*, 349 U.S. 294 (1955).

10. Alexander Bickel, *The Least Dangerous Branch: The Supreme Court at the Bar of Politics* (1962), 247–54.

11. Derrick Bell, "Serving Two Masters: Integration Ideals and Client Interests in School Desegregation Litigation," *Yale Law Journal* 85 (1976): 470.

12. Comment, "Brown v. Board of Education and the Interest-Convergence Dilemma," *Harvard Law Review* 93 (1980): 518.

13. See Derrick Bell, *Race, Racism and American Law*, 2nd ed. (1980), 2–44.

14. Ibid., 33.

15. Gary Becker, *The Economics of Discrimination*, 2nd ed. (1971). See, for example, Richard Epstein, *Forbidden Grounds: The Case Against Employment Discrimination Laws* (1992); Richard A. Posner, *Economic Analysis of Law*, 3rd ed. (1986), 621–23; John J. Donohue, "Is Title VII Efficient?" *University of Pennsylvania Law Review* 134 (1986): 1411; Richard A. Posner, "The Efficiency and Efficacy of Title VII," *University of Pennsylvania Law Review* 136 (1987): 513; John J. Donohue, "Further Thoughts on Employment Discrimination Legislation: A Reply to Judge Posner," *University of Pennsylvania Law Review* 136 (1987): 523; and Strauss, "Law and Economics." See also John J. Donohue and Peter Siegelman, "The Changing Nature of Employment Discrimination Litigation," *Stanford Law Review* 43 (1991): 983; John J. Donohue and James J. Heckman, "Re-Evaluating Federal Civil Rights Policy," *Georgetown Law Journal* 79 (1991): 1713.

16. Donohue, "Is Title VII Efficient?" 1411–12.

17. Posner, "Efficiency and Efficacy of Title VII, 513, 521.

18. Ibid., 516.

19. David A. Strauss, "The Law and Economics of Racial Discrimination in Employment: The Case for Numerical Standards" *Georgetown Law Journal* 79 (1991): 1619, 1630.

20. Matthew Goldberg, "Discrimination, Nepotism, and Long-Run Wage Differentials," *Quarterly Journal of Economics* 97 (1982): 307.

21. See *Economic Report of the President*, H.R. Doc. No. 28, 92d Cong., 1st Sess. 119 (1971).

22. See Conn. Gen. Stat. Sec. 22a-6b (West Supp. 1990).

23. Act of 7 August 1977, Pub. L. No. 95–96, 91 Stat. 714, codified as amended at 42 U.S.C. Sec. 7420(2)(A) (1988 & Supp. 1990).

24. Act of 7 August 1977, as amended at 42 U.S.C. Sec. 7503(1)(A) (1988).

25. "There's Another Way to Honor King," *Chicago Tribune*, 18 November 1990, sec. 4, p. 3.

26. George Will, "Bush's Blunder on Racial Scholarships," *Newsday* 27 December 1990, p. 95 (characterizing Fiesta Bowl officials' actions as a "penance for the sin of playing football in Arizona").

27. See Nell Painter, *Standing at Armageddon: The United States, 1877–1919* (1987), 110–44, 163–69.

28. Herbert Wechsler, "Toward Neutral Principles of Constitutional Law," *Harvard Law Review* 73 (1959): 1 (suggesting that the *Brown* decision may have arbitrarily traded the rights of whites not to associate with blacks in favor of the rights of blacks to associate with whites).

29. For a summary of black reparations efforts in both the nineteenth and the twentieth centuries, see Bell, *Race, Racism*, 44–47.

30. Herbert Wechsler, "Toward Neutral Principles," *Harvard Law Review* 73 (1959): 1, 34.

THE FUTURE OF ANTIRACISMS

Eileen O'Brien

WHO IS A WHITE ANTIRACIST? DEFINING TERMS

When the word "feminist" is uttered, most people at least conjure up an image of someone or something focused on rejecting sexism. Certainly, there are many different images of feminists in American popular culture—from the most radical "bra-burners" or "male bashers" to the more liberal supporters of "women's issues." Volumes have been written on the varieties of feminisms and the images and stereotypes associated with the word "feminist." Everyone from politicians to academics draws parallels between sexism and racism, so one might expect that a word like "antiracist" might be equally familiar. Yet I have lost count of how often I have had to explain the topic of my research—"white antiracists"—to people who inquire about it. Hearing the words "white" and "racist" in the same breath, especially if the word "activist" is included as a descriptor, people have tended to picture a white Ku Klux Klan or neo-Nazi activist when I have told them the topic of my research. Not only is the word "antiracist" not easily recognizable, but the coupling of the word "white" with "antiracist" makes for an even more unfamiliar designation. Who are we talking about here?

Antiracists, quite simply, are people who have committed themselves, in thought, action and practice, to dismantling racism. In our culture, "I'm not a racist" rolls off the tongues of many people, often right before they make incredibly derogatory or racially stereotypic remarks, so it is important to distinguish between "nonracists" and "antiracists." Joe Barndt has written: "Nonracists try to deny that the prison exists. Antiracists work for the prison's eventual destruction" (1991, 65). Rather than trying to minimize the significance of racism in the United States, for themselves and others, antiracists make it a point to notice and address racism regularly. I also borrow from bell hooks [*sic*] to develop this definition:

a white antiracist is someone who "daily vigilantly resist[s] becoming reinvested in white supremacy" (1995, 157–158). So in saying that an antiracist notices and addresses racism regularly, I mean that this effort is daily and vigilant. As I sought people to interview for this research, I made them aware of this definition and relied upon their own self-definitions. For the whites whose names (or pseudonyms) appear here, being an "antiracist" by the above definition was an important part of their identities. To find out what whites can do about racism today, one of the best places to look for answers is in the lives of those who now practice antiracism as an ongoing, vigilant part of their day.

Although I have been using the terms "racism" and "white supremacy" interchangeably thus far, it is important to discuss their meanings, since racism and white supremacy (and their elimination) are the daily focus of an antiracist identity. Racism and white supremacy should not be confused, in and of themselves, with the ideology and practices of the Ku Klux Klan or other extremists. Although such an overt and even hostile stance of white racial superiority is indeed racist and white supremacist, it is only one of many dimensions of racism or white supremacy. Racism and white supremacy are manifested in blatant ways, but they also work in covert and subtle ways, and the latter are much more common in today's society than the former. Tatum (1997) has defined racism as a system of advantage, and for the duration of the United States's history that system of advantage has legally, politically, socially, and economically favored white Americans. So, certainly, any clear act of prejudice or discrimination—someone who says whites are naturally more intelligent than blacks or black homeseekers who are denied a mortgage due to their race—would be an example of racism. However, subtle and unintended actions might also be considered examples of racism, such as a television network which does not feature any actors of color in its prime time shows.

So racism is a system of many different beliefs and practices (individual and institutional, intentional and unintentional) which result in a collective advantage of one "race" over another.

That advantaged race has always been the white in our society, which is why people like bell hooks and others prefer the term "white supremacy" instead of racism. Because racism is often thought of as a "black problem," using the term white supremacy instead of racism shifts the focus towards whites' advantages and away from people of color's disadvantages (and also away from any advantages individual people of color may have over individual whites). The term white supremacy also reminds us that white advantage can be bolstered even when people of color are not present or not even mentioned—when "race" seems to not be an issue. Because my definition of the term "racism" includes the focus on systemic white advantages which "white supremacy" seeks to incorporate, I will be using them both interchangeably throughout this work.

The final note that should be made about definitions is that to be "white," or any "race" for that matter, is a social and cultural construct that has no true basis in biology, and is fairly recent in human history. Whole volumes have also been devoted to this idea, so I will not belabor it here except to paraphrase W. I. Thomas—even though the concepts of "black," "white," or any other "race" are not real, they are real in their consequences. It is in that spirit that I use any racial category throughout this work.

. . .

I interviewed thirty North American white antiracists for this study, between 1996 and 1999. The respondents were selected using a purposive snowball sampling technique. My purpose was to gather as wide a variety of white antiracists as possible, in terms of geographic region, age, and socioeconomic status. I also deliberately selected an even number of men and women for the study (fifteen each) because the scant research done previously on white antiracists in the 1990s usually relied solely on women and feminist networks (e.g., Eichstedt 1997; Feagin and Vera 1995; Frankenberg 1993). . . .

There were some aspects of interviewing protocol for white antiracists which are not at all addressed in most traditional methods handbooks. One thing that was particularly important to nearly all of these respondents was knowing about my own identity as an antiracist. Not only did they want to know whether I was antiracist, but they also wanted to know *why* I was, and what had motivated me to be so— some as a condition of being interviewed, others as a condition of being more open and candid during the interview process. Additionally, a statement in the "informed consent" form assuring the respondents that their real name would not be used in my reports, which might ordinarily result in more comfort and candor with the interview, actually left many interviewees disappointed. Given the historical amnesia about white antiracists I have already discussed here, a good number of the respondents felt strongly that their real names *should* be used if at all possible. They expressed the hope that they could connect with other antiracists, build networks, and become known for the work they were proud of doing. In this way, the project departed somewhat from traditional research methods in order to allow for more comfort for the respondents, but more importantly to form community—between myself and other white antiracists as well as between the respondents and any other antiracists who might read the book (including other respondents). This was in keeping with the larger goal of the study: to facilitate visibility and connection between white antiracists so they would not need to reinvent the wheel.

Although the interviews make up the bulk of the data used here, the analysis would not have been complete without the archival analysis and participant observation I did with antiracist groups and their members. Half (fifteen) of the respondents belonged to one of two antiracist organizations—Anti-Racist Action (ARA) or the People's Institute for Survival and Beyond (PI)—which are described in detail in the next section. As a participant observer, I joined ARA in protesting a KKK demonstration in Ohio in 1996. Then, in 1997, I accompanied one ARA organizer to a concert in which he distributed information about ARA and signed up people on the mailing list to receive *ARA News*, its free biannual publication. As part of that effort, I answered questions and provided information about the group and offered information about how they could join. In 1998 one other white person and I coordinated an ARA chapter in Florida for the duration of one semester, which included many efforts of recruitment ("tabling") like that which I participated in at the concert, as well as updating phone lists and presiding over meetings. I also participated in one of PI's intense two-and-one-half-day Undoing Racism workshops in 1998.

To get to know these organizations, their missions and practices as clearly as possible, I also reviewed any written materials they produced, including brochures, pamphlets, newsletters, and books. Additionally, I exchanged written correspondence with key organizers from each group as we dialogued about their philosophies. Even when interviewees did not belong to ARA or PI, they sometimes provided me with written information about their own activities in groups, such as New Abolitionists, Race Traitors, and Institutes for the Healing of Racism. While I do not make these groups a key part of the analysis here, reading about them helped me to reach a greater understanding of the diversity of antiracist experiences and to see more clearly the origins of these particular individuals' motivations and philosophies. It will become evident throughout this text that it is impossible to fully comprehend the experiences of white antiracist activists without factoring in the organizations which have inspired and shaped them. In this work I focus on ARA and PI to illuminate this point.

ANTI-RACIST ACTION AND THE PEOPLE'S INSTITUTE FOR SURVIVAL AND BEYOND

Anti-Racist Action (ARA) was officially founded in the early 1990s in the cities of Columbus, Ohio; Minneapolis; and Toronto, mostly by white individuals to counteract Ku Klux Klan and neo-Nazi activity in their communities (see Novick 1997; Franklin 1998). Counterdemonstrations at Klan rallies drew initial memberships, and youths wanting to protest right wing hate groups that were forming at their schools followed suit. Now there are close to a

hundred chapters in the United States alone. Although ARA is sometimes criticized for its focus on the racism of these "fringe" groups, the *ARA News* exposes how these groups are not so "fringe" after all. This newsletter, with subscribers in the tens of thousands, also serves to educate about racism (and other forms of hatred) happening around the country through its collage of newspaper clippings and commentaries. Another from of education ARA provides to the community is its visits to local schools to give presentations. ARA focuses predominantly on frontline activism, and its newest and most famous such project is Copwatch—a system of videotaping and police misconduct litigation that "polices the police" in urban neighborhoods (Selena and Katrina 1996). ARA's emphasis on overt forms of racism is evident in the four main principles all of its various chapters abide by:

1. We go where they go. Whenever racists/fascists are organizing or active in public, we confront them and do our best to stop them.

2. We don't rely on the cops or courts to do our work or to protect us.

3. We defend and support each other in spite of our differences.

4. We are active with the goal of building a movement against racism, sexism, anti-Semitism, homophobia and discrimination against the disabled, the oldest, the youngest and the weakest of our society (from an organizational memo "What to Do: An Introduction to ARA").

Although ARA is a network of many different chapters with different foci and expertise, they all agree to uphold these four principles.

The People's Institute for Survival and Beyond (PI) was originally founded in 1980 in New Orleans by Jim Dunn and Ron Chisom, two African American men, as a training institute for those in social service professions which served primarily communities of color. PI is most noted for its Undoing Racism workshops, which are now offered on a national scale and serve as transformative experiences for whites confronting racism. Perhaps the best way to explain the workshop is to list what it is *not*: "The Undoing Racism workshop is not . . . a quick fix, a sensitivity session, a guilt trip, a sexism/classism workshop, a training in reducing individual acts of prejudice, [or] a lecture" (Chisom and Washington 1997, 88–89). While ARA concentrates on more overt acts of racism, one of PI's workshop topics is "how well-intentioned individuals and institutions unwittingly maintain racist policies, biases, systems and benefits" (Chisom and Washington 1997, 87); this indicates attention to covert and unintentional forms of racism. Focusing on institutionalized racism as a barrier to community organizing, the workshop trainers delve extensively into historical and contemporary race relations and rely on a Malcolm X-like philosophy that whites should be doing separate work in their own communities. As such, PI has a white subsidiary group called European Dissent ("dissenting what has been done in the European name") of which all of the PI respondents here are members. PI also has four principles:

1. That racism has historically been the most critical barrier to unity in this country. It continues to be the primary cause of our failure to overcome poverty and bring about justice.

2. That culture is the life support system of the community. Organizers must understand and respect indigenous culture and cultural diversity.

3. That *militarism* is applied racism. It is a pervasive cultural, economic, and political force that undercuts all efforts to work for justice and peace.

4. That *history* is a guide to the future. We take seriously the notion that those who fail to learn from history are condemned to repeat it (from an informational brochure).

These principles indicate that, compared to ARA, PI is dedicated toward understanding/education as opposed to action. While ARA also does education and PI also does action, these are not the primary foci of their principles. Further, a comparison of the two organizations' principles reveals that ARA sees other "isms" as just as important, while PI sees them as secondary and racism as "primary." The organizations also differ in that PI makes explicit acknowledgment of race differences within their movement while ARA does not.

Both ARA and PI are antiracist organizations which draw large proportions of white members. As such, they were an ideal source for obtaining sizable numbers of white antiracists to interview. At the beginning of my research, as places to find respondents seemed to me to be their only relevance to my work. However, once I began analyzing what those respondents had to say about being antiracist—from what inspired them to become antiracists to what they did every day—it became evident that what they did and how they did it had everything to do with the role of ARA or PI in their lives. How these groups "frame" racism and what we can do about it will become a recurring influence throughout the text.

. . .

Two major antiracist organizations share the common goal of fighting racism. They share the goal of wanting to involve more and more people in their struggles, and just by being active in their communities they have done so. Their white members share passions about wanting to reduce the daily assaults on the humanity of other members of our society. Yet they differ on nearly everything else. From where they focus their efforts to even the definition of racism itself, in some ways they are as opposite as night and day. This makes it increasingly difficult to visualize a unified antiracist movement toward which aspiring white antiracists can look. Since white antiracists are few and far between as it is, the lack of a common language among them poses a challenge for any quest for complete unity. However, there is potential for coalition building among these groups as well as among those who do not have access to any such group in their immediate surroundings. The key to this potential lies in defining racism as broadly as possible, even as the differences between white antiracists lie in how they define racism. Competing frames of racism separate the two organizations, yet fitting each of these frames into a larger frame of which they each hold a part opens up possibilities in which all white antiracists, regardless of organizational affiliation (or lack thereof) can be included.

STRENGTHS THAT ORGANIZATIONS SHARE

Although in some ways as different as night and day, ARA and PI do both provide some similar resources to members. For one thing, they both make antiracism a visible option in their communities, regardless of what form that antiracism takes. Several of the activists I interviewed stressed ARA or PI "recruitment" (for lack of a better word) as crucial to their becoming antiracists in the first place. For example, Jason began going to ARA meetings with a friend. Ani picked up some literature about ARA and its meeting time at a local concert, and then attended as part of a course assignment to participate in a social movement. Holly embarked upon a trial-and-error search for someplace to be an activist when she finally settled on ARA, which was well publicized in her area. Pam, Rosalind, Henry, and Mike all attended the PI Undoing Racism workshop on the recommendation of friends. None of these individuals had any strong commitments to antiracism before their involvement with these groups. This lends support to the argument that more whites would become antiracist if only they just knew where to go or what to do. Organizations thus serve as these "role model" examples.

Additionally, regardless of its frame of racism, being a member of a local organization appears to protect white antiracists from job- or life-threatening repercussions for their work. . . . Certainly, it is easier for those who wish to penalize antiracists to direct their disapproval at a single individual rather than a group. But we also must consider the organization as a supportive resource for planning successful actions. For example, if Amy had consulted a larger group about how to respond to the racist fraternity at her school, they might have advised her not to put her name and home phone number on the signs; ARA encourages chapters to use post office boxes as contact information rather than home addresses or numbers precisely for this reason. If she had worked in conjunction with ARA for this action, undoubtedly they would have alerted her to this fact and saved her from threatening phone calls. Similarly, when David made the decision to

take his students to a civil rights demonstration, if he had consulted a group like PI first, they might have first asked him who else at the school might be supportive, and advised him to act in conjunction with these individuals or with certain community groups. Then he might have been less likely to have been isolated and fired. Organizations serve as a contact point, especially for new activists, to connect with more veteran activists on what works and what does not work. This expertise and foresight contributes to the buffer effect that organizations have in protecting against the more serious "occupational hazards" of antiracism.

The recruitment potential and the "safety effect" of both ARA and PI were the most notable similarities between the two. Again, it is also evident that both groups share a passion for organizing against the atrocious effects that racism has on society, perhaps the most important and crucial concurrence. What the organizations share in common is important to keep in mind, because sometimes the differences seem almost overwhelming.

DIFFERENT FRAMES, DIFFERENT PICTURES

The different frames that ARA and PI use to define racism were made evident throughout this text, so I will summarize them only briefly. ARA focuses on "hate in any form" and targets mainly neo-Nazi groups, the Ku Klux Klan, and police brutality in terms of their organizing efforts. PI defines racism as "race prejudice plus power" and targets everyday institutions such as school and government in their organizing efforts. These overall organizing frames result in several practical differences between the two groups. Although both groups do well at "recruiting" new members, it is interesting to note how the competing frames result in differences even here. ARA seems more focused on raising the sheer numbers of ARA members and is not as concerned about educating them into any particular framework, provided they agree to the four principles. . . . On the other hand, PI sees their two-and-one-half-day Undoing Racism workshop as crucial, because they claim there are many people who may think they are

Table 10.1   Similarities and Differences Between Antiracist Organizations

	PI	*ARA*	*Both Organizations*
Becoming involved	Quality of "recruits" paramount	Quantity of "recruits" paramount	Provide visible place to start; recruitment when friends ask others to join
Frame of racism	Covert racism perpetuated by members of everyday institutions; reflexive race cognizance	Overt racism perpetuated by hate groups and police; selective race cognizance	
Individual actions	More likely to use long-term strategy of building relationship with perpetrator; "maintain relationships"	More likely to confront head-on	
Institutional actions	Use own positions within institutions to bring about change; "gatekeepers"	Challenge institutions in which they are not members, such as the police	Provide buffer against repercussions; less likely to have individual jobs/lives threatened
Emotional struggles	Provide context within which to interpret distrust; "authentic relationships"; "accountability"	Personal struggles and relationships not a primary focus	

antiracist but are actually doing more harm than good in the communities where they think they are helping. If forced to choose between two hundred people who have not done their workshop but want to help their community and twenty people who still want to help *and* have done the workshop, they may go with the latter since there would be no way of guaranteeing that the former would not simply result in more damage to the community. In Table 10.1, I have summarized this difference as quantity versus quality, noting simply what is *most* important to each. Ideally, of course, both would prefer quantity *and* quality of membership, but the frame dictates on what they will spend more time and energy. ARA spends a lot of time tabling (collecting names) and PI spends a lot of time holding workshops (educating).

The way ARA and PI have framed antiracism also affects how members see race itself, in terms of how they claim to perceive themselves and people of color. PI members tend to be *reflexively* race cognizant, whereas ARA members tend to be *selectively* race cognizant. This

means that PI members are explicit about noticing their own race and a person of color's race, while ARA members recognize how "racists" use race as a way of dispensing power and privilege but strive not to notice race in their own interactions. In this respect, it is as if the two groups are speaking different languages. For ARA members, colorblindness is a desired goal for all, while for PI members, colorblindness is described as "denial" and even as a form of racism itself. This is hardly a matter of semantics since it has everything to do with their organizing efforts. To ARA members, prejudice in any form is the target, and the race of the perpetrator is of no concern. As Travis put it, racists come in "every color and every nationality." Further, the members' own racial backgrounds matter little in how they organize. While ARA is predominantly white, it does have members of color, but no difference is articulated about how those members should proceed in terms of their actions. The guidelines for protesting and issues one will face as an antiracist are not separated out by race. This contrasts with PI, which has a separate group for whites called European Dissent and stresses that the issues whites face and people of color face when doing antiracism are very different. Being reflexive, PI members also speak about working on their "own racism," as distinct from ARA members who focus on the "hatemongers" (which do not include themselves).

This focus on their "own racism" on the part of PI bespeaks humility, and this has an outcome on how they react to racism at the individual level. Perhaps because they see themselves as not so far removed from anyone who could make a racist comment or joke, PI members tend to take actions that will result in befriending that person rather than insulting him or her. ARA member Holly felt free to boldly call individuals out on a streetcar, perhaps because she saw them as "hatemongers" of which she did not feel a part. In contrast, PI members are taught to "maintain relationships" with other white people, and to see themselves as part of a "white collective" (another reflexive outlook). Thus, they are more likely to formulate long-term strategies for developing a relationship with the perpetrator of a racist comment or joke, in hopes of persuading the person to think about it differently, and maybe even to come to a workshop.

Again, being reflexively race cognizant allows whites to see themselves as participants in racism in a way that being selectively race cognizant would not. As such, when focusing on institutional racism, PI members struggle to bring change into the institutions where they live, work, and worship, while ARA members challenge institutions such as the police force, which they explicitly advocate in their principles should not be considered *allies*, much less should ARA members consider *being* police officers. In evaluating their successes, then, it is notable that PI members tend to stress changes in their own institutions (adding "antiracist" to Kendra's church mission statement; adding a multicultural arts program to Pam's school) while ARA members point to high attendance at protest events as a success. The latter perspective not only emphasizes resistance against an entity of which one is not a member (for example, the KKK), but it also reminds us of the focus on quantity as opposed to quality.

Finally, being reflexive means that personal struggles with emotions and relationships are much more of a concern. I never asked my respondents to talk about feelings specifically, so the fact that PI members brought emotions up more regularly into our discussions indicates that they see emotions as more of a part of antiracism than do ARA members. Further, PI members relied on specific terminology such as accountability and authentic relationships when describing these personal struggles, so even the terminology itself invites PI members to reflect on their own personal relationships as a part of antiracism. This focus on terminology brings us back to a key point: that these two organizations sometimes may as well be speaking different languages.

NONORGANIZATIONAL MEMBERS: MORE LIKE PI THAN ARA

Many of the voices I have drawn upon in this analysis were not members of ARA or PI, so I would be remiss in omitting them from this discussion. It became evident throughout the analysis here that those who were not affiliated with either ARA or PI were more likely to be reflexively than selectively race cognizant. Even though their journey to that point might have been self-described as longer than that of PI members, most had made it there by the time our interview took place. The similarity of those who were not exposed to PI's philosophy to PI members themselves can only be explained by examining the different frames involved.

PI's and ARA's different frames of who is the antagonist, and where one's actions should be directed, have everything to do with why individuals acting alone are less likely to model ARA's selective race cognizance. Framing racism as part of everyday institutions (as does reflexive race cognizance) means it is easier for whites to participate in the absence of an organization; challenging a group like neo-Nazis is less inviting of a task to take on by oneself. Even though institutions are seen as larger than life, and neo-Nazis seen as isolated crazies, in reality neo-Nazis seldom practice in isolation. They recruit members just like ARA or PI does, by encouraging friends of the virtues of the group. Thus, a single individual who wishes to counterdemonstrate against neo-Nazis or KKK members finds himself or herself up against a pack of people for which she or he is no match. Further, one actually has to research when a right-wing group is going to demonstrate, or else rely upon an antiracist group for information on when they think the group will demonstrate. This again places emphasis on the group, whereas people are always at their job, church, school, or home and can regularly observe racism in those areas without consulting others. Although a group might help advise individuals on how to challenge that racism in those areas without ending up threatened or fired, there are many less risky things one can do in those settings without needing the backing of a group. Therefore, the very nature of being an isolated antiracist lends itself to being reflexive about one's involvement in racism, hence the closer resemblance to PI's reflexively race cognizant frame.

SAME FRAME, DIFFERENT PICTURES

While throughout this work I have used the social movements concept of framing, it will be useful when considering the future of antiracism to think literally of frames and pictures for the sake of analogy. There is one style of picture frame that allows for two or three or more pictures to be put in it, due to the way the matting is cut. These are sometimes referred to as collage frames. It is this type of frame that I will use as my analogy to discuss the possibility of coalition building between multiple antiracist groups that is necessary if we are to ever see a strong white antiracist presence in our society.

The discrepant frames between ARA and PI are directly related to how they define racism. ARA says racists are other, hateful people, while PI says racists are all whites since institutions lean toward privileging them. Due to the inclusion of all whites in the latter definition, white PI members posit themselves in that definition. All the differences in organizing tactics and foci of energy then flow from those competing frames. If ARA members talked about being colorblind, PI members would see them as racist, while if PI members said all whites are

racist and people of color cannot be racist, ARA would find this in itself to be a racist and prejudicial statement. Although my research did not involve members of the two groups directly dialoging about the other's frame of racism, disagreements were directly implicated in many of their respective statements. With these two diametrically opposing frames, the outlook for coalition building between the two groups seems pessimistic, to say the least.

However, if frames of antiracism are based on one's definition of racism, let us conceptualize a definition within which both groups could work inside the same frame. Racism is a system of advantage for those of the privileged "race" (which would be whites in the context of the United States) which has both overt and covert manifestations and occurs at both individual and institutional levels. Within this all-inclusive definition, it is evident that all of the white antiracists interviewed for this study are at least working on *some* aspect of racism. This is an important point, since there are those who may argue that anyone who says they do not notice their own race, or that of others, cannot truly be antiracist. They may question whether some ARA members are actually antiracist, if they are focusing only on overt acts of prejudice. However, since racism is maintained through a combination of overt and covert acts, and through a combination of individual and institutional levels, to say that ARA is an antiprejudice, but not an antiracist, group is incorrect. They do indeed focus on *part* of racism. Indeed it would be impossible to focus on every aspect of racism simultaneously. It is a multifaceted problem, to be sure.

Yet it is unclear whether ARA subscribes to this definition, and is just choosing to focus on one aspect for the sake of practicality, or whether its members are guided by a limited view of racism. If we examine the only four principles that all ARA chapters must agree to . . . , they begin with the commitment to publicly challenge "racists/fascists" whenever they are organizing in public. "We go where they go," it reads. Are the only racists those who stand on a street corner and proclaim their prejudices unabashedly? The second and third principles refer to using grassroots tactics and agreeing to disagree among chapters, so it is not until the fourth and final principle that we see an actual broadening of focus. The fourth principle mentions "discrimination," but this word is immediately followed by "against the disabled, the oldest, the youngest and the weakest of our society." Thus, this alerts us to a wider range of "isms" than just racism, but it does not necessarily point to a broader conceptualization of racism itself.

Notably, the *ARA News* edition circulated by the Columbus, Ohio, chapter features clippings of newspaper articles highlighting various forms of discrimination, including job-based civil rights lawsuits like a black fast-food worker being fired because of her braids. Mac was responsible for collecting these articles. It is evident from the excerpts of Mac's interview that Mac had a different perspective than most ARA members. He was considerably older, having lived through the civil rights movement, and he was reflexive in terms of thinking about his own role in racism in a way that other ARA members were not. Mac attempted to infuse a more inclusive definition of racism into this particular publication, but my interviews with other ARA members did not clearly indicate that anyone else had picked up on this wider perspective. All of the articles in *ARA News* which highlighted activism focused on the efforts of Copwatch or on neo-Nazi groups. While Mac's approach of getting members' "foot-in-the-door" and educating them later may have its advantages in terms of *quantity* of membership, members may be left with limited understandings of racism that will not help them to see it when it is going on in their midst (including when they themselves are the culprits).

Conversely, PI members may not often focus on "hate groups," but they recognize they are one aspect of racism at least. The European Dissent press conference about the racist fraternity . . . was one of the rare times that PI members focused on overt racist acts. For the most part, they do their antiracist work within their own places of work and worship, usually focusing on more covert dimensions of racism. However, the educational aspect of PI provided by the Undoing Racism workshop allows for racism to actually be defined for members in a way that is never done by ARA. This meant that everyone I interviewed from PI gave me similar

definitions of racism when asked, but ARA members each presented their own unique definition. Travis focused on "hate-mongering," while Tim also mentioned "outward hatred" but then admitted there were more subtle things like the internal discomfort he sometimes got around people of color since he so rarely sees them where he lives. So ARA members differed in the degree to which they included covert aspects of racism, while PI members were unanimous about racism having multiple manifestations. The white antiracists who were not members of either group provided definitions similar to those given by PI members. They consistently included "unintentional" (covert) aspects of racism like white privilege in their definitions in a way that ARA members did not. In our society, we often agree that something is racist if it is overt, yet we have a harder time agreeing upon the less overt manifestations of racism. This disagreement is no less present among the white antiracists featured in this study.

Keeping the all-encompassing definition of racism as an overarching frame, there could be room for certain antiracist groups to work on overt hate groups while others work on covert racism in less public settings. That is, within the frame of racism, particular antiracist groups could focus on different issues within this frame. Yet this is not exactly what is happening on the current antiracist scene. Instead, there is a lack of agreement upon the definition of racism, so some antiracists are taking a myopic view and not even realizing that they are working on but one piece of a much larger puzzle. . . . Selective race cognizance can be used as a strategy—that is, language which reflects this myopic view of racism (e.g., color-blindness) could be used as a tool to engage mainstream whites with antiracism as an initial step. However, when antiracists continue to conceptualize racism as mainly overt acts only, even after some time with an antiracist organization, it becomes less plausible to regard the limited frame as solely strategic. Acknowledging all facets of racism while strategically directing tactics at one aspect of it is quite different from directing tactics at one aspect of racism while ignoring its other manifestations. In order for these antiracists to be working within the same frame with their different tactics, those who focus on overt acts would have to be cognizant of their own role in racist institutions even if that is not where they chose to direct their antiracist energies. If these changes were made, coalition building among white antiracists would be a more foreseeable part of the future of antiracism.

This is not to suggest that all social movement organizations within a movement should share a common ideology. Indeed, this has never been the case with any social justice movement. Historically, such organizations have ranged from the most liberal to the most radical within almost any movement, from civil rights and feminism to environmental and labor movements. Organizations have combined forces, tackling different aspects of the problem, and often vehemently disagreeing with each other on whose area of focus is more necessary. However, when we consider the situation of white antiracists, their organizational rifts present a more serious challenge than mere *tactical* differences, because *framing* differences between white antiracists revolve around how they define their *own* relationship to the problem. African Americans may find themselves disagreeing on whether to use violent or nonviolent tactics, for example, but they are less likely to disagree on the fundamental issue of whether they are impacted by racism themselves. Following the frame and picture analogy, they would be working within the same definitional frame of the problem but selecting different areas of focus or different pictures within the frame. This is the most common type of difference we see historically between social movement organizations. The framing issue is particularly central for white antiracists precisely because they are privileged resisters— they stand to benefit from racism in ways their allies of color do not. Therefore, working in different frames altogether comes out of whites' struggle with conceptualizing their own role in racism. While in any social movement there is undoubtedly room for disagreement about where one's energies are best focused, coalition building would be enhanced if there were minimal agreement on the frame of the problem, particularly members' own relationship to it.

What Whites Can Do About Racism

Ideally, coalition building would be so successful that there would be visible antiracist groups with sizeable white involvement in nearly every community. Yet this vision is undoubtedly futuristic, perhaps distantly so. Immediately, however, there are still many ways whites can become active in fighting racism, and the data presented here attest to those multiple possibilities. While those possibilities are endless, they can be summarized in three key areas: finding strength in numbers, strategizing actions for maximum effectiveness, and striving for humility.

Finding Strength in Numbers

We know that the most effective antiracist actions have not occurred in isolation. There are many antiracist organizations across the United States and Canada in which whites can take part. . . . If available, whites can get involved with a local organization. Membership grows by member referral. White antiracists should remind themselves that part of their antiracist work includes reaching out to others, particularly other whites, so inviting others to meetings and workshops with their organization would be a crucial way of extending this work. Also, white antiracists may want to be proactive in seeing to it that their organization is aware of all manifestations of racism, both overt and covert, and make sure white members are mindful of the ways in which they participate in racism themselves from day to day.

White antiracists can also find strength in numbers even outside of any antiracist organization. If they are interested in fighting racism in the areas where they live and work, they should talk to others in those areas who they think might be sympathetic to such work. This kind of networking may include passing on particularly influential readings or other forms of expression which could be influential in making those other people aware of the reality of modern racism and its effects, if they are not already aware. Again, one undertakes this work cognizant of overt and covert levels of racism. Certainly, if racism in manifesting itself overtly in one's home community, there are readily visible places to begin. However, there are many other necessary tasks for white antiracists to take on, even in seemingly benign areas. Is there token integration, no integration, or integration at a surface level while covert racism lurks below the surface? We know that some antiracists have begun their work with these very questions about their churches, workplaces, gyms, and even their own families. The key in addressing all these issues is to not go at it alone. Transforming these institutions requires the complicity of more than just one of their members. Developing a cadre of allies will be a necessary first step.

Strategizing Actions for Maximum Effectiveness

At both individual and institutional levels, we have seen that white antiracists can make a difference. Clearly, taking antiracist action goes far beyond merely having good intentions. White antiracists most often develop some kind of strategy whereby change would be most likely to occur, keeping in mind that change is not immediate nor should it be postponed indefinitely, whether out of fear or out of privilege. Privileged resistance means that whites have a wider range of options to choose from for fighting racism than people of color do. They are more likely to be seen, heard, and believed, and less likely to suffer repercussions for their actions. With this wider range of choices also comes responsibilities. Several white antiracists have learned through decades of experience that effective action requires a balance between (1) courage to speak out in difficult situations and (2) diplomacy enough to maintain relationships with those in whom change is desired. Effective antiracist action should not result in severing ties with either individuals or institutions who could be sources of antiracist change. By the same token, one should not be so preoccupied with pleasing everyone that no action is ever taken. Simply put, diplomacy should not be confused with complacency. Each situation an antiracist encounters will have to be evaluated, since what constitutes effectiveness in one setting may not be in another. Regardless of the situational specifics, however, keeping away

from the two extreme poles of complacency and of aggressively alienating others is the key to developing effective white antiracist strategies.

Striving for Humility

Even when white antiracists gather in large numbers, and strategize for maximum effectiveness, they will undoubtedly make mistakes and in some cases even cause more harm than good. Those white antiracists who recognize the inevitability of these "minefields" that they will face along the way will be more apt to sustain their commitment to antiracism and continue their work despite these setbacks. There is no room for an "ego" in white antiracist work. Whites undergo socialization from birth, which prepares them to effectively uphold the racial status quo and which alone cannot immediately chip these layers of socialization away. The sooner white antiracists accept the lifetime of learning that is ahead of them, the easier it will be for them to be open to criticism and self-improvement, without defensiveness or deflection onto others. As one activist of color put it, "humility is something white people need, big time!" Having white antiracists striving to be humble is crucial in maintaining the commitment to antiracism over the long haul that will be needed in order to incorporate succeeding generations into the process.

Humility with respect to antiracism is especially a challenge because of the individualistic society in which we live. Individualism places emphasis on the ability to control one's own fate. Whites may feel a loss of that sense of control to which they have become accustomed when even their best laid plans come under scrutiny. However, it is important to recognize that we have all inherited a system of racism which was laid in place well before our time. Those white antiracists who are able to maintain humility without defensiveness understand that whatever racial perspectives they have internalized which may end up being responsible for their mistakes originated from the workings of that historical system and not from a personal character flaw. While they do not personalize the *origins* of their mistakes, they still take personal responsibility for learning from them and striving not to repeat them. No matter how many years they have been working at it, truly humble white antiracists acknowledge they have a lifetime of "minefields" ahead. As Lisa stated, "It's taken hundreds of years for this system to be put in place, and you can't fix it in thirty years or even sixty years . . . this just takes a long time, this is a lifetime commitment."

Anti-Racist Action (ARA)
www.aranet.org
to locate a chapter near you

People's Institute for Survival and Beyond
7166 Crowder Blvd Suite 100
New Orleans, LA 70127
(504) 241-7452
www.thepeoplesinstitute.org
to locate trainings near you

References

Barndt, Joseph. 1991. *Dismantling Racism: The Continuing Challenge to White America*. Minneapolis, Minn.: Augsberg Fortress.

Chisom, Ronald, and Michael Washington. 1997. *Undoing Racism: A Philosophy of International Social Change*, 2nd ed. New Orleans: The People's Institute Press.

Eichstedt, Jennifer L. 1997. White Identities and Anti-Racism Activism. Paper presented at the annual meeting of the American Sociological Association, August, Toronto, Ontario.

Feagin, Joe R., and Herrán, Vera. 1995. *White Racism: The Basics*. New York: Routledge.

Frankenberg, Ruth. 1993. *White Women, Race Matters: The Social Construction of Whiteness*. Minneapolis, Minn.: University of Minnesota Press.

Franklin, Jonathan. 1998. Skinnin' Heads. *Vibe* (June–July): 84–85.

hooks, bell. 1995. *Killing Rage: Ending Racism*. New York: Henry Holt.

Novick, Michael. 1997. Anti-Racist Action on the Move. *Turning the Tide: Journal of Anti-Racist Activism Research and Education* 10, no. 2:1–2.

Selena and Katrina. 1996. Copwatch. *Race Traitor* 6:18–23.

Tatum, Beverly Daniel. 1997. *Why Are All the Black Kids Sitting Together in the Cafeteria?* New York: Basic Books.

Abolish the White Race by Any Means Necessary

Noel Ignatiev and John Garvey

The white race is a historically constructed social formation—historically constructed because (like royalty) it is a product of some people's responses to historical circumstances; a social formation because it is a fact of society corresponding to no classification recognized by natural science.

The white race cuts across ethnic and class lines. It is not coextensive with that portion of the population of European descent, since many of those classified as "colored" can trace some of their ancestry to Europe, while African, Asian, or American Indian blood flows through the veins of many considered white. Nor does membership in the white race imply wealth, since there are plenty of poor whites, as well as some people of wealth and comfort who are not white.

The white race consists of those who partake of the privileges of the white skin in this society. Its most wretched members share a status higher, in certain respects, than that of the most exalted persons excluded from it, in return for which they give their support to the system that degrades them.

The key to solving the social problems of our age is to abolish the white race. Until that task is accomplished, even partial reform will prove elusive, because white influence permeates every issue in U.S. society, whether domestic or foreign.

Advocating the abolition of the white race is distinct from what is called "antiracism." The term "racism" has come to be applied to a variety of attitudes, some of which are mutually incompatible, and has been devalued to mean little more than a tendency to dislike some people for the color of their skin. Moreover, antiracism admits the natural existence of "races" even while opposing social distinctions among them. The abolitionists maintain, on the contrary, that people were not favored socially because they were white; rather they were defined as "white" because they were favored. Race itself is a product of social discrimination; so long as the white race exists, all movements against racism are doomed to fail.

The existence of the white race depends on the willingness of those assigned to it to place their racial interests above class, gender, or any other interests they hold. The defection of enough of its members to make it unreliable as a determinant of behavior will set off tremors that will lead to its collapse.

Race Traitor aims to serve as an intellectual center for those seeking to abolish the white race. It will encourage dissent from the conformity that maintains it and popularize examples of defection from its ranks, analyze the forces that hold it together and those that promise to tear it apart. Part of its task will be to promote debate among abolitionists. When possible, it will support practical measures, guided by the principle, *treason to whiteness is loyalty to humanity.*

Dissolve the Club

The white race is a club that enrolls certain people at birth, without their consent, and brings them up according to its rules. For the most part the members go through life accepting the benefits of membership, without thinking about the costs. When individuals question the rules, the officers are quick to remind them of all they owe to the club, and warn them of the dangers they will face if they leave it.

Race Traitor aims to dissolve the club, to break it apart, to explode it. Some people who sympathize with our aim have asked us how we intend to win over the majority of so-called whites to anti-racism. Others, usually less friendly, have asked if we plan to exterminate physically millions, perhaps hundreds of millions, of people. Neither of these plans is what we have in mind. The weak point of the club is its need for unanimity. Just as the South, on launching the Civil War, declared that it needed its entire territory and would have it, the white race must have the support of all those it has designated as its constituency, or it ceases to exist.

Before the Civil War, the leading spokesmen for the slaveholders acknowledged that the majority of white northerners, swayed above all by the presence of the fugitive slave, considered slavery unjust. The Southerners also understood that the opposition was ineffective; however much the white people of the north disapproved of the slave system, the majority went along with it rather than risk the ordinary comforts of their lives, meager as they were in many cases.

When John Brown attacked Harpers Ferry, Southern pro-slavery leaders reacted with fury: they imposed a boycott on northern manufacturers, demanded new concessions from the government in Washington, and began to prepare for war. When they sought to portray John Brown as a representative of northern opinion, Southern leaders were wrong; he represented only a small and isolated minority. But they were also right, for he expressed the hopes that still persisted in the northern population despite decades of cringing before the slaveholders. Virginia did not fear John Brown and his small band of followers, but rather his soul that would go marching on, though his body lay a-mould'rin' in the grave.

When the South, in retaliation for Harpers Ferry, sought to further bully northern opinion, it did so not out of paranoia but out of the realistic assessment that only a renewal of the national pro-slavery vows could save a system whose proud facade concealed a fragile foundation. By the arrogance of their demands, the Southern leaders compelled the people of the north to resist. Not ideas but events were in command. Each step led inexorably to the next: Southern land-greed, Lincoln's victory, secession, war, blacks as laborers, soldiers, citizens, voters. And so the war that began with not one person in a hundred foreseeing the end of slavery was transformed within two years into an anti-slavery war.

It is our faith—and with those who do not share it we shall not argue—that the majority of so-called whites in this country are neither deeply nor consciously committed to white supremacy; like most human beings in most times and places, they would do the right thing if it were convenient. As did their counterparts before the Civil War, most go along with a system that disturbs them, because the consequences of challenging it are terrifying. They close their eyes to what is happening around them, because it is easier not to know.

At rare moments their nervous peace is shattered, their certainty is shaken, and they are compelled to question the common sense by which they normally live. One such moment was in the days immediately following the Rodney King verdict, when a majority of white Americans were willing to admit to polltakers that black people had good reasons to rebel, and some joined them. Ordinarily the moments are brief, as the guns and reform programs are moved up to restore order and the confidence that matters are in good hands and they can go back to sleep. Both the guns and the reform programs are aimed at whites as well as blacks—the guns as a warning and the reform programs as a salve to their consciences.

Recently, one of our editors, unfamiliar with New York City traffic laws, made an illegal right turn there on a red light. He was stopped by two cops in a patrol car. After examining his license, they released him with a courteous admonition. Had he been black, they probably would have ticketed him, and might even have taken him down to the station. A lot of history was embodied in that small exchange: the cops treated the miscreant leniently at least in part because they assumed, looking at him, that he was white and therefore loyal. Their courtesy was a habit meant both to reward good conduct and induce future cooperation.

Had the driver cursed them, or displayed a bumper sticker that said, "Avenge Rodney King," the cops might have reacted differently.

We admit that neither gesture on the part of a single individual would in all likelihood be of much consequence. But if enough of those who looked white broke the rules of the club to make the cops doubt their ability to recognize a white person merely by looking at him or her, how would it affect the cops' behavior? And if the police, the courts, and the authorities in general were to start spreading around indiscriminately the treatment they normally reserve for people of color, how would the rest of the so-called whites react?

How many dissident so-called whites would it take to unsettle the nerves of the white executive board? It is impossible to know. One John Brown—against a background of slave resistance—was enough for Virginia. Yet it was not the abolitionists, not even the transcendent John Brown, who brought about the mass shifts in consciousness of the Civil War period. At most, their heroic deeds were part of a chain of events that involved mutual actions and reactions on a scale beyond anything they could have anticipated—until a war that began with both sides fighting for slavery (the South to take it out of the Union, the North to keep it in) ended with a great army marching through the land singing, "As He died to make men holy, let us fight to make men free."

The moments when the routine assumptions of race break down are the seismic promise that somewhere in the tectonic flow a new fault is building up pressure, a new Harpers Ferry is being prepared. Its nature and timing cannot be predicted, but of its coming we have no doubt. When it comes, it will set off a series of tremors that will lead to the disintegration of the white race. We want to be ready, walking in Jerusalem just like John.

Being an Ally

Paul Kivel

What Does an Ally Do?

Being allies to people of color in the struggle to end racism is one of the most important things

that white people can do. There is no one correct way to be an ally. Each of us is different. We have different relationships to social organizations, political processes, and economic structures. We are more or less powerful because of such factors as our gender, class, work situation, family, and community participation. Being an ally to people of color is an ongoing strategic process in which we look at our personal and social resources, evaluate the environment we have helped to create, and decide what needs to be done.

This book is filled with things to do and ways to get involved. These suggestions are not prioritized because they cannot be. Times change and circumstances vary. What is a priority today may not be tomorrow. What is effective or strategic right now may not be next year. We need to be thinking with others and noticing what is going on around us so we will know how to put our attention, energy, time, and money toward strategic priorities in the struggle to end racism and other injustices.

This includes listening to people of color so that we can support the actions they take, the risks they bear in defending their lives and challenging white hegemony. It includes watching the struggle of white people to maintain dominance and the struggle of people of color to gain equal opportunity, justice, safety, and respect.

We don't need to believe or accept as true everything people of color say. There is no one voice in any community, much less in the complex and diverse communities of color spanning our country. We do need to listen carefully to the voices of people of color so that we understand and give credence to their experience. We can then evaluate the content of what they are saying by what we know about how racism works and by our own critical thinking and progressive political analysis.

It is important to emphasize this point because often we become paralyzed when people of color talk about racism. We are afraid to challenge what they say. We will be ineffective as allies if we give up our ability to analyze and think critically, if we simply accept everything that a person of color states as truth.

Listening to people of color and giving critical credence to their experience is not easy for us because of the training we have received. Nevertheless, it is an important first step. When we hear statements that make us want to react defensively, we can instead keep the following points in mind as we try to understand what is happening and determine how best to be allies.

We have seen how racism is a pervasive part of our culture. Therefore we should always assume that racism is at least part of the picture. In light of this assumption, we should look for the patterns involved rather than treating most events as isolated occurrences.

Since we know that racism is involved, we know our whiteness is also a factor. We should look for ways we are acting from assumptions of white power or privilege. This will help us acknowledge any fear or confusion we may feel. It will allow us to see our tendencies to defend ourselves or our tendencies to assume we should be in control. Then we may want to talk with other white people both to express our feelings and to get support so our tendencies towards defensiveness or controlling behavior don't get in the way of our being effective allies.

We have many opportunities to practice these critical listening and thinking skills because we are all involved in a complex web of interpersonal and institutional relationships. Every day we are presented with opportunities to analyze what is going on around us and to practice taking direct action as allies to people of color.

People of color will always be on the front lines fighting racism because their lives are at stake. How do we act and support them effectively, both when they are in the room with us and when they are not?

Basic Tactics

Every situation is different and calls for critical thinking about how to make a difference. Taking the statements above into account, I have compiled some general guidelines.

1. **Assume racism is everywhere, every day.** Just as economics influences everything we do, just as our gender and gender politics influence everything we do, assume that racism is affecting whatever is going on. We assume this because it's true and because one of the privileges of being white is not having to see or deal with racism all the time. We have to learn to see the effect that racism has.

Notice who speaks, what is said, how things are done and described. Notice who isn't present. Notice code words for race, and the implications of the policies, patterns, and comments that are being expressed. You already notice the skin color of everyone you meet and interact with—now notice what difference it makes.

2. **Notice who is the center of attention and who is the center of power.** Racism works by directing violence and blame toward people of color and consolidating power and privilege for white people.

3. **Notice how racism is denied, minimized, and justified.**

4. **Understand and learn from the history of whiteness and racism.** Notice how racism has changed over time and how it has subverted or resisted challenges. Study the tactics that have worked effectively against it.

5. **Understand the connections between racism, economic issues, sexism, and other forms of injustice.**

6. **Take a stand against injustice.** Take risks. It is scary, difficult, and may bring up feelings of inadequacy, lack of self-confidence, indecision, or fear of making mistakes, but ultimately it is the only healthy and moral human thing to do. Intervene in situations where racism is being passed on.

7. **Be strategic.** Decide what is important to challenge and what's not. Think about strategy in particular situations. Attack the source of power.

8. **Don't confuse a battle with the war.** Behind particular incidents and interactions are larger patterns. Racism is flexible and adaptable. There will be gains and losses in the struggle for justice and equality.

9. **Don't call names or be personally abusive.** Since power is often defined as power over others—the ability to abuse or control people—it is easy to become abusive ourselves. However, we usually end up abusing people who have less power than we do because it is less dangerous. Attacking people doesn't address the systemic nature of racism and inequality.

10. **Support the leadership of people of color.** Do this consistently, but not uncritically.

11. **Learn something about the history of white people who have worked for racial justice.** There is a long history of white people who have fought for racial justice. Their stories can inspire and sustain you.

12. **Don't do it alone.** You will not end racism by yourself. We can do it if we work together. Build support, establish networks, and work with already established groups.

13. **Talk with your children and other young people about racism.**

GETTING INVOLVED

It can be difficult for those of us who are white to know how to be strong allies for people of color when discrimination occurs. In the following interaction, imagine that Roberto is a young Latino just coming out of a job interview with a white recruiter from a computer company. Let's see how one white person might respond.

Roberto is angry, not sure what to do next. He walks down the hall and meets a white teacher who wants to help.

Teacher: *Hey, Roberto, how's it going?*

Roberto: *That son of a bitch! He wasn't going to give me no job. That was really messed up.*

Teacher: *Hold on there, don't be so angry. It was probably a mistake or something.*

Roberto: *There was no mistake. The racist bastard. He wants to keep me from getting a good job. Rather have us all on welfare or doing maintenance work.*

Teacher: *Calm down now or you'll get yourself in more trouble. Don't go digging a hole for yourself. Maybe I could help you if you weren't so angry.*

Roberto: *That's easy for you to say. This man was discriminating against me. White folks are all the same. They talk about equal opportunity, but it's the same old shit.*

Teacher: *Wait a minute. I didn't have anything to do with this. Don't blame me, I'm not responsible.*

If you wouldn't be so angry maybe I could help you. You probably took what he said the wrong way. Maybe you were too sensitive.

Roberto: *I could tell. He was racist. That's all. (He storms off.)*

What did you notice about this scene? The teacher is concerned and is trying to help, but his intervention is not very effective. He immediately downplays the incident, discounting Roberto's feelings and underestimating the possibility of racism. He seems to think that racism is unlikely—that it was just a misunderstanding, or that Roberto was being too sensitive.

The teacher is clearly uncomfortable with Roberto's anger. He begins to defend himself, the job recruiter, and white people. He ends up feeling attacked for being white. Rather than talking about what happened, he focuses on Roberto's anger and his generalizations about white people. He threatens to get Roberto in trouble himself if Roberto doesn't calm down. As he walks away, he may be thinking it's no wonder Roberto didn't get hired for the job.

You probably recognize some of the tactics described. . . . The teacher denies or minimizes the likelihood of racism, blames Roberto, and eventually counterattacks, claiming to be a victim of Roberto's anger and racial generalizations.

This interaction illustrates some of the common feelings that can get in the way of intervening effectively where discrimination is occurring. First is the feeling that we are being personally attacked. It is difficult to hear the phrases "all white people" or "you white people." We want to defend ourselves and other whites. We don't want to believe that white people could intentionally hurt others. Or we may want to say, "Not me, I'm different."

There are some things we should remember when we feel attacked. First, this is a question of injustice. We need to focus on what happened and what we can do about it, not on our feelings of being attacked.

Second, someone who has been the victim of injustice is legitimately angry and may or may not express that anger in ways we like. Criticizing the way people express their anger deflects attention and action away from the injustice that was committed. After the injustice has been dealt with, if you still think it's worthwhile and not an attempt to control the situation yourself, you can go back and discuss ways of expressing anger.

Often, because we are frequently complacent about injustice that doesn't affect us directly, it takes a lot of anger and aggressive action to bring attention to a problem. If we were more proactive about identifying and intervening in situations of injustice, people would not have to be so "loud" to get our attention in the first place.

Finally, part of the harm that racism does is that it forces people of color to be wary and mistrustful of all white people, just as sexism forces women to mistrust all men. People of color face racism every day, often from unexpected quarters. They never know when a white friend, co-worker, teacher, police officer, doctor, or passerby may discriminate, act hostile, or say something offensive. They have to be wary of all white people, even though they know that not all white people will mistreat them. They have likely been hurt in the past by white people they thought they could trust, and therefore they may make statements about all white people. We must remember that although we want to be trustworthy, trust is not the issue. We are not fighting racism so that people of color will trust us. Trust builds over time through our visible efforts to be allies and fight racism. Rather than trying to be safe and trustworthy, we need to be more active, less defensive, and put issues of trust aside.

When people are discriminated against they may feel unseen, stereotyped, attacked, or as if a door has been slammed in their face. They may feel confused, frustrated, helpless, or angry. They are probably reminded of other similar experiences. They may want to hurt someone in return, or hide their pain, or simply forget about the whole experience. Whatever the response, the experience is deeply wounding and painful. It is an act of emotional violence.

It's also an act of economic violence to be denied access to a job, housing, educational program, pay raise, or promotion that one deserves. It is a practice that keeps economic resources in the hands of one group and denies them to another.

When a person is discriminated against it is a serious event and we need to treat it seriously. It is also a common event. For instance, the government estimates that there are over 2 million acts of race-based housing discrimination every year—20 million every decade. We know that during their lifetime, every person of color will probably have to face such discriminatory experiences in school, work, housing, and community settings.

People of color do not protest discrimination lightly. They know that when they do, white people routinely deny or minimize it, blame them for causing trouble, and then counterattack. This is the "happy family" syndrome [described earlier].

People of color are experts in discrimination resulting from racism. Most experience it regularly and see its effects on their communities. Not every complaint of discrimination is valid, but most have some truth in them. It would be a tremendous step forward if we assumed that there was some truth in every complaint of racial discrimination, even when other factors may also be involved. At least then we would take it seriously enough to investigate fully.

How could the teacher in the above scenario be a better ally to Roberto? We can go back to the guidelines suggested earlier for help. First, he needs to listen much more carefully to what Roberto is saying. He should assume that Roberto is intelligent, and if he says there was racism involved then there probably was. The teacher should be aware of his own power and position, his tendency to be defensive, and his desire to defend other white people or presume their innocence. It would also be worthwhile to look for similar occurrences because racism is usually not an isolated instance but a pattern within an organization or institution.

Let's see how these suggestions might operate in a replay of this scene.

Teacher: Hey, Roberto, what's happening?

Roberto: That son of a bitch! He wasn't going to give me no job. He was messin' with me.

Teacher: You're really upset. Tell me what happened.

Roberto: He was discriminating against me. Wasn't going to hire me cause I'm Latino. White folks are all alike. Always playing games.

Teacher: This is serious. Why don't you come into my office and tell me exactly what happened.

Roberto: Okay. This company is advertising for computer programmers and I'm qualified for the job. But this man tells me there aren't any computer jobs, and then he tries to steer me toward a janitor job. He was a racist bastard.

Teacher: That's tough. I know you would be good in that job. This sounds like a case of job discrimination. Let's write down exactly what happened, and then you can decide what you want to do about it.

Roberto: I want to get that job.

Teacher: If you want to challenge it, I'll help you. Maybe there's something we can do.

This time the teacher was being a strong, supportive ally to Roberto.

AN ALLY MAKES A COMMITMENT

Nobody needs fly-by-night allies, those who are here today and gone tomorrow. Being an ally takes commitment and perseverance. It is a life-long struggle to end racism and other forms of social injustice. People of color know this well because they have been struggling for generations for recognition of their rights and the opportunity to participate fully in our society. The struggle to abolish slavery took over 80 years. Women organized for over 60 years to win the right to vote. I was reminded about the long haul recently when my sister sent me a news clipping about my old high school in Los Angeles, Birmingham High.

The clipping was about the 17-year struggle to change the "Birmingham Braves" name and caricatured image of an "Indian" used by the school teams to something that did not insult Native Americans. I was encouraged to hear that the name and mascot were now being changed, but was upset to read that there was an alumni group resisting the change and filing a lawsuit to preserve the old name.

Soon after receiving the article I had the good fortune to talk with a white woman who had been involved with the struggle over the mascot. The challenge had originated with a group of Native Americans in the San Fernando Valley. This woman decided to join the group—the only white person to do so. She started attending meetings. For the first two or three years all she did was listen, and the group hardly spoke to her. After a time, members of the group began to acknowledge her presence, talk with her, and include her in their activities. This woman learned a tremendous amount about herself, the local Native cultures, and the nature of white resistance during the 15 years she was involved with this group. They tried many different strategies and eventually, because they met with so much intransigence at the high school, they went to the Los Angeles school board.

When the school board made its decision to eliminate Native-American names and logos in school programs, it affected every school in the Los Angeles area. Subsequently the decision became a model for the Dallas school district's policy and is being considered for adoption in other school districts across the country.

This was a long struggle, but much public education was accomplished in the process. This work is part of a national effort by Native Americans and their allies to get sports teams and clubs to relinquish offensive names and mascots.

If the woman I talked with had been discouraged or offended because nobody welcomed her or paid her special attention during those first meetings, or if she felt that after a year or two nothing was going to be accomplished, or if she had not listened and learned enough to be able to work with and take leadership from the Native American community involved in this struggle, she would have gone home and possibly talked about how she had tried but it hadn't worked. She would not have been transformed by the struggle the way she had been; she would not have contributed to and been able to celebrate the success of this struggle for Native-American dignity and respect. Her work as an ally reminded me of what commitment as an ally really means.

DISCUSSION QUESTIONS

1. Why does Williams state that colorblindness is a fiction? If a truly color-blind society is the eventual goal, why do scholars like Williams, Bell, and others advocate color-conscious policies for ending inequality? Is it possible to craft feasible solutions for racism that do not acknowledge race, knowing that modern racism often occurs without mentioning race? Which type of approach do you think would be more effective for ending racism (color-blind or color-conscious policy) and why?

2. Do you think overt or covert racism is easier to fight, and why? Since our legal structure deals mainly with overt racism, what policy suggestions can you offer for dealing with covert racism, including that which is perpetrated unintentionally? Should people be punished similarly whether they intended to be discriminatory or not, if the effect is the same on the perpetrator? (Hint: Think of how the law treats other crimes.)

3. Do you think whites' energies are better spent working with other whites (that is, being "race traitors," challenging whites who give them privileges) or as allies to people of color? What are the benefits and drawbacks of each approach? If you are a person of color, what would you prefer to see whites do and why? If you are a white person, which would be easier and which would be harder for you to do and why?

4. What kinds of activities do you think you can do in your daily life to end oppression? Are there things you do already, or things you would like to do more of? Think of the last time you witnessed racism and were not pleased with how you handled the situation. Consider what you would have done differently. What kinds of things can you do, even in the absence of such incidents, to help reduce oppression in society? If you cannot think of anything you would be willing to do, what is it that holds you back?

COMMITMENT TO COMBAT RACISM

Judith Katz

Sheet 1

Indicate whether you have taken action on the items listed below. Check appropriate item.

Yes	No	
		1. Have I aggressively sought out more information in an effort to enhance my own awareness and understanding of racism (talking with others, reading, listening)?
		2. Have I spent some time recently looking at my own racist attitudes and behavior as they contribute to or combat racism around me?
		3. Have I reevaluated my use of terms or phrases that may be perceived by others as degrading or hurtful?
		4. Have I openly disagreed with a racist comment, joke, or action among those around me?
		5. Have I made a personal contract with myself to take a positive stand, even at some possible risk, when the chance occurs?
		6. Have I become increasingly aware of racist TV programs, advertising, news broadcasts, etc.? Have I complained to those in charge?
		7. Have I realized that White Americans are trapped by their own school, homes, media, government, etc., even when they choose not to be openly racist?
		8. Have I suggested and taken steps to implement discussions or workshops aimed at understanding racism with friends, colleagues, social clubs, or church groups?
Yes	No	9. Have I been investigating political candidates at all levels in terms of their stance and activity against racist government practices?
		10. Have I investigated curricula of local schools in terms of their treatment of the issue of racism (also textbooks, assemblies, faculty, staff, administration)?
		11. Have I contributed time and/or funds to an agency, fund, or program that actively confronts the problems of racism?
		12. Have my buying habits supported nonracist shops, companies, or personnel?
		13. Is my school or place of employment a target for my educational efforts in responding to racism?
		14. Have I become seriously dissatisfied with my own level of activity in combating racism?

SOURCE: Developed by James Edler, University of Maryland.

Sheet 2

1. Educating roommates, close friends.

2. Raising issues in the dorm with reads of residence, resident directors, counseling staff, students, student government.

3. Providing information services—changing what normally appears on bulletin boards and walls to provocative posters, handouts, and other materials relevant to racism.

4. Being a referral resource—directing others to people or groups who might be of assistance.

5. Acting as a race model, questioning the White power structure.

6. Establishing discussion groups, colloquia.

7. Finding films to expose racism, developing new directions and strategies.

8. Finding out how dorm money is spent, using it to demonstrate meaningful concern about racism.

9. Working as a counselor with people who are genuinely interested in making sense of racial issues.

INDEX

ABOUT THE EDITORS

Joseph F. Healey, Ph.D., is Professor and Chair of Sociology and Social Work at Christopher Newport University. He is the author of *Race, Ethnicity and Gender in the United States* (1996), *Statistics: A Tool for Social Research, 6th edition* (2001), *Race, Ethnicity, Gender and Class, 3rd edition* (2003), and *Diversity and Society* (2004). He is also coeditor with York Bradshaw of *Sociology for a New Century* (2001) and coauthor with Earl Babbie and Fred Halley of *Exploring Social Issues: Using SPSS for Windows* (1997). He received A.B. and M.A. degrees from The College of William and Mary (Sociology and Anthropology) and a Ph.D. from University of Virginia (Sociology and Anthropology). In his spare time, he plays and records music for hammer dulcimer, banjo, and concertina.

Eileen O'Brien is Visiting Assistant Professor at the College of William and Mary, where her teaching and research interests range from introductory sociology to courses on race, ethnicity, gender, social class, and theory. She authored *Whites Confront Racism* (2001) and has coauthored *White Men on Race* (2003) with Joe Feagin, a preeminent scholar on race and ethnic relations. She received her Ph.D. from the University of Florida in 1999 and an M.A. from Ohio State University in 1996; both degrees in Sociology. In her spare time, she enjoys African drumming, playing Scrabble, and teaching aerobics, but mostly just being in awestruck love with her new daughter, Kaya.